BOLLINGEN SERIES

IBN KHALDÛN

THE MUQADDIMAH

An Introduction to History

TRANSLATED AND INTRODUCED BY

FRANZ ROSENTHAL

ABRIDGED AND EDITED BY

N. J. DAWOOD

With a new introduction by Bruce B. Lawrence

BOLLINGEN SERIES
PRINCETON UNIVERSITY PRESS
PRINCETON AND OXFORD

First edition, 1967
First Princeton/Bollingen Paperback printing, 1969
New introduction by Bruce B. Lawrence, 2005
First Princeton Classics edition, 2015

This is an abridgment of the three-volume edition translated, and with an
introduction, by Franz Rosenthal, published by Pantheon Books as
Bollingen Series XLIII and copyright © 1958 by Bollingen Foundation,
Inc., New York, NY. A second edition, with corrections and augmented
bibliography, was published by Princeton University Press in 1967. In the
present edition, the notes to the main text are Professor Rosenthal's unless
otherwise noted.

The abridged edtion was originally published in 1967 jointly by
Routledge & Kegan Paul Ltd. and Martin Secker and Warburg Ltd.,
London.

Paperback ISBN: 978-0-691-16628-5

Library of Congress Control Number: 2015930405

British Library Cataloging-in-Publication Data is available

Printed on acid-free paper. ∞

press.princeton.edu

Printed in the United States of America

7 9 10 8 6

Contents

CONTENTS

INTRODUCTION TO THE 2005 EDITION

by Bruce B. Lawrence

This is the abridged version of the only complete English translation of the *Muqaddimah* (introduction), which was published in
1958 in three volumes for the Bollingen Foundation. The *Muqaddimah* is the most significant, and challenging, Islamic history of
the premodern world. Its author was the fourteenth-century
Mediterranean scholar Ibn Khaldûn (1332–1406).

Ibn Khaldûn was a man of his time, but he was not like others of
his time. He was marked by travel, even before he was born. In the
eighth century his ancestors emigrated from Southern Arabia, or
Yemen, to Andalusia, or southern Spain, then a part of the Muslim
world. His full name attests to his Yemeni roots: 'Abd-ar-Rahmân
Abû Zayd ibn Muhammad ibn Muhammad ibn Khaldûn al-
Hadramî. Al-Hadramî links its bearer to Hadramut, a part of
Yemen. Other privileged members of Andalusian society were also
Arab immigrants, though many, including Ibn Khaldûn's forbears,
had intermarried with indigenous Berbers. What distinguished
Ibn Khaldûn was neither his Arab lineage nor his linkage to
Berbers via marriage but his Mediterranean location. At the intersection of Jewish, Christian, and Muslim influences, heir to Greek
science and Arabic poetry, and connected by trade and history to
Asia, the Mediterranean Sea had become the nexus of Muslim cos-
mopolitanism by the fourteenth century. Social mobility as well as
physical travel animated Mediterranean Muslims, especially those,
like Ibn Khaldûn, who rose to high posts in government, law, and
education. Travel (*rihlah*) became the model for his autobiography, *At-Ta'rîf bi-Ibn Khaldûn wa-rihlatuhu gharban wa-sharqan*, or
Biography of Ibn Khaldûn and His Travel in the West and in the East
(hereafter referred to as *Autobiography*).[1] Though other Muslims

---

[1] The original Arabic version was edited by Muhammad Tawit at-Tanjî and pub-
lished in 1370 in Cairo. It was reprinted in 1951 and translated into French by
Abdesselam Cheddadi as *Le Voyage d'Occident et d'Orient* (Paris: Sindbad, 1980).
Regrettably, as noted by the translator of the English edition, Franz Rosenthal,
Cheddadi omitted almost all of the poetry that Ibn Khaldûn quoted (Rosenthal,
"Ibn Khaldûn in His Time," in *Ibn Khaldûn and Islamic Ideology*, ed. Bruce B.
Lawrence [Leiden: E. J. Brill, 1984], 25n.11).

vii

wrote autobiographies prior to Ibn Khaldûn's,[2] his is unusual because he attempts to place his own life squarely at the intersection of East and West. Begun in the last decade of his life and continuing up through his meeting with Tamerlane (in 1401), it situates him in the midst of the political activities of his time, but even more, it stresses how crucial is the awareness of geographical/ historical factors in assessing political events and their consequences. What made Ibn Khaldûn different was not travel per se but rather his ability to travel in the imagination of his own world, to create another perspective that at once linked him to his contemporaries yet set him apart from them. Whether we call this disposition quirkiness or eccentricity, narcissism or genius,[3] we must recognize it as the critical element of Ibn Khaldûn that made it possible for him to conceive, then write the *Muqaddimah*, a study which the twentieth-century doyen of British historians, Arnold J. Toynbee, has called "undoubtedly the greatest work of its kind that has ever yet been created by any mind in any time or place."[4]

Marking himself as different was almost reflexive for Ibn Khaldûn. He was different not just in his thought and speech but also in his dress. When he served as a judge in Cairo, he continued to wear Maghribi (or North African) robes instead of the lighter

---

[2] See Walter J. Fischel, *Ibn Khaldûn and Tamerlane* (Berkeley: University of California Press, 1952), 14–17. As Fischel makes clear, the *Autobiography* was initially conceived of as an addendum, integral to the larger work *Kitâb al-'Ibar* (*History*). Only toward the end of his life did Ibn Khaldûn make it into an independent work, though without a proper introduction and with the title itself an afterthought.

[3] A study of Ibn Khaldûn's relationship to Sufism, or Islamic mysticism, begins with the observation that his character reflected "many discrepancies between his ideas and his actions, the contrast between his attempts at social reform and his own transgressions of social codes, his public sense and his pronounced egotism, his scientific impartiality and his very obvious personal preferences, his wide comprehension and his personal vanity," yet the same author concludes that "most of these contradictions can be ascribed to the dualistic character of all genius" (M. Syrier, "Ibn Khaldûn and Islamic Mysticism," *Islamic Culture* 21 [1947]: 264, as cited in Fischel, *Ibn Khaldûn and Tamerlane*, 28n.66).

[4] A. J. Toynbee, *A Study of History*, vol. 3, *The Growths of Civilizations*, 2d ed. (London: Oxford University Press, 1935), 322. Cited in Franz Rosenthal, translator's introduction to *The Muqaddimah: An Introduction to History*, by Ibn Khaldûn (New York: Pantheon Books, 1958), 1:cxv. While Toynbee's praise may seem excessive, it reflects the broad reception of the *Muqaddimah* and the deep engagement with Ibn Khaldûn's thought, in both Arabic and European sources, among

robes of Egyptian judges. Though he may have been uncomfortable, he was indicating pride in his Andalusian roots, without, however, suggesting that he was less than a faithful, observant Muslim or other than an obedient, subservient officer of the Egyptian state.[5]

In his writing Ibn Khaldûn also expressed difference, but always within limits and often by inference. It must be remembered that he was not employed to be a historian. He was a juridical activist with a secondary interest in history. Particularly in the odd circumstances of his own life experience did he hope to find lessons (*'ibar*) that would be instructive for others. While his *Autobiography* ranges over many moments, none is more poignant, or more instructive, than his meetings with Tamerlane. The year was 1401. The place was Damascus. Tamerlane had just laid siege to the Mamluk city, which had not yet surrendered. During the previous twenty years Tamerlane had become the most feared and successful warrior from the East after the Mongol chieftain Chingiz Khan. Tamerlane was heir to Chingiz Khan in a double sense. Though Turkish and Muslim, he also had Mongol lineage, with shamanic loyalties, through his mother. Even more important, Tamerlane had inherited the Mongol ideal of universal sovereignty via military conquest. He had been systematic in his plundering and massacres, from Moscow in the north to Delhi in the south to Izmir in the west. No one was spared: all those conquered, whether Muslim or not, were treated as prisoners. Some were tortured, many were slain, all were at risk.

Muslims as well as non-Muslims. The major sources till the late 1950s have been noted in Walter J. Fischel, selected bibliography to *The Muqaddimah*, trans. Franz Rosenthal (New York: Pantheon Books, 1958), 3:485–512. An updated bibliography, which alas includes a gratuitous critique of Fischel's bibliography, is to be found in Aziz Al-Azmeh, *Ibn Khaldûn in Modern Scholarship: A Study in Orientalism* (London: Third World Centre for Research and Publication, 1981), 231–318. Not all readers, of course, are convinced by Ibn Khaldûn's novel and complex thesis. Even Toynbee qualified his commendation, observing that "a modern Western critic may feel that Ibn Khaldûn's empirical foundation is rather too narrow to bear the weight or to justify the range of his masterly generalization"(*A Study of History*, 3:475).

[5] For more extensive annotation of Ibn Khaldûn as self-consciously marked by his difference from contemporaries, see Fischel, *Ibn Khaldûn and Tamerlane*, 70–71n.54, and also Rosenthal, "Ibn Khaldûn in His Time," 16–24.

When Ibn Khaldûn was summoned by Tamerlane in January 1401, he met him outside Damascus, where the conqueror had camped while his army laid siege to the city. Ibn Khaldûn feared for his life. Yet he also knew from reports that Tamerlane could be indulgent as well as cruel, and that he had befriended scholars and mystics on previous occasions.[6] Ibn Khaldûn won Tamerlane's confidence, so much so that the account of their meetings justified his supplementary labor as a historian. Not only did Ibn Khaldûn claim a role in gaining pardon for Mamluk prisoners of Tamerlane, but he also saw in the Central Asian world conqueror a Turco-Mongol vindication of his own thesis, to wit, that civilization is always and everywhere marked by the fundamental difference between urban and primitive, producing a tension that is also an interplay between nomad and merchant, desert and city, orality and literacy. Ibn Khaldûn may have been projecting his own life's ambition in the subsequent portrait he provided of "Timur," or Tamerlane:

> This king Timur is one of the greatest and mightiest of kings. Some attribute to him knowledge, others attribute to him heresy because they note his preference for "members of the House (of 'Ali)," still others attribute to him the employment of magic and sorcery, but in all this there is nothing; it is simply that he is highly intelligent and perspicacious, addicted to debate and argumentation about what he knows and also about what he does not know.[7]

The final part of this description could have served as an epitaph for Ibn Khaldûn, even without the legacy of his *Muqaddimah*: "he is highly intelligent and perspicacious, addicted to debate and argumentation about what he knows and also about what he does

---

[6] Though Ibn Khaldûn had heard of the torture of a prominent Damascene judge at the hands of Tamerlane prior to their meeting (Fischel, *Ibn Khaldûn and Tamerlane*, 78–79n.81), he also knew that the first successful approach for amnesty to Tamerlane had come from a group of Damascene notables, led by a Sufi master (ibid., 30, 64–65n.32). The subsequent plunder of Damascus, once the city fell to the Mongol siege, is recounted in sparse detail by Ibn Khaldûn. He does condemn the outcome, though not without qualification: "This was an absolutely dastardly and abominable deed, but changes in affairs are in the hands of Allah—He does with His creatures as He wishes, and decides in His kingdom as He wills" (ibid., 39).

[7] Fischel, *Ibn Khaldûn and Tamerlane*, 47.

not know." It is his ability to test the limits of what is known and knowable that makes Ibn Khaldûn an explorer of the mind and not a conventional intellectual in the terms of either his own time or later times in the history of Muslim civilization.

The biggest difference between Ibn Khaldûn and the cosmopolitan elites of his generation was his orientation to *adab*.[8] Though trained as a *faqîh*, or jurist, and familiar with all the ancillary sciences of *fiqh* (jurisprudence), Ibn Khaldûn was also an *adîb*, or littérateur. A littérateur is attentive to words, to their expression in both speech and writing but above all, to their polyvalence. Words can mean many things in different times, places, and contexts. Though this may seem a truism today, it was far from accepted knowledge or the dominant outlook, even among the notables whom Ibn Khaldûn knew and whom he engaged in discussion or debate.

As a littérateur Ibn Khaldûn was especially concerned with poetry and prose. It is crucial to recognize, for instance, that he was engaged by the lyrical tones of verse, that he saw poetry as a register of local identity, and that he himself had poetic aspirations.[9] As a littérateur, he also moved beyond the range of what is usually thought to be literature. He engaged the full spectrum of sciences that were known in Arabic translations from Greek sources by the ninth century and which were then expanded through experiment and study by Muslim scientists during subsequent centuries. By the time of Ibn Khaldûn, scientific activity had been professionalized—so much so that "most of the distinguished physicians and astronomers of twelfth- and thirteenth-century Syria and Cairo were employed as jurists, teachers in madrasa-like medical

---

[8] For the first and fullest development of Ibn Khaldûn as an *adîb*, see miriam cooke, "Ibn Khaldûn and Language: From Linguistic Habit to Philological Craft," in Lawrence, *Ibn Khaldûn and Islamic Ideology*, 27–36. There is no single English equivalent of *adab*, and so I leave it untranslated, yet for stylistic ease I have taken the liberty of rendering *adîb*, one who practices and pursues *adab*, as "littérateur" throughout.

[9] It is Ibn Khaldûn's contemporary, Ibn al-Khaṭîb, who remarks on "his promising bid for recognition as a poet," at the same time that Ibn al-Khaṭîb praises Ibn Khaldûn for the latter's partial commentary on a poem that he (Ibn al-Khaṭîb) had composed on the principles of jurisprudence. See citations in Rosenthal, translator's introduction to *The Muqaddimah*, 1:xliv–xlv.

xi

institutions, or timekeepers in the region's major mosques."[10] At first, it may seem odd that his treatment of the sciences would be delayed until the sixth and final chapter of the *Muqaddimah*. It is not because sciences are unimportant, or of second order importance, to Muslim elites, but rather because sciences are not integral to urban life. Like other aspects of urban society, sciences are a luxury or convenience neither natural nor necessary. Sciences are unlike crafts. Crafts are a necessity. They are linked to gainful occupations, and because they are, Ibn Khaldûn introduces, then analyzes them in chapter 5 of the *Muqaddimah*, prior to his enumeration and assessment of the sciences.

Both the placement of science and the distinction between crafts and sciences reveal the organizational vision of Ibn Khaldûn about his new science. It builds materially from manual, physical labor to refined, intellectual pursuits. It builds thematically from desert to sedentary civilization. It builds diachronically from notions of statecraft that relate to religious norms at different angles: peripheral in tribal dynasties, central in the caliphate, then asymmetric in the royal/military empires that followed the caliphate. The six chapters of the *Muqaddimah* sort out from the most general to the most specific:

(1) On human civilization and the part of the earth that is civilized
(2) On desert civilization, among tribes and savage nations
(3) On dynasties, the caliphate, and royal authority
(4) On sedentary civilization, countries, and cities
(5) On crafts and ways of making a living
(6) On sciences, their acquisition and study. (43)[11]

In assessing the *Muqaddimah* in general and its organizational structure in particular, one must remember that Ibn Khaldûn was more than a jurist and a littérateur—he was also a teacher. Teachers repeat, not to be redundant but to communicate the same thought on different occasions and often to different audiences. A practic-

---

[10] Ahmad Dallal, "Science, Medicine, and Technology: The Making of a Scientific Culture," in *The Oxford History of Islam*, ed. John L. Esposito (New York: Oxford University Press, 1999), 213.
[11] This list has been modified slightly here for rhetorical effect. Hereafter parenthetical citations of page numbers refer to the present edition of the *Muqaddimah*.

ing jurist fond of *adab*, Ibn Khaldûn wrote as he taught. He propounded novel ideas that he both documented and qualified. He repeated himself, often with different examples or sources, in order to make the same point in multiple contexts, and perhaps for multiple audiences.[12]

It is the principle of Ibn Khaldûn's argumentation that remains the same. To appreciate that principle in its stark originality, however, we need to consider two crucial instances relating the bases of jurisprudence to the laws of evidence in depicting historical data. As a jurist he approaches his new science within the parameters of juridical reasoning, yet precisely because jurisprudence too is a science it is not till chapter 6 that Ibn Khaldûn discusses the relationship between it and his own method. Jurisprudence is the crucial science for Ibn Khaldûn. To understand his persistent, foundational use of juridical logic, one must first grasp what he says in chapter 6 about jurisprudence as a science and then return to chapter 1, where he introduces the decisive distinction between two terms that pervades his entire book but only makes sense from the perspective of juridical logic. The two terms are *khabar*, or Event, and *hadîth*, or Tradition.[13]

For Ibn Khaldûn jurisprudence is both a science and a pedagogical tool. Though its provenance is religious law, its practice also informs linguistics or rather lexicography. In chapter 6 the connection of these two scientific fields, *fiqh* and *lugha*, jurisprudence and lexicography, is made in compelling argumentation, at once novel and subtle. After establishing that *ijmâ'*, or consensus, is a third kind of evidence (after the Qur'ân and the Sunnah) for jurisprudence, Ibn Khaldûn explains:

> Now many of the things that happened after the Prophet are not included in the established texts [the Qur'ân and

---

[12] Muhsin Mahdi depicts this practice as an expedient strategy for Ibn Khaldûn: "It was necessary for Ibn Khaldûn to use a specific style of writing through which he could successfully impart to the intimate circle of the few the doctrines intended for it without allowing the many to suspect even the existence of such doctrines in the *'Ibar* [the larger project to which *The Muqaddimah* is an introduction]" (Mahdi, *Ibn Khaldûn's Philosophy of History* [London: George Allen & Unwin, 1957], 117).

[13] Because of their central role in Ibn Khaldûn's method, these two words, Event (*khabar*) and Tradition (*hadîth*), will be capitalized throughout the remainder of this essay.

the Sunnah]. Therefore, they [religious scholars] compared and combined them with the established evidence that is found in the texts, (and drew their conclusions from analogy) according to certain rules that governed their combinations. This assured the soundness of their comparison of two similar (cases), so that it could be assumed that one and the same divine law covered both cases. This became (another kind of) legal evidence, because the (early Muslims) all agreed upon it [*bi-ijmâ'ihim 'alayhi*]. This is analogy [*qiyâs*], the fourth kind of evidence. (347)[14]

The subtlety of this approach is its connection of analogy to consensus as part of a continuous process. Earlier, in the case for upholding the Sunnah, Ibn Khaldûn had also argued that "the Sunnah, as it has been transmitted to us, is justified by the general consensus (to the effect) that Muslims must act in accordance with traditions that are sound."[15] There are four elements without which law could not be law in an Islamic key: the Qur'ân, the Sunnah, consensus, and analogy. Though the Qur'ân would seem to be prior to consensus, it is in fact the consensus of the Community of Believers in Allah and His Last Prophet who confirm that the Book is the Revealed Word to Muḥammad, just as the Sunnah becomes forceful because it too reflects this same consensus. Nor can analogy work, as the above quotation makes clear, except as a further application of the principle of consensus. Consensus, in short, is the glue, the cohesive element, that informs and fortifies every step of the judicial process that safeguards Islam as a divinely guided community.

To a person who has heard the lectures or read the book that became the *Muqaddimah*, it is evident that Ibn Khaldûn is investing *ijmâ'*, or consensus, with a special property, a collective will, an *'aṣabîyah*.

'Aṣabîyah is the major neologism permeating all of Ibn Khaldûn's work. Franz Rosenthal translates it throughout as 'group feeling.' Some have criticized that standardized rendition of

[14] Words or phrases given in parentheses are the translator's, while those in brackets are mine. For further explanation of the use of parentheses in both the 1958 edition of the *Muqaddimah* and in the abridged one, see pages xxxii and xliii, in the present edition.
[15] Rosenthal, *The Muqaddimah*, 3:25.

ʿaṣabîyah, considering it too static and natural an English equivalent of what remains for Ibn Khaldûn a variable pinned between the state (*dawlah*) and religion (*dîn*). Moḥammed Talbi, for instance, defines *ʿaṣabîyah* as "at one and the same time the cohesive force of the group, the conscience that it has of its own specificity and collective aspirations, and the tension that animates it and impels it ineluctably to seek power through conquest."[16] The last element—the drive to power through conquest—seems to fall outside the juridical realm, unless one realizes that the law also is an instrument of power, whether through persuasion or domination. Jon Anderson comes closest to understanding the itinerancy of Ibn Khaldûn's usage when he writes that "*ʿaṣabîyah* seems to be a concept of relation by sameness, opposed both to the state (*dawlah*) based on relations of difference or complementarity, and to religion (*dîn*), which alone supercedes it."[17] Religion does supercede *ʿaṣabîyah,* but it does so by redefining it rather than denying it. The concept of consensus, valorized as the glue or binding element of Islamic law, functions with the force of *ʿaṣabîyah,* at least during the period of the early caliphate.

And so it is not ambiguous but ambivalent use of language that characterizes Ibn Khaldûn. As a jurist who is also a littérateur, he does not employ a technical term out of context; rather he applies a concept to fit the argument at hand. As miriam cooke has observed, for Ibn Khaldûn "a word used metaphorically may convey the meaning more clearly than a conventional word, because it conveys itself and also a 'possible consequence,' i.e., the double/multiple level of meaning prized by writers."[18] The same may be said of his coining of new terms. He coins new terms like *ʿaṣabîyah* or *ʿumrân* or *badâwah* with a specific range of meanings, one of which may be to amplify the notion of a known word, as *ʿaṣabîyah* deftly does with the juridical concept of consensus.

Reliance on metaphor also allows Ibn Khaldûn to demonstrate how the same word, like the same event or person, can be viewed differently over time, and also from different places in the same

---

[16] Moḥammed Talbi, *Ibn Khaldûn: Sa Vie—Son Oeuvre* (Tunis: Maison Tunisienne de l'Edition, 1973), 44.

[17] Jon W. Anderson, "Conjuring with Ibn Khaldûn," in Lawrence, *Ibn Khaldûn and Islamic Ideology,* 120.

[18] cooke, "Ibn Khaldûn and Language," 36n.27.

time frame. Perhaps the most crucial argument that Ibn Khaldûn makes on behalf of history as an Islamic science is that historians alone among Muslim scientists can explain how Islam arose out of a context of orality and nomadism/primitivism (*badâwah*) to become a proponent of both writing and civilization (*ḥaḍârah*). What had been speech and a habit became writing and a craft.[19] Yet the very lifeline of Islam depended on maintaining the connection between literacy and orality, between writing and speech, as also between civilized and nomad. In short, analogy, while it had its most immediate application in law, could, and should, also be applied to the understanding of the laws of history—above all, the history of Muslim civilization.

> Now, when speech was a habit of those who used it [the pagan Arabs and early Muslims], these (linguistic matters) were neither sciences nor norms. At that time, jurists did not need them, because linguistic matters were familiar to them by natural habit. But when the habit of the Arabic language was lost, the experts who made it their speciality determined it once and for all with the help of a sound tradition and of sound rules of *analogy* they evolved. (Linguistic matters) thus became sciences the jurists had to master, in order to know the divine laws. (347–48; emphasis added)

Analogy applied to history is not the same as analogy applied to law, however. The strategy of one science is imported to the practice of another. It is crucial to understand how the connection emerged and developed in Ibn Khaldûn's imagination, for the same term when used in divergent contexts also embraces new connotations.

Put differently, new connotations require new facts which analogy itself cannot provide. On this point Ibn Khaldûn is clear,

---

[19] It may be confusing to speak of writing as a craft when the sciences include the sciences linked to the Arabic language—grammar, lexicography, syntax, style, and criticism as well as literature. But Ibn Khaldûn's unwavering criterion is manual labor, so that both the art of writing and book production are listed as crafts (chap. 5, pp. 327–28), while not only medieval Arabic language but also Qur'ânic Arabic (Muḍar), South Arabian Arabic (Himyarite), and Spanish Arabic are treated, along with poetry and the distinction between poetry and prose, in chapter 6 as instances of scientific production.

though his clarity as a historian has always to be qualified by his status as a jurist. As he writes in chapter 6,

> the meanings of words cannot be established by analogy, if their usage is not known, although, for jurists, their usage may be known by virtue of (the existence of) an inclusive (concept) that attests to the applicability of (a wider meaning) to the first (word). . . . (This is so) only because the use of analogy (in this case) is attested by the religious law, which deduces the soundness of (the application of) analogy (in this case) from the (general norms) on which it is based. *We do not have anything like it in lexicography.* There, only the intellect can be used, which means (relying on) judgment. . . . It should not be thought that the establishment of word meanings falls under the category of word definitions. A definition indicates (the meaning of) a given idea by showing that the meaning of an unknown and obscure word is identical with the meaning of a clear and well-known word. Lexicography, on the other hand, affirms that such-and-such a word is used to express such-and-such an idea. The difference here is very clear.[20]

What Ibn Khaldûn is explaining comes closest to what modern linguists call the distinction between stipulative and conventional definitions. Elsewhere, Ibn Khaldûn notes that "knowledge of the conventional meanings in general is not sufficient for [jurisprudence]."[21] Lexical or conventional definitions link a specific word to a known idea, creating synonyms within a familiar realm of limited association, while stipulative or juridical definitions take an unknown and obscure word and link it to the meaning of a clear and well-known word, enlarging the connotative range of the latter while adding heuristic value to the former because of its novelty. While the difference is far from clear to most people, it is both clear and compelling to Ibn Khaldûn: stipulative definitions become the hallmark of his new science.

---

[20] Rosenthal, *The Muqaddimah,* 3:331–32 (emphasis added). The connection between 'aṣabîyah (group feeling) and ijmâ' (consensus) discussed earlier relies on just this distinction: ijmâ' is not identical with 'aṣabîyah, yet 'aṣabîyah in Ibn Khaldûn's use of the word does convey the force of ijmâ'.

[21] Rosenthal, *The Muqaddimah,* 3:26.

The key strategy for students of Ibn Khaldûn is always and every-where to recall that he is at once a jurist and a littérateur. His move to the latter, as in the above excerpt, does not falsify his standing in the former. He is not trying to undercut the Islamic juridical tra-dition or to disparage the history of Muslim civilization. He is try-ing to forge a new science that at once makes Islamic law more ex-pansive and Muslim civilization more resilient, at the same time that it foregrounds him as the interpreter who facilitates and pro-tects both!

Having followed the linguistic turn in juridical logic outlined in chapter 6, we can now return to the beginning of the *Muqaddimah*. The major lexical term is *khabar*, or Event. Ibn Khaldûn already highlights it in the full title for the larger book to which the *Mu-qaddimah* was intended as an introduction (though chapter 1 was later incorporated along with the introduction into what now ap-pears as the *Muqaddimah*).[22] The crucial comparison is Event to Tradition. Trained as a jurist, Ibn Khaldûn understood both the importance of Tradition and the danger of generalizing its usage. While it was impossible for him to write the history of Islam with-out attention to the religious sciences, he also deemed it impossi-ble to do justice to the scope and depth of Muslim civilization if re-stricted to the religious sciences.

Ibn Khaldûn strove to be different, to be a man of his times and more: to grasp a point of balance or measurement (*mi'yâr*) be-tween the norms of belief, religion, and law (*da'wah*) and the demands of state, science, and practical reason (*dawlah*). In schematizing his view of history, he relied on observation and ar-gumentation to offset a blind acceptance of stories, even those that could be confirmed by a 'sound' chain of transmitters. He used the methodology of Tradition scholars but did not accept its claim to be universal in scope. To the claims of Tradition he counter-posed Event, the sort of evidence that can be proven or disproven by independent inquiry.

The term Event, however, is itself open to qualification. In Arabic, the full title of *Kitâb al-'Ibar* reads: *Kitâb al-'ibar wa-dîwân al-mubtada' wa-l-khabar fî ayyâm al-'Arab wal-'Ajam wal-Barbar wa-man*

22 See Rosenthal, translator's introduction to *The Muqaddimah*, 1:lxviii, for an ex-planation of how the original introduction and chapter 1 of the *Kitâb al-'Ibar* (*History*) became one book, known collectively as *The Muqaddimah*.

'asarahum min dhawî as-sultân al-akbar. In translation the title becomes: *The Book of Lessons and Archive of Early and Subsequent History, Dealing with Political Events Concerning Arabs, non-Arabs, and Berbers, and with Their Contemporary Supreme Rulers.* If Ibn Khaldûn hopes to offer *'ibar* (instructions or lessons), their content revolves around understanding Event. What is *dîwân al-mubtada' wa-l-khabar*? They are the bookends of history, the beginning and the end, with *khabar* having a multilayered meaning. It is both Event and outcome or sequel. Given Ibn Khaldûn's disposition to use linguistics in the service of his new science, *al-mubtada' wa-l-khabar* are framed as grammatical terms, specifically, the subject and the predicate, that is the beginning and the sequel or end, of a nominal sentence. The subject becomes the early conditions, or first instances, of social organization, namely, *badâwah* or desert civilization, which sets the stage for what follows it, namely, the emergence of world civilization (*'umrân*) through sedentary or urban civilization. From the very title of *Kitâb al-'Ibar, khabar* becomes the key word, or signifier, the cipher, for what will be the showcase of his new science, namely, the interplay of oral and written, primitive and cosmopolitan, Arab and non-Arab, in the making of oecumenical or world civilization. *Khabar* is at once Event, sequel, outcome, civilization.

At the same time, however, Event retains another, more juridically weighted meaning. Event is integral to Tradition scholarship but as a subsidiary link: Events were the accounts of the persons whose integrity was being reviewed in order to verify or disqualify what they reported as Tradition. For Ibn Khaldûn, the grammatical and juridical meanings of Event expand into something more vital and visionary: the surplus of labor, but also of thought, that produces a model of civilization across time and space. The linchpin to transforming Event into this new conceptual domain was *mutâbaqa,* or conformity. Even while eschewing the idea that all forms are external, Ibn Khaldûn did believe in conformity, namely, the correspondence between what one remembered as Event and historical reports of what others witnessed as Event.

Methodologically, the passage linking Tradition to Event while also distinguishing between them is the most crucial one in the *Muqaddimah.* It occurs at the outset of chapter 1, where Ibn Khaldûn sets forth the criteria of assessment for his own historical project. Here he pits knowledge of the nature of civilization against criticism of the personalities of transmitters. It is a double move: he is not saying that the appraisal or criticism of the personalities of transmitters is invalid or useless, but he is saying that its use should be limited to norms and values. While crucial to laying out a religious system, it cannot, and should not, guide historical inquiry.

Though Rosenthal's translation is apt, it is best comprehended within the larger argument about the rules of scholarly inquiry that separate law from history, Tradition from Event:

> Personality criticism is taken into consideration *only* in connection with the soundness (or lack of soundness) of Muslim religious information. . . . [For Events, by contrast,] a requirement to consider is the conformity (or lack of conformity of the reported information with general conditions). . . . [And so] the correct notion about something that *ought to be* [*inshâ'*] can [only] be derived from (personality criticism), while the correct notion about something that *was* [*khabar*] can [and should] be derived from (personality criticism) and external (evidence) by (checking) the conformity (of the historical report with general conditions).[23]

The difficulty of this passage is precisely its pithy understatement. At first glance, it seems to be just a matter of tenses, the shift between subjunctive (normative) and indicative (past/present/future). The Moroccan historian Abdallah Laroui has provided a straightforward translation that reflects this level of reading: "The normative draws its sense solely from itself, while the account, which is indicative, draws its sense both from itself and from an ex-

---

[23] Rosenthal, *The Muqaddimah*, 1:76–77 (emphasis added). "Personality criticism" is Rosenthal's choice to define the subdiscipline of *ḥadîth* scholarship known as *'ilm al-jarḥ wal-ta'dîl*. Ibn Khaldûn provides perhaps his best explanation of this term in examining the appeal of the Mahdî among the Fâṭimids by surveying all the *ḥadîth* relating to the Mahdî. In introducing this long and often convoluted section (51) of chapter 3, he notes that "*ḥadîth* scholars acknowledge negative criticism [of the personalities of *ḥadîth* transmitters] to have precedence over positive criticism" ['*inda ahl al-ḥadîth anna al-jarḥ muqaddamun 'alâ al-ta'dîl*] (Rosenthal, *The Muqaddimah*, 2:158). The one exception, of course, is the *Saḥîḥayn*, the two *Ṣaḥîḥs* of al-Bukhârî and Muslim, which, though still open to criticism, are considered to be at a different, higher order of soundness than other Sunni collections.

ternal fact which corresponds to it." Laroui is condensing the earlier, more complex analysis of another North African historian, the Tunisian Moḥammed Talbi. Talbi, like Laroui, agrees that this passage is the decisive methodological statement in the entire *Muqaddimah*. Yet Talbi explains the intricacy of this phrase as turning on a linguistic usage, in this case not grammatical but rhetorical. "Arab rhetoricians," observes Talbi, "divide language into two categories: *inshâ'* and *khabar*. What is prescribed as a norm or Tradition (*inshâ'*) cannot be qualified with any other datum: it functions as a command or a query, while Event (*khabar*) is open to either confirmation, qualification, or refutation by other sources both internal and external to itself."[24]

For Talbi, the introduction of *inshâ'* as Tradition is yet another application of analogy by Ibn Khaldûn. In other words, its rhetorical use is extended to a new field of inquiry, the demarcation of historical inquiry from juridical investigation. Since no scholar before Ibn Khaldûn had summarized the process of *ḥadîth* verification as *inshâ'*, its use here stamps Ibn Khaldûn as radically different; it demarcates his new science from the efforts of all his predecessors. But precisely because neither the dyad of Tradition/Event nor its importance will be transparent to nonspecialists reading the *Muqaddimah*, it seems necessary to frame the context in which this crucial use of analogy takes place.

The practice of law depends on the soundness of characters in the chain of transmitters. The core methodology for juridical scholars is the integrity or soundness of those who claim to have received the report of an esteemed person, in this case, the Prophet Muḥammad, whose words and deeds become the Sunnah, or model for Islamic law, during all the successive generations of devout Muslims. To understand the centrality of Tradition studies, one need only consider the commendation of Tradition offered by Shah Wali Allah Dihlawi, one of its most renowned and cosmopolitan advocates:

> There is no way for us to obtain knowledge of the divine laws . . . except through the report of the Prophet. . . . There

[24] For Abdallah Laroui, see *Islam et l'Histoire* (Paris: Flammarion, 1999), 144n.11. Moḥammed Talbi's *Ibn Khaldûn: Sa Vie—Son Oeuvre* (see note 16) remains one of the outstanding introductory books on the distinctive terminology and the even more distinctive historical vision of Ibn Khaldûn. The quotation here is taken from page 33, note 1.

is also no way for us to have knowledge of the sayings of the Prophet . . . , except by receiving reports which go back to him by successive links and transmission, whether they are in his words; or they are interrupted Traditions whose transmission was verified by a group of the Companions and the Successors . . . and in our time there is no way to receive these reports except to follow the literature written in the science of Tradition.[25]

Even though the author of this passage lived in the eighteenth century, 300 years after Ibn Khaldûn, he was reflecting a comparable worldview. Observance of the law was the backbone of collective Muslim life. Jurists had to make decisions based on Islamic principles, and those revolved around a double axis: the Messenger and the Message, the Prophet and the Qur'ân, each reinforcing the other, but with different textual domains. While the Qur'ân exceeds 6,600 verses, most Muslim jurists and scholars agree that only some 500 verses have a legal content. Though these verses, often quite long, do provide elements for a coherent legal system, they need to be supplemented in a society based on divine law. And so the locus of attention became the vast legacy of attributions to the Prophet. Collecting, verifying, and systematizing Traditions occupied enormous scholarly labor in the aftermath of the rapid expansion, then consolidation of an Islamic polity.

Among the four schools of Sunni jurisprudence that evolved, the eponymous founder of one, Aḥmad ibn Ḥanbal, was renowned for both his knowledge of Tradition and his skill in applying Tradition to the demands of jurisprudence. Once, we are told, Aḥmad ibn Ḥanbal was asked how many Traditions a scholar needed to know in order to give a *fatwa*, or authoritative legal opinion. His response was 300,000–500,000![26] Even if we were to accept the middle figure of 400,000 Traditions as the baseline of knowledge requisite for juridical scholars issuing *fatwas*, the dedication to Tradition dwarfs the attention to Qur'ânic data, despite the towering importance of the latter.

---

[25] Marcia K. Hermansen, trans., *The Conclusive Argument from God: Shah Wali Allah of Delhi's "Hujjat Allah al-Baligha"* (Leiden: E. J. Brill, 1995), 387.
[26] Ibid., 445.

Perhaps even more daunting than the task of mastering Tradition was the subsidiary task of winnowing out the true from the false. By the third century after the *hijrah* (exodus),[27] the tracing of *isnâd*, or chains of transmission, had become a fixed part of Islamic legal training. One book catalogs all the various categories of malfeasants who make up Traditions. They range from atheists and heretics to outright falsifiers of Traditions, including those who would invent Traditions in order to embellish religious stories they told in mosques and hence collect larger donations from gullible believers![28]

In order to establish his new science, Ibn Khaldûn the jurist had to both affirm his own practice of Tradition criticism[29] while also allowing for another way to approach human social organization, which for him is the basis of global or world civilization (*'umrân al-'âlam*). Hence it is crucial to understand how his forensic skill as a littérateur allowed him to cite Event, itself an ancillary part of Tradition scholarship, as an independent term conveying the surplus of meaning that he wanted to impart to the study of human social organization or the history of world civilization. Demarcating Tradition from Event, while affirming both, became the pathway to his new science.

As crucial as is the distinction between Tradition and Event, it is important not to overanalyze Ibn Khaldûn's motives for invoking, then pursuing this distinction. Was he smuggling philosophical reason into the domain of law and history? Was he a secularist undermining transcendental absolutes with pragmatic alternatives? Was he a crypto-Sufi jurist offsetting external formalism with internal dynamism? Even while all these speculations have circulated about Ibn Khaldûn, their confirmation, or disavowal, depends on

[27] That is, the exodus of the Prophet Muḥammad from Mecca to Medina, due to the threats on his life, and those of his followers, from hostile Quraysh. It occurred in 622 C.E. and became the baseline for measuring years and centuries in the lunar, or Islamic, calendar.

[28] Farhat J. Ziadeh, "Integrity ('*Adalah*) in Classical Islamic Law," quoting al-Busti, *Kitâb al-majrûḥîn*, in *Islamic Law and Jurisprudence: Studies in Honor of Farhat J. Ziadeh*, ed. Nicholas Heer (Seattle: University of Washington Press, 1990), 89.

[29] *Ḥadîth* criticism is in effect the science of personality criticism ('*ilm al-jarḥ wal-ta'dîl*), as explained *supra* in note 23. Though introduced at the outset of Book One of *Kitâb al-'Ibar* (see p. 35n.1), it is not fully explained till much later, requiring the reader to make explicit the connection that is left implicit by Ibn Khaldûn.

a prior question: what difference did Ibn Khaldûn project between himself and most of his predecessors as well as his contemporaries? Above all, he was a littérateur cast as a jurist. His novelty was linguistic: (a) to use old terms in new ways and (b) to introduce new terms that might reflect the deeper layers of actual experience. He remained engaged by dyads or binary expressions of major phenomena, even as he often invoked dyads in order to qualify or even invert them. The intricate relationship of crafts to sciences, earlier discussed, is but one major instance of dyadic logic pushed to new limits. Crafts are a crucial category, related to custom yet different from it. Crafts, like custom, may be practiced everyday, but the former are also marked as intrinsically useful. They are indispensable to science and the sciences, even when the latter seem to distance themselves from their material origins. In the same way, Ibn Khaldûn seems to privilege writing over orality when, toward the end of chapter 5, he asserts that "writing is the most useful craft" (331). Writing allows for calculation and scientific inquiry. It permits one to move over the range of symbols. It makes possible "the habit of intellection" (332). Because writing emerges at the core of urban cosmopolitan life, it, rather than poetry or oral communication, would seem to be the centerpiece of world civilization. Yet poetry remains a desideratum at the heart of sedentary culture, and the final sections of the final chapter (6.51–59) of the *Muqaddimah* are devoted to extolling the benefits, and clarifying the challenge, of poetry for city dwellers, whether they be Arabs or non-Arabs.

No one will ever know the full set of conversations between Ibn Khaldûn and Tamerlane.[30] Addicted, as both were, to debate and argumentation, they must have discussed the nature of dynastic power, the collective urge to control (*'aṣabîyah*), and also the relationship between primitive/nomadic life (*badâwah*) and the demands of urban civilization (*ḥaḍârah*). Samarqand and the splen-

---

[30] Fischel, *Ibn Khaldûn and Tamerlane*, 29–48, provides an English translation of Ibn Khaldûn's summary accounts of his meetings with Timur, but they are clearly just that, summaries, at the same time that the larger report to which they allude was cast in the form of a letter to the Marinid ruler, Abu Sa'id, of Fez, and so are designed to please, or at least not alarm, the ruler of the region where Ibn Khaldûn's closest personal and professional ties remained till the end of his life (Fischel, *Ibn Khaldûn and Tamerlane*, 110–12n.199–201).

dors of its courtly life remain the legacy of Timur's cultural sophistication and organizational prowess; the *Muqaddimah* and, in its shadow, *Kitâb al-'Ibar* remain the legacy of Ibn Khaldûn's juridically inspired and linguistically channeled genius.[31] If you cannot travel to Samarqand, you can read the *Muqaddimah*. In it you will discover the marvel of a civilizational vision that exceeds both time and space, precisely because it is so attentive to each.

[31] The modern Syrian playwright Sa'dallah Wannus imagines a parallel declaration from Ibn Khaldûn, though his is penned as a retort by Ibn Khaldûn to one of his students (Sharaf ad-dîn) who is critical of his collaboration with Tamerlane: "History will not remember except the science which I have created and the book which I have written" (Sa'dallah Wannus, "Munamnamât tâ'rîkhîyah," [Historical Miniatures] in *Al-a'mâl al-kâmilah* [Damascus: Ahâli, 1996], 418).

FROM THE TRANSLATOR'S INTRODUCTION
TO THE 1958 UNABRIDGED EDITION

(1) The first complete translation of the *Muqaddimah* ever pub lished was a Turkish version. In the year 1730 Pirizade Effendi (1674–1749) translated the *Muqaddimah* from the beginning through the fifth chapter. This Turkish text was published in Cairo in 1275 [1859],[1] in a lithographed edition of 617 pages in large format; the translation ended on p. 522. On the remaining pages, the work was completed by a reproduction of the Arabic text based on the first Bulaq edition. A few pages on Ibn Khaldûn's life serve as introduction, compiled by Ahmet Jevdet Effendi, later Pasha (1822–95). The latter also translated the remaining sixth chapter of the *Muqaddimah*, which was published in Istanbul in 1277 [1860/61],[2] accompanied by copious explanatory notes.

(2) A complete French translation, under the title of *Pro-légomènes historiques d' Ibn Khaldoun*, was published by William MacGuckin de Slane on the basis of Quatremère's edition and with comparison of the Paris manuscripts used by Quatremère, the first Bulaq edition, and the Turkish translation (in part). The three volumes appeared in Paris in the years 1862, 1865, and 1868, as Vols. XIX to XXI of the *Notices et Extraits des manuscrits de la Bibliothèque Impériale*.

De Slane did an altogether admirable job of presenting a highly readable and, in the main, accurate translation of the work. The

Excerpted from pages cvii to cxv of Franz Rosenthal's introduction to *The Mu-qaddimah: An Introduction to History*, by Ibn Khaldûn (3 vols., Pantheon Books, 1958). Where the Rosenthal's introduction cross-referenced portions of text not included in the present edition, a clarification has been given in square brackets. In addition, the original footnotes 153 to 165 have been renumbered 1 to 13 for ease of reading.

[1] F. Babinger, *Die Geschichtsschreiber der Osmanen*, pp. 282 f., mentions an edition (Bulaq, 1274) of 626 pp. I have no further information about it. M. Mostafa Ziada refers to a Turkish translation of the *Muqaddimah* made for Muḥammad 'Alî of Egypt [?]. Cf. *Middle Eastern Affairs*, IV (1953), 267.

[2] According to Babinger, this is the third volume of a complete edition of the Turkish translation, begun in 1275 [1858/59]. I am familiar only with the volume containing the sixth chapter. For the work on the *'Ibar* by 'Abd-al-Laṭîf Ṣubḥî Pasha (1818–1886), published in Istanbul in 1276 [1859/60], cf. Babinger, pp. 368–70.

"freedom" of his version has often been unjustly censured, for it was intentional, and a "free" translation is perfectly legitimate for a work with the stylistic character of the *Muqaddimah*. There are occasional mistakes of translation, some of them caused by the difficulty of the subject matter and the language, others of a sort that might easily have been avoided. Explanatory footnotes are sparse, and de Slane usually did not bother to indicate the sources for his statements. However, the concluding words of R. Dozy's review of de Slane's work still stand: "Rarely has so difficult a book been translated so well."[3]

A photomechanical reproduction of de Slane's translation was published in Paris in 1934–38, with a brief preface by G. Bouthoul. Important corrections to the translation were provided by R. Dozy in the review by him which appeared in *Journal asiatique*, XIV[6] (1869), 133–218. More recently, a number of valuable corrections were published by A. Bombaci, "Postille alla traduzione De Slane della *Muqaddimah* di Ibn Ḫaldûn," in *Annali dell' Istituto Universitario Orientale di Napoli*, N.S. III (1949), 439–72.

For many years after the publication of de Slane's translation, scholars, almost to a man, relied on it for their quotations from the *Muqaddimah*. The occasional exceptions have been noted in footnotes to this translation at the appropriate passages. Only in recent years have fresh translations of comparatively large sections of the *Muqaddimah* begun to be made.[4]

(3) In English, there are a few brief passages in R. A. Nicholson, *Translations of Eastern Poetry and Prose* (Cambridge, 1922). Recently, a rather large selection of brief excerpts was published by Charles Issawi, under the title of *An Arab Philosophy of History* (London, 1950).

(4) The book by Erwin Rosenthal, entitled *Ibn Khalduns Gedanken über den Staat* (Munich and Berlin, 1932), consists largely of excerpts from the *Muqaddimah*, in German translation. A large volume of selections in German translation was published by A. Schimmel in Tübingen in 1951, under the title of *Ibn Chaldun: Ausgewählte Abschnitte aus der muqaddima*.

(5) A short selection of Arabic passages with accompanying

---

[3] In *Journal asiatique*, XIV[6] (1869), 218.
[4] For early partial translations, see [Rosenthal, translator's introduction to *The Muqaddimah*, 1:c].

French translation was published by G. Surdon and L. Bercher under the title of *Recueil de textes de sociologie et de droit public musulman contenus dans les "Prolégomènes" d' Ibn Khaldoun*, "Bibliothèque de l'Institut d'Etudes Supérieures Islamiques d'Alger," No. 6 (Algiers, 1951). The translators profess their particular concern for bringing out the basically juridical flavor of Ibn Khaldûn's terminology.

THE PRESENT TRANSLATION

A work such as the *Muqaddimah*, modern in thought yet alien in language and style, may be presented to the modern reader in one of three ways. It may be translated as literally as the second language permits. The translator may go farther and use modern phraseology and style. Or, finally, the work may be recast and given the form it would have had it been written by a contemporary author in the second language.

If a translation is to impress the modern reader with the full worth and significance of the original, the last-mentioned approach would seem to be the ideal one. Realizing this, scholars have frequently chosen to publish selected and rearranged passages of the *Muqaddimah*. However, a complete rewriting in this manner, besides being hardly practicable, would almost necessarily produce a subjective interpretation of the *Muqaddimah*, and thereby obscure Ibn Khaldûn's thought.

The second approach to translation was what de Slane attempted. It, too, has pitfalls. One is the danger of distorting the author's ideas by modernizing them, and thereby attributing to him thoughts that were utterly foreign to him. Moreover, a work dealing with a great variety of subjects, and the *Muqaddimah* is certainly such a work, depends to a great extent in its formal and intellectual organization upon the threads of association that the author's particular terminology and way of expression provide.

The drawback of any completely literal translation is obvious: it may easily be incomprehensible to the general reader. Further, a literal translation often entirely perverts the literary character of the original. It is transformed from a literary product using the normal and accepted forms of its own language into a work rendered strained and unnatural by not conforming to the style of the language into which it was translated.

The present translation was begun in the belief that a mixture of the literal and modernizing types of rendering would produce the most acceptable result. Yet, it must be confessed that with each successive revision, the translator has felt an irresistible urge to follow ever more faithfully the linguistic form of the original.

The literalness of the present version is intended to reduce to a minimum the amount of interpretation always necessary in any translation. The reader unfamiliar with the Arabic original ought to be encumbered by no more than an unavoidable minimum of subjective interpretation. Moreover, Ibn Khaldûn's particular terminology, which he evolved with great pains for his "new science," had to be preserved as far as possible; to some degree, it must have impressed his contemporary readers as unusual. Therefore, at least the outstanding terms, such as 'umrân, 'aṣabîyah, badâwah, were preserved in the translation by rather artificial loan renderings ("civilization," "group spirit," "desert life or attitude"). This involved the occasional occurrence of expressions such as "large civilization." But any other procedure would irrevocably have destroyed the essential unity of Ibn Khaldûn's work, which is one of its main claims to greatness.[5] For the sake of literalness, an attempt has been made to translate passages that are repeated in the original, in identical or nearly identical words, in the same fashion each time. However, since such repetitions occur frequently in the text of the Muqaddimah, the attempt probably remained unsuccessful, or, at best, only partly successful. Some modernizing tendency remains in the translation but it chiefly affects syntactical and stylistic features, and only very rarely the vocabulary.

Ibn Khaldûn's contemporaries praised the literary quality of the Muqaddimah highly. Ibn Khaldûn himself, in a poetical dedication of his History, used rather exuberant language in speaking of the linguistic perfection of his work:

---

[5] It seems regrettable, and in some ways definitely misleading, that it was not possible to give a uniform translation to such commonly used words as nasab "descent, pedigree, lineage, family," sirr "secret," fann "branch," and many others. In quite a few cases, as, for instance, in the case of sulṭân "government, authority, ruler, Sultan," it may seem advisable to add the Arabic at each occurrence. I decided against such a procedure, and only very rarely will the reader find an Arabic word added in brackets in the text of the translation.

I tamed rude speech. It may be said that
Refractory language becomes in (my work)
amenable to the words I utter.[6]

This self-praise was, of course, a routine authors had to follow in
the past when the advertising methods of the modern publishing
business were as yet unknown. But others chimed in with their
praise. The style of the *Muqaddimah* was said to be "more brilliant
than well-strung pearls and finer than water fanned by the zephyr."
It was called a "Jâḥiẓian" style, reminiscent of the verbal fireworks
of al-Jâḥiẓ, the celebrated model of good Arabic style.[7] All these
testimonies may have been rather perfunctory; still, they certainly
have some basis in fact. It is true, as has often been remarked, that
Ibn Khaldûn did not always adhere strictly to the accepted norms
and rules of classical Arabic, which were artificial to him and remote from the speech habits of his time. But Ibn Khaldûn's long,
rolling, involved sentences, his skillful and yet restrained application of rhetorical figures, and his precise use of a large, though not
farfetched, vocabulary make it indeed a pleasure to read the
Muqaddimah, or to hear it read aloud.[8]

However, the modern translator's agreement with such positive
appraisals of the linguistic and stylistic qualities of the *Muqaddimah*
is somewhat forced. For, alas! all the factors that enhance the
beauty of the work in its original language and justified the admiration of Ibn Khaldûn's contemporaries, are so many thorns in the
translator's flesh. His long sentences have constantly to be broken
up into smaller units, and the cohesiveness of the author's style is
thereby loosened. In keeping with a common stylistic feature of
Arabic speech, Ibn Khaldûn could repeat pronouns through
whole pages, thus confronting his translator with the task of sup-
plying the appropriate nouns. Ibn Khaldûn also was extremely
fond of a threefold *parallelismus membrorum*, another source of em-
barrassment to the translator. The ordinary twofold parallelism,
well known from the Bible, is difficult enough to translate, an imitation of the threefold one practically impossible. Sometimes, one
word or phrase may do as a translation of all three members, but

---

[6] Cf. *Autobiography*, p. 240, l. 10.
[7] Cf. F. Rosenthal, *A History of Muslim Historiography*, p. 419 (n. 7).
[8] See [Rosenthal, translator's introduction to *The Muqaddimah*, 1.lxviii f.]

more often than not, the threefold parallelism can only be broken up into seemingly redundant phrases. Another stylistic feature is a kind of inversion by means of which later elements of a story are given first, and the earlier elements are given later, in a sentence introduced by "after." This can be brilliant in Arabic but is most often unpalatable in modern English translation (although it would have been somewhat more acceptable in another age, in the eighteenth century, for instance).

The large number of parentheses (in the translation) is the result of the need for clarifying stylistic changes. These parentheses have been used in order to indicate to the reader that in these passages the translator has added something that is not literally found in the Arabic text. They may be disregarded, and the text enclosed by them should be considered an integral part of the context. In a few cases, however, the words in parentheses serve another purpose, namely, that of explaining the preceding words.

In the choice of explanatory footnotes the translator has more leeway. Ibn Khaldûn's own ideas and the way he expressed them offer no particular difficulties to the understanding. But the numerous passages where technical details are discussed or earlier authors are quoted sorely try the translator's knowledge of words and things. Incidentally, Ibn Khaldûn himself is on record as admitting that he did not quite understand the text he copied [at 2:224 and 3:183 of the 3-volume unabridged edition]. Like many other Arabic works, the *Muqaddimah* contains some passages where it obviously was much easier for the author to copy his source than it is for the translator to find out the meaning of the text copied. In general, where the translator has succeeded in understanding Ibn Khaldûn's text correctly, very little in the way of added explanation is necessary.

However, historical understanding and interpretation of the work pose greater problems. The *Muqaddimah* was composed nearly at the end of the intellectual development of medieval Islam, and the work covers practically all its aspects. A well-nigh incalculable number of notes and excursuses would be required if one were to comment on the historical significance of Ibn Khaldûn's statements and put each of them in proper perspective. Nearly a century ago de Slane felt that he could provide unlimited notes and explanations to his translation (cf. his introduction, p.

ii), but he refrained from doing so for the sake of brevity. In the end, he did very little indeed in the way of annotation.[9] Since his time, the material that has a sound claim to consideration in the notes has grown immeasurably. A hundred years ago, very few printed Arabic texts existed, and nearly all the pertinent information was still buried in manuscripts. Even nowadays, when a good part of Arabic literature has become available in printed form, it is often necessary, in connection with the *Muqaddimah*, to refer to manuscripts. In fact, our knowledge has outgrown the stage where the historical problems of a work like the *Muqaddimah*, considered in its entirety, can be elucidated by means of footnotes. The important task of interpretation must be left to monographs on individual sections of the text, a scholarly labor that has been attempted so far only on a very small scale.[10] In the notes to this translation, the major problem has been one of selection, that of providing references that give the fullest possible information in easily accessible form.

In some respects, it has been possible to be briefer than de Slane. Nowadays, many of Ibn Khaldûn's examples from political history no longer require comment, nor, from the point of view of modern historiography and sociology, does the acceptability of Ibn Khaldûn's historical interpretations have to be argued.[11]

A reference to C. Brockelmann, *Geschichte der arabischen Literatur*, where authors and works of literature are concerned, makes it possible to dispense with further references, save, perhaps, for very recent bibliographical material, which has been carefully examined before inclusion. The *Encyclopaedia of Islam* and that splendid time-saving tool, the *Concordance et Indices de la tradition musulmane*, were also, in many cases, considered sufficient as guides to further study.

---

[9] See p. [xxviii], above.

[10] Cf., for instance, the article by Renaud quoted [in vol. 3], n. 616 to Ch. VI. For earlier attempts in this direction by S. van den Bergh, J.-D. Luciani, and H. Frank, see nn. 1, 263, and 454 to Ch. VI.

[11] The total number of "mistakes" of one kind or another in the *Muqaddimah* is astonishingly small. Vico's *La scienza nuova*, by comparison, is full of wrong and outdated statements; cf. the translation by T. G. Bergin and M. H. Fisch (Ithaca, N. Y., 1948), p. VIII. Naturally, Vico was handicapped by his age's predilection for learned information. The desire to show off one's learning led to committing many blunders, but also prepared the soil for a tremendous growth of true learning, such as the prudent and staid civilization of Ibn Khaldûn would never have contemplated.

Apart from obvious references of this kind, and a certain amount of necessary philological comment,[12] the selection of notes has been guided by one dominant consideration. Works that Ibn Khaldûn himself knew, knew about, or may reasonably be supposed to have known or known about, have been emphasized. Knowledge of Ibn Khaldûn's sources is of immeasurable assistance in better understanding his historical position and significance. While a very small start in this direction could be made in the footnotes to this translation, I am convinced that this kind of comment should be given preference over any other.

When I had completed my version, I compared it with the previous translations as carefully as possible, giving particular attention to de Slane's. I have not considered it necessary to acknowledge de Slane's help whenever I have corrected mistakes of my own. Nor have I felt it necessary to signal passages where I think de Slane erred. The reader ignorant of Arabic may be slightly puzzled when he observes the divergencies, often considerable, between this translation and that of de Slane. Nonetheless, my hope is that he will put greater reliance in the present translation, although its recent origin, of course, is no guarantee of its correctness.

Rendering proper names is a minor problem in all translations from the Arabic, as here. Arabic proper names can easily be transcribed, and the method of transcription employed here needs no special comment. However, foreign proper names, and especially place names in northwestern Africa (the Maghrib), make for complications. European place names, Spanish ones most notably, have been translated into their accepted English or current native form. Place names from the East are given in transcription, except when a generally accepted English form exists. There may, however, be differences of opinion as to what constitutes a generally accepted English form. Thus, some of the proper names as well as generally known Arabic terms retained in the translation have been deprived of their macrons or circumflexes, while others, with perhaps an equal claim to such distinction, have been left untouched; as a rule, preference has been given to accurate transcription. With a very few exceptions, place names from north-

---

[12] Variant readings of the MSS have, however, not been indicated with any degree of consistency. Cf. [Rosenthal, translator's introduction to *The Muqaddimah*, 1:lxxxix].

western Africa have been given in what may be considered the most widely used and acceptable of the various French forms; usually, a transcription of the Arabic form has been added. In the case of Berber names, we will know how Ibn Khaldûn pronounced them, once a study of the manuscripts of the *'Ibar* has been made. For the time being, we know his pronunciation only in those cases where the manuscripts of the *Muqaddimah* and the *Autobiography* indicate it, and his pronunciation has, of course, been followed. In modern scholarly literature, there seems to be little agreement on the finer points of the transcription of ancient Berber tribal and personal names.

Much more might be said about technical details arising out of the present translation. However, if they were wrongly handled, mere knowledge of that fact would not repair the harm done to, nor, if they were correctly applied, increase by itself the usefulness of, the translation of what has been called with little, if any, exaggeration, "undoubtedly the greatest work of its kind that has ever yet been created by any mind in any time or place."[13]

---

[13] A. J. Toynbee, *A Study of History* (2d ed.; London, 1935), III, 322.

THE MUQADDIMAH

The Introduction and Book One
of the World History, entitled
Kitâb al-'Ibar
of Ibn Khaldûn

IN THE NAME OF GOD, THE COMPASSIONATE, THE MERCIFUL. PRAY, O GOD, FOR OUR MASTER MUḤAMMAD, HIS FAMILY, AND THE MEN AROUND HIM

The Servant of God who needs the mercy of God who is so rich in His kindness, 'Abd-ar-Raḥmân b. Muḥammad b. Khaldûn al-Ḥaḍramî—God give him success!—says:

Praised be God! He is powerful and mighty. In His hand, He holds royal authority and kingship. His are the most beautiful names and attributes. His knowledge is such that nothing, be it revealed in secret whispering or left unsaid, remains strange to Him. His power is such that nothing in heaven or on earth is too much for Him or escapes Him.

He created us from the earth as living, breathing creatures. He made us to settle on it as races and nations. From it, He gave us sustenance and provisions.

Our mothers' wombs, and then houses, are our abode. Sustenance and food keep us alive. Time wears us out. Our lives' final terms, the dates of which have been fixed for us in the Book (of Destiny), claim us. But He lasts and endures. He is the Living One who does not die.

Prayer and blessings upon our Lord and Master, Muḥammad, the Arab prophet, whom Torah and Gospel have mentioned and described; for whose birth the world that is was already in labour before Sundays followed upon Saturdays in regular sequence and before Saturn and Behemoth had become separated; to whose truthfulness pigeon and spider bore witness.

Prayer and blessings also upon his family and the men around him who, by being his companions and followers, gained wide influence and fame, and who by supporting him found unity while their enemies were weakened through dispersion. Pray, O God, for him and them, for as long as Islam shall continue to enjoy its lucky fortune and the frayed rope of unbelief shall remain cut! Manifold blessings upon them all!

FOREWORD

History is a discipline widely cultivated among nations and races. It is eagerly sought after. The men in the street, the ordinary people, aspire to know it. Kings and leaders vie for it.

Both the learned and the ignorant are able to understand it. For on the surface history is no more than information about political events, dynasties, and occurrences of the remote past, elegantly presented and spiced with proverbs. It serves to entertain large, crowded gatherings and brings to us an understanding of human affairs. It shows how changing conditions affected (human affairs), how certain dynasties came to occupy an ever wider space in the world, and how they settled the earth until they heard the call and their time was up.

The inner meaning of history, on the other hand, involves speculation and an attempt to get at the truth, subtle explanation of the causes and origins of existing things, and deep knowledge of the how and why of events. History, therefore, is firmly rooted in philosophy. It deserves to be accounted a branch of it.

The outstanding Muslim historians made exhaustive collections of historical events and wrote them down in book form. But, then, persons who had no right to occupy themselves with history introduced into those books untrue gossip which they had thought up or freely invented, as well as false, discredited reports which they had made up or embellished. Many of their successors followed in their steps and passed that information on to us as they had heard it. They did not look for, or pay any attention to, the causes of events and conditions, nor did they eliminate or reject nonsensical stories.

Little effort is being made to get at the truth. The critical eye, as a rule, is not sharp. Errors and unfounded assumptions are closely allied and familiar elements in historical information. Blind trust in tradition is an inherited trait in human beings. Occupation with the (scholarly) disciplines on the part of those who have no genuine claim to them is widespread. But the pasture of stupidity is unwholesome for mankind. No one can stand up against the authority of truth, and the evil of falsehood is to be fought with enlightening speculation. The reporter merely dictates and passes on (the material). It takes critical insight to sort out the hidden truth; it takes knowledge to lay truth bare and polish it so that critical insight may be applied to it.

Many systematic historical works have been composed, and the history of nations and dynasties in the world has been compiled and written down. But there are very few historians who have become so well known as to be recognized as authorities, and who have replaced the products of their predecessors by their own works. They

5

can almost be counted on the fingers. There are, for instance, Ibn Isḥâq;[1] aṭ-Ṭabarî;[2] Ibn al-Kalbî;[3] Muḥammad b. 'Umar al-Wâqidî;[4] Sayf b. 'Umar al-Asadî;[5] al-Mas'ûdî;[6] and other famous historians who are distinguished from the general run.

It is well known to competent persons and reliable experts that the works of al-Mas'ûdî and al-Wâqidî are suspect and objectionable in certain respects. However, their works have been distinguished by universal acceptance of the information they contain and by adoption of their methods and their presentation of material. The discerning critic is his own judge as to which part of their material he finds spurious, and which he gives credence to. Civilization, in its different conditions, contains different elements to which historical information may be related and with which reports and historical material may be checked.

Most of the histories by these authors cover everything because of the universal geographical extension of the two earliest Islamic dynasties[7] and because of the very wide selection of sources of which they did or did not make use. Some of these authors, such as al-Mas'ûdî and historians of his type, gave an exhaustive history of pre-Islamic dynasties and nations and other affairs in general. Some later historians, on the other hand, showed a tendency towards greater restriction, hesitating to be so general and comprehensive. They brought together the happenings of their own period and gave exhaustive historical information about their own part of the world. They restricted themselves to the history of their own dynasties and cities. This was done by Ibn Ḥayyân, the historian of Spain and the Spanish Umayyads,[8] and by Ibn ar-Raqîq, the historian of Ifrîqiyah[9] and the dynasty in Kairouan (al-Qayrawân).[10]

The later historians were all tradition-bound and dull of nature and intelligence, or did not try to avoid being dull. They merely copied their predecessors and followed their example. They disregarded the changes in conditions and in the customs of nations and

---

[1] Muḥammad b. Isḥâq, author of the famous biography (sîrah) of Muhammad. He died in 150 or 151 [A.D. 767/68].
[2] Muḥammad b. Jarîr, author of the Annals, 224/25–310 [839–923].
[3] Hishâm b. Muḥammad, d. 204 or 206 [819/20 or 821/22].
[4] The biographer of Muḥammad and historian of early Islam, 130–207 [747–823].
[5] He died in 180 [796/97].
[6] 'Alî b. al-Ḥusayn, d. 345 or 346 [956 or 957].
[7] The Umayyads and the 'Abbâsids.
[8] Ḥayyân b. Khalaf, 377–469 [987/88–1076].
[9] Ifrîqiyah reflects the name of the Roman province of Africa. This geographical term is commonly used by Ibn Khaldûn and has been retained in the translation.
[10] Ibrâhîm b. al-Qâsim, who lived ca. A.D. 1000.

races that the passing of time had brought about. Thus, they presented historical information about dynasties and stories of events from the earliest times as mere forms without substance, blades without scabbards; as knowledge that must be considered ignorance, because it is not known what of it is extraneous and what is genuine. It concerns happenings, the origins of which are not known. It concerns species, the genera of which are not taken into consideration, and whose specific differences are not verified. They neglected the importance of change over the generations in their treatment of (historical material), because they had no one who could interpret it for them. Their works, therefore, give no explanation for it. When they then turn to the description of a particular dynasty, they report the historical information parrot-like and take care to preserve it as it had been passed down to them, whether imaginary or true. They do not turn to the beginning of the dynasty. Nor do they tell why it unfurled its banner and was able to give prominence to its emblem, or what caused it to come to a stop when it had reached its term. The student, thus, has still to search for the beginnings of conditions and for (the principles of) organization adopted by the various dynasties. He must himself inquire.why the various dynasties brought pressure to bear upon each other and why they succeeded each other. He must search for a convincing explanation of the elements that made for mutual separation or contact among the dynasties. All this will be dealt with in the Introduction to this work.

Other historians, then, came with too brief a presentation. They went to the extreme of being satisfied with the names of kings, without any genealogical or historical information, and with only a numerical indication of the length of their reigns. This was done by Ibn Rashîq in the *Mîzân al-'amal*,[1] and by those lost sheep who followed his method. No credence can be given to what they say. They are not considered trustworthy, nor is their material considered worthy of transmission, for they caused useful material to be lost and damaged the methods and customs acknowledged to be sound and practical by historians.

When I had read the works of others and probed into the recesses of yesterday and today, I shook myself out of that drowsy complacency and sleepiness. Although not much of a writer, I exhibited my own literary ability as well as I could, and, thus, composed a book on history. In this book I lifted the veil from conditions as they arose in the various generations. I arranged it methodically in chapters dealing with historical facts and reflections. In it I showed how and why dynasties and civilization originated. I based the work on the history of the two races that constitute the population of the

[1] Ḥasan b. Rashîq, 390 to 456 or 463 [1000 to 1064 or 1070/71].

Maghrib at this time and people its various regions and cities, and on that of their ruling houses, both long- and short-lived, including the rulers and allies they had in the past. These two races are the Arabs and the Berbers. They are the two races known to have resided in the Maghrib for such a long time that one can hardly imagine they ever lived elsewhere, for its inhabitants know no other human races.

I corrected the contents of the work carefully and presented it to the judgment of scholars and the elite. I followed an unusual method of arrangement and division into chapters. From the various possibilities, I chose a remarkable and original method. In the work, I commented on civilization, on urbanization, and on the essential characteristics of human social organization, in a way that explains to the reader how and why things are as they are, and shows him how the men who constituted a dynasty first came upon the historical scene. As a result, he will wash his hands of any blind trust in tradition. He will become aware of the conditions of periods and races that were before his time and that will obtain thereafter.

I divided the work into an introduction and three books:

The Introduction deals with the great merit of historiography, offers an appreciation of its various methods, and cites historians' errors.

The First Book deals with civilization and its essential characteristics, namely, royal authority, government, gainful occupations, ways of making a living, crafts, and sciences, as well as with the causes and reasons thereof.

The Second Book deals with the history, races, and dynasties of the Arabs, from the beginning of creation down to this time. This will include references to such famous nations and dynasties contemporaneous with them, as the Nabataeans, the Syrians, the Persians, the Israelites, the Copts, the Greeks, the Byzantines, and the Turks.

The Third Book deals with the history of the Berbers and of the Zanâtah who are part of them; with their origins and races; and, in particular, with the royal houses and dynasties of the Maghrib.

Later on, there was my trip to the East, to seek the manifold illumination it offers and to fulfil the religious duty and custom of circumambulating the Ka'bah and visiting Medina, as well as to study the systematic works on history. As a result, I was able to fill the gaps in my historical information about the non-Arab (Persian) rulers of those lands, and about the Turkish dynasties in the regions over which they ruled. I added this information to what I had written here. I inserted it into the treatment of the nations of the various districts and rulers of the various cities and regions that were contemporary with those races. In this connection I was brief and

8

concise and preferred the easy goal to the difficult one. I proceeded from genealogical tables to detailed historical information. Thus, this work contains an exhaustive history of the world. It forces stubborn stray wisdom to return to the fold. It gives causes and reasons for happenings in the various dynasties. It turns out to be a vessel for philosophy, a receptacle for historical knowledge. The work contains the history of the Arabs and the Berbers, both the sedentary groups and the nomads. It also contains references to the great dynasties that were contemporary with them, and, moreover, clearly points out memorable lessons to be learned from early conditions and from subsequent history. Therefore, I called the work 'Book of Lessons and Archive of Early and Subsequent History, Dealing with the Political Events concerning the Arabs, Non-Arabs, and Berbers, and the Supreme Rulers who were Contemporary with them.'

I omitted nothing concerning the origin of races and dynasties, the synchronism of the earliest nations, the reasons for change and variation in past periods and within religious groups; also concerning dynasties and religious groups, towns and hamlets, strength and humiliation, large numbers and small numbers, sciences and crafts, gains and losses, changing general conditions, nomadic and sedentary life, actual events and future events—all things expected to occur in civilization. I treated everything comprehensively and exhaustively and explained the arguments and reasons for its existence.

As a result, this book has become unique, as it contains unusual knowledge and familiar if hidden wisdom. Still, after all has been said, I am conscious of imperfections when I look at the work of scholars past and present. I confess my inability to penetrate so difficult a subject. I wish that men of scholarly competence and wide knowledge would look at the book with a critical, rather than a complacent eye, and silently correct and overlook the mistakes they come upon. The capital of knowledge that an individual scholar has to offer is small. Admission (of one's shortcomings) saves from censure. Kindness from colleagues is hoped for. It is God whom I ask to make our deeds acceptable in His sight. He is a good protector.

THE INTRODUCTION

The excellence of historiography. An appreciation of the various approaches to history. A glimpse of the different kinds of errors to which historians are liable. Why these errors occur.

It should be known that history is a discipline that has a great number of approaches. Its useful aspects are very many. Its goal is distinguished.

History makes us acquainted with the conditions of past nations as they are reflected in their national character. It makes us acquainted with the biographies of the prophets and with the dynasties and policies of rulers. Whoever so desires may thus achieve the useful result of being able to imitate historical examples in religious and worldly matters.

The (writing of history) requires numerous sources and much varied knowledge. It also requires a good speculative mind and thoroughness, which lead the historian to the truth and keep him from slips and errors. If he trusts historical information in its plain transmitted form and has no clear knowledge of the principles resulting from custom, the fundamental facts of politics, the nature of civilization, or the conditions governing human social organization, and if, furthermore, he does not evaluate remote or ancient material through comparison with near or contemporary material, he often cannot avoid stumbling and slipping and deviating from the path of truth. Historians, Qur'ân commentators and leading transmitters have committed frequent errors in the stories and events they reported. They accepted them in the plain transmitted form, without regard for its value. They did not check them with the principles underlying such historical situations, nor did they compare them with similar material. Also, they did not probe with the yardstick of philosophy, with the help of knowledge of the nature of things, or with the help of speculation and historical insight. Therefore, they strayed from the truth and found themselves lost in the desert of baseless assumptions and errors.

This is especially the case with figures, either of sums of money or of soldiers, whenever they occur in stories. They offer a good opportunity for false information and constitute a vehicle for nonsensical statements. They must be controlled and checked with the help of known fundamental facts.

For example, al-Mas'ûdî and many other historians report that Moses counted the army of the Israelites in the desert. He had all those able to carry arms, especially those twenty years and older, pass muster. There turned out to be 600,000 or more. In this connection, al-Mas'ûdî forgets to take into consideration whether Egypt and Syria could possibly have held such a number of soldiers. Every realm may have as large a militia as it can hold and support, but no more. This fact is attested by well-known customs and familiar conditions. Moreover, an army of this size cannot march or fight as a unit. The whole available territory would be too small for it. If it were in battle formation, it would extend two, three, or more times beyond the field of vision. How, then, could two such parties fight with each other, or one battle formation gain the upper hand when one flank does not know what the other flank is doing! The situation at the present day testifies to the correctness of this statement. The past resembles the future more than one drop of water another.

Furthermore, the realm of the Persians was much greater than that of the Israelites. This fact is attested by Nebuchadnezzar's victory over them. He swallowed up their country and gained complete control over it. He also destroyed Jerusalem, their religious and political capital. And he was merely one of the officials of the province of Fârs. It is said that he was the governor of the western border region. The Persian provinces of the two 'Irâqs,[1] Khurâsân, Transoxania, and the region of Derbend on the Caspian Sea were much larger than the realm of the Israelites. Yet, the Persian army did not attain such a number or even approach it. The greatest concentration of Persian troops, at al-Qâdisîyah, amounted to 120,000 men, all of whom had their retainers. This is according to Sayf, who said that with their retainers they amounted to over 200,000 persons. According to 'Â'ishah and az-Zuhrî, the troop concentration with which Rustum advanced against Sa'd at al-Qâdisîyah amounted to only 60,000 men, all of whom had their retainers.

Then, if the Israelites had really amounted to such a number, the extent of the area under their rule would have been larger, for the size of administrative units and provinces under a particular dynasty is in direct proportion to the size of its militia and the groups that support the dynasty. Now, it is well known that the territory of the Israelites did not comprise an area larger than the Jordan province and Palestine in Syria and the region of Medina and Khaybar in the Hijâz. Also, there were only three generations between Moses and Israel, according to the best-informed scholars. Moses was the son of Amram, the son of Kohath, the son of Levi, the son of Jacob who is Israel-Allâh. This is Moses' genealogy in the Torah.[2] The length of time between Israel and Moses was indicated by al-Mas'ûdî when

---

[1] That is, Mesopotamia and north-western Persia adjacent to it.

[2] Exod. 6: 16 ff.

he said: 'Israel entered Egypt with his children, the tribes, and their children, when they came to Joseph numbering seventy souls. The length of their stay in Egypt until they left with Moses for the desert was two hundred and twenty years. During those years, the kings of the Copts, the Pharaohs, passed them on (as their subjects) one to the other.' It is improbable that the descendants of one man could branch out into such a number within four generations.

It has been assumed that this number of soldiers applied to the time of Solomon and his successors. Again, this is improbable. Between Solomon and Israel, there were only eleven generations, that is: Solomon, the son of David, the son of Jesse, the son of Obed, the son of Boaz, the son of Salmon, the son of Nahshon, the son of Amminadab, the son of Ram, the son of Hezron, the son of Perez, the son of Judah, the son of Jacob. The descendants of one man in eleven generations would not branch out into such a number, as has been assumed. They might, indeed, reach hundreds or thousands. This often happens. But an increase beyond that to higher figures is improbable. Comparison with observable present-day and well-known nearby facts proves the assumption and report to be untrue. According to the definite statement of the Israelite stories,[1] Solomon's army amounted to 12,000 men, and his horses numbered 1,400, which were stabled at his palace. This is the correct information. No attention should be paid to nonsensical statements by the common run of informants. In the days of Solomon, the Israelite state saw its greatest flourishing and their realm its widest extension.

Whenever contemporaries speak about the dynastic armies of their own or recent times, and whenever they engage in discussions about Muslim or Christian soldiers, or when they get to figuring the tax revenues and the money spent by the government, the outlays of extravagant spenders, and the goods that rich and prosperous men have in stock, they are quite generally found to exaggerate, to go beyond the bounds of the ordinary, and to succumb to the temptation of sensationalism. When the officials in charge are questioned about their armies, when the goods and assets of wealthy people are assessed, and when the outlays of extravagant spenders are looked at in ordinary light, the figures will be found to amount to a tenth of what those people have said. The reason is simple. It is the common desire for sensationalism, the ease with which one may just mention a higher figure, and the disregard of reviewers and critics. This leads to failure to exercise self-criticism about one's errors and intentions, to demand from oneself moderation and fairness in reporting, to reapply oneself to study and research. Such historians let themselves

[1] Cf. I Kings 10: 26. As a rule, Muslim scholars gave an unpleasant connotation to the term 'Israelite stories', as mere fiction presented as history.

go and made a feast of untrue statements. 'They procure for themselves entertaining stories in order to lead others away from the path of God.'[1] This is a bad enough business.

It may be said that the increase of descendants to such a number would be prevented under ordinary conditions which, however, do not apply to the Israelites. The increase in their case would be a miracle in accordance with the tradition which said that one of the things revealed to their forefathers, the prophets Abraham, Isaac, and Jacob, was that God would cause their descendants to increase until they were more numerous than the stars of heaven and the pebbles of the earth. God fulfilled this promise to them as an act of divine grace bestowed upon them and as an extraordinary miracle in their favour. Thus, ordinary conditions could not hinder it and nobody should speak against it.

Someone might come out against this tradition with the argument that it occurs only in the Torah which, as is well known, was altered by the Jews. The reply to this argument would be that the statement concerning the alteration of the Torah by the Jews is unacceptable to thorough scholars and cannot be understood in its plain meaning, since custom prevents people who have a revealed religion from dealing with their divine scriptures in such a manner. Thus, the great increase in numbers in the case of the Israelites would be an extraordinary miracle. Custom, in the proper meaning of the word, would prevent anything of the sort from happening to other peoples.

It is true that a movement of (such a large group) would hardly be possible, but none took place, and there was no need for one. It is also true that each realm has only its particular number of militia. But the Israelites at first were no militiamen and had no dynasty. Their numbers increased that much, so that they could gain power over the land of Canaan which God had promised them and the territory of which He had purified for them. All these things are miracles. God guides to the truth.

The history of the Tubba's, the kings of the Yemen and of the Arabian Peninsula, as it is generally transmitted, is another example of silly statements by historians. It is said that from their home in the Yemen, the Tubba's used to raid Ifrîqiyah and the Berbers of the Maghrib. Afrîqus b. Qays b. Ṣayfî, one of their great early kings who lived in the time of Moses or somewhat earlier, is said to have raided Ifrîqiyah. He caused a great slaughter among the Berbers. He gave them the name of Berbers when he heard their jargon and asked what that barbarah was. This gave them the name which has remained with them since that time. When he left the Maghrib, he is said to have concentrated some Ḥimyar tribes there. They remained

[1] Qur'ân 31. 6 (5).

14

there and mixed with the native population. Their descendants are the Ṣinhâjah and the Kutâmah. This led aṭ-Ṭabarî, al-Mas'ûdî, and others to make the statement that the Ṣinhâjah and the Kutâmah belong to the Ḥimyar. The Berber genealogists do not admit this, and they are right. Al-Mas'ûdî also mentioned that one of the Ḥimyar kings after Afrîqus, Dhû l-Adh'âr, who lived in the time of Solomon, raided the Maghrib and forced it into submission. Something similar is mentioned by al-Mas'ûdî concerning his son and successor, Yâsir. He is said to have reached the Sand River in the Maghrib and to have been unable to find passage through it because of the great mass of sand. Therefore, he returned.

Likewise, it is said that the last Tubba', As'ad Abû Karib, who lived in the time of the Persian Kayyanid king Yastâsb, ruled over Mosul and Azerbaijan. He is said to have met and routed the Turks and to have caused a great slaughter among them. Then he raided them again a second and a third time. After that, he is said to have sent three of his sons on raids, (one) against the country of Fârs, one against the country of the Soghdians, one of the Turkish nations of Transoxania, and one against the country of the Rûm (Byzantines). The first brother took possession of the country up to Samarkand and crossed the desert into China. There, he found his second brother who had raided the Soghdians and had arrived in China before him. The two together caused a great slaughter in China and returned together with their booty. They left some Ḥimyar tribes in Tibet. They have been there down to this time. The third brother is said to have reached Constantinople. He laid siege to it and forced the country of the Rûm into submission. Then, he returned.

All this information is remote from the truth. It is rooted in baseless and erroneous assumptions. It is more like the fiction of storytellers. The realm of the Tubba's was restricted to the Arabian Peninsula. Their home and seat was Ṣan'â' in the Yemen. The Arabian Peninsula is surrounded by the ocean on three sides: the Indian Ocean on the south, the Persian Gulf jutting out of the Indian Ocean to Baṣrah on the east, and the Red Sea jutting out of the Indian Ocean to Suez in Egypt on the west. This can be seen on the map. There is no way from the Yemen to the Maghrib except via Suez. The distance between the Red Sea and the Mediterranean is two days' journey or less. It is unlikely that the distance could be traversed by a great ruler with a large army unless he controlled that region. This, as a rule, is impossible. In that region there were the Amalekites and Canaan in Syria, and, in Egypt, the Copts. Later on, the Amalekites took possession of Egypt, and the Israelites of Syria. There is, however, no report that the Tubba's ever fought against one of these nations or that they had possession of any part of this region. Furthermore, the distance from the Yemen to the Maghrib is great, and an army requires much food and fodder. Soldiers travelling in regions other than their own have to requisition grain and livestock and to plunder the countries they pass through. As a rule, such a procedure does not yield enough food and fodder. On the other hand, if they attempted to take along enough provisions from their own region, they would not have enough animals for transportation. So, their whole line of march necessarily takes them through regions they must take possession of and force into submission in order to obtain provisions from them. Again, it would be a most unlikely and impossible assumption that such an army could pass through all those nations without disturbing them, obtaining its provisions by peaceful negotiation. This shows that all such information is silly or fictitious.

Mention of the allegedly impassable Sand River has never been heard in the Maghrib, although the Maghrib has often been crossed and its roads have been explored by travellers and raiders at all times and in every direction. Because of the unusual character of the story, there is much eagerness to pass it on.

With regard to the supposed raid of the Tubba's against the countries of the East and the land of the Turks, it must be admitted that the line of march in this case is wider than the (narrow) passage at Suez. The distance, however, is greater, and the Persian and Byzantine nations are interposed on the way to the Turks. There is no report that the Tubba's ever took possession of the countries of the Persians and Byzantines. They merely fought the Persians on the borders of the 'Irâq and of the Arab countries between al-Baḥrayn and al-Ḥîrah, which were border regions common to both nations.[1] It would, however, ordinarily have been impossible for the Tubba's to traverse the land of the Persians on their way to raid the countries of the Turks and Tibet, because of the nations that are interposed on the way to the Turks, because of the need for food and fodder, as well as the great distance, mentioned before. All information to this effect is silly and fictitious. Even if the way this information is transmitted were sound, the points mentioned would cast suspicion upon it. All the more then must the information be suspect since the manner in which it has been transmitted is not sound. In connection with Yathrib (Medina) and the Aws and Khazraj, Ibn Isḥâq says that the last Tubba' travelled eastward to the 'Irâq and Persia, but a raid by the Tubba's against the countries of the Turks and Tibet is in no way confirmed by the established facts. Assertions to this

[1] Al-Ḥîrah on the Euphrates was the capital of the Lakhmid buffer state under Persian control. Al-Baḥrayn (Bahrain) included the country on the north-western shore of the Persian Gulf, and not only the islands today known under that name.

effect should not be trusted; all such information should be investigated and checked with sound norms. The result will be that it will most beautifully be demolished.

Even more unlikely and more deeply rooted in baseless assumptions is the common interpretation of the following verse of the *Sûrat al-Fajr*: 'Did you not see what your Lord did with 'Âd—Iram, that of the pillars?'[1]

The commentators consider the word Iram the name of a city which is described as having pillars, that is, columns. They report that 'Âd b. 'Ûṣ b. Iram had two sons, Shadîd and Shaddâd, who ruled after him. Shadîd perished. Shaddâd became the sole ruler of the realm, and the kings there submitted to his authority. When Shaddâd heard a description of Paradise, he said: 'I shall build something like it.' And he built the city of Iram in the desert of Aden over a period of three hundred years. He himself lived nine hundred years. Iram is said to have been a large city, with castles of gold and silver and columns of emerald and hyacinth, containing all kinds of trees and freely-flowing rivers. When the construction of the city was completed, Shaddâd went there with the people of his realm. But when he was the distance of only one day and night away from it, God sent a clamour from heaven, and all of them perished. This is reported by aṭ-Ṭabarî, ath-Tha'âlibî, az-Zamakhsharî, and other Qur'ân commentators. They transmit the following story on the authority of one of the men around Muḥammad, 'Abdallâh b. Qilâbah. When he went out in search of some of his camels, he came upon the city and took away from it as much as he could carry. His story reached Mu'âwiyah, who had him brought to him, and he told the story. Mu'âwiyah sent for Ka'b al-aḥbâr and asked him about it. Ka'b said, 'It is Iram, that of the pillars. Iram will be entered in your time by a Muslim who is of a reddish, ruddy colour, and short, with a mole at his eyebrow and one on his neck, who goes out in search of some of his camels.' He then turned around and, seeing Ibn Qilâbah, he said: 'Indeed, he is that man.'

No information about this city has since become available anywhere on earth. The desert of Aden where the city is supposed to have been built lies in the middle of the Yemen. It has been inhabited continuously, and travellers and guides have explored its roads in every direction. Yet, no information about the city has been reported. No antiquarian, no nation has mentioned it. If (the Qur'ân commentators) said that it had disappeared like other antiquities, the story would be more likely, but they expressly say that it still exists. Some identify it with Damascus, because Damascus was in the

[1] Qur'ân 89. 6–7 (5–6).

possession of the people of 'Âd. Others go so far in their crazy talk as to maintain that the city lies hidden from sensual perception and can be discovered only by trained magicians and sorcerers. All these are assumptions that would better be termed nonsense.

All these suggestions proffered by Qur'ân commentators were the result of grammatical considerations, for Arabic grammar requires the expression, 'that of the pillars', to be an attribute of Iram. The word 'pillars' was understood to mean columns. Thus, Iram was narrowed down in its meaning to some sort of building. (The commentators) were influenced in their interpretation by the reading of Ibn az-Zubayr who read a genitive construction: 'Âd of Iram. They then adopted these stories, which are better called fictitious fables.

In fact, however, the 'pillars' are tent poles. If 'columns' were intended by the word, it would not be far-fetched, as the power of (the people of 'Âd) was well known, and they could be described as people with buildings and columns in the general way. But it would be far-fetched to say that a special building in one or another specific city (was intended). If it is a genitive construction, as would be the case according to the reading of Ibn az-Zubayr, it would be a genitive construction used to express tribal relationships, such as, for instance, the Quraysh of Kinânah, or the Ilyâs of Muḍar, or the Rabî'ah of Nizâr. There is no need for such an implausible interpretation which uses for its starting point silly stories of the sort mentioned, which cannot be imputed to the Qur'ân because they are so implausible.

Another fictitious story of the historians, which they all report, concerns the reason for ar-Rashîd's destruction of the Barmecides. It is the story of al-'Abbâsah, ar-Rashîd's sister, and Ja'far b. Yaḥyâ b. Khâlid, his minister. Ar-Rashîd is said to have worried about where to place them when he was drinking wine with them. He wanted to receive them together in his company. Therefore, he permitted them to conclude a marriage that was not consummated. Al-'Abbâsah then tricked Ja'far in her desire to be alone with him, for she had fallen in love with him. Ja'far finally had intercourse with her—it is assumed, when he was drunk—and she became pregnant. The story was reported to ar-Rashîd who flew into a rage.

This story is irreconcilable with al-'Abbâsah's position, her religiousness, her parentage, and her exalted rank. She was a descendant of 'Abdallâh b. 'Abbâs and separated from him by only four generations, and they were the most distinguished and greatest men in Islam after him. Al-'Abbâsah was the daughter of Muḥammad al-Mahdî, the son of Abû Ja'far 'Abdallâh al-Manṣûr, the son of Muḥammad as-Sajjâd, the son of the Father of the Caliphs 'Alî.

'Alî was the son of 'Abdallâh, the Interpreter of the Qur'ân, the son of the Prophet's uncle, al-'Abbâs. Al-'Abbâsah was the daughter of a caliph and the sister of a caliph. She was born to royal power, into the prophetical succession (the caliphate), and was descended from the men around Muḥammad and his uncles. She was connected by birth with the leadership of Islam, the light of the revelation, and the place where the angels descended to bring the revelation. She was close in time to the desert attitude of true Arabism, to that simple state of Islam still far from the habits of luxury and lush pastures of sin. Where should one look for chastity and modesty, if she did not possess them? Where could cleanliness and purity be found, if they no longer existed in her house? How could she link her pedigree with that of Ja'far b. Yaḥyâ and stain her Arab nobility with a Persian client? His Persian ancestor had been acquired as a slave, or taken as a client, by one of her ancestors, an uncle of the Prophet and noble Qurashite, and all Ja'far did was that he together with his father was drawn along (by the growing fame of) the 'Abbâsid dynasty and thus prepared for and elevated to a position of nobility. And how could it be that ar-Rashîd, with his high-mindedness and great pride, would permit himself to become related by marriage to Persian clients! If a critical person looks at this story in all fairness and compares al-'Abbâsah with the daughter of a great ruler of his own time, he must find it disgusting and unbelievable that she could have done such a thing with one of the clients of her dynasty and while her family was in power. He would insist that the story be considered untrue. And who could compare with al-'Abbâsah and ar-Rashîd in dignity!

The reason for the destruction of the Barmecides was their attempt to gain control over the dynasty and their retention of the tax revenues. This went so far that when ar-Rashîd wanted even a little money, he could not get it. They took his affairs out of his hands and shared with him in his authority. He had no say with them in the affairs of his realm. Their influence grew, and their fame spread. They filled the positions and ranks of the government with their own children and creatures who became high officials, and thus barred all others from the positions of wazir, secretary, army commander, doorkeeper, and from the military and civilian administration. It is said that in the palace of ar-Rashîd, there were twenty-five high officials, both military and civilian, all children of Yaḥyâ b. Khâlid. There, they crowded the people of the dynasty and pushed them out by force. They could do that because of the position of their father, Yaḥyâ, mentor to Hârûn both as crown prince and as caliph. Hârûn practically grew up in his lap and got all his education from him. Hârûn let him handle his affairs and used to call him 'father'. As a result, the Barmecides, and not the government, wielded all the

19

influence. Their presumption grew. Their position became more and more influential. They became the centre of attention. All obeyed them. All hopes were addressed to them. From the farthest borders, presents and gifts of rulers and amirs were sent to them. The tax money found its way into their treasury, to serve as an introduction to them and to procure their favour. They gave gifts to and bestowed favours upon the men of the Shī'ah and upon important relatives of the Prophet. They gave the poor from the noble families related to the Prophet something to earn. They freed the captives. Thus, they were given praise as was not given to their caliph. They showered privileges and gifts upon those who came to ask favours from them. They gained control over villages and estates in the open country and near the main cities in every province.

Eventually, the Barmecides irritated the inner circle. They caused resentment among the elite and aroused the displeasure of high officials. Jealousy and envy of all sorts began to show themselves, and the scorpions of intrigue crept into their soft beds in the government. The Qaḥṭabah family, Ja'far's maternal uncles, led the intrigues against them. Feelings for blood ties and relationship could not move or sway the Qaḥṭabahs from the envy which was so heavy on their hearts. This joined with their master's incipient jealousy, with his dislike of restrictions and high-handedness, and with his latent resentment aroused by small acts of presumptuousness on the part of the Barmecides. When they continued to flourish, as they did, they were led to gross insubordination.

Ja'far himself paved the way for his own and his family's undoing, which ended with the collapse of their exalted position, with the heavens falling in upon them and the earth's sinking with them and their house. Their days of glory became a thing of the past, an example to later generations.

Close examination of their story, scrutinizing the ways of government and their own conduct, discloses that all this was natural and is easily explained. One understands that it was only jealousy and struggle for control on the part of the caliph and his subordinates that killed them. Another factor was the verses that enemies of the Barmecides among the inner circle surreptitiously gave the singers to recite, with the intention that the caliph should hear them and his stored-up animosity against them be aroused. These are the verses:

> Would that Hind could fulfil her promise to us
> And deliver us from our predicament,
> And for once act on her own.
> The impotent person is he who never acts on his own.[1]

[1] The verses are by 'Umar b. Abî Rabî'ah who lived *ca.* A.D. 700.

When ar-Rashîd heard these verses, he exclaimed: 'Indeed, I am just such an impotent person.' By this and similar methods, the enemies of the Barmecides eventually succeeded in arousing ar-Rashîd's latent jealousy and in bringing his terrible vengeance upon them. God is our refuge from men's desire for power and from misfortune.

The stupid story of ar-Rashîd's winebibbing and his getting drunk in the company of boon companions is really abominable. It does not in the least agree with ar-Rashîd's attitude toward the fulfilment of the requirements of religion and justice incumbent upon caliphs. He consorted with religious scholars and saints. He wept when he heard their sermons. Then, there is his prayer in Mecca when he circumambulated the Ka'bah. He was pious, observed the times of prayer, and attended the morning prayer at its earliest hour. He used to go on raids (against unbelievers) one year and to make the pilgrimage to Mecca the next. He once rebuked his jester, Ibn Abî Maryam, who made an unseemly remark to him during prayer. When Ibn Abî Maryam heard ar-Rashîd recite: 'How is it that I should not worship Him who created me?'[1] he said: 'Indeed, I do not know why.' 'Jokes even at prayer?' he said. 'Beware, beware of the Qur'ân and Islam. Apart from that, you may do whatever you wish.'

Furthermore, ar-Rashîd possessed a good deal of learning and simplicity, because his epoch was close to that of his forebears who had those qualities. The time between him and his grandfather, al-Manṣûr, was not a long one. He was a young lad when al-Manṣûr died. Al-Manṣûr possessed a good deal of learning and religion.

His son, al-Mahdî, ar-Rashîd's father, experienced the austerity of al-Manṣûr, who would not use public funds to provide new clothes for his family. One day, al-Mahdî came to him when he was at his office discussing with the tailors the patching of his family's worn garments. Al-Mahdî did not relish that and said: 'O Commander of the Faithful, this year I shall pay for the family's clothes from my own income.' Al-Manṣûr's reply was: 'Do that.' He did not prevent him from paying himself but would not permit any public Muslim money to be spent for that purpose.

Ar-Rashîd was very close in time to that caliph and to his forebears. He was reared under the influence of such and similar conduct in his own family, so that it became his own nature. How could such a man have been a winebibber and have drunk wine openly? It is well known that noble pre-Islamic Arabs avoided wine. The vine was not one of the plants cultivated by them. Most of them considered it reprehensible to drink wine. Ar-Rashîd and his forebears

[1] Qur'ân 36. 22 (21).

21

were very successful in avoiding anything reprehensible in their religious or worldly affairs and in making all praiseworthy actions and qualities of perfection, as well as the aspirations of the Arabs, their own nature. . . .

It is a well-established fact that ar-Rashîd had consented to keep Abû Nuwâs[1] imprisoned until he repented and gave up his ways, because he had heard of the latter's excessive winebibbing. Ar-Rashîd used to drink a date liquor, according to the 'Irâqî legal school whose *responsa* (concerning the permissibility of that drink) are well known. But he cannot be suspected of having drunk pure wine. Silly reports to this effect cannot be credited. He was not the man to do something that is forbidden and considered by Muslims as one of the greatest of capital sins. Not one of (the early 'Abbâsids) had anything to do with effeminate prodigality or luxury in matters of clothing, jewellery, or the kind of food they took. They still retained the tough desert attitude and the simple state of Islam. Could it be assumed they would do something that would lead from the lawful to the unlawful and from the licit to the illicit? Historians such as aṭ-Ṭabarî, al-Mas'ûdî, and others are agreed that all the early Umayyad and 'Abbâsid caliphs used to ride out with only light silver ornamentation on their belts, swords, bridles, and saddles, and that the first caliph to originate riding out in golden apparel was al-Mu'tazz b. al-Mutawakkil, the eighth caliph after ar-Rashîd. The same applied to their clothing. Could one, then, assume any differently with regard to what they drank? This will become still clearer when the nature of dynastic beginnings in desert life and modest circumstances is understood. . . .

A current story explains how al-Ma'mûn came to be al-Ḥasan b. Sahl's son-in-law by marrying his daughter Bûrân. One night, on his rambles through the streets of Baghdad, al-Ma'mûn is said to have come upon a basket that was being let down from one of the roofs by means of pulleys and twisted cords of silk thread. He seated himself in the basket and grabbed the pulley, which started moving. He was taken up into a chamber of extraordinary magnificence. Then, a woman of uncommonly seductive beauty is said to have come out from behind curtains. She greeted al-Ma'mûn and invited him to keep her company. He drank wine with her the whole night long. In the morning he returned to his companions at the place where they had been awaiting him. He had fallen so much in love with the woman that he asked her father for her hand. How does all this accord with al-Ma'mûn's well-known religiosity and learning, his emulation of the way of life of his forefathers, the right-guided ('Abbâsid) caliphs, his adoption of the way of life of those pillars of

[1] Poet (d. A.D. 810).

22

Islam, the first four caliphs, his respect for religious scholars, or his observance in his prayers and legal practice of the norms established by God! How could it be correct that he would act like one of those wicked scoundrels who amuse themselves by rambling about at night, entering strange houses in the dark, and engaging in nocturnal trysts in the manner of Bedouin lovers! And how does that story fit with the position and noble character of al-Ḥasan b. Sahl's daughter, and with the firm morality and chastity that reigned in her father's house!

There are many such stories. They are always cropping up in the works of the historians. The incentive for inventing and reporting them shows a tendency to forbidden pleasures and for smearing the reputation of others. People justify their own subservience to pleasure by citing the supposed doings of men and women of the past. Therefore, they often appear very eager for such information and are alert to find it when they go through the pages of published works.

I once criticized a royal prince for being so eager to learn to sing and play the strings. I told him it was not a matter that should concern him and that it did not befit his position. He referred me to Ibrâhîm b. al-Mahdî[1] who was the leading musician and best singer of his time. I replied: 'For heaven's sake, why do you not rather follow the example of his father or his brother? Do you not see how that pursuit prevented Ibrâhîm from attaining their position?' The prince, however, was deaf to my criticism and turned away.

Further silly information is accepted by many historians. They do not care to consider the factual proofs and circumstantial evidence that require us to recognize that the contrary is true. . . .

Dynasty and government serve as the world's market-place, attracting to it the products of scholarship and craftsmanship alike. Wayward wisdom and forgotten lore turn up there. In this market stories are told and items of historical information are delivered. Whatever is in demand on this market is in general demand everywhere else. Now, whenever the established dynasty avoids injustice, prejudice, weakness, and double-dealing, with determination keeping to the right path and never swerving from it, the wares on its market are as pure silver and fine gold. However, when it is influenced by selfish interests and rivalries, or swayed by vendors of tyranny and dishonesty, the wares of its market-place become as dross and debased metals. The intelligent critic must judge for

[1] The son of the caliph al-Mahdî, who was for a short time considered by some groups as caliph. 162–224 [779–839].

himself as he looks around, examining this, admiring that, and choosing the other. . . .

Lengthy discussion of these mistakes has taken us rather far from the purpose of this work. However, many competent persons and expert historians slipped in connection with such stories and assertions, and they stuck in their minds. Many weak-minded and uncritical men learned these things from them, and even (competent historians) accepted them without critical investigation, and thus (strange stories) crept into their material. In consequence, historiography became nonsensical and confused, and its students fumbled around. Historiography came to be considered a domain of the common people. Therefore, today, the scholar in this field needs to know the principles of politics, the nature of things, and the differences among nations, places, and periods with regard to ways of life, character qualities, customs, sects, schools, and everything else. He further needs a comprehensive knowledge of present conditions in all these respects. He must compare similarities or differences between present and past conditions. He must know the causes of the similarities in certain cases and of the differences in others. He must be aware of the differing origins and beginnings of dynasties and religious groups, as well as of the reasons and incentives that brought them into being and the circumstances and history of the persons who supported them. His goal must be to have complete knowledge of the reasons for every happening, and to be acquainted with the origin of every event. Then, he must check transmitted information with the basic principles he knows. If it fulfils their requirements, it is sound. Otherwise, the historian must consider it as spurious and dispense with it. It was for this reason alone that historiography was highly esteemed by the ancients, so much so that aṭ-Ṭabarî, al-Bukhârî, and, before them, Ibn Isḥâq and other Muslim religious scholars, chose to occupy themselves with it. Most scholars, however, forgot this, the secret of historiography, with the result that it became a stupid occupation. Ordinary people as well as scholars who had no firm foundation of knowledge, considered it a simple matter to study and know history, to delve into it and sponge on it. Strays got into the flock, bits of shell were mixed with the nut, truth was adulterated with lies. 'The final outcome of things is up to God.'[1]

A hidden pitfall in historiography is disregard for the fact that conditions within nations and races change with the change of periods and the passage of time. This is a sore affliction and is deeply hidden, becoming noticeable only after a long time, so that rarely do more than a few individuals become aware of it.

[1] Qur'ân 31. 22 (21).

This is as follows. The condition of the world and of nations, their customs and sects, does not persist in the same form or in a constant manner. There are differences according to days and periods, and changes from one condition to another. Such is the case with individuals, times, and cities, and it likewise happens in connection with regions and districts, periods and dynasties.

The old Persian nations, the Syrians, the Nabataeans, the Tubba's, the Israelites, and the Copts, all once existed. They all had their own particular institutions in respect of dynastic and territorial arrangements, their own politics, crafts, languages, technical terminologies, as well as their own ways of dealing with their fellow men and handling their cultural institutions. Their historical relics testify to that. They were succeeded by the later Persians, the Byzantines, and the Arabs. The old institutions changed and former customs were transformed, either into something very similar, or into something distinct and altogether different. Then, there came Islam. Again, all institutions underwent another change, and for the most part assumed the forms that are still familiar at the present time as the result of their transmission from one generation to the next.

Then, the days of Arab rule were over. The early generations who had cemented Arab might and founded the realm of the Arabs were gone. Power was seized by others, by non-Arabs like the Turks in the east, the Berbers in the west, and the European Christians in the north. With their passing, entire nations ceased to exist, and institutions and customs changed. Their glory was forgotten, and their power no longer heeded.

The widely accepted reason for changes in institutions and customs is the fact that the customs of each race depend on the customs of its ruler. As the proverb says: 'The common people follow the religion of the ruler.'[1]

When politically ambitious men overcome the ruling dynasty and seize power, they inevitably have recourse to the customs of their predecessors and adopt most of them. At the same time, they do not neglect the customs of their own race. This leads to some discrepancies between the customs of the new ruling dynasty and the customs of the old race.

The new power, in turn, is taken over by another dynasty, and customs are further mixed with those of the new dynasty. More discrepancies come in, so that the contrast between the new dynasty and the first one is much greater than that between the second and the first one. Gradual increase in the degree of discrepancy continues. The eventual result is an altogether distinct (set of customs and

[1] *Dīn* 'religion' is here used in the more general sense of 'way of doing things'.

institutions). As long as there is this continued succession of different races to royal authority and government, changes in customs and institutions will not cease to occur.

Analogical reasoning and comparison are well known to human nature. They are not safe from error. Together with forgetfulness and negligence, they sway man from his purpose and divert him from his goal. Often, someone who has learned a good deal of past history remains unaware of the changes that conditions have undergone. Without a moment's hesitation, he applies his knowledge (of the present) to historical information, and measures such information by the things he has observed with his own eyes, although the difference between the two is great. Consequently, he falls into an abyss of error.

This may be illustrated by what the historians report concerning al-Ḥajjâj.[1] They state that his father was a schoolteacher. At the present time, teaching is a craft and serves to make a living. It is a far cry from the pride of group feeling. Teachers are weak, indigent, and rootless. Many weak professional men and artisans who work for a living aspire to positions for which they are not fit but which they believe to be within their reach. They are misled by their desires, a rope which often slips from their hands and precipitates them into the abyss of ruinous perdition. They do not realize that what they desire is impossible for men like them to attain. They do not realize that they are professional men and artisans who work for a living. And they do not know that at the beginning of Islam and under the (Umayyad and 'Abbâsid) dynasties, teaching was something different. Scholarship, in general, was not a craft in that period. Scholarship consisted of transmitting statements that people had heard the Lawgiver (Muḥammad) make. It was the teaching of religious matters that were not known, by way of oral transmission. Persons of noble descent and people who shared in the group feeling and directed the affairs of Islam were the ones who taught the Book of God and the Law of the Prophet, (and they did so) as one transmits traditions, not as one gives professional instruction. The Qur'ân was their Scripture, revealed to the Prophet in their midst. It constituted their guidance, and Islam was their religion, and for it they fought and died. It distinguished them from the other nations and ennobled them. They wished to teach it and make it understandable to the Muslims. They were not deterred by censure coming from pride, nor were they restrained by criticism coming from arrogance. This is attested by the fact that the Prophet sent the most important of the men around him with his embassies to the Arabs, in order to teach them the norms of Islam and the religious laws he brought.

[1] Al-Ḥajjâj b. Yûsuf, the great governor of 'Irâq (ca. 660–714).

He sent his ten Companions[1] and others after them on this mission.

Then, Islam became firmly established and securely rooted. Far-off nations accepted Islam at the hands of the Muslims. With the passing of time, the situation of Islam changed. Many new laws were evolved from the (basic) texts as the result of numerous and unending developments. A fixed norm was required to keep (the process) free from error. Scholarship came to be a habit. For its acquisition, study was required. Thus, scholarship developed into a craft and profession.

The men who controlled the group feeling now occupied themselves with directing the affairs of royal and governmental authority. The cultivation of scholarship was entrusted to others. Thus, scholarship became a profession that served to make a living. Men who lived in luxury and were in control of the government were too proud to do any teaching. Teaching came to be an occupation restricted to weak individuals. As a result, its practitioners came to be despised by the men who controlled the group feeling and the government.

Now, Yûsuf, the father of al-Ḥajjâj, was one of the lords and nobles of the Thaqîf, well known for their share in the Arab group feeling and for their rivalry with the nobility of the Quraysh. Al-Ḥajjâj's teaching of the Qur'ân was not the same as the teaching of the Qur'ân is at this time, namely, a profession that serves to make a living. His teaching was the kind practised at the beginning of Islam, and as we have just described.

Another illustration of the same (kind of error) is the baseless conclusion critical readers of historical works draw when they hear about the position of judges, leadership in war, and the command of armies that judges exercised. Their misguided thinking leads them to aspire to similar positions. They think that the office of judge at the present time is as important as it was formerly. When they hear that the father of Ibn Abî 'Âmir, who had complete control over Hishâm, and that the father of Ibn 'Abbâd, one of the rulers of Sevilla, were judges, they assume that they were like present-day judges. They are not aware of the change in customs that has affected the office of judge. Ibn Abî 'Âmir and Ibn 'Abbâd belonged to Arab tribes that supported the Umayyad dynasty in Spain and represented the group feeling of the Umayyads, and it is known how important their positions were. The leadership and royal authority they attained did not derive from the rank of the judgeship as such. In the ancient administrative organization, the office of judge was given by the dynasty and

[1] The 'asharah al-mubashsharah, the ten early Muslims to whom Paradise was guaranteed.

its clients to men who shared in the group feeling (of the dynasty), as is done in our age with the wazirate in the Maghrib. One has only to consider the fact that (in those days judges) accompanied the army on its summer campaigns and were entrusted with the most important affairs, such as are entrusted only to men who can command the group feeling needed for their execution.

Hearing such things, some people are misled and get the wrong idea about conditions. At the present time, weak-minded Spaniards are especially given to errors in this respect. The group feeling has been lost in their country for many years, as the result of the annihilation of the Arab dynasty in Spain and the emancipation of the Spaniards from the control of Berber group feeling. The Arab descent has been remembered, but the ability to gain power through group feeling and mutual co-operation has been lost. In fact, the (Spaniards) came to be like (passive) subjects, without any feeling for the obligation of mutual support. They were enslaved by tyranny and had become fond of humiliation, thinking that their descent, together with their share in the ruling dynasty, was the source of power and authority. Therefore, among them, professional men and artisans are to be found pursuing power and authority and eager to obtain them. On the other hand, those who have experience with tribal conditions, group feeling, and dynasties along the western shore, and who know how superiority is achieved among nations and tribal groups, will rarely make mistakes or give erroneous interpretations in this respect.

Another illustration of the same kind of error is the procedure historians follow when they mention the various dynasties and enumerate the rulers belonging to them. They mention the name of each ruler, his ancestors, his mother and father, his wives, his surname, his seal ring, his judge, doorkeeper, and wazir. In this respect, they blindly follow the tradition of the historians of the Umayyad and 'Abbâsid dynasties, without being aware of the purpose of those historians. Their predecessors wrote their histories for members of the ruling dynasty, whose children wanted to learn about the lives and circumstances of their ancestors, so that they might be able to follow in their steps and to do what they did, even down to such details as obtaining servants from among those who were left over from the previous dynasty and giving ranks and positions to the descendants of its servants and retainers. Judges, too, shared in the group feeling of the dynasty and enjoyed the same importance as wazirs, as we have just mentioned. Therefore, the historians of that time had to mention all these details.

Later on, however, various distinct dynasties made their appearance. The time intervals became longer and longer. Historical

28

interest now was concentrated on the rulers themselves and on the mutual relationships of the various dynasties in respect to power and predominance. (The problem now was) which nations could stand up (to the ruling dynasty) and which were too weak to do so. Therefore, it is pointless for an author of the present time to mention the sons and wives, the engraving on the seal ring, the surname, judge, wazir, and doorkeeper of an ancient dynasty, when he does not know the origin, descent, or circumstances of its members. Present-day authors mention all these things in mere blind imitation of former authors. They disregard the intentions of the former authors and forget to pay attention to historiography's purpose.

An exception are the wazirs who were very influential and whose historical importance overshadowed that of the rulers. Such wazirs as, for instance, al-Ḥajjâj, the Banû Muhallab, the Barmecides, the Banû Sahl b. Nawbakht, Kâfûr al-Ikhshîdî, Ibn Abî 'Âmir, and others should be mentioned. There is no objection to dealing with their lives or referring to their conditions for in importance they rank with the rulers.

An additional note to end this discussion may find its place here.

History refers to events that are peculiar to a particular age or race. Discussion of the general conditions of regions, races, and periods constitutes the historian's foundation. Most of his problems rest upon that foundation, and his historical information derives clarity from it. It forms the topic of special works, such as the *Murûj adh-dhahab* of al-Mas'ûdî. In this work, al-Mas'ûdî commented upon the conditions of nations and regions in the West and in the East during his period, the three hundred and thirties [the nine hundred and forties]. He mentioned their sects and customs. He described the various countries, mountains, oceans, provinces, and dynasties. He distinguished between Arab and non-Arab groups. His book, thus, became the basic reference work for historians, their principal source for verifying historical information.

Al-Mas'ûdî was succeeded by al-Bakrî,[1] who did something similar for routes and provinces, to the exclusion of everything else, because, in his time, not many transformations or great changes had occurred among the nations and races. However, at the present time—that is, at the end of the eighth [fourteenth] century—the situation in the Maghrib, as we can observe, has taken a turn and changed entirely. The Berbers, the original population of the Maghrib, have been

---

[1] The geographer, 'Abdallâh b. Muḥammad, 432–487 [1040/41–1094]. He is repeatedly quoted by Ibn Khaldûn. A new edition of al-Bakrî's geographical dictionary, *Mu'jam mâ sta'jam*, appeared in Cairo in 1945–51. His *Routes and Provinces* (*al-Masâlik wa-l-mamâlik*) is still unpublished except for some sections.

replaced by an influx of Arabs (that began in) the fifth [eleventh] century. The Arabs outnumbered and overpowered the Berbers, stripped them of most of their lands, and also obtained a share of those that remained in their possession. This was the situation until, in the middle of the eighth [fourteenth] century, civilization both in the East and the West was visited by a destructive plague which devastated nations and caused populations to vanish. It swallowed up many of the good things of civilization and wiped them out. It overtook dynasties at the time of their senility, when they had reached the limit of their duration. It lessened their power and curtailed their influence. It weakened their authority. Their situation approached the point of annihilation and dissolution. Civilization decreased with the decrease of mankind. Cities and buildings were laid waste, roads and way signs were obliterated, settlements and mansions became empty, dynasties and tribes grew weak. The entire inhabited world changed. The East, it seems, was similarly visited, though in accordance with and in proportion to (its more affluent) civilization. It was as if the voice of existence in the world had called out for oblivion and restriction, and the world had responded to its call. God inherits the earth and all who dwell upon it.

When there is a general change of conditions, it is as if the entire creation had changed and the whole world been altered, as if it were a new and repeated creation, a world brought into existence anew. Therefore, there is need at this time that someone should systematically set down the situation of the world among all regions and races, as well as the customs and sectarian beliefs that have changed for their adherents, doing for this age what al-Mas'ûdî did for his. This should be a model for future historians to follow. In this book of mine, I shall discuss as much of that as will be possible for me here in the Maghrib. I shall do so either explicitly or implicitly in connection with the history of the Maghrib, in conformity with my intention to restrict myself in this work to the Maghrib, the circumstances of its races and nations, and its subjects and dynasties, to the exclusion of any other region.[1] (This restriction is necessitated) by my lack of knowledge of conditions in the East and among its nations, and by the fact that secondhand information would not give the essential facts I am after. Al-Mas'ûdî's extensive travels in various countries enabled him to give a complete picture, as he mentioned in his work. Nevertheless, his discussion of conditions in the Maghrib is incomplete. God is the ultimate repository of all knowledge. Man is weak and deficient. Admission (of one's ignorance) is a specific (religious) duty. He whom God helps finds his way made easy and his

[1] Ibn Khaldûn soon changed his mind and added the history of the East to his work at a very early stage in its preparation.

efforts and quests successful. We seek God's help for the goal to which we aspire in this work. God gives guidance and help. He may be trusted.

It remains for us to explain the method of transcribing non-Arabic sounds whenever they occur in this book of ours:

It should be known that the letters (sounds)[1] of speech are modifications of sounds that come from the larynx. These modifications result from the fact that the sounds are broken up in contact with the uvula and the sides of the tongue in the throat, against the palate or the teeth, and also through contact with the lips. The sound is modified by the different ways in which such contact takes place. As a result, the sounds become distinct. Their combination constitutes the word that expresses what is in the mind.

Not all nations have the same sounds in their speech. One nation has sounds different from those of another. The sounds of the Arabic alphabet are twenty-eight, as is known. The Hebrews have sounds that are not to be found in our language. In our language, in turn, there are (sounds) that are not in theirs. The same applies to the European Christians, the Turks, the Berbers, and other non-Arabs.

In order to express their audible sounds, literate Arabs chose to use conventional letters written individually separate, such as ', b, j, r, ṭ, and so forth through all the twenty-eight letters. When they come upon a letter for which there is no phonetic equivalent in their language, it is not indicated in writing and not clearly expressed. Scribes sometimes express it by means of the letter which is closest to it in our language, the one either preceding or following it. This is not a satisfactory way of indicating a sound but a complete replacement of it.

Our book contains the history of the Berbers and other non-Arabs. In their names and in some of their words, we came across (sounds) that have no equivalents in our written language and conventional orthography. Therefore, we were forced to indicate such sounds (by special signs). As we said, we did not find it satisfactory to use the letters closest to them, because in our opinion this is not a satisfactory indication. In my book, therefore, I have chosen to represent such non-Arabic (sounds) in such a way as to indicate the two (sounds) closest to it, so that the reader may be able to pronounce it somewhere in the middle between the sounds represented by the two letters and thus reproduce it correctly.

I derived this idea from the way the Qur'ân scholars write sounds that are not sharply defined, such as occur, for instance, in aṣ-ṣirâṭ according to Khalaf's reading. The ṣ is to be pronounced somehow

[1] The written symbol is considered to be identical with the sound indicated by it.

between ꜱ and ẕ. In this case, they spell the word with ꜱ and write a ẕ into it. They thus indicate a pronunciation somewhere in the middle between the two sounds.

In the same way, I have indicated every letter that is to be pronounced somehow in the middle between two of our letters. The Berber *k*, for instance, which is pronounced midway between our clear *k* and *g* or *q*, as, for instance, in the name Buluggîn, is spelled by me with a *k* with the addition of one dot—from the *g* —below, or one dot or two—from the *q* on top of it. This indicates that the sound is to be pronounced midway between *k* and *g* or *q*. This sound occurs most frequently in the Berber language. In the other cases, I have spelled each sound that is to be pronounced midway between two sounds of our language, with a similar combination of two letters. The reader will thus know that it is an intermediate sound and pronounce it accordingly. In this way, we have indicated it satisfactorily.

God gives success.

BOOK ONE OF THE
KITÂB AL-'IBAR

The nature of civilization. Bedouin and
settled life, the achievement of superiority,
gainful occupations, ways of making a living,
sciences, crafts, and all the other things that
affect civilization.
The causes and reasons thereof

It should be known that history, in matter of fact, is information about human social organization, which itself is identical with world civilization. It deals with such conditions affecting the nature of civilization as, for instance, savagery and sociability, group feelings, and the different ways by which one group of human beings achieves superiority over another. It deals with royal authority and the dynasties that result in this manner and with the various ranks that exist within them. Also with the different kinds of gainful occupations and ways of making a living, with the sciences and crafts that human beings pursue as part of their activities and efforts, and with all the other institutions that originate in civilization through its very nature.

Untruth naturally afflicts historical information. There are various reasons that make this unavoidable. One of them is partisanship for opinions and schools. If the soul is impartial in receiving information, it devotes to that information the share of critical investigation the information deserves, and its truth or untruth thus becomes clear. However, if the soul is infected with partisanship for a particular opinion or sect, it accepts without a moment's hesitation the information that is agreeable to it. Prejudice and partisanship obscure the critical faculty and preclude critical investigation. The result is that falsehoods are accepted and transmitted.

Another reason making untruth unavoidable in historical information is reliance upon transmitters. Investigation of this subject belongs to (the discipline) of personality criticism.[1]

Another reason is unawareness of the purpose of an event. Many a transmitter does not know the real significance of his observations or of the things he has learned about orally. He transmits the information, attributing to it the significance he assumes or imagines it to have. The result is falsehood.

Another reason is unfounded assumption as to the truth of a thing. This is frequent. It results mostly from reliance upon transmitters.

Another reason is ignorance of how conditions conform with reality. Conditions are affected by ambiguities and artificial distortions. The informant reports the conditions as he saw them, but on account of artificial distortions he himself has no true picture of them.

[1] 'Personality criticism' (al-jarḥ wa-t-taʿdīl) is concerned with investigating the reliability or unreliability of the transmitters of traditions. Ibn Khaldûn often has occasion to refer to it.

Another reason is the fact that people as a rule approach great and high-ranking persons with praise and encomiums. They embellish conditions and spread their fame. The information made public in such cases is not truthful. Human souls long for praise, and people pay great attention to this world and the positions and wealth it offers. As a rule, they feel no desire for virtue and have no special interest in virtuous people.

Another reason making untruth unavoidable—and this one is more powerful than all the reasons previously mentioned—is ignorance of the nature of the various conditions arising in civilization. Every event (or phenomenon), whether (it comes about in connection with some) essence or (as the result of) action, must inevitably possess a nature peculiar to its essence as well as to the accidental conditions that may attach themselves to it. If the student knows the nature of events and the circumstances and requirements in the world of existence, it will help him to distinguish truth from untruth in investigating the historical information critically. This is more effective in critical investigation than any other aspect that may be brought up in connection with it.

Students often happen to accept and transmit absurd information that, in turn, is believed on their authority. Al-Mas'ûdî, for instance, reports such a story about Alexander. Sea monsters prevented Alexander from building Alexandria. He took a wooden container in which a glass box was inserted, and dived in it to the bottom of the sea. There he drew pictures of the devilish monsters he saw. He then had metal effigies of these animals made and set them up opposite the place where building was going on. When the monsters came out and saw the effigies, they fled. Alexander was thus able to complete the building of Alexandria.

It is a long story, made up of nonsensical elements which are absurd for various reasons. Thus, (Alexander is said) to have taken a glass box and braved the sea and its waves in person. Now, rulers would not take such a risk. Any ruler who would attempt such a thing would work his own undoing and provoke the outbreak of revolt against himself, and be replaced by the people with someone else. That would be his end. People would not wait one moment for him to return from the risk he is taking.

Furthermore, the jinn are not known to have specific forms and effigies. They are able to take on various forms. The story of the many heads they have is intended to indicate ugliness and frightfulness. It is not meant to be taken literally.

All this throws suspicion upon the story. Yet, the element in it that makes the story absurd for reasons based on the facts of existence is more convincing than all the other arguments. Were one to go down deep into the water, even in a box, one would have too little air for natural breathing. Because of that, one's spirit[1] would quickly become hot. Such a man would lack the cold air necessary to maintain a well-balanced humour of the lung and the vital spirit. He would perish on the spot. This is the reason why people perish in hot baths when cold air is denied to them. It also is the reason why people who go down into deep wells and dungeons perish when the air there becomes hot through putrefaction, and no winds enter those places to stir the air up. Those who go down there perish immediately. This also is why fish die when they leave the water, for the air is not sufficient for a fish to balance its lung. The fish is extremely hot, and the water to balance its humour is cold. The air into which the fish now comes is hot. Heat, thus, gains power over its animal spirit, and it perishes at once. This also is the reason for sudden death, and similar things.

Al-Mas'ûdî reports another absurd story, that of the Statue of the Starling in Rome. On a fixed day of the year, starlings gather at that statue bringing olives from which the inhabitants of Rome get their oil. How little this has to do with the natural procedure of getting oil!

Another absurd story is reported by al-Bakrî. It concerns the way the so-called 'Gate City' was built. That city had a circumference of more than a thirty days' journey and had ten thousand gates. Now, cities are used for security and protection. Such a city, however, could not be controlled and would offer no security or protection.

Then, there is also al-Mas'ûdî's story of the 'Copper City'. This is said to be a city built wholly of copper in the desert of Sijilmâsah which Mûsâ b. Nuṣayr[2] crossed on his raid against the Maghrib. The gates of this city are said to be closed. When the person who climbs its walls, in order to enter it, reaches the top, he claps his hands and throws himself down and never returns. All this is an absurd story. It belongs to the idle talk of storytellers. The desert of Sijilmâsah has been crossed by travellers and guides. They have not come across any information about such a city. All the details mentioned about it are absurd. They contradict the natural facts that apply to the building and planning of cities. Metal exists at best in quantities sufficient for utensils and furnishings. It is clearly absurd and unlikely that there would be enough to cover a city with it.

There are many similar things. Only knowledge of the nature of

[1] The 'vital spirit' which, according to Galenic and Muslim medicine, was believed to originate in the left cavity of the heart.
[2] The great general (A.D. 640–716/17) who completed the conquest of the Muslim West.

civilization makes critical investigation of them possible. It is the best and most reliable way to investigate historical information critically and to distinguish truth from falsehood. It is superior to investigations that rely upon criticism of the personalities of trans-mitters. Such personality criticism should not be resorted to until it has been ascertained whether a specific piece of information is in itself possible, or not. If it is absurd, there is no use engaging in personality criticism. Critical scholars consider absurdity inherent in the literal meaning of historical information, or an interpretation not acceptable to the intellect, as something that makes such information suspect. Personality criticism is taken into consideration only in con-nection with the soundness (or lack of soundness) of Muslim religious information, because this religious information mostly concerns in-junctions in accordance with which the Lawgiver (Muḥammad) enjoined Muslims to act whenever it can be presumed that the information is genuine. The way to achieve presumptive soundness is to ascertain the probity ('adâlah) and exactness of the transmitters.

On the other hand, to establish the truth and soundness of in-formation about factual happenings, a requirement to consider is the conformity (or lack of conformity of the reported information with general conditions). Therefore, it is necessary to investigate whether it is possible that the (reported facts) could have happened. This is more important than, and has priority over, personality criticism. For the correct notion about something that ought to be can be derived only from (personality criticism), while the correct notion about something that was can be derived from (personality criticism) and external (evidence) by (checking) the conformity (of the histori-cal report with general conditions).

If this is so, the normative method for distinguishing right from wrong in historical information on the grounds of inherent possi-bility or absurdity is to investigate human social organization, which is identical with civilization. We must distinguish the conditions that attach themselves to the essence of civilization as required by its very nature; the things that are accidental and cannot be counted on; and the things that cannot possibly attach themselves to it. If we do that, we shall have a normative method for distinguishing right from wrong and truth from falsehood in historical information by means of a logical demonstration that admits of no doubts. Then, whenever we hear about certain conditions occurring in civilization, we shall know what to accept and what to declare spurious. We shall have a sound yardstick with the help of which historians may find the path of truth and correctness where their reports are concerned.

Such is the purpose of this first book of our work. (The subject) is in a way an independent science with its own peculiar object—that is, human civilization and social organization. It also has its own peculiar problems—that is, explaining in turn the conditions that attach themselves to the essence of civilization. Thus, the situation is the same with this science as it is with any other science, whether it be a conventional or an intellectual one.

It should be known that the discussion of this topic is something new, extraordinary, and highly useful. Penetrating research has shown the way to it. It does not belong to rhetoric, one of the logical disciplines (represented in Aristotle's *Organon*), which are concerned with convincing words whereby the mass is moved to accept or reject a particular opinion. It is also not politics, because politics is concerned with the administration of home or city in accordance with ethical and philosophical requirements, for the purpose of directing the mass toward a behaviour that will result in the preservation and permanence of the species.

The subject here is different from those two disciplines which, however, are often similar to it. In a way, it is an entirely original science. In fact, I have not come across a discussion along these lines by anyone. I do not know if this is because people have been unaware of it, but there is no reason to suspect them of having been unaware of it. Perhaps they have written exhaustively on this topic, and their work did not reach us. There are many sciences. There have been numerous sages among the nations of mankind. The knowledge that has not come down to us is larger than the knowledge that has. Where are the sciences of the Persians that 'Umar ordered to be wiped out at the time of the conquest? Where are the sciences of the Chaldaeans, the Syrians, and the Babylonians, and the scholarly products and results that were theirs? Where are the sciences of the Copts, their predecessors? The sciences of only one nation, the Greeks, have come down to us, because they were translated through al-Ma'mûn's efforts. He was successful in this direction because he had many translators at his disposal and spent much money in this connection. Of the sciences of others, nothing has come to our attention.

The accidents involved in every manifestation of nature and intellect deserve study. Any topic that is understandable and real requires its own special science. In this connection, scholars seem to have been interested in the results (of the individual sciences). As far as the subject under discussion is concerned, the result, as we have seen, is just historical information. Although the problems it raises are important, both essentially and specifically, (exclusive concern for it) leads to one result only: the mere verification of historical information. This is not much. Therefore, scholars might have avoided the subject.

God knows better. 'And you were given but little knowledge.'[1]

In the field under consideration here, we encounter certain problems, treated incidentally by scholars among the arguments applicable to their particular sciences, but that in object and approach are of the same type as the problems we are discussing. In connection with the arguments for prophecy, for instance, scholars mention that human beings co-operate with each other for their existence and, therefore, need men to arbitrate among them and exercise a restraining influence. Or, in the science of the principles of jurisprudence, in the chapter of arguments for the necessity of languages, mention is made of the fact that people need means to express their intentions because by their very nature, co-operation and social organization are made easier by proper expressions. Or, in connection with the explanation that laws have their reason in the purposes they are to serve, the jurists mention that adultery confuses pedigrees and destroys the species; that murder, too, destroys the human species; that injustice invites the destruction of civilization with the necessary consequence that the species will be destroyed. Other similar things are stated in connection with the purposes embedded in laws, which are based upon the effort to preserve civilization. Therefore they apply to things that belong to civilization. This is obvious from our references to these problems which are mentioned as representative of the general situation.

We also find a few of the problems of the subject under discussion treated in scattered statements by the sages of mankind. However, they did not exhaust the subject. For instance, we have the speech of the Môbedhân[2] before Bahrâm b. Bahrâm in the story of the owl reported by al-Mas'ûdî. It runs: 'O king, the might of royal authority materializes only through the religious law, obedience toward God, and compliance with His commands and prohibitions. The religious law persists only through royal authority. Mighty royal authority is accomplished only through men. Men persist only with the help of property. The only way to property is through cultivation. The only way to cultivation is through justice. Justice is a balance set up among mankind. The Lord set it up and appointed an overseer for it, and that overseer is the ruler.'

There also is a statement by Anôsharwân[3] to the same effect: 'Royal authority exists through the army, the army through money, money through taxes, taxes through cultivation, cultivation through justice, justice through the improvement of officials, the improve-

---

[1] Qur'ân 17. 85 (87).
[2] Môbedh (< magupat) is the title of the Zoroastrian priest. Môbedhân actually is the Persian plural of the word.
[3] Anôsharwân is the celebrated Sassanian ruler Khosraw I, A.D. 531–579.

ment of officials through the forthrightness of wazirs, and the whole thing in the first place through the ruler's personal supervision of his subjects' condition and his ability to educate them, so that he may rule them, and not they him.'

In the *Book on Politics* that is ascribed to Aristotle and has wide circulation, we find a good deal about our subject. The treatment, however, is not exhaustive, nor is the topic provided with all the arguments it deserves, and it is mixed with other things. In the book, the author referred to such general ideas as we have reported on the authority of the Môbedhân and Anôsharwân. He arranged his statement in a remarkable circle that he discussed at length. It runs as follows: 'The world is a garden the fence of which is the dynasty. The dynasty is an authority through which life is given to proper behaviour. Proper behaviour is a policy directed by the ruler. The ruler is an institution supported by the soldiers. The soldiers are helpers who are maintained by money. Money is sustenance brought together by the subjects. The subjects are servants who are protected by justice. Justice is something familiar,[1] and through it, the world persists. The world is a garden . . .'—and then it begins again from the beginning. These are eight sentences of political wisdom. They are connected with each other, the end of each one leading into the beginning of the next. They are held together in a circle with no definite beginning or end. The author was proud of what he had hit upon and made much of the significance of the sentences.

When our discussion in the section on royal authority and dynasties has been studied and due critical attention given to it, it will be found to constitute an exhaustive, very clear, fully substantiated interpretation and detailed exposition of these sentences. We became aware of these things with God's help and without the instruction of Aristotle or the teaching of the Môbedhân.

The statements of Ibn al-Muqaffa'[2] and the excursions on political subjects in his treatises also touch upon many of the problems of our work. However, he did not substantiate his statements with arguments as we have done. He merely mentioned them in passing in the flowing prose style and eloquent verbiage of the rhetorician.

Judge Abû Bakr aṭ-Ṭurṭûshî[3] also had the same idea in the *Kitâb Sirâj al-Mulûk*. He divided the work into chapters that come close to the chapters and problems of our work. However, he did not achieve his aim or realize his intention. He did not exhaust the problems and did not bring clear proofs. He sets aside a special chapter for a

---

[1] *Ma'lûf* 'familiar' may here possibly mean 'harmonious'. Arabic *ta'lîf* translates Greek ἁρμονία.

[2] 'Abdallâh b. al-Muqaffa', d. 142 [759/60].

[3] Muḥammad b. al-Walîd, *ca.* 451 to 520 or 525 [1059 to 1126 or 1131].

particular problem, but then he tells a great number of stories and traditions and he reports scattered remarks by Persian sages such as Buzurjmihr[1] and the Môbedhân, and by Indian sages, as well as material transmitted on the authority of Daniel, Hermes, and other great men. He does not verify his statements or clarify them with the help of natural arguments. The work is merely a compilation of transmitted material similar to sermons in its inspirational purpose. In a way, aṭ-Ṭurṭûshî aimed at the right idea, but did not hit it. He did not realize his intention or exhaust his problems.

We, on the other hand, were inspired by God. He led us to a science whose truth we ruthlessly set forth. If I have succeeded in presenting the problems of this science exhaustively and in showing how it differs in its various aspects and characteristics from all other crafts, this is due to divine guidance. If, on the other hand, I have omitted some point, or if the problems have got confused with something else, the task of correcting remains for the discerning critic, but the merit is mine since I cleared and marked the way.

God guides with His light whom He will.[2]

In this book, now, we are going to explain such various aspects of civilization that affect human beings in their social organization, as royal authority, gainful occupation, sciences, and crafts, all in the light of various arguments that will show the true nature of the varied knowledge of the elite and the common people, repel misgivings, and remove doubts.

We say that man is distinguished from the other living beings by certain qualities peculiar to him, namely: (1) The sciences and crafts which result from that ability to think which distinguishes man from the other animals and exalts him as a thinking being over all creatures. (2) The need for restraining influence and strong authority, since man, alone of all the animals, cannot exist without them. It is true, something has been said in this connection about bees and locusts. However, if they have something similar, it comes to them through inspiration,[3] not through thinking or reflection. (3) Man's efforts to make a living and his concern with the various ways of obtaining and acquiring the means of life. This is the result of man's need for food to keep alive and subsist, which God instilled in him, guiding him to desire and seek a livelihood. God said: 'He gave every thing its natural characteristics, and then guided it.'[4] (4) Civilization.

[1] The wazir of Khosraw I Anôsharwân who appears in Arabic literature and is the chief representative of Persian wisdom.

[2] Cf. Qur'ân 24. 35 (35).

[3] Arabic uses the same word (*waḥy*) for Prophetical 'inspiration' and for what we would translate in this context as 'instinct'. The 'inspiration' of bees is mentioned in Qur'ân 16. 68 (70).

[4] Qur'ân 20. 50 (52).

This means that human beings have to dwell in common and settle together in cities and hamlets for the comforts of companionship and for the satisfaction of human needs, as a result of the natural disposition of human beings toward co-operation in order to be able to make a living, as we shall explain. Civilization may be either desert (Bedouin) civilization as found in outlying regions and mountains, in hamlets (near) pastures in waste regions, and on the fringes of sandy deserts; or it may be sedentary civilization as found in cities, villages, towns, and small communities that serve the purpose of protection and fortification by means of walls. In all these different conditions, there are things that affect civilization essentially in as far as it is social organization.

Consequently, the discussion in this work falls naturally under six chapter headings:

(1) On human civilization in general, its various kinds, and the portion of the earth that is civilized.

(2) On desert civilization, including a report on the tribes and savage nations.

(3) On dynasties, the caliphate, and royal authority, including a discussion of government ranks.

(4) On sedentary civilization, countries, and cities.

(5) On crafts, ways of making a living, gainful occupations, and their various aspects. And

(6) On the sciences, their acquisition and study.

I have discussed desert civilization first, because it is prior to everything else, as will become clear later on. The discussion of royal authority was placed before that of countries and cities for the same reason. The discussion of ways of making a living was placed before that of the sciences, because making a living is necessary and natural, whereas the study of science is a luxury or convenience. Anything natural has precedence over luxury. I lumped the crafts together with gainful occupations, because they belong to the latter in some respects as far as civilization is concerned, as will become clear later.

God gives success and support.

Chapter 1

Human civilization in general

Human social organization is something necessary. The philosophers expressed this fact by saying: 'Man is "political" by nature.' That is, he cannot do without the social organization for which the philosophers use the technical term 'town' (*polis*).

This is what civilization means. (The necessary character of human social organization or civilization) is explained by the fact that God created and fashioned man in a form that can live and subsist only with the help of food. He guided man to a natural desire for food and instilled in him the power that enables him to obtain it.

However, the power of the individual human being is not sufficient for him to obtain (the food) he needs, and does not provide him with as much food as he requires to live. Even if we assume an absolute minimum of food—that is, food enough for one day, (a little) wheat, for instance—that amount of food could be obtained only after much preparation such as grinding, kneading, and baking. Each of these three operations requires utensils and tools that can be provided only with the help of several crafts, such as the crafts of the blacksmith, the carpenter, and the potter. Assuming that a man could eat unprepared grain, an even greater number of operations would be necessary in order to obtain the grain: sowing and reaping, and threshing to separate it from the husks of the ear. Each of these operations requires a number of tools and many more crafts than those just mentioned. It is beyond the power of one man alone to do all that, or part of it, by himself. Thus, he cannot do without a combination of many powers from among his fellow beings, if he is to obtain food for himself and for them. Through co-operation, the needs of a number of persons, many times greater than their own number, can be satisfied.

Likewise, each individual needs the help of his fellow beings for his defence. When God fashioned the natures of all living beings and divided the various powers among them, many dumb animals were given more perfect powers than God gave to man. The power of a horse, for instance, is much greater than the power of a man, and so

45

is the power of a donkey or an ox. The power of a lion or an elephant is many times greater than the power of man.

Aggressiveness is natural in living beings. Therefore, God gave each of them a special limb for defence against aggression. To man, instead, He gave the ability to think, and the hand. With the help of the ability to think, the hand is able to prepare the ground for the crafts. The crafts, in turn, procure for man the instruments that serve him instead of limbs, which other animals possess for their defence. Lances, for instance, take the place of horns for goring, swords the place of claws to inflict wounds, shields the place of thick skins, and so on. There are other such things. They were all mentioned by Galen in *De usu partium*.[1]

The power of one individual human being cannot withstand the power of any one dumb animal, especially the power of the predatory animals. Man is generally unable to defend himself against them by himself. Nor is his unaided power sufficient to make use of the existing instruments of defence, because there are so many of them and they require so many crafts and things. It is absolutely necessary for man to have the co-operation of his fellow men. As long as there is no such co-operation, he cannot obtain any food or nourishment, and life cannot materialize for him, because God fashioned him so that he must have food if he is to live. Nor, lacking weapons, can he defend himself. Thus, he falls prey to animals and dies much before his time. Under such circumstances, the human species would vanish. When, however, mutual co-operation exists, man obtains food for his nourishment and weapons for his defence. God's wise plan that mankind should subsist and the human species be preserved will be fulfilled.

Consequently, social organization is necessary to the human species. Without it, the existence of human beings would be incomplete. God's desire to settle the world with human beings and to leave them as His representatives on earth[2] would not materialize. This is the meaning of civilization, the object of the science under discussion.

The aforementioned remarks have been in the nature of establishing the existence of the object in this particular field. A scholar in a particular discipline is not obliged to do this, since it is accepted in logic that a scholar in a particular science does not have to establish the existence of the object in that science.[3] On the other hand,

---

[1] At the beginning of the work, ed. C. G. Kühn (Leipzig, 1821–33), III, 2.

[2] Cf. Qur'ân 2. 30 (28).

[3] The 'object' (*mawḍûʿ*) of a science is the fundamental elements at its basis, such as quantities (measurements) in geometry, numbers in arithmetic, substances in physics, and so on. The object of Ibn Khaldûn's new science is human social organization, or civilization.

logicians do not consider it forbidden to do so. Thus, it is a voluntary contribution.

God, in His grace, gives success.

When mankind has achieved social organization, as we have stated, and when civilization in the world has thus become a fact, people need someone to exercise a restraining influence and keep them apart, for aggressiveness and injustice are in the animal nature of man. The weapons made for the defence of human beings against the aggressiveness of dumb animals do not suffice against the aggressiveness of man to man, because all of them possess those weapons. Thus, something else is needed for defence against the aggressiveness of human beings toward each other. It could not come from outside, because all the other animals fall short of human perceptions and inspiration. The person who exercises a restraining influence, therefore, must be one of themselves. He must dominate them and have power and authority over them, so that no one of them will be able to attack another. This is the meaning of royal authority.

It has thus become clear that royal authority is a natural quality of man which is absolutely necessary to mankind. The philosophers mention that it also exists among certain dumb animals, such as the bees and the locusts. One discerns among them the existence of authority and obedience to a leader. They follow one who is distinguished as their leader by his natural characteristics and body. However, outside of human beings, these things exist as the result of natural disposition and divine guidance, and not as the result of an ability to think or to administrate.

The philosophers go further. They attempt to give logical proof of the existence of prophecy and to show that prophecy is a natural quality of man. In this connection, they carry the argument to its ultimate consequences and say that human beings absolutely require some authority to exercise a restraining influence. They go on to say that such restraining influence exists through the religious law ordained by God and revealed to mankind by a human being. He is distinguished from the rest of mankind by special qualities of divine guidance that God gave him, in order that he might find the others submissive to him and ready to accept what he says. Eventually, the existence of an authority among them and over them becomes a fact that is accepted without the slightest disapproval or dissent.

This proposition of the philosophers is not logical, as one can see. Existence and human life can materialize without (the existence of prophecy) through injunctions a person in authority may devise on his own or with the help of a group feeling that enables him to force the others to follow him wherever he wants to go. People who have a (divinely revealed) book and who follow the prophets are few in number in comparison with the Magians[1] who have none. The latter constitute the majority of the world's inhabitants. Still, they have possessed dynasties and monuments, not to mention life itself. They still possess these things at this time in the intemperate zones to the north and the south. This is in contrast with human life in the state of anarchy, with no one to exercise a restraining influence. That would be impossible.

This shows that the philosophers are wrong when they assume that prophecy exists by necessity. The existence of prophecy is not required by logic. Its (necessary character) is indicated by the religious law, as was the belief of the early Muslims.

God gives success and guidance.

[1] 'Magians' originally meant the Zoroastrians. In later Islam they were considered as people who followed a kind of prophet but did not have Scriptures like the Christians and the Jews. Thus, they occupied a position somewhere between the latter and polytheists. The term was eventually used to denote the general idea of pagans.

*The parts of the earth where civilization is found. Some
information about oceans, rivers, and zones*

In the books of philosophers who speculated about the condition of
the world, it has been explained that the earth has a spherical shape
and is enveloped by the element of water. It may be compared to a
grape floating upon water.

The water withdrew from certain parts of the earth, because God
wanted to create living beings upon it and settle it with the human
species that rules as His representative over all other beings. One
might from this get the impression that the water is below the earth.
This is not correct. The natural 'below' of the earth is the core and
middle of its sphere, the centre to which everything is attracted by
its gravity. All the sides of the earth beyond that and the water
surrounding the earth are 'above'. When some part of the earth is
said to be 'below', it is said to be so with reference to some other
region.

The part of the earth from which the water has withdrawn is one-
half the surface of the sphere of the earth. It has a circular form and
is surrounded on all sides by the element of water which forms a sea
called 'the Surrounding Sea'.

The part of the earth that is free from water (and thus suitable) for
human civilization has more waste and empty areas than (habitable)
areas. The empty area in the south is larger than that in the north.
The cultivated part of the earth extends more toward the north. In
the shape of a circular plane it extends in the south to the equator
and in the north to a circular line, behind which there are mountains
separating (the cultivated part) from the elemental water.

The part of the earth that is free from water is said to cover one-
half or less of the sphere. The cultivated part covers one-fourth of it.
It is divided into seven zones.[1]

The equator divides the earth into two halves from west to east. It
represents the length of the earth. It is the longest line on the sphere
of the earth, just as the ecliptic and the equinoctial lines are the
longest on the firmament. The ecliptic is divided into 360 degrees.
The geographical degree is twenty-five parasangs, the parasang
being 12,000 cubits or three miles, since one mile has 4,000 cubits.
The cubit is twenty-four fingers, and the finger is six grains of barley
placed closely together in one row. The distance of the equinoctial
line, parallel to the equator of the earth and dividing the firmament

[1] *Iqlîm,* Greek κλίμα, 'clime'.

into two parts, is ninety degrees from each of the two poles. However, the cultivated area north of the equator is only sixty-four degrees. The rest is empty and uncultivated because of the bitter cold and frost, exactly as the southern part is altogether empty because of the heat. We shall explain it all, if God wills.

Information about the cultivated part and its boundaries and about the cities, towns, mountains, rivers, waste areas, and sandy deserts it contains, has been given by men such as Ptolemy in the *Geography* and, after him, by the author of the *Book of Roger*.[1] These men divided the cultivated area into seven parts which they called the seven zones. The borders of the seven zones are imaginary. They extend from east to west. In latitudinal extension they are identical, in logitudinal extension different. The first zone is longer than the second. The same applies to the second zone, and so on. The seventh zone is the shortest. This is required by the circular shape that resulted from the withdrawal of the water from the sphere of the earth.

According to these scholars, each of the seven zones is divided from west to east into ten contiguous sections. Information about general conditions and civilization is given for each section.

(The geographers) mention that the Mediterranean which we all know branches off from the Surrounding Sea in the western part of the fourth zone. It begins at a narrow straits about twelve miles wide between Tangier and Tarifa, called the Street (of Gibraltar). It then extends eastward and opens out to a width of 600 miles. It terminates at the end of the fourth section of the fourth zone, a distance of 1,160 parasangs from its starting point. There, it is bordered by the coast of Syria. On the south, it is bordered by the coast of the Maghrib, beginning with Tangier at the Straits, then Ifrîqiyah, Barqah, and Alexandria. On the north, it is bordered by the coast of Constantinople, then Venice, Rome, France, and Spain, back to Tarifa at the Street (of Gibraltar) opposite Tangier. The Mediterranean is also called the Roman Sea or the Syrian Sea. It contains many populous islands. Some of them are large, such as Crete, Cyprus, Sicily, Majorca, and Sardinia.

In the north, they say, two other seas branch off from the Mediterranean through two straits. One of them is opposite Constantinople. It starts at the Mediterranean in a narrow straits, only an arrow-shot in width. It flows for a three days' run and touches Constantinople. Then, it attains a width of four miles. It flows in this channel for sixty miles, where it is known as the Straits of Constantinople. Through a mouth six miles wide, it then flows into the Black Sea,

[1] By Muḥammad al-Idrîsî, *ca.* A.D. 1099/1100–1162, who wrote this important geographical work for Roger II of Sicily (1129–1154).

and becomes a sea that, from there, turns eastward in its course. It passes the land of Heracleia (in Bithynia) and ends at the country of the Khazars, 1,300 miles from its mouth. Along its two coasts live the Byzantine, the Turkish, the Bulgar, and the Russian nations.

The second sea that branches off from the two straits of the Mediterranean is the Gulf of Venice. It emerges from Byzantine territory at its northern limit. Then, from Sant' Angelo (de' Lombardi), its western boundary extends from the country of the Venetians to the territory of Aquileia, 1,100 miles from where it started. On its two shores live the Venetians, the Byzantines, and other nations. It is called the Gulf of Venice (Adriatic Sea).

From the Surrounding Sea, they say, a large and wide sea flows on the east at thirteen degrees north of the equator. It flows a little toward the south, entering the first zone. Then it flows west within the first zone until it reaches the country of the Abyssinians and the Negroes and Bâb al-Mandeb in the fifth section of the first zone, 4,500 parasangs from its starting point. This sea is called the Chinese, Indian, or Abyssinian Sea (Indian Ocean). It is bordered on the south by the country of the Negroes and the country of Berbera which Imru'ul-Qays mentioned in his poem. These 'Berbers' do not belong to the Berbers who make up the tribes in the Maghrib. The sea is then bordered by the area of Mogadishu, Sufâlah, and the land of al-Wâqwâq, and by other nations beyond which there is nothing but waste and empty areas. On the north, where it starts, it is bordered by China, then by Eastern and Western India, and then by the coast of the Yemen—that is, al-Aḥqâf, Zabîd, and other cities. Where it ends, it is bordered by the country of the Negroes, and, beyond them, the Beja.

Two other seas, they say, branch off from the Indian Ocean. One of them branches off where the Indian Ocean ends, at Bâb al-Mandeb. It starts out narrow, then flows widening toward the north and slightly to the west until it ends at the city of al-Qulzum in the fifth section of the second zone, 1,400 miles from its starting point. This is the Sea of al-Qulzum or Sea of Suez (Red Sea). From the Red Sea at Suez to Fusṭâṭ[1] is the distance of a three days' journey. The Red Sea is bordered on the east by the coast of the Yemen, the Ḥijâz, and Jiddah, and then, where it ends, by Midyan, Aila, and Fârân. On the west, it is bordered by the coast of Upper Egypt, 'Aydhâb, Suakin, and Zayla', and then, where it begins, by the country of the Beja. It ends at al-Qulzum. It would reach the Mediterranean at al-'Arîsh. The distance between the Red Sea and the Mediterranean is a six days' journey. Many rulers, both Muslim

[1] The mention of Fusṭâṭ shows that, basically, the information presented here goes back to a time before the foundation of Cairo in 969/70.

and pre-Islamic, have wanted to cut through the intervening territory but this has not been achieved.

The second sea branching off from the Indian Ocean and called the Persian Gulf (the Green Gulf), branches off at the region between the west coast of India and al-Aḥqâf in the Yemen. It flows toward the north and slightly to the west until it ends at al-Ubullah on the coast of al-Baṣrah in the sixth section of the second zone, 440 parasangs from its starting point. It is called the Persian Gulf (Persian Sea). It is bordered on the east by the coast of Western India, Mukrân, Kirmân, Fârs, and al-Ubullah where it ends. On the west, it is bordered by the coast of al-Baḥrayn, the Yamâmah, Oman, ash-Shiḥr, and al-Aḥqâf where it starts. Between the Persian Gulf and al-Qulzum lies the Arabian Peninsula, jutting out from the mainland into the sea. It is surrounded by the Indian Ocean to the south, by the Red Sea to the west, and by the Persian Gulf to the east. It adjoins the 'Irâq in the region between Syria and al-Baṣrah, where the distance between Syria and the 'Irâq is 1,500 miles. In the 'Irâq are al-Kûfah, al-Qâdisîyah, Baghdad, the Reception Hall of Khosraw (at Ctesiphon), and al-Ḥîrah. Beyond that live non-Arab nations such as the Turks, the Khazars, and others. The Arabian Peninsula comprises the Ḥijâz in the west, the Yamâmah, al-Baḥrayn, and Oman in the east, and in the south the Yemen along the coast of the Indian Ocean.

In the cultivated area, they say, there is another sea to the north in the land of the Daylam. This sea has no connection with the other seas. It is called the Sea of Jurjân and Ṭabaristân (Caspian Sea). Its length is 1,000 miles, and its width 600. To the west of it lie Azerbaijan and the Daylam territory; to the east of it the land of the Turks and Khuwârizm; to the south of it Ṭabaristân; and to the north of it the land of the Khazars and the Alans.

These are all the famous seas mentioned by the geographers.

They further say that in the cultivated part of the earth, there are many rivers. The largest among them are four in number, namely, the Nile, the Euphrates, the Tigris, and the River of Balkh which is called Oxus (Jayḥûn).

The Nile begins at a large mountain, sixteen degrees beyond the equator at the boundary of the fourth section of the first zone. This mountain is called the Mountain of the Qumr. No higher mountain is known on earth. Many springs issue from the mountain, some of them flowing into one lake there, and some of them into another lake. From these two lakes, several rivers branch off, and all of them flow into a lake at the equator which is at the distance of a ten days' journey from the mountain. From that lake, two rivers issue. One of them flows due north, passing through the country of the Nûbah and then through Egypt. Having traversed Egypt, it divides into many branches lying close to each other. Each of these is called a 'channel'. All flow into the Mediterranean at Alexandria. This river is called the Egyptian Nile. It is bordered by Upper Egypt on the east, and by the oases on the west. The other river turns westward, flowing due west until it flows into the Surrounding Sea. This river is the Sudanese Nile. All the Negro nations live along its borders.

The Euphrates begins in Armenia in the sixth section of the fifth zone. It flows south through Byzantine territory (Anatolia) past Malatya to Manbij, and then passes Ṣiffîn, ar-Raqqah, and al-Kûfah until it reaches the Marsh (al-Baṭḥâ') between al-Baṣrah and Wâsiṭ. From there it flows into the Indian Ocean. Many rivers flow into it along its course. Other rivers branch off from it and flow into the Tigris.

The Tigris originates in a number of springs in the country of Khilâṭ, which is also in Armenia. It passes on its course southward through Mosul, Azerbaijan, and Baghdad to Wâsiṭ. There, it divides into several channels, all of which flow into the Lake of al-Baṣrah and join the Persian Gulf. The Tigris flows east of the Euphrates. Many large rivers flow into it from all sides. The region between the Euphrates and the Tigris, where it is first formed, is the Jazîrah of Mosul, facing Syria on both banks of the Euphrates, and facing Azerbaijan on both banks of the Tigris.

The Oxus originates at Balkh, in the eighth section of the third zone, in a great number of springs there. Large rivers flow into it, as it follows a course from south to north. It flows through Khurâsân, then past Khurâzân to Khuwârizm in the eighth section of the fifth zone. It flows into Lake Aral (the Lake of Gurganj) which is situated at the foot of the city of Gurganj. In length as in width, it extends the distance of one month's journey. The river of Farghânah and Tash-kent (ash-Shâsh), which comes from the territory of the Turks, flows into it. West of the Oxus lie Khurâsân and Khuwârizm. East of it lie the cities of Bukhârâ, at-Tirmidh, and Samarkand. Beyond that are the country of the Turks, Farghânah, the Kharlukh, and other non-Arab nations.

All this was mentioned by Ptolemy in his work and by the Sharîf al-Idrîsî in the *Book of Roger*. All the mountains, seas, and rivers to be found in the cultivated part of the earth are depicted on maps and exhaustively treated in geography. We do not have to go any further into it. It is too lengthy a subject, and our main concern is with the Maghrib, the home of the Berbers, and the Arab home countries in the East.

God gives success.

*The northern quarter of the earth has more civilization
than the southern quarter. The reason thereof*

We know from observation and from continuous tradition that the first and the second of the cultivated zones have less civilization than the other zones. The cultivated area in the first and second zones is interspersed with empty waste areas and sandy deserts and has the Indian Ocean to the east. The nations and populations of the first and second zones are not excessively numerous. The same applies to the cities and towns there.

The third, fourth, and subsequent zones are just the opposite. Waste areas there are few. Sandy deserts also are few or non-existent. The nations and populations are tremendous. Cities and towns are exceedingly numerous. Civilization has its seat between the third and the sixth zones. The south is all emptiness.

Many philosophers have mentioned that this is because of the excessive heat and slightness of the sun's deviation from the zenith in the south. Let us explain and prove this statement. The result will clarify the reason why civilization in the third and fourth zones is so highly developed and extends also to the fifth, sixth, and seventh zones.

We say: When the south and north poles of heaven are upon the horizon, they constitute a large circle that divides the firmament into two parts. It is the largest circle and runs from west to east. It is called the equinoctial line. In astronomy, it has been explained in the proper place that the highest sphere moves from east to west in a daily motion by means of which it also forces the spheres enclosed by it to move. This motion is perceptible to the senses. It has also been explained that the stars in their spheres have a motion that is contrary to this motion and is, therefore, a motion from west to east. The periods of this movement differ according to the different speeds of the motions of the stars.

Parallel to the courses of all these stars in their spheres, there runs a large circle which belongs to the highest sphere and divides it into two halves. This is the ecliptic (zodiac). It is divided into twelve 'signs'. As has been explained in the proper place, the equinoctial line intersects the ecliptic at two opposite points, namely, at the beginning of Aries and at the beginning of Libra. The equinoctial line divides the zodiac into two halves. One of them extends northward from the equinoctial line and includes the signs from the

54

beginning of Aries to the end of Virgo. The other half extends southward from it and includes the signs from the beginning of Libra to the end of Pisces.

When the two poles fall upon the horizon among all the regions of the earth, a line is formed upon the surface of the earth that faces the equinoctial line and runs from west to east. This line is called the equator. According to astronomical observation, this line is believed to coincide with the beginning of the first of the seven zones. All civilization is to the north of it.

The north pole gradually ascends on the horizon of the cultivated area of the earth until its elevation reaches sixty-four degrees. Here, all civilization ends. This is the end of the seventh zone. When its elevation reaches ninety degrees on the horizon—that is the distance between the pole and the equinoctial line—then it is at its zenith, and the equinoctial line is on the horizon. Six of the signs of the zodiac, the northern ones, remain above the horizon, and six, the southern ones, are below it.

Civilization is impossible in the area between the sixty-fourth and the ninetieth degrees, for no admixture of heat and cold occurs there because of the great time interval between them. Generation, therefore, does not take place.

The sun is at its zenith on the equator at the beginning of Aries and Libra. It then declines from its zenith down to the beginning of Cancer and Capricorn. Its greatest declination from the equinoctial line is twenty-four degrees.

Now, when the north pole ascends on the horizon, the equinoctial line declines from the zenith in proportion to the elevation of the north pole, and the south pole descends correspondingly, as regards the three (distances constituting geographical latitude). Scholars who calculate the prayer times call this the latitude of a place. When the equinoctial line declines from the zenith, the northern signs of the zodiac gradually rise above it, proportionately to its rise, until the beginning of Cancer is reached. Meanwhile, the southern signs of the zodiac correspondingly descend below the horizon until the beginning of Capricorn is reached, because of the inclination of the (two halves of the zodiac) upward or downward from the horizon of the equator, as we have stated.

The northern horizon continues to rise, until its northern limit, which is the beginning of Cancer, is in the zenith. This is where the latitude is twenty-four degrees in the Ḥijâz and the territory adjacent. This is the declination from the equinoctial at the horizon of the equator at the beginning of Cancer. With the elevation of the north pole Cancer rises, until it attains the zenith. When the pole rises more than twenty-four degrees, the sun descends from the zenith and continues to do so until the elevation of the pole is sixty-four degrees, and the sun's descent from the zenith, as well as the depression of the south pole under the horizon, is the same distance. Then, generation stops because of the excessive cold and frost and the long time without any heat.

At and nearing its zenith, the sun sends its rays down upon the earth at right angles. In other positions, it sends them down at obtuse or acute angles. When the rays form right angles, the light is strong and spreads out over a wide area, in contrast to what happens in the case of obtuse and acute angles. Therefore, at and nearing its zenith, the heat is greater than in other positions, because the light (of the sun) is the reason for heat and calefaction. The sun reaches its zenith at the equator twice a year in two points of Aries and Libra. No declination (of the sun) goes very far. The heat hardly begins to become more temperate, when the sun has reached the limit of its declination at the beginning of Cancer or Capricorn and begins to rise again toward the zenith. The perpendicular rays then fall heavily upon the horizon there and hold steady for a long time, if not permanently. The air gets burning hot, even excessively so. The same is true whenever the sun reaches the zenith in the area between the equator and latitude twenty-four degrees, as it does twice a year. The rays exercise almost as much force upon the horizon there as they do at the equator. The excessive heat causes a parching dryness in the air that prevents generation. As the heat becomes more excessive, water and all kinds of moisture dry up, and the power of generation is destroyed in minerals, plants, and animals, because generation depends on moisture.

Now, when the beginning of Cancer declines from the zenith at the latitude of twenty-five degrees and beyond, the sun also declines from its zenith. The heat becomes more or less temperate. Then, generation can take place. This goes on until the cold becomes excessive, due to the lack of light and the obtuse angles of the rays of the sun. Then generation again decreases and is destroyed. However, the destruction caused by great heat is greater than that caused by great cold, because heat brings about desiccation faster than cold brings about freezing.

Therefore, there is little civilization in the first and second zones. There is a medium degree of civilization in the third, fourth, and fifth zones, because the heat there is temperate owing to the decreased amount of light. There is a great deal of civilization in the sixth and seventh zones because of the decreased amount of heat there. At first, cold does not have the same destructive effect upon the power of generation as heat; it causes desiccation only when it becomes excessive and thus has dryness added. This is the case beyond the seventh zone. All this, then, is why civilization is stronger and more abundant in the northern quarter. And God knows better!

The philosophers concluded from these facts that the region at the equator and beyond it was empty. On the strength of observation and continuous tradition, it was argued against them that it was cultivated. How would it be possible to prove this? It is obvious that the philosophers did not mean to deny entirely the existence of civilization there, but their argumentation led them to (infer) that the power of generation must, to a large degree, be destroyed there because of the excessive heat. Consequently, civilization there would be either impossible, or only minimally possible. This is so. The region at the equator and beyond it, even if it has civilization as has been reported, has only a very little of it.

Averroës[1] assumed that the equator is in a symmetrical position and that what is beyond the equator to the south corresponds to what is beyond it to the north; consequently, as much of the south would be cultivated as of the north. His assumption is not impossible, so far as the argument of the destruction of the power of generation is concerned. However, as to the region south of the equator, it is made impossible by the fact that the element of water covers the face of the earth in the south, where the corresponding area in the north admits of generation. On account of the greater amount of water in the south, Averroes' assumption of the symmetrical (position of the equator) thus turns out to be impossible. Everything else follows, since civilization progresses gradually and begins its gradual progress where it can exist, not where it cannot exist.

The assumption that civilization cannot exist at the equator is contradicted by continuous tradition. And God knows better!

After this discussion, we wish to draw a map of the earth, as was done by the author of the *Book of Roger*. . . . [2]

[1] Muḥammad b. Aḥmad b. Rushd, 520–595 [1126–1198].
[2] Here follows a detailed description of the map of the world (not reproduced in this edition).

The temperate and the intemperate zones.

The influence of the air upon the colour of human beings and
upon many other aspects of their condition

We have explained that the cultivated region of that part of the earth which is not covered by water has its centre toward the north, because of the excessive heat in the south and the excessive cold in the north. The north and the south represent opposite extremes of cold and heat. It necessarily follows that there must be a gradual decrease from the extremes toward the centre, which, thus, is moderate. The fourth zone is the most temperate cultivated region. The bordering third and fifth zones are rather close to being temperate. The sixth and second zones which are adjacent to them are far from temperate, and the first and seventh zones still less so. Therefore, the sciences, the crafts, the buildings, the clothing, the foodstuffs, the fruits, even the animals, and everything that comes into being in the three middle zones are distinguished by their temperate (well-proportioned) character. The human inhabitants of these zones are more temperate in their bodies, colour, character qualities, and general conditions. They are found to be extremely moderate in their dwellings, clothing, foodstuffs, and crafts. They use houses that are well constructed of stone and embellished by craftsmanship. They rival each other in production of the very best tools and implements. Among them one finds the natural minerals, such as gold, silver, iron, copper, lead, and tin. In their business dealings they use the two precious metals (gold and silver). They avoid intemperance quite generally in all their conditions. Such are the inhabitants of the Maghrib, of Syria, the two 'Irâqs, Western India, and China, as well as of Spain; also the European Christians near by, the Galicians, and all those who live together with these peoples or near them in the three temperate zones. The 'Irâq and Syria are directly in the middle and therefore are the most temperate of all these countries.

The inhabitants of the zones that are far from temperate, such as the first, second, sixth, and seventh zones, are also farther removed from being temperate in all their conditions. Their buildings are of clay and reeds. Their foodstuffs are durra and herbs. Their clothing is the leaves of trees, which they sew together to cover themselves, or animal skins. Most of them go naked. The fruits and seasonings of their countries are strange and inclined to be intemperate. In their business dealings, they do not use the two noble metals, but copper,

58

iron, or skins, upon which they set a value for the purpose of business dealings. Their qualities of character, moreover, are close to those of dumb animals. It has even been reported that most of the Negroes of the first zone dwell in caves and thickets, eat herbs, live in savage isolation and do not congregate, and eat each other. The same applies to the Slavs. The reason for this is that their remoteness from being temperate produces in them a disposition and character similar to those of the dumb animals, and they become correspondingly remote from humanity. The same also applies to their religious conditions. They are ignorant of prophecy and do not have a religious law, except for the small minority that lives near the temperate regions: for instance, the Abyssinians, who are neighbours of the Yemenites and have been Christians from pre-Islamic and Islamic times down to the present; and the Mâlî, the Gawgaw, and the Takrûr who live close to the Maghrib and, at this time, are Muslims. They are said to have adopted Islam in the seventh [thirteenth] century. Or, in the north, there are those Slav, European Christian, and Turkish nations that have adopted Christianity. All the other inhabitants of the intemperate zones in the south and in the north are ignorant of all religion. (Religious) scholarship is lacking among them. All their conditions are remote from those of human beings and close to those of wild animals.

The foregoing statement is not contradicted by the existence of the Yemen, the Ḥaḍramawt, al-Aḥqâf, the Ḥijâz, the Yamâmah, and adjacent regions of the Arabian Peninsula in the first and second zones. As we have mentioned, the Arabian Peninsula is surrounded by the sea on three sides. The humidity of the sea influences the humidity in the air. This diminishes the dryness and intemperance that the heat would cause. Because of the humidity from the sea, the Arabian Peninsula is to some degree temperate.

Genealogists who had no knowledge of the true nature of things imagined that Negroes were the children of Ham, the son of Noah, and that they were singled out to be black as the result of Noah's curse, which produced Ham's colour and the slavery God inflicted upon his descendants. It is mentioned in the Torah[1] that Noah cursed his son Ham. No reference is made there to blackness. The curse included no more than that Ham's descendants should be the slaves of his brothers' descendants. To attribute the blackness of the Negroes to Ham, reveals disregard of the true nature of heat and cold and of the influence they exercise upon the climate and upon the creatures that come into being in it. The black skin common to the inhabitants of the first and second zones is the result of the composition of the air in which they live, and which comes about

[1] Cf. Gen. 9: 25.

under the influence of the greatly increased heat in the south. The sun is at the zenith there twice a year at short intervals. In all seasons, the sun is in culmination for a long time. The light of the sun, thereiore, is plentiful. People there go through a very severe summer, and their skins turn black because of the excessive heat. Something similar happens in the two corresponding zones to the north, the seventh and sixth zones. There, a white skin is common among the inhabitants, likewise the result of the composition of the air in which they live, and which comes about under the influence of the excessive cold in the north. The sun is always on the horizon within the visual field, or close to it. It never ascends to the zenith, nor even gets close to it. The heat, therefore, is weak in this region, and the cold severe in all seasons. In consequence, the colour of the inhabitants is white, and they tend to have little body hair. Further consequences of the excessive cold are blue eyes, freckled skin, and blond hair.

The fifth, fourth, and third zones occupy an intermediate position. They have an abundant share of temperance, which is the golden mean. The fourth zone, being the one most nearly in the centre, is as temperate as can be. We have mentioned that before. The physique and character of its inhabitants are temperate to the degree necessitated by the composition of the air in which they live. The third and fifth zones lie on either side of the fourth, but they are less centrally located. They are closer to the hot south beyond the third zone and the cold north beyond the fifth zone. However, they do not become intemperate.

The four other zones are intemperate, and the physique and character of their inhabitants show it. The first and second zones are excessively hot and black, and the sixth and seventh zones cold and white. The inhabitants of the first and second zones in the south are called the Abyssinians, the Zanj, and the Sudanese. These are synonyms used to designate the particular nation that has turned black. The name 'Abyssinians', however, is restricted to those Negroes who live opposite Mecca and the Yemen, and the name 'Zanj' is restricted to those who live along the Indian Sea. These names are not given to them because of an alleged descent from a black human being, be it Ham or anyone else. Negroes from the south who settle in the temperate fourth zone or in the seventh zone that tends toward whiteness, are found to produce descendants whose colour gradually turns white in the course of time. Vice versa, inhabitants from the north or from the fourth zone who settle in the south produce descendants whose colour turns black. This shows that colour is conditioned by the composition of the air.

The inhabitants of the north are not called by their colour, because the people who established the conventional meanings of words were themselves white. Thus, whiteness was something usual and common to them, and they did not see anything sufficiently remarkable in it to cause them to use it as a specific term.

The inhabitants of the middle zones are temperate in their physique and character and in their ways of life. They have all the natural conditions necessary for a civilized life, such as ways of making a living, dwellings, crafts, sciences, political leadership, and royal authority. They thus have had prophecy, religious groups, dynasties, religious laws, sciences, countries, cities, buildings, horticulture, splendid crafts, and everything else that is temperate.

Now, among the inhabitants of these zones about whom we have historical information are, for instance, the Arabs, the Byzantines (Rûm), the Persians, the Israelites, the Greeks, the Indians, and the Chinese. When genealogists noted differences between these nations, their distinguishing marks and characteristics, they considered these to be due to their different descents. They declared all the Negro inhabitants of the south to be descendants of Ham. They had misgivings about their colour and therefore undertook to report the aforementioned silly story. They declared all or most of the inhabitants of the north to be the descendants of Japheth, and they declared most of the temperate nations, who inhabit the central regions, who cultivate the sciences and crafts, and who possess religious groups and religious laws as well as political leadership and royal authority, to be the descendants of Shem. Even if the genealogical construction were correct, it would be the result of mere guesswork, not of cogent, logical argumentation. It would merely be a statement of fact. It would not imply that the inhabitants of the south are called 'Abyssinians' and 'Negroes' because they are descended from 'black' Ham. The genealogists were led into this error by their belief that the only reason for differences between nations is in their descent. This is not so. Distinctions between races or nations are in some cases due to a different descent, as in the case of the Arabs, the Israelites, and the Persians. In other cases, they are caused by geographical location and physical marks, as in the case of the Zanj, the Abysinians, the Slavs, and the Sudanese Negroes. Again, in other cases, they are caused by custom and distinguishing characteristics, as well as by descent, as in the case of the Arabs. Or, they may be caused by anything else among the conditions, qualities, and features peculiar to the different nations. But to generalize and say that the inhabitants of a specific geographical location in the south or in the north are the descendants of such-and-such a well-known person because they have a common colour, trait, or physical mark which that forefather had, is one of those errors caused by disregard, both of the true nature of created beings and of geographical facts. (There also is disregard of the fact that the physical circumstances and environment) are subject to changes that affect later generations.

The influence of climate upon human character

We have seen that Negroes are in general characterized by levity, excitability, and great emotionalism. They are found eager to dance whenever they hear a melody. They are everywhere described as stupid. The real reason for these opinions is that, as has been shown by philosophers in the proper place, joy and gladness are due to expansion and diffusion of the animal spirit. Sadness is due to the opposite, namely, contraction and concentration of the animal spirit. It has been shown that heat expands and rarefies air and vapours and increases their quantity. A drunken person experiences inexpressible joy and gladness, because the vapour of the spirit in his heart is pervaded by natural heat, which the power of the wine generates in his spirit. The spirit, as a result, expands, and there is joy. Likewise, when those who enjoy a hot bath inhale the air of the bath, so that the heat of the air enters their spirits and makes them hot, they are found to experience joy. It often happens that they start singing, as singing has its origin in gladness.

Now, Negroes live in the hot zone. Heat dominates their temperament and formation. Therefore, they have in their spirits an amount of heat corresponding to that in their bodies and that of the zone in which they live. In comparison with the spirits of the inhabitants of the fourth zone, theirs are hotter and, consequently, more expanded. As a result, they are more quickly moved to joy and gladness, and they are merrier. Excitability is the direct consequence.

In the same way, the inhabitants of coastal regions are somewhat similar to the inhabitants of the south. The air in which they live is very much hotter because of the reflection of the light and rays of the sun from the surface of the sea. Therefore, their share in the qualities resulting from heat, that is, joy and levity, is larger than that of the inhabitants of cold and hilly or mountainous countries. To a degree, this may be observed in the inhabitants of the Jarîd in the third zone. There is much heat there, since it lies south of the coastal plains and hills. Another example is furnished by the Egyptians. Egypt lies at about the same latitude as the Jarîd. The Egyptians are dominated by joyfulness, levity, and disregard for the future. They store no provisions of food, neither for a month nor a year ahead, but purchase most of it in the market. Fez in the Maghrib, on the other hand, lies inland and is surrounded by cold hills. Its inhabitants can be observed to look sad and gloomy and to be too much concerned for the future. Although a man in Fez might have provisions of wheat stored, sufficient to last him for years, he always goes to the market early to buy his food for the day, because he is afraid to consume any of his hoarded food.

If one pays attention to this sort of thing in the various zones and countries, the influence of the varying quality of the climate upon the character of the inhabitants will become apparent.

Al-Mas'ûdî undertook to investigate the reason for the levity, excitability, and emotionalism in Negroes, and attempted to explain it. However, he did no better than to report, on the authority of Galen and Ya'qûb b. Ishâq al-Kindî, that the reason is a weakness of their brains which results in a weakness of their intellect. This is an inconclusive and unproven statement.

*Differences with regard to abundance and scarcity
of food in the various inhabited regions and how they affect
the human body and character*

It should be known that not all the temperate zones have an abundance of food, nor do all their inhabitants lead a comfortable life. In some parts, the inhabitants enjoy an abundance of grain, seasonings, wheat, and fruits, because the soil is well balanced and favourable to plants and there is an abundant civilization. And then, in other parts, the land is strewn with rocks, and no seeds or herbs grow at all. There, the inhabitants have a very hard time. Instances of such people are the inhabitants of the Ḥijâz and the Yemen, or the Veiled Ṣinhâjah who live in the desert of the Maghrib on the fringes of the sandy wastes which lie between the Berbers and the Sudanese Negroes. All of them lack grain and seasonings. Their nourishment and food consist of milk and meat. Another such people are the Arabs who roam the waste regions. They may get grain and seasonings from the hills, but this is the case only at certain times and is possible only under the eyes of the militia which protects (those parts). Whatever they get is little, because they have little money. They obtain no more than the bare necessity, and sometimes less, and in no case enough for a comfortable or abundant life. They are mostly found restricted to milk, which is for them a very good substitute for wheat. In spite of this, the desert people who lack grain and seasonings are found to be healthier in body and better in character than the hill people who have plenty of everything. Their complexions are clearer, their bodies cleaner, their figures more perfect, their character less intemperate, and their minds keener as far as knowledge and perception are concerned. This is attested by experience in all these groups. There is a great difference in this respect between the Arabs and Berbers (on the one hand), and the Veiled (Berbers) and the inhabitants of the hills (on the other). This fact is known to those who have investigated the matter.

As to the reason for it, it may be tentatively suggested that a great amount of food and the moisture it contains generate pernicious superfluous matters in the body, which, in turn, produce a disproportionate widening of the body, as well as many corrupt, putrid humours. The result is a pale complexion and an ugly figure, because the person has too much flesh, as we have stated. When the moisture with its evil vapours ascends to the brain, the mind and the ability to think are dulled. The result is stupidity, carelessness, and a general intemperance. This can be exemplified by comparing the animals of waste regions and barren habitats, such as gazelles, wild cows, ostriches, giraffes, onagers, and wild buffaloes, with their counterparts among the animals that live in hills, coastal plains, and fertile pastures. There is a big difference between them with regard to the glossiness of their coat, their shape and appearance, the proportions of their limbs, and their sharpness of perception. The gazelle is the counterpart of the goat, and the giraffe that of the camel; the onagers and wild buffaloes are identical with domestic donkeys and cattle. Still, there is a wide difference between them. The only reason for it is the fact that the abundance of food in the hills produces pernicious superfluous matters and corrupt humours in the bodies of the domestic animals, the influence of which shows on them. Hunger, on the other hand, may greatly improve the physique and shape of the animals of the waste regions.

The same observations apply to human beings. We find that the inhabitants of fertile zones where the products of agriculture and animal husbandry as well as seasonings and fruits are plentiful, are, as a rule, described as stupid in mind and coarse in body. This is the case with those Berbers who have plenty of seasonings and wheat, as compared with those who lead a frugal life and are restricted to barley or durra, such as the Maṣmûdah Berbers and the inhabitants of as-Sûs and the Ghumârah. The latter are superior both intellectually and physically. The same applies in general to the inhabitants of the Maghrib who have plenty of seasonings and fine wheat, as compared with the inhabitants of Spain in whose country butter is altogether lacking and whose principal food is durra. The Spaniards are found to have a sharpness of intellect, a nimbleness of body, and a receptivity for instruction such as no one else has. The same also applies to the inhabitants of rural regions of the Maghrib as compared with the inhabitants of settled areas and cities. Both use many seasonings and live in abundance, but the town dwellers only use them after they have been prepared and cooked and softened by admixtures. They thus lose their heaviness and become less substantial. Principal foods are the meat of sheep and chickens. They do not use butter because of its tastelessness. Therefore the moisture in their food is small, and it brings only a few pernicious superfluous matters into their bodies. Consequently, the bodies of the urban population are found to be more delicate than those of the inhabitants of the desert who live a hard life. Likewise, those inhabitants of the desert who are used to hunger are found to have in their bodies no superfluous matters, thick or thin.

It should be known that the influence of abundance upon the body is apparent even in matters of religion and divine worship. The frugal inhabitants of the desert and those of settled areas who have accustomed themselves to hunger and to abstinence from pleasures are found to be more religious and more ready for divine worship than people who live in luxury and abundance. Indeed, it can be observed that there are few religious people in towns and cities, inasmuch as people there are for the most part obdurate and careless, which is connected with the use of much meat, seasonings, and fine wheat. The existence of pious men and ascetics is, therefore, restricted to the desert, whose inhabitants eat frugally. Likewise, the condition of the inhabitants within a single city can be observed to differ according to the different distribution of luxury and abundance.

It can also be noted that those people who, whether they inhabit the desert or settled areas and cities, live a life of abundance and have all the good things to eat, die more quickly than others when a drought or famine comes upon them. This is the case, for instance, with the Berbers of the Maghrib and the inhabitants of the city of Fez and, as we hear, of Cairo. It is not so with the Arabs who inhabit waste regions and deserts, or with the inhabitants of regions where the date palm grows and whose principal food is dates, or with the present-day inhabitants of Ifrîqiyah whose principal food is barley and olive oil, or with the inhabitants of Spain whose principal food is durra and olive oil. When a drought or a famine strikes them, it does not kill as many of them as of the other group of people, and few, if any, die of hunger. As a reason for that, it may tentatively be suggested that the stomachs of those who have everything in abundance and are used to seasonings and, in particular, to butter, acquire moisture in addition to their basic constitutional moisture, and the moisture they are used to eventually becomes excessive. Then, when eating habits are thwarted by small quantities of food, by lack of seasonings, and by the use of coarse food to which it is unaccustomed, the stomach, which is a very weak part of the body and for that reason considered one of the vital parts, soon dries out and contracts. Sickness and sudden death are prompt consequences to the man whose stomach is in this condition. Those who die in famines are victims of their previous habitual state of satiation, not of the hunger that now afflicts them for the first time. In those who are accustomed to thirst and to doing without seasonings and butter, the basic moisture, which is good for all natural foods, always stays within its proper limits and does not increase. Thus, their stomachs are not affected by dryness or intemperance in consequence of a change of nourishment. As a rule, they escape the fate that awaits others on account of the abundance of their food and the great amount of seasonings in it.

The basic thing to know is that foodstuffs, and whether to use or not to use them, are matters of custom. Whoever accustoms himself to a particular type of food that agrees with him becomes used to it. He finds it painful to give it up or to make any changes, provided (the food in question) is not something that does not fulfil the purpose of food, such as poison, or alkaloids, or anything excessively intemperate. Whatever can be used as food and is agreeable may be used as customary food. If a man accustoms himself to milk and vegetables instead of wheat, milk and vegetables become for him his habitual food, and he definitely has no longer any need for wheat or grains.

The same applies to those who have accustomed themselves to suffer hunger and do without food. Such things are reported about the trained (ascetics). We hear remarkable things about men of this type. Those who have no knowledge of things of the sort can scarcely believe them. The explanation lies in custom. Once the soul gets used to something, it becomes part of its make-up and nature, because the soul is able to take on many colourings. If through gradual training it has become used to hunger, (hunger) becomes a natural habit of the soul.

The assumption of physicians that hunger causes death is not correct, except when a person is exposed suddenly to hunger and is entirely cut off from food. Then, the stomach is isolated, and contracts an illness that may be fatal. When, however, the amount of food one eats is slowly decreased by gradual training, there is no danger of death. The adepts of Sufism practise (such gradual abstinence). Gradualness is also necessary when one gives up the training. Were a person suddenly to return to his original diet, he might die. Therefore, he must end the training as he started it, that is, gradually.

We personally saw a person who had taken no food for forty or more consecutive days. Our *shaykhs* were present at the court of Sultan Abû l-Ḥasan[1] when two women from Algeciras and Ronda were presented to him, who had for years abstained from all food. Their story became known. They were examined, and the matter was found to be correct. The women continued this way until they died. Many persons we used to know restricted themselves to goat's milk. They drank from the udder some time during the day or at breakfast. This was their only food for fifteen years.

It should be known that everybody who is able to suffer hunger or eat only little, is physically better off if he stays hungry than if he eats too much. Hunger has a favourable influence on the health and well-being of body and intellect, as we have stated. This may be exemplified by the different influence of various kinds of food upon

[1] The Merinid of Fez who ruled from 1331 to 1351 and was the predecessor of Abû 'Inân, under whom Ibn Khaldûn came to Fez.

the body. We observe that those persons who live on the meat of strong, large-bodied animals grow up as a (strong and large-bodied) race. Comparison of the inhabitants of the desert with those of settled areas shows this. The same applies to persons who live on the milk and meat of camels. This influences their character, so that they become patient, persevering, and able to carry loads, as is the case with camels. Their stomachs also grow to be healthy and tough as the stomachs of camels. They are not beset by any feebleness or weakness, nor are they affected by unwholesome food, as others are. They may take strong (alkaloid) cathartics unadulterated to purify their bellies, such as, for instance, unripe colocynths, the deadly carrot, and Euphorbia. Their stomachs do not suffer any harm from them. But if the inhabitants of settled areas, whose stomachs have become delicate because of their soft diet, were to partake of them, death would come to them instantly, because these cathartics have poisonous qualities.

An indication of the influence of food upon the body is a fact that has been mentioned by agricultural scholars and observed by men of experience, that when the eggs of chickens which have been fed on grain cooked in camel dung, are set to hatch, the chicks come out as large as can be imagined. One does not even have to cook any grain to feed them; one merely smears camel dung on the eggs set to hatch, and the chickens that come out are extremely large. There are many similar things.

When we observe the various ways in which food exercises an influence upon bodies, there can be no doubt that hunger also exercises an influence upon them, because two opposites follow the same pattern. Hunger influences the body in that it keeps it free from corrupt superfluities and mixed fluids that destroy body and intellect, in the same way that food influenced the original existence of the body.

God knows all.

The various types of human beings who have
supernatural perception either through natural disposition or
through exercise, preceded by a discussion of inspiration
and dream visions

It should be known that God has chosen certain individuals. He honoured them by addressing them. He created them so that they might know Him. He made them connecting links between Himself and His servants. These individuals are to acquaint their fellow men with what is good for them and to urge them to let themselves be guided aright. They are to make it their task to keep their fellow men out of the fire of Hell and to show them the path to salvation. The knowledge that God gave them, and the wonders He manifested through their statements, indicated that there exist things beyond the reach of man that can be learned only from God through the mediation of such individuals, and that these individuals themselves cannot know unless God instruct them. Muḥammad said: 'Indeed, I know only what God taught me.' It should be known that the information they give is intrinsically and necessarily true, as will become clear when the reality of prophecy is explained.

The sign by which such human beings can be recognized is that, in the state of inspiration, they seem to be remote from those present. This is accompanied by a feeling of being choked that looks like swooning or unconsciousness but has nothing to do with either. In reality, it is an immersion in and encounter with the spiritual kingdom, the result of perceptions congenial to them but entirely foreign to the ordinary perceptions of men. (These extraordinary perceptions) are then brought down to the level of human perceptions in the form of some speech sound the person who receives the revelation hears and is able to understand, or in the form of an individual delivering the divine message to him. This state then leaves him, but he retains the content of the given revelation. When Muḥammad was asked about revelation, he said: 'At times, it comes to me like the ringing of a bell. This affects me most. When it leaves me, I have retained what was said. At other times, the angel appears to me in the form of a man. He talks to me, and I retain the things he says.' During that (process, the inspired person) shows inexplicable signs of strain and choking. 'Ā'ishah said: 'The revelation would come to him on very cold days. Nevertheless, when it left him, there was sweat on his forehead.' God says in the Qur'ân: 'We shall lay upon you a weighty message.'

Because the act of receiving revelations leads to such conditions, the idolaters used to accuse the prophets of being possessed. The outward appearance of the condition they observed misled them.

Another sign by which inspired human beings can be recognized is the fact that even before receiving revelations, they are good, innocent men, averse to any blameworthy or sinful action. This is what is meant by 'infallibility'. It looks as if, by nature, they were disposed to avoid and shun base actions, and as if such actions were the negation of their very nature. . . .

Another sign is that they seek to propagate religion and divine worship by means of prayer, almsgiving, and chastity. Khadîjah, as well as Abû Bakr, took that conduct as proof of Muḥammad's truthfulness. They did not need any further proof of his mission beyond his conduct and character. It is said that when Heraclius received the Prophet's letter in which he was asked to become a Muslim, he called the Qurashites who could be found in his country, among them Abû Safyân, and questioned them about Muḥammad. One of the questions he asked concerned the things Muḥammad commanded them to do. Abû Sufyân's reply was: 'Prayer, almsgiving, charity, and chastity.' Similar replies were given to all the other questions Heraclius asked. Heraclius' comment was: 'If it is all really as you say, he is a prophet and he will take possession of this very ground upon which I am standing.' The 'chastity' to which Heraclius referred is infallibility. It is worth noting that Heraclius consider infallibility and propaganda for religion and divine worship as proofs of the genuineness of a prophetical mission, and did not require a miracle. This story, therefore, is proof that these qualities are among the signs of prophecy.

Another sign is the prestige they have among their people. (It is said that) Abû Sufyân replied to Heraclius' question concerning Muḥammad's standing among the Qurashites, by saying that he had prestige among them. Whereupon Heraclius said, 'Whenever messengers are sent, they have prestige among their people.' That means that (such a man) has group feeling and influence which protect him from harm at the hands of unbelievers, until he has delivered the messages of his Lord and achieved the degree of complete perfection with respect to his religion and religious organization that God intended for him.

Another sign is that they work wonders which attest to their truthfulness. 'Wonders' are actions the like of which it is impossible for other human beings to achieve. They are, therefore, called 'miracles'. They are not within the ability of men, but beyond their power. There is a difference of opinion as to how they occur and as to how they prove the truth of the prophets. Speculative theologians

71

base themselves on the doctrine of the 'voluntary agent' and say that miracles occur through the power of God, and not through the action of the prophet. The Mu'tazilah[1] maintain that human actions proceed from man himself. Still, miracles do not belong to the type of actions that human beings perform. According to all schools, the prophet's place in the performance of miracles is circumscribed by the 'advance challenge' which he offers by divine permission. That is, the prophet uses the miracles before they occur as proof of the truth of his claims. They thus take the place of an explicit statement from God to the effect that a particular prophet is truthful, and they are definite proof of the truth. An evidential miracle is the combination of a wonder and the advance challenge. Therefore, the latter constitutes part of the miracle.

In the opinion of those who admit the existence of acts of divine grace, if an advance challenge occurs in connection with them, and if it is proof of them, it is proof only of saintliness, which is different from prophecy. This is why Professor Abû Isḥâq and others did not admit the occurrence of wonders as acts of divine grace. They wanted to avoid confusion between the advance challenge of the saint and prophecy. We, however, have just shown that there is a difference between the two. The advance challenge of a saint is concerned with other things than that of a prophet. There can be no doubt that the report on the authority of Professor Abû Isḥâq is not clear and has often led to denying that the wonders of the prophets could have been wrought by saints, on the grounds that each of the two groups has its own kind of wonders.

It is absurd to believe that miracles could be produced fraudulently by a liar. According to the Ash'arites, this is absurd because the essential part of a miracle is defined as 'confirmation of truthfulness and right guidance'. Were a miracle to occur under the contrary conditions, proof would become doubt, guidance misguidance, and, I might add, the confirmation of truthfulness, untruth. Realities would become absurdities, and the essential qualities would be turned upside down. Something, the occurrence of which would be absurd, cannot be possible.

The philosophers hold that wonders are acts of the prophet, even though they have no place in his own power. This is based upon their doctrine of an essential and necessary (causality) and of events developing out of each other according to conditions and reasons that (always) come up anew and, in the last instance, go back to the Necessary *per se* that acts *per se* and not by choice. In their opinion, the prophetical soul has special essential qualities which

[1] The Mu'tazilah is the theological school whence came the speculative dogmatics of Islam.

produce wonders, with the help of the power of (the Necessary *per se*) and the obedience of the elements to Him for purposes of generation. In their opinion the role of the prophet (in this process) is that through those qualities which God put into him, he is by nature fitted for being active among all created things, whenever he addresses himself to them and concentrates on them. They hold that wonders are wrought by the prophet himself, whether there is an advance challenge or not. They are evidence of the prophet's truthfulness, inasmuch as they prove that he is active among the created things, such activity constituting a special quality of the prophetic soul, not because they take the place of a clear assertion of his truthfulness. In their opinion, therefore, wonders are no definitive proof (of the prophet's truthfulness), as they are in the opinion of the speculative theologians. 'Advance awareness', for them, does not constitute part of the miracle. It does not stand out as the thing that differentiates (miracles) from acts of divine grace. They hold that (miracles) are differentiated from sorcery by the fact that a prophet is by nature fitted for good actions and averse to evil deeds. Therefore, he could not do evil through the wonders he works. The opposite is the case with the sorcerer. All his actions are evil and done for evil purposes. Further, (miracles) are differentiated from acts of divine grace by the fact that the wonders of a prophet are of an unusual character, such as ascending to heaven, passing through solid bodies, reviving the dead, conversing with angels, and flying through the air. The wonders of a saint, on the other hand, are of a lower order, such as making much out of little, speaking about something that will happen in the future, and similar things inferior to the power of action of prophets. A prophet can produce the wonders of saints, but a saint is not able to produce anything like the wonders of prophets. This has been confirmed by the Sufis in what they have written about the mystic path and reported of their ecstatic experiences.

Now that this has been established, it should be known that the evidence of the Qur'ân, which was revealed to our Prophet, is the greatest, noblest, and clearest miracle. Wonders are as a rule wrought by a prophet separately and apart from the revelation he receives. The miracle comes as evidence for its truthfulness. The Qur'ân, on the other hand, is in itself the claimed revelation. It is itself the wondrous miracle. It is its own proof. It requires no outside proof, as do the other wonders wrought in connection with revelations. It is the clearest proof that can be, because it unites in itself both the proof and what is to be proved. This is the meaning of Muḥammad's statement, 'Every prophet was given signs likely to provide reassurance for mankind. What I have been given is a revelation that was revealed to me. Therefore, I hope to have the greatest number of followers on the day of resurrection.' He refers to the fact that a miracle identical with the revelation (confirmed by it) is of such clarity and force of evidence that it will be found truthful, because of its clarity, by the greatest number of people. Therefore, many are those who consider the Prophet truthful, and believe. They are the 'followers', the nation of Islam.

All this indicates that the Qur'ân is alone among the divine books, in that our Prophet received it directly in the words and phrases in which it appears. In this respect, it differs from the Torah, the Gospel, and other heavenly books. The prophets received them in the form of ideas during the state of revelation. After their return to a human state, they expressed those ideas in their own ordinary words. Therefore, those books do not have the attribute of 'inimitability'. Inimitability is restricted to the Qur'ân. The other prophets received their books in a manner similar to that in which our Prophet received ideas that he attributed to God, such as are found in many traditions. The fact that he received the Qur'ân directly, in its literal form, is attested by the following statement of Muḥammad on the authority of his Lord who said: 'Do not move your tongue too fast to con this revelation. We Ourself shall see to its collection and recital.'[1]

Many verses of the Qur'ân show that He directly and literally revealed the Qur'ân, of which every *sûrah* is inimitable. Our Prophet wrought no greater miracle than the Qur'ân and the fact that he united the Arabs in his mission. 'Had you given away all the riches of the earth, you could not have so united them. But God has united them.'[2]

This should be known. It should be pondered. It will then be found to be correct, exactly as I have stated. One should also consider the evidence that lies in the superiority of Muḥammad's rank over that of the other prophets and in the exaltedness of his position.

We shall now give an explanation of the real meaning of prophecy as interpreted by many thorough scholars. We shall then mention the real meaning of soothsaying, dream vision, divination, and other supernatural ways of perception. We say:

(*The real meaning of prophecy*)

This world with all the created things in it has a certain order and solid construction. It shows nexuses between causes and things caused, combinations of some parts of creation with others, and transformations of some existent things into others, in a pattern that

---

[1] Qur'ân 75. 16f.   [2] Qur'ân 8. 63 (64).

is both remarkable and endless. Beginning with the world of the body and sensual perception, and therein first with the world of the visible elements, one notices how these elements are arranged gradually and continually in an ascending order, from earth to water, to air, and to fire. Each one of the elements is prepared to be transformed into the next higher or lower one, and sometimes is transformed. The higher one is always finer than the one preceding it. Eventually, the world of the spheres is reached. They are finer than anything else. They are in layers which are interconnected, in a shape which the senses are able to perceive only through the existence of motions. These motions provide some people with knowledge of the measurements and positions of the spheres, and also with knowledge of the existence of the essences beyond, the influence of which is noticeable in the spheres through the fact that they have motion.

One should then look at the world of creation. It started out from the minerals and progressed, in an ingenious, gradual manner, to plants and animals. The last stage of minerals is connected with the first stage of plants, such as herbs and seedless plants. The last stage of plants, such as palms and vines, is connected with the first stage of animals, such as snails and shellfish which have only the power of touch. The word 'connection' with regard to these created things means that the last stage of each group is fully prepared to become the first stage of the next group.

The animal world then widens, its species become numerous, and, in a gradual process of creation, it finally leads to man, who is able to think and to reflect. The higher stage of man is reached from the world of the monkeys, in which both sagacity and perception are found, but which has not reached the stage of actual reflection and thinking. At this point we come to the first stage of man. This is as far as our (physical) observation extends.

Now, in the various worlds we find manifold influences. In the world of sensual perception there are certain influences of the motions of the spheres and the elements. In the world of creation there are certain influences of the motions of growth and perception. All this is evidence of the fact that there is something that exercises an influence and is different from the bodily substances. This is something spiritual. It is connected with the created things, because the various worlds must be connected in their existence. This spiritual thing is the soul, which has perception and causes motion. Above the soul there must exist something else that gives the soul the power of perception and motion, and that is also connected with it. Its essence should be pure perception and absolute intellection. This is the world of the angels. The soul, consequently, must be prepared

75

to exchange humanity for angelicality, in order actually to become part of the angelic species at certain times in the flash of a moment. This happens after the spiritual essence of the soul has become perfect in actuality, as we shall mention later on.

The soul is connected with the stage next to it, as are all the orders of the *existentia*, as we have mentioned before. It is connected both upward and downward. Downward, it is connected with the body, thus acquiring the sense perceptions by which it is prepared for actual intellection. Upward, it is connected with the stage of the angels. There, it acquires scientific and supernatural perceptions, for knowledge of the things that come into being exists timelessly in the intellections of (the angels). This is in consequence of the well-constructed order of existence mentioned above, which requires that the essences and powers of (the world of existence) be connected with one another.

The human soul cannot be seen, but its influence is evident in the body, as if all its parts, in combination or separately, were organs of the soul and its powers. The powers of action are touching with the hand, walking with the foot, speaking with the tongue, and the total combined motion with the body.

The powers of sensual perception are graded and ascend to the highest power, that is, the power of thinking, for which there exists the term 'rational power'. Thus, the powers of external sense perception, with the organs of vision, hearing, and all the other (organs), lead up to inward (perception).

The first (inward sense) is the 'common sense', that is, the power that simultaneously perceives all objects of sensual perception, whether they belong to hearing, seeing, touching, or anything else. In this respect, it differs from the power of external sense perception, as the objects of sensual perception do not all crowd upon external sense perception at one and the same time.

The common sense transfers (the perceptions) to the imagination, which is the power that pictures an object of sensual perception in the soul, as it is, abstracted from all external matter. The organ for the activity of these two powers (common sense and imagination) is the first cavity of the brain. The front part of that cavity is for the common sense, and the back part for the imagination.

Imagination leads up to the estimative power and the power of memory. The estimative power serves for perceiving ideas that refer to individualities, such as the hostility of Zayd, the friendship of 'Amr, the compassion of the father, or the savagery of the wolf. The power of memory serves as a repository for all objects of perception, whether they are imagined or not. It is like a storehouse that preserves them for the time when they are needed. The organ for the activity of these two powers is the back cavity of the brain. The front part of that cavity is for the estimative power, and the back for the power of memory.

All these powers then lead up to the power of thinking. Its organ is the middle cavity of the brain. It is the power that causes reflection to be set in motion and leads toward intellection. The soul is constantly moved by it, as the result of its constitutional desire to think. It wants to be free from the grip of (the lower human) powers and the human kind of preparedness. It wants to proceed to active intellection by assimilating itself to the highest spiritual group (that of the angels), and to get into the first order of the *spiritualia* by perceiving them without the help of bodily organs. Therefore, the soul is constantly moving in that direction. It exchanges all humanity and human spirituality for angelicality of the highest stage, without the help of any acquired faculty but by virtue of a primary natural disposition that God has placed in it.

Human souls are of three kinds. One is by nature too weak to arrive at spiritual perception. Therefore, it is satisfied to move downward toward the perceptions of the senses and imagination and the formation of ideas with the help of the power of memory and the estimative power, according to limited rules and a special order. In this manner, people acquire perceptive and apperceptive knowledge, which is the product of thinking in the body. All this is (the result of the power of) imagination and is limited in extent, since from the way it starts it can reach the primary (*intelligibilia*) but cannot go beyond them. Also, if they are corrupt, everything beyond them is also corrupt. This, as a rule, is the extent of human corporeal perception. It is the goal of the perceptions of scholars. It is in it that scholars are firmly grounded.

A (second) kind (of soul), through thinking, moves in the direction of spiritual intellection and (a type of) perception that does not need the organs of the body, because of its innate preparedness for it. The perceptions of this kind of soul extend beyond the primary (*intelligibilia*) to which primary human perception is restricted, and cover the ground of inward observations, which are all intuitive. They are unlimited as to their beginning and their end. They are the perceptions of saints, of men of mystical learning and divine knowledge. The blessed obtain them after death, in Purgatory.

A (third) kind is by nature suited to exchange humanity altogether, both corporeal and spiritual humanity, for angelicality of the highest stage, so that it may actually become an angel in the flash of a moment, glimpse the highest group within their own stage, and listen to essential speech and divine address during that moment. (Individuals possessing this kind of soul) are prophets. God implanted and formed in them the natural ability to slough off humanity in that moment which is the state of revelation. God freed them from the lets and hindrances of the body, by which they were afflicted as human beings. He did this by means of 'iṣmah (infallibility) and straightforwardness, which He implanted in them and which gave them that particular outlook, and by means of a desire for divine worship which He centred in them and which converges from all sides toward that goal. They thus move toward the angelic, sloughing off humanity at will, by virtue of their natural constitution, and not with the help of any acquired faculty or craft.

The prophets move in that direction, slough off their humanity, and, once among the highest group (of angels), learn all that may there be learned. They then bring what they have learned back down to the level of the powers of human perception, as this is the way in which it can be transmitted to human beings. At times, this may happen in the form of a noise the prophet hears. It is like indistinct words from which he derives the idea conveyed to him. As soon as the noise has stopped, he retains and understands (the idea). At other times, the angel who conveys (the message) to the prophet appears to him in the form of a man who talks to him, and the prophet comprehends what he says. Learning the message from the angel, reverting to the level of human perception, and understanding the message conveyed to him—all this appears to take place in one moment, or rather, in a flash. It does not take place in time, but everything happens simultaneously. . . .

It should be known that, in general, the state of revelation presents difficulties and pains throughout. Revelation means leaving one's humanity, in order to attain angelic perceptions and to hear the speech of the soul. This causes pain, since it means that an essence leaves its own essence and exchanges its own stage for the ultimate stage. This is the meaning of the choking feeling which Muḥammad referred to in connection with the beginning of revelation in his statement: 'And he (Gabriel) choked me until it became too much for me; then he released me. Then he said, "Read", and I replied, "I cannot read." ' He did this a second and a third time, as the tradition tells.

Gradual habituation to the process of revelation brings some relief. It is for this reason that the earliest passages, sûrahs, and verses of the Qur'ân, revealed to Muḥammad in Mecca, are briefer than those revealed to him in Medina. This may serve as a criterion for distinguishing the Meccan sûrahs and verses from the Medinese. God leads to that which is correct. This is the quintessence of prophecy.

(Soothsaying)

Soothsaying (kahânah) is also one of the particular qualities of the human soul. This is as follows.

In the previous discussion, we stated that the human soul is prepared to exchange its humanity for the spirituality that lies above. Human beings have an intimation of that (exchange) in prophets who are by nature fitted to achieve it. It has been established that they neither need acquired qualities, nor are they dependent on any help from perceptions, notions, bodily activities, be they speech or motion, or anything else. It is a natural change from humanity to angelicality in the flash of a moment.

If this is so and if such preparedness exists in human nature, logical classification requires that there must be another kind of human beings, as inferior to the first kind as anything that has something perfect as its opposite must be inferior to that opposite. Independence from all help in (achieving contact with the supernatural) is the opposite of dependence on help in connection with it. They are two very different things.

Now, the classification of the world of existence requires that there must be a kind of human beings fitted by nature for the process of thinking voluntarily under the impulse of their rational power, whenever that power has a desire for it. (But the rational power) is not by nature capable of (supernatural perception). Thus, when its weakness keeps it from (contact with the supernatural), it is natural for it to get involved with particulars, either of sensual perception or of the imagination, such as transparent bodies, animal bones, speech in rhymed prose, or whatever bird or animal may present itself. (A person whose rational power is thus engaged) attempts to retain such sensual or imaginary perceptions, since he depends on their help in attaining the supernatural perception he desires. They give him a sort of assistance.

The power which in (such persons) constitutes the starting point of supernatural perception is soothsaying. The souls of such persons are inferior by nature and unable to attain perfection. Therefore, they have a better perception of particulars than of universals. They get involved with the former and neglect the latter. Therefore, the power of imagination is most strongly developed in those persons, because it is the organ of the particulars. (The particulars) completely pervade (the power of the imagination), both in the sleeping and the waking state. They are ever ready and present in it. The power of imagination brings (the particulars) to the attention of (those persons) and serves as a mirror in which they are seen constantly.

79

The soothsayer is not able to achieve perfection in his perception of the *intelligibilia*, because the revelation he receives is inspired by devils. The highest state this type of person can reach is to achieve disregard for the senses, with the help of rhymed prose and the use of words of an identical structure at the end of successive cola, and thereby to attain an imperfect contact of the sort described. From that motion and the foreign support that accompanies it, his heart receives some inspiration to express itself in words. The soothsayer, thus, often speaks the truth and agrees with reality. Often, however, what he says are falsehoods, because he supplements his deficiency with something foreign to, different from, and incompatible with, his perceptive essence. Thus, truth and falsehood are jumbled together in him, and he is not trustworthy. He often takes refuge in guesses and hypotheses, because, in his self-deception, he desires to have supernatural perception and is willing to cheat those who ask him for information.

Men who use such rhymed prose are distinguished by the name of soothsayers. They rank highest among their kind. Prophecy is a direct and independent contact of the essence of the prophet with (the angels). Because of his weakness, the soothsayer depends on the help of foreign notions. These enter into his perception and mingle with the perception toward which he aspires. He thus becomes confused by them. So it is that falsehood makes its way to his (door). It is, therefore, impossible (for his activity) to be prophecy. . . .

Soothsayers who are a prophet's contemporaries are aware of the prophet's truthfulness and the significance of his miracle, since they derive some intuitive experience from prophecy, such as every human being derives from sleep. Intellectual awareness of this relationship is stronger in the soothsayer than in the sleeper. What prevents soothsayers from acknowledging the truthfulness of the prophet, and causes them to deny him, is simply their misguided desire to be prophets themselves. This leads them to spiteful opposition. But when faith gains the upper hand and they stop aspiring to become prophets themselves, they make the most faithful of believers.

(Dream visions)

Real dream vision is an awareness on the part of the rational soul in its spiritual essence, of glimpses of the forms of events. While the soul is spiritual, the forms of events have actual existence in it, as is the case with all spiritual essences. The soul becomes spiritual through freeing itself from bodily matters and corporeal perceptions. This happens to the soul (in the form of) glimpses through the agency of sleep, whereby it gains the knowledge of future events that it desires and regains the perceptions that belong to it. When this process is weak and indistinct, the soul applies to it allegory and imaginary pictures, in order to gain (the desired knowledge). Such allegory, then, necessitates interpretation. When, on the other hand, this process is strong, it can dispense with allegory. Then, no interpretation is necessary, because the process is free from imaginary pictures.

The occurrence, in the soul, of such glimpses is caused by the fact that the soul is potentially a spiritual essence, supplemented by the body and the perceptions of the body. Its essence, thus, eventually becomes pure intellection, and its existence becomes perfect in actuality. The soul, now, is a spiritual essence having perception without the help of any of the bodily organs. However, among the *spiritualia*, it is of a lower species than the angels, who inhabit the highest stage, and who never had to supplement their essences with corporeal perceptions or anything else. The preparedness (for spirituality) comes to (the soul) as long as it is in the body. There is a special kind (of preparedness), such as saints have, and there is a general kind common to all human beings. This is what 'dream vision' means.

In the case of the prophets, this preparedness is a preparedness to exchange humanity for pure angelicality, which is the highest rank of *spiritualia*. It expresses itself repeatedly during revelations. It exists when (the prophet) returns to the level of corporeal perceptions. Whatever perception he has at that moment is clearly similar to what happens in sleep, even though sleep is much inferior to (revelation).

Because of this similarity, Muḥammad defined dream vision as being the forty-sixth—or, according to other recensions, the forty-third, or the seventieth—part of prophecy. None of these fractions is meant to be taken literally. They are to indicate the great degree of difference between the various stages of supernatural perception. This is shown by the reference to 'seventy' in one of the recensions. The number 'seventy' is used by the Arabs to express the idea of a large number.

The remote preparedness is commonly found among human beings. However, there are many obstacles and hindrances that prevent man from translating it into actuality. One of the greatest hindrances is the external senses. God, therefore, created man in such a way that the veil of the senses could be lifted through sleep, which is a natural function of man. When that veil is lifted, the soul is ready to learn the things it desires to know in the world of Truth. At times, it catches a glimpse of what it seeks.

The reason the veil of the senses is lifted in sleep is as follows. The perceptions and actions of the rational soul are the result of the corporeal animal spirit. This spirit is a fine vapour concentrated in the left cavity of the heart, as is stated in the anatomical works of Galen and others. It spreads with the blood in the veins and arteries, and makes sensual perception, motion, and all the other corporeal actions possible. Its finest part goes up to the brain. There, it is tempered by the coldness of (the brain), and it effects the actions of the powers located in the cavities of the brain. The rational soul perceives and acts only by means of that vaporous spirit. It is connected with it, being the result of the wisdom of creation which requires that nothing fine can influence anything coarse. Of all the corporeal matters, only the animal spirit is fine. Therefore, it is receptive to the influence of the essence, which differs from it only in respect of corporeality, that is, the rational soul. Thus, through the medium of (the animal spirit), the influence of the rational soul reaches the body.

We have stated before that the perception of the rational soul is of two kinds. There is an external perception through the five senses, and an inward perception through the cerebral powers. All these perceptions divert the rational soul from the perception for which it is prepared by nature—that of the essences of the *spiritualia*, which are higher than it.

Since the external senses are corporeal, they are subject to weakness and lassitude as the result of exertion and fatigue, and to spiritual exhaustion through too much activity. Therefore, God gave them the desire to rest, so that perfect perception may be renewed afterwards. This is accomplished by the retirement of the animal spirit from all the external senses and its return to the inward sense. This process is supported by the cold that covers the body during the night. Under the influence of the cold of the night, the natural heat repairs to the innermost recesses of the body and turns from its exterior to the interior. It thus guides its vehicle, the animal spirit, into the interior of the body. This is the reason why human beings, as a rule, sleep only at night.

The spirit, thus, withdraws from the external senses and returns to the inward powers. The preoccupations and hindrances of sensual perception lessen their hold over the soul, and it now returns to the forms that exist in the power of memory. Then, through a process of synthesis and analysis, (these forms) are shaped into imaginary pictures. Most of these pictures are customary ones, because (the soul) has only shortly before withdrawn from the conventional objects of sensual perception. It now transmits them to the common sense, which combines all the five external senses, to be perceived in the manner of those five senses. Frequently, however, the soul turns to its spiritual essence in concert with the inward powers. It then accomplishes the spiritual kind of perception for which it is fitted by nature. It takes up some of the forms of things that have become inherent in its essence at that time. Imagination seizes on those perceived forms, and pictures them in the customary moulds either realistically or allegorically. Pictured allegorically, they require interpretation. The synthetic and analytic activity which (the soul) applies to the forms in the power of memory, before it perceives what it can (of the supernatural), is what is called in the Qur'ân 'confused dreams'.

Clear dream visions are from God. Allegorical dream visions, which call for interpretation, are from the angels. And 'confused dreams' are from Satan, because they are altogether futile, as Satan is the source of futility.

This is what 'dream vision' really is, and how it is caused and encouraged by sleep. It is a particular quality of the human soul common to all mankind. Nobody is free from it. Every human being has, more than once, seen something in his sleep that turned out to be true when he awakened. He knows for certain that the soul must necessarily have supernatural perception in sleep. If this is possible in the realm of sleep, it is not impossible in other conditions, because the perceiving essence is one and its qualities are always present. God guides toward the truth.

('Dream words')

Note: Most of the (aforementioned supernatural perception by means of dream visions) occurs to human beings unintentionally and without their having power over it. The soul occupies itself with a thing. As a result, it obtains that glimpse (of the supernatural) while it is asleep, and it sees that thing. It does not plan it that way.

In the *Ghâyah*[1] and other books by practitioners of magic, reference is made to words that should be mentioned on falling asleep so as to cause the dream vision to be about the things one desires. These words are called 'dream words'. In the *Ghâyah*, Maslamah mentioned a dream word that he called 'the dream word of the perfect nature'. It consists of saying, upon falling asleep and after obtaining freedom of the inner senses and finding one's way clear (for supernatural perception), the following non-Arabic words: *tamâghis ba'dân yaswâdda waghdâs nawfanâ ghâdis.*[2] The person should then mention what he wants, and the thing he asks for will be shown to him in his sleep.

[1] The *Ghâyat al-ḥakîm*, ascribed to the famous tenth-century Spanish scientist Maslamah b. Aḥmad al-Majrîṭî.
[2] These magical words seem to be Aramaic.

With the help of these words, I have myself had remarkable dream visions, through which I learned things about myself that I wanted to know. However, (the existence of such dream words) is no proof that the intention to have a dream vision can produce it. The dream words produce a preparedness in the soul for the dream vision. If that preparedness is a strong one, (the soul) will be more likely to obtain that for which it is prepared. A person may arrange for whatever preparedness he likes, but that is no assurance that the thing for which preparations have been made will actually happen. The power to prepare for a thing is not the same as power over the thing itself. This should be known and considered in similar cases.

(Other types of divination)

In the human species we find individuals who foretell things before they take place. They have a special natural aptitude for it. Through that aptitude, they are distinguished from all other human beings. They do not have recourse to a craft for their predictions, nor do they get them with the help of astral influences or anything else. Their forecasts are the necessary result of their natural disposition. Among such people are diviners: men who gaze into transparent bodies such as mirrors or bowls of water; men who examine the hearts, livers, and bones of animals; men who draw auguries from birds and wild animals; and men who cast pebbles, grains of wheat, or date pits. All these things are found among mankind; no one can deny them or be ignorant of them. Statements concerning supernatural things are also placed upon the tongues of the insane, who are thus able to give information about (supernatural things). Sleeping and dying persons, being about to die or to fall asleep, likewise speak about supernatural things. Men who have followed Sufi training have, as is well known, as acts of divine grace, obtained perceptions of supernatural things.

(The different kinds of supernatural perception)

. . . All the kinds of (supernatural) perception mentioned are found in man. The Arabs used to repair to soothsayers in order to learn about forthcoming events. They consulted them in their quarrels, to learn the truth by means of supernatural perception. Their literature contains much information about this matter. . . .

Some people have another way of supernatural perception. It occurs in the stage of transition from waking to sleeping, and is in (the form of unconsciously) speaking about the thing one wants to know and thereby obtaining supernatural knowledge of the matter

84

as desired. This happens only during the transition from waking to sleeping, when one has lost the power to control one's words. Such a person talks as if by innate compulsion. The most he can do is to hear and understand what he says.

Words of a similar nature come from those who are about to be killed, at the moment when their heads are being severed from their trunks. We have been informed that certain criminal tyrants used to kill their prisoners in order to learn their own future from the words the prisoners would utter when they were about to be killed. It was unpleasant information they received from them.

In the *Ghâyah*, Maslamah similarly mentioned that when a human being is placed in a barrel of sesame oil and kept in it for forty days, is fed with figs and nuts until his flesh is gone and only the arteries and sutures of the skull remain, and is then taken out of the oil and exposed to the drying action of the air, he will answer all special and general questions regarding the future that may be asked. This is detestable sorcery. However, it shows what remarkable things exist in the world of man.

There are men who attempt to obtain supernatural perception through exercise. They attempt an artificial (state of) death through self-mortification. They kill all corporeal powers (in themselves), and wipe out all influences of those powers that colour the soul in various ways. This is achieved by concentrated thinking, and doing without food for long periods. It is definitely known that when death descends upon the body, sensual perception and the veil it constitutes disappear, and the soul beholds its essence and its world. (These men) attempt to produce, artificially before death, the experience they will have after death, and to have their soul behold the supernatural.

Other such people are the men who train themselves in sorcery. They train themselves in these things, in order to be able to behold the supernatural and to be active in the various worlds. Most such live in the intemperate zones of the north and the south, especially in India, where they are called yogis. They possess a large literature on how such exercises are to be done. The stories about them in this connection are remarkable.

The Sufi training is a religious one. It is free from any such reprehensible intentions. The Sufis aspire to total concentration upon God and upon the approach to Him, in order to obtain the mystical experiences of gnosis and Divine oneness. In addition to their training in concentration and hunger, the Sufis feed on exercises by which their devotion to that training can fully materialize. When the soul is reared on such exercises, it comes closer to the gnosis of God, whereas, without it, it comes to be a Satanic one.

Whatever supernatural knowledge or activity is achieved by the

Sufis is accidental, and was not originally intended. Had it been intentional, the devotion of the Sufis would have been directed toward something other than God, namely, toward supernatural activity and vision. What a losing business that would have been! In reality, it would have been polytheism. Through their devotion, (Sufis) intend (to come near) the Master, and nothing else. If, meanwhile, some (supernatural perception) is obtained, it is accidental and unintentional. Many (Sufis) shun (supernatural perception) when it accidentally happens to them, and pay no attention to it. They want God only for the sake of His essence, and nothing else. It is well known that (supernatural perception) occurs among the (Sufis). They call their supernatural experiences and mind-reading 'physiognomy' and 'uncovering'. Their experiences of supernatural activity they call 'acts of divine grace'. None of these things is unworthy of them. . . .

Among the adepts of mysticism are fools and imbeciles who are more like insane persons than like rational beings. None the less, they deservedly attained stations of sainthood and the mystic states of the righteous. The persons with mystical experience who learn about them know that such is their condition, although they are not legally responsible. The information they give about the supernatural is remarkable. They are not bound by anything. They speak absolutely freely about it and tell remarkable things. When jurists see they are not legally responsible, they frequently deny that they have attained any mystical station, since sainthood can be obtained only through divine worship. This is an error. The attainment of sainthood is not restricted to the correct performance of divine worship, or anything else. When the human soul is firmly established as existent, God may single it out for whatever gifts of His He wants to give it. The rational souls of such people are not non-existent, nor are they corrupt, as is the case with the insane. They merely lack the intellect that is the basis of legal responsibility. That intellect is a special attribute of the soul. It means various kinds of knowledge that are necessary to man and that guide his speculative ability and teach him how to make a living and organize his home. One may say that if he knows how to make a living, he has no excuse left not to accept legal responsibility, so that he may prepare for his life after death. Now, a person who lacks that special attribute of the soul called intellect still does not lack the soul itself, and has not forgotten his reality. He has reality, though he lacks the intellect entailing legal responsibility, that is, the knowledge of how to make a living. This is not absurd. God does not select His servants for gnosis only on the basis of the performance of some legal duty.

If this is correct, it should be known that the state of these men is frequently confused with that of the insane, whose rational souls are corrupted and who belong to the category of animals. There are signs by which one can distinguish the two groups. One of them is that fools are found devoting themselves constantly to certain exercises and divine worship, though not in the way the religious law requires, since, as we have stated, they are not legally responsible. The insane, on the other hand, have no particular devotion whatever.

Another sign is that fools were created stupid, and were stupid from their earliest days. The insane, on the other hand, lose their minds after some portion of their life has passed, as the result of natural bodily accidents. When this happens to them and their rational souls become corrupt, they are lost.

A further sign is the great activity of fools among men. It may be good or bad. They do not have to have permission, because for them there is no legal responsibility. The insane, on the other hand, show no such activity.

The course of our discussion caused us to insert the preceding paragraph. God leads toward that which is correct.

(Other alleged ways of supernatural perception)

Some people think that there are ways of supernatural perception not involving remoteness from sensual perception. Such are the astrologers who believe in astrological indications, consequences of the positions of (stars) in the firmament, influences of (the stars) upon the elements, and results from the tempering of the natures of (the stars) when they look at each other, as well as effects of such tempers upon the air. Astrologers have nothing to do with the supernatural. All is guesswork and conjecture based upon (the assumed existence of) astral influence, and a resulting conditioning of the air. (Such guesswork) is accompanied by an additional measure of sagacity enabling scholars to determine the distribution (of astral influence) upon particular individuals in the world, as Ptolemy said. We shall explain the futility of astrology in the proper place, if God wills. It has nothing whatever to do with the supernatural perception we have mentioned.

(Geomancy)

Other such people include certain men of the common people who, to discover the supernatural and know the future, invented a craft they called 'sand writing' (geomancy) after the material one uses for it. This craft consists in forming combinations of dots in four 'ranks'.

The sand diviners have given different names to the different combinations and classified them as lucky or unlucky, as is done with the stars. They have invented a discipline that runs parallel to astrology and the system of astrological judgments. However, astrological judgments are based upon natural indications, as Ptolemy assumes. The indications of sand writing, on the other hand, are conventional.

Ptolemy discussed only nativities and conjunctions which, in his opinion, come within the influence of the stars and the positions of the spheres upon the world of the elements. Subsequent astrologers, however, discussed questions (*interrogationes*), in that they attempted to discover the innermost thoughts by attributing them to the various houses of the firmament and drawing conclusions concerning them, according to the judgments governing each particular astral house. They are those mentioned by Ptolemy.

It should be known that innermost thoughts concern psychic knowledge, which does not belong to the world of the elements. They do not come within the influence of the stars or the positions of the spheres, nor do (the stars and the positions of the spheres) give any indications with regard to them. The branch of questions (*interrogationes*) has indeed been accepted in astrology as a way of making deductions from the stars and positions of the spheres. However, it is used where it is not natural for it to be used.

Some sand diviners attempt supernatural perception, in that they occupy their senses with study of the combinations of figures. They thus reach a state of preparedness, like those who are by nature fitted for preparedness, as we shall mention later on. These men are the noblest class of sand diviners. . . .

Geomancy is prevalent in civilized regions. There exists a literature dealing with it. Outstanding ancient and modern personalities were famous for it. But it is obviously based on arbitrary notions and wishful thinking. The truth that should be present to one's mind is that the supernatural cannot be perceived by any craft at all. The only people who can acquire knowledge of the supernatural are those distinguished human beings who are fitted by nature to return from the world of sensual perception to the world of the spirit. The astrologers, therefore, called all such people 'Venusians', with reference to Venus, because they assumed that the position of Venus in the nativities of these people indicates their ability to have supernatural perception.

The sign by which persons who are disposed by nature to supernatural perceptions can be recognized is this: When these persons devote themselves to acquiring a knowledge of things, they suffer a departure from their natural condition. They yawn and stretch, and show symptoms of remoteness from sensual perception. These vary in intensity according to the different degrees to which they possess this natural disposition. Those in whom this sign is not found have nothing to do with supernatural perception. They are merely trying to spread the falsehoods to which they are committed.

There are others who also lay down certain rules for the discovery of the supernatural. Their rules do not belong to the first category, that which has to do with the spiritual perceptions of the soul, and also differ from speculations based upon astral influences, as assumed by Ptolemy, as well as from the guesswork and conjecturing with which the diviners work. They are nothing but fallacies thrown out like snares for weak-minded people. . . .

And God knows better how it may be.

All these ways of perceiving the supernatural are based upon no proof, and are not verifiable. The reader should investigate this matter critically, if he is a well-grounded scholar. . . .

It is obvious that it is from the relations existing among the data that one finds out the unknown from the known. This, however, applies only to events occurring in the world of existence or in science. Things of the future belong to the supernatural and cannot be known unless the causes for their happening are known and we have trustworthy information about it. . . .

Chapter 2

*Bedouin civilization, savage nations and tribes
and their conditions of life, including
several basic and explanatory statements*

1   Both Bedouins and sedentary people are natural groups

It should be known that differences of condition among people are
the result of the different ways in which they make their living. Social
organization enables them to co-operate toward that end and to start
with the simple necessities of life, before they get to conveniences and
luxuries.

Some people live by agriculture, the cultivation of vegetables and
grains; others by animal husbandry, the use of sheep, cattle, goats,
bees, and silkworms, for breeding and for their products. Those who
live by agriculture or animal husbandry cannot avoid the call of the
desert, because it alone offers the wide fields, pastures for animals,
and other things that the settled areas do not offer. It is therefore
necessary for them to restrict themselves to the desert. Their social
organization and co-operation for the needs of life and civilization,
such as food, shelter, and warmth, do not take them beyond the bare
subsistence level, because of their inability (to provide) for anything
beyond those (things). Subsequent improvement of their conditions
and acquisition of more wealth and comfort than they need, cause
them to rest and take it easy. Then, they co-operate for things beyond the bare necessities. They use more food and clothes, and take
pride in them. They build large houses, and lay out towns and cities
for protection. This is followed by an increase in comfort and ease,
which leads to formation of the most developed luxury customs.
They take the greatest pride in the preparation of food and a fine
cuisine, in the use of varied splendid clothes of silk and brocade and
other (fine materials), in the construction of ever higher buildings
and towers, in elaborate furnishings for the buildings, and the most
intensive cultivation of crafts in actuality. They build castles and
mansions, provide them with running water, build their towers
higher and higher, and compete in furnishing them (most elaborately). They differ in the quality of the clothes, the beds, the vessels,
and the utensils they employ for their purposes. 'Sedentary people'

means the inhabitants of cities and countries, some of whom adopt the crafts as their way of making a living, while others adopt commerce. They earn more and live more comfortably than Bedouins, because they live on a level beyond the level of bare necessity, and their way of making a living corresponds to their wealth.

It has thus become clear that Bedouins and sedentary people are natural groups which exist by necessity, as we have stated.

2 The Bedouins are a natural group in the world

We have mentioned in the previous section that the inhabitants of the desert adopt the natural manner of making a living, namely, agriculture and animal husbandry. They restrict themselves to the necessary in food, clothing, and mode of dwelling, and to the other necessary conditions and customs. They do not possess conveniences and luxuries. They use tents of hair and wool, or houses of wood, or of clay and stone, which are not furnished (elaborately). The purpose is to have shade and shelter, and nothing beyond that. They also take shelter in caverns and caves. The food they take is either little prepared or not prepared at all, save that it may have been touched by fire.

For those who make their living through the cultivation of grain and through agriculture, it is better to be stationary than to travel around. Such, therefore, are the inhabitants of small communities, villages, and mountain regions. These people make up the large mass of the Berbers and non-Bedouins.

Those who make their living from animals requiring pasturage, such as sheep and cattle, usually travel around in order to find pasture and water for their animals, since it is better for them to move around in the land. They are called 'sheepmen', that is, men who live on sheep and cattle. They do not go deep into the desert, because they would not find good pastures there. Such people include the Berbers, the Turks, the Turkomans and the Slavs, for instance.

Those who make their living by raising camels move around more. They wander deeper into the desert, because the hilly pastures with their plants and shrubs do not furnish enough subsistence for camels. They must feed on the desert shrubs and drink the salty desert water. They must move around the desert regions during the winter, in flight from the harmful cold to the warm desert air. In the desert sands, camels can find places to give birth to their young ones. Of all animals, camels have the hardest delivery and the greatest need for warmth in connection with it. (Camel nomads) are therefore forced to make excursions deep (into the desert). Frequently, too, they are driven from the hills by the militia, and they penetrate farther into the desert, because they do not want the militia to mete out justice to them or to punish them for their hostile acts. As a result, they are the most savage human beings that exist. Compared with sedentary people, they are on a level with wild, untamable animals and dumb beasts of prey. Such people are the Bedouins. In the West, the nomadic Berbers and the Zanâtah are their counterparts, and in the East, the Kurds, the Turkomans, and the Turks. The Bedouins, however, make deeper excursions into the desert and are more rooted in desert life because they live exclusively on camels, while the other groups live on sheep and cattle, as well as camels.

It has thus become clear that the Bedouins are a natural group which by necessity exists in civilization.

3 Bedouins are prior to sedentary people. The desert is the basis and reservoir of civilization and cities

We have mentioned that the Bedouins restrict themselves to the bare necessities in their way of life and are unable to go beyond them, while sedentary people concern themselves with conveniences and luxuries in their conditions and customs. The bare necessities are no doubt prior to the conveniences and luxuries. Bare necessities, in a way, are basic, and luxuries secondary. Bedouins, thus, are the basis of, and prior to, cities and sedentary people. Man seeks first the bare necessities. Only after he has obtained the bare necessities does he get to comforts and luxuries. The toughness of desert life precedes the softness of sedentary life. Therefore, urbanization is found to be the goal to which the Bedouin aspires. Through his own efforts, he achieves what he proposes to achieve in this respect. When he has obtained enough to be ready for the conditions and customs of luxury, he enters upon a life of ease and submits himself to the yoke of the city. This is the case with all Bedouin tribes. Sedentary people, on the other hand, have no desire for desert conditions, unless they are motivated by some urgent necessity or they cannot keep up with their fellow city dwellers.

Evidence for the fact that Bedouins are the basis of, and prior to, sedentary people is furnished by investigating the inhabitants of any given city. We shall find that most of its inhabitants originated among Bedouins dwelling in the country and villages of the vicinity. Such Bedouins became wealthy, settled in the city, and adopted a life of ease and luxury, such as exists in the sedentary environment.

All Bedouins and sedentary people differ also among themselves in their conditions of life. Many a clan is greater than another, many a tribe greater than another, many a city larger than another, and many a town more populous than another. . . .

4 Bedouins are closer to being good than sedentary people

The reason for this is that the soul in its first natural state of creation is ready to accept whatever good or evil may arrive and leave an imprint upon it. Muḥammad said: 'Every infant is born in the natural state. It is his parents who make him a Jew or a Christian or a heathen.' To the degree the soul is first affected by one of the two qualities, it moves away from the other and finds it difficult to acquire it. When customs proper to goodness have been first to enter the soul of a good person, and his (soul) has thus acquired the habit of (goodness, that person) moves away from evil and finds it difficult to do anything evil. The same applies to the evil person.

Sedentary people are much concerned with all kinds of pleasures. They are accustomed to luxury and success in worldly occupations and to indulgence in worldly desires. Therefore, their souls are coloured with all kinds of blameworthy and evil qualities. The more of them they possess, the more remote do the ways and means of goodness become to them. Eventually they lose all sense of restraint. Many of them are found to use improper language in their gatherings as well as in the presence of their superiors and womenfolk. They are not deterred by any sense of restraint, because the bad custom of behaving openly in an improper manner in both words and deeds has taken hold of them. Bedouins may be as concerned with worldly affairs as (sedentary people are). However, such concern would touch only the necessities of life and not luxuries or anything causing, or calling for, desires and pleasures. The customs they follow in their mutual dealings are, therefore, appropriate. As compared with those of sedentary people, their evil ways and blameworthy qualities are much less numerous. They are closer to the first natural state and more remote from the evil habits that have been impressed upon the souls (of sedentary people) through numerous and ugly, blameworthy customs. Thus, they can more easily be cured than sedentary people. This is obvious. It will later on become clear that sedentary life constitutes the last stage of civilization and the point where it begins to decay. It also constitutes the last stage of evil and of remoteness from goodness. Clearly, the Bedouins are closer to being good than sedentary people. . . .

5 Bedouins are more disposed to courage than sedentary people

The reason for this is that sedentary people have become used to laziness and ease. They are sunk in well-being and luxury. They have entrusted the defence of their property and their lives to the governor and ruler who rules them, and to the militia which has the task of guarding them. They find full assurance of safety in the walls that surround them, and the fortifications that protect them. No noise disturbs them, and no hunting occupies their time. They are carefree and trusting, and have ceased to carry weapons. Successive generations have grown up in this way of life. They have become like women and children, who depend upon the master of the house. Eventually, this has come to be a quality of character that replaces natural disposition.

The Bedouins, on the other hand, live apart from the community. They are alone in the country and remote from militias. They have no walls or gates. Therefore, they provide their own defence and do not entrust it to, or rely upon others for it. They always carry weapons. They watch carefully all sides of the road. They take hurried naps only when they are together in company or when they are in the saddle. They pay attention to the most distant barking or noise. They go alone into the desert, guided by their fortitude, putting their trust in themselves. Fortitude has become a character quality of theirs, and courage their nature. They use it whenever they are called upon or roused by an alarm. When sedentary people mix with them in the desert or associate with them on a journey, they depend on them. They cannot do anything for themselves without them. This is an observed fact. (Their dependence extends) even to knowledge of the country, the directions, watering places, and crossroads. Man is a child of the customs and the things he has become used to. He is not the product of his natural disposition and temperament. The conditions to which he has become accustomed, until they have become for him a quality of character and matters of habit and custom, have replaced his natural disposition. If one studies this in human beings, one will find much of it, and it will be found to be a correct observation.

6 The reliance of sedentary people upon laws destroys their fortitude and power of resistance

Not everyone is master of his own affairs. Chiefs and leaders who are masters of the affairs of men are few in comparison with the rest. As a rule, man must by necessity be dominated by someone else. If the domination is kind and just and the people under it are not oppressed by its laws and restrictions, they are guided by the courage or cowardice that they possess in themselves. They are satisfied with the absence of any restraining power. Self-reliance eventually becomes a quality natural to them. They would not know anything else. If, however, the domination with its laws is one of brute force and intimidation, it breaks their fortitude and deprives them of their power of resistance as a result of the inertness that develops in the souls of the oppressed, as we shall explain.

When laws are (enforced) by means of punishment, they completely destroy fortitude, because the use of punishment against someone who cannot defend himself generates in that person a feeling of humiliation that, no doubt, must break his fortitude.

When laws are (intended to serve the purposes of) education and instruction and are applied from childhood on, they have to some degree the same effect, because people then grow up in fear and docility and consequently do not rely on their own fortitude.

Thus, greater fortitude is found among the savage Arab Bedouins than among people who are subject to laws. Furthermore, those who rely on laws and are dominated by them from the very beginning of their education and instruction in the crafts, sciences, and religious matters, are thereby deprived of much of their own fortitude. They can scarcely defend themselves at all against hostile acts. This is the case with students, whose occupation it is to study and to learn from teachers and religious leaders, and who constantly apply themselves to instruction and education in very dignified gatherings. This situation and the fact that it destroys the power of resistance and fortitude must be understood.

It is no argument that the men around Muḥammad observed the religious laws, and yet did not experience any diminution of their fortitude, but possessed the greatest possible fortitude. When the Muslims got their religion from Muḥammad, the restraining influence came from themselves, as a result of the encouragement and discouragement he gave them in the Qur'ân. It was not a result of technical instruction or scientific education. The laws were the laws and precepts of the religion that they received orally and which their firmly rooted belief in the truth of the articles of faith caused them to observe. Their fortitude remained unabated, and it was not corroded by education or authority. 'Umar said, 'Those who are not (disciplined) by the religious law are not educated by God.' 'Umar's desire was that everyone should have his restraining influence in himself. His certainty was that Muḥammad knew best what is good for mankind.

(The influence of) religion, then, decreased among men, and they came to use restraining laws. The religious law became a branch of learning and a craft to be acquired through instruction and education. People turned to sedentary life and assumed the character trait of submissiveness to law. This led to a decrease in their fortitude.

Clearly, then, governmental and educational laws destroy fortitude, because their restraining influence is something that comes from outside. The religious laws, on the other hand, do not destroy fortitude, because their restraining influence is something inherent. Therefore, govermental and educational laws influence sedentary people, in that they weaken their souls and diminish their stamina, because they have to suffer them both as children and as adults. The bedouins, on the other hand, are not in the same position, because they live far away from the laws of government, instruction, and education. . . .

7 Only tribes held together by group feeling can live in the desert

It should be known that God put good and evil into the nature of man. Thus, He says in the Qur'ân: 'We led him along the two paths.'[1] He further says: 'And inspired the soul with wickedness as well as fear of God.'[2]

Evil is the quality that is closest to man when he fails to improve his customs and when religion is not used as the model to improve him. The great mass of mankind is in that condition, with the exception of those to whom God gives success. Evil qualities in man are injustice and mutual aggression. He who casts his eye upon the property of his brother will lay his hand upon it to take it, unless there is a restraining influence to hold him back. The poet thus says:

> Injustice is a human trait. If you find
> A moral man, there is some reason why he is not unjust

Mutual aggression of people in towns and cities is averted by the authorities and the government, which hold back the masses under their control from attacks and aggression upon each other. They are thus prevented by the influence of force and governmental authority from mutual injustice, save such injustice as comes from the ruler himself.

Aggression against a city from outside may be averted by walls, in the event of unpreparedness, a surprise attack at night, or inability (of the inhabitants) to withstand the enemy during the day. Or it may be averted with the help of government auxiliary troops, if (the inhabitants are) prepared and ready to offer resistance.

The restraining influence among Bedouin tribes comes from their *shaykh*s and leaders. It results from the great respect and veneration they generally enjoy among the people. The hamlets of the Bedouins are defended against outside enemies by a tribal militia composed of noble youths of the tribe who are known for their courage. Their defence and protection are successful only if they are a closely knit group of common descent. This strengthens their stamina and makes them feared, since everybody's affection for his family and his group

[1] Qur'ân 90. 10 (10).   [2] Qur'ân 91. 8 (8).

is more important (than anything else). Compassion and affection for one's blood relations and relatives exist in human nature as something God put into the hearts of men. It makes for mutual support and aid, and increases the fear felt by the enemy.

Those who have no one of their own lineage (to care for) rarely feel affection for their fellows. If danger is in the air on the day of battle, such a man slinks away and seeks to save himself, because he is afraid of being left without support. Such people, therefore, cannot live in the desert, because they would fall prey to any nation that might want to swallow them up.

If this is true with regard to the place where one lives, which is in constant need of defence and military protection, it is equally true with regard to every other human activity, such as prophecy, the establishment of royal authority, or propaganda. Nothing can be achieved in these matters without fighting for it, since man has the natural urge to offer resistance. And for fighting one cannot do without group feeling, as we mentioned at the beginning.

8 Group feeling results only from blood relationship or something corresponding to it

(Respect for) blood ties is something natural among men, with the rarest exceptions. It leads to affection for one's relations and blood relatives, (the feeling that) no harm ought to befall them nor any destruction come upon them. One feels shame when one's relatives are treated unjustly or attacked, and one wishes to intervene between them and whatever peril or destruction threatens them. This is a natural urge in man, for as long as there have been human beings. If the direct relationship between persons who help each other is very close, so that it leads to close contact and unity, the ties are obvious and clearly require the (existence of a feeling of solidarity) without any outside (prodding). If, however, the relationship is somewhat distant, it is often forgotten in part. However, some knowledge of it remains and this causes a person to help his relatives for the known motive, in order to escape the shame he would feel in his soul were a person to whom he is somehow related treated unjustly.

Clients and allies belong in the same category. The affection everybody has for his clients and allies results from the feeling of shame that comes to a person when one of his neighbours, relatives, or a blood relation in any degree is humiliated. The reason for it is that a client(-master) relationship leads to close contact exactly, or approximately in the same way, as does common descent. It is in that sense that one must understand Muḥammad's remark, 'Learn as much of your pedigrees as is necessary to establish your ties of kindred.' It means that pedigrees are useful only in so far as they imply the close contact that is a consequence of blood ties and that eventually leads to mutual help and affection. Anything beyond that is superfluous. For a pedigree is something imaginary and devoid of reality. Its usefulness consists only in the resulting connection and close contact. If the fact of (common descent) is obvious and clear, it evokes in man a natural affection, as we have said. If, however, its existence is known only from remote history, it moves the imagination but faintly. Its usefulness is gone, and preoccupation with it becomes gratuitous, a kind of game, and as such is not permissible. In this sense, one must understand the remark, 'Genealogy is something which is of no use to know and which it does no harm not to know.' This means that when common descent is no longer clear and has become a matter of scientific knowledge, it can no longer move the imagination and is denied the affection caused by group feeling. It has become useless.

9 Purity of lineage is found only among the savage Arabs of the desert and other such people

This is because of the poor life, hard conditions, and bad habitats that are peculiar to the Bedouins. They are the result of necessity, inasmuch as their subsistence depends on camels and camel breeding and pasturage. The camels are the cause of the Bedouins' savage life in the desert, since they feed on desert shrubs and give birth in the desert sands. The desert is a place of hardship and starvation, but to them it has become familiar and accustomed. Generations of Bedouins grew up in the desert. Eventually, they became confirmed in their character and natural qualities. No member of any other nation was disposed to share their conditions. No member of any other race felt attracted to them. But if one of them were to find ways and means of fleeing from these conditions, he would not give them up. Therefore, their pedigrees can be trusted not to have been mixed up and corrupted. They have been preserved pure in unbroken lines. This is the case, for instance, with Muḍar tribes such as the Quraysh, the Kinânah, the Thaqîf, the Banû Asad, the Hudhayl, and their Khuzâ'ah neighbours. They lived a hard life in places where there was no agriculture or animal husbandry. They lived far from the fertile fields of Syria and the 'Irâq, far from the sources of seasonings and grains. How pure have they kept their lineages! These are unmixed in every way, and are known to be unsullied.

Other Arabs lived in the hills and at the sources of fertile pastures and plentiful living. Among these Arabs were the Ḥimyar and the Kahlân, such as the Lakhm, the Judhâm, the Ghassân, the Ṭayy, the Quḍâ'ah, and the Iyâd. Their lineages were mixed up, and their groups intermingled. It is known that (genealogists) differ with respect to each one of these families. This came about as the result of intermixture with non-Arabs. They did not pay any attention to preserving the (purity of) lineage of their families and groups. This was done only by (true) Arabs. Furthermore, the Arabs of the fertile fields were affected by the general human trend toward competition for the fat soil and the good pastures. This resulted in intermingling and much mixture of lineages. Even at the beginning of Islam, people occasionally referred to themselves by their places of residence. They referred to the Districts of Qinnasrîn, of Damascus, or of the 'Awâṣim (the border region of northern Syria). This custom was then transferred to Spain. It happened not because the Arabs rejected genealogical considerations, but because they acquired particular places of residence after the conquest. They eventually became known by their places of residence. These became a distinguishing mark, in addition to the pedigree, used by the Arabs to identify themselves in the presence of their amirs. Later on, sedentary Arabs mixed with Persians and other non-Arabs. Purity of lineage was completely lost, and its fruit, the group feeling, was lost and rejected. The tribes, then, disappeared and were wiped out, and with them, group feeling was wiped out. But (the earlier situation) remained unchanged among the Bedouins.

God inherits the earth and all that is upon it.

10 How lineages become confused

It is clear that a person of a certain descent may become attached to people of another descent, either because he feels well-disposed toward them, or because there exists an alliance or client(-master) relationship, or yet because he had to flee from his own people by reason of some crime he committed. Such a person comes to be known as having the same descent as those to whom he is attached and is counted one of them with respect to the things that result from (common descent), such as affection, the rights and obligations concerning talion and blood money, and so on. When the things resulting from common descent are there, it is as if (common descent) itself were there, because the only meaning of belonging to one or another group is that one is subject to its laws and conditions, as if one had come into close contact with it. In the course of time, the original descent is almost forgotten. Those who knew about it have passed away, and it is no longer known to most people. Family lines in this manner continually changed from one tribal group to another, and some people developed close contact with others (of a different descent). This happened both in pre-Islamic and in Islamic times, and between both Arabs and non-Arabs. . . .

11 Leadership over people who share in a given group feeling cannot be vested in those not of the same descent

This is because leadership exists only through superiority, and superiority only through group feeling. Leadership over people, therefore, must, of necessity, derive from a group feeling that is superior to each individual group feeling. Each individual group feeling that becomes aware of the superiority of the group feeling of the leader is ready to obey and follow him.

Now, a person who has become attached to people of a common descent usually does not share the group feeling that derives from their common descent. He is merely attached to them. The firmest connection he has with the group is as client and ally. This in no way guarantees him superiority over them. Assuming that he has developed close contact with them, that he has mixed with them, that the fact that he was originally merely attached to them has been forgotten, and that he has become one of their kin and is addressed as one having the same descent as they, how could he, or one of his forebears, have acquired leadership before that process had taken place, since leadership is transmitted in one particular branch that has been marked for superiority through group feeling? The fact that he was merely attached to the tribe was no doubt known at an earlier stage, and at that time prevented him (or rather, his forebears) from assuming leadership. Thus, it could not have been passed on by a man who was still merely attached (to the tribe). Leadership must of necessity be inherited from the person who is entitled to it, in accordance with the fact, which we have stated, that superiority results from group feeling.

Many leaders of tribes or groups are eager to acquire certain pedigrees. They desire them because persons of that particular descent possessed some special virtue, such as bravery, or nobility, or fame, however this may have come about. They go after such a family and involve themselves in claims to belong to a branch of it. They do not realize that they thus bring suspicion upon themselves with regard to their leadership and nobility. . . .

These pedigrees are invented by people to get into the good graces of rulers, through (sycophantic) behaviour and through the opinions they express. Their (fabrications) eventually become so well known as to be irrefutable. . . .

12 Only those who share in a group feeling can have a 'house' and nobility in the basic sense and in reality, while others have it only in a metaphorical and figurative sense

This is because nobility and prestige are the result of (personal) qualities. A 'house' means that a man counts noble and famous men among his forebears. The fact that he is their progeny and descendant gives him great standing among his fellows, for his fellows respect the great standing and nobility that his ancestors acquired through their qualities.

We have explained that the advantage of a (common) descent consists in the group feeling that derives from it and that leads to affection and mutual help. Wherever the group feeling is truly formidable and its soil kept pure, the advantage of a common descent is most evident, and the (group feeling) is more effective. It is an additional advantage to have a number of noble ancestors. Thus, prestige and nobility become firmly grounded in those who share in the group feeling (of a tribe), because there exists the result of (common) descent. The nobility of a 'house' is in direct proportion to the different degrees of group feeling, because (nobility) is the secret of (group feeling).

Isolated inhabitants of cities can have a 'house' only in a metaphorical sense. The assumption that they possess one is a specious claim. Seen in its proper light, prestige means to the inhabitants of cities that some of them count among their forefathers men who had good (personal) qualities and who mingled with good people, and (that, in addition, they) try to be as decent as possible. This is different from the real meaning of group feeling, as group feeling derives from descent and a number of forefathers. The terms 'prestige' and 'house' are used metaphorically in this connection, because there exists in this case a number of successive ancestors who consistently performed good deeds. This is not true and unqualified prestige.

A 'house' possesses an original nobility through group feeling and personal qualities. Later on, the people (who have a 'house') divest themselves of that nobility when group feeling disappears as the result of sedentary life, and they mingle with the common people. A certain delusion as to their former prestige remains in their souls and leads them to consider themselves members of the most noble houses. They are, however, far from that (status), because their group feeling has completely disappeared. Many inhabitants of cities who had their origins in noble Arab or non-Arab 'houses' share such delusions.

The Israelites are the most firmly misled in this delusion. They originally had one of the greatest 'houses' in the world, first, because of the great number of prophets and messengers born among their ancestors, extending from Abraham to Moses, the founder of their religious group and law, and next, because of their group feeling and the royal authority that God had promised and granted them by means of that group feeling. Then, they were divested of all that, and they suffered humiliation and indigence. They were destined to live as exiles on earth. For thousands of years, they knew only enslavement and unbelief. Still, the delusion of (nobility) has not left them. They can be found saying: 'He is an Aaronite'; 'He is a descendant of Joshua'; 'He is one of Caleb's progeny'; 'He is from the tribe of Judah.' This in spite of the fact that their group feeling has disappeared and that for many long years they have been exposed to humiliation. Many other inhabitants of cities who hold (noble) pedigrees but no longer share in any group feeling are inclined to similar nonsense.

Abû l-Walîd b. Rushd (Averroës) erred in this respect. He mentioned prestige in the *Rhetoric*. 'Prestige', he states, 'belongs to people who are ancient settlers in a town.' He did not consider the things we have just mentioned. I should like to know how long residence in a town can help (anyone to gain prestige), if he does not belong to a group that makes him feared and causes others to obey him. Averroës considers prestige as depending exclusively on the number of forefathers. Yet, rhetoric means to sway the opinions of those whose opinions count, that is, the men in command. It takes no notice of those who have no power. They cannot sway anyone's opinions, and their own opinions are not sought. The sedentary inhabitants of cities fall into that category. It is true that Averroes grew up in a generation and a place where people had no experience of group feeling and were not familiar with the conditions governing it. Therefore, he did not progress beyond his well-known (definition of) 'house' and prestige as something depending merely on the number of one's ancestors, and did not refer to the reality of group feeling and its influence among men.

13 'House' and nobility come to clients and followers only through their masters and not through their own descent

This is because, as we have mentioned before, only those who share in a group feeling have basic and true nobility. When such people take people of another descent as followers, or when they take slaves and clients into servitude, and enter into close contact with them, as we have said, the clients and followers share in the group feeling of their masters and take it on as if it were their own group feeling. By taking their special place within the group feeling, they participate to some extent in the descent to which that particular group feeling belongs.

His own descent and birth are of no help as regards the group feeling of (the master), since that group feeling has nothing to do with his own descent. The group feeling that belonged to his own family is lost, because its influence disappeared when he entered into close contact with that other family and lost contact with the men whose group feeling he had formerly shared. He thus becomes one of the others and takes his place among them. If a number of his ancestors also shared the group feeling of these people, he comes to enjoy among (these other people) a certain nobility and 'house', in keeping with his position as their client and follower. However, he does not come to be as noble as they are, but remains inferior to them.

This is the case with clients of dynasties and with all servants. They acquire nobility by being firmly rooted in their client relationship, and by their service to their particular dynasty, and by having a large number of ancestors who had been under its protection. One knows that the Turkish clients of the 'Abbâsids and, before them, the Barmecides, as well as the Banû Nawbakht, thus achieved 'house' and nobility and created glory and importance for themselves by being firmly rooted in their relationship to the ('Abbâsid) dynasty. Ja'far b. Yaḥyâ b. Khâlid had the greatest possible 'house' and nobility. This was the result of his position as a client of ar-Rashîd and his family. It was not the result of his own (noble) descent among the Persians. The same is the case with clients and servants under any dynasty. They have 'house' and prestige by being firmly rooted in their client relationship with a particular dynasty and by being its faithful followers. Their original descent disappears if it is not that of (the dynasty). It remains under cover and is not considered in connection with their importance and glory. The thing that is considered is their position as clients and followers, because this accords with that secret of group feeling which produces 'house' and nobility.

The nobility of (a client) is, in a way, derived from the nobility of his masters, and his 'house' is derived from what they have built. His own descent and birth do not help him. His glory is built upon his relationship as client to a particular dynasty, and upon his close contact with it as a follower and product of its education. His own original descent may have implied close contact with some group feeling and dynasty. If that (close contact) is gone and the person in question has become a client and follower of another (dynasty), his original (descent) is no longer of any use to him, because its group feeling has disappeared. The new (relationship) becomes useful to him, because (its group feeling) exists.

This applies to the Barmecides. It has been reported that they belonged to a Persian 'house', the members of which had been guardians of the Persian fire temples. When they became clients of the 'Abbâsids, their original (descent) was not taken into consideration. Their nobility resulted from their position as clients and followers of the ('Abbâsid) dynasty.

All other notions are unsupported and unrealistic delusions prompted by undisciplined souls. The facts of existence confirm our remarks.

14 Prestige lasts at best four generations in one lineage

The world of the elements and all it contains comes into being and decays. Minerals, plants, all the animals including man, and the other created things come into being and decay, as one can see with one's own eyes. The same applies to the conditions that affect created things, and especially the conditions that affect man. Sciences grow up and then are wiped out. The same applies to crafts, and to similar things.

Prestige is an accident that affects human beings. It comes into being and decays inevitably. No human being exists who possesses an unbroken pedigree of nobility from Adam down to himself. The only exception was made in the case of the Prophet, as a special act of divine grace to him, and as a measure designed to safeguard his true character.

Nobility originates in the state of being outside. That is, being outside of leadership and nobility and being in a base, humble station, devoid of prestige. This means that all nobility and prestige is preceded by the non-existence of nobility and prestige, as is the case with every created thing.

It reaches its end in a single family within four successive generations. This is as follows: The builder of the family's glory knows what it cost him to do the work, and he keeps the qualities that created his glory and made it last. The son who comes after him had personal contact with his father and thus learned those things from him. However, he is inferior to him in this respect, inasmuch as a person who learns things through study is inferior to a person who knows them from practical application. The third generation must be content with imitation and, in particular, with reliance upon tradition. This member is inferior to him of the second generation, inasmuch as a person who relies upon tradition is inferior to a person who exercises independent judgment.

The fourth generation, then, is inferior to the preceding ones in every respect. Its member has lost the qualities that preserved the edifice of its glory. He despises (those qualities). He imagines that the edifice was not built through application and effort. He thinks that it was something due his people from the very beginning by virtue of the mere fact of their descent, and not something that resulted from group (effort) and (individual) qualities. For he sees the great respect in which he is held by the people, but he does not know how that respect originated and what the reason for it was. He imagines that it is due to his descent and nothing else. He keeps away from those in whose group feeling he shares, thinking that he is better than they. He trusts that (they will obey him because) he was brought up to take their obedience for granted, and he does not know the qualities that made obedience necessary. Such qualities are humility (in dealing) with (such men) and respect for their feelings. Therefore, he considers them despicable, and they, in turn, revolt against him and despise him. They transfer leadership from him and his direct lineage to some other related branch, in obedience to their group feeling, after they have convinced themselves that the qualities of the (new leader) are satisfactory to them. His family then grows, whereas the family of the original (leader) decays and the edifice of his 'house' collapses.

That is the case with rulers who have royal authority. It also is the case with all the 'houses' of tribes, of amirs, and of everybody else who shares in a group feeling, and then also with the 'houses' among the urban population. When one 'house' goes down, another one rises in another group of the same descent.

The rule of four (generations) with respect to prestige usually holds true. It may happen that a 'house' is wiped out, disappears, and collapses in fewer than four, or it may continue unto the fifth and sixth generations, though in a state of decline and decay. The four generations can be defined as the builder, the one who has personal contact with the builder, the one who relies on tradition, and the destroyer.

Muḥammad said: 'The noble son of the noble father of the noble grandfather of the noble great-grandfather: Joseph, the son of Jacob, the son of Isaac, the son of Abraham.' This indicates that Joseph had reached the limit in glory.

In the Torah, there is the following passage: 'God, your Lord, is powerful[1] and jealous, visiting the sins of the fathers upon the children unto the third and the fourth generations.' This shows that

[1] De Slane makes the important observation that the addition of 'powerful' in Exod. 20: 5 is found only in the Vulgate, which, therefore, must have been the ultimate source of Ibn Khaldûn's quotation.

four generations in one lineage are the limit in extent of ancestral prestige. . . .

15 Savage nations are better able to achieve superiority than others

Since desert life no doubt is the source of bravery, savage groups are braver than others. They are, therefore, better able to achieve superiority and to take away the things that are in the hands of other nations. The situation of one and the same group changes, in this respect, with the change of time. Whenever people settle in fertile plains and amass luxuries and become accustomed to a life of abundance and refinement, their bravery decreases to the degree that their wildness and desert habits decrease.

This is exemplified by dumb animals, such as gazelles, wild buffaloes, and donkeys, that are domesticated. When they cease to be wild as the result of contact with human beings, and when they have a life of abundance, their vigour and violence undergo change. This affects even their movements and the beauty of their coat. The same applies to savage human beings who become sociable and friendly.

The reason is that familiar customs determine human nature and character. Superiority comes to nations through enterprise and courage. The more firmly rooted in desert habits and the wilder a group is, the closer does it come to achieving superiority over others, if both (parties) are approximately equal in number, strength, and group feeling.

In this connection, one may compare the Muḍar with the Ḥimyar and the Kahlân before them, who preceded them in royal authority and in the life of luxury, and also with the Rabî‘ah who settled in the fertile fields of the ‘Irâq. The Muḍar retained their desert habits, and the others embarked upon a life of abundance and great luxury before they did. Desert life prepared the Muḍar most effectively for achieving superiority. They took away and appropriated what the other groups had in their hands. . . .

16 The goal to which group feeling leads is royal authority

This is because group feeling gives protection and makes possible mutual defence, the pressing of claims, and every other kind of social activity. By dint of their nature, human beings need someone to act as a restraining influence and mediator in every social organization, in order to keep its members from (fighting) with each other. That person must, by necessity, have superiority over the others in the matter of group feeling. If not, his power cannot be effective. Such superiority is royal authority. It is more than leadership. Leadership means being a chieftain, and the leader is obeyed, but he has no power to force others to accept his rulings. Royal authority means superiority and the power to rule by force.

When a person sharing in the group feeling has reached the rank of chieftain and commands obedience, and when he then finds the way open toward superiority and the use of force, he follows that way, because it is something desirable. He cannot completely achieve his (goal) except with the help of the group feeling, which causes (the others) to obey him. Thus, royal superiority is a goal to which group feeling leads, as one can see.

Even if an individual tribe has different 'houses' and many diverse group feelings, still, there must exist a group feeling that is stronger than all the other group feelings combined, that is superior to them all and makes them subservient, and in which all the diverse group feelings coalesce, as it were, to become one greater group feeling. Otherwise, splits would occur and lead to dissension and strife.

Once group feeling has established superiority over the people who share in it, it will, by its very nature, seek superiority over people who have other group feelings unrelated to the first. If the one (group feeling) is the equal of the other or is able to stave off (its challenge), the (competing people) are even with and equal to each other. Each group feeling maintains its sway over its own domain and people, as is the case with tribes and nations all over the earth. However, if the one group feeling overpowers the other and makes it subservient to itself, the two group feelings enter into close contact, and the (defeated) group feeling gives added power to the (victorious) group feeling, which, as a result, sets its goal of superiority and domination higher than before. In this way, it goes on until the power of that particular group feeling equals the power of the ruling dynasty. Then, when the ruling dynasty grows senile and no defender arises from among its friends who share in its group feeling, the (new group feeling) takes over and deprives the ruling dynasty of its power, and, thus, obtains complete royal authority.

The power of (a given group feeling) may reach its peak when the ruling dynasty has not yet reached senility. (This stage) may coincide with the stage at which (the ruling dynasty) needs to have recourse to the people who represent the various group feelings (in order to master the situation). In such a case, the ruling dynasty includes (the people who enjoy the powerful group feeling) among those of its clients whom it uses for the execution of its various projects. This, then, means (the formation of) another royal authority, inferior to that of the controlling royal authority. This was the case with the Turks under the 'Abbâsids.

It is thus evident that royal authority is the goal of group feeling. When it attains that goal, the tribe (representing that particular group feeling) obtains royal authority, either by seizing actual control or by giving assistance (to the ruling dynasty) according to the circumstances prevailing. If the group feeling encounters obstacles on its way to the goal, it stops where it is, until God decides its fate.

17 Obstacles on the way toward royal authority are luxury and the submergence of the tribe in a life of prosperity

This is because, when a tribe has achieved a certain measure of superiority with the help of its group feeling, it gains control over a corresponding amount of wealth and comes to share prosperity and abundance with those who have been in possession of these things. It shares in them to the degree of its power and usefulness to the ruling dynasty. If the ruling dynasty is so strong that no one thinks of depriving it of its power or of sharing with it, the tribe in question submits to its rule and is satisfied with whatever share in the dynasty's wealth and tax revenue it is permitted to enjoy. Hopes would not go so high as to think of royal prerogatives or ways to obtain (royal authority). (Members of the tribe) are merely concerned with prosperity, gain, and a life of abundance. (They are satisfied) to lead an easy, restful life in the shadow of the ruling dynasty, and to adopt royal habits in building and dress, a matter they stress and in which they take more and more pride, the more luxuries and plenty they acquire, as well as all the other things that go with luxury and plenty.

As a result, the toughness of desert life is lost. Group feeling and courage weaken. Members of the tribe revel in the well-being that God has given them. Their children and offspring grow up too proud to look after themselves or to attend to their own needs. They have disdain also for all the other things that are necessary in connection with group feeling. This finally becomes a character trait and natural characteristic of theirs. Their group feeling and courage decrease in the next generations. Eventually, group feeling is altogether destroyed. They thus invite their own destruction. The greater their luxury and the easier the life they enjoy, the closer they are to extinction, not to mention (their lost chance of securing) royal authority. The things that go with luxury and submergence in a life of ease break the vigour of the group feeling, which alone produces superiority. When group feeling is destroyed, the tribe is no longer able to protect itself, let alone press any claims. It will be swallowed up by other nations.

*18 Meekness and docility to outsiders that may come to be found in a
tribe are obstacles on the way toward royal authority*

This is because meekness and docility break the vigour of group
feeling. If people are meek and docile (their group feeling) is lost.
They do not become fond of meekness until they are too weak to
defend themselves. Those who are too weak to defend themselves are
all the more weak when it comes to withstanding their enemies and
pressing their claims.

The Israelites are a good example. Moses urged them to go and
become rulers of Syria. He informed them that God had made this
their destiny. But the Israelites were too weak for that. They said:
'There are giants in that country, and we shall not enter it until the
giants have departed.'[1] That is, until God has driven them out by
manifesting His power, without the application of our group feeling,
and that will be one of your miracles, O Moses. And when Moses
urged them on, they persisted and became rebellious, and said:
'Go yourself and your Lord, and fight.'[2]

They had become used to being too weak to offer opposition and
to press claims. The verse must be interpreted in that manner.
(This situation) was the result of the quality of docility and the
longing to be subservient to the Egyptians, which the Israelites had
acquired through many long years and which led eventually to the
complete loss of their group feeling. In addition, they did not really
believe what Moses told them, namely, that Syria would be theirs
and that the Amalekites who were in Jericho would fall prey to
them, by virtue of the divine decree that God had made in favour of
the Israelites. They were unable to do (what they were asked to do)
and felt too weak to do it. They realized that they were too weak to
press any claims, because they had acquired the quality of meekness.
They suspected the story their prophet told them and the command
he gave them. For that, God punished them by obliging them to
remain in the desert. They stayed in the desert between Syria and
Egypt for forty years. They had no contact with civilization nor did
they settle in any city,[3] as it is told in the Qur'ân. This was because
of the harshness the Amalekites in Syria and the Copts in Egypt had
practised against them. Thus, they thought themselves too weak to
oppose them. From the context and meaning of the verse, it evidently
refers to the implication of such a sojourn in the desert, namely, the
disappearance of the generation whose character had been formed
and whose group feeling had been destroyed by the humiliation,
oppression, and force from which it had escaped, and the eventual
appearance in the desert of another powerful generation that knew

[1] Qur'ân 5. 22 (25).   [2] Qur'ân 5. 24 (27).   [3] Qur'ân 5. 26 (29).

neither laws nor oppression and did not have the stigma of meekness. Thus, a new group feeling could grow up, and that enabled them to press their claims and to achieve superiority. This makes it evident that forty years is the shortest period in which one generation can disappear and a new generation can arise. Praised be the Wise, all-knowing One.

This shows most clearly what group feeling means. Group feeling produces the ability to defend oneself, to offer opposition, to protect oneself, and to press one's claims. Whoever loses it is too weak to do any of these things.

The subject of imposts and taxes belongs to this discussion of the things that force meekness upon a tribe.

A tribe paying imposts did not do that until it became resigned to meek submission with respect to paying them. Imposts and taxes are a sign of oppression and meekness that proud souls do not tolerate, unless they consider (paying them) easier than being killed and destroyed. In such a case, the group feeling (of a tribe) is too weak for its own defence and protection. People whose group feeling cannot defend them against oppression certainly cannot offer any opposition or press any claims. They have submitted to meekness, and, as we have mentioned before, meekness is an obstacle. When one sees a tribe humiliated by the payment of imposts, one cannot hope that it will ever achieve royal authority. . . .

19 A sign of royal authority is a person's eager desire to acquire praiseworthy qualities, and vice versa

Royal authority is something natural to human beings, because of its social implications. In view of his natural disposition and his power of logical reasoning, man is more inclined toward good qualities than toward bad qualities, because the evil in him is the result of the animal powers in him, and inasmuch as he is a human being, he is more inclined toward goodness and good qualities. Now, royal and political authority come to man *qua* man, because it is something peculiar to man and is not found among animals. Thus, the good qualities in man are appropriate to political and royal authority since goodness is appropriate to political authority.

We have already noted that glory has a basis upon which it is built and through which it achieves its reality: group feeling and the tribal group.

Glory also depends upon a detail that completes and perfects its existence: (an individual's personal) qualities. Royal authority is a goal of group feeling. Thus, it is likewise a goal of the perfecting details, namely, the personal qualities. The existence of (royal authority without the perfecting details would be like the existence of a person with his limbs cut off, or it would be like appearing naked before people.

The existence of group feeling without the practice of praiseworthy qualities would be a defect among people who possess a 'house' and prestige. All the more so would it be a defect in men who are invested with royal authority, the greatest possible kind of glory and prestige. Furthermore, political and royal authority are God's guarantee to mankind and serve as a representation of God among men with respect to His laws. Now, divine laws affecting men are all for their good and envisage their interests. This is attested by the religious law. Bad laws, on the other hand, all result from stupidity and from Satan, in opposition to the predestination and power of God. He makes both good and evil and predetermines them, for there is no maker except Him.

He who thus obtained group feeling guaranteeing power, and who is known to have good qualities appropriate for the execution of God's laws concerning His creatures, is ready to act as His substitute and guarantor among mankind. He has the qualifications for that. This proof is more reliable and solid than the first one.

It has thus become clear that good qualities attest the (potential) existence of royal authority in a person who possesses group feeling. Whenever we observe people who possess group feeling and who have gained control over many lands and nations, we find in them an eager desire for goodness and good qualities, such as generosity, the forgiveness of error, tolerance toward the weak, hospitality toward guests, the support of dependants, maintenance of the indigent, patience in adverse circumstances, faithful fulfilment of obligations, liberality with money for the preservation of honour, respect for the religious law and for the scholars who are learned in it, observation of the things to be done or not to be done that those scholars prescribe for them, thinking highly of religious scholarship, belief in and veneration for men of religion and a desire to receive their prayers, great respect for old men and teachers, acceptance of the truth in response to those who call to it, fairness to and care for those who are too weak to take care of themselves, humility toward the poor, attentiveness to the complaints of supplicants, fulfilment of the duties of the religious law and divine worship in all details, avoidance of fraud, cunning, deceit, and shirking of obligations, and similar things. Thus, we know that these are the qualities of leadership, which (persons qualified for royal authority) have obtained and which have made them deserving of being the leaders of the people under their control, or to be leaders in general. It is something good that God has given them, corresponding to their group feeling and superiority.

Vice versa, when God wants a nation to be deprived of royal authority, He causes (its members) to commit blameworthy deeds and to practise all sorts of vices. This will lead to the complete loss of their political virtues, which will continue to be destroyed until they no longer exercise royal authority. Someone else will exercise it in their stead. This is to constitute an insult to them, in that the royal authority God has given them and the good things He has placed at their disposal are taken away from them. Upon close investigation, many such instances will be found among the nations of the past.

It should be known that a quality belonging to perfection, which tribes possessing group feeling are eager to cultivate and which attests to their (right to) royal authority, is respect for scholars, pious men, noble (relatives of the Prophet), well-born persons, and the different kinds of merchants and foreigners, as well as the ability to assign everybody to his proper station. The respect shown by tribes and persons (in control) of group feelings and families, for men of comparable nobility, tribal position, group feeling, and rank, is something natural. It mostly results from the desire for rank, or from fear of the people of the person to whom respect is paid, or from a wish for reciprocal treatment. However, in the case of people who have no group feeling to make themselves feared, and who have no rank (to bestow) for which one might hope, there can be no doubt as to why they are respected, and it is quite clear what one seeks through them, namely, glory, perfection in personal qualities, and total progress toward political leadership. Respect for one's rivals and equals must exist in connection with the special political leadership that concerns one's tribe and its competitors (and equals). Respect for excellent and particularly qualified strangers means perfection in general political leadership. The pious are thus respected for their religion; scholars, because they are needed for establishing the statutes of the religious law; merchants, in order to give encouragement (to their profession), so that their usefulness may be as widespread as possible. Strangers are respected out of generosity and in order to encourage them to undertake certain kinds (of activity). Assigning everybody to his proper station is done out of fairness, and fairness means justice. When people who possess group feeling have that, one knows that they are ready for general political leadership, which means royal authority. God permits (political leadership) to exist among them, because the sign of (political leadership) exists among them. Therefore, the first thing to disappear in a tribe that exercises royal authority, when God wants to deprive its members of their royal and governmental authority, is respect for such people. When a nation is observed to have lost it, it should be realized that its virtues have begun to go, and it can be expected that royal authority will cease to exist in it.

20 While a nation is savage, its royal authority extends farther

This is because such a nation is better able to achieve superiority and full control, and to subdue other groups. The members of such a nation have the strength to fight other nations, and they are among human beings what beasts of prey are among dumb animals. The Bedouins and the Zanâtah and similar groups, for instance, are such nations, as are the Kurds, the Turkomans, and the Veiled Şinhâjah.

These savage peoples, furthermore, have no homelands that they might use as a fertile (pasture), and no fixed place to which they might repair. All regions and places are the same to them. Therefore, they do not restrict themselves to possession of their own and neighbouring regions. They do not stop at the borders of their horizon. They swarm across distant zones and achieve superiority over faraway nations. . . .

21 As long as a nation retains its group feeling, royal authority that disappears in one branch will, of necessity, pass to some other branch of the same nation

The reason for this is that (the members of a particular nation) acquire royal authority only after (proving their) forcefulness and finding other nations obedient to them. A (few) are singled out to become the actual rulers and to be directly connected with the throne. It could not be all of them, because there is not enough room for all to compete, and because the existence of jealousy cuts short the aspirations of many of those who aspire to high office.

Those who are singled out to support the dynasty indulge in a life of ease and sink into luxury and plenty. They make servants of their fellows and contemporaries and use them to further the various interests and enterprises of the dynasty. Those who are far away from the government and who are thus prevented from having a share in it, remain in the shadow of the dynastic power. They share in it by virtue of their descent; they are not affected by senility, because they remain far from the life of luxury and the things that produce luxury.

Time gets the upper hand over the original group (in power). Their prowess disappears as the result of senility. (The duties of) the dynasty saps their energy. Time feasts on them, as their energy is exhausted by well-being and their vigour drained by the nature of luxury. They reach their limit, the limit that is set by the nature of human urbanization and political superiority. At that moment, the group feeling of other people (within the same nation) is strong. Their force cannot be broken. Their emblem is recognized to be victorious. As a result, their hopes of achieving royal authority, from which they had been kept until now by a superior power within their own group, are high. Their superiority is recognized, and, therefore, no one disputes their claim to royal authority. They seize power. They then have the same experience as (their predecessors) at the hands of those other groups within the nation that remain away from (the government). Royal authority thus continues in a particular nation until the force of its group feeling is broken and gone, or until all its groups have ceased to exist. That is how God proceeds with regard to life in this world.

This can be illustrated by what happened among the nations. When the royal authority of 'Âd was wiped out, their brethren, the Thamûd, took over. They were succeeded, in turn, by the Amalekites; the Amalekites were succeeded by the Ḥimyar; the Ḥimyar by the Tubba's, who belonged to the Ḥimyar. They, likewise, were succeeded by the Adhwâ'. Then, the Muḍar came to power.

The same was the case with the Persians. When the Kayyanid rule was wiped out, the Sassanians ruled after them. Eventually, God permitted them all to be destroyed by the Muslims.

The same was also the case with the Greeks. Their rule was wiped out and transferred to the Rûm (Romans).

This is how God proceeds with His servants and creatures.

All this has its origin in group feeling, which differs in different groups. Luxury wears out royal authority and overthrows it. When a dynasty is wiped out, power is taken away from that dynasty by those whose group feeling has a share in the (established) group feeling, since it is recognized that people submit and are subservient to (the established group feeling) and since people are used to the fact that this has superiority over all other group feelings. (The same group feeling), now, exists only in those people who are closely related (to the outgoing dynasty), because group feeling is proportionate to the degree of relationship. Eventually, a great change takes place in the world, such as the transformation of a religion, or the disappearance of a civilization, or something else willed by the power of God. Then, royal authority is transferred from one group to another—to the one that God permits to effect that change.

22   *The vanquished always want to imitate the victor in his distinctive characteristics, his dress, his occupation, and all his other conditions and customs*

The reason for this is that the soul always sees perfection in the person who is superior to it and to whom it is subservient. It considers him perfect, either because it is impressed by the respect it has for him, or because it erroneously assumes that its own subservience to him is not due to the nature of defeat but to the perfection of the victor. If that erroneous assumption fixes itself in the soul, it becomes a firm belief. The soul, then, adopts all the manners of the victor and assimilates itself to him. This, then, is imitation.

Or, the soul may possibly think that the superiority of the victor is not the result of his group feeling or great fortitude, but of his customs and manners. This also would be an erroneous concept of superiority, and (the consequences) would be the same as in the former case.

Therefore, the vanquished can always be observed to assimilate themselves to the victor in the use and style of dress, mounts, and weapons; indeed, in everything.

In this connection, one may compare how children constantly imitate their fathers. They do that only because they see perfection in them. One may also compare how almost everywhere people are dominated (in fashion) by the dress of the militia and the government forces, because they are ruled by them.

This goes so far that a nation dominated by another, neighbouring nation will show a great deal of assimilation and imitation. At this time, this is the case in Spain. The Spaniards are found to assimilate themselves to the Galician nations in their dress, their emblems, and most of their customs and conditions. This goes so far that they even draw pictures on the walls and have them in buildings and houses. The intelligent observer will draw from this the conclusion that it is a sign of being dominated by others.

In this light, one should understand the secret of the saying, 'The common people follow the religion of the ruler.' (This saying) belongs to the subject under discussion. The ruler dominates those under him. His subjects imitate him, because they see perfection in him, exactly as children imitate their parents, or students their teachers.

God is wise and all-knowing.

*23 A nation that has been defeated and has come under the rule of
another nation will quickly perish*

The reason for this may possibly lie in the apathy that comes over
people when they lose control of their own affairs and, through enslavement, become the instrument of others and dependent upon
them. Hope diminishes and weakens. Now, propagation and an
increase in civilization (population) take place only as the result of
strong hope and of the energy that hope creates in the animal powers
(of man). When hope and the things it stimulates are gone through
apathy, and when group feeling has disappeared under the impact
of defeat, civilization decreases and business and other activities
stop. With their strength dwindling under the impact of defeat,
people become unable to defend themselves. They become the victims of anyone who tries to dominate them, and a prey to anyone
who has the appetite. It makes no difference whether they have
already reached the limit of their royal authority or not.

Here, we possibly learn another secret, namely, that man is a
natural leader by virtue of the fact that he has been made a representative (of God on earth). When a leader is deprived of his
leadership and prevented from exercising all his powers, he becomes
apathetic, even down to such matters as food and drink. This is in
the human character. A similar observation may be made with
regard to beasts of prey. They do not cohabit when they are in
human captivity. The group that has lost control of its own affairs
thus continues to weaken and to disintegrate until it perishes. God
alone endures.

This may be illustrated by the Persian nation. In the past, the
Persians filled the world with their great numbers. When their
military force was annihilated by the Arabs, they were still very
numerous. It is said that Saʿd b. Abî Waqqâṣ counted (the population) beyond Ctesiphon. It numbered 137,000, including 37,000
heads of families. But when the Persians came under the rule of the
Arabs and were subjugated, they lasted only a short while and were
wiped out as if they had never been. One should not think that this
was the result of some persecution or aggression perpetrated against
them. The rule of Islam is known for its justice. Such (disintegration)
is in human nature. It happens when people lose control of their own
affairs and become the instrument of someone else.

Therefore, the Negro nations are, as a rule, submissive to slavery,
because (Negroes) have little that is (essentially) human and possess
attributes that are quite similar to those of dumb animals, as we
have stated.

24 Bedouins can gain control only over flat territory

On account of their savage nature, the Bedouins are people who plunder and cause damage. They plunder whatever they are able to lay their hands on without having to fight or to expose themselves to danger. They then retreat to their pastures in the desert. They do not attack or fight except in self-defence. Every stronghold or (locality) that seems difficult to attack, they by-pass in favour of some less difficult (enterprise). Tribes that are protected by inaccessible mountains are safe from their mischief and destructiveness. The Bedouins would not cross hills or undergo hardship and danger in order to get to them.

Flat territory. on the other hand, falls victim to their looting and prey to their appetite whenever they can gain power over it, when there is no militia, or when the dynasty is weak. Then they raid, plunder, and attack that territory repeatedly, because it is easily (accessible) to them. Eventually, its inhabitants succumb utterly to the Bedouins and then are pushed around by them in accordance with changes of control and shifts in leadership. Eventually, their civilization is wiped out. God has power over His creatures.

25 Places that succumb to the Bedouins are quickly ruined

The reason for this is that the Bedouins are a savage nation, fully accustomed to savagery and the things that cause it. Savagery has become their character and nature. They enjoy it, because it means freedom from authority and no subservience to leadership. Such a natural disposition is the negation and antithesis of civilization. All the customary activities of the Bedouins lead to wandering and movement. This is the antithesis and negation of stationariness, which produces civilization. For instance, they need stones to set them up as supports for their cooking-pots. So, they take them from buildings which they tear down to get the stones, and use them for that purpose. Wood, too, is needed by them for props for their tents and for use as tent poles for their dwellings. So, they tear down roofs to get the wood for that purpose. The very nature of their existence is the negation of building, which is the basis of civilization. This is the case with them quite generally.

Furthermore, it is their nature to plunder whatever other people possess. Their sustenance lies wherever the shadow of their lances falls. They recognize no limit in taking the possessions of other people. Whenever their eyes fall upon some property, furnishings, or utensils, they take them. When they acquire superiority and royal authority, they have complete power to plunder (as they please).

There no longer exists any political (power) to protect property, and civilization is ruined.

Furthermore, since they use force to make craftsmen and professional workers do their work, they do not see any value in it and do not pay them for it. Now, labour is the real basis of profit. When labour is not appreciated and is done for nothing, the hope for profit vanishes, and no (productive) work is done. The sedentary population disperses, and civilization decays.

Furthermore, the Bedouins are not concerned with laws, or with deterring people from misdeeds or with protecting some against others. They care only for the property that they might take away from people through looting and imposts. When they have obtained that, they have no interest in anything further, such as taking care of people, looking after their interests, or forcing them not to commit misdeeds. They often impose fines on property, because they want to get some advantage, some tax, or profit out of it. This is their custom. It does not help to prevent misdeeds or to deter those who undertake to commit them. On the contrary, it increases (misdeeds), because as compared to getting what one wants, the possible financial loss through fines is insignificant.

Under the rule of Bedouins, their subjects live as in a state of anarchy, without law. Anarchy destroys mankind and ruins civilization, since, as we have stated, the existence of royal authority is a natural quality of man. It alone guarantees their existence and social organization.

Furthermore, every Bedouin is eager to be the leader. There is scarcely one among them who would cede his power to another, even to his father, his brother, or the eldest member of his family. That happens only in rare cases and under pressure of considerations of decency. There are numerous authorities and amirs among them. The subjects have to obey many masters in connection with the control of taxation and law. Civilization decays and is wiped out.

It is noteworthy how civilization always collapsed in places the Bedouins took over and conquered, and how such settlements were depopulated and laid in ruin. The Yemen where Bedouins live is in ruins, except for a few cities. Persian civilization in the Arab 'Irâq is likewise completely ruined. The same applies to contemporary Syria. Formerly, the whole region between the Sudan and the Mediterranean was settled. This is attested to by the relics of civilization there, such as monuments, architectural sculpture, and the visible remains of villages and hamlets.

26 Bedouins can acquire royal authority only by making use of some religious colouring, such as prophethood, or sainthood, or some great religious event in general

The reason for this is that because of their savagery, the Bedouins are the least willing of nations to subordinate themselves to each other, as they are rude, proud, ambitious, and eager to be the leaders. Their individual aspirations rarely coincide. But when there is religion (among them) through prophethood or sainthood, then they have some restraining influence in themselves. The qualities of haughtiness and jealousy leave them. It is, then, easy for them to subordinate themselves and to unite (as a social organization). This is achieved by the common religion they now have. It causes rudeness and pride to disappear and exercises a restraining influence on their mutual envy and jealousy. When there is a prophet or saint among them, who calls upon them to fulfil the commands of God, rids them of blameworthy qualities, and causes them to adopt praiseworthy ones, and who prompts them to concentrate all their strength in order to make the truth prevail, they become fully united and acquire superiority and royal authority. Besides, no people are as quick to accept (religious) truth and right guidance, because their natures have been preserved free from distorted habits and uncontaminated by base qualities. The only (difficulty) lies in the quality of savagery, which, however, is easily taken care of and which is ready to admit good (qualities), as it has remained in its first natural state, remote from the ugly customs and bad habits that leave their impress upon the soul.

27 The Bedouins are of all nations the one most remote from royal leadership

The reason for this is that the Bedouins are more rooted in desert life and penetrate deeper into the desert than any other nation. They have less need of the products and grain of the hills, because they are used to a tough, hard life. Therefore, they can dispense with other people. It is difficult for them to subordinate themselves to each other, because they are not used to (any control) and because they are in a state of savagery. Their leader needs them mostly for the group spirit that is necessary for purposes of defence. He is, therefore, forced to rule them kindly and to avoid antagonizing them. Otherwise, he would have trouble with the group spirit, resulting in his undoing and theirs. Royal leadership and government, on the other hand, require the leader to exercise a restraining influence by force. If not, his leadership would not last.

Furthermore, it is the nature of the Bedouins not only to appropriate the possessions of other people but, beyond that, to refrain from arbitrating among them and to fail to keep them from (fighting) each other. When they have taken possession of a nation, they make it the goal of their rule to profit (from their position) by taking away the property of the members of that nation. They often punish crimes by fines on property, in their desire to increase the tax revenues and to obtain some (pecuniary) advantage. That is no deterrent. It is often an incentive to it, in view of the fact that incentives to commit misdeeds (may be very strong) and that, in the opinion of (the criminal), payment of a fine is insignificant, weighed against getting what he wants. Thus, misdeeds increase, and civilization is ruined. A nation dominated by the Bedouins is in a state no different from anarchy, where everybody is set against the others. Such a civilization cannot last and goes quickly to ruin, as would be the case in a state of anarchy, as we have mentioned before.

The Bedouins are by nature remote from royal leadership. They attain it once their nature has undergone a complete transformation under the influence of some religious colouring that wipes out all such (qualities) and causes the Bedouins to have a restraining influence on themselves and to keep people apart from each other.

This is illustrated by the Arab dynasty in Islam. Religion cemented their leadership with the religious law and its ordinances, which, explicitly and implicitly, are concerned with what is good for civilization. The caliphs succeeded one another. As a result, the royal authority and government of the Arabs became great and strong.

Later on, the Arabs were cut off from the dynasty for generations. They neglected religion. Thus, they forgot political leadership and returned to their desert. They were ignorant of the connection of their group feeling with the people of the ruling dynasty, because subservience and lawful (government) had become strange to them. They became once again as savage as they had been before. The epithet 'royal' was no longer applicable to them, except in so far as it applied to the caliphs who were (Arab) by race. When the caliphate disappeared and was wiped out, governmental power passed altogether out of their hands. Non-Arabs took over their power, and they remained as Bedouins in the desert, ignorant of royal authority and political leadership. Most Arabs do not even know that they possessed royal authority in the past, or that no nation had ever exercised such (sweeping) royal authority as had their race. The dynasties of 'Âd and Thamûd, the Amalekites, the Ḥimyar, and the Tubba's testify to that statement, and then, there was the Muḍar dynasty in Islam, the Umayyads and the 'Abbâsids. But when the Arabs forgot their religion, they no longer had any connection with political leadership, and they returned to their desert origins. At times, they achieve superiority over weak dynasties, as is the case in the contemporary Maghrib. But their domination leads only to the ruin of the civilization they conquer, as we have stated before.

28 Desert tribes and groups are dominated by the urban population

We have said before that desert civilization is inferior to urban civilization, because not all the necessities of civilization are to be found among the people of the desert. They do have some agriculture at home but do not possess the materials that belong to it, most of which (depend on) crafts. They do not have any carpenters, tailors, blacksmiths, or others (who) would provide them with the necessities required for making a living in agriculture and other things.

Likewise, they do not have (coined) money. They have the equivalent of it in harvested grain, in animals, and in animal products such as milk, wool, (camel's) hair, and hides, which the urban population needs and pays the Bedouins money for. However, while (the Bedouins) need the cities for their necessities of life, the urban population needs (the Bedouins) for conveniences and luxuries. Thus, as long as they live in the desert and have not acquired royal authority and control of the cities, the Bedouins need the inhabitants (of the latter). They must be active in behalf of their interests and obey them whenever (the cities) ask and demand obedience from them.

When there is a ruler in the city, the submissiveness and obedience of (the Bedouins) is the result of the ruler's superiority. When there is no ruler in the city, some political leadership and control by some of the inhabitants over the remainder must, of necessity, exist there. If not, the civilization of the city would be wiped out. Such a leader makes (the Bedouins) obey him and exert themselves in behalf of his interests. He does so either by persuasion, in that he distributes money among them and lets them have the necessities they need from his city, which enables their civilization to subsist; or, if he has the power to do so, he forces them to obey him, even if he has to cause discord among them so as to get the support of one party, with the help of which he will then be able to overcome the remainder and thus force the others to obey him, since they fear the decay of their civilization as the result of (the unstable situation). (These Bedouins) often cannot leave particular districts (and go) to other regions, because all of them are (already) inhabited by (other) Bedouins who usurped them and kept others out of them. They have, therefore, no hope of survival except by being obedient to the city. Thus, they are of necessity dominated by the urban population.

Chapter 3

On dynasties, royal authority, the caliphate, government ranks, and all that goes with these things. The chapter contains basic and supplementary propositions

1 Royal authority and large-scale dynastic power are attained only through a group and group feeling

This is because aggressive and defensive strength is obtained only through group feeling which means affection and willingness to fight and die for each other.

Now, royal authority is a noble and enjoyable position. It comprises all the good things of the world, the pleasures of the body, and the joys of the soul. Therefore, there is, as a rule, great competition for it. It rarely is handed over (voluntarily), but it may be taken away. Thus, discord ensues. It leads to war and fighting, and to attempts to gain superiority. Nothing of all this comes about except through group feeling, as we have also mentioned.

This situation is not at all understood by the great mass. They forget it, because they have forgotten the time when the dynasty first became established. They have grown up in settled areas for a long time. They have lived there for successive generations. Thus, they know nothing about what took place with God's help at the beginning of the dynasty. They merely notice that the colouring of the men of the dynasty is determined, that people have submitted to them, and that group feeling is no longer needed to establish their power. They do not know how it was at the beginning and what difficulties had to be overcome by the founder. The inhabitants of Spain especially have forgotten group feeling and its influence, because so long a time has passed, and because as a rule they have no need of the power of group feeling, since their country has been annihilated and is depleted of tribal groups.

2 When a dynasty is firmly established, it can dispense with group feeling

The reason for this is that people find it difficult to submit to general dynastic (power) at the beginning, unless they are forced into

123

submission by strong superiority. The new government is something strange. People are not familiar with, or used to, its rule. But once leadership is firmly vested in the members of the family qualified to exercise royal authority in the dynasty, and once (royal authority) has been passed on by inheritance over many generations and through successive dynasties, the beginnings are forgotten, and the members of that family are clearly marked as leaders. It has become a firmly established article of faith that one must be subservient and submissive to them. People will fight with them in their behalf, as they would fight for the articles of faith. By this time, (the rulers) will not need much group (feeling to maintain) their power. It is as if obedience to the government were a divinely revealed book that cannot be changed or opposed.

(The rulers) maintain their hold over the government and their own dynasty with the help, then, either of clients and followers who grew up in the shadow and power of group feeling, or of tribal groups of a different descent who have become their clients.

Something of the sort happened to the 'Abbâsids. The group feeling of the Arabs had been destroyed by the time of the reign of al-Mu'taṣim and his son, al-Wâthiq. They tried to maintain their hold over the government thereafter with the help of Persian, Turkish, Daylam,[1] Saljûq, and other clients. Then, the (non-Arabs) and their clients gained power over the provinces (of the realm). The influence of the dynasty grew smaller, and no longer extended beyond the environs of Baghdad. Eventually, the Daylam closed in upon and took possession of (that area). The caliphs were ruled by them. Then (the Daylam), in turn, lost control. The Saljûqs seized power after the Daylam, and the (caliphs) were ruled by them. Then (the Saljûqs), in turn, lost control. Finally, the Tatars closed in. They killed the caliph and wiped out every vestige of the dynasty.

The same happened to the Umayyad dynasty in Spain. When its Arab group feeling was destroyed, small princes seized power and divided the territory among themselves. In competition with each other, they distributed among themselves the realm of the Umayyad dynasty. Each one of them seized the territory under his control and aggrandized himself. (These rulers) learned of the relations that existed between the non-Arabs (in the East) and the 'Abbâsids. (Imitating them), they adopted royal surnames and used royal trappings. There was no danger that anyone would take (the prerogatives they claimed) away from them or alter (the situation in this respect), because Spain was no longer the home of groups and tribes.

[1] Daylam is the name of the region along the southern shore of the Caspian Sea and of the ethnic stock living there, which provided the 'Abbâsid caliphate with a large group of powerful mercenaries.

They tried to maintain their power with the help of clients and followers and with that of the Zanâtah and other Berber tribes which infiltrated Spain from the (African) shore. They imitated the way the Umayyad dynasty in its last stages had tried to maintain its power with their help. (These newcomers) founded large states. Each one of them had control over a section of Spain. They also had a large share of royal authority, corresponding to (that of) the dynasty they had divided up. They thus remained in power until the Almoravids, who shared in the strong Lamtûnah group feeling, crossed the sea. The latter came and replaced and dislodged them from their centres. They obliterated all traces of (the small princes) who were unable to defend themselves because they had no (longer any) group feeling. . . .

3 Members of a royal family may be able to found a dynasty that can dispense with group feeling

This is because the group feeling in which (a member of a royal family) shares may have much power over nations and races, and the inhabitants of remote regions who support his power may be obedient (to that family) and submissive. So, when such a person secedes, leaving the seat of his rule and the home of his might, and joins those inhabitants of remote regions, they adopt him. They support his rule and help him. They take care of establishing his dynasty on a firm basis. They hope that he will be confirmed in his family (rights) and take the power away from his kinsmen. They do not desire to share in any way in his rule, as they subject themselves to his group feeling and submit to the colouring of material superiority firmly belonging to him and his people. They believe, as in an article of faith, in being obedient to (him and his people). Were they to desire to share his rule with him or to rule without him, 'the earth would be shaken'. . . .[1]

4 Dynasties of wide power and large royal authority have their origin in religion based either on prophethood or on truthful propaganda.

This is because royal authority results from superiority. Superiority results from group feeling. Only by God's help in establishing His religion do individual desires come together in agreement to press their claims, and hearts become united. The secret of this is that when hearts succumb to false desires and are inclined toward the world, mutual jealousy and widespread differences arise. When they

[1] Qur'ân 99. 1 (1).

are turned toward the truth and reject the world and whatever is false, and advance toward God, they become one in their outlook. Jealousy disappears. Mutual co-operation and support flourish. As a result, the extent of the state widens, and the dynasty grows, as we shall explain now.

5 Religious propaganda gives a dynasty at its beginning another power in addition to that of the group feeling it possessed as the result of the number of its supporters

As we have mentioned before, the reason for this is that religious colouring does away with mutual jealousy and envy among people who share in a group feeling, and causes concentration upon the truth. When people come to have the (right) insight into their affairs, nothing can withstand them, because their outlook is one and their object one of common accord. They are willing to die for (their objectives). The members of the dynasty they attack may be many times as numerous as they. But their purposes differ, inasmuch as they are false purposes, and (the people of the worldly dynasty) come to abandon each other, since they are afraid of death. Therefore, they do not offer resistance to (the people with a religious colouring), even if they themselves are more numerous. They are overpowered by them and quickly wiped out, as a result of the luxury and humbleness existing among them, as we have mentioned before.

This happened to the Arabs at the beginning of Islam during the Muslim conquests. The armies of the Muslims at al-Qâdisîyah and at the Yarmûk numbered some 30,000 in each case, while the Persian troops at al-Qâdisîyah numbered 120,000, and the troops of Heraclius, according to al-Wâqidî, 400,000. Neither of the two parties was able to withstand the Arabs, who routed them and seized what they possessed.

This can also be illustrated (by the situation existing at the time) when the religious colouring changes and is destroyed. The power (of the ruling dynasty) is then wiped out. Superiority exists then merely in proportion to (the existing) group feeling, without the additional (power of) religion. As a result, the dynasty is overpowered by those groups (up to this time) under its control, that are equal or superior to it in strength. It had formerly overpowered the groups that had a stronger group feeling and were more deeply rooted in desert life, with the help of the additional power that religion had given it. . . .

6 *Religious propaganda cannot materialize without group feeling*

This is because every mass (political) undertaking by necessity requires group feeling. This is indicated in Muḥammad's saying: 'God sent no prophet who did not enjoy the protection of his people.' If this was the case with the prophets, who are among human beings those most likely to perform wonders, one would (expect it to apply) all the more so to others. One cannot expect them to be able to work the wonder of achieving superiority without group feeling.

To this chapter belong cases of revolutionaries from among the common people and of jurists who undertake to reform evil practices. Many religious people who follow the ways of religion come to revolt against unjust amirs. They call for a change in, and prohibition of, evil practices. They hope for a divine reward for what they do. They gain many followers and sympathizers among the great mass of the people, but they risk being killed, and most of them actually do perish in consequence of their activities as sinners, unrewarded, because God had not destined them for such (activities). He commands such activities to be undertaken only where there exists the power to bring them to a successful conclusion. Muḥammad said: 'Should one of you see evil activities, he should change them with his hand. If he cannot do that, he should change them with his tongue. And if he cannot do that, he should change them with his heart.'

Rulers and dynasties are strongly entrenched. Their foundations can be undermined and destroyed only through strong efforts backed by the group feeling of tribes and families, as we have mentioned before. Similarly, prophets in their religious propaganda depended on groups and families, though they were the ones who could have been supported by God with anything in existence, if He had wished, but in His wisdom He permitted matters to take their customary course.

If someone who is on the right path were to attempt (religious reforms) in this way, his isolation would keep him from (gaining the support of) group feeling, and he would perish. If someone merely pretends to (achieve religious reforms) in order to gain (political) leadership, he deserves to be hampered by obstacles and to fall victim to perdition. (Religious reforms) are a divine matter that materializes only with God's pleasure and support, through sincere devotion for Him and in view of good intentions toward the Muslims. No Muslim, no person of insight, could doubt this. . . .

Many deluded individuals took it upon themselves to establish the truth. They did not know that they would need group feeling for that.

They did not realize how their enterprise must necessarily end and what they would come to. Toward such people it is necessary to adopt one of the following courses. One may either treat them, if they are insane, or one may punish them either by execution or beatings when they cause trouble, or one may ridicule them and treat them as buffoons.

At the beginning of this century, a man known as al-'Abbâs appeared among the Ghumârah. The lowest among the stupid and imbecile members of those tribes followed his blethering. He marched on Bâdis, one of the (Ghumârah) cities, and entered it by force. He was then killed, forty days after the start of his mission. He perished like those before him.

There are many similar cases. Their mistake is that they disregard the significance of group feeling (for success) in such matters. If deceit is involved, it is better that such a person should not succeed and be made to pay for his crime.

7 Each dynasty has a certain amount of provinces and lands, and no more.

The reason for this is that the group to which a given dynasty belongs and the people who support and establish it, must of necessity be distributed over the provinces and border regions which they reach and take into possession. Only thus is it possible to protect them against enemies and to enforce the laws of the dynasty relative to the collection of taxes, restrictions, and other things.

When the (various) groups have spread over the border regions and provinces, their numbers are necessarily exhausted. This, then, is the time when the territory (of the dynasty) has reached its farthest extension, where the border regions form a belt around the centre of the realm. If the dynasty then undertakes to expand beyond its holdings, its widening territory remains without military protection and is laid open to any chance attack by enemy or neighbour. This has the detrimental result for the dynasty of the creation of boldness toward it and of diminished respect for it. If the group is a very large one and its numbers are not exhausted when distributed over border regions and territories, the dynasty retains the strength to go beyond the limit (so far reached), until its expansion has gone as far as possible.

The natural reason for this (situation) lies in the fact that the power of group feeling is one of the natural powers. Any power resulting in any kind of action must proceed in its action in such manner.

A dynasty is stronger at its centre than it is at its border regions. When it has reached its farthest expansion, it becomes too weak and incapable to go any farther. This may be compared to light rays that spread from their centres, or to circles that widen over the surface of the water when something strikes it.

When the dynasty becomes senile and weak, it begins to crumble at its extremities. The centre remains intact until God permits the destruction of the whole dynasty. Then, the centre is destroyed. But when a dynasty is overrun from the centre, it is of no avail to it that the outlying areas remain intact. It dissolves all at once. The centre is like the heart from which the (vital) spirit spreads. Were the heart to be overrun and captured, all the extremities would be routed.

This may be observed in the Persian dynasty. Its centre was al-Madâ'in (Ctesiphon). When the Muslims took over al-Madâ'in, the whole Persian empire dissolved. Possession of the outlying provinces of the realm was of no avail to Yazdjard.

Conversely, the centre of the Byzantine dynasty in Syria was in Constantinople. When the Muslims took Syria away from the Byzantines, the latter repaired to their centre in Constantinople. The loss of Syria did not harm them. Their rule continued there without interruption until God permitted it to be ended.

Another example is the situation of the Arabs at the beginning of Islam. Since they were a very large group, they very quickly overran neighbouring Syria, 'Irâq, and Egypt. Then, they penetrated Western India (as-Sind), Abyssinia, Ifrîqiyah, and the Maghrib, and later Spain. Their numbers were exhausted by that expansion. No further conquests could be made by them, and the Muslim empire reached its farthest extension.

The situation of later dynasties was the same. Each dynasty depended on the numerical strength of its supporters. When its numbers were exhausted through expansion, no further conquest or extension of power was possible. This is how God proceeds with His creatures.

8 The greatness of a dynasty, the extent of its territory, and the length of its duration depend upon the numerical strength of its supporters

The reason for this is that royal authority exists only through group feeling. Representatives of group feeling are the militiamen who settle in the provinces and territories of the dynasty and are spread over them. The more numerous the tribes and groups of a large dynasty are, the stronger and larger are its provinces and lands. Their royal authority, therefore, is wider.

An example of this was the Muslim dynasty when God united the power of the Arabs in Islam. The number of Muslims who participated in the raid against Tabûk, the Prophet's last raid, was 110,000 Muḍar and Qaḥṭân horsemen and foot soldiers. That number was augmented by those who became Muslims after the (raid) and down to the time of the Prophet's death. When (all these people) then set out to seek for themselves the royal authority held by (other) nations, there was no protection against them or refuge. They were allowed (to take possession of) the realms of the Persians and the Byzantines who were the greatest dynasties in the world at that time, (as well as the realms) of the Turks in the East, of the European Christians and Berbers in the West (Maghrib), and of the Goths in Spain. They went from the Ḥijâz to as-Sûs in the far west, and from the Yemen to the Turks in the farthest north. They gained possession of all seven zones.

Thus, the expansion and power of a dynasty correspond to the numerical strength of those who obtain superiority at the beginning of the rule. The length of its duration also depends upon it. The life of anything that comes into being depends upon the strength of its temper. The temper of dynasties is based upon group feeling. If the group feeling is strong, the (dynasty's) temper likewise is strong, and its life of long duration. Group feeling, in turn, depends on numerical strength.

The real reason why (large dynasties last longer) is that when collapse comes it begins in the outlying regions, and the large dynasty has many such provinces far from its centre. Each defection that occurs necessarily requires a certain time. The time required (for collapse) will be long in such cases, because there are many provinces, each of which collapses in its own good time. The duration of a large dynasty, therefore, is long.

This may be observed in the Arab Muslim dynasty. It lasted the longest of (all Muslim) dynasties, counting both the 'Abbâsids in the centre and the Umayyads far away in Spain. Their rule collapsed only after the fourth [tenth] century.

Thus, the life of a dynasty depends upon (the number of) its supporters.

9 *A dynasty rarely establishes itself firmly in lands with many different tribes and groups*

This is because of differences in opinions and desires. Behind each opinion and desire, there is a group feeling defending it. At any time, therefore, there is much opposition to a dynasty and rebellion against it, even if the dynasty possesses group feeling, because each group feeling under the control of the ruling dynasty thinks that it has in itself enough strength and power.

One may compare what has happened in this connection in Ifrîqiyah and the Maghrib from the beginning of Islam to the present time. The inhabitants of those lands are Berber tribes and groups. The first (Muslim) victory over them and the European Christians (in the Maghrib) was of no avail. They continued to rebel and apostatized time after time. The Muslims massacred many of them. After the Muslim religion had been established among them, they went on revolting and seceding, and they adopted dissident religious opinions many times. They remained disobedient and unmanageable. The 'Irâq at that time was different, and so was Syria. The militia there consisted of Persians and Byzantines respectively. All the inhabitants were a mixed lot of town and city dwellers. When the Muslims deprived them of their power, there remained no one capable of making a defence or of offering opposition.

The Berber tribes in the West are innumerable. All of them are Bedouins and members of groups and families. Whenever one tribe is destroyed, another takes its place and is as refractory and rebellious as the former one had been. Therefore, it has taken the Arabs a long time to establish their dynasty in the land of Ifrîqiyah and the Maghrib.

In the age of the Israelites, the same was the case in Syria, where there existed a very large number of tribes with a great variety of group feelings, such as the tribes of Palestine and Canaan, the children of Esau, the Midyanites, the children of Lot, the Edomites, the Armenians [!], the Amalekites, Girgashites, and the Nabataeans from the Jazîrah and Mosul. Therefore, it was difficult for the Israelites to establish their dynasty firmly. Time after time, their royal authority was endangered. The (spirit of) opposition (in the country) communicated itself to (the Israelites). They opposed their own government and revolted against it. They thus never had a continuous and firmly established royal authority. Eventually they were overpowered, first by the Persians, then by the Greeks, and finally by the Romans, when their power came to an end in the Diaspora.

On the other hand, it is easy to establish a dynasty in lands that are free from group feelings. Government there will be a tranquil affair, because rebellions are few, and the dynasty there does not need much group feeling. This is the case in contemporary Egypt and Syria. They are free from tribes and group feelings; indeed, one would never suspect that Syria had once been a mine of them, as we have stated. Royal authority in Egypt is most peaceful and firmly rooted, because Egypt has few dissidents or people who represent tribal groups. Egypt has a sultan and subjects. Its ruling dynasty consists of the Turkish rulers and their groups. They succeed each other in power, and the rule circulates among them, passing from one branch to another. The caliphate belongs in name to an

'Abbâsid, a descendant of the 'Abbâsid caliphs of Baghdad. The same is the case in contemporary Spain. . . .

10 By its very nature, royal authority claims all glory for itself and goes in for luxury and prefers tranquillity and peace

As to claiming all glory for itself, this is because, as we have mentioned before, royal authority exists through group feeling. Group feeling is something composite that results from (amalgamating) many groups, one of which is stronger than all the others. Thus, (a group feeling) is able to overcome and gain power over (all the others), and, eventually, brings them all under its sway. In this way, social organization and superiority over men and dynasties come about. The secret here is that a group feeling extending over the entire tribe corresponds to the temper in the things that come into being. Temper is the product (of the mingling) of the elements. When the elements are combined in equal proportions, no mixing can take place. One (element) must be superior to the others, and when (it exercises) its superiority over them, mixing occurs. In the same way, one of the various tribal group feelings must be superior to all, in order to be able to bring them together, to unite them, and to weld them into one group feeling comprising all the various groups. All the various groups are then under the influence of the superior group feeling.

This highest group feeling can go only to people who have a 'house' and leadership among (the tribe). One of those people must be the leader who has superiority over them. He is singled out as leader of all the various group feelings, because he is superior to all the others by birth. When he is singled out for (leadership), he is too proud to let others share in his leadership and control or to let them participate in it, because the qualities of haughtiness and pride are innate in animal nature. Thus, he develops the quality of egotism, innate in human beings.

Moreover, politics requires that only one person exercise control. Were various persons, liable to differ among each other, to exercise it, destruction of the whole could result.

Thus, the aspirations of the various group feelings are blunted. People become tame and do not aspire to share with the leader in the exercise of control. Their group feeling is forced to refrain (from such aspirations). The leader takes charge all by himself, as far as possible. Eventually, he leaves no part in his authority to anyone else. He thus claims all the glory for himself and does not permit the people to share in it. This may come to pass already with the first ruler of a dynasty, or it may come to pass only with the second or the third, depending on the resistance and strength of the various group feelings, but it is something unavoidable in a dynasty.

As to going in for luxury, this is because, when a nation has gained the upper hand and taken possession of the holdings of its predecessors who had royal authority, its prosperity and well-being grow. People become accustomed to a great number of things. From the necessities of life and a life of austerity, they progress to the luxuries and a life of comfort and beauty. They come to adopt the customs and (enjoy) the conditions of their predecessors. Luxuries require development of the customs necessary to produce them. People then also tend toward luxury in food, clothing, furnishings and household goods. They take pride in such things and vie with other nations in delicacies, gorgeous raiment, and fine mounts. Every new generation wants to surpass the preceding one in this respect, and so it goes right down to the end of the dynasty. The larger the realm ruled by a dynasty, the greater is the share of its people in these luxuries. The limit eventually to be reached is set for a particular dynasty by its own power and by the customs of its predecessors.

As to preferring tranquillity and peace, this is because a nation acquires royal authority only by pressing its claims, having in mind the purpose of obtaining superiority and royal authority. When this purpose is accomplished, all efforts cease.

When people have acquired royal authority, they no longer do the tiresome chores they had been used to undertake while still in search of it. They prefer rest and quiet and tranquillity. Now they seek to enjoy the fruits of royal authority, such as buildings, dwellings, and clothing. They build castles and install running water. They plant gardens and enjoy life. They take pride in clothing, food, household goods, and furnishings, as much as possible. They get used to this attitude and pass it on to later generations. It continues to grow in their midst, until God permits His command to be executed.

11 When the natural tendencies of royal authority to claim all glory for itself and to acquire luxury and tranquillity have been firmly established, the dynasty approaches senility

This can be explained in several ways.

First: As we have stated, (royal authority), by its very nature, must claim all glory for itself. As long as glory was the common (property) of the group, and all members of the group made an identical effort, their aspirations to gain the upper hand over others and to defend their own possessions were expressed in exemplary unruliness and lack of restraint. They all aimed at fame. Therefore, they considered death encountered in pursuit of glory, sweet, and they preferred annihilation to the loss of (glory). Now, however, when one of them claims all glory for himself, he treats the others severely and holds them in check. Further, he excludes them from possessing property and appropriates it for himself. People, thus, become too lazy to care for fame. They become dispirited and come to love humbleness and servitude.

The next generation grows up in this (condition). They consider their allowances the government's payment to them for military service and support. No other thought occurs to them, (but) a person would rarely hire himself out to sacrifice his life. This (situation) debilitates the dynasty and undermines its strength. Its group feeling decays because the people who represent the group feeling have lost their energy. As a result, the dynasty progresses toward weakness and senility.

Second: As we have said before, royal authority by its very nature requires luxury. People get accustomed to a great number of things. Their expenses are higher than their allowances and their income is not sufficient to pay for their expenditure. Those who are poor perish. Spendthrifts squander their income on luxuries. This (condition) becomes aggravated in the later generations. Eventually, all their income cannot pay for the luxuries and other things they have become used to. They grow needy. When their rulers urge them to defray the costs of raids and wars, they cannot get around it. Therefore, (the rulers) impose penalties on the (people) and deprive many of them of their property, either by appropriating it for themselves or by handing it over to their own children and supporters in the dynasty. In that way, they make the people too weak to keep their own affairs going, and their weakness then recoils upon the ruler and weakens him.

Also, when luxury increases in a dynasty and people's income becomes insufficient for their needs and expenses, the ruler, that is, the government, must increase their allowances in order to tide them over and remedy their unsound condition. The amount of tax revenue, however, is a fixed one. It neither increases nor decreases. When it is increased by new customs duties, the amount to be collected as a result of the increase has fixed limits (and cannot be increased again). And when the tax revenues must go to pay for recently increased allowances that had to be increased for everybody in view of new luxuries and great expenditure, the militia decreases in number from what it had been before the increase in allowances.[1]

Luxury, meanwhile, is still on the increase. As a result, allowances become larger, and the militia decreases in number. This happens a

[1] That is, since the allowances to be paid are higher than before, and the tax income has not increased, fewer men can be hired.

third and a fourth time. Eventually, the army is reduced to the smallest possible size. The result is that the military defence of the dynasty is weakened and the power of the dynasty declines. Neighbouring dynasties, or groups and tribes under the control of the dynasty itself, become bold and attack it, and God permits it to suffer the destruction that He has destined for His creatures.

Furthermore, luxury corrupts the character, through luxury the soul acquiring diverse kinds of evil and sophisticated customs, as will be mentioned in the section on sedentary culture. People lose the good qualities that were a sign and indication of royal authority. They adopt the contrary bad qualities. This points toward retrogression and ruin, according to the way God (has planned) for His creatures in this connection. The dynasty shows symptoms of dissolution and disintegration. It becomes affected by the chronic diseases of senility and finally dies.

Third: As we have mentioned, royal authority, by its very nature, requires tranquillity. When people become accustomed to tranquillity and rest and adopt them as character traits, they become part of their nature. This is the case with all the things to which one grows accustomed.

The new generations grow up in comfort and the ease of luxury and tranquillity. The trait of savagery (that former generations had possessed) undergoes transformation. They forget the customs of desert life that enabled them to achieve royal authority, such as great energy, the habit of rapacity, and the ability to travel in the wilderness and find one's way in waste regions. No difference remains between them and ordinary city dwellers, except for their fighting skill and emblems. Their military defence weakens, their energy is lost, and their strength is undermined. The evil effects of this situation on the dynasty show themselves in the form of senility.

People, meanwhile, continue to adopt ever newer forms of luxury and sedentary culture and of peace, tranquillity, and softness in all their conditions, and to sink ever deeper into them. They thus become estranged from desert life and desert toughness. Gradually, they lose more and more of the old virtues. They forget the quality of bravery that was their protection and defence. Eventually, they come to depend upon some other militia, if they have one.

An example of this is the nations whose history is available in the books you have. What I have said will be found to be correct and admitting of no doubt.

In a dynasty affected by senility as the result of luxury and rest, it sometimes happens that the ruler chooses helpers and partisans from groups not related to the ruling dynasty but used to toughness. He uses them as an army which will be better able to suffer the hardships of wars, hunger, and privation. This could prove a cure for the senility of the dynasty when it comes, but only until God permits His command regarding the dynasty to be executed.

That was what happened to the Turkish dynasty in the East. Most members of its army were Turkish clients. The rulers then chose horsemen and soldiers from among the white slaves (Mamelukes) who were brought to them. They were more eager to fight and better able to suffer privations than the children of the earlier white slaves who had grown up in easy circumstances as a ruling class in the shadow of the government.

The same was the case with the Almohad dynasty in Ifrîqiyah. Their rulers often selected their armies from the Zanâtah and the Arabs. They used many of them, and disregarded their own people who had become used to luxury. Thus, the dynasty obtained another, new life, unaffected by senility.

12 Dynasties have a natural life span like individuals

In the opinion of physicians and astrologers, the natural life span of individuals is one hundred and twenty years, that is, the period astrologers call the great lunar year. Within the same generation, the duration of life differs according to the conjunctions. It may be either more or less than one hundred and twenty years. The life span of persons who are under some particular conjunction will be a full hundred years. Of others, it will be fifty, or eighty, or seventy years, accordingly as the indications of conjunctions noted by these observers may require. The life of a Muslim lasts between sixty and seventy years. The natural life span of one hundred and twenty years is surpassed only on the occasion of rare configurations and extraordinary positions on the firmament. Such was the case with Noah and with a few among the peoples of 'Âd and Thamûd.

The same applies to the life span of dynasties. Their duration may differ according to the conjunctions. However, as a rule no dynasty lasts beyond the life span of three generations.[1] A generation is identical with the average duration of the life of a single individual, namely, forty years, the time required for growth to be completed and maturity reached.

Our statement is confirmed by the significance of the (forty-year) sojourn of the children of Israel in the desert. Those forty years were intended to bring about the disappearance of the generation then alive and the growth of another generation, one that had not witnessed and felt the humiliation in Egypt. This is proof of the assump-

[1] The following assumption of a period of forty years does not square with the remarks Ibn Khaldûn makes here about the length of human life.

tion that forty years, which is identical with the (average) life of a single individual, must be considered the duration of a generation.

We have stated that the life of a dynasty does not as a rule extend beyond three generations. The first generation retains the desert qualities, desert toughness, and desert savagery. (Its members are used to) privation and to sharing their glory (with each other); they are brave and rapacious. Therefore, the strength of group feeling continues to be preserved among them. They are sharp and greatly feared. People submit to them.

Under the influence of royal authority and a life of ease, the second generation changes from the desert attitude to sedentary culture, from privation to luxury and plenty, from a state in which everybody shared in the glory to one in which one man claims all the glory for himself while the others are too lazy to strive for glory, and from proud superiority to humble subservience. Thus, the vigour of group feeling is broken to some extent. People become used to lowliness and obedience. But many of the old virtues remain in them, because they had had direct personal contact with the first generation and its conditions, and had observed with their own eyes its prowess and striving for glory and its intention to protect and defend (itself). They cannot give all of it up at once, although a good deal of it may go. They live in hope that the conditions that existed in the first generation may come back, or they live under the illusion that those conditions still exist.

The third generation, then, has (completely) forgotten the period of desert life and toughness, as if it had never existed. They have lost (the taste for) the sweetness of fame and for group feeling, because they are dominated by force. Luxury reaches its peak among them, because they are so much given to a life of prosperity and ease. They become dependent on the dynasty and are like women and children who need to be defended. Group feeling disappears completely. People forget to protect and defend themselves and to press their claims. With their emblems, apparel, horseback-riding, and (fighting) skill, they deceive people and give them the wrong impression. For the most part, they are more cowardly than women upon their backs. When someone comes and demands something from them, they cannot repel him. The ruler, then, has need of other, brave people to support him. He takes many clients and followers. They help the dynasty to some degree, until God permits it to be destroyed, and it goes with everything it stands for.

As one can see, we have there three generations. In the course of these three generations, the dynasty grows senile and is worn out. Therefore, it is in the fourth generation that (ancestral) prestige is destroyed.

Three generations last one hundred and twenty years, as stated before. As a rule, dynasties do not last longer than that many years, a few more or a few less, save when, by chance, no one appears to attack them. When senility becomes preponderant, there may be no claimant (for dynastic power, and then nothing will happen), but if there should be one, he will encounter no one capable of repelling him. If the time is up, (the end of the dynasty) cannot be put off for a single hour, nor can it be advanced.

In this way, the life span of a dynasty corresponds to the life span of an individual; it grows up and passes into an age of stagnation and thence into retrogression. Therefore, people commonly say that the life span of a dynasty is one hundred years. . . .

13   The transition of dynasties from desert life to sedentary culture

It should be known that these stages are natural for the growth of dynasties. The superiority through which royal authority is achieved is the result of group feeling and of the great energy and rapacious habits which go with it. As a rule, these things are possible only in connection with desert life. The first stage of dynasties, therefore, is that of desert life.

When royal authority is acquired, it is accompanied by a life of ease and increased opportunities. Sedentary culture is merely a diversification of luxury and a refined knowledge of the crafts employed for its diverse aspects and ways. This concerns, for instance, food, clothing, building, carpets, utensils, and other household needs. Each one of these things requires special interdependent crafts serving to refine and improve it. These increase in number with the variety of pleasures and amusements and ways and means to enjoy the life of luxury the soul desires, and (with the growing number of) different things to which people get used.

The sedentary stage of royal authority follows the stage of desert life. It does so of necessity, as a result of the fact that royal authority is necessarily accompanied by a life of ease. In the sedentary stage and under (sedentary) conditions, the people of a given dynasty always follow the traditions of the preceding dynasty. They observe with their own eyes the circumstances (under which the preceding dynasty lived), and, as a rule, learn from them.

Something of the sort happened to the Arabs during the conquest by which they came to rule the Persians and Byzantines and made their daughters and sons their servants. At that time, the Arabs had no sedentary culture at all. The story goes that when they were given a pillow they supposed it was a bundle of rags. The camphor they found in the treasuries of the Persian king was used by them as salt in their dough. There are many similar things. The Arabs, then, enslaved the people of the former dynasties and employed them in their occupations and their household needs. From among them, they selected skilled masters of the various (crafts), and were in turn taught by them to handle, master, and develop these for themselves. In addition, the circumstances of the Arabs' life widened and became more diversified. Thus, they reached the limit in this respect. They entered the stage of sedentary culture, of luxury and refinement in food, drink, clothing, building, weapons, carpets, household goods, music, and all other commodities and furnishings. The same (perfection they showed) on their gala days, banquets, and wedding nights. In this respect, they surpassed the limit.

Looking at the reports of al-Mas'ûdî, aṭ-Ṭabarî, and other (historians) concerning the wedding of al-Ma'mûn to Bûrân, daughter of al-Ḥasan b. Sahl, one will be amazed. They tell about the gifts Bûrân's father made to the retinue of al-Ma'mûn when the caliph came by boat to (al-Ḥasan's) house in Fumm aṣ-ṣilḥ to ask for Bûrân's hand. They tell about the expenditure for the wedding and the gifts al-Ma'mûn gave her. On the wedding day, al-Ḥasan b. Sahl gave a lavish banquet that was attended by al-Ma'mûn's retinue. To members of the first class, al-Ḥasan distributed lumps of musk wrapped in papers granting farms and estates to the holders. Each obtained what chance and luck gave him. To the second class, he distributed bags each of which held 10,000 dinars. To the third class, he distributed bags with the same amount in dirhams. In addition to all this, he had already spent many times as much when al-Ma'mûn had stayed in his house. Also, al-Ma'mûn gave Bûrân a thousand hyacinths (rubies) as her wedding gift on the wedding night. He burned candles of amber each of which weighed one hundred *mann*—a *mann* being one and two-thirds pounds. He had laid down for her carpets woven with threads of gold and adorned with pearls and hyacinths. One hundred and forty mule-loads of wood had been brought three times a day for a whole year to the kitchen in readiness for the wedding night. All that wood was consumed that very night. Palm twigs were set alight by pouring oil on them. Boatmen were ordered to bring boats to transport the distinguished guests on the Tigris. The boats prepared for that purpose numbered 30,000, and they carried people back and forth all day long. There were many other such things.

A similar occasion was the wedding of al-Ma'mûn b. Dhî n-nûn in Toledo.

All these people had previously been in the first stage of desert life. They had been completely incapable of such things, because, in

139

their low standard of living and their simplicity, they lacked both the means and the people with technical ability. . . .

Sedentary culture was always transferred from the preceding dynasty to the later one. The sedentary culture of the Persians was transferred to the Arab Umayyads and 'Abbâsids. The sedentary culture of the Umayyads in Spain was transferred to the Almohad and Zanâtah kings of the contemporary Maghrib. That of the 'Abbâsids was transferred, successively, to the Daylam, to the Saljûq Turks, to the Turks in Egypt, and to the Tatars in the two 'Irâqs.

The larger a dynasty, the more important is its sedentary culture. For sedentary culture is the consequence of luxury; luxury is the consequence of wealth and prosperity; and wealth and prosperity are the consequences of royal authority and related to the extent of territorial possessions which the people of a particular dynasty have gained. All the elements of sedentary culture are, thus, proportionate to the greater or smaller extent of royal authority. Upon close and careful examination this will be found to be a correct statement as regards civilization and dynasties.

14 Luxury will at first give additional strength to a dynasty.

The reason for this is that a tribe that has acquired royal authority and luxury is prolific and produces many children, so that the community grows. Thus, the group grows. Furthermore, a greater number of clients and followers is acquired. The new generations grow up in a climate of prosperity and luxury. Through them, (the dynasty) gains in numbers and in strength, because a great number of groups form at that time as the result of the numerical increase. When the first and second generations are gone and the dynasty starts to become senile, its followers and clients cannot do anything on their own to put the dynasty and its royal authority on a firmer basis, because they never had authority of their own but were dependent on the men of (the dynasty) and (merely) supported it. When the roots are gone, the branches cannot be strong on their own, but disappear completely, and the dynasty no longer retains its former strength.

This is exemplified by what happened to the Arab dynasty in Islam. The Arabs at the time of the Prophet and the early caliphs numbered approximately 150,000 Muḍar and Qaḥtân (tribesmen). The life of luxury reached its climax in the dynasty. The (population) grew rapidly with the growth of prosperity. The caliphs acquired many clients and followers. Thus, the (original) number increased many times. It is said that during the conquest of Amorium, al-Mu'taṣim laid siege to the city with 900,000 men. This number can hardly fail being correct, if one thinks of (the large size of) the Muslim militia of the border regions both far and near, in both the East and the West, and adds the soldiers directly in the service of the ruler, together with all the clients and followers. . . .

15 *The stages of dynasties. How the desert attitude differs among the people in the different stages*

A dynasty goes through different stages and encounters new conditions. Through the conditions that are peculiar to a particular stage, the supporters of the dynasty acquire in that stage traits of character such as do not exist in any other stage. Traits of character are the natural result of the peculiar situations in which they are found.

The conditions and stages of a dynasty are as a rule no more than five (in number).

The first stage is that of success, the overthrow of all opposition, and the appropriation of royal authority from the preceding dynasty. In this stage, the ruler serves as model to his people by the manner in which he acquires glory, collects taxes, defends property, and provides military protection. He does not claim anything exclusively for himself to the exclusion of (his people), because (such an attitude) is dictated by group feeling, (and it was group feeling) that gave superiority (to the dynasty), and (group feeling) still continues to exist as before.

The second stage is the one in which the ruler gains complete control over his people, claims royal authority all for himself, excluding them, and prevents them from trying to have a share in it. In this stage, the ruler of the dynasty is concerned with gaining adherents and acquiring clients and followers in great numbers, so as to be able to blunt the aspirations of the people who share in his group feeling and belong to his group, who are of the same descent as he himself and have the same claim to royal authority as he has. He keeps them from power and bars them from its sources. He stops them from getting to it, and, eventually, all the power is in the hands of his family. He reserves all the glory that he is building up to the members of his own house. He takes as much, or more, care to keep his people at a distance and to subdue them, as the first members of the dynasty did in the search for power. The first members of the dynasty kept strangers away, and all the people who shared in their group feeling supported them in this. He, on the other hand, keeps his relatives away, and he is supported in this effort only by a very small number of people, who are not related to him. Thus, he undertakes a very difficult task.

The third stage is one of leisure and tranquillity in which the fruits of royal authority are enjoyed: the things that human nature desires, such as acquisition of property, creation of lasting monuments, and fame. All the ability (of the ruler) is expended on collecting taxes; regulating income and expenses, bookkeeping and planning expenditure; erecting large buildings, big constructions, spacious cities, and lofty monuments; presenting gifts to embassies of nobles from (foreign) nations and tribal dignitaries; and dispensing bounty to his own people. In addition, he supports the demands of his followers and retinue with money and positions. He inspects his soldiers, pays them well, and distributes fairly their allowances every month. Eventually, the result of this (liberality) shows itself in their dress, their fine equipment, and their armour on parade days. The ruler thus can impress friendly dynasties and frighten hostile ones with (his soldiers). This stage is the last during which the ruler is in complete authority. Throughout this and the previous stages, the rulers are independent in their opinions. They build up their strength and show the way for those after them.

The fourth stage is one of contentment and peacefulness. The ruler is content with what his predecessors have built. He lives in peace with all his royal peers. He adopts the tradition of his predecessors and follows closely in their footsteps. He imitates their ways most carefully. He thinks that to depart from tradition would mean the destruction of his power and that they knew better (what is good for the preservation of) the glory they themselves had built.

The fifth stage is one of waste and squandering. In this stage, the ruler wastes on pleasures and amusements (the treasures) accumulated by his ancestors, through (excessive) generosity to his inner circle. Also, he acquires bad, low-class followers to whom he entrusts the most important matters (of state), which they are not qualified to handle by themselves, not knowing which of them they should tackle and which they should leave alone. The ruler seeks to destroy the great clients of his people and followers of his predecessors. Thus they come to hate him and conspire to refuse support to him. He loses a number of soldiers by spending their allowances on his pleasures (instead of paying them) and by refusing them access to his person and not supervising them (properly). Thus, he ruins the foundations his ancestors had laid and tears down what they had built up. In this stage, the dynasty is seized by senility and the chronic disease from which it can hardly ever rid itself, for which it can find no cure, and, eventually, it is destroyed.

16 The monuments of a given dynasty are proportionate to its original power

The reason for this is that monuments owe their origin to the power that brought the dynasty into being. The impression the dynasty leaves is proportionate to that power.

The monuments of a dynasty are its buildings and large (edifices). They are proportionate to the original power of the dynasty. They can materialize only when there are many workers and united action and co-operation. When a dynasty is large and far-flung, with many provinces and subjects, workers are very plentiful and can be brought together from all sides and regions. Thus, even the largest edifice can be constructed.

Think of the works of the people of 'Âd and Thamûd, about which the Qur'ân tells. Or, one should see with one's own eyes the Reception Hall of Khosraw, that powerful achievement of Persian (architecture). Ar-Rashîd intended to tear it down and destroy it. He could not do so for all his trouble. He began the work, but then was not able to continue. It is worth noting that one dynasty was able to construct a building that another dynasty was unable to tear down, even though destruction is much easier than construction. That illustrates the great difference between the two dynasties.

One may also compare the Mosque of al-Walîd in Damascus, the Umayyad Mosque in Córdoba, the bridge over the river at Córdoba, and, as well, the arches of the aqueduct over which water is brought into Carthage, the monuments of Cherchel in the Maghrib, the pyramids of Egypt, and many other such monuments that may still be seen. They illustrate differences in strength and weakness that have existed among the various dynasties.

All these works of the ancients were possible only through engineering skill and the concerted labour of many workers. Only thus could these monuments and works be constructed. One should not think, as the common people do, that it was because the ancients had bodies larger in size than our own. Human beings do not differ in this respect as much as monuments and relics differ. Storytellers have seized upon the subject and used it to make exaggerated (fables). One of the strangest of these stories is about Og, the son of Anak, one of the Canaanites against whom the children of Israel fought in Syria. According to these storytellers, he was so tall that he took fish out of the ocean and held them up to the sun to be cooked. To their ignorance of human affairs, the storytellers here add ignorance of astronomical matters. They believe that the sun is heat and that the heat of the sun is greatest close to it. They do not know that the heat of the sun is its light and that its light is stronger near the earth (than it is near the sun) because of the reflection of the rays from the surface of the earth when it is hit by the light. Therefore, the heat here is many times greater (than near the sun). When the zone in which the reflected rays are effective is passed, there will be no heat there, and it will be cold. (That is) where the clouds are. The sun itself is neither hot nor cold, but a simple uncomposed substance that gives light.

The error of (storytellers) results from the fact that they admired the vast proportions of the monuments left by nations (of the past), but did not understand the different situation in which dynasties may find themselves with respect to social organization and co-operation. They did not understand that (superior social organization) together with engineering skill made the construction of large monuments possible. Therefore, they ascribed such monuments to a strength and energy derived by the peoples of the past from the large size of their bodies. But this is not so. . . .

Another (kind of) monument (to the greatness) of a dynasty is the way it handled weddings and banquets, as we have mentioned.

Another monument of a dynasty is the gifts it made. Gifts are proportionate to (the importance of a dynasty). This holds true even when the dynasty is close to senility.

The way the Barmecides gave allowances and gifts and spent their money illustrates this. Whenever they provided for a needy person, it meant property, high office, and prosperity for that person for ever after. It was not just an allowance that was spent in a day or sooner. . . .

A person who looks at these (data) should bear in mind the relative (importance) of the various dynasties. He should not reject (data) for which he finds no observable parallels in his own time. Otherwise, many things that are possible would (be considered impossible by him and) escape his attention. Many excellent men, hearing stories of this kind about past dynasties, have not believed them. This is not right. Conditions in the world and in civilization are not (always) the same. He who knows a low or medium (level of civilization) does not know all of them. When we consider our information about the 'Abbâsids, the Umayyads, and the 'Ubaydid (-Fâṭimids), and when we compare what we know to be sound in it with our own observations of the less important dynasties (of today), then we find a great difference between them. That difference results from differences in the original strength of (those dynasties) and in the civilizations (of their realms). As we have stated before, all the monuments of a dynasty are proportionate to its original strength. We are not entitled to reject any such (information) about them. Much of it deals with matters that are extremely well known and obvious. Part of it is traditional information known through a continuous tradition. Part of it is direct information based upon personal observation of architectural monuments and other such things.

One should think of the various degrees of strength and weakness, of bigness and smallness, in the various dynasties as they are known through tradition, and compare that information with the following interesting story. In the times of the Merinid Sultan, Abû 'Inân, a *shaykh* from Tangier, by name Ibn Baṭṭûtah,[1] came back to the Maghrib. Twenty years before, he had left for the East and journeyed through the countries of the 'Irâq, the Yemen, and India. He had come to the city of Delhi, the seat of the ruler of India, the Sultan Muḥammad Shâh.[2] (The ruler) esteemed Ibn Baṭṭûtah highly and employed him as Mâlikite judge in his domain. He then returned to the Maghrib and made contact with the Sultan Abû 'Inân. He used to tell about experiences he had had on his travels and about the remarkable things he had seen in different realms. He spoke mostly about the ruler of India. He reported things about him that his listeners considered strange. That, for instance, when the ruler of India went on a trip, he counted the inhabitants of his city, men, women, and children, and ordered that their requirements for (the next) six months be paid them out of his own income. When he returned from his trip and entered (the city), it was a festive day. All the people went out into the open country and strolled about. In front of (the ruler), in the crowd, mangonels were set up on the backs of pack animals.[3] From the mangonels, bags of dirhams and dinars were shot out over the people, until the ruler entered his audience hall.

Ibn Baṭṭûtah told other similar stories, and people in (high positions) whispered to each other that he must be a liar. During that time, one day I met the Sultan's famous wazir, Fâris b. Wadrâr. I talked to him about this matter and intimated to him that I did not believe that man's stories, because people in the dynasty were in general inclined to consider him a liar. Whereupon the wazir Fâris said to me: 'Be careful not to reject such information about the conditions of dynasties, because you have not seen such things yourself. You would then be like the son of the wazir who grew up in prison. The wazir had been imprisoned by his ruler and remained in prison several years. His son grew up in prison. When he reached the age of reason, he asked his father about the meat which he had been

[1] Muḥammad b. 'Abdallâh, 703–779 [1304–1377].
[2] Muḥammad Shâh ruled from 1325 to 1351, and it was during his reign that Ibn Baṭṭûtah was in Delhi.
[3] These, of course, were elephants.

eating. (His father) told him that it was mutton, and he asked him what that was. When his father described a sheep to him in all details, (the son) said, "Father, you mean, it looks like a rat?" His father was angry with him and said, "What has a sheep to do with a rat?" The same happened later about beef and camel meat. The only animals he had seen in prison were rats, and so he believed that all animals were of the same species as rats.'

It often happens that people are (incredulous) with regard to historical information, just as it also happens that they are tempted to exaggerate certain information, in order to be able to report something remarkable. We stated this earlier at the beginning of the book. Therefore, a person should look at his sources and rely upon himself. With a clear mind and straightforward, natural (common sense) he should distinguish between the nature of the possible and the impossible. Everything within the sphere of the possible should be accepted, and everything outside it should be rejected. We do not have in mind 'possible' in the absolute sense of what is intellectually possible. That covers a very wide range, so that it cannot be used to determine what is possible in actual fact. What we have in mind is the possibility inherent in the matter that belongs to a given thing. When we study the origin of a thing, its genus, (specific) difference, size, and strength, we can draw conclusions as to (the possibility or impossibility) of the data (reported in connection with it). We adjudge to be impossible everything outside the sphere of (the possible, in this sense).

17   The ruler seeks the help of clients and followers against the men of his own people and group feeling

A ruler can achieve power only with the help of his own people. They are his group and his helpers in his enterprise. He uses them to fight against those who revolt against his dynasty. It is they with whom he fills the administrative offices, whom he appoints as wazirs and tax collectors. They help him to achieve superiority. They participate in the government. They share in all his other important affairs.

This applies as long as the first stage of a dynasty lasts, as we have stated. With the approach of the second stage, the ruler shows himself independent of his people, claims all the glory for himself, and pushes his people away from it with the palms of his hands. As a result, his own people become, in fact, his enemies. In order to prevent them from seizing power, and in order to keep them away from participation in it, the ruler needs other friends, not of his own kin, whom he can use against (them) and who will be his friends in their place. These become closer to him than anyone else. They deserve better than anyone else to be close to him and to be his followers, as well as to be preferred and to be given high positions, because they are willing to give their lives for him, preventing his own people from regaining the power that had been theirs and from occupying with him the rank to which they had been used.

In this (situation), the ruler cares only for his new followers. He singles them out for preference and for many honours. He distributes among them as much (property) as (he does among) most of his own people. He confers upon them the most important administrative positions, such as the offices of wazir, general, and tax collector, as well as royal titles which are his own prerogative, and which he does not share with his own people. (He does this) because they are now his closest friends and most sincere advisers. This, then, announces the destruction of the dynasty and indicates that chronic disease has befallen it, the result of the loss of the group feeling on which the (dynasty's) superiority had been built. The feelings of the people of the dynasty become diseased as a result of the contempt in which they are held and the hostility of the ruler. They hate him and await the opportunity of a change in his fortune. The great danger inherent in this situation reverts upon the dynasty. There can be no hope it will recover from that illness. The (mistakes of the) past grow stronger with each successive generation and lead eventually to loss of the (dynasty's) identity.

This is exemplified by the Umayyad dynasty. For their wars and for administrative purposes, they had recourse to the support of Arabs such as 'Amr b. Sa'd b. Abî Waqqâṣ, 'Ubaydallâh b. Ziyâd b. Abî Sufyân, al-Ḥajjâj b. Yûsuf, and others. For a while the 'Abbâsid dynasty, too, used the support of Arab personalities. But when the dynasty came to claim all the glory for itself and kept the Arabs from aspiring to administrative positions, the wazirate fell to non-Arabs such as the Barmecides and others. Thus, the dynasty came to belong to people other than those who had established it. Power went to people other than those who had first won it.

This is how God proceeds with His servants.

18 The situation of clients and followers in dynasties

Followers occupy different positions in a dynasty depending on whether their close contact with the ruler is of old or of recent standing. The reason for this is that the purpose of group feeling, which is defence and aggression, can be fulfilled only with the help of a common descent. For, as we have stated before, blood relations and other close relatives help each other, while strangers and outsiders do not. Client relationships and contacts with slaves or allies have the same effect as (common descent). The consequences of common descent, though natural, still are something imaginary. The real thing to bring about the feeling of close contact is social intercourse, friendly association, long familiarity, and the companionship that results from growing up together, having the same wet nurse, and sharing the other circumstances of death and life. If close contact is established in such a manner, the result will be affection and co-operation. Observation of people shows this to be so.

Something similar can be observed in connection with the relation between master and follower. Between the two, there develops a special closeness of relationship which has the same effect (as common descent) and strengthens the close contact. Even though there is no common descent, the fruits of common descent are there.

Whenever such a client relationship exists between a tribe and its clients before the tribe has acquired royal authority, the roots of the relationship are more firmly intertwined, the feelings and beliefs involved are more sincere, and the relationship itself is more clearly defined, for two reasons.

First: Before people acquire royal authority, they are a model in their ways. Only in the rarest cases is a distinction made between common descent and the client relationship. The position (of clients) is the same as that of close or blood relatives. However, if they choose followers after they have acquired royal authority, their royal rank causes them to make a distinction between master and client, and another between close relatives and clients or followers. The conditions of leadership and royal authority require this in view of distinctions and differences in rank. The situation (of followers), therefore, is different. They are now on the same level as strangers. The close contact between (the ruler and his followers) weakens, and co-operation, therefore, becomes less likely. This means that followers are now less (close) than they were before (he acquired) royal authority.

Second: Followers from before (the time the ruler acquired) royal authority had the status of followers long before the dynasty (came to power). It is, thus, no longer clear (to contemporaries) how the close contact came about. As a rule, it is supposed to be a case of common descent, and in this case the group feeling is strengthened. On the other hand, (follower relationships formed) after (the ruler has acquired) royal authority are of recent date and equally well known to most people. (The origin of) the close contact is clear, and it is clearly distinguishable from common descent. The group feeling, in the latter case, is weak in comparison with the group feeling that results from the client relationship that existed before the dynasty (came to power).

148

A look at dynasties and other cases of (political) leadership will show this to be so. Follower relationships formed before leadership and royal authority were secured, will be found to show a stronger and closer contact between masters and followers. The latter occupy the same position with their master as do his children, his brothers, and other blood relatives. On the other hand, follower relationships formed after royal authority and political leadership were acquired do not show the same close connection that exists in the first (group).

At the end of their power, dynasties eventually resort to employing strangers and accepting them as followers. These people, however, do not acquire any such glory as the men who had become followers of the dynasty before it came to power were able to build up for themselves. Their status as followers is too recent in origin. Also, the destruction of the dynasty is imminent. Therefore, they occupy a very low and humble position. In taking them on as followers and re-placing his old clients and original followers by them, the ruler is motivated by the fact that (his old clients and followers) have become overbearing. They show little obedience to him. They look at him in the same way as his own tribe and relatives do. Close contact existed between him and them for a very long time. They had grown up together with him, had had connections with his ancestors and older members of his family, and were aligned with the great men of his house. As a result, they become proud and overbearing towards him. This is why the ruler comes to shun them and use others in their place. It has been only for a short time that he has come to care for these others and to use them as followers. Therefore, they do not attain positions of glory but retain their position as outsiders.

This is the case with dynasties at their end. As a rule, the words 'followers' and 'clients' are used for the first group. The more recent followers are called 'servants' and 'helpers'.

19 Seclusion of, and control over, the ruler (by others) may occur in dynasties

When royal authority is firmly established in one particular family and branch of the tribe supporting the dynasty, and when that family claims all royal authority for itself and keeps the rest of the tribe away from it, and when the children of that family succeed to royal authority in turn, by appointment, then it often happens that their wazirs and entourage gain power over the throne. This occurs most often when a little child or a weak member of the family is appointed successor by his father or made ruler by his creatures and servants. It becomes clear that he is unable to fulfil the functions of ruler. Therefore, they are fulfilled by his guardian, one of his father's wazirs, someone from his entourage, one of his clients, or a member of his tribe. (That person) gives the impression that he is guarding the power of the (child ruler) for him. Eventually, it becomes clear that it is he who exercises control, using the fact as a tool to achieve royal authority. He keeps the child away from his people. He accustoms him to the pleasures of a life of luxury and gives him every possible opportunity to indulge in them. He causes him to forget to look at government affairs. Eventually, he gains full control over him. He accustoms the (child ruler) to believe that the ruler's share in royal authority consists merely in sitting on the throne, shaking hands, being addressed as Sire, and sitting with the women in the seclusion of the harem. All (exercise of the) actual executive power, and the personal handling and supervision of matters that concern the ruler, such as inspection of the army, finances, and (defence of) the border regions, are believed (by the child ruler) to belong to the wazir. He defers to him in all these things. Eventually the wazir definitely adopts the colouring of the leader, of the man in control. The royal authority comes to be his. He reserves it for his family and his children after him.

Such was the case with the Bûyids and the Turks, with Kâfûr al-Ikhshîdî and others in the East, and with al-Manṣûr b. Abî 'Âmir in Spain.

It may happen that a ruler who is secluded and deprived of authority becomes aware of his situation and contrives to escape from it. He thus regains royal authority for his family. He stops the person who has gained power over it, either by killing him or by merely deposing him. However, this happens very rarely. Once a dynasty has fallen into the hands of wazirs and clients, it remains in that situation. Rarely is it able to escape from it, because (such control by others) is mostly the result of living in luxury and of the fact that the royal princes have grown up immersed in prosperity. They have forgotten the ways of manliness and have become accustomed to the character traits of wet nurses, and they have grown up that way. They do not desire leadership. They are not used to exercising sole power, the prerogative of superiority. All their ambition requires is the satisfactions of pomp and having a great variety of pleasures and luxuries. Clients and followers gain superiority when the family of the ruler is in sole control over its people and claims all royal authority for itself to their exclusion. This is something that happens to dynasties of necessity, as we have stated before.

These are two diseases of dynasties which cannot be cured, except in very rare cases.

20 Those who gain power over the ruler do not share with him in the special title that goes with royal authority

This is because the first men to achieve royal and governmental authority at the beginning of the dynasty do so with the help of the group feeling of their people and with the help of their own group feeling which causes their people to follow them until they and their people have definitely adopted the colouring of royal authority and superiority. The colouring, then, continues to exist. Through it the identity and persistence of the dynasty are assured.

The person who gains superiority (over the ruler) may have a share in the group feeling that belongs to the tribe which has gained royal authority or to its clients and followers. However, his group feeling still is comprised by, and subordinate to, the group feeling of the family of the ruler. He cannot (take on) the colouring of royal authority. Thus, in gaining control, he does not plan to appropriate royal authority for himself openly, but only to appropriate its fruits, that is, the exercise of administrative, executive, and all other power. He gives the people of the dynasty the impression that he merely acts for the ruler and executes the latter's decisions from behind the curtain. He carefully refrains from using the attributes, emblems, or titles of royal authority. He avoids throwing any suspicion upon himself in this respect, even though he exercises full control. For, in his exercise of full control, he takes cover behind the curtain the ruler and his ancestors had set up to protect themselves from their own tribe when the dynasty came into being. He disguises his exercise of control under the form of acting as the ruler's representative.

Should he undertake to adopt (any of the royal prerogatives), the people who represent the group feeling and tribe of the ruler would resent it and contrive to appropriate (such prerogatives) for themselves, to his exclusion. He has no definite colouring to (make him appear suited for the royal prerogatives) or cause others to submit to him and obey him. (Any attempt by him to appropriate the royal prerogatives) would, thus, instantly precipitate his doom. . . .

21 The true character and different kinds of royal authority

Royal authority is an institution that is natural to mankind. We have explained before that human beings cannot live and exist except through social organization and co-operation for the purpose of obtaining their food and other necessities of life. When they have organized, necessity requires that they deal with each other and satisfy their needs. Each one will stretch out his hand for whatever he needs and (try simply to) take it, since injustice and aggressiveness are in the animal nature. The others, in turn, will try to prevent him from taking it, motivated by wrathfulness and spite and the strong human reaction when one's own property is menaced. This causes dissension, which leads to hostilities, and hostilities lead to trouble and bloodshed and loss of life, which lead to the destruction of the species. Now, (the human species) is one of the things the Creator has especially (enjoined us) to preserve.

People, thus, cannot persist in a state of anarchy and without a ruler who keeps them apart. Therefore, they need a person to restrain them. He is their ruler. As is required by human nature, he must be a forceful ruler, one who exercises authority. In this connection, group feeling is absolutely necessary, for as we have stated before, aggressive and defensive enterprises can succeed only with the help of group feeling. As one can see, royal authority of this kind is a noble institution, toward which all claims are directed, and one that needs to be defended. Nothing of the sort can materialize except with the help of group feelings, as has been mentioned before.

Group feelings differ. Each group feeling exercises its own authority and superiority over the people and family adhering to it. Not every group feeling has royal authority. Royal authority, in reality, belongs only to those who dominate subjects, collect taxes, send out (military) expeditions, protect the frontier regions, and have no one over them who is stronger than they. This is generally accepted as the real meaning of royal authority.

There are people whose group feeling falls short of accomplishing (one or another of these things which constitute) part of (real royal authority), such as protecting the frontier regions, or collecting taxes, or sending out (military) expeditions. Such royal authority is defective and not royal authority in the real meaning of the term.

Then, there are people whose group feeling is not strong enough to gain control over all the other group feelings or to stop everyone, so that there exists an authority superior to theirs. Their royal authority is also defective, and not royal authority in the real meaning of the term. It is exercised, for instance, by provincial amirs and regional chieftains who are all under one dynasty. This situation is often found in far-flung dynasties. I mean that there are rulers of provincial and remote regions who rule their own people but also obey the central power of the dynasty.

22   Exaggerated harshness is harmful to royal authority and in most cases causes its destruction

The interest subjects have in their ruler is not interest in his person and body, for example, in his good figure, handsome face, large frame, wide knowledge, good handwriting, or acute mind. Their interest in him lies in his relation to them. Royal and governmental authority is something relative, a relationship between ruler and subjects. Government becomes a reality when (a ruler) rules over subjects and handles their affairs. A ruler is he who has subjects, and subjects are persons who have a ruler. The quality accruing to the ruler from the fact of his correlative relation with his subjects is called 'rulership'. That is, he rules them, and if such rulership and its concomitants are of good quality, the purpose of government is most perfectly achieved. If such rulership is good and beneficial, it will serve the interests of the subjects. If it is bad and unfair, it will be harmful to them and cause their destruction.

Good rulership is equivalent to mildness. If the ruler uses force and is ready to mete out punishment and eager to expose the faults of people and to count their sins, (his subjects) become fearful and depressed and seek to protect themselves against him through lies, ruses, and deceit. This becomes a character trait of theirs. Their mind and character become corrupted. They often abandon (the ruler) on the battlefield and (fail to support his) defensive enterprises. The decay of (sincere) intentions causes the decay of (military) protection. The subjects often conspire to kill the ruler. Thus, the dynasty decays, and the fence (that protects it) lies in ruin. If the ruler continues to keep a forceful grip on his subjects, group feeling will be destroyed. If the ruler is mild and overlooks the bad sides of his subjects, they will trust him and take refuge with him. They love him heartily and are willing to die for him in battle against his enemies. Everything is then in order in the state.

The concomitants of good rulership are kindness to, and protection of, one's subjects. The true meaning of royal authority is realized when the ruler defends his subjects. To be kind and beneficent toward them is part of being mild to them and showing an interest in the way they live. These things are important for the ruler in gaining the love of his subjects.

An alert and very shrewd person rarely has the habit of mildness. Mildness is usually found in careless and unconcerned persons. The least (of the many drawbacks) of alertness (in a ruler) is that he imposes tasks upon his subjects that are beyond their ability, because he is aware of things they do not perceive and, through his genius, foresees the outcome of things at the start. (The ruler's excessive demands) may lead to his subjects' ruin. Muḥammad said: 'Follow the pace of the weakest among you.'

Muḥammad therefore made it a condition that the ruler should not be too shrewd. For this quality is accompanied by tyrannical and bad rulership and by a tendency to make the people do things that it is not in their nature to do.

The conclusion is that it is a drawback in a political leader to be (too) clever and shrewd. Cleverness and shrewdness imply that a person thinks too much, just as stupidity implies that he is too rigid. In the case of all human qualities, the extremes are reprehensible, and the middle road is praiseworthy. This is, for instance, the case with generosity in relation to waste and stinginess, or with bravery in relation to foolhardiness and cowardice. And so it is with all the other human qualities. For this reason, the very clever person is said to have the qualities of a devil. He is called a 'satan', or 'a would-be satan', and the like.

23 The meaning of caliphate and imamate

Royal authority implies a form of organization necessary to mankind. It requires superiority and force, which express the wrathfulness and animality (of human nature). The decisions of the ruler will therefore, as a rule, deviate from what is right. They will be ruinous to the worldly affairs of the people under his control, since, as a rule, he forces them to execute his intentions and desires, and this may be beyond their ability. This situation will differ according to the intentions to be found in different generations. It is for this reason difficult to be obedient to the ruler. Disobedience makes itself noticeable and leads to trouble and bloodshed.

Therefore, it is necessary to have reference to ordained political norms, which are accepted by the mass and to whose laws it submits. The Persians and other nations had such norms. The dynasty that does not have a policy based on such (norms) cannot fully succeed in establishing the supremacy of its rule.

If these norms are ordained by the intelligent and leading personalities and minds of the dynasty, the result will be a political (institution) with an intellectual (rational) basis. If they are ordained by God through a lawgiver who establishes them as (religious) laws, the result will be a political (institution) with a religious basis, which will be useful for life in both this and the other world.

This is because the purpose of human beings is not only their worldly welfare. This entire world is trifling and futile. It ends in death and annihilation. The purpose (of human beings) is their religion, which leads them to happiness in the other world. Therefore, religious laws have as their purpose to cause (them) to follow such a course in all their dealings with God and their fellow men. This (situation) also applies to royal authority, which is natural in human social organization. (The religious laws) guide it along the path of religion, so that everything will be under the supervision of the religious law. Anything (done by royal authority) that is dictated by force, superiority, or the free play of the power of wrathful-ness, is tyranny and injustice and considered reprehensible by (the religious law), as it is also considered reprehensible by the require-ments of political wisdom. Likewise, anything (done by royal authority) that is dictated by considerations of policy or political deci-sions without supervision of the religious law, is also reprehensible, because it is vision lacking the divine light. At the Resurrection, the actions of human beings, whether they had to do with royal authority or anything else, will all come back to them.

Political laws consider only worldly interests. On the other hand, the intention the Lawgiver has concerning mankind is their welfare in the other world. Therefore, it is necessary, as required by the religious law, to cause the mass to act in accordance with the religious laws in all their affairs touching both this world and the other world. The au-thority to do so was possessed by the representatives of the religious law, the prophets; then by those who took their place, the caliphs.

This makes it clear what the caliphate means. (To exercise) natural royal authority means to cause the masses to act as required by purpose and desire. (To exercise) political (royal authority) means to cause the masses to act as required by intellectual (rational) insight into the means of furthering their worldly interests and avoid-ing anything that is harmful in that respect. (To exercise) the cali-phate means to cause the masses to act as required by religious insight into their interests in the other world as well as in this world. (Worldly interests) have bearing upon (the interests in the other world), since according to Muḥammad all worldly conditions are to be considered in their relation to their value for the other world. Thus, (the caliphate) in reality is a substitute for Muḥammad inas-much as it serves, like him, to protect the religion and to exercise leadership of the world.

24 *The differences of Muslim opinion concerning the laws and conditions governing the caliphate*

We have explained the real meaning of the (caliphate). It is a sub-stitute for Muḥammad inasmuch as it serves, like him, to preserve the religion and to exercise (political) leadership of the world. (The institution) is called 'the caliphate' or 'the imamate'. The person in charge of it is called 'the caliph' or 'the imam'.

In later times, he has been called 'the sultan', when there were numerous (claimants to the position) or when, in view of the dis-tances (separating the different regions) and in disregard of the conditions governing the institution, people were forced to render the oath of allegiance to anybody who seized power. . . .

The position of imam is a necessary one. The consensus of the men around Muḥammad and the men of the second generation shows that (the imamate) is necessary according to the religious law. At the death of the Prophet, the men around him proceeded to render the oath of allegiance to Abû Bakr and to entrust him with the supervision of their affairs. And so it was at all subsequent periods. In no period were the people left in a state of anarchy. This was so by general consensus, which proves that the position of imam is a necessary one.

Some people have expressed the opinion that the necessity of the imamate is apparent for rational reasons, and that the consensus which happens to exist merely confirms the authority of the intellect in this respect. As they say, what makes (the imam rationally) necessary is the need of human beings for social organization and the impossibility of their living and existing by themselves. One of the necessary consequences of social organization is disagreement, because of the pressure of cross-purposes. As long as there is no ruler who exercises a restraining influence, this leads to trouble which, in turn, may lead to the destruction and uprooting of mankind. Now, the preservation of the species is one of the necessary intentions of the religious law.

This very idea is the one the philosophers had in mind when they considered prophethood as something (intellectually) necessary for mankind. We have already shown the incorrectness of their reasoning. One of its premises is that the restraining influence comes into being only through a religious law from God, to which the mass submits as a matter of belief and religious creed. This premise is not acceptable. The restraining influence comes into being as the result of the impetus of royal authority and the forcefulness of the mighty, even if there is no religious law. This was the case among heathens and other nations who had no scriptures and had not been reached by a prophetic mission.

Or, we might say: In order to remove disagreement, it is sufficient that every individual should know that injustice is forbidden him by the authority of the intellect. Then, their claim that the removal of disagreement takes place only through the existence of the religious law in one case, and the position of the imam in another case, is not correct. It may (be removed) as well through the existence of powerful leaders, or through the people refraining from disagreement and mutual injustice, as through the position of the imam. Thus, the intellectual proof based upon that premise does not stand up. This shows that the necessity of (an imam) is indicated by the religious law, that is, by the consensus, as we have stated before.

Some people have taken the exceptional position of stating that the position of imam is not necessary at all, neither according to the intellect nor according to the religious law. People who have held that opinion include the Mu'tazilah al-Aṣamm and certain Khârijites, among others. They think that it is necessary only to observe the religious laws. When Muslims agree upon (the practice of) justice and observance of the divine laws, no imam is needed, and the imamate is not necessary. Those (who so argue) are refuted by the consensus. They adopted such an opinion because they were (attempting to) escape the royal authority and its overbearing, domineering, and worldly ways. They had seen that the religious law was full of censure and blame for such things and for the people who practised them, and that it encouraged the desire to abolish them.

The religious law does not censure royal authority as such and does not forbid its exercise. It merely censures the evils resulting from it, such as tyranny, injustice, and pleasure-seeking. Here, no doubt, we have forbidden evils. They are the concomitants of royal authority. The religious law praises justice, fairness, the fulfilment of religious duties, and the defence of religion. It states that these things will of necessity find their reward (in the other world). Now, all these things are concomitants of royal authority, too. Thus, censure attaches to royal authority only on account of some of its qualities and conditions, not others. (The religious law) does not censure royal authority as such, nor does it seek to suppress it entirely. It also censures concupiscence and wrathfulness in responsible persons, but it does not want to see either of these qualities relinquished altogether, because necessity calls for their existence. It merely wants to see that proper use is made of them. David and Solomon possessed royal authority such as no one else ever possessed, yet they were divine prophets and belonged, in God's eyes, among the noblest human beings that ever existed.

Furthermore, we say to them: The (attempt to) dispense with royal authority by (assuming) that the institution (of the imamate) is not necessary does not help you at all. You agree that observance of the religious laws is a necessary thing. Now, that is achieved only through group feeling and power, and group feeling, by its very nature, requires royal authority. Thus, there will be royal authority, even if no imam is set up. Now, that is just what you (wanted to) dispense with.

If it has been established that the institution (of the imamate) is necessary by the consensus, (it must be added that this institution) is a community duty and is left to the discretion of all competent Muslims. It is their obligation to see to it that (the imamate) is set up, and everybody has to obey (the imam) in accordance with the verse of the Qur'ân, 'Obey God, and obey the apostle and the people in authority among you.'[1]

It is not possible to appoint two men to the position (of imam) at the same time. Religious scholars generally are of this opinion, on the basis of certain traditions.

Others hold that (the prohibition against two imams) applies only to two imams in one locality, or where they would be close to each other. When there are great distances and the imam is unable to control the farther region, it is permissible to set up another imam there to take care of public interests. . . .

The pre-requisites governing the institution of (the imamate) are four: (1) knowledge, (2) probity, (3) competence, and (4) freedom of the senses and limbs from any defect that might affect judgment and action. There is a difference of opinion concerning a fifth pre-requisite, that is, (5) Qurashite descent.

(1) The necessity of knowledge as a pre-requisite is obvious. The imam can execute the divine laws only if he knows them. Those he does not know, he cannot properly present. His knowledge is satisfactory only if he is able to make independent decisions. Blind acceptance of tradition is a shortcoming, and the imamate requires perfection in all qualities and conditions.

(2) Probity is required because (the imamate) is a religious institution and supervises all the other institutions that require (this quality). There is no difference of opinion as to the fact that his probity is nullified by the actual commission of forbidden acts and the like. But there is a difference of opinion on the question of whether it is nullified by innovations in dogma.

(3) Competence means that he is willing to carry out the punishments fixed by law and to go to war. He must understand warfare and be able to assume responsibility for getting the people to fight. He also must know about group feeling and the fine points (of diplomacy). He must be strong enough to take care of political duties. All of which is to enable him to fulfil his functions of protecting religion, leading in the holy war against the enemy, maintaining the (religious) laws, and administering the (public) interests.

(4) Freedom of the senses and limbs from defects or disabilities such as insanity, blindness, muteness, or deafness, and from any loss of limbs affecting (the imam's) ability to act, such as missing hands, feet, or testicles, is a pre-requisite of the imamate, because all such defects affect his full ability to act and to fulfil his duties. Even in the case of a defect that merely disfigures the appearance, as, for instance,

[1] Qur'ân 4. 59 (62).

loss of one limb, the condition of freedom from defects (remains in force as a condition in the sense that it) aims at his perfection.

Lack of freedom of action is connected with loss of limbs. Such a lack may be of two kinds. One is forced (inaction) and complete inability to act through imprisonment or the like. (Absence of any restriction upon freedom of action) is as necessary a condition (of the imamate) as freedom from bodily defects. The other kind is in a different category. (This lack of freedom of action implies that) some of (the imam's) men may gain power over him, although no disobedience or disagreement may be involved, and keep him in seclusion. Then, the problem is shifted to the person who has gained power. If he acts in accordance with Islam and justice and praiseworthy policies, it is permissible to acknowledge (him). If not, Muslims must look for help from persons who will restrain him and eliminate the unhealthy situation created by him, until the caliph's power of action is re-established.

(5) The pre-requisite of a Qurashite origin is based upon the consensus on this point that obtained in the men around Muḥammad on the day of Abû Bakr's elevation to the caliphate. . . .

Among those who deny that Qurashite descent is a condition of the imamate is Judge Abû Bakr al-Bâqillânî. The Qurashite group feeling had come to disappear and dissolve (in his day), and non-Arab rulers controlled the caliphs. Therefore, when he saw what the condition of the caliphs was in his day, he dropped the pre-requisite of a Qurashite origin.

Scholars in general, however, retain Qurashite descent as a condition (of the imamate). (They maintain that) the imamate rightly belongs to a Qurashite, even if he is too weak to handle the affairs of the Muslims. Against them is the fact that this involves dropping the pre-requisite of competence, which requires that he have the power to discharge his duties. If his strength has gone with the disappearance of group feeling, his competence, too, is gone. And if the condition of competence be eliminated, that will reflect further upon knowledge and religion. (In this case, then, all) the conditions governing the institution would no longer be considered, and this would be contrary to the consensus. . . .

When one considers what God meant the caliphate to be, nothing more needs (to be said) about it. God made the caliph his substitute to handle the affairs of His servants. He is to make them do the things that are good for them and forbid them to do those that are harmful. He has been directly told so. A person who lacks the power to do a thing is never told directly to do it. The religious leader, Ibn al-Khaṭîb, said that most religious laws apply to women as they do to men. However, women are not directly told (to follow the religious laws) by express reference to them in the text, but, in (Ibn al-Khaṭīb's) opinion, they are included only by way of analogical reasoning. That is because women have no power whatever. Men control their (actions), except in as far as the duties of divine worship are concerned, where everyone controls his own. Therefore, women are directly told (to fulfil the duties of divine worship) by express reference to them in the text, and not (merely) by way of analogical reasoning.

Furthermore, (the world of) existence attests to (the necessity of group feeling for the caliphate). Only he who has gained superiority over a nation or a race is able to handle its affairs. The religious law would hardly ever make a requirement in contradiction to the requirements of existence. . . .

26 The transformation of the caliphate into royal authority

Royal authority is the natural goal of group feeling. It results from group feeling, not by choice but through (inherent) necessity and the order of existence, as we have stated before. All religious laws and practices and everything that the masses are expected to do requires group feeling. Only with the help of group feeling can a claim be successfully pressed, as we have stated before.

Group feeling is necessary to the Muslim community. Its existence enables (the community) to fulfil what God expects of it. Still, we find that Muḥammad censured group feeling and urged us to reject it and to leave it alone. He said: 'God removed from you the arrogance of pre-Islamic times and its pride in ancestry. You are the children of Adam, and Adam was made of dust.' God said: 'Most noble among you in God's eyes is he who fears God most.'[1]

We also find that Muḥammad censured royal authority and its representatives. He blamed them because of their enjoyment of good fortune, their senseless waste, and their deviations from the path of God. He enjoined friendship among all Muslims and warned against discord and dissension.

It should be known that in Muḥammad's opinion, all of this world is a vehicle for transport to the other world. He who loses the vehicle can go nowhere. When Muḥammad forbids or censures certain human activities or urges their omission, he does not want them to be neglected altogether. Nor does he want them to be completely eradicated, or the powers from which they result to remain altogether unused. He wants those powers to be employed as much as possible for the right aims. Every intention should thus eventually

[1] Qur'ân 49. 13 (13).

become the right one and the direction of all human activities one and the same.

Muḥammad did not censure wrathfulness with the intention of eradicating it as a human quality. If the power of wrathfulness were no longer to exist in man, he would lose the ability to help the truth become victorious. There would no longer be holy war or glorification of the word of God. Muḥammad censured the wrathfulness that is in the service of Satan and reprehensible purposes, but the wrathfulness that is one in God and in the service of God deserves praise. Such praiseworthy wrathfulness was one of the qualities of Muḥammad.

Likewise, when he censures the desires, he does not want them to be abolished altogether, for a complete abolition of concupiscence in a person would make him defective and inferior. He wants the desires to be used for permissible purposes to serve the public interests, so that man becomes an active servant of God who willingly obeys the divine commands.

Likewise, when the religious law censures group feeling and says: 'Neither your blood relatives nor your children will be of use to you (on the Day of Resurrection)',[1] (such a statement) is directed against a group feeling that is used for worthless purposes, as was the case in pre-Islamic times. It is also directed against a group feeling that makes a person proud and superior. For an intelligent person to take such an attitude is considered a gratuitous action, which is of no use for the other world, the world of eternity. On the other hand, a group feeling that is working for the truth and for fulfilment of the divine commands is something desirable. If it were gone, religious laws would no longer be, because they materialize only through group feeling, as we have stated before.

Likewise, when Muḥammad censures royal authority, he does not censure it for gaining superiority through truth, for forcing the great mass to accept the faith, nor for looking after the (public) interests. He censures royal authority for achieving superiority through worthless means and for employing human beings for indulgence in (selfish) purposes and desires, as we have stated. If royal authority would sincerely exercise its superiority over men for the sake of God and so as to cause those men to worship God and to wage war against His enemies, there would not be anything reprehensible in it. . . .

When the Messenger of God was about to die, he appointed Abû Bakr as his representative to (lead the) prayers, since (prayer) was the most important religious activity. People were, thus, content to accept him as caliph, that is, as the person who causes the great mass to act according to the religious laws. No mention was made of royal

[1] Qur'ân 60. 3 (3).

authority, because royal authority was suspected of being worthless, and because at that time it was the prerogative of unbelievers and enemies of Islam. Abû Bakr discharged the duties of his office in a manner pleasing to God, following the traditions of his master. He fought against apostates until all the Arabs were united in Islam. He then appointed 'Umar his successor. 'Umar followed Abû Bakr's example and fought against (foreign) nations. He defeated them and permitted the Arabs to appropriate their worldly possessions and their royal authority, and the Arabs did that.

The caliphate, then, went to 'Uthmân b. 'Affân and 'Alî. All these caliphs renounced royal authority and kept apart from its ways. They were strengthened in this attitude by the low standard of living in Islam and the desert outlook of the Arabs. The world and its luxuries were more alien to them than to any other nation, on account of their religion, which inspired asceticism where the good things of life were concerned, and on account of the desert outlook and habitat and the rude, severe life to which they were accustomed. No nation was more used to a life of hunger than the Muḍar. In the Ḥijâz, the Muḍar inhabited a country without agricultural or animal products. They were kept from the fertile plains, rich in grain, because the latter were too far away and were monopolized by the Rabî'ah and Yemenites who controlled them. They had no envy of the abundance of (those regions). They often ate scorpions and beetles. They were proud to eat *'ilhiz*, that is, camel hair ground with stones, mixed with blood, and then cooked. The Quraysh were in a similar situation with regard to food and housing.

Finally, the group feeling of the Arabs was consolidated in Islam through the prophethood of Muḥammad with which God honoured them. They then advanced against the Persians and Byzantines, and they looked for the land that God had truthfully promised and destined to them. They took away the royal authority of (the Persians and the Byzantines) and confiscated their worldly possessions. They amassed enormous fortunes. It went so far that one horseman obtained, as his share in one of the raids, about 30,000 gold pieces. The amounts they got were enormous. Still, they kept to their rude way of life. 'Umar used to patch his (only) garment with pieces of leather. 'Alî used to say: 'Gold and silver! Go and lure others, not me!' Abû Mûsâ refrained from eating chicken, because chickens were very rare among the Arabs of that time and not (generally) known to them. Sieves were altogether nonexistent among (the Bedouins), and they ate wheat kernels with the bran. Yet, the gains they made were greater than any ever made by other human beings.

Al-Mas'ûdî says: 'In the days of 'Uthmân, the men around

Muḥammad acquired estates and money. On the day 'Uthmân was killed, 150,000 dinars and 1,000,000 dirhams were in the hands of his treasurer. The value of his estates in Wâdî l-Qurâ and Ḥunayn and other places was 200,000 dinars. He also left many camels and horses. The eighth part of the estate of az-Zubayr after his death amounted to 50,000 dinars. He also left 1,000 horses and 1,000 female servants. Ṭalḥah's income from the 'Irâq was 1,000 dinars a day, and his income from the region of ash-Sharâh was more than that. The stable of 'Abd-ar-Raḥmân b. 'Awf contained 1,000 horses. He also had 1,000 camels and 10,000 sheep. One-fourth of his estate after his death amounted to 84,000. Zayd b. Thâbit left silver and gold that was broken into pieces with pickaxes, in addition to the (other) property and estates that he left, in the value of 100,000 dinars. Az-Zubayr built himself a residence in al-Baṣrah and other residences in Egypt and al-Kûfah and Alexandria. Ṭalḥah built one in al-Kûfah and had his residence in Medina improved. He used plaster, bricks, and teakwood. Sa'd b. Abî Waqqâṣ built himself a residence in al-'Aqîq, (a suburb of Medina). He made it high and spacious, and had balustrades put on top of it. Al-Miqdâd built his residence in Medina and had it plastered inside and out. Ya'lâ b. Munyah left 50,000 dinars and estates and other things the value of which amounted to 300,000 dirhams.' End of the quotation from al-Mas'ûdî.

Such were the gains people made. Their religion did not blame them for (amassing so much), because, as booty, it was lawful property. They did not employ their property wastefully but in a planned way in all their conditions, as we have stated. Amassing worldly property is reprehensible, but it did not reflect upon them, because blame attaches only to waste and lack of planning, as we have indicated. Since their expenditure followed a plan and served the truth and its ways, amassing (so much property) helped them along on the path of truth and served the purpose of attaining the other world.

Soon, the desert attitude of the Arabs and their low standard of living approached its end. The nature of royal authority—which is the necessary consequence of group feeling as we have stated—showed itself, and with it, there came superiority and force. Royal authority, as (the early Muslims) saw it, belonged in the same category as luxury and amassed property. They did not apply their superiority to worthless things, and they did not abandon the intentions of their religion or the ways of truth.

When trouble arose between 'Alî and Mu'âwiyah as a necessary consequence of group feeling, they were guided in (their dissensions) by the truth and by independent judgment. They did not fight for any worldly purpose or over preferences of no value, or for reasons of personal enmity. This might be suspected, and heretics might like to think so. However, what caused their difference was their independent judgment as to where the truth lay. It was on this matter that each side opposed the point of view of the other. Even though 'Alî was in the right, Mu'âwiyah's intentions were not evil. He wanted the truth, but missed it. Each was right in so far as his intentions were concerned. Now, the nature of royal authority requires that one person claim all the glory for himself and appropriate it to himself. It was not for Mu'âwiyah to deny (the natural requirement of royal authority) to himself and his people. (Royal authority) was a natural thing that group feeling, by its very nature, brought in its train. Even the Umayyads and those of their followers who were not after the truth like Mu'âwiyah felt that. They banded together around him and were willing to die for him. Had Mu'âwiyah tried to lead them on another course of action, had he opposed them and not claimed all the power for (himself and them), it would have meant the dissolution of the whole thing that he had consolidated. It was more important to him to keep it together than to bother about a course of action that could not entail much criticism.

When royal authority is obtained and we assume that one person has it all for himself, no objection can be raised if he uses it for the various ways and aspects of the truth. Solomon and his father David had the royal authority of the Israelites for themselves, as the nature of royal authority requires, and it is well known how great a share in prophecy and truth they possessed.

Likewise, Mu'âwiyah appointed Yazîd as his successor, because he was afraid of the dissolution of the whole thing, inasmuch as the Umayyads did not like to see the power handed over to any outsider. Had Mu'âwiyah appointed anyone else his successor, the Umayyads would have been against him. Moreover, they had a good opinion of Yazîd. Mu'âwiyah would not have been the man to appoint Yazîd his successor, had he believed him to be really so wicked. Such an assumption must be absolutely excluded in Mu'âwiyah's case.

The same applies to Marwân b. al-Ḥakam and his sons. Even though they were kings, their royal ways were not those of worthless men and oppressors. They complied with the intentions of the truth with all their energy, except when necessity caused them to do something (unworthy). Such (a necessity existed) when there was fear that the whole thing might face dissolution. (To avoid that) was more important to them than any (other) intention. That this was (their attitude) is attested by the fact that they followed and imitated (the early Muslims).

Then came the later Umayyads. As far as their worldly purposes and intentions were concerned, they acted as the nature of royal authority required. They forgot the deliberate planning and the reliance upon the truth that had guided the activities of their predecessors. This caused the people to censure their actions and to accept the 'Abbâsid propaganda in the place of the Umayyads'. Thus, the 'Abbâsids took over the government. The probity of the 'Abbâsids was outstanding. They used their royal authority to further, as far as possible, the different aspects and ways of the truth. (The early 'Abbâsids) eventually were succeeded by the descendants of ar-Rashîd. Among them there were good and bad men. Later on, when the power passed to their descendants, they gave royal authority and luxury their due. They became enmeshed in worldly affairs of no value and turned their backs on Islam. Therefore, God permitted them to be ruined, and the Arabs to be completely deprived of their power, which He gave to others. Whoever considers the biographies of these caliphs and their different approaches to truth and worthlessness knows that what we have stated is correct. . . .

It has thus become clear how the caliphate was transformed into royal authority. The form of government in the beginning was a caliphate. Everybody had his restraining influence in himself, that is, (the restraining influence of) Islam. They preferred (Islam) to their worldly affairs, even if (the neglect of worldly affairs) led to their own destruction.

When 'Uthmân was besieged in his house, al-Ḥasan, al-Ḥusayn, 'Abdallâh b. 'Umar, Ibn Ja'far, and others came and offered to defend him. But he refused and did not permit swords to be drawn among Muslims. He feared a split and wanted to preserve the harmony that would keep the whole thing intact, even if it could be done only at the cost of his own destruction.

At the beginning of his (term of) office, 'Alî himself was advised by al-Mughîrah to leave az-Zubayr, Mu'âwiyah, and Ṭalḥah in their positions, until the people had agreed to render the oath of allegiance to him and the whole thing was consolidated. After that, he might do what he wanted. That was good power politics. 'Alî, however, refused. He wanted to avoid deceit, because deceit is forbidden by Islam. Al-Mughîrah came back to him the following morning and said: 'I gave you that advice yesterday, but then I reconsidered it and realized that it was neither right nor good advice. You were right.' 'Alî replied: 'Indeed, no. I know that the advice you gave me yesterday was good advice and that you are deceiving me today. However, regard for the truth prevented me from following your good advice.' To such a degree were these early Muslims concerned with improving their religion at the expense of their worldly affairs.

It has thus been shown how the form of government came to be royal authority. However, there remained the traits that were characteristic of the caliphate, namely, preference for Islam and its ways, and adherence to the path of truth. A change became apparent only in the restraining influence that had been Islam and now came to be group feeling and the sword. That was the situation in the time of Mu'âwiyah, Marwân, his son 'Abd-al-Malik, and the first 'Abbâsid caliphs down to ar-Rashîd and some of his sons. Then, the characteristic traits of the caliphate disappeared, and only its name remained. The form of government came to be royal authority pure and simple. Superiority attained the limits of its nature and was employed for particular (worthless) purposes, such as the use of force and the arbitrary gratification of desires and for pleasure.

This was the case with the successors of the sons of 'Abd-al-Malik and the 'Abbâsids after al-Mu'taṣim and al-Mutawakkil. They remained caliphs in name, because the Arab group feeling continued to exist. In these two stages caliphate and royal authority existed side by side. Then, with the disappearance of Arab group feeling and the annihilation of the race and complete destruction of (Arabism), the caliphate lost its identity. The form of government remained royal authority pure and simple.

This was the case, for instance, with the non-Arab rulers in the East. They showed obedience to the caliph in order to enjoy the blessings (involved in that), but royal authority belonged to them with all its titles and attributes. The caliph had no share in it.

It is thus clear that the caliphate at first existed without royal authority. Then, the characteristic traits of the caliphate became mixed up and confused. Finally, when its group feeling had separated from the group feeling of the caliphate, royal authority came to exist alone.

27 The meaning of the oath of allegiance

It should be known that the *bay'ah* (oath of allegiance) is a contract to render obedience. It is as though the person who renders the oath of allegiance made a contract with his amir, to the effect that he surrenders supervision of his own affairs and those of the Muslims to him and that he will not contest his authority and that he will obey him by (executing) all the duties with which he might be charged, whether agreeable or disagreeable.

When people rendered the oath of allegiance to the amir and concluded the contract, they put their hands into his hand to confirm the contract. This was considered to be something like the action of buyer and seller (after concluding a bargain). Therefore, the oath of allegiance was called *bay'ah,* the infinitive of *bâ'a* 'to sell (or buy)'. The *bay'ah* was a handshake. Such is its meaning in customary linguistic terminology and the accepted usage of the religious law.

The oath of allegiance that is common at present is the Persian custom of greeting kings by kissing the earth, or their hand, their foot, or the lower hem of their garment. The term *bay'ah,* which means a contract to render obedience, was used metaphorically to denote this, since such an abject form of greeting and politeness is one of the consequences and concomitants of obedience. (The practice) has become so general that it has become customary and has replaced the handshake which was originally used, because shaking hands with everybody meant that the ruler lowered himself and made himself cheap, things that are detrimental to leadership and the dignity of the royal position. However, (the handshake is practised) by a very few rulers who want to show themselves humble and who, therefore, themselves shake hands with their nobles and with famous divines among their subjects.

This customary meaning of the oath of allegiance should be understood. A person must know it, because it imposes upon him certain duties toward his ruler and imam. His actions will thus not be frivolous or gratuitous. This should be taken into consideration in one's dealings with rulers.

28 The succession

We have been discussing the imamate and mentioned the fact that it is part of the religious law because it serves the (public) interest. (We have stated) that its real meaning is the supervision of the interests of the Muslim nation in both their worldly and their religious affairs. (The caliph) is their guardian and trustee. He looks after their (affairs) as long as he lives. It follows that he should also look after their (affairs) after his death, and, therefore, should appoint someone to take charge of them as he had done, someone they can trust to look after them as they had trusted him then.

The appointment of a successor is recognized as part of the religious law through the consensus of the (Muslim) nation, (which says) that it is permissible and binding when it occurs. Thus, Abû Bakr appointed 'Umar as his successor in the presence of the men around Muḥammad. They considered (this appointment) permissible and considered themselves obliged by it to render obedience to 'Umar. Likewise, 'Umar appointed six persons to be members of (an electoral) council.

No suspicion of the imam is justified in this connection, even if he appoints his father or his son his successor. He is trusted to look after the affairs of the Muslims as long as he lives. He is all the more responsible for not tolerating while he is (alive the possibility that there might arise evil) developments after his death. This is against those who say that he is suspect with regard to (the appointment of) his son or father, and also against those who consider him suspect with regard to the (appointment of) his son only, not his father. In fact, he could hardly be suspected in this respect in any way. Especially if there exists some reason for (the appointment of a successor), such as a desire to promote the (public) interest or fear that some harm might arise (if no successor were appointed), suspicion of the imam is out of the question.

This, for instance, was the case with Mu'âwiyah's appointment of his son Yazîd. The action met with agreement of the people, and, therefore, is in itself an argument for the problem under discussion. But Mu'âwiyah himself preferred his son Yazîd to any other successor, because he was concerned with the (public) interest of preserving unity and harmony among the people, since the men who possessed executive authority, that is, the Umayyads, agreed at that time upon Yazîd. No other motive could be expected of Mu'âwiyah. His probity and the fact that he was one of the men around Muḥammad preclude any other explanation.

After Mu'âwiyah, caliphs who were used to choosing the truth and to acting in accordance with it, acted similarly. Such caliphs included the Umayyads 'Abd-al-Malik and Sulaymân and the 'Abbâsids as-Saffâḥ, al-Manṣûr, al-Mahdî, and ar-Rashîd, and others like them whose probity, and whose care and concern for the Muslims are well known. They cannot be blamed because they gave preference to their own sons and brothers, in that respect departing from the Sunnah of the first four caliphs. Their situation was different from that of the (four) caliphs who lived in a time when royal authority as such did not yet exist, and the restraining influence was religious. Thus, everybody had his restraining influence in himself. Consequently, they appointed the person who was acceptable to Islam, and preferred him over all others. They trusted every aspirant to have his own restraining influence.

After them, from Mu'âwiyah on, the group feeling (of the Arabs) approached its final goal, royal authority. The restraining influence of religion had weakened. The restraining influence of government and group was needed. If, under those circumstances, someone not acceptable to the group had been appointed as successor, such an appointment would have been rejected by it. The (chances of the appointee) would have been quickly demolished, and the community would have been split and torn by dissension.

Someone asked 'Alî: 'Why do the people disagree concerning you, and why did they not disagree concerning Abû Bakr and 'Umar?' 'Alî replied: 'Because Abû Bakr and 'Umar were in charge of men like me, and I today am in charge of men like you.' He referred to the restraining influence of Islam.

When al-Ma'mûn appointed 'Alî b. Mûsâ b. Ja'far aṣ-Ṣâdiq his successor and called him ar-Riḍâ, the 'Abbâsids greatly disapproved of the action. They declared invalid the oath of allegiance that had been rendered to al-Ma'mûn, and took the oath of allegiance to his uncle Ibrâhîm b. al-Mahdî. There was so much trouble, dissension, and interruption of communications, and there were so many rebels and seceders, that the state almost collapsed. Eventually, al-Ma'mûn went from Khurâsân to Baghdad and brought matters back to their former condition.

Such (differences as the one just cited between caliphate and royal authority) must be taken into consideration in connection with (the problem of) succession. Times differ according to differences in affairs, tribes, and group feelings, which come into being during those (times). Differences in this respect produce differences in (public) interests, and each (public interest) has its own particular laws.

However, Islam does not consider preservation of (the ruler's) inheritance for his children the proper purpose of appointing a successor. Succession to the rule is something that comes from God who distinguishes by it whomsoever He wishes.

In (appointing a successor), it is necessary to be as well-intentioned as possible. Otherwise, there is danger that one may trifle with religious institutions. . . .

Some wrongly assume the imamate to be one of the pillars of the faith. It is one of the general (public) interests. The people are delegated to take care of it. If it were one of the pillars of the faith, it would be something like prayer, and Muhammad would have appointed a representative, exactly as he appointed Abû Bakr to represent him at prayer. (Had he done so), it would have become generally known, as was the case with prayer. That the men around Muhammad considered the caliphate as something analogous to prayer and on the strength of that attitude argued in favour of Abû Bakr's caliphate, is merely another proof of the fact that no appointment of an heir had taken place. It also shows that the question of the imamate and succession to it was not as important then as it is today. Group feeling, which determines unity and disunity in the customary course of affairs, was not of the same significance then as it was to be later on. Islam was winning the hearts of the people and causing them to be willing to die for it in a way that disrupted the customary course of affairs. That happened because people observed with their own eyes the presence of angels to help them, the repeated appearance of heavenly messages among them, and the constant (Qur'ânic) recitation of divine pronouncements to them in connection with every happening. Thus, it was not necessary to pay any attention to group feeling. Men generally had the qualities of submissiveness and obedience. They were thoroughly frightened and perturbed by a sequence of extraordinary miracles and other divine happenings, and by frequent visitations of angels. Such questions as that of the caliphate, of royal authority, succession, group feeling, and other such matters, were submerged in this turmoil the way it happened.

These helpful (circumstances) passed with the disappearance of miracles and the death of the generations that had witnessed them with their own eyes. The qualities mentioned changed little by little. The impression the wonders had made passed, and affairs took again their ordinary course. The influence of group feeling and of the ordinary course of affairs manifested itself in the resulting good and bad institutions. The (questions of) caliphate and royal authority and that of the succession to both became very important affairs in the opinion of the people. Their importance increased somewhat during the time of the (early) caliphs because there arose certain needs in connection with military protection, the holy war, the apostasy (of Arab tribes after Muḥammad's death), and the conquests. The (first caliphs) could decide whether they would (appoint successors) or not. Subsequently, as at the present time, the matter has become most important in connection with harmony in (military) protection and the administration of public interests. Group feeling has come to play a role in it. (Group feeling is) the secret divine (factor that) restrains people from splitting up and abandoning each other. It is the source of unity and agreement, and the guarantor of the intentions and laws of Islam. When this is understood, God's wise plans with regard to His creation and His creatures will become manifest.

As regards the wars that took place in Islam among the men around Muḥammad and the men of the second generation, those differences concerned religious matters only, and arose from independent interpretation of proper arguments and considered insights. Differences may well arise among people who use independent judgment. They were no more than differences in the independent interpretation of equivocal religious problems, and they have to be considered in this light. . . .

29 The functions of the religious institution of the caliphate

It has become clear that to be caliph in reality means acting as substitute for the Lawgiver (Muḥammad) with regard to the preservation of the religion and the political leadership of the world. The Lawgiver was concerned with both things, with religion in his capacity as the person commanded to transmit the duties imposed by the religious laws to the people and to cause them to act in accordance with them, and with worldly political leadership in his capacity as the person in charge of the (public) interests of human civilization.

We have mentioned before that civilization is necessary to human beings and that care for the (public) interests connected with it is likewise (necessary), if mankind is not to perish of neglect. We have also mentioned before that royal authority and its impetus suffice to create (the institutions serving) the (public) interest, although they would be more perfect if they were established through religious laws, because they understand the (public) interests better.

Royal authority, if it be Muslim, falls under the caliphate and is one of its concomitants. (The royal authority) of a non-Muslim nation stands alone. But in any case, it has its subordinate ranks and dependent positions which relate to particular functions. The people of the dynasty are given offices, and each one of them discharges (the duties) of his office as directed by the ruler who controls them all. Thus, the power of the ruler fully materializes, and he is well able to discharge his governmental (duties).

Even though the institution of the caliphate includes royal authority in the sense mentioned, its religious character brings with it special functions and ranks peculiar to the Muslim caliphs. We are going to mention the religious functions peculiar to the caliphate, and we shall come back later on to the functions of royal government.

All the religious functions of the religious law, such as prayer, the office of judge, the office of mufti, the holy war, and market supervision fall under the 'great imamate', which is the caliphate. (The caliphate) is a kind of great mainspring and comprehensive basis, and all these (functions) are branches of it and fall under it because of the wide scope of the caliphate, its active interest in all conditions of the Muslim community, both religious and worldly, and its general power to execute the religious laws relative to both (religious and worldly affairs).

(The leadership of prayer)

The leadership of prayer is the highest of these functions and higher than royal authority as such, which, like (prayer), falls under the caliphate. This is attested by the (circumstance) that the men around Muḥammad deduced from the fact that Abû Bakr had been appointed Muḥammad's representative as prayer leader, the fact that he had also been appointed his representative in political

171

leadership. They said: 'The Messenger of God found him acceptable for our religion. So, why should we not accept him for our worldly affairs?' If prayer did not rank higher than political leadership, the analogical reasoning would not have been sound.

The laws and conditions governing the office of (prayer leader) and the person entrusted with it are known from the law books. The first caliphs did not delegate the leadership of prayer. The fact that certain of the caliphs were stabbed in the mosque during the call to prayer, being expected by the assassins to be there at the prayer times, shows that the caliphs personally led the prayer and were not represented by others. This custom was continued by the Umayyads later on. They considered it their exclusive privilege and a high office to lead the prayer.

Later, when the nature of royal authority, with its qualities of harshness and unequal treatment of the people in their religious and worldly affairs, made itself felt, (the rulers) chose men to represent them as prayer leaders. They reserved for themselves the leadership of prayer at certain times and on general (festive) occasions, such as the two holidays and the Friday service. This was for purposes of display and ostentation.

(The office of mufti)

As to the office of mufti, the caliph must examine the religious scholars and teachers and entrust it only to those who are qualified for it. He must help them in their task, and he must prevent those who are not qualified for the office from attaining it. The office of mufti is one of the public interests of the Muslim religious community. (The caliph) has to take care, lest unqualified persons undertake to act as mufti and so lead the people astray.

Teachers have the task of teaching and spreading religious knowledge and of holding classes for that purpose in the mosques. If the mosque is one of the great mosques under the administration of the ruler, where the ruler looks after the prayer leaders, teachers must ask the ruler for permission to (teach there). If it is one of the general mosques, no permission is needed. However, teachers and muftis must have some restraining influence in themselves that tells them not to undertake something for which they are not qualified, so that they may not lead astray those who ask for the right way or cause to stumble those who want to be guided.

(The office of judge)

The office of judge is one of the positions that come under the caliphate. It is an institution that serves the purpose of settling suits and resolving disputes and dissensions. It proceeds, however, along the lines of the religious laws laid down by the Qur'ân and the Sunnah. Therefore, it is one of the positions that belongs to the caliphate and falls under it generally.

At the beginning of Islam, the caliphs exercised the office of judge personally. They did not permit anyone else to function as judge in any matter. The first caliph to charge someone else with exercise of this office was 'Umar. He appointed Abû d-Dardâ' to be judge with him in Medina, he appointed Shurayḥ as judge in al-Baṣrah, and Abû Mûsâ al-Ash'arî as judge in al-Kûfah. On appointing Abû Mûsâ, he wrote him the famous letter that contains all the laws that govern the office of judge, and is the basis of them. He says in it:

Now, the office of judge is a definite religious duty and a generally followed practice.

Understand the depositions that are made before you, for it is useless to consider a plea that is not valid.

Consider all the people equal before you in your court and in your attention, so that the noble will not expect you to be partial and the humble will not despair of justice from you.

The claimant must produce evidence; from the defendant, an oath may be exacted.

Compromise is permissible among Muslims, but not any agreement through which something forbidden would be permitted, or something permitted forbidden.

If you gave judgment yesterday, and today upon reconsideration come to the correct opinion, you should not feel prevented by your first judgment from retracting; for justice is primeval, and it is better to retract than to persist in worthlessness.

Use your brain about matters that perplex you and to which neither Qur'ân nor Sunnah seem to apply. Study similar cases and evaluate the situation through analogy with them.

If a person brings a claim, which he may or may not be able to prove, set a time limit for him. If he brings proof within the time limit, you should allow his claim, otherwise you are permitted to give judgment against him. This is the better way to forestall or clear up any possible doubt.

All Muslims are acceptable as witnesses against each other, except such as have received a punishment provided for by the religious law, such as are proved to have given false witness, and such as are suspected (of partiality) on (the ground of) client status or relationship, for God, praised be He, forgives when sworn testimony is rendered and postpones (punishment) in face of the evidence.

Avoid fatigue and weariness and annoyance at the litigants.

For establishing justice in the courts of justice, God will grant you a rich reward and give you a good reputation. Farewell.

Although the personal exercise of the office of judge was to have been the task of the caliphs, they entrusted others with it because they were too busy with general politics and too occupied with the holy war, conquests, defence of the border regions, and protection of the centre. These were things which could not be undertaken by anyone else because of their great importance. They considered it an easy matter to act as judge in litigation among the people and, therefore, had themselves represented by others in the exercise of (the office of judge), so as to lighten their own (burden). Still, they always entrusted the office only to people who shared in their group feeling either through common descent or their status as clients. They did not entrust it to men who were not close to them in this sense.

In the period of the caliphs, the duty of the judge was merely to settle suits between litigants. Gradually, later on, other matters were referred to him more and more often as the preoccupation of the caliphs and rulers with high policy grew. Finally, the office of judge came to include, in addition to the settling of suits, certain general concerns of the Muslims, such as supervision of the property of insane persons, orphans, bankrupts, and incompetents who are under the care of guardians; supervision of wills and mortmain donations and of the marrying of marriageable women without guardians to give them away, according to the opinion of some authorities; supervision of (public) roads and buildings; examination of witnesses, attorneys, and court substitutes, to acquire complete knowledge and full acquaintance relative to their reliability or unreliability. All these things have become part of the position and duties of a judge.

Former caliphs had entrusted the judge with the supervision of torts. This is a position that combines elements both of government power and judicial discretion. It needs a strong hand and much authority to subdue the evildoer and restrain the aggressor among two litigants. In a way, it serves to do what the judges and others are unable to do. It is concerned with the examination of evidence, with punishments not foreseen by the religious law, with the use of indirect and circumstantial evidence, with the postponement of judgment until the legal situation has been clarified, with attempts to bring about reconciliation between litigants, and with the swearing in of witnesses. This is a wider field than that with which the judges are concerned.

The first caliphs exercised that function personally until the days of the 'Abbâsid al-Muhtadî. They also often entrusted the judges with leadership of the holy war in summer campaigns. Making appointments to these functions was the task of the caliphs or of those to whom they entrusted it, such as a minister to whom full powers were delegated, or a ruler who had gained superiority.

(The police)

In the 'Abbâsid dynasty and in the dynasties of the Umayyads in Spain and under the 'Ubaydid(-Fâṭimids) in Egypt and the Maghrib, the control of crimes and imposition of punishments required by the religious law was also a special task and was delegated to the chief of police. The police is another religious function that under these dynasties belonged to the positions connected with the religious law. Its field is somewhat wider than that of the office of judge. It makes it possible for suspects to be brought into court. It decides upon preventive punishments before crimes have been committed. It imposes the punishments required by the religious law where they are due, and determines compensation in cases of bodily injury where the law of talion applies. It imposes punishments not provided for by the religious law, and provides for corrective measures against those who did not execute the crimes (they had planned).

The proper functions of the police and of torts were forgotten during the dynasties in which the nature of the caliphate was no longer remembered. Torts were transferred to the ruler whether he had been delegated by the caliph to take care of them or not. The police function was split into two parts. One of them was that of taking care of suspects, imposing the punishments required by the religious law, and amputating (criminals condemned for crimes punishable by the amputation of a limb), and seeing to it that the laws of talion were applied where appropriate. For these duties, the dynasties appointed an official who exercised his office in the service of the political (establishment) without reference to the religious laws. He was sometimes called *wâlî* (governor), and sometimes *shurṭah* (police). The remaining former police functions dealt with punishments not provided for by the religious law and the imposition of punishments for crimes fixed by the religious law. They were combined with the functions of judge previously mentioned. They became part of the official duties of the (judge), and have so remained down to this time.

This position was taken away from the people who shared in the group feeling of the dynasty. When there was a religious caliphate, the caliphs entrusted the function, since it was a religious office, only to Arabs or to clients—allies, slaves, or followers—who shared in their group feeling and upon whose ability and competence to execute the tasks they could rely.

175

When the character and appearance of the caliphate changed and royal and government authority took over, the religious functions lost to some degree their connection with (the powers in control), inasmuch as they did not belong among the titles and honours of royal authority. The Arabs later on lost all control of the government. Royal authority fell to Turkish and Berber nations. These caliphal functions, as far as their character and the group feeling that belonged to them was concerned, were even more remote from them (than from their predecessors). This was because the Arabs had been of the opinion that the religious law was their religion and that the Prophet was one of them and that his religious laws distinguished them in their thought and action from other nations. The non-Arabs did not think that way. If they had some respect for (these functions) it was merely because they had become Muslims. Therefore, they came to entrust them to men outside their own group who had become familiar with (these functions) in the dynasties of former caliphs. Under the influence of the luxury of the dynasties to which they had been accustomed for hundreds of years, these people had forgotten the old desert period and desert toughness. They had acquired sedentary culture, luxurious customs, tranquillity, and lack of ability to take care of themselves. In the kingdoms that succeeded the (rule of the) caliphs, the functions of the caliphate became the prerogative of this kind of urban weakling. They were no longer exercised by people of prestige, but by persons whose qualifications were limited, both by their descent and by the sedentary culture to which they had become accustomed. They were despised as sedentary people are, who live submerged in luxury and tranquillity, who have no connection with the group feeling of the ruler, and who depend on others for protection. Their position in the dynasty derives from the fact that it takes care of the Muslim religious community and follows the religious laws, and that these persons know the laws and can interpret them through legal decisions. They have no standing in the dynasty because they are honoured as personalities. Their standing merely reflects an affectation of respect for their position in the royal councils, where it is desired to make a show of reverence for the religious ranks. They do not have executive authority to make decisions in (these councils). If they participate in (the making of decisions), it is just as a matter of form, with no reality behind it. Executive authority in reality belongs to those who have the power to enforce (their decisions). Those who do not have the power (to enforce their decisions) have no executive authority. They are merely used as authorities on religious law, and their legal decisions are accepted.

Some scholars think that this is not right, and that rulers who keep jurists and judges out of their councils act wrongly, since Muḥammad said, 'The scholars are the heirs of the prophets.' However, royal and governmental authority is conditioned by the natural require- ments of civilization; were such not the case, it would have nothing to do with politics. The nature of civilization does not require that (jurists and scholars) have any share (in authority). Advisory and executive authority belongs only to the person who controls the group feeling and is by it enabled to exercise authority, to do things or not do them. Those who do not have group feeling, who have no control over their own affairs, and who cannot protect themselves, are dependent upon others. How, then, could they participate in councils, and why should their advice be taken into consideration? Their advice as derived from their knowledge of the religious laws (is taken into consideration) only in so far as they are consulted for legal decisions. Advice on political matters is not their province, because they have no group feeling and do not know the conditions and laws which govern (group feeling). To honour (jurists and scholars) is an act of kindness on the part of rulers and amirs. It testifies to their high regard for Islam and to their respect for men who are in any way concerned with it. . . .

The position of official witness

This is a religious position depending on the office of judge and connected with court practice. The men who hold it give testimony —with the judge's permission—for or against people's (claims). They serve as witnesses when testimony is to be taken, testify during a lawsuit, and fill in the registers which record the rights, possessions, and debts of people and other legal transactions.

We have mentioned 'the judge's permission' because people may have become confused, and then only the judge knows who is reliable and who is not. Thus, in a way, he gives permission to those of whose probity he is sure, so that people's affairs and transactions will be properly safeguarded.

The prerequisite governing this position is the incumbent's posses- sion of the quality of probity according to the religious law, his freedom from unreliability. Furthermore, he must be able to fill in the (court) records and make out contracts in the right form and proper order and correctly, (observing) the conditions and stipula- tions governing them from the point of view of the religious law. Thus, he must have such knowledge of jurisprudence as is necessary for the purpose. Because of these conditions and the experience and practice required, (the office) came to be restricted to persons of probity. Probity came to be (considered) the particular quality of persons who exercise this function. But this is not so. Probity is one of the prerequisites qualifying them for the office.

The judge must examine their conditions and look into their way of life, to make sure that they fulfil the condition of probity. He must not neglect to do so, because it is his duty to safeguard the rights of the people. The responsibility for everything rests with him, and he is accountable for the outcome.

Once (official witnesses) have been shown clearly to be qualified for the position, they become more generally useful (to the judges). (They can be used) to find out about the reliability of other men whose probity is not known to the judges, because of the large size of cities and their confused conditions. In assessing the reliability of (the evidence), they usually count upon these professional witnesses. In every city, they have their own shops and benches where they always sit, so that people who have transactions to make can engage them to function as witnesses and register the (testimony) in writing.

The term 'probity' ('*adâlah*) thus came to be used both for the position whose significance has just been explained and for 'probity (reliability)' as required by the religious law, which is used paired with 'unreliability'. The two are the same, but still, they are different.

Market supervision

The office of market supervisor is a religious position. It falls under the religious obligation 'to command to do good and forbid to do evil', which rests with the person in charge of the affairs of the Muslims. He appoints to the position men whom he considers qualified for it. The obligation thus devolves upon the appointee. He may use other men to help him in his job. He investigates abuses and applies the appropriate punishments and corrective measures. He sees to it that the people act in accord with the public interest in the town. For instance, he prohibits the obstruction of roads. He forbids porters and boatmen to carry too heavy loads. He orders the owners of buildings threatening to collapse to tear them down and thus remove the possibility of danger to passers-by. He prevents teachers in schools and other places from beating young pupils too much. His authority is not restricted to cases of quarrels or complaints, but he must look after, and rule on, everything of the sort that comes to his knowledge or is reported to him. He has no authority over legal claims in general but he has authority over everything relating to fraud and deception in connection with food and other things and in connection with weights and measures. Among his duties is that of making dilatory debtors pay what they owe, and similar things that do not require hearing of evidence or a legal verdict, in other words, cases with which a judge would have nothing to do because they are so common and simple. These, therefore, are referred to the person who holds the office of market supervisor to take care of them. The position, consequently, is subordinate to the office of judge. In many Muslim dynasties, such as the dynasties of the 'Ubaydid-Fâṭimids in Egypt and the Maghrib and that of the Umayyads in Spain, (the office of market supervisor) fell under the general jurisdiction of the judge, who could appoint anyone to the office at discretion. Then, when the position of ruler became separated from the caliphate and when (the ruler) took general charge of all political matters, the office of market supervisor became one of the royal positions and a separate office.

The mint

The office of the mint is concerned with the coins used by Muslims in (commercial) transactions, with guarding against possible falsification or substandard quality (clipping) when the number of coins (and not the weight of their metal) is used in transactions, and with all else relating to (monetary matters). Further, the office is concerned with putting the ruler's mark upon the coins, thus indicating their good quality and purity. The mark is impressed upon the coins with an iron seal that is especially used for the purpose and that has special designs (legends) on it. It is placed upon the dinar and the dirham after their proper weight has been established, and is then beaten with a hammer until the designs have been impressed upon the coin. This then indicates the good quality of the coin according to the best methods of melting and purification customary among the inhabitants of a particular region under the ruling dynasty. (The metal standard) is not something rigidly fixed but depends upon independent judgment. Once the inhabitants of a particular part or region have decided upon a standard of purity, they hold to it and call it the 'guide' or 'standard'. They use it to test their coins. If they are substandard, they are bad.

Supervision of all these things is the duty of the holder of the office (of the mint). In this respect, it is a religious office and falls under the caliphate. It used to belong to the general jurisdiction of the judge but now has become a separate office, as is the case with that of market supervision.

This is all that is to be said about caliphal positions. There were other positions that disappeared when the things that were their concern disappeared. Further, there are positions that became positions of rulers other than the caliph. Such are the positions of amir and wazir, and those concerned with warfare and taxation. They will be discussed later on in their proper places.

The position concerned with (prosecution of) the holy war ceased to exist when the holy war was no longer waged, save in a few dynasties which, as a rule, classify the laws governing it under the governmental (and not the caliphal) authority. Likewise, the office of marshal of the nobility consisting of relatives of the caliphs, whose descent gives them a claim to the caliphate or to an official pension, disappeared when the caliphate ceased.

In general, the honours and positions of the caliphate merged with those of royal authority and political leadership. This is the present situation in all dynasties.

30 The title of 'Commander of the Faithful', which is characteristic of the caliph

It was created in the period of the first four caliphs. This is because the men around Muḥammad and all the other early Muslims called Abû Bakr, when he received the oath of allegiance, 'representative' (khalîfah, caliph) of the Messenger of God. This form of address was used until he died. Then, the oath of allegiance was rendered to 'Umar who was appointed by Abû Bakr, and people called 'Umar 'Representative of the Representative of the Messenger of God'. However, they considered the title somewhat cumbersome. It was long and had a succession of genitives. (With successive caliphs) it would become longer and longer and end up as a tongue twister, and it would no longer be distinct and recognizable because of the great number of dependent genitives. Therefore, they tried to replace the title by some other one appropriate to a (caliph).

The leaders of (military) missions used to be called 'amîrs'. Before becoming Muslims, people used to call the Prophet 'Amir of Mecca' and 'Amir of the Ḥijâz'.

Now, it so happened that one of the men around Muḥammad addressed 'Umar as 'Commander of the Faithful'. People liked (this form of address) and approved it. Thus, they called 'Umar by this title. The caliphs who succeeded him inherited the title as a characteristic which no other person shared with them. . . .

The caliphs inherited the title of Commander of the Faithful from each other. It became a characteristic of the ruler of the Ḥijâz, Syria, and the 'Irâq, the regions that were the home of the Arabs and the centres of the Muslim dynasty and the bases of Islam and Muslim conquest. Therefore, (it was no longer distinctive) when the ('Abbâsid) dynasty reached its flowering and prime, and another style of address gained currency, one that served to distinguish them

from each other, inasmuch as the title of Commander of the Faithful
was one they all had. The 'Abbâsids took surnames such as as-Saffâḥ,
al-Manṣûr, al-Mahdî, al-Hâdî, ar-Rashîd, and so on, and thus
created a sort of cover to guard their proper names against abuse by
the tongues of the common people and protect them against profana-
tion. (They continued with that custom) down to the end of the
dynasty. The 'Ubaydid(-Fâṭimids) in Ifrîqiyah and Egypt followed
their example.

The Umayyads refrained from that (for a long time). The earlier
Umayyads in the East had done so, in keeping with their austerity
and simplicity. Arab manners and aspirations had not yet been
abandoned in their time, and (the Umayyads) had not yet exchanged
Bedouin characteristics for those of sedentary culture. The Umayyads in Spain also refrained from such titles, because they followed
the tradition of their ancestors. Moreover, they were conscious of
their inferior position, since they did not control the caliphate which
the 'Abbâsids had appropriated, and had no power over the Ḥijâz,
the mainspring of the Arabs and Islam, and were remote from the
seat of the caliphate around which the (Arab) group feeling centred.
By being rulers of a remote region, they merely protected themselves
against the persecution of the 'Abbâsids. Finally, however, it became
known how greatly the liberty of the caliphate in the East had been
curtailed and how the clients of the 'Abbâsids had taken control of
the dynasty and had achieved complete power to depose, replace,
kill, or blind the caliphs. 'Abd-ar-Raḥmân III, therefore, adopted
the ways of the caliphs in the East and in Ifrîqiyah: he had himself
called Commander of the Faithful and assumed the surname of an-
Nâṣir-li-dîn-Allâh. This custom, which he was the first to practise,
was followed and became an established one.

This situation prevailed down to the time when Arab group feeling
was completely destroyed and the caliphate lost its identity. Non-
Arab clients gained power over the 'Abbâsids; followers of their own
making gained power over the 'Ubaydid-Fâṭimids in Cairo; the
Ṣinhâjah gained power over the realm of Ifrîqiyah; the Zanâtah
gained power over the Maghrib; and the *reyes de taïfas* (small princes)
in Spain gained power over the Umayyads. (Each of) these (groups)
took over part of (the caliphate). The Muslim empire dissolved. The
rulers in the West and the East adopted different titles. Formerly,
they had all been called by the name of *Sulṭân*.

The non-Arab rulers in the East were distinguished by the caliphs
with special honorific surnames indicating their subservience and
obedience and their good status as officials. When these men gained
control over the caliphs, they were satisfied to keep these surnames
and did not adopt caliphal titles out of deference to the institution

and in order to avoid any usurpation of its peculiar characteristics, as is customary among those who gain power and control over an existing institution. However, later on, the non-Arabs in the East strengthened their grip on royal authority and became more and more prominent in state and government. The group feeling of the caliphate vanished and dissolved completely. At that time, these non-Arabs were inclined to adopt titles that were characteristic of royal authority, such as an-Nâṣir and al-Manṣûr. This was in addition to the titles they had previously held and which indicated that they were no longer clients and followers.

The *reyes de taïfas* in Spain, who had a powerful grip on (the caliphate) by virtue of the fact that they shared in its tribal group feeling, divided up and distributed among themselves the caliphal titles.

The Ṣinhâjah restricted themselves to the display titles that the 'Ubaydid-Fâṭimid caliphs had given them. Later on, as the distance between them and the caliphate grew, they forgot these titles and restricted themselves to the name of Sultan. The same was the case with the Maghrâwah rulers in the Maghrib. The only title they adopted was that of Sultan, in accordance with Bedouin custom and desert austerity.

At the time when the name of the caliphate had become extinct and its influence non-existent, the Almoravid ruler Yûsuf b. Tâshfîn made his appearance among the Berber tribes in the Maghrib. He became the ruler of both shores. He was a good and conservative man who, consequently, in order to comply with all the formalities of his religion, wished to submit to the caliphal authority. He addressed himself to the 'Abbâsid al-Mustaẓhir and sent to him two *shaykh*s from Sevilla as his ambassadors, 'Abdallâh b. al-'Arabî and 'Abdallâh's son, Judge Abû Bakr. They were to transmit the oath of allegiance to al-Mustaẓhir and were to ask him to appoint and invest Ibn Tâshfîn as ruler over the Maghrib. They returned with the caliphal appointment of Ibn Tâshfîn as ruler over the Maghrib and with permission to use the caliphal style in dress and flag. In (the document, the caliph) addressed Ibn Tâshfîn as 'Commander of the Muslims', in order to honour and distinguish him. Ibn Tâshfîn, therefore, took that as his title.

The Mahdî (of the Almohads) followed upon the (Almoravids). He made propaganda for the truth. He called his followers Almohads (champions of the strict oneness of God). He followed the opinion of the 'Alids with regard to 'the Infallible Imam' who must exist in every age and whose existence preserves the order of the world. Al-Mahdî was at first called Imam, in accordance with the aforementioned Shî'ah practice with regard to the title of their caliphs.

The word *al-ma'ṣûm* (infallible) was linked with Imam to indicate his tenet.

When governmental authority in the Maghrib lapsed and the Zanâtah took power, their first rulers continued the ways of desert life and simplicity and followed the Almoravids in using the title of Commander of the Muslims, out of deference to the high rank of the caliphate. The later (Zanâtah) rulers aspired to the title of Commander of the Faithful, and are using it at this time to comply fully with royal aspirations and the ways and characteristics of royal authority.

31 Remarks on the words 'Pope' and 'Patriarch' in the Christian religion and on the word 'Kohen' used by the Jews

It should be known that after the removal of its prophet, a religious group must have someone to take care of it. Such a person must cause the people to act according to the religious laws. In a way, he stands to them in the place of their prophet, inasmuch as he enjoins the obligations which the prophet had imposed upon them. Furthermore, in accordance with the aforementioned need for political leadership in social organization, the human species must have a person who will cause them to act in accordance with what is good for them and who will prevent them by force from doing things harmful to them. Such a person is the one who is called ruler.

In the Muslim community, the holy war is a religious duty, because of the universalism of the Muslim mission and (the obligation to) convert everybody to Islam either by persuasion or by force. Therefore, caliphate and royal authority are united in Islam, so that the person in charge can devote the available strength to both of them at the same time.

The other religious groups did not have a universal mission, and the holy war was not a religious duty to them, save only for purposes of defence. It has thus come about that the person in charge of religious affairs in (other religious groups) is not concerned with power politics at all. (Among them) royal authority comes to those who have it—by accident and in some way that has nothing to do with religion. It comes to them as the necessary result of group feeling, which by its very nature seeks to obtain royal authority, as we have mentioned before, and not because they are under obligation to gain power over other nations, as is the case with Islam. They are merely required to establish their religion among their own people.

This is why the Israelites after Moses and Joshua remained unconcerned with royal authority for about four hundred years. Their only concern was to establish their religion. The person from among them who was in charge of their religion was called the Kohen. He was in a way the representative (caliph) of Moses. He regulated the prayers and sacrifices of the Israelites. They made it a condition for him to be a descendant of Aaron, as it had been destined for him and his children by divine revelation. For (supervision of the) political matters which naturally arise among human beings, the Israelites selected seventy elders who were entrusted with a general legal authority. The Kohen was higher in religious rank than they and more remote from the turbulent legal authority. This continued to obtain (among the Israelites) until the nature of group feeling made itself fully felt and all power became political. The Israelites dispossessed the Canaanites of the land that God had given them as their heritage in Jerusalem and the surrounding region, as it had been explained to them through Moses. The nations of the Philistines, the Canaanites, the Armenians [!], the Edomites, the Ammonites, and the Moabites fought against them. During that time political leadership was entrusted to the elders among them. The Israelites remained in that condition for about four hundred years. They did not have any royal power and were harassed by attacks from foreign nations. Therefore, they asked God through Samuel, one of their prophets, that He permit them to make someone king over them. Thus, Saul became their king. He defeated the foreign nations and killed Goliath, the ruler of the Philistines. After Saul, David became king, and then Solomon. His kingdom flourished and extended to the borders of the Ḥijâz and further to the borders of the Yemen and to the borders of the land of the Byzantines. After Solomon, the tribes split into two dynasties. This was in accordance with the necessary consequence of group feeling in dynasties, as we have mentioned before. One of the dynasties was that of the ten tribes in the region of Nablus, the capital of which is Samaria (Sabasṭiyah), and the other that of the children of Judah and Benjamin in Jerusalem. Nebuchadnezzar, the king of Babylon, then deprived them of their royal authority. He first (dealt with) the ten tribes in Samaria, and then with the children of Judah in Jerusalem. Their royal authority had had an uninterrupted duration of a thousand years. Now he destroyed their temple, burnt their Torah, and killed their religion. He deported the people to Iṣfahân and the 'Irâq. Eventually, one of the Persian Kayyanid (Achaemenid) rulers brought them back to Jersualem, seventy years after they had left it. They rebuilt the temple and re-established their religion in its original form with priests only. The royal authority belonged to the Persians.

Alexander and the Greeks then defeated the Persians, and the Jews came under Greek domination. The Greek rule then weakened, and, with the help of their natural group feeling, the Jews rose against the Greeks and made an end to their domination over them. Jewish royal authority was in charge of their Hasmonean priests. The Hasmoneans fought the Greeks. Eventually, their power was destroyed. The Romans defeated them, and the Jews came under Roman domination. The Romans advanced toward Jerusalem, the seat of the children of Herod, relatives by marriage of the Hasmoneans and the last remnant of the Hasmonean dynasty. They laid siege to them for a time, finally conquering Jerusalem by force in an orgy of murder, destruction, and arson. They laid Jerusalem in ruins and exiled the Jews to Rome and the regions beyond. This was the second destruction of the temple. The Jews call it 'the Great Exile'. After that, they had no royal authority, because they had lost their group feeling. They remained afterwards under the domination of the Romans and their successors. Their religious affairs were taken care of by their head, called the Kohen.

The Messiah (Jesus) brought the Jews his religion, as is known. He abolished some of the laws of the Torah. He performed marvellous wonders, such as healing the insane and reviving the dead. Many people joined him and believed in him. The largest group among his following were his companions, the Apostles. There were twelve of them. He sent some of them as messengers to all parts of the world. They made propaganda for his religious group. That was in the days of Augustus, the first of the Roman emperors, and during the time of Herod, the king of the Jews, who had taken away royal authority from the Hasmoneans, his relatives by marriage. The Jews envied Jesus and declared him a liar. Their king, Herod, wrote to the Roman Emperor, Augustus, and incited him against Jesus. The Roman Emperor gave the Jews permission to kill him, and the story of Jesus as recited in the Qur'ân occurred.

The Apostles divided into different groups. Most of them went to the country of the Romans and made propaganda for the Christian religion. Peter was the greatest of them. He settled in Rome, the seat of the Roman emperors. They then wrote down the Gospel that had been revealed to Jesus, in four recensions according to their different traditions. Matthew wrote his Gospel in Jerusalem in Hebrew. It was translated into Latin by John, the son of Zebedee, one of the Apostles. Luke wrote his Gospel in Latin for a Roman dignitary. John, the son of Zebedee, wrote his Gospel in Rome. Peter wrote his Gospel in Latin and ascribed it to his pupil Mark. These four recensions of the Gospel differ from each other. Not all of it is pure revelation, but the Gospels have an admixture of the words of Jesus and of the Apostles. They consist chiefly of sermons and stories. There are very few laws in them.

The Apostles came together at that time in Rome and laid down the rules of the Christian community. They entrusted them to Clement, a pupil of Peter, noting in them the list of books that are to be accepted and in accordance with which one must act.

The books which belong to the old religious law of the Jews are the following:

> The Torah, which consists of five volumes.
> The Book of Joshua.
> The Book of Judges.
> The Book of Ruth.
> The Book of Judith.
> The four Books of Kings.
> The Book of Chronicles.
> The three Books of Maccabees, by Ibn Gorion.
> The Book of Ezra, the religious leader.
> The Book of Esther and the story of Haman.
> The Book of Job the Righteous.
> The Psalms of David.
> The five Books of David's son, Solomon.
> The sixteen Prophecies of the major and minor prophets.
> The Book of Jesus, the son of Sira, the minister of Solomon.

The books of the religious law of Jesus that was received by the Apostles are the following:

> The four recensions of the Gospel.
> The Book of Paul which consists of fourteen epistles.
> The Katholika (General Epistles) which consist of seven epistles, the eighth being the Praxeis (Acts), stories of the Apostles.
> The Book of Clement which contains the laws.
> The Book of the Apocalypse (Revelation) which contains the vision of John, the son of Zebedee.

The attitude of the Roman emperors toward Christianity varied. At times, they adopted it and honoured its adherents. At other times, they did not recognize it and persecuted its adherents and killed and exiled them. Finally, Constantine appeared and adopted Christianity. From then on, all (the Roman emperors) were Christians.

The head of the Christian (community) and the person in charge of (Christian religious) institutions is called Patriarch. He is their religious head and the representative (caliph) of the Messiah among them. He sends his delegates and representatives to the remote Christian nations. They are called 'bishop', that is, delegate of the

Patriarch. The man who leads the prayers and makes decisions in religious matters is called 'priest'. The person who withdraws from society and retires into solitude for worship is called 'monk'. The latter usually seeks solitude in monastic cells.

The Apostle Peter, the chief Apostle and oldest of the disciples, was in Rome and established the Christian religion there. Nero, the fifth Roman emperor, killed him. Successor to Peter at the Roman see was Arius.

Mark the Evangelist spent seven years in Alexandria and Egypt and the Maghrib making propaganda. After him came Ananias, who was called Patriarch. He was the first Patriarch there. He appointed twelve priests to be with him, and it was arranged that when the Patriarch died, one of the twelve should take his place, and one of the faithful be elected to take his place as the twelfth priest. Thus, the patriarchate fell to the priests.

Later on, dissension broke out among the Christians with regard to the basic principles and articles of their religion. They assembled in Nicaea in the days of Constantine, in order to lay down (the doctrine of) true Christianity. Three hundred and eighteen bishops agreed upon one and the same doctrine of Christianity. They wrote it down and called it 'the Creed'. They made it the fundamental principle to which they would all have reference. Among the things they set down in writing was that with respect to the appointment of the Patriarch as the head of Christianity, no reference should be made to the independent judgment of the priests, as Ananias, the disciple of Mark, had prescribed. That point of view was abolished. The Patriarch was to come from a large group and to be elected by the leaders and chiefs of the believers. It has been so ever since. Later on, other dissensions arose concerning the basic principles of Christianity. Synods concerned with regulating (the religion) were assembled, but there was no dissension with regard to the basic principles of the method of selecting the Patriarch. It has remained the same ever since.

The Patriarchs always appointed bishops as their delegates. The bishops used to call the Patriarch 'Father', as a sign of respect. The priests similarly came to call the bishop 'Father', when he was not together with the Patriarch, as a sign of respect. This caused confusion in the use of the title over a long period, ending, it is said, with the Patriarchate of Heraclius in Alexandria. It was considered desirable to distinguish the Patriarch from the bishop in the matter of respect (shown to him by style of address). Therefore, the Patriarch was called 'Pope', that is, 'Father of fathers'. The name first appeared in Egypt, according to the theory expressed by Jirjis b. al-'Amîd in his *History*. It was then transferred to the occupant of the most important see, the see of Rome, which was the see of the Apostle Peter, as we have mentioned before. The title of Pope has remained characteristic of the see of Rome down to this day.

Thereafter, there were dissensions among the Christians with regard to their religion and to Christology. They split into groups and sects, which secured the support of the various Christian rulers against each other. At different times there appeared different sects. Finally, these sects crystallized into three groups, which constitute the Christian sects. Others have no significance. These are the Melchites, the Jacobites, and the Nestorians. We do not think that we should blacken the pages of this book with discussion of their dogmas of unbelief. In general, they are well known. All of them are unbelief. This is clearly stated in the noble Qur'ân. To discuss or argue those things with them is not for us. It is (for them to choose between) conversion to Islam, payment of the poll tax, or death.

Later on, each sect had its own Patriarch. The Patriarch of Rome is today called 'Pope'. He is of the Melchite persuasion. Rome belongs to the European Christians. Their royal authority is established in that region.

The Patriarch of the Christian subjects in Egypt is of the Jacobite persuasion. He resides among them. The Abyssinians follow the religion of (the Egyptian Christians). The Patriarch of Egypt delegates bishops to the Abyssinians, and these bishops arrange religious affairs in Abyssinia. The name of 'Pope' is specially reserved for the patriarch of Rome at this time. The Jacobites do not call their patriarch 'Pope'. The word is pronounced *Pappa*.

It is the custom of the Pope with respect to the European Christians to urge them to submit to one ruler and have recourse to him in their disagreements and agreements, in order to avoid the dissolution of the whole thing. His purpose is to have the group feeling that is the strongest among them (concentrated upon one ruler), so that he has power over all of them. The ruler is called 'Emperor'. (The Pope) personally places the crown upon the head of (the emperor), in order to let him have the blessing implied (in that ceremony). The emperor, therefore, is called 'the crowned one'. Perhaps that is the meaning of the word 'emperor'.

This, briefly, is our comment on the two words Pope and Kohen.

32 The ranks of royal and governmental authority and the titles that go with those ranks

It should be known that, by himself, the ruler is weak, and carries a heavy burden. He must look for help from his fellow men. He needs their help for the necessities of life and for all his other requirements. How much more, then, does he need it to exercise political leadership over his own species, over the creatures and servants of God whom God entrusted to him as subjects. He must defend and protect the community from its enemies. He must enforce restraining laws among the people, in order to prevent mutual hostility and attacks upon property. This includes improving the safety of the roads. He must cause the people to act in their own best interests, and he must supervise such general matters involving their livelihood and mutual dealings as foodstuffs and weights and measures, in order to prevent cheating. He must look after the mint, in order to protect from fraud the currency used by the people in their mutual dealings. He must exercise political leadership and get people to submit to him to the degree he desires and be satisfied, both with his intentions regarding them and with the fact that he alone has all the glory and they have none. This requires an extraordinary measure of psychology. A noble sage has said: 'Moving mountains from their places is easier for me than to influence people psychologically.'

It is better that such help be sought from persons close to the ruler through common descent, common upbringing, or old attachment to the dynasty. This makes such persons and the ruler work together in the same spirit.

The person from whom the ruler seeks help may help him with the sword, or with the pen, or with advice and knowledge, or by keeping the people from crowding upon him and diverting him from the supervision of their affairs. (The ruler may) also entrust the supervision of the whole realm to him and rely upon his competence and ability for the task. Therefore, the help the ruler seeks may be given by one man, or it may be distributed among several individuals.

Each of the different (instruments) through which help may be given has many different subdivisions. 'The pen' has such subdivisions, for instance, as 'the pen of letters and correspondence', 'the pen of diplomas and fiefs', and 'the pen of bookkeeping', which means the offices of chief of tax collections and allowances and of minister of the army. 'The sword' includes such subdivisions, for instance, as the offices of chief of military operations, chief of police, chief of the postal service, and administration of the border regions.

It should further be known that governmental positions in Islam fell under the caliphate, because the institution of the caliphate was both religious and worldly. The religious laws govern all (governmental positions) and apply to each one of them in all its aspects, because the religious law governs all the actions of human beings.

189

Jurists, therefore, are concerned with the rank of ruler or sultan and with the conditions under which it is assumed, whether by gaining control over the caliphate—this is what is meant by sultan—or by the caliph delegating (power)—that is what they mean by wazir, as will be mentioned. (They are also concerned with) the extent of (the ruler's) jurisdiction over legal, financial, and other political matters, which may be either absolute or circumscribed. Furthermore, (they are concerned with the causes) that necessitate (the ruler's) removal, should (such causes) present themselves, and with other things connected with the ruler or sultan. Jurists are likewise concerned with all the positions under the ruler and sultan, such as the wazirate, the tax collector's office, and the administrative functions. Jurists must concern themselves with all these things, because, as we have mentioned before, in Islam the caliphate is an institution of the Muslim religious law, and as such determines the position of the ruler or sultan.

However, when we discuss royal and governmental positions, it will be as something required by the nature of civilization and human existence. It will not be under the aspect of particular religious laws. This, one knows, is not our intention in this book. The subject is fully treated in books on administration. If we discuss the caliphal positions and treat them individually, it is only in order to make the distinction between them and the governmental positions clear, and not in order to make a thorough study of their legal status. This is not the purpose of our book. Thus, we shall discuss those matters only as the necessary result of the nature of civilization in human existence.

The wazirate

The wazirate is the mother of governmental functions and royal ranks. The name itself simply means 'help'.

We mentioned before, at the beginning of this section, that the conditions and activities of the ruler are restricted to four fields:

(1) (They) may concern ways and means of protecting the community, such as the supervision of soldiers, armaments, war operations, and other matters connected with military protection and aggression. The person in charge is the wazir, as the term was customarily used in the old dynasties in the East, and as it is still used at this time in the West.

(2) Or, they may concern correspondence with persons far away from the ruler in place or in time, and the execution of orders concerning persons with whom the ruler has no direct contact. The man in charge is the secretary.

(3) Or, they may concern matters of tax collection and expendi-

ture, and the safe handling of these things in all their aspects. The man in charge is the chief of tax and financial matters. In the contemporary East, he is called the wazir.

(4) Or, they may concern ways to keep petitioners away from the ruler, so that they do not crowd upon him and divert him from his affairs. This task reverts to the doorkeeper, who guards the door.

The (ruler's) activities do not extend beyond these four fields. Each royal and governmental function belongs to one of them. However, the most important field is the one that requires giving general assistance in connection with everything under the ruler's direct control. This means constant contact with the ruler and participation in all his governmental activities. (All functions) that concern some particular group of people or some particular department are of lower rank. (Among these are) the (military) leadership of a border region, the administration of some special tax, or the supervision of some particular matter, such as surveillance of foodstuffs, or supervision of the mint. All these activities are concerned with particular conditions. The persons in charge are, therefore, subordinate to those in general supervision, and the latter outrank them.

It was this way throughout the whole pre-Islamic period. When Islam appeared on the scene and power was vested in the caliph, the forms of royal authority no longer existed, and all its functions disappeared, except for some advisory and consultative ones that were natural and continued to exist because they were unavoidable. The Prophet used to ask the men around him for advice and to consult them on both general and special (private) matters. In addition, he discussed other very special affairs with Abû Bakr. Certain Arabs familiar with the situation in the Persian, Byzantine, and Abyssinian dynasties, called Abû Bakr, therefore, Muḥammad's 'wazir'. The word *wazîr* was not known (originally) among the Muslims, because the simplicity of Islam had done away with royal ranks.

No specific ranks existed among the (early Muslims) in the fields of tax collection, expenditure, and bookkeeping. The Muslims were illiterate Arabs who did not know how to write and keep books. For bookkeeping they employed Jews, Christians, or certain non-Arab clients versed in it. (Bookkeeping) was little known among them. Their nobles did not know it well, because illiteracy was their distinctive characteristic.

Likewise, no specific rank existed among (the early Muslims) in the field of (official) correspondence and (the transmission in writing) of orders to be executed. They were illiterate, and everyone could be trusted to keep a statement secret and to forward it safely (to its destination). Also, there were no political matters that would have required the use of (confidential secretaries), because the caliphate was a religious matter and had nothing to do with power politics. Furthermore, secretarial skill had not yet become a craft, with its best features sought by the caliph. Every individual was capable of explaining what he wanted in the most eloquent manner. The only thing lacking was the (technical ability to) write. For this, the caliph always appointed someone who knew how to write well, to do such writing as there was occasion for.

Keeping petitioners away from the gates (of the caliph's court) was something that the religious law forbade, and they did not do it. However, when the caliphate changed to royal authority and when royal forms and titles made their appearance, the first thing the dynasty did was to bar the masses from access (to the ruler). The rulers feared that their lives were in danger from attacks by rebels and others, such as had happened to 'Umar, to 'Alî, to Mu'âwiyah, to 'Amr b. al-'Âṣ, and to others. Furthermore, were the people given free access (to the ruler), they would crowd upon him and divert him from state affairs. Therefore, the ruler appointed some person to take care of this for him and called him 'doorkeeper'.

Afterwards, royal authority flourished. The (official) councillor and assistant for tribal and group affairs made his appearance. For him, the name of wazir was used. Bookkeeping remained in the hands of clients, Jews, and Christians. For (official) documents, a special secretary was appointed, as a precaution against possible publication of the ruler's secrets, something that would be disastrous to his role as political leader. This secretary was not as important as the wazir, because he was needed only for written matters, and not for matters that could be discussed orally. At that time, speech still preserved its old position and was uncorrupted. Therefore, the wazirate was the highest rank throughout the Umayyad dynasty. The wazir had general supervision of all matters delegated to him and in which he acted in a consultative capacity, as well as all other matters of a defensive or offensive nature. This also entailed the supervision of the ministry of the army, the assignment of military allowances at the beginning of each month, and other matters.

Then the 'Abbâsid dynasty made its appearance. Royal authority flourished. The royal ranks were many and high ones. At that time, the position of wazir assumed an added importance. He became the delegate (of the caliph) as executive authority. His rank in the dynasty became conspicuous. Everyone looked toward the wazirate and submitted to it. Supervision of the bookkeeping office was entrusted to (the wazir), because his function required him to distribute the military allowances. Thus, he had to supervise the collection and distribution of (the money). Furthermore, supervision of 'the pen' and (official) correspondence was entrusted to him, in order to protect the ruler's secrets and to preserve good style, since the language of the great mass had (by that time) become corrupt. A seal was made to be placed upon the documents of the ruler, in order to preserve them from becoming public. This was also entrusted to (the wazir).

Thus, the name of wazir came to include the functions of both 'the sword' and 'the pen', in addition to all the other things for which the wazirate stood and in addition to its function of giving assistance (to the ruler). In the days of ar-Rashîd, Ja'far b. Yaḥyâ was actually called 'sultan', an indication of the general extent of his supervisory powers and control of the dynasty. The only governmental rank that he did not hold was the office of doorkeeper, and he did not hold it because he disdained to accept such an office.

Then the 'Abbâsid dynasty entered the period when control over the caliphs was exercised (by others). That control was at times in the hands of the wazir. At other times, it was in the hands of the ruler. When the wazir gained control, it was necessary for him to be appointed the caliph's delegate to comply fully with the religious laws. At that time, the wazirate was divided into an 'executive wazirate'—this happened when the ruler was in control of his affairs and the wazir executed his decisions—and a 'delegated wazirate'—which happened when the wazir controlled the ruler and the caliph delegated all the affairs of the caliphate, leaving them to his supervision and independent judgment. This has caused a difference of opinion as to whether two wazirs could be appointed at the same time to the 'delegated wazirate'.

(The ruler) continued to be controlled in this way. Non-Arab rulers seized power. The identity of the caliphate was lost. The usurpers were not interested in adopting the caliphal titles, and they disdained to share the same title with the wazirs, because the wazirs were their servants. Therefore, they used the names 'amir' and 'sultan'. Those in control of the dynasty were called amîr al-umarâ' or sulṭân, in addition to the ornamental titles which the caliph used to give them. They left the name wazir to those who held the office in the private retinue of the caliph. So remained the case down to the end of the 'Abbâsid dynasty.

In the course of this long period, language had become corrupt. It became a craft practised by certain people. Thus, it came to occupy an inferior position, and the wazirs were too proud to bother with it. Also, the wazirs were non-Arab, and neither eloquence (nor good style) could be expected of their language. People from other classes were chosen for this function. It was their specialty, and it came to be something that was at the service of the wazir.

The name *amîr* was restricted to the men in charge of war operations and the army and related matters, although (the amir) had power over the other ranks and exercised control over everything, either as (the ruler's) delegate or through being in control (of the government). This remained the situation.

Very recently, the Turkish dynasty has made its appearance in Egypt. (The Turkish rulers) noticed that the wazirate had lost its identity, because the (amirs) had been too proud to accept it and had left it to men who were inclined to hold it in the service of the secluded (and powerless) caliph. The authority of the wazir had become secondary to that of the amir. (The wazirate) had become a subordinate, ineffectual office. Consequently, the persons who held high rank in the dynasty, (as, for example, the amirs), disdained to use the name of wazir. The person in charge of legal decisions and supervision of the army at the present time, they call 'deputy' (*nâ'ib*). They used the name wazir to designate (the person in charge of) tax collection.

The Umayyads in Spain at first continued to use the name wazir in its original meaning. Later, they subdivided the functions of the wazir into several parts. For each function, they appointed a special wazir. They appointed a wazir to furnish an accounting of (government) finances; another for (official) correspondence; another to take care of the needs of those who had suffered wrongs; and another to supervise the situation of people in the border regions. A house was prepared for (all these wazirs). There, they sat upon carpets spread out for them and executed the orders of the ruler, each in the field entrusted to him. One of the wazirs was appointed liaison officer between the wazirs and the caliph. He had a higher position than the others, because he had constant contact with the ruler. His seat was higher than that of the other wazirs. He was distinguished by the title of 'doorkeeper' (*hâjib*). So it continued down to the end of the Umayyad dynasty. The function and rank of *hâjib* took precedence over the other ranks. Eventually, the *reyes de taïfas* came to adopt the title. The most important among them at that time was called 'doorkeeper'.

Then, the Shî'ah dynasty (the 'Ubaydid-Fâṭimids) made its appearance in Ifrîqiyah and al-Qayrawân. The people who supported it were firmly rooted in desert life. Therefore, they at first neglected such functions and did not use the proper names for them. Eventually, however, the dynasty reached the stage of sedentary culture, and (people) came to follow the tradition of the two preceding dynasties with regard to the use of titles, as the dynasty's history reveals.

When, later on, the Almohad dynasty made its appearance, it at first neglected the matter because of its desert attitude, but eventually it, too, adopted names and titles. The name wazir was used in its original meaning. Later the tradition of the (Spanish) Umayyad dynasty was followed with regard to government matters and the name wazir was used for the person who guarded the ruler in his court and saw to it that embassies and visitors to the ruler used the proper forms of greeting and address, and that the requisite manners were observed in his presence. The office of doorkeeper was considered by (the later Almohads) a much higher one. It has continued to be this way down to the present time.

In the Turkish dynasty in the East, the (official) who sees to it that people use the proper modes of address and greeting at court and when embassies are presented to the ruler, is called the *dawâdâr*. His office includes control of the 'private secretary' and of the (intelligence agents) who are active in the ruler's interest both far and near. Such is the condition of the Turkish dynasty at this time.

The office of doorkeeper

We have already mentioned that in the Umayyad and 'Abbâsid dynasties the title of doorkeeper was restricted to the person who guarded the ruler from the common people and would not give them access to him, or only in such ways, and at such times, as he determined. The office of doorkeeper was lower in rank at that time than the other functions and subordinate to them, because the wazir could intervene whenever he saw fit. This was the situation during the whole 'Abbâsid period, and the situation still persists at this time. In Egypt, (the doorkeeper) is subordinate to the person in charge of the highest function there, who is called 'deputy' (*nâ'ib*).

In the Umayyad dynasty in Spain, the doorkeeper was the person who guarded the ruler from his entourage and from the common people. He was the liaison officer between the ruler and the wazirs and lower officials. In the Umayyad dynasty, the office of doorkeeper was an extremely high position.

Later, when the Umayyad dynasty came under the control of others, the person in control was called doorkeeper (*hâjib*), because the office of doorkeeper had been such a distinguished one. The most powerful of the *reyes de taïfas* used the royal style and titles, and then inevitably mentioned the titles *hâjib* and *dhû l-wizâratayn* (Holder of the Two Wazirates), meaning the wazirates of 'the sword' and 'the pen'.

In the dynasties of the Maghrib and Ifrîqiyah, no mention was made of the title of (doorkeeper), on account of their Bedouin attitude. Occasionally, but rarely, it is found in the 'Ubaydid (-Fâṭimid) dynasty in Egypt. That was at the time when (the 'Ubaydid-Fâṭimids) had become powerful and used to sedentary culture.

In the Almohad dynasty, sedentary culture, which calls for the use of titles and the separation of government functions with distinctive names, only later on became firmly established. The only rank they had at first was that of wazir, which they used for the secretary who participated with the ruler in the administration of his private affairs. He also had to take care of bookkeeping and all the financial business. Later on, the name of wazir was given to relatives of the Almohad dynasty.

In the Ḥafṣid dynasty of Ifrîqiyah, the top position was at first in the hands of a wazir who gave advice and counsel. He was called 'Shaykh of the Almohads'. He had to take care of appointments and dismissals, the leadership of the army, and war operations. Bookkeeping and the ministry of tax collection were another, separate rank. The person in charge of it was called Ṣâḥib al-ashghâl (manager of financial affairs). He had complete charge of income and expenditure. He audited the finances, collected payments, and punished defaulters. One condition was that he be an Almohad. 'The pen' was also a separate office under the Almohads. It was only entrusted to a person with good knowledge of (official) correspondence and who could be trusted with secrets. Since people (of consequence in the dynasty) had no professional knowledge of writing and the proper use of their language for (official) correspondence, a particular descent was not a condition of appointment to that office.

The royal authority of the Ḥafṣid ruler was very far-flung, and a great number of dependants lived in his house. Therefore, he needed a steward to be in charge of his house, who had the duty properly of apportioning and fixing the salaries, allowances, garments, kitchen and stable expenditure, and other things. He was in control of the stores in the treasuries and had the duty of telling the tax collectors to provide for (the quantities and amounts of money) needed. He was called doorkeeper. Occasionally, the function of signing documents was added to his duties, if he happened to have a good knowledge of writing. However, that function was occasionally given to somebody else. It continued to be this way. The ruler stayed in seclusion, and the doorkeeper became the liaison officer between the people and all the officials. In the later (years) of the dynasty, the offices of 'the sword' and of war operations were added to his duties. At this time it also became his duty to give advice and counsel.

Thus, his office became the highest in rank and included all government functions. For some time after (the reign of) the twelfth ruler of the Ḥafṣids, the government was controlled by others, and the ruler kept in seclusion. Afterwards, his grandson Sultan Abû l-'Abbâs regained control of his affairs. He removed the vestiges of seclusion and (outside) control by abolishing the office of doorkeeper, which had been the stepping-stone toward (control of the government). He handled all his affairs himself without asking anyone else for help. This is the situation at the present time.

There is no trace of the title of doorkeeper among the Zanâtah dynasties in the Maghrib, of which the most important is the dynasty of the Merinids. Leadership of war operations and of the army belongs to the wazir. The rank of 'the pen', as far as it is concerned with bookkeeping and (official) correspondence, goes to the person who knows these things well, even though it may be in the private possession of certain houses among followers of the dynasty. Sometimes, (the office) is kept in (the same family), sometimes it is shared with others. . . .

Present-day Spaniards call the person in charge of bookkeeping and of the ruler's activities and of all the other financial matters, wakîl (manager). The wazir has the same duties as the wazir (usually has), but he is also in charge of (official) correspondence. The ruler puts his signature to all documents. Thus, the Spaniards do not have a separate office of signer of documents ('alâmah) as other dynasties have.

In the Turkish dynasty in Egypt, the name of doorkeeper (ḥâjib) is used for persons of authority (ḥâkim) among the men who hold power, that is, the Turks. These persons have to enforce the law among the people in the town. There are numerous ḥâjibs. The office of ḥâjib among the Turks is lower than that of nâ'ib, which has general jurisdiction over both the ruling class and the common people. The nâ'ib has the authority to appoint and remove certain officials at the proper times. He may grant and fix small salaries. His orders and decrees are executed as those of the ruler. He is the ruler's delegate in every respect. The doorkeepers (ḥâjib), on the other hand, have jurisdiction over the various classes of common people and over the soldiers only when a complaint is lodged against them. They can use force against those who do not want to submit to (their) judgment.

In the Turkish dynasty, the wazir is the person in charge of collecting all the different kinds of taxes: the land tax, customs duties, and the poll tax. He also (is in charge of) the disposition of (the tax revenue) for government expenditure and the fixed stipends (for soldiers and government employees). In addition, he can appoint or remove all officials, whatever their rank and description, who are concerned with tax collection and disbursement. It is a custom of the Turks that the wazir be appointed from among the Copts in charge of the office of bookkeeping and tax collection, because in Egypt they have been familiar with these matters since ancient times. Occasionally, the ruler appoints to that office a member of the ruling group, one of the Turkish grandees or one of their descendants, as occasion may arise.

The ministry of financial operations and taxation

The ministry of taxation is an office that is necessary to the royal authority. It is concerned with tax operations. It guards the rights of the dynasty in the matters of income and expenditure. It takes a census of the names of all soldiers, fixes their salaries, and pays out their allowances at the proper times. In this connection recourse is had to rules set up by the chiefs of (tax) operations and the stewards of the dynasty. They are all written down in a book which gives all the details concerning income and expenditure. It is based upon a good deal of accounting, which is mastered only by those who have considerable skill in (tax) operations. The book is called the dîwân. At the same time, (the word dîwân) designates the place where the officials concerned with these matters have their offices.

One person is in charge of this office. He supervises all the operations of this kind. Each branch has its own supervisor. In some dynasties supervision of the army, of military fiefs, of keeping count of allowances, and of other (such) things, is constituted as separate offices.

The office of (tax collections) originates in dynasties only when their power and superiority and their interest in the different aspects of royal authority and in the ways of efficient administration have become firmly established. The first to set up the dîwân in the Muslim dynasty was 'Umar. The reason is said to have been the arrival of Abû Hurayrah with money from al-Baḥrayn. The Muslims thought that it was a very large sum, and they had trouble with its distribution. They tried to count the money and to establish how it should be paid out for allowances and claims. On that occasion, Khâlid b. al-Walîd advised the use of the dîwân. He said: 'I have seen the rulers of Syria keeping a dîwân.' 'Umar accepted the idea from Khâlid.

It has also been said that the person who advised 'Umar to introduce the dîwân was al-Hurmuzân.[1] He noticed that (military) missions were dispatched without a dîwân (a muster roll). He asked

[1] The ruler of al-Ahwâz, who was captured during the conquest of the 'Irâq.

'Umar: 'Who would know if some of (the soldiers) disappeared? Those who remain behind might leave their places and abscond with the money that had been given to them for their services (if they could assume that their desertion would not be noticed). Such things should be noted down exactly in a book. Therefore, establish a *dîwân* for them.' 'Umar asked what the word *dîwân* meant, and it was explained to him. He ordered his men to write down the *dîwân* of the Muslim army. (It was arranged) according to family relationships and began with the relatives of the Prophet and continued according to the degree of relationship. This was the beginning of the ministry *dîwân* of the army.

At first the ministry (*dîwân*) of the land tax and tax collections in the 'Irâq used Persian, and in Syria Byzantine Greek. The secretaries of the *dîwâns* were Muslim subjects of the two groups. Then, with the appearance of 'Abd-al-Malik b. Marwân, the form of the state became that of royal authority. People turned from the low standard of desert life to the splendour of sedentary culture and from the simplicity of illiteracy to the sophistication of literacy. Experts in writing and bookkeeping made their appearance among the Arabs and their clients. Thus, 'Abd-al-Malik ordered Sulaymân b. Sa'd, then governor of the Jordan province, to introduce the use of Arabic in the *dîwân* of Syria. Sulaymân completed the task in exactly one year to the day.

Al-Ḥajjâj ordered his secretary Ṣâliḥ b. 'Abd-ar-Raḥmân to introduce the use of Arabic, instead of Persian, in the *dîwân* of the 'Irâq. Ṣâliḥ knew how to write both Arabic and Persian. (Ṣâliḥ now carried out al-Ḥajjâj's order and introduced the use of Arabic in the *dîwân*), overcoming the reluctance of the Persian secretaries.

Later on, in the 'Abbâsid dynasty, the office was added to the duties of (the wazir) who supervised the man in charge of it. This was the case under the Barmecides and other 'Abbâsid wazirs.

This office constitutes a large part of all royal authority. In fact, it is the third of its basic pillars. Royal authority requires soldiers, money, and the means to communicate with those who are absent. The ruler, therefore, needs persons to help him in the matters concerned with 'the sword', 'the pen', and finances. Thus, the person who holds the office (of tax collections) has (a good) part of the royal authority for himself.

This was the case under the Umayyad dynasty in Spain and under its successors, the *reyes de taïfas*. In the Almohad dynasty, the man in charge of (the office) was an Almohad. He had complete freedom to levy, collect, and handle money, to control the activities of officials and agents in this connection, and then to make disbursements in the proper amounts and at the proper times. He was known as

Ṣāḥib al-ashghāl (financial affairs manager). Occasionally, in some places, the office was held by persons who had a good understanding of it, but were not Almohads.

The Ḥafṣids gained control over Ifrîqiyah at the time when the exodus from Spain took place. Exiled Spanish notables came to the Ḥafṣids. Among them, there were some who had been employed in this (type of work) in Spain, such as the Banû Sa'îd, the lords of Alcalá near Granada, who were known as the Banû Abî l-Ḥusayn. The Ḥafṣids entrusted them with the supervision of (tax) affairs, which was what they had been doing in Spain. They employed them and the Almohads alternately for this purpose. Later on, the accountants and secretaries took the office over for themselves, and the Almohads lost it. As the position of doorkeeper (*ḥājib*) became more and more important, and as his executive power came to extend over all government affairs, the institution of the *Ṣāḥib al-ashghāl* ceased to be influential. The person in charge of it was dominated by the doorkeeper and became (no more than) a mere tax collector. He lost the authority he had formerly had in the dynasty.

In the contemporary Merinid dynasty, the accounting of the land tax and (military) allowances is in the hands of one man. He audits all accounts. Recourse is had to his *dîwân*, and his authority is second only to the authority of the ruler or wazir. His signature attests to the correctness of the accounts dealing with the land tax and (military) allowances.

These are the principal governmental ranks and functions. They are high ranks, involving the exercise of general authority and direct contact with the ruler.

In the Turkish dynasty, these functions are divided. The person in charge of the *dîwân* of (military) allowances is known as inspector of the army (*nâẓir al-jaysh*). The person in charge of finances is called the wazir. He has supervision over the dynasty's *dîwân* of general tax collection. This is the highest rank among the men who are in charge of financial matters. Among the Turks, supervision of financial matters is spread over many ranks, because the dynasty rules a large (territory) and exercises great powers, and its finances and taxes are too vast to be handled by one man all by himself, however competent. Therefore, for the general supervision of (financial affairs), the man known as wazir is appointed. In spite of his (important position), he is second to one of the clients of the ruler who shares in the ruler's group feeling and belongs to the military (caste) and who is called *Ustâdh-ad-dâr*. This official outranks the wazir, who does all he can to do his bidding. He is one of the great amirs of the dynasty and belongs to the army and the military (caste).

Other functions are subordinate to that of (the wazir) among the

Turks. All of them have reference to financial matters and book-keeping, and are restricted in their authority to particular matters. There is, for instance, the inspector of the privy purse (*nâẓir al-khâṣṣ*) —that is, the person who handles the ruler's private finances, such as concern his fiefs or his shares in the land tax and taxable lands that are not part of the general Muslim fisc. He is under the control of the amir, the *Ustâdh-ad-dâr*, but if the wazir is an army man, the *Ustâdh-ad-dâr* has no authority over him. The inspector of the privy purse also is under the control of the treasurer of the finances of the ruler, one of the latter's mamelukes, who is called *Khâzindâr* (treasurer), because his office is concerned with the private property of the ruler. Such is the nomenclature used in connection with the function of (financial administration) in the Turkish dynasty in the East.

The ministry of official correspondence and writing

This office is not required by the nature of royal authority. Many dynasties were able to dispense with it completely, as, for example, the dynasties rooted in the desert and which were not affected by the refinements of sedentary culture and high development of the crafts.

In the Muslim dynasty, the Arabic language situation and (the custom of) expressing what one wanted to express in good form intensified the need for the office. Thus, writing came to convey, as a rule, the essence of a matter in better stylistic form than was possible in oral expression. The secretary to an (Arab) amir was customarily a relative and one of the great of his tribe. This was the case with the caliphs and leading personalities among the men around Muḥammad in Syria and the 'Irâq, because of the great reliability and genuine discretion (of relatives and tribesmen).

When the language became corrupt and a craft (that had to be learned), (the office) was entrusted to those who knew Arabic well. Under the 'Abbâsids, it was a high office. The secretary issued documents freely, and put his own signature to them at the end. He sealed them with the seal of the ruler, which was a signet upon which the name of the ruler or his emblem was engraved. It was impressed on a red clay mixed with water and called sealing clay. The document was folded and glued, and then both sides were sealed. Later on, documents were issued in the name of the ruler, and the secretary affixed his signature ('*alâmah*) to them at the beginning or end. He could choose where he wanted to put it as well as its wording.

The office then lost standing through the fact that officials of other government ranks gained in the ruler's esteem or because the wazir gained control over (the ruler). The signature of a secretary became ineffective (as a sign of authority) and was replaced by the signature of his superior, and this was now considered decisive. (The secretary) affixed his official signature, but the signature of his superior made the document valid. This happened in the later years of the Ḥafṣid dynasty, when the office of doorkeeper gained in esteem, and the doorkeeper became the delegate of the ruler and then came to control him. The signature of the secretary became ineffective (as a sign of authority) but was still affixed to documents, in acknowledgment of its former importance. The doorkeeper made it a rule for the secretary to sign letters of his by affixing a handwritten (note) for which he could choose any formula of ratification he wished. The secretary obeyed him and affixed the usual mark. As long as the ruler was in control of his own affairs, he saw to the matter himself and made it a rule for the secretary to affix the signature.

One of the functions of the secretary's office is the *tawqî'*. It means that the secretary sits in front of the ruler during his public audiences and notes down, in the most concise and stylistically most perfect manner, the decisions he receives from the ruler concerning the petitions presented to him. These decisions are then issued as they are, or they are copied in a document which must be in the possession of the petitioner. The person who formulates a *tawqî'* needs a great deal of stylistic skill. Ja'far b. Yaḥyâ used to write *tawqî'*s on petitions for ar-Rashîd and to hand the petition (with the *tawqî'*) back to the petitioner. Stylists vied with each other to obtain his *tawqî'*s, in order to learn the different devices and kinds of good style from them. It has even been said that such petitions (with Ja'far's *tawqî'* on them) were sold for a dinar. Things were handled in this manner in (various) dynasties.

The person in charge of this function must be selected from among the upper classes and be a refined gentleman of great knowledge and with a good deal of stylistic ability. He will have to concern himself with the principal branches of scholarship, because such things may come up in the gatherings and audiences of the ruler. In addition, to be a companion of kings calls for good manners and the possession of good qualities of character. And he must know all the secrets of good style, to be able to write letters and find the words that conform to the meaning intended.

In some dynasties, the rank (of secretary) is entrusted to military men, since those dynasties, by their very nature, have no regard for scholarship, on account of the simplicity of group feeling (prevailing in them). The ruler gives his government offices and ranks to men who share in his group feeling. Appointments to the financial administration, to 'the sword', and to the office of secretary, are made from among them. 'The sword' requires no learning. But the financial administration and the secretaryship need it, for the latter requires a good style and the former requires accounting skill. Therefore, (rulers) select people from the (learned) class for the office of secretary, when there is need for it, and entrust it to them. However, the secretary is subordinate to the higher authority exercised by the men who share in the ruler's group feeling, and his authority derives from that of his superior. This is the case with the Turkish dynasty in the East at this time. The office of chief secretary belongs to the 'secretary of state' (*Ṣâḥib al-inshâ*'). However, the secretary of state is under the control of an amir from among the men who share in the group feeling of the ruler. This man is known as the *Dawîdâr*. The ruler usually relies upon him, trusts him, and confides in him, whereas he relies upon the (secretary) for matters that have to do with good style and the conformity of the expression to what one wants to express, and other, related matters.

The ruler who selects and picks a (secretary) from the rank and file has many conditions to consider. These are best and most completely presented in the *Epistle* that the secretary 'Abd-al-Ḥamîd[1] addressed to his fellow secretaries. It runs as follows:

And now: May God guard you who practise the craft of secretaryship, and may He keep you and give you success and guidance. There are prophets and messengers and highly honoured kings. After them come different kinds of men, all of them made by God. They are of different kinds, even if they are all alike in fact. God occupied them with different kinds of crafts and various sorts of businesses, so that they might be able to make a living and earn their sustenance. He gave to you, secretaries, the great opportunity to be men of education and gentlemen, to have knowledge and good judgment. You bring out whatever is good in the caliphate and straighten out its affairs. Through your advice, God improves the government for the benefit of human beings and makes their countries civilized. The ruler cannot dispense with you. You alone make him a competent ruler. Your position with regard to rulers is that you are the ears through which they hear, the eyes through which they see, the tongues through which they speak, and the hands through which they touch. May God give you, therefore, enjoyment of the excellent craft with which He has distinguished you, and may He not deprive you of the great favours that He has shown you.

No craftsman needs more than you to combine all praiseworthy good traits and all memorable and highly regarded excellent qualities, O secretaries, if you aspire to fit the description given of you in this letter. The secretary needs on his own account, and his master, who trusts him with his important affairs, expects him, to be mild where mildness is needed, to be understanding where judgment is needed, to be enterprising where enterprise is needed, to be hesitant

1 'Abd-al-Ḥamîd b. Yaḥyâ perished in the debacle of his Umayyad masters in 132 [750].

where hesitation is needed. He must prefer modesty, justice, and fairness. He must keep secrets. He must be faithful in difficult circumstances. He must know (beforehand) about the calamities that may come. He must be able to put things in their proper places and misfortunes into their proper categories. He must have studied every branch of learning and must know it well, and if he does not know it well, he must at least have acquired an adequate amount of it. By virtue of his natural intelligence, good education, and outstanding experience, he must know what is going to happen to him before it happens, and he must know the result of his actions before action starts. He must make the proper preparations for everything, and he must set up everything in its proper, customary form.

Therefore, assembled secretaries, vie with each other to acquire the different kinds of education and to gain an understanding of religious matters. Start with knowledge of the Book of God and religious duties. Then, study the Arabic language, as that will give you a cultivated form of speech. Then, learn to write well, as that will be an ornament to your letters. Transmit poetry and acquaint yourselves with the rare expressions and ideas that poems contain. Acquaint yourselves also with both Arab and non-Arab political events, and with the tales of (both groups) and the biographies describing them, as that will be helpful to you in your endeavours. Do not neglect to study accounting, for it is the mainstay of the land tax register. Detest prejudices with all your heart, lofty ones as well as low ones, and all idle and contemptible things, for they bring humility and are the ruin of secretaryship. Do not let your craft be a low one. Guard against backbiting and calumny and the actions of stupid people. Beware of haughtiness, foolishness, and pride, for they mean acquiring hostility without (even the excuse of) hatred. Love each other in God in your craft. Advise your colleagues to practise it in a way befitting your virtuous, fair, and gifted predecessors.

If times go hard for one of you, be kind to him and console him, until everything be well with him again. Should old age make one of you unable to get around and pursue his livelihood and meet his friends, visit him and honour him and consult him, and profit from his outstanding experience and mature knowledge. Everyone of you should be more concerned for his assistants, who may be useful when needed, then for his own children or brothers. Should some praise come (to one of you) in the course of his work, he should ascribe the merit to his colleague; any blame he should bear all by himself. He should beware of mistakes and slips and of being annoyed when conditions change. You know that everyone of you has a master, one who gives from his own as much as can be expected, and (everyone of you) has the obligation to repay him, since he deserves it, with fidelity, gratefulness, tolerance, patience, good counsel, discretion, and active interest in his affairs, and to show (his good intentions) by his actions whenever his master needs him and his resources. Be conscious of (your obligations)—God give you success—in good and bad circumstances, in privation as in munificence and kindness, in happiness as in misfortune. Any member of this noble craft who has all these qualities has good qualities indeed.

If any one of you be appointed to an office, or if some matter that concerns God's children be turned over to one of you, he should think of God and choose obedience to Him. He should be kind to the weak and fair to those who have been wronged. All creatures are God's children. He loves most those who are kindest to His children. Furthermore, he should judge with justice, he should honour the noble (descendants of Muḥammad), augment the booty (gained in wars against infidels), and bring civilization to the country. He should be friendly to the subjects, and refrain from harming them. He should be humble and mild in his office. He should be kind in handling the land tax registers and in calling in outstanding claims.

You should explore the character of him with whom you associate. When his good and bad sides are known, you will be able to help him to do the good things that agree with him, and be able to contrive to keep him from the bad things he desires. You must be able to do that in the subtlest and best manner. You know that a person who is in charge of an animal and understands his job, endeavours to know the character of the animal. If it is inclined to gallop, he does not goad it when he is riding it. If it is inclined to kick, he takes precautions with its forelegs. If he fears that it will shy, he takes precautions with its head. If it is restive, he gently subdues its desire to go where it wants to go. If it still continues, he pulls it slightly to the side, then has its halter loosened. This description of how to take care of an animal contains good points for those who want to lead human beings and deal with them, serve them, and have intimate contact with them. The secretary, with his excellent education, his noble craft, his subtlety, his frequent dealings with people who confer with him and discuss things with him and learn from him or fear his severity, needs to be kind to his associates, to flatter them, and to supply their wants, even more than the person in charge of an animal which cannot answer, does not know what is right, does not understand what is said to it, and goes only where its master who rides upon it makes it go. Be kind—God show you mercy—when you look after things. Use as much reflection and thought as possible. God permitting, you will thus escape harshness, annoyance, and rudeness on the part of your associates. They will be in agreement with you, and you will have their friendship and protection, if God wills.

None of you should have too sumptuous an office or go beyond the proper limits in his dress, his mount, his food, his drink, his house, his servants, or in the other things pertaining to his station, for, despite the nobility of the craft by which God has distinguished you, you are servants who are not permitted to fall short in their service. You are caretakers whom one does not permit to be wasteful or spendthrift. Try to preserve your modesty by planned moderation in all the things I have mentioned and told you. Beware of the wastefulness of prodigality and the bad results of luxury. They engender poverty and bring about humiliation. People (prodigal and living in luxury) are put to shame, especially if they be secretaries and men of education.

Things repeat themselves. One thing contains the clue to another. Let yourselves be guided in your future undertakings by your previous experience. Then, choose the method of doing things that is most definite, most accurate, and that promises the best result. You should know that there is something that defeats accomplishment, namely, talking about things. The person who does it is prevented from using his knowledge and his ability to think. Therefore, everyone of you, while he is in his office, should endeavour to talk no more than is sufficient; he should be concise in the matters he brings up and in the answers he gives; and he should give thought to all the arguments he advances. His work will profit from that. It will prevent too much preoccupation with other things. He should implore God to grant him success and to support him with His guidance, for he must fear making mistakes that might hurt his body and (cast doubt upon) his intelligence and education. When anyone of you says or thinks that the high quality and efficiency of his work is obviously the result of his own cleverness and knowledge of how to do things, he provokes God. God will let him depend upon himself alone, and then he will find that he is not adequate to his task. This is no secret to those who reflect.

None of you should say that he has a better understanding of affairs, or knows better how to handle difficult matters, than other members of his craft, than those who serve together with him. Of two persons, discerning people consider him the more intelligent who throws off conceit and thinks his colleagues more intelligent and more skilful than he. But at any rate, both parties should acknowledge the excellence of God's favours. No one should let himself be deceived by his own opinions and consider himself free from mistakes. Nor should he strive to outdo his friends, equals, colleagues, or his family. Everybody must give praise to God, in humility in the face of His greatness, in meekness in the face of His might, and in fulfilment of the command to speak of God's favours.

In this letter of mine, let me refer to the old proverb: 'He who accepts good advice is successful.' This is the essence of this letter and the best that is said in it, after the references to God it contains. Therefore, I have placed it at the end, and I close the letter with it. May God take care of us and of you, assembled students and secretaries, in the same way He takes care of those whom, as He knows in His prescience, He will make happy and guide aright. He can do it. It is in His hand.

Farewell, and God's mercy and blessings upon you.

The police

In Ifrîqiyah, the holder (of the office of chief of police) is at this time called the 'magistrate' (*ḥâkim*). In Spain, he is called the 'town chief' (*ṣâḥib al-madînah*). In the Turkish dynasty (in Egypt), he is called the 'governor' (*wâlî*). It is an office that is subordinate to the person in charge of 'the sword' in the dynasty, who at times uses the (chief of police) to execute his orders.

The office of (chief of) police was originally created by the 'Abbâsid dynasty. The person who held it had (a twofold duty). He had, firstly, to concern himself with crimes in the investigating stage, and, secondly, to execute the legal punishments. The religious law cannot concern itself with suspicions of possible criminal acts. It can concern itself only with executing the legal punishments. Political leadership, on the other hand, has to concern itself with the investigating stage, in which is (ascertained the commission of crimes) necessitating (legal punishments). It does this through the magistrate, who, being in the possession of all the circumstantial evidence, forces (the criminal) to confess, as is required by the general (public) interest. The person in charge of the investigating stage and of executing afterwards the legal punishments due, when the judge has no longer anything to do with (the case), was called 'chief of police'. Occasionally, he was given sole jurisdiction over capital crimes and legal punishments, and those matters were taken away from the judge's jurisdiction. This rank was considered one of great reputation, and was entrusted to high military leaders and important clients of the court entourage. It implied no general executive power over all classes, its jurisdiction extending only over low and suspect elements and (involving) the restraining of turbulent and criminal people.

Among the Spanish Umayyads, the office acquired great celebrity. It was divided into a 'great police' and a 'small police'. The jurisdiction of the 'great police' was made to extend over both the upper and the lower classes. It had jurisdiction over government dignitaries, and, in cases of wrongdoing, could restrain them, their relatives, and other persons of rank who were connected with them as clients. The chief of the 'small police' was concerned only with the common people. The chief of the 'great police' had his seat at the gate of the palace of the ruler. He had footmen (*rajl*) who occupied places near him, which they did not leave except to go about his business. (The office) was entrusted only to great personalities of the dynasty. It even became a stepping-stone to the wazirate and to the office of doorkeeper.

In the Almohad dynasty in the Maghrib, (the office) enjoyed a certain reputation, even though it did not have general (jurisdiction).

It was entrusted only to important Almohad personalities. It did not have authority over government dignitaries. Nowadays, its importance has greatly decreased. It no longer is the preserve of Almohad personalities, and may be entrusted to any follower (of the dynasty able to) take charge of it.

In the Merinid dynasty at this time in the West, (the office) is vested in the houses of Merinid clients and followers.

In the Turkish dynasty in the East, (the office is entrusted) to Turkish persons or to descendants of the people of the preceding Kurdish dynasty. They are chosen for (the office) according to the energy and resolution they show in enforcing the law. The purpose is to cut down corruption, to stamp out criminality, to destroy and dissolve the homes and centres of criminal activity, and to enforce the punishments imposed by the religious law and by the political authorities, as concern for the general (public) interests in a town requires.

The admiralty

(The admiralty) is one of the ranks and functions of the dynasty in the realm of the Maghrib and Ifrîqiyah. It is subordinate to the person in charge of 'the sword' and comes under his authority in many respects. In customary usage, the person in charge of the admiralty is called *Almiland*, with an emphatic *l*. (The word) is derived from the language of the European Christians. It is the technical term for the office in their language.

The rank (of admiral) is restricted to the realm of Ifrîqiyah and the Maghrib, because both Ifrîqiyah and the Maghrib are on the southern shore of the Mediterranean. Along its southern shore the lands of the Berbers extend from Ceuta to Alexandria and on to Syria. Along its northern shore are the countries of Spain and of the European Christians (Franks), the Slavs, and the Byzantines, also extending to Syria. It is called the Byzantine Sea or the Syrian Sea, according to the people who inhabit its shores. Those who live along the coast and on the shores of both sides of the Mediterranean are more concerned with (maritime) conditions than any other maritime nation.

The Byzantines, the European Christians, and the Goths lived on the northern shore of the Mediterranean. Most of their wars and most of their commerce was by sea. They were skilled in navigating (the Mediterranean) and in naval war. When these people coveted the possession of the southern shore, as the Byzantines (coveted) Ifrîqiyah and as the Goths the Maghrib, they crossed over in their fleets and took possession of it. Thus, they achieved superiority over the Berbers and deprived them of their power. They had populous cities there, such as Carthage, Sbeitla, Jalûlâ, Murnâq, Cherchel, and Tangier. The ancient master of Carthage used to fight the master of Rome and to send fleets loaded with armies and equipment to wage war against him. Thus, (seafaring) is a custom of the inhabitants of both shores of the Mediterranean, which was known in ancient as in modern times.

When the Muslims took possession of Egypt, 'Umar b. al-Khaṭṭâb wrote to 'Amr b. al-'Âṣ and asked him to describe the sea to him. 'Amr replied: 'The sea is a great creature upon which weak creatures ride—like worms upon a piece of wood.' Thus, he recommended at that time that the Muslims be kept away from seafaring. No Arab travelled by sea save those who did so without 'Umar's knowledge and were punished by him for it. Thus it remained until Mu'âwiyah's reign. He permitted the Muslims to go by sea and to wage the holy war in ships. The reason for this was that on account of their Bedouin attitude, the Arabs were at first not skilled in navigation and seafaring, whereas the Byzantines and the European Christians, on account of their experience of the sea and the fact that they had grown up travelling in ships, were used to the sea and well trained in navigation.

The royal and governmental authority of the Arabs became firmly established and powerful at that time. The non-Arab nations became servants of the Arabs and were under their control. Every craftsman offered them his best services. They employed seagoing nations for their maritime needs. Their own experience of the sea and of navigation grew, and they turned out to be very expert. They wished to wage the holy war by sea. They constructed ships and galleys and loaded the fleet with men and weapons. They embarked the army and warriors to fight against the unbelievers across the sea. This was the special concern of the provinces and border regions closest to the shores of the Mediterranean, such as Syria, Ifrîqiyah, the Maghrib, and Spain. The caliph 'Abd-al-Malik recommended to Ḥassân b. an-Nu'mân, the governor of Ifrîqiyah, that a shipyard be set up in Tunis for the production of maritime implements, as he was desirous of waging the holy war. From there, the conquest of Sicily was achieved.

Thereafter, under the 'Ubaydid(-Fâṭimids) and the (Spanish) Umayyads, the fleets of Ifrîqiyah and Spain constantly attacked each other's countries in civil war operations, and they thoroughly devastated the coastal regions. In the days of 'Abd-ar-Raḥmân an-Nâṣir, the Spanish fleet had grown to about two hundred vessels, and the African fleet to the same number, or close to it. The fleet admiral in Spain was Ibn Rumâḥis. The ports used by (the Spanish fleet) for docking and hoisting sail were Pechina and Almería. The fleet was assembled from all the provinces. Each region where ships were used contributed one unit under the supervision of a commander in charge of everything connected with fighting, weapons and combatants alike. There also was a captain who directed the movement of the fleet, using either the wind or oars. He also directed its anchoring in port. When the whole fleet was assembled for a large-scale raid or for important government business, it was manned in its home port. The ruler loaded it with men from his best troops and clients, and placed them under the supervision of one commander, who belonged to the highest class of the people of his realm and to whom all were responsible. He then sent them off, and awaited their victorious return with booty.

During the time of the Muslim dynasty, the Muslims gained control over the whole Mediterranean. Their power and domination over it was vast. The Christian nations could do nothing against the Muslim fleets, anywhere in the Mediterranean. All the time, the Muslims rode its wave for conquest. There occurred then many well-known episodes of conquest and plunder. The Muslims took possession of all the islands that lie off its shores, such as Mallorca, Minorca, Ibiza, Sardinia, Sicily, Pantelleria, Malta, Crete, Cyprus, and of all the other (Mediterranean) provinces of the Byzantines and the European Christians. Abû l-Qâsim ash-Shî'î[1] and his descendants sent their fleets on raids against the island of Genoa from al-Mahdîyah. They returned victorious with booty. Mujâhid al-'Âmirî, the master of Denia, one of the *reyes de taïfas*, conquered the island of Sardinia with his fleet in the year 405 [1014/15]. The Christians reconquered it in due course.

During all that time, the Muslims were gaining control over the largest part of the high sea. Their fleets kept coming and going, and the Muslim armies crossed the sea in ships from Sicily to the great mainland opposite Sicily, on the northern shore. They fell upon the European Christian rulers and made massacres in their realms. This happened in the days of the Banû Abî l-Husayn,[2] the rulers of Sicily, who supported the 'Ubaydid(-Fâṭimid) propaganda there. The Christian nations withdrew with their fleets to the north-eastern side of the Mediterranean, to the coastal regions inhabited by the European Christians and the Slavs, and to the Aegean islands, and did not go beyond them. The Muslim fleet had pounced upon them as eagerly as lions upon their prey. They covered most of the surface of the Mediterranean with their equipment and numbers and travelled its lanes (on missions both) peaceful and warlike. Not a single Christian board floated on it.

[1] Al-Qâ'im, the second Fâṭimid, who ruled from 934 to 946.
[2] The Kalbite governors of Sicily in the latter part of the tenth and the beginning of the eleventh century.

Eventually, however, the 'Ubaydid(-Fâṭimid) and Umayyad dynasties weakened and softened and were affected by infirmity. Then, the Christians reached out for the eastern islands of the Mediterranean, such as Sicily, Crete, and Malta, and took possession of them. They pressed on against the shores of Syria during this interval, and took possession of Tripoli, Ascalon, Tyre, and Acco. They gained control over all the seaports of Syria. They conquered Jerusalem and built there a church as an outward manifestation of their religion and worship. They deprived the Banû Khazrûn of Tripolitania and (conquered) Gabès and Sfax, and imposed a poll tax upon their inhabitants. Then they took possession of al-Mahdîyah, the (original) seat of the 'Ubaydid(-Fâṭimids), and took it away from the descendants of Buluggîn b. Zîrî. In the fifth [eleventh] century, they had the lead in the Mediterranean. In Egypt and Syria, interest in the fleet weakened and eventually ceased to exist. Since then, they have shown no concern for the naval matters with which they had been so exceedingly concerned under the 'Ubaydid (-Fâṭimid) dynasty. In consequence, the identity of the office of the admiralty was lost in those countries. It remained in Ifrîqiyah and the Maghrib, but only there. At the present time, the western Mediterranean has large fleets and is very powerful. No enemy has trespassed on it or been able to do anything there.

In (Almoravid) times, the admirals of the fleet in (the West) were the Banû Maymûn, chieftains from the peninsula of Cadiz, which they (later on) handed over to (the Almohad) 'Abd-al-Mu'min, to whom they paid obedience. Their fleets, from the countries on both shores, reached the number of one hundred.

In the sixth [twelfth] century, the Almohad dynasty flourished and had possession of both shores. The Almohads organized their fleet in the most perfect manner ever known and on the largest scale ever observed. Their admiral was Aḥmad aṣ-Ṣiqillî. The Christians had captured him, and he had grown up among them. The ruler of Sicily (Roger II) selected him for his service and employed him in it, but he died and was succeeded by his son, whose anger (Aḥmad) somehow aroused. He feared for his life and went to Tunis, where he stayed with the chief of Tunis. He went on to Marrakech, and was received there by the caliph Yûsuf al-'Ashrî b. 'Abd-al-Mu'min with great kindness and honour. (The caliph) gave him many presents and entrusted him with command of his fleet. (As commander of the fleet) he went to wage the holy war against the Christian nations. He did noteworthy and memorable deeds during the Almohad dynasty.

In his time, the Muslim fleet was of a size and quality never, to our knowledge, attained before or since. When Ṣalâḥ-ad-dîn Yûsuf b. Ayyûb, the ruler of Egypt and Syria at this time, set out to recover the ports of Syria from the Christian nations and to cleanse Jerusalem of the abomination of unbelief and to rebuild it, one fleet of unbelievers after another came to the relief of the ports, from all the regions near Jerusalem which they controlled. They supported them with equipment and food. The fleet of Alexandria could not stand up against them. (The Christians) had had the upper hand in the eastern Mediterranean for so long, and they had numerous fleets there. The Muslims, on the other hand, had for a long time been too weak to offer them any resistance there, as we have mentioned. In this situation, Ṣalâḥ-ad-dîn sent 'Abd-al-Karîm b. Munqidh, a member of the family of the Banû Munqidh, the rulers of Shayzar, as his ambassador to Ya'qûb al-Manṣûr, the Almohad ruler of the Maghrib at that time, asking for the support of his fleets, to prevent the fleets of the unbelievers from achieving their desire of bringing relief to the Christians in the Syrian ports. Al-Manṣûr sent him back to Ṣalâḥ-ad-dîn, and did not comply with his request.

This is evidence that the ruler of the Maghrib alone possessed a fleet, that the Christians controlled the eastern Mediterranean, and that the dynasties in Egypt and Syria at that time and later were not interested in naval matters or in building up government fleets.

Ya'qûb al-Manṣûr then died, and the Almohad dynasty became infirm. The Galician nations seized control of most of Spain. The Muslims sought refuge in the coastal region and took possession of the islands of the western Mediterranean. They regained their former strength, and their power on the surface of the Mediterranean grew. Their fleets increased, and the strength of the Muslims became again equal to that of (the Christians). This happened in the time of (the Merinid) Sultan, Abû l-Ḥasan,[1] the Zanâtah ruler in the Maghrib. When he desired to wage the holy war, his fleet was as well equipped and numerous as that of the Christians.

Then, the naval strength of the Muslims declined once more, because of the weakness of the ruling dynasty. Maritime habits were forgotten under the impact of the strong Bedouin attitude prevailing in the Maghrib, and as the result of the discontinuance of Spanish habits. The Christians resumed their former, famous maritime training, and (renewed) their constant activity in the Mediterranean and their experience with conditions there. (They again showed) their former superiority over others on the high seas and in (Mediterranean) shipping. The Muslims came to be strangers to the Mediterranean. The only exceptions are a few inhabitants of the coastal regions. They ought to have many assistants and supporters, or they ought to have support from the dynasties to enable them to recruit help and to work toward the goal of (increased seafaring activities).

---

[1] Abû l-Ḥasan ruled from 1331 to 1351.

The rank (of admiral) has been preserved to this day in the dynasties of the Maghrib. There, the identity (of the admiralty is still preserved), and how to take care of a fleet, how to build ships and navigate them, is known. Perhaps some political opportunity will arise in the coastal countries, and the Muslims will ask the wind to blow against unbelief and unbelievers. The inhabitants of the Maghrib have it on the authority of the books of predictions that the Muslims will yet have to make a successful attack against the Christians and conquer the lands of the European Christians beyond the sea. This, it is said, will take place by sea.

33 The different importance of the ranks of 'the sword' and 'the pen' in the dynasties

It should be known that both 'the sword' and 'the pen' are instruments for the ruler to use in his affairs. However, at the beginning of a dynasty, so long as its people are occupied in establishing power, the need for 'the sword' is greater than that for 'the pen'. In that situation, 'the pen' is merely a servant and agent of the ruler's authority, whereas 'the sword' contributes active assistance.

The same is the case at the end of a dynasty when its group feeling weakens and its people decrease in number under the influence of senility. The dynasty then needs the support of the military. The dynasty's need of the military for the purpose of protection and defence is as strong then as it was at the beginning of (the dynasty) for the purpose of getting established. In these two situations, 'the sword', thus, has the advantage over 'the pen'. At that time, the military have the higher rank. They enjoy more benefits and more splendid fiefs.

In mid-term of the dynasty, the ruler can to some degree dispense with 'the sword'. His power is firmly established. His only remaining desire is to obtain the fruits of royal authority, such as collecting taxes, holding (property), excelling other dynasties, and enforcing the law. 'The pen' is helpful in all that. Therefore, the need for using it increases. The swords stay unused in their scabbards, unless something happens and they are called upon to repair a breach. In this situation, the men of the pen have more authority. They occupy a higher rank. They enjoy more benefits and greater wealth and have a closer and more frequent and intimate contact with the ruler. At such a time, the wazirs and the military can be dispensed with. They are kept away from the intimate circle of the ruler and have to beware of his moods.

34 The characteristic emblems of royal and government authority

It should be known that the ruler has emblems and arrangements that are the necessary result of pomp and ostentation. They are restricted to him, and by their use he is distinguished from his subjects, his intimates, and all other leaders in his dynasty.

We shall mention the best-known emblems as well as our knowledge permits.

Trumpets and banners

One of the emblems of royal authority is the display of banners and flags and the beating of drums and the blowing of trumpets and horns. In the *Book on Politics* ascribed to Aristotle, he notes that its real significance is to frighten the enemy in war. Frightful sounds do have the psychological effect of causing terror. Indeed, as everyone knows from his own experience, this is an emotional element that plays a role on battlefields. The explanation given by Aristotle—if it was he who gave it—is correct in some respects. But the truth is that listening to music and sounds no doubt causes pleasure and emotion in the soul. The spiritual temper of man is thereby affected by a kind of elation, which causes him to make light of difficulties and to be willing to die in the very condition in which he finds himself. This (state of affairs) exists even in dumb animals. Camels are influenced by the driver's call, and horses are influenced by whistling and shouting, as everyone knows. The effect is greater when the sounds are harmonious ones, as in the instance of music. It is known what happens to people who listen to music. The non-Arabs, therefore, take musical instruments, drums or trumpets, onto the battlefield with them. Singers with instruments surround the cavalcade of the ruler and sing. Thus, they move the souls of brave men emotionally and cause them to be willing to die.

In the wars of the Arabs (in north-western Africa), we have seen persons in front of the cavalcade sing poetical songs and make music. The minds of heroes were stirred by the contents of the songs. They hurried to the battleground, and everybody went forth eagerly to meet his rival.

The origin of it all is the cheerfulness created in the soul (through music). It leads to bravery, just as drunkenness does, as the result of the cheerfulness which it produces.

The great number of flags, their manifold colours, and their length, are intended to cause fright, nothing more. Fright produces greater aggressiveness in the soul. Psychological conditions and reactions are strange.

The various rulers and dynasties differ in their use of such emblems. Some of them use a great many, others few, according to the extent and importance of the given dynasty.

Flags have been the insignia of war since the creation of the world. The nations have always displayed them on battlefields and during raids. This was also the case in the time of the Prophet and that of the caliphs who succeeded him.

The Muslims, however, refrained from beating drums and blowing trumpets at the beginning of Islam. They wanted to avoid the coarseness of royal authority and do without royal customs. They also despised pomp, which has nothing whatever to do with the truth. The caliphate then came to be royal authority, and the Muslims learned to esteem the splendour and luxury of this world. Persian and Byzantine clients, subjects of the preceding (pre-Islamic) dynasties, mixed with them and showed them their ways of ostentation and luxury. Among the things the Muslims came to like were those emblems. Therefore, they used them, and permitted their officials to use them, to increase the prestige of royal authority and its representatives. 'Abbâsid or 'Ubaydid(-Fâṭimid) caliphs would often grant permission to display their flags to officials such as the master of a border region or the commander of an army. Such officials then, setting out on a mission or going from the house of the caliph or from their own houses to their offices, were accompanied by a cavalcade of people carrying flags and trumpets. The only distinction between the cavalcade of an official and that of the caliph was the number of flags, or the use of particular colours for the caliph's flag. Thus, black was used for the flags of the 'Abbâsids. Their flags were black as a sign of mourning for the martyrs of their family, the Hâshimites, and as a sign of reproach directed against the Umayyads who had killed them.

When the Hâshimites divided into factions and the 'Alids went against the 'Abbâsids on every possible occasion, they wanted to differ from them in the colour of their flag, and so they used white flags. White was used by the 'Alids throughout the reign of the 'Ubaydid(-Fâṭimids). It was also used by the 'Alids who seceded at that time in the East. When al-Ma'mûn gave up wearing black and using the (black) insignia of his dynasty, he turned to green and used green flags. . . .

The contemporary Galicians, a European Christian nation in Spain, use only a few flags, which fly high in the air. In addition, they make a kind of music with string and wind instruments on the battlefields. This is all the information we have about them and the non-Arab rulers who live beyond them.

The throne

Throne, dais, couch, chair—they all mean pieces of wood or ottomans set up for the ruler, so that he may have a higher seat than the other people at court and so that he will not be on the same level with them. This has always been a royal custom, even before Islam and in the non-Arab dynasties. (Pre-Islamic rulers) sat upon thrones of gold. Solomon, the son of David, had a throne of ivory overlaid with gold. However, dynasties use a throne only after they have become flourishing and luxurious, as is the case with all pomp. Dynasties that are in the initial stage and still keep the Bedouin attitude do not desire it.

The first to use a throne in Islam was Mu'âwiyah. He asked the people for permission to use one, saying that he had become corpulent. So they permitted him to use one, and he did. His example was followed by (all the later) Muslim rulers. (The use of an ornate throne) came to indicate a tendency toward pomp.

One day 'Amr b. al-'Âṣ was in his castle in Egypt, sitting on the ground with the Arabs. The Muqawqis[1] came to the castle. He had men carry out a throne of gold, so that he could sit upon it like a king. He sat on it in front of the Arabs. They were not jealous of him, because they felt that they had to give him the protection upon which they had agreed, and because they rejected royal pomp. Later on, the 'Abbâsids, the 'Ubaydid(-Fâṭimids), and all the other Muslim rulers in both the East and the West, had thrones, daises, and couches that eclipsed (in splendour those of) the Persian and Roman Emperors.

The mint

(The mint) is concerned with the stamping of the dinars and dirhams used in (commercial) transactions. This is done with a die of iron, upon which pictures or words are engraved in reverse. The stamp is pressed upon the dinar or the dirham, and the designs (legends) of those engravings appear on the coin clearly and correctly. Before this is done, the standard of purity of the particular coin, the result of repeated refinings, is taken into consideration, and the individual dinars and dirhams are given the proper, fixed weight that has been agreed upon. Then, the number of coins (and not their weight only) can be made use of in transactions. If the individual pieces have not been given the weight fixed upon, then the weight of the coins must be taken into consideration.

The word sikkah (mint) refers to the stamp, that is, the piece of

[1] The celebrated, though still rather enigmatic personality who corresponds to the historical Cyrus, governor of Egypt at the end of the Byzantine domination.

iron used for the purpose (of stamping the coins). The word was then used to designate the result of (the application of the stamp), that is, the engravings that appear upon dinars and dirhams. The word was further used to designate control of (the process of engraving) and supervision of the whole operation, of everything dealing with coinage and all the conditions that govern it. Such (control and supervision) is (exercised by) the office (of the mint). The word has thus come to designate (that office), and is customarily so used in governmental usage. It is an office that is necessary to the royal authority, for it enables people to distinguish between good and bad coins in their transactions. That they are not bad is guaranteed by the engravings known to have been stamped upon them by the ruler.

The non-Arabs used coins and engraved special pictures on them —for example, a picture of the ruler at the time of issue, a fortress, some animal or product, or something else. This remained the practice of the non-Arabs down to the end of their power. When Islam appeared, the practice was discontinued, because of the simplicity of Islam and the Bedouin attitude of the Arabs. In their transactions, they used gold and silver according to weight. They also had Persian dinars and dirhams. They used them, too, according to weight and employed them as their medium of exchange. The government paid no attention to the matter. As a result, the frauds practised with dinars and dirhams eventually became very serious. According to reports, 'Abd-al-Malik ordered al-Ḥajjâj to coin dirhams, and bad coins (began to) be distinguished from good ones. This took place in 74 [693/94], or in 75 [694/95]. In the year 76 [695/96], 'Abd-al-Malik ordered that dirhams be coined in all the other regions.

Later on, in the days of Yazîd b. 'Abd-al-Malik, Ibn Hubayrah became governor of the 'Irâq and improved the mint. Then Khâlid al-Qasrî, and after him Yûsuf b. 'Umar, made great efforts to improve it. . . .

When 'Abd-al-Malik saw fit to use the mint to protect against fraud the two coins (the gold dinar and the silver dirham) that were current in Muslim transactions, he determined their values as what they had been in the time of 'Umar. He used the iron stamp, but engraved words on it, rather than pictures, because eloquent words were obviously more congenial to the Arabs. Moreover, the religious law forbids pictures.

After ('Abd-al-Malik), the coinage remained the same for the whole Muslim period. Both the dinar and the dirham were round. The inscription on them was written in concentric circles. On one side, the legend included the names of God with the formulas: 'There is no god but God' and 'Praised be God', and the prayer for the Prophet and his family; on the other side, it included the date

217

and the name of the caliph. (Coins were of) this type during the period of the 'Abbâsids, the 'Ubaydid(-Fâṭimids), and the (Spanish) Umayyads. The Ṣinhâjah had no mint except at the end of their rule when al-Manṣûr, the master of Bougie, used one.

For the Almohads, al-Mahdî set the precedent of coining square dirhams and engraving a square on the round dinar. He covered one side of the coins with formulas: 'There is no god but God' and 'Praised be God', and the other with a legend of several lines containing his name, (replaced by) his successors with their names. This became the practice of the Almohads. Their coinage has kept that shape down to this time. It has been reported that before al-Mahdî came forth, he was described as 'master of the square dirham' by the practitioners of magic who predicted the coming of his dynasty.

The present-day inhabitants of the East have no coinage of fixed value. For their transactions, they use dinars and dirhams by weight, and their value is determined through standard weights corresponding to so-and-so many dirhams, or dinars. The mint engraves on them the formula 'There is no god but God' and the prayer for the Prophet, as well as the ruler's name, as is also the practice of the Maghribîs. . . .

The seal

(Use of) the seal is one of the government functions and a royal office. The sealing of letters and diplomas was known to rulers before and after Islam. It has been established that when the Prophet wanted to write to the Byzantine Emperor, he was told that the non-Arabs accepted only sealed letters. Thus, he took a silver seal (ring) and had the following legend engraved upon it: 'Muḥammad, the Messenger of God.' Muḥammad said: 'No one else should use a similar legend.' Abû Bakr, 'Umar, and 'Uthmân have been said to have continued to use that ring for sealing. . . .

The process of sealing expresses the idea of 'end' or 'completion', in the sense that a writing thus sealed is correct and valid. A particular letter somehow becomes effective through the use of such a signature. Without it, it would be invalid and imperfect. The sealing may also be (effected) through something written by hand at the end or the beginning of a letter, some well-chosen words of praise and glory, or the name of the ruler or amir, or of the writer of the letter, whoever he may have been, or through terms descriptive of the writer. Such (formulas) written by hand indicate the correctness and validity of the letter. They are commonly known under the name of 'signature', but are also called 'seal' because they are compared to the impression of the seal ring.

The 'seal' the judge sends to litigants is connected with this usage. That 'seal' is his signature and hand, validating his decisions. The 'seal' of the ruler or caliph, that is, his signature, is also connected with the usage referred to.

It is also possible to impress a seal upon some soft substance, so that the letters of the legend appear on that substance, and to place the substance (with the seal impression) on the knots (of the strings with) which letters are tied, and upon places for deposits (such as storehouses, strong boxes, etc.).

The first to introduce the sealing of letters, that is, the use of signature, was Mu'âwiyah. He also introduced the ministry of the seal. It is composed of the secretaries who see to it that the letters of the ruler are expedited and sealed, either by means of a signature, or by tying them.

Letters are tied either by piercing the paper and tacking (the letter) together (with a string), as is the custom of the secretaries of the Maghrib, or by glueing the top of the sheet to the part of the letter over which the top is folded, as is the custom of the people in the East. Over the place where the letter is pierced and tacked, or where it is glued, a signature is placed. It guarantees that the letter has not been opened and that its contents have not been read. The people of the Maghrib place a piece of wax where the letter is pierced and tacked, and seal it with a seal upon which some signature is engraved for use in sealing, and the engraving is impressed upon the wax. In the old dynasties of the East, the place where the letter was glued was also sealed with an engraved seal that was put into a red paste of clay prepared for that purpose. The engraving of the seal was impressed upon the clay. Under the 'Abbâsid dynasty, this clay was called 'sealing clay'.

(The use of) the seal was peculiar to the ministry of correspondence. In the 'Abbâsid dynasty, it belonged to the wazir. Later on, custom differed. It went to those who were in charge of (official) correspondence and the office of the secretaries in the (various) dynasties. In the Maghrib, people came to consider the seal ring as one of the royal marks and emblems. They made artistic seal rings of gold inlaid with gems of hyacinth (ruby), turquoise, and emerald. The ruler according to their custom wore the seal ring as an insignia.

The ṭirâz

It is part of royal and governmental pomp and dynastic custom to have the names of rulers or their peculiar marks embroidered on the silk, brocade, or pure silk garments that are prepared for their wearing. The writing is brought out by weaving a gold thread or some other coloured thread of a colour different from that of the fabric itself into it. (Its execution) depends upon the skill of the weavers in designing and weaving it. Royal garments are embroidered with such a *ṭirâz*, in order to increase the prestige of the ruler or the person of lower rank who wears such a garment, or in order to increase the prestige of those whom the ruler distinguishes by bestowing upon them his own garment when he wants to honour them or appoint them to one of the offices of the dynasty.

The pre-Islamic non-Arab rulers used to make a *ṭirâz* of pictures and figures of kings, or figures and pictures specifically (designed) for it. The Muslim rulers later on changed that and had their own names embroidered together with other words of good omen or prayer. In the Umayyad and 'Abbâsid dynasties, the *ṭirâz* was one of the most splendid things and honours. The houses within the palaces in which such garments were woven were called '*ṭirâz* houses'. The person who supervised them was called '*ṭirâz* master'. He was in charge of the craftsmen, the implements, and the weavers in (the *ṭirâz* houses), the payment of their wages, the care of their implements, and the control of their work. (The office of *ṭirâz* master) was entrusted by the 'Abbâsids to their intimates and their most trusted clients. The same was the case with the Umayyads in Spain and their successors, the *reyes de taïfas*, as well as with the 'Ubaydid(-Fâṭimids) in Egypt and the eastern non-Arab rulers contemporary with them. When luxury and cultural diversity receded with the receding power of the (great) dynasties, and when the number of (small) dynasties grew, the office and its administration completely ceased to exist in most dynasties. When, at the beginning of the sixth [twelfth] century, the Almohads succeeded the Umayyads, they did not have the *ṭirâz* at the beginning of their dynasty, because they had been taught by their imam Muḥammad b. Tûmart al-Mahdî the ways of religion and simplicity. They were too austere to wear garments of silk and gold. The office (of the *ṭirâz*), therefore, had no place in their dynasty. Their descendants in the later (years) of the dynasty, however, reestablished it in part, but it was not nearly so splendid.

At the present time, we have personally seen quite a lot of (*ṭirâz* manufacture) in the flourishing and proud Merinid dynasty in the Maghrib. The Merinids had learned it from the contemporary dynasty of the Ibn al-Aḥmar (Naṣrids) in Spain. They (in turn) followed the *ṭirâz* customs of the *reyes de taïfas* and achieved in this respect something that speaks for itself.

In the contemporary Turkish dynasty of Egypt and Syria, the *ṭirâz* is very much cultivated in accordance with the importance of the realm (of that dynasty) and the civilization of its country. However, the *ṭirâz* is not produced within the houses and palaces of the dynasty, and it is not an office of the dynasty. (The *ṭirâz*) required by the dynasty is woven by craftsmen familiar with the craft, from silk and pure gold. They call it *zarkash*, a Persian word. The name of the ruler or amir is embroidered on it. It is made by craftsmen for the dynasty, together with other fine products.

Large tents and tent walls

It should be known that among the emblems of royal authority and luxury are small and large tents and canopies of linen, wool, and cotton, with linen and cotton ropes. They are used for display on journeys. They are of different kinds, large or small, according to the affluence of the dynasty. At the beginning of the dynasty, the same type of housing used by the people of the dynasty before they have achieved royal authority, continues to be used. At the time of the first Umayyad caliphs, the Arabs continued to use the dwellings they had, tents of leather and wool. Only a very few of the Arabs had at that date ceased to live in the Bedouin manner. When they went on raids or went to war, they travelled with all their camels, their nomad households, and their dependent women and children, as is still the case with the Arabs at this time. Their armies, therefore, consisted of many nomad households, and the distance between the encampments was great. The groups were widely separated, and each group was too far away to see the other.

The Arab dynasty then adopted diverse ways of sedentary culture and ostentation. People settled in towns and cities. They were transformed from tent dwellers into palace dwellers. They exchanged the camel for the horse and the donkey as riding animals. Now, they used linen fabrics for their dwellings on their journeys, fashioning them into houses (tents) of various shapes and sizes, round, oblong, or square. In this connection, they displayed the greatest possible pomp and art.

Luxurious living then caused women and children to stay behind in their palaces and mansions. People, therefore, travelled light. The spaces between the encampments of the army became less far apart. Army and ruler encamped in one and the same camp, which was completely within the field of vision (of a single observer). It was a pretty sight because of the various colours. This remained the way dynasties displayed their luxury.

It has also been this way in the Almohad and Zanâtah dynasties whose shadow extends over us. At the beginning of their power, when they travelled they used the ordinary sleeping tents they had used before they achieved royal authority. However, eventually, the dynasty adopted the ways of luxury, and people began to dwell in palaces. Then, they turned to using tents both large and small to a greater extent than they had (first) intended.

It is a great luxury. However, armies become more vulnerable to night attacks when they are assembled in one place, where a sudden attack may involve them all. Furthermore, they do not have their families and children with them, and it is for their families and children they would be willing to die. Therefore, other protective measures are needed in this connection.

The prayer enclosure (maqṣûrah) and the prayer during the Friday sermon

These two things are caliphal prerogatives and royal emblems in Islam. They are not known in non-Muslim dynasties.

The enclosure for the ruler to pray in is a latticed screen around the prayer niche (*miḥrâb*), and the space immediately adjacent. The first to use one was Muʿâwiyah b. Abî Sufyân, after a Khârijite had stabbed him. It is also said that the first to use one was Marwân b. al-Ḥakam, after a Yemenite had stabbed him. Afterwards, all the caliphs used it. It became a custom distinguishing the ruler from the rest of the people during prayer. It arises only when dynasties are luxurious and flourishing, as is the case with all pomp.

It remained this way in all Muslim dynasties when the ʿAbbâsid dynasty dissolved and the number of different dynasties in the East grew. It also remained so in Spain when the Umayyad dynasty was destroyed and the *reyes de taïfas* became numerous. As for the Maghrib, the Aghlabids used it in al-Qayrawân. It was used later on by the ʿUbaydid(-Fâṭimid) caliphs and by their Ṣinhâjah governors of the Maghrib. When the Almohads then took possession of all the Maghrib and Spain, they abolished the institution of (the prayer enclosure) in accordance with the desert attitude that characterized them. But then the dynasty flourished and acquired its share of luxury. When the third Almohad ruler, Yaʿqûb al-Manṣûr, appeared, he used a prayer enclosure. Afterwards, its use remained a custom of the rulers of the Maghrib and of Spain. The same was the case with all other dynasties.

As to the prayer from the pulpit (*minbar*) during the Friday sermon, it should be said that the caliphs at first directed the prayers themselves. Therefore, they used to say a prayer (for themselves), after the obligatory prayer for the Prophet and the blessings for the men around him had been spoken.

The first to use a pulpit was ʿAmr b. al-ʿÂṣ when he built his mosque in Egypt. ʿUmar b. al-Khaṭṭâb wrote to him: 'And now: I have heard that you use a pulpit and thus raise yourself above the necks of the Muslims. Is it not sufficient for you that you are standing while the Muslims are at your heels? Therefore, I urge you to smash it to bits.'

When pomp came into being and the caliphs came to be prevented from (personally delivering) the sermon and leading the prayer, they appointed delegates for both tasks. The preacher mentioned the caliph from the pulpit. He mentioned his name in praise and prayed for him, because God had appointed him in the interest of the world, and because a prayer at such an hour was thought likely to be heard.

Only the caliph was (mentioned). But when the time came that the caliphs were secluded and under the control of others, the men who were in control of the dynasties often shared the (prayer) with the caliph, and their names were mentioned after his.

When these dynasties disappeared, (the custom) also disappeared. Only the ruler was privileged to be mentioned in the prayer from the pulpit, and no one else. No one was permitted to share that privilege with the ruler or to aspire to do so.

The founders of dynasties often neglected this institution when the dynasty still had a low standard of living and preserved the negligent and coarse Bedouin attitude. They were satisfied with a summary, anonymous reference to the one entrusted with the affairs of the Muslims. . . .

But when their political eyes were opened and they looked toward all the aspects of royal authority and perfected the details of sedentary culture and the ideas of ostentation and pomp, they adopted all the external attributes (of royal authority) and exhausted all the possibilities in this respect. They disliked the idea that anyone else might share in them, and they were afraid that they might lose them and that their dynasty would be deprived of the effect of them.

35 Wars and the methods of waging war practised by the various nations

Wars and different kinds of fighting have always occurred in the world since God created it. The origin of war is the desire of certain human beings to take revenge on others. Each (party) is supported by the people sharing in its group feeling. When they have sufficiently excited each other for the purpose and the two parties confront each other, one seeking revenge and the other trying to defend itself, there is war. It is something natural among human beings. No nation and no race (generation) is free from it.

The reason for such revenge is as a rule either jealousy and envy, or hostility, or zeal in behalf of God and His religion, or zeal in behalf of royal authority and the effort to found a kingdom.

The first (kind of war) usually occurs between neighbouring tribes and competing families.

The second (kind)—war caused by hostility—is usually found among savage nations living in the desert, such as the Arabs, the Turks, the Turkomans, the Kurds, and similar peoples. They earn their sustenance with their lances and their livelihood by depriving other people of their possessions. They declare war against those who defend their property against them. They have no further desire for rank and royal authority. Their minds and eyes are set only upon depriving other people of their possessions.

The third is the (kind) the religious law calls 'the holy war'.

The fourth (kind), finally, is dynastic war against seceders and those who refuse obedience.

These are the four kinds of war. The first two are unjust and lawless, the other two are holy and just wars.

Since the beginning of men's existence, war has been waged in the world in two ways. One is by advance in closed formation. The other is the technique of attack and withdrawal.

The advance in closed formation has been the technique of all the non-Arabs throughout their entire existence. The technique of attack and withdrawal has been that of the Arabs and of the Berbers of the Maghrib.

Fighting in closed formation is more steady and fierce than fighting with the technique of attack and withdrawal. That is because in fighting in closed formation, the lines are orderly and evenly arranged, like arrows or like rows of worshippers at prayers. People advanced in closed lines against the enemy. This makes for greater steadiness in assault and for better use of the proper tactics. It frightens the enemy more. A closed formation is like a long wall or a well-built castle which no one could hope to move.

It is obvious what great wisdom there is in requiring that the lines be kept steady and in forbidding anyone to fall back during an attack. Those who turn their backs to the enemy bring disorder into the line formation. They are guilty of the crime of causing a rout. Fighting in closed formation was more important (than any other kind) in the opinion of Muḥammad.

Fighting with the technique of attack and withdrawal is not as fierce or as secure against the possibility of rout, as is fighting in closed formation, unless there is set up a steady line formation to the rear, to which the fighting men may fall back in attack and withdrawal throughout the fighting. Such a line formation would take the place of the closed formation.

The ancient dynasties had many soldiers and a vast realm. They subdivided their armies into smaller units. The reason for this was that their soldiers grew exceedingly numerous and were assembled from the most remote regions. This made it unavoidable that some of the soldiers would not know others, when they mingled on the field of battle and engaged the enemy in shooting and close fighting. It was feared lest, on such occasions, they would fall to fighting each other because of the existing confusion and their ignorance of each other. Therefore, they divided the armies into smaller units and put men who knew each other together. They arranged the units in an arrangement resembling the natural one of the four directions of the compass. The chief of all the armies, either the ruler himself or a general, was in the centre. This arrangement was called 'the battle order'. It is mentioned in the history of the Persians, that of the Byzantines, and that of the (Umayyad and 'Abbâsid) dynasties at the beginning of Islam. In front of the ruler stood one army with its own battle lines, its own general and its own flag. It was called 'the advance guard'. Then, to the right of the place where the ruler was, stood another army. It was called 'the right flank'. There was another army to the left, called 'the left flank'. Then, there was another army behind the main army, called 'the rear guard'. The ruler and his entourage stood at the middle of these four (armies). The place where he was, was called the centre. When this ingenious arrangement was completed—covering an area within the field of vision (of a single observer) or extending over a wider area but with at most one or two days' (journey) between each of the two armies, and utilizing the possibilities suggested by the greater or smaller number of soldiers—then, when the battle order was thus set up, the advance in closed formation could begin. This may be exemplified by the history of the (Muslim) conquests and the history of the (Umayyad and 'Abbâsid) dynasties.

Much the same sort of arrangement was also to be found among the Spanish Umayyads. It is not known among us now, because we live in a time when dynasties possess small armies which cannot mistake each other on the field of battle. Most of the soldiers of both parties together could nowadays be assembled in a hamlet or a town. Everyone of them knows his comrade and calls him by his name and surname in the thick of battle. Therefore, this particular battle order can be dispensed with.

One of the techniques of the people who use the method of attack and withdrawal, is to set up, behind their armies, a (barricade) of solid objects and dumb animals to serve as a refuge for the cavalry during attack and withdrawal. It is intended to steady the fighters, so that they will fight more persistently and have a better chance of winning.

Those who fight in closed formation do the same, in order to increase their steadfastness and power. The Persians who fought in closed formation used to employ elephants in their wars. They made them carry wooden towers like castles, loaded with combatants, weapons, and flags. They disposed them in successive lines behind them in the thick of battle, as if they were fortresses. This fortified them psychologically and gave them added confidence.

In this connection, one may compare what happened at al-Qâdisîyah. On the third day, the Persians pressed the Muslims hard with (the elephants). Eventually, some outstanding Arabs counterattacked, infiltrated among the elephants, and struck them on the trunk with their swords. (The elephants) fled and turned back to their stables in al-Madâ'in. This paralysed the Persian camp, and they fled on the fourth day.

The Byzantines, the Gothic rulers in Spain, and most other non-Arab peoples used to employ thrones for the purpose of steadying the battle lines. A throne would be set up for the ruler in the thick of battle and surrounded by those of the ruler's servants, entourage, and soldiers who were thought to be willing to die for him. Flags were run up at the corners of the throne. A further wall of sharpshooters and foot soldiers was put around it. The throne thus assumed considerable dimensions. It became, for the fighters, a place to fall back upon and a refuge in attack and withdrawal. This was what the Persians did in the battle of al-Qâdisîyah. Rustum sat upon a throne that had been set up for him there. Finally, the Persian lines became disordered, and the Arabs penetrated to his throne. He abandoned it and went to the Euphrates, where he was killed.

The Arabs and most other Bedouin nations that move about and employ the technique of attack and withdrawal, dispose their camels and the pack animals carrying their litters in lines to steady the fighting men. (Such lines) become for them a place to fall back upon. Every nation that follows this technique can be observed to be more steady in battle and to be better protected against being surprised and routed. This is a well-attested fact, but it has been altogether neglected by the contemporary dynasties. Instead, they dispose the pack animals carrying their baggage and large tents behind them, as a rear guard. These animals cannot take the place of elephants and camels. Therefore, the armies are exposed to the danger of being routed, and they are always ready to flee in combat.

At the beginning of Islam, all battles were fought in closed formation, although the Arabs knew only the technique of attack and withdrawal. Two things at the beginning of Islam caused them to (fight in closed formation). First, their enemies fought in closed formation, and they were thus forced to fight them in the same way. Second, they were willing to die in the holy war, because they wished to prove their endurance and were very firm in their belief. Now, the closed formation is the fighting technique most suitable for one willing to die.

When luxury penetrated the various dynasties, the use of the rally line behind the fighters was forgotten. This was because when they were Bedouins and lived in tents, they had many camels, and the women and children lived in camp with them. Then they achieved royal luxury and became used to living in palaces and in a sedentary environment and they abandoned the ways of the desert and waste regions. At that time, they forgot the period of camels and litters, and it was difficult for them to use them. When they travelled, they left their women behind. Royal authority and luxury caused them to use tents both large and small. They restricted themselves to pack animals carrying baggage and tents. They used these things to form their (protective) line in war. It was by no means sufficient. These things, unlike one's own family and property, do not inspire any willingness to die. People, therefore, have little endurance. The turmoil of the battle frightens them, and their lines crumble.

We have mentioned the strength that a line formation behind the army gives to the fighters who use the technique of attack and withdrawal. Therefore the Maghribî rulers have come to employ groups of European Christians in their army, and they are the only ones to have done that, for their compatriots know only the technique of attack and withdrawal. The position of the ruler is strengthened by establishing a line formation in support of the fighting men ahead of it. The men in such a line formation must be people who are used to hold firm in closed formation. If not, they will run away like the men who use the technique of attack and withdrawal, and, when they run away, the ruler and the army will be routed. Therefore, the rulers of the Maghrib had to use soldiers from a nation used to hold firm in closed formation. That nation was the European Christians. The Maghribî rulers do that despite the fact that it means utilizing the aid of unbelievers. They fear that their own line formation might run away, and (they know that) the European Christians know only how to hold firm, because it is their custom to fight in closed formation. They are, therefore, more suitable for the purpose than others. However, the Maghribî rulers employ (such European Christians) only in wars against Arab and Berber nations, in order to force them into submission. They do not use them for the holy war, because they are afraid that they might take sides against the Muslims. Such is the situation in the Maghrib at this time.

We hear that the fighting (technique) of the contemporary Turkish nations is the shooting of arrows. Their battle order consists of a line formation. They divide their army into three lines, one placed behind the other. They dismount from their horses, empty their quivers on the ground in front of them, and then shoot from a sitting position. Each line protects the one ahead of it against being overrun by the enemy, until victory is assured for one party. This is a very good and remarkable battle order.

In war, the ancients followed the method of digging trenches around their camps when they were about to attack, because they were afraid of treacherous night attacks and assaults by night upon the camp, since darkness and wildness multiply fear. Under such conditions, the soldiers might seek refuge in flight and would find in the darkness a psychological protection against the shame of (fleeing). If all the soldiers were to do the same, the camp would be dis-organized, and there would be a rout. Therefore, they were accustomed to dig trenches around the camp. They set up their tents and made trenches all around them on every side, lest the enemy be able to get through them in a night attack, in which case they would abandon each other.

Dynasties were able to do such things involving large concentrations of manpower, wherever they settled, because civilization was prosperous and royal authority impressive. But when civilization was ruined, and (strong dynasties) were succeeded by weak dynasties with few soldiers and no workers, the thing was altogether forgotten, as if it had never been.

One should think of the admonitions and encouragement that 'Alî gave his men on the day of Ṣiffîn. One will find in them a good deal of military knowledge. No one had better insight into military matters than 'Alî. He said in one of his speeches: 'Straighten out your lines like a strongly constructed building.

'Place the armed men in front, and those who are not armed in the rear.

'Bite on your molars. This makes it harder for sword blows to harm the head.

'Keep something wrapped around the tips of your spears. This preserves the sharpness of their points.

'Keep your eyes down. This keeps the soul more concentrated and gives greater peace to the heart.

'Do not hold your flags inclined and do not remove them. Place them in the hands only of those among you who are brave.

'Call upon truth and endurance for aid, for "after endurance there is victory". . . .'

There is no certainty of victory in war, even when the equipment and the numerical (superiority) that cause victory exist. Victory and superiority in war come from luck and chance. This is explained by the fact that the causes of superiority are, as a rule, a combination of several factors. There are external factors, such as the number of soldiers, the perfection and good quality of weapons, the number of brave men, (skilful) arrangement of the line formation, the proper tactics, and similar things. Then, there are hidden factors. These may be the result of human trickery, such as spreading alarming news and rumours to cause defections (in the ranks of the enemy); occupying high points, so that one is able to attack from above, which surprises those below and causes them to abandon each other; hiding in thickets or depressions and concealing oneself from the enemy in rocky terrain, so that one's own armies suddenly appear when (the enemy) is in a precarious situation, and he must then flee to safety (instead of defending himself), and similar things. These hidden factors may also be celestial matters, which man has no power to produce for himself. They affect people psychologically, and thus generate fear in them. They cause confusion in the centres of armies, and there are routs. Routs very often are the result of hidden causes, because both parties make much use of (the opportunities offered by) them in their desire for victory. One of them must by necessity be successful in their use. Muḥammad said: 'War is trickery.' An Arab proverb says: 'Many a trick is worth more than a tribe.'

It is thus clear that superiority in war is, as a rule, the result of hidden causes, not of external ones. The occurrence of opportunities as the result of hidden causes is what is meant by the word 'luck'. This explains Muḥammad's victory with small numbers over the polytheists during his lifetime, and the victories of the Muslims during the Muslim conquests after Muḥammad's death. Terror in the hearts of their enemies was why there were so many routs during the Muslim conquests, but it was a factor concealed from men's eyes.

Aṭ-Ṭurṭûshî mentions that one of the reasons for victory in war is that one side may have a larger number of brave and famous knights than the other. For instance, one side may have ten or twenty famous heroes, and the other only eight or sixteen. The side that has more, even if only one more, will be victorious. He states this very emphatically. He is referring to the external causes we have mentioned before, but he is not right. What is the fact proven to make for superiority is the situation with regard to group feeling. If one side has a group feeling comprising all, while the other side is made up of numerous different groups, and if both sides are approximately the same in numbers, then the side with a united group feeling is stronger than, and superior to, the side that is made up of several different groups. . . .

36 Taxation and the reason for low and high tax revenues

It should be known that at the beginning of a dynasty, taxation yields a large revenue from small assessments. At the end of the dynasty, taxation yields a small revenue from large assessments.

The reason for this is that when the dynasty follows the ways of Islam, it imposes only such taxes as are stipulated by the religious law, such as charity taxes, the land tax, and the poll tax. These have fixed limits that cannot be exceeded.

When the dynasty follows the ways of group feeling and (political) superiority, it necessarily has at first a desert attitude, as has been mentioned before. The desert attitude requires kindness, reverence, humility, respect for the property of other people, and disinclination to appropriate it, except in rare instances. Therefore, the individual imposts and assessments, which together constitute the tax revenue, are low. When tax assessments and imposts upon the subjects are low, the latter have the energy and desire to do things. Cultural enterprises grow and increase, because the low taxes bring satisfaction. When cultural enterprises grow, the number of individual imposts and assessments mounts. In consequence, the tax revenue, which is the sum total of (the individual assessments), increases.

When the dynasty continues in power and their rulers follow each other in succession, they become sophisticated. The Bedouin attitude and simplicity lose their significance, and the Bedouin qualities of moderation and restraint disappear. Royal authority with its tyranny and sedentary culture that stimulates sophistication, make their appearance. The people of the dynasty then acquire qualities of character related to cleverness. Their customs and needs become more varied because of the prosperity and luxury in which they are immersed. As a result, the individual imposts and assessments upon the subjects, agricultural labourers, farmers, and all the other taxpayers, increase. Every individual impost and assessment is greatly increased, in order to obtain a higher tax revenue. Customs duties are placed upon articles of commerce and (levied) at the city gates. Then, gradual increases in the amount of the assessments succeed each other regularly, in correspondence with the gradual increase in the luxury customs and many needs of the dynasty and the spending required in connection with them. Eventually, the taxes will weigh heavily upon the subjects and overburden them. Heavy taxes become an obligation and tradition, because the increases took place gradually, and no one knows specifically who increased them or levied them. They lie upon the subjects like an obligation and tradition.

The assessments increase beyond the limits of equity. The result is that the interest of the subjects in cultural enterprises disappears, since when they compare expenditures and taxes with their income and gain and see the little profit they make, they lose all hope. Therefore, many of them refrain from all cultural activity. The result is that the total tax revenue goes down, as individual assessments go down. Often, when the decrease is noticed, the amounts of individual imposts are increased. This is considered a means of compensating for the decrease. Finally, individual imposts and assessments reach their limit. It would be of no avail to increase them further. The costs of all cultural enterprise are now too high, the taxes are too heavy, and the profits anticipated fail to materialize. Finally, civilization is destroyed, because the incentive for cultural activity is gone. It is the dynasty that suffers from the situation, because it profits from cultural activity.

If one understands this, he will realize that the strongest incentive for cultural activity is to lower as much as possible the amounts of individual imposts levied upon persons capable of undertaking cultural enterprises. In this manner, such persons will be psychologically disposed to undertake them, because they can be confident of making a profit from them.

37 In the later years of dynasties, customs duties are levied

At the beginning, dynasties maintain the Bedouin attitude. Therefore, they have few needs, since luxury and the habits that go with it do not yet exist. Expenses and expenditures are small. At that time, revenue from taxes pays for much more than the necessary expenditure, and there is a large surplus.

The dynasty, then, soon starts to adopt the luxury and luxury customs of sedentary culture, and follows the course that had been taken by previous dynasties. The result is that the expenses of the people of the dynasty grow. Especially do the expenses of the ruler mount excessively, on account of his expenditure for his entourage and the great number of allowances he has to grant. The revenue from taxes cannot pay for all that. Therefore, the dynasty must increase its revenues, because the militia needs ever larger allowances and the ruler needs more money to meet his expenditure. At first, the amounts of individual imposts and assessments are increased; then, as expenses and needs increase under the influence of the gradual growth of luxury customs and additional allowances for the militia, the dynasty is affected by senility. Its people are too weak to collect the taxes from the provinces and remote areas. Thus, the revenue from taxes decreases, while the habits (requiring money) increase. As they increase, salaries and allowances to the soldiers also increase. Therefore, the ruler must invent new kinds of taxes. He levies them on commerce. He imposes taxes of a certain amount on prices realized in the markets and on the various (imported) goods at the city gates. (The ruler) is, after all, forced to this because people have become spoiled by generous allowances, and because of the growing numbers of soldiers and militiamen. In the later (years) of a dynasty, (taxation) may become excessive. Business falls off, because all hopes (of profit) are destroyed, permitting the dissolution of civilization and reflecting upon (the status of) the dynasty. This (situation) becomes more and more aggravated, until the dynasty disintegrates.

Much of this sort happened in the Eastern cities during the later days of the 'Abbâsid and 'Ubaydid-Fâṭimid dynasties. Taxes were levied even upon pilgrims making the pilgrimage. The same also happened in Spain at the time of the *reyes de taïfas*

38 Commercial activity on the part of the ruler is harmful to his subjects and ruinous to the tax revenue

A dynasty may find itself in financial straits, as we have mentioned before, on account of the number of (its luxurious) habits and on account of its expenditure and the insufficiency of the tax revenue to pay for its needs. It may require more money and higher revenues. Then, it sometimes imposes customs duties on the commercial activities of its subjects. Sometimes, it increases the kinds of customs duties, if (customs duties as such) had been introduced before. Sometimes, it applies torture to its officials and tax collectors and sucks their bones dry. (This happens) when officials and tax collectors are observed to have appropriated a good deal of tax money, which their accounts do not show.

Sometimes, the ruler himself may engage in commerce and agriculture, from desire to increase his revenues. He sees that merchants and farmers make (large) profits and have plenty of property and that their gains correspond to the capital they invest. Therefore, he starts to acquire livestock and fields in order to cultivate them for profit, purchase goods, and expose himself to fluctuations of the market. He thinks that this will improve his revenues and increase his profits.

However, this is a great error. It causes harm to the subjects in many ways. First, farmers and merchants will find it difficult to buy livestock and merchandise and to procure cheaply the things that belong to (farming and commerce). The subjects have all the same or approximately the same amount of wealth. Competition between them already exhausts, or comes close to exhausting, their financial resources. Now, when the ruler, who has so much more money than they, competes with them, scarcely a single one of them will any longer be able to obtain the things he wants, and everybody will become worried and unhappy.

Furthermore, the ruler can appropriate much of (the agricultural produce and the available merchandise), if it occurs to him. (He can do this) by force or by buying things up at the cheapest possible price. Further, there may be no one who would dare to bid against him. Thus, he will be able to force the seller to lower his price. Further, when agricultural products such as corn, silk, honey, and sugar, etc., or goods of any kind, become available, the ruler cannot wait for a favourable market and a boom, because he has to take care of government needs. Therefore, he forces the merchants or farmers who deal in these particular products to buy from him. He will be satisfied only with the highest prices and more. (The merchants and farmers, on the other hand), will exhaust their liquid capital in such transactions. The merchandise they thus acquire will remain useless on their hands. They themselves will no longer be able to trade, which is what enables them to earn something and make their living. Often, they need money. Then, they have to sell the goods (that they were forced to buy from the ruler), at the lowest prices, during a slump in the market. Often, the merchant or farmer has to do the same thing over again. He thus exhausts his capital and has to go out of business.

This becomes an oft-repeated process. The trouble and financial difficulties and the loss of profit that it causes the subjects take away from them all incentives to effort, thus ruining the fiscal (structure). Most of the revenue from taxes comes from farmers and merchants, especially once customs duties have been introduced and the tax revenue has been augmented by means of them. Thus, when the farmer gives up agriculture and the merchant goes out of business, the revenue from taxes vanishes altogether or becomes dangerously low.

Were the ruler to compare the revenue from taxes with the small profits (he reaps from trading himself), he would find the latter negligible in comparison with the former. Even if (his trading) were profitable, it would still deprive him of a good deal of his revenue from taxes, so far as commerce is concerned. It is unlikely that customs duties would be levied on (the ruler's commercial activities). If, however, the same deals were made by others, the customs duties would be included in the tax total.

Furthermore, (the trading of the ruler) may cause the destruction of civilization and hence the disintegration of the dynasty. When the subjects can no longer make their capital larger through agriculture and commerce, it will decrease and disappear as the result of expenditure. This will ruin their situation.

The Persians made no one king except members of the royal house. Further, they chose him from among those who possessed virtue, religion, education, liberality, bravery, and nobility. Then, they stipulated in addition that he should be just. Also, he was not to take a farm, as this would harm his neighbours. He was not to engage in trade, as this would of necessity raise the prices of all goods. And he was not to use slaves as servants, since they would not give good and beneficial advice.

It should be known that the finances of a ruler can be increased, and his financial resources improved, only through the revenue from taxes. This can be improved only through the equitable treatment of people with property and regard for them, so that their hopes rise, and they have the incentive to start making their capital bear fruit and grow. This, in turn, increases the ruler's revenues in taxes.

Amirs and other men in power in a country who engage in commerce and agriculture, reach a point where they undertake to buy agricultural products and goods from their owners who come to them, at prices fixed by themselves as they see fit. Then, they resell these things to the subjects under their control, at the proper times, at prices fixed by themselves. This is even more dangerous, harmful, and ruinous for the subjects than the aforementioned (procedure). The ruler is often influenced to choose such a (course) by those sorts of people—I mean, merchants and farmers—who bring him into contact with the profession in which they have been reared. They work with him, but for their own profit, to garner quickly as much money as they may wish, especially through profits reaped from doing business without having to pay taxes and customs duties. Exemption from taxes and customs duties is more likely than anything else to cause one's capital to grow, and it brings quick profits. These people do not understand how much damage is caused the ruler by each decrease in the revenue from taxes. The ruler, therefore, must guard against such persons, and not pay any attention to suggestions that are harmful to his revenues and his rule.

*39   The ruler and his entourage are wealthy only in the middle period
of the dynasty*

The reason for this is that at the beginning of the dynasty, the
revenues are distributed among the tribe and the people who share
in the ruler's group feeling, in accordance with their usefulness and
group feeling and because they are needed to establish the dynasty.
Under these circumstances, their leader refrains in their favour from
(claiming) the revenues which they would like to have. He feels
compensated by the control over them that he hopes to establish.
They can put pressure on him, and he needs them. His share of the
revenues is restricted to the very small (amounts) he needs. Consequently, the members of his entourage and company, his wazirs,
secretaries, and clients, usually can be observed to be destitute. Their
position is restricted, because it depends on the position of their
master, and his authority is narrowed down by the competition of
the people who share in his group feeling.

Then, when royal authority has come into its own and the ruler
has obtained control over his people, he prevents them from getting
(any part of) the revenues, beyond their official shares. Their portions shrink, because their usefulness to the dynasty has diminished.
Their influence has been checked, and clients and followers have
come to share with them in the support of the dynasty and the
establishment of its power. At this time, the ruler disposes alone of
the whole income from taxes, or the greater part of it. He keeps this
money, and holds it for spending on important projects. His wealth
grows. His treasuries are filled. The authority of his position expands,
and he dominates all his people. As a consequence, the men of his
entourage and retinue, the wazir, the secretary, the doorkeeper, the
client, and the policeman, all become more important, and their
positions expand. They acquire property and enrich themselves.

Then, when the dynasty starts to become senile, as the result of
the dissolution of group feeling and the disappearance of the tribe
that founded it, the ruler needs supporters and helpers, because there
are then many seceders, rivals, and rebels, and there is the fear of
destruction. His revenues then go to his allies and supporters, military men who have their own group feelings. He spends his treasures
and revenues on attempts to restore (the power of) the dynasty.
Moreover, the revenue from taxes decreases, because there are many
allowances to be paid and expenditure to be made. The revenues
from the land tax decrease. The dynasty's need for money becomes
more urgent. The intimates, the doorkeepers, and the secretaries no
longer live under the shadow of prosperity and luxury, as their
positions lose importance and the authority of the ruler shrinks.

The ruler's need for money at this time becomes even more urgent. The new generation within his inner circle and entourage spend the money with which their fathers had enriched themselves, for a purpose for which it was not intended, namely, that of helping the ruler. They begin to be no longer as sincerely loyal as their fathers and ancestors had been. The ruler, in turn, becomes of the opinion that he is more entitled than they to the wealth that was acquired during the reign of his predecessors and with the help of their position. He takes it and appropriates it for himself, gradually and according to their ranks. Thus the dynasty makes itself unpopular with them. It loses its entourage and great personalities and its rich and wealthy intimates. A great part of the edifice of glory crumbles, after having been supported and built up to a great height by those who shared in it.

Anticipating such dangerous situations, most of the people in the dynasty try to avoid holding any government position. They try to escape from government control and go to some other region with the government property they have acquired. They are of the opinion that this will be more wholesome for them and give them the opportunity to spend and enjoy (their money) in greater safety. This assumption is a great mistake and a self-deception that will ruin them materially.

It should be known that it is difficult and impossible to escape (from official life) after having once been in it. When the person who has such intentions is the ruler himself, his subjects and the people who share in his group feeling and crowd around him will not for a moment permit him to escape. If any such (intention) on his part becomes visible, it means the destruction of his realm and his own ruin, the usual result in such a case, for it is difficult to escape from the servitude of royal authority, especially when the dynasty has reached its peak and its authority is shrinking, and it is becoming more remote from glory and good qualities, and acquiring bad qualities.

If the person who intends to escape is one of the ruler's inner circle and entourage or one of the dignitaries in his dynasty, he rarely is given the opportunity to do so. The reason is, in the first place, that rulers consider their people and entourage and, indeed, all their subjects as slaves familiar with their thoughts and sentiments. Therefore, they are not disposed to loosen the bonds of servitude binding those persons. They want to avoid the chance that someone (outside) might come to know (their secrets) and their circumstances (through such persons), and they are averse to letting them become the servants of others.

The Spanish Umayyads thus prevented their people from going abroad to fulfil the duty of the pilgrimage. They were afraid they might fall into the hands of the 'Abbâsids. During all their days, none of their people made the pilgrimage. The pilgrimage was again permitted to (Spaniards) who belonged to the dynasties in Spain, only after the Umayyad rule had come to an end, and Spain had reverted to control of the *reyes de taïfas*.

In the second place, even if rulers were kind enough to loosen the bonds (of a person who intended to escape from their control), their kindness would not extend to leaving his property alone. They consider it part of their own wealth—in the same way that its owner has been part of their dynasty—inasmuch as it was obtained only through the dynasty and under the shadow of its authority. Therefore, they are most eager to take his property and to let it remain as it is, as something belonging to the dynasty that they are entitled to use.

Furthermore, assuming that he gets away with his property to some other region, which happens in very rare cases, (he is not safe there either, because) the eyes of the rulers in that region fall on him, and they dispossess him by indirect threats and intimidation or by open force. They consider (his property) as revenue or as government property, which should be spent in the public interest. If the eyes of (rulers) can fall upon rich and wealthy people who have acquired their money in the exercise of a profession, it is all the more understandable that their eyes can fall upon tax moneys and government property, to which they have access by law and custom. . . .

40 Curtailment of the allowances given by the ruler implies curtailment of the tax revenue

The reason for this is that dynasty and government serve as the world's greatest market-place, providing the substance of civilization. Now, if the ruler holds on to property and revenue, or they are lost or not properly used by him, then the property in the possession of the ruler's entourage will be small. The gifts which they, in their turn, had been used to give to their entourage and people, stop, and all their expenditure is cut down. They constitute the greatest number of people (who make expenditures), and their expenditure provides more of the substance of trade than that of any other (group). (When they stop spending), business slumps and commercial profits decline because of the shortage of capital. Revenues from the land tax decrease, because the land tax and taxation depend on cultural activity, commercial transactions, business prosperity, and the people's demand for gain and profit. It is the dynasty that suffers

237

from the situation, because under these circumstances the property of the ruler decreases in consequence of the decrease in revenues from the land tax. The dynasty is the greatest market, the mother and base of all trade, the substance of income and expenditure. If government business slumps and the volume of trade is small, the dependent markets will naturally show the same symptoms, and to a greater degree. Furthermore, money circulates between subjects and ruler, moving back and forth. Now, if the ruler keeps it to himself, it is lost to the subjects.

41 Injustice brings about the ruin of civilization

Attacks on people's property remove the incentive to acquire and gain property. People, then, become of the opinion that the purpose and ultimate destiny of (acquiring property) is to have it taken away from them. The extent and degree to which property rights are infringed upon determines the extent and degree to which the efforts of the subjects to acquire property slacken. When attacks on (property) are extensive and general, affecting all means of making a livelihood, business inactivity, too, becomes general. If the attacks upon property are but light, the stoppage of gainful activity is correspondingly slight. Civilization and its well-being as well as business prosperity depend on productivity and people's efforts in all directions in their own interest and profit. When people no longer do business in order to make a living, and when they cease all gainful activity, the business of civilization slumps, and everything decays. People scatter everywhere in search of sustenance, to places outside the jurisdiction of their present government. The population of the particular region becomes sparse. The settlements there become empty. The cities lie in ruins. The disintegration causes the disintegration of the status of dynasty and ruler, because (their peculiar status) constitutes the form of civilization and the form necessarily decays when its matter (in this case, civilization) decays.

One may compare here the story that al-Mas'ûdî tells in connection with the history of the Persians. In the days of King Bahrâm b. Bahrâm, the Môbedhân, the chief religious dignitary among the Persians, expressed to the King his disapproval of the latter's injustice and indifference to the consequences that his injustice must bring upon the dynasty. He did this through a parable, which he placed in the mouth of an owl. The King, hearing an owl's cry, asked the Môbedhân whether he understood what it was saying. He replied: 'A male owl wanted to marry a female owl. The female owl, as a condition prior to consent, asked the male owl for the gift of twenty villages ruined in the days of Bahrâm, that she might hoot in them. (The male owl) accepted her condition and said to her: "If the King continues to rule, I shall give you a thousand ruined villages. This is of all wishes the easiest to fulfil." '

The King was stirred out of his negligence by that story. He had a private (talk) with the Môbedhân and asked him what he had in mind. He replied: 'O King, the might of royal authority materializes only through the religious law, obedience toward God, and compliance with His commands and prohibitions. The religious law persists only through royal authority. Mighty royal authority is achieved only through men. Men persist only with the help of property. The only way to property is through cultivation. The only way to cultivation is through justice. Justice is a balance set up among mankind. The Lord set it up and appointed an overseer of it, and that is the ruler. You, O King, went after the farms and took them away from their owners and cultivators. They are the people who pay the land tax and from whom one gets money. You gave their farms as fiefs to your entourage and servants and to sluggards. They did not cultivate them and did not heed the consequences. (They did not look for the things) that would be good for the farms. They were leniently treated with regard to the land tax (and were not asked to pay it), because they were close to the king. The remaining landowners who did pay the land tax and cultivated their farms had to carry an unjust burden. Therefore, they left their farms and abandoned their settlements. They took refuge in farms that were far away or difficult (of access), and lived on them. Thus, cultivation slackened, and the farms were ruined. There was little money, and soldiers and subjects perished. Neighbouring rulers coveted the Persian realm, because they were aware of the fact that the basic materials that alone maintain the foundation of a realm had been cut off.'

When the King heard that, he proceeded to look into (the affairs of) his realm. The farms were taken away from the intimates of the ruler and restored to their owners. They were again treated, as they had formerly been treated. They began again to cultivate (their farms). Those who had been weak gained in strength. The land was cultivated, and the country became prosperous. There was much money for the collectors of the land tax. The army was strengthened. The enemies' sources of (strength) were cut off. The frontier garrisons were manned. The ruler proceeded to take personal charge of his affairs. His days were prosperous, and his realm was well organized.

The lesson this teaches is that injustice ruins civilization, which has as its consequence the complete destruction of the dynasty. In this connection, one should disregard the fact that dynasties (centred) in great cities often infringe upon justice and still are not ruined. It should be known that this is the result of a relationship that exists between such infringements and the situation of the urban population. When a city is large and densely populated and unlimited in the variety of its conditions, the loss it suffers from hostile acts and injustice is small, because such losses take place gradually. Because of the great variety of conditions and the manifold productivity of a particular city, any loss may remain concealed. Its consequences will become visible only after some time. Thus, the dynasty which committed the infringements (of justice) may be replaced before the city is ruined. Another dynasty may make its appearance and restore the city with the help of its wealth. Thus, the (previous) loss which had remained concealed is made up and is scarcely noticed. This, however, happens only rarely. The proven fact is that civilization inevitably suffers losses through injustice and hostile acts, as we have mentioned, and it is the dynasty that suffers consequently.

Injustice should not be understood to imply only the confiscation of money or other property from the owners, without compensation and without cause. It is commonly understood in that way, but it is something more general than that. Whoever takes someone's property, or uses him for forced labour, or presses an unjustified claim against him, or imposes upon him a duty not required by the religious law, does an injustice to that particular person. People who collect unjustified taxes commit an injustice. Those who infringe upon property commit an injustice. Those who take away property commit an injustice. Those who deny people their rights commit an injustice. Those who, in general, take property by force, commit an injustice. It is the dynasty that suffers from all these acts, inasmuch as civilization, which is the substance of the dynasty, is ruined when people have lost all incentive.

This is what Muḥammad actually had in mind when he forbade injustice. He meant the resulting destruction and ruin of civilization, which ultimately permits the eradication of the human species. This is what the religious law quite generally and wisely aims at in emphasizing five things as necessary: the preservation of (1) religion, (2) the soul (life), (3) the intellect, (4) progeny, and (5) property.

Since, as we have seen, injustice calls for the eradication of the species by leading to the ruin of civilization, it contains in itself a good reason for being prohibited. Consequently, it is important that it be forbidden.

If injustice were to be committed by every individual, the list of deterring punishments that would then have been given for it (in the religious law) would be as large as that given for the other (crimes) which lead to the destruction of the human species and which everybody is capable of committing, such as adultery, murder, and drunkenness. However, injustice can be committed only by persons who cannot be touched, only by persons who have power and authority. Therefore, injustice has been very much censured, and repeated threats against it have been expressed in the hope that perhaps the persons who are able to commit injustice will find a restraining influence in themselves.

One of the greatest injustices and one contributing most to the destruction of civilization is the unjustified imposition of tasks and the use of the subjects for forced labour. This is so because labour belongs to the things that constitute capital. Gain and sustenance represent the value realized from labour among civilized people. By their efforts and all their labours they (acquire) capital and (make a) profit. They have no other way to make a profit except (through labour). Subjects employed in cultural enterprises gain their livelihood and profit from such activities. Now, if they are obliged to work outside their own field and are used for forced labour unrelated to their (ordinary ways of) making a living, they no longer have any profit and are thus deprived of the price of their labour, which is their capital (asset). They suffer, and a good deal of their livelihood is gone, or even all of it. If this occurs repeatedly, all incentive to cultural enterprise is destroyed, and they cease utterly to make an effort. This leads to the destruction and ruin of civilization.

An injustice even greater and more destructive of civilization and the dynasty is the appropriation of people's property by buying their possessions as cheaply as possible and then reselling the merchandise to them at the highest possible prices by means of forced sales and purchases. Often, people have to accept (high) prices with the privilege of later payment. They console themselves for the loss they suffer with the hope that the market will fluctuate in favour of the merchandise that had been sold to them at such a high price, and that their loss will be cancelled later on. But then, they are required to make payment at once, and they are forced to sell the merchandise at the lowest possible price. The loss involved in the two transactions affects their capital.

This (situation) affects all kinds of merchants, those resident in town and those who import merchandise from elsewhere, the pedlars and shopkeepers who deal in food and fruit, and the craftsmen who deal in the instruments and implements that are in general use. The loss affects all professions and classes quite generally. This goes on from hour to hour. It causes capital funds to dwindle. The only possibility that remains is for the merchants to go out of business, because their capital is gone, as it can no longer be restored by the profits. Merchants who come from elsewhere for the purchase and sale of merchandise are slow to come, because of that situation. Business declines, and the subjects lose their livelihood, which, generally, comes from trading. Therefore, if no (trading) is being done in the markets, they have no livelihood, and the tax revenue of the ruler decreases or deteriorates, since, in the middle (period) of a dynasty and later on, most of the tax revenue comes from customs duties on commerce. This leads to the dissolution of the dynasty and the decay of urban civilization. The disintegration comes about gradually and imperceptibly.

This happens whenever the ways and means of seizing property described above are used. On the other hand, if it is taken outright and if the hostile acts are extended to affect the property, the wives, the lives, the skins, and the honour of people, it will lead to sudden disintegration and decay and the quick destruction of the dynasty. It will result in disturbances leading to complete destruction.

On account of these evil consequences, all such (unfair activities) are prohibited by the religious law. The religious law legalizes the use of cunning in trading, but forbids depriving people of their property illegally. The purpose is to prevent such evil (consequences), which would lead to the destruction of civilization through disturbances or the lack of opportunity to make a living.

It should be known that all these (practices) are caused by the need for more money on the part of dynasty and ruler, because they have become accustomed to luxurious living. Their expenditure increases, and much spending is done. Their ordinary income does not meet (the expenditures). Therefore, the ruler invents new sorts and kinds of taxes, in order to increase the revenues and to be able to balance the budget. But luxury continues to grow, and spending increases on account of it. The need for (appropriating) people's property becomes stronger and stronger. In this way, the authority of the dynasty shrinks until its influence is wiped out and its identity lost and it is defeated by an attacker.

42 How it happens that access to the ruler becomes restricted in the dynasty. Such restriction becomes important when the dynasty grows senile

At the beginning, the dynasty is remote from royal aspirations. It needs group feeling through which its power and domination can materialize, and the desert attitude is characteristic of group feeling.

A dynasty based upon religion is remote from royal aspirations. In one based exclusively upon superior (political) power, the desert attitude, through which superiority is achieved, likewise is remote from royal aspirations and ways.

Now, if a dynasty at the beginning of its rule is a Bedouin one, the ruler possesses austerity and the desert attitude. He is close to the people and easily accessible. Then, when his power is firmly established, he comes to claim all the glory for himself. He needs to keep away from the people and to remain aloof with his friends, in order to be able to talk with them about his (private) affairs, since his following has by then become large. Therefore, he seeks to keep away from the common people as much as possible. He employs someone at his door to admit those of his friends and of the people of the dynasty whom he cannot avoid, and to prevent people (in general) from having access to him.

Then, when royal authority flourishes and royal ways and aspirations make their appearance, the ruler adopts royal character qualities. They are strange, peculiar qualities. They must be carefully dealt with in the proper way by those who are in contact with them. Persons in contact with (rulers) often do not know about these qualities and may do something that (rulers) do not like. He may become displeased with them and get into the mood of punishing them. Thus, knowledge of manners to be used in intercourse with (rulers) became the sole property of their special friends. (The rulers) kept all except their intimates from meeting them at all times, so as to protect themselves against noticing anything that might displease them and in order to protect the people against exposing themselves to punishment. Thus, (they) introduced another entrance restriction even more selective than the first. The first concerns the ruler's special friends and prevents everyone else's admission. The second restriction concerns the meetings with those friends and prevents admission of everyone else from among the common people.

The first entrance restriction originated in the days of Mu'âwiyah and 'Abd-al-Malik and the Umayyad caliphs. Then, the 'Abbâsid dynasty made its appearance. Its famous luxury and power came into being, and the royal qualities reached their proper perfection in it. This called for the second entrance restriction. The name of 'doorkeeper' was restricted to it. The court of the caliphs contained two buildings to house their retinue, one for the special group and another for the common people. This is stated in 'Abbâsid history.

In the later dynasties, a third entrance restriction came into being. It was even more selective than the two previous ones. This occurred at the period when the attempt was made to seclude the ruler. It resulted from the fact that the first step taken by the men of the dynasty and intimates of the ruler who set up the young princes and attempted to gain control over them, was to keep the inner circle and the special friends of (the young ruler's) father away from him. The person who attempted to gain control over the young ruler suggested to him that it would diminish respect for him and would

243

destroy the rules of etiquette if these men were to be in contact with him. His purpose was to keep the young ruler from meeting anybody else and see to it that he would become so used to him that he would not want to replace him with anybody else until he securely dominated him. An entrance restriction such as (the third) was obviously required under these circumstances. It indicates the senility and decline of the dynasty. It is one of the things that the members of dynasties are afraid of. Those who support the dynasty will naturally attempt such a thing when the dynasty reaches senility and later-born members of the ruling family lose control. Human beings love very much to gain control over royal authority, especially when the soil is prepared and all the requirements and symptoms are there.

43 The division of one dynasty into two

It should be known that the first (perceptible) consequence of a dynasty's senility is that it splits. This is because, when royal authority comes into its own and achieves the utmost luxury and prosperity and when the ruler controls all the glory and has it all for himself, he is too proud to let anyone share in it. As far as possible, he eliminates all claims in this direction by destroying those of his relatives who are possible candidates for his position and whom he suspects.

Those who participate with the ruler in this (activity) often fear for their own (safety) and take refuge in remote parts of the realm. People who are in the same situation as they of running a risk and becoming suspect, join them there and gather around them. At that time the authority of the dynasty has already begun to shrink and to withdraw from the remote parts of the realm. Thus, the refugee related (to the dynasty) gains control. His power grows continually, while the authority of the dynasty shrinks. Eventually he becomes, or almost becomes, an equal partner in the dynasty.

This may be observed in the Arab Muslim dynasty. Its power was great and concentrated and its authority far-flung. Then the Umayyads lost control, and the 'Abbâsids took over. The Arab dynasty had, by that time, achieved the utmost superiority and luxury, and was beginning to shrink. 'Abd-ar-Rahmân I ad-Dâkhil took refuge in Spain, the most remote region of the Muslim dynasty. He founded a realm there and severed it from the 'Abbâsid cause. Thus, he made two dynasties out of one. Then, Idrîs took refuge in the Maghrib and seceded and seized power there.

Later on, the 'Abbâsid dynasty shrank more and more. The Aghlabids were stirred up to resist it. Then, the Shî'ah (the 'Ubaydid-Fâṭimids) seceded. The Kutâmah and the Ṣinhâjah supported them, and they took possession of Ifrîqiyah and the Maghrib, and then conquered Egypt, Syria, and the Ḥijâz. They defeated the Idrîsids and divided the ('Abbâsid) dynasty into two more, so that the Arab ('Abbâsid) dynasty now consisted of three (independent) dynasties: the 'Abbâsids at the centre and base of the Arab world and at the source of Islam; the Umayyads, who had renewed their old royal authority and caliphate of the East in Spain; and the 'Ubaydid (-Fâṭimids) in Ifrîqiyah, Egypt, Syria, and the Ḥijâz. These dynasties continued to exist until their destruction was imminent or complete. . . .

The process of splitting may lead to the formation of more than two or three dynasties that are not controlled by members of the (original) ruling family. This was the case with the *reyes de taïfas* in Spain, with the non-Arab rulers in the East, and in other realms. . . .

44 Once senility has come upon a dynasty, it cannot be warded off

We have already cited the symptoms and causes of senility, one by one. We have explained that it is natural for the causes of senility to affect the dynasty. If, then, senility is something natural to the life of the dynasty, it must come about in the same way natural things come about, exactly as senility affects the temper of living beings. Senility is a chronic disease that cannot be cured or made to disappear because it is something natural, and natural things do not change.

Many a politically conscious person among the people of the dynasty becomes alert to it and notices the symptoms and causes of senility that have affected his dynasty. He considers it possible to make that senility disappear. Therefore, he takes it upon himself to repair the dynasty and relieve its temper of senility. He supposes that it resulted from shortcomings or negligence on the part of former members. This is not so. These things are natural to the dynasty. Customs that have developed prevent him from repairing it. Customs are like a second nature. A person who, for instance, has seen his father and the older members of his family wear silk and brocade and use gold ornaments for weapons and mounts and be inaccessible to the people in their salons and at prayer, will not be able to diverge from the customs of his forebears in this respect. He will not be able to use coarse dress and apparel and mingle with the people. Custom would prevent him and expose him if he were to do this. Were he to do it, he would be accused of madness for his brusque disregard of custom. There is the danger that it would have bad consequences for his government.

One might contrast (this with) the disregard for custom and

245

opposition to it shown by the prophets. However, the prophets had divine support and celestial help.

Group feeling has often disappeared (when the dynasty has grown senile), and pomp has taken the place it occupied in the souls of men. Now, when in addition to the weakening of group feeling, pomp, too, is discontinued, the subjects grow audacious vis-à-vis the dynasty. Therefore, the dynasty shields itself by holding on to pomp as much as possible, until everything is finished.

At the end of a dynasty, there often also appears some (show of) power that gives the impression that the senility of the dynasty has been made to disappear. It lights up brilliantly just before it is extinguished, like a burning wick the flame of which leaps up brilliantly a moment before it goes out, giving the impression it is just starting to burn, when in fact it is going out.

45 How disintegration befalls dynasties

Any royal authority must be built upon two foundations. The first is might and group feeling, which finds its expression in soldiers. The second is money, which supports the soldiers and provides the whole structure needed by royal authority. Disintegration befalls the dynasty at these two foundations.

We shall mention first the disintegration that comes about through might and group feeling, and then, we shall come back and discuss the one that comes about through money and taxation.

A dynasty can be founded and established only with the help of group feeling. There must be a major group feeling uniting all the group feelings subordinate to it. This (major group feeling) is the family and tribal group feeling peculiar to the ruler.

When the natural luxury of royal authority makes its appearance in the dynasty, and when the people who share in the group feeling of the dynasty are humiliated, the first to be humiliated are the members of the ruler's family and his relatives who share with him in the royal name. They are much more humiliated than anyone else. Moreover, luxury has a greater hold on them than on anyone else, because they have a share in royal authority, power, and superiority. Thus, two agents of destruction surround them, luxury and force. (The use of) force eventually leads to their being killed. They become sick at heart when they see the ruler firmly established in royal authority. His envy of them then changes to fear for his royal authority. Therefore, he starts to kill and humiliate them and to deprive them of the prosperity and luxury to which they had become in large measure accustomed. They perish, and become few in number. The group feeling that the ruler had through them is destroyed.

It dissolves and its grip weakens. Its place is taken by the inner circle of clients and followers who enjoy the favours and benefactions of the ruler. A (new) group feeling is derived from them. However, (this new group feeling) does not have anything like the powerful grip (of the other), because it lacks direct and close blood relationships.

The ruler thus isolates himself from his family and helpers, those who have natural affection for him. This is sensed by the people of other groups. Very naturally, they become audacious *vis-à-vis* the ruler and his inner circle. Therefore, the ruler destroys them and persecutes and kills them, one after the other. The later people of the dynasty follow the tradition of the former in that respect. In addition, they are exposed to the detrimental effect of luxury that we have mentioned before. Thus, destruction comes upon them through luxury and through being killed. Eventually, they no longer have the colouring of their group feeling. They forget the affection and strength that used to go with it. They become hirelings for the military protection (of the dynasty). They thus become few in number. As a consequence, the militia settled in the remote and frontier regions becomes numerically weak. This, then, emboldens the subjects in the remote regions to abandon the (dynastic) cause there. Rebels—members of the ruling family and others—go out to these remote regions. They hope that under these circumstances, they will be able to reach their goal by obtaining a following among the inhabitants of the remote regions of the realm, will be secure from capture by the (government) militia. This keeps on and the authority of the ruling dynasty continues gradually to shrink until the rebels reach places extremely close to the centre of the dynasty. The dynasty then often splits into two or three dynasties, depending on its original strength. People who do not share in the group feeling take charge of (dynastic) affairs, though they obey the people who do share in the (dynastic) group feeling and accept their acknowledged superiority.

This may be exemplified by the Arab Muslim dynasty. At the beginning it reached as far as Spain, India, and China. The Umayyads had complete control of all the Arabs through the group feeling of 'Abd-Manâf. It was even possible for Sulaymân b. 'Abd-al-Malik in Damascus to order the killing of 'Abd-al-'Azîz b. Mûsâ b. Nuṣayr in Córdoba. He was killed, and Sulaymân's order was not disobeyed. Then, luxury came to the Umayyads, and their group feeling was wiped out. The Umayyads were destroyed, and the 'Abbâsids made their appearance. They curbed[1] the Hâshimites. They killed

[1] Lit., 'lowered the reins', a phrase which is explained to mean gentling a horse. Here Ibn Khaldûn was apparently thinking of his theory that a dynasty tends to repress the members of its own family.

all the descendants of Abû Ṭâlib and exiled them. In consequence, the group feeling of 'Abd-Manâf dissolved and was wiped out. The Arabs grew audacious *vis-à-vis* the 'Abbâsids. People in the remote regions of the realm, such as the Aghlabids in Ifrîqiyah and the inhabitants of Spain and others, gained control over them, and the dynasty split. Then, the Idrîsids seceded in the Maghrib. The Berbers supported them, in obedience to their group feeling. Also, they were secure from capture by the soldiers or militiamen of the dynasty.

Men with a cause, for which they make propaganda, eventually secede. They gain control over border areas and remote regions. There, they are able to make propaganda for their cause and achieve royal authority. As a result, the dynasty splits. As the dynasty shrinks more and more, this process often continues until the centre is reached. The inner circle, thereafter, weakens, because luxury undermines it. It perishes and dissolves. The whole divided dynasty weakens. Occasionally, it lingers on long after that. (The dynasty) can dispense with group feeling now, because it has coloured the souls of its subject people with the habit of subservience and submission for so many long years that no one alive can think back to its beginning and origin. They cannot think of anything except being submissive to the ruler. Therefore, he can dispense with group strength. In order to establish his power, hired soldiers and mercenaries are sufficient. The submissiveness generally found in the human soul helps in this respect. Should anyone think of disobedience or secession—which hardly ever happens—the great mass would disapprove of him and oppose him. Thus, he would not be able to attempt such a thing, even if he should try very hard. In this situation, the dynasty often becomes more secure, as far as rebels and rivals are concerned, because submissiveness is firmly established. Individuals would scarcely admit to themselves the least thought of opposition, and the idea of straying from obedience would not enter anybody's mind. (The dynasty), therefore, is safer (than ever) so far as the trouble and destruction that come from groups and tribes are concerned. The dynasty may continue in this condition, but its substance dwindles, like natural heat in a body that lacks nourishment. Eventually, (the dynasty) reaches its destined time.

As for the disintegration that comes through money, it should be known that at the beginning the dynasty has a desert attitude, as was mentioned before. It has the qualities of kindness to subjects, planned moderation in expenditure, and respect for other people's property. It avoids onerous taxation and the display of cunning or

AND ALL THAT GOES WITH THESE THINGS

shrewdness in the collection of money and the accounting (required) from officials. Nothing at this time calls for extravagant expenditure. Therefore, the dynasty does not need much money.

Later come domination and expansion. Royal authority flourishes. This calls for luxury, which causes increased spending. The expenditure of the ruler, and of the people of the dynasty in general, grows. This (tendency) spreads to the urban population. It calls for increases in soldiers' allowances and in the salaries of the people of the dynasty. Extravagant expenditure mounts. It spreads to the subjects, because people follow the (ways) and customs of the dynasty.

The ruler, then, must impose duties on articles sold in the markets, in order to improve his revenues; he sees the luxury of the urban population testifying to their prosperity, and because he needs the money for the expenditure of his government and the salaries of his soldiers. Habits of luxury, then, further increase. The customs duties no longer pay for them. The dynasty, by this time, is flourishing in its power and its forceful hold over the subjects under its control. Its hand reaches out to seize some of the property of the subjects, either through customs duties, or through commercial transactions, or, in some cases, merely by hostile acts directed against (property holdings), on some pretext or even with none.

At this stage, the soldiers have already grown bold against the dynasty, because it has become weak and senile as far as its group feeling is concerned. (The dynasty) expects that from them, and attempts to remedy and smooth over the situation through generous allowances and much spending for (the soldiers). It cannot get around that.

At this stage, the tax collectors in the dynasty have acquired much wealth, because vast revenues are in their hands and their position has widened in importance for this reason. Suspicions of having appropriated tax money, therefore, attach to them. It becomes common for one tax collector to denounce another, because of their mutual jealousy and envy. One after another is deprived of his money by confiscation and torture. Eventually, their wealth disappears, and they are ruined. The dynasty loses the pomp and magnificence it had possessed through them.

After their prosperity is destroyed, the dynasty goes farther afield and approaches its other wealthy subjects. At this stage, feebleness has already afflicted its former might. (The dynasty) has become too weak to retain its power and forceful hold. The policy of the ruler, at this time, is to handle matters diplomatically by spending money. He considers this more advantageous than the sword, which is of little use. His need for money grows beyond what is needed for expenditure and soldiers' salaries. He never gets enough. Senility affects the dynasty more and more. The people of other regions grow bold against it.

46 The authority of the dynasty at first expands to its limit and then is narrowed down in successive stages, until the dynasty dissolves and disappears

Each dynasty has its specific share of provinces and districts, and no more. (Its expansion) depends on the distribution of the dynasty's group (strength) for the protection of its territory and regions. Wherever its numbers go, their advance (eventually) comes to a stop at the 'border region'. This surrounds the dynasty on all sides like a belt. Its farthest extension may coincide with the original 'belt' of authority of the preceding dynasty. Or it may be still wider, if the numerical (strength) of the (new) group is greater than that of the preceding dynasty.

All this takes place while the dynasty has the characteristics of desert life and rude courage.

Subsequently, power and superiority come into their own. Bounties and salaries become abundant as a result of improved revenues. Luxury and sedentary culture abound. New generations grow up accustomed to this situation. The character of the militia softens, and they lose their toughness. This makes them cowards and lazy fellows. It causes them to shed the characteristics of courage and manliness. They give up the desert attitude and desert toughness and seek power through assiduous competition for leadership. This causes some of them to kill others. The ruler prevents them from doing that, by killing their great men and destroying their leaders. Thus, amirs and great men no longer exist, and the number of followers and subordinates grows. This blunts the sharp edges of the dynasty and decreases its strength.

This is paralleled by extravagance in expenditure. The people of the dynasty suffer from the pomp of power and limitless ostentation as they compete with each other in matters of food, clothing, large palaces, good weapons, and the horses in their stables. At this time, the income of the dynasty is too small to pay for such expenditure, and thus the second element of disintegration afflicts the dynasty, that which comes through money and taxation. Weakness and destruction are the results of these two elements of disintegration.

The leaders of (the dynasty) often compete with each other. They quarrel, and are too weak to stand up and defend themselves against rivals and neighbours. The people of the border and remote regions often sense the weakness of the dynasty at their backs, and they show their strength. They eventually gain independent control over the districts in their possession. The ruler is too weak to force them back on the (right) path. Thus, the authority of the dynasty becomes narrower than it had been at the beginning. The administration restricts itself to a smaller area. Eventually, the same weakness, laziness with regard to group strength, and the shortage of money and revenue that had come about in the first, larger, area also come about in the second, smaller, area.

The person in charge of the dynasty now undertakes to change the norms the dynasty had adopted as its policy with regard to soldiers, money, and administrative functions. The purpose is to have norms suitable for balancing the budget, satisfying the militia, safeguarding the administrative districts, distributing the tax revenue for the (soldiers') salaries in the proper manner, and readjusting (the new conditions) to those that had existed at the beginning of the dynasty. However, evil happenings can still be expected from every quarter.

At this later stage, what had happened before in the first stage happens again. The ruler now considers the same (measures) that the first ruler had considered, and applies the old yardstick to the new conditions of the dynasty. He intends to repel the evil consequences of disintegration, which reappears at every stage and affects every part of the realm until the area of the dynasty is again narrower than it had been before, and what had happened before happens again.

Each of the persons who change the previous (dynastic) norms is in a way the builder of a new dynasty and the founder of a new realm. However, the dynasty is eventually destroyed. The nations around it push on to gain superiority over it. They then found a new dynasty of their own.

This may be exemplified by the Muslim dynasty. Through its conquests and victories its authority expanded. Its militia then increased, and its numerical (strength) grew as the result of the bounties and salaries to (the soldiers). Eventually, the power of the Umayyads was destroyed. The 'Abbâsids gained the upper hand. Luxury, then, increased. Sedentary culture emerged, and disintegration made its appearance. The creation of the Marwânid (Umayyad Spanish) and 'Alid (Idrîsid) dynasties cut down the authority of the 'Abbâsids in Spain and the Maghrib. These two border regions were cut off from 'Abbâsid authority.

Then, dissension arose among the sons of ar-Rashîd. 'Alid propagandists appeared in every region, and 'Alid dynasties were founded. Then, after the death of al-Mutawakkil, the amirs gained control over the caliphs and kept them in seclusion. Provincial governors in the outlying regions became independent, and the land tax from there did not come in any longer. Luxury still increased. Al-Mu'taḍid appeared. He changed the norms of the dynasty and adopted another policy. He gave the outlying regions, over which the governors had won control, to them as fiefs. Then, the power of the Arabs was broken up. The non-Arabs achieved superiority. Then arose the dynasty of the Saljûq Turks. The Saljûqs gained domination over the Muslim empire. They kept the caliphs in seclusion, until their dynasties were destroyed. From the time of an-Nâṣir[1] on, the caliphs were in control of an area smaller than the ring around the moon. The dynasty continued in that manner until the power of the caliphs was destroyed by Hûlâgû, the ruler of the Tatars and Mongols. They defeated the Saljûqs and took possession of the part of the Muslim empire that had been theirs.

Thus, the authority of the dynasty becomes successively narrower than it had been at the beginning. (This process) continues, stage by stage, until the dynasty is destroyed.

47 How a new dynasty originates

When the ruling dynasty starts on the road to senility and destruction, the rise of the new dynasty takes place in two ways:

(One way is) for provincial governors to gain control over remote regions when (the dynasty) loses its influence there. Each one of them founds a new dynasty for his people and a realm to be perpetuated in his family. His children or clients inherit it from him. Gradually, they have a flourishing realm. They often compete bitterly with each other and aspire to gain sole possession of it. The one who is stronger than his rival will gain the upper hand and take away what the other had.

This happened in the 'Abbâsid dynasty when it started on the road to senility and its shadow receded from the remote regions. The same thing happened in the Umayyad dynasty in Spain. Their realm was divided among the *reyes de taïfas* who had been their provincial governors. It was divided into several dynasties with several rulers, who passed their realms on after their death to their relatives or clients. This way of forming a new dynasty avoids the possibility of war between the (new rulers) and the ruling dynasty. (These new rulers) are already firmly established in their leadership and do not want to gain domination over the ruling dynasty. The latter is affected by senility, and its shadow recedes from the remote regions of the realm and can no longer reach them.

The other way is for some rebel from among the neighbouring nations and tribes to revolt against the dynasty. He either makes

[1] The 'Abbâsid who reigned from 1180 to 1225.

propaganda for some particular cause to which he intends to win the people, or he possesses great power and a great group feeling among his people. His power is already flourishing among them, and now he aspires with the help of (his people) to gain royal authority. They are convinced that they will obtain it, because they feel that they are superior to the ruling dynasty, which is affected by senility. Thus, to (the rebel) and his people, it is a fact that they will gain domination over it. They constantly attack it, until they defeat it and inherit its power.

48 A new dynasty gains domination over the ruling dynasty through perseverance, and not through sudden action

We have mentioned the two ways new dynasties originate. The first applies to governors of outlying regions when the shadow of the ruling dynasty recedes from those regions and its waves are rolled back. As a rule, they do not attack the dynasty, because they are satisfied with what they already have. The second applies to men who make propaganda for some cause or rebel against the dynasty. It is inevitable that they attack it, because their power warrants it. They (revolt) only when they have a family with sufficient group feeling and strength to give them success. Indecisive battles take place between them and the ruling dynasty. (Such battles) are repeated and continued, until by perseverance they achieve domination and victory. As a rule, they do not gain victory through sudden action.

Victory in war as a rule is the result of imaginary psychological factors. Numbers, weapons, and proper tactics may guarantee (victory). However, as has been mentioned above, (all these things) are less effective than the factors above-mentioned. Trickery is one of the most useful things employed in warfare. It is the thing most likely to bring victory.

Accepted custom has made obedience to the ruling dynasty a necessity and an obligation. This puts many hindrances in the way of the founder of a new dynasty. It discourages his followers and supporters. His closest intimates may be fully intent upon obeying him and helping him, but there are others more numerous who are affected by weakness and laziness under the influence of the belief that they owe submission to the ruling dynasty. Their zeal slackens. Therefore, the founder of a new dynasty is hardly able to make a stand against the established one. Consequently, he falls back on patience and perseverance, until the senility of the ruling dynasty has become obvious. Then his people lose the belief that they owe submission to the ruling dynasty. They become sufficiently spirited to make an open attack in concert with (the founder of the new dynasty). Victory and domination are the result.

Furthermore, the ruling dynasty enjoys many luxuries. The authority of its members had been firmly established. To the exclusion of others, they had appropriated a good deal of the revenues from taxes. Thus, they have many horses in their stables and good weapons. There is much royal pomp among them. Gifts from their rulers, given either voluntarily or under constraint, have been showered upon them. With all this, they frighten their enemies.

The members of the new dynasty lack such things. They have the desert attitude and are poor and indigent. This leaves them unprepared. What they hear about the conditions and excellent state of preparedness of the ruling dynasty makes them apprehensive. Therefore, their leader is forced to wait until senility takes hold of the ruling dynasty and its group feeling and fiscal structure are disintegrating. Then, the founder of the new dynasty seizes the opportunity to gain the upper hand, quite some time after his attack had begun.

The men of the new dynasty differ from those of the ruling dynasty with regard to descent, customs, and all other things. (Persistent) attacks and their desire to gain the upper hand estrange them more and more from the men of the ruling dynasty. Consequently, the people of the two dynasties become thoroughly estranged from each other, inwardly and outwardly. No information about the ruling dynasty, either secretly or openly, reaches the would-be dynasty, such as might enable them to find some unpreparedness among them, because all connection and intercourse between the two dynasties has been cut off. They thus continue to exert pressure but they are in a state of fear and shy away from sudden action.

Eventually, God permits the ruling dynasty to end, its life to stop, and disintegration to afflict it from all sides. Its senility and decay, which had been concealed from the people of the new dynasty, now become clear to them. In the meantime, their strength has grown, because they had cut off and taken away outlying regions. Thus, they become spirited enough (to attempt) sudden action, and this finally brings domination.

This may be exemplified by the emergence and beginnings of the 'Abbâsid dynasty. The ('Abbâsid) Shî'ah remained in Khurâsân for ten years or more after the ('Abbâsid) propaganda had consolidated, and (the 'Abbâsids) had gathered for attack. Then, their victory materialized, and they gained the upper hand over the Umayyads....

A constant struggle marked by (constant) attacks and long perseverance, is characteristic of the relationship between new and ruling dynasties. This is how God proceeds with His servants.

The events of the Muslim conquests cannot be used as an argument against (the preceding remarks). (The Muslims) gained the upper hand over the Persians and the Byzantines in the three or four years that followed the death of the Prophet, and there was no long waiting period. It should be realized that this was one of the miracles of our Prophet. The secret of it lay in the willingness of the Muslims to die in the holy war against their enemies because of their feeling that they had the right religious insight, and in the corresponding fear and defeatism that God put into the hearts of their enemies. All these (miraculous facts) broke through the known custom of a long wait between new and ruling dynasties. (Such miracles) in Islam are generally acknowledged. Miracles cannot be used as analogies for ordinary affairs and constitute no argument against them.

49 There is overpopulation at the end of dynasties, and pestilences and famines frequently occur then

It has been established that, at the beginning, dynasties are inevitably kind in the exercise of their power and just in their administration. The reason is either their religion, when (the dynasty) is based upon religious propaganda, or their noble and benevolent attitude toward others, which is required by the desert attitude that is natural to dynasties (at the beginning).

A kind and benevolent rule serves as an incentive to the subjects and gives them energy for cultural activities. (Civilization) becomes abundant, and procreation vigorous. All this takes place gradually. The effects will become noticeable after one or two generations at best. At the end of two generations, the dynasty approaches the limit of its natural life. At that time, civilization has reached the limit of its abundance and growth.

It should not be objected here that it was stated before that in the later years of a dynasty, there will be coercion of the subjects and bad government. This is correct, but it does not contradict what we have just said. Even though coercion makes its appearance at that time and the revenues decrease, the destructive influences of this situation on civilization will become noticeable only after some time, because things in nature all have a gradual development.

In the later years of dynasties, famines and pestilences become numerous. As far as famines are concerned, the reason is that most people at that time refrain from cultivating the soil. For, in the later years of dynasties, there occur attacks on property and tax revenue and, through customs duties, on trading. Or, trouble occurs as the result of the unrest of the subjects and the great number encouraged by the senility of the dynasty to rebel. Therefore, as a rule, little grain is stored. The grain and harvest situation is not always good and stable from year to year. The amount of rainfall in the world differs by nature. The rainfall may be little or much. Grain, fruits, and the amount of milk given by animals vary correspondingly. Still, for their food requirements, people put their trust in what it is possible to store. If nothing is stored, people must expect famines. The price of grain rises. Indigent people are unable to buy any and perish. If for some years nothing is stored, hunger will be general.

The large number of pestilences are caused by the famines just mentioned; or by the many disturbances that result from the disintegration of the dynasty. There is much unrest and bloodshed, and plagues occur. The principal reason for the latter is the corruption of the air by overpopulation, and the putrefaction and the many evil moistures with which the air has contact (in a densely populated region). Now, air nourishes the animal spirit and is constantly with it. When it is corrupted, corruption affects the temper of the spirit. If the corruption is strong, the lung is afflicted with disease. This results in epidemics, which affect the lung in particular. Even if the corruption is not strong, putrefaction grows and multiplies, resulting in many fevers that affect the tempers, and the bodies become sick and perish. The reason for the growth of putrefaction and evil moistures is invariably a dense and abundant civilization such as exists in the later years of a dynasty. Such civilization is the result of the good government, the kindness, the safety, and the light taxation that existed at the beginning of the dynasty. This is obvious. Therefore, science has made it clear that it is necessary to have empty spaces and waste regions interspersed between urban areas. This makes circulation of the air possible. It removes the corruption and putrefaction affecting the air after contact with living beings, and brings healthy air. This also is the reason why pestilences occur much more frequently in densely populated cities than elsewhere, as, for instance, in Cairo in the East and Fez in the Maghrib.

50 Human civilization requires political leadership for its organization

We have mentioned before in more than one place that human social organization is something necessary. It is the thing that is meant by 'the civilization' which we have been discussing. (People) in any social organization must have someone who exercises a restraining influence and rules them and to whom recourse may be had. His rule over them is sometimes based upon a divinely revealed religious law. They are obliged to submit to it in view of their belief in reward and punishment in the other world. Sometimes, (his rule is based) upon rational politics. People are obliged to submit to it in view of the reward they expect from the ruler after he has become acquainted with what is good for them.

The first (type of rule) is useful for this world and for the other world, because the lawgiver knows the ultimate interest of the people and is concerned with the salvation of man in the other world. The second is useful only for this world.

We do not mean here that which is known as 'political utopianism'. By that, the philosophers mean the disposition of soul and character which each member of a social organization must have, if, eventually, people are completely to dispense with rulers. They call the social organization that fulfils these requirements the 'ideal city'. The norms observed in this connection are called 'political utopias'. They do not mean the kind of politics that the members of a social organization are led to adopt through laws for the common interest. That is something different. The 'ideal city' (of the philosophers) is something rare and remote. They discuss it as a hypothesis.

Now, the aforementioned rational politics may be of two types. The first type of rational politics may concern itself with the general interest, and with the ruler's interest in connection with the administration of his realm, in particular. This was the politics of the Persians. It is something related to philosophy. God made this type of politics superfluous for us in Islam at the time of the caliphate. The religious laws take its place in connection with both general and (particular) interests, for they also include the maxims (of the philosophers) and the rules of royal authority.

The second type (of rational politics) is the one concerned with the interest of the ruler and how he can maintain his rule through the forceful use of power. The general interest is, here, secondary. This is the type of politics practised by all rulers, whether they are Muslims or unbelievers. Muslim rulers, however, practise this type of politics in accordance with the requirements of the Muslim religious law, as much as they are able to. Therefore, the political norms here are a mixture of religious laws and ethical rules, norms that are natural in social organization together with a certain necessary concern for strength and group feeling. . . .

51 The Mahdî. The opinions of the people about him. The truth about the matter

It has been (accepted) by all Muslims in every epoch, that at the end of time a man from the family (of the Prophet) will without fail make his appearance, one who will strengthen Islam and make justice triumph. Muslims will follow him, and he will gain domination over the Muslim realm. He will be called the Mahdî. Following him, the Antichrist will appear, together with all the subsequent signs of the Day of Judgment. After the Mahdî, Jesus will descend and kill the Antichrist. Or, Jesus will descend together with the Mahdî, and help him kill the Antichrist.

Such statements have been found in the traditions that religious leaders have published. They have been (critically) discussed by those who disapprove of them and have often been refuted by means of certain traditions. . . .

More recent Sufis have other theories concerning the Mahdî. The time, the man, and the place are clearly indicated in them. But the (predicted) time passes, and there is not the slightest trace of (the prediction coming true). Then, some new suggestion is adopted which is based upon linguistic equivocations, imaginary ideas, and astrological judgments. The life of every one of those people is spent on such suppositions.

Most of our contemporary Sufis refer to the (expected) appearance of a man who will renew the Muslim law and the ordinances of the truth. They assume that his appearance will take place at some time near our own period. Some of them say that he will be one of the descendants of Fâṭimah. Others speak about him only in general terms.

The truth one must know is that no religious or political propaganda can be successful, unless power and group feeling exist to support the religious and political aspirations and to defend them against those who reject them.

The group feeling of the Fâṭimids and the Ṭâlibids, indeed, that of all the Quraysh, has everywhere disappeared. There are other nations whose group feeling has gained the upper hand over that of the Quraysh. The only exception is a remnant of the Ṭâlibids—in the Ḥijâz, in Mecca, al-Yanbu', and Medina. They are spread over these regions and dominate them. They are Bedouin groups. They are settled and rule in different places and hold divergent opinions. They number several thousands. If it is correct that a Mahdî is to appear, there is only one way for his propaganda to make its appearance. He must be one of them, and God must unite them in the intention to follow him, until he gathers enough strength and group feeling to gain success for his cause and to move the people to support him. Any other way—such as a Fâṭimid who would make propaganda for (the cause of the Mahdî) among people anywhere at all, without the support of group feeling and power, by merely relying on his relationship to the family of Muḥammad—will not be feasible or successful, for the sound reasons that we have mentioned previously.

The common people, the stupid mass, who make claims with respect to the Mahdî and who are not guided in this connection by any intelligence or helped by any knowledge, assume that the Mahdî may appear in a variety of circumstances and places. They do not understand the real meaning of the matter. They mostly assume that the appearance will take place in some remote province out of the reach of the (ruling) dynasties and outside their authority. Therefore, they firmly imagine that the Mahdi will appear there, since these regions are not under the control of dynasties and out of the reach of law and force. Many weak-minded people go to those places in order to support a deceptive cause that the human soul in its delusion and stupidity leads them to believe capable of succeeding. Many of them have been killed. . . .

52 *Forecasting the future of dynasties and nations, including a discussion of predictions and an exposition of the subject called 'divination'*

It should be known that one of the qualities of the human soul is the desire to learn the outcome of affairs that concern (human beings) and to know what is going to befall them, whether it be life or death, good or evil. (This desire is) especially great with regard to events of general importance, and one wants to know, for instance, how long the world or certain dynasties are going to last. Curiosity in this respect is human nature and innate in human beings. Therefore, many people are found who desire to learn about these things in their sleep (through dreams). Stories of soothsayers being approached by rulers and commoners alike, with the request for predictions, are well known.

In the towns, we find a group of people who try to make a living out of predicting the future, because they realize that the people are most eager to know it. Therefore, they set themselves up in the streets and in shops and offer themselves to those who (wish to) consult them. All day long, women and children of the town and, indeed, many weak-minded men as well, come and ask them to foretell the future for them, how it will affect their business, their rank, their friendships, their enmities, and similar things. There are those who make their predictions by writing on sand (geomancy), those who cast pebbles and grains (of wheat), and those who look into mirrors and into water. These things are very common in cities, and their reprehensible character is established by the religious law.

Rulers and amirs who want to know the duration of their own dynasties show the greatest concern for these things. Therefore, the interest of scholars has been directed to the subject of predicting the duration of dynasties. Every nation has had its soothsayers, its astrologers, and its saints, who have spoken about things of this kind; of wars and battles with nations that were going to occur, about how long the ruling dynasty would last, how many rulers it would have, and they have also attempted to give the names. The Arabs had soothsayers and diviners to whom they had recourse in this respect. They forecast the royal authority and dynasty the Arabs were going to have. . . .

During the Muslim dynasty many such predictions were made. Some predictions had reference to how long the world in general would last. Others had reference to a particular dynasty and its particular life.

At the beginning of Islam, (predictions) were based upon statements reported on the authority of the men around Muḥammad and, especially, on that of Jewish converts to Islam.

After the early years of Islam, people applied themselves to the sciences and the technical terminologies. The books of the (Greek) philosophers were translated into Arabic. The main basis for predictions now were astrological discussions. Matters concerning royal authority and dynasties and all other matters of general importance were considered as depending on the conjunctions of the stars. Nativities and interrogations and all other private matters were considered to depend on people's 'ascendants'—that is, on the constellations of the firmament at the time when (these matters) were brought up.

With regard to how long Islam and the world in general will last, traditionists accepted the prediction that the world will last five hundred years after the coming of Islam. Since it has become obvious that this is not true, the theory has been demolished. . . .

As a basis for specific forecasts concerning dynasties, the *Kitâb al-Jafr* is used. People think that it contains information in the form of traditions or astrological (predictions). They do not (think) beyond that, and they do not know its origin nor its basis. The book contained remarkable statements concerning the interpretation of the Qur'ân and its inner meaning, transmitted on the authority of Ja'far aṣ-Ṣâdiq. The book has not come down through continuous transmission and is not known as a book as such. . . .

Astrologers, in making forecasts concerning dynasties, base themselves upon astrological judgments. For matters of general importance such as royal authority and dynasties, they use the conjunctions, especially those of the two superior planets, Saturn and Jupiter.

The conjunctions of the two superior planets are divided into great, small, and medium. The great conjunction is the meeting of the two superior planets in the same degree of the firmament, which reoccurs after 960 years. The medium conjunction is the conjunction of the two superior planets in each triplicity with its twelve repetitions; after 240 years, they move on to another triplicity. The small conjunction is the conjunction of the two superior planets in the same sign; after twenty years, they have a conjunction in another sign in trine dexter at the same degree and minute.

The great conjunction indicates great events, such as a change in royal authority or dynasties, or a transfer of royal authority from one people to another. The medium conjunction (indicates) the appearance of persons in search of superiority and royal authority; the small conjunction indicates the appearance of rebels or propagandists, and the ruin of towns or of their civilization.

In between these conjunctions, there occurs the conjunction of the two unlucky planets Saturn and Mars in the sign of Cancer once every thirty years. The sign of Cancer is the ascendant of the world. This conjunction strongly indicates disturbances, wars, bloodshed, the appearance of rebels, the movement of armies, the disobedience of soldiers, plagues, and drought. These things persist, or come to an end, depending on the luck or ill luck at the time of conjunction of (the two unlucky planets). . . .

Ya'qûb b. Isḥâq al-Kindî, astrologer to ar-Rashîd and al-Ma'mûn, composed a book on the conjunctions affecting Islam. He is said to have made complete forecasts concerning the 'Abbâsid dynasty. He indicated that its destruction and the fall of Baghdad would take place in the middle of the seventh [thirteenth] century.

We have not found any information concerning al-Kindî's book, and we have not seen anyone who has seen it. Perhaps it was lost with those books which Hûlâgû, the ruler of the Tatars, threw into the Tigris when the Tatars took possession of Baghdad and killed the last caliph, al-Musta'ṣim. . . .

Chapter 4

Countries and cities, and all other forms of sedentary civilization. The conditions occurring there. Primary and secondary considerations in this connection

1 Dynasties are prior to towns and cities. Towns and cities are secondary products of royal authority

The explanation for this is that building and city planning are features of sedentary culture brought about by luxury and tranquillity, as we have mentioned before. They come after Bedouin life and the features that go with it.

Furthermore, towns and cities with their monuments, vast constructions, and large buildings, are set up for the masses and not for the few. Therefore, united effort and much co-operation are needed for them. They are not among the things that are necessary matters of general concern to human beings, in the sense that all human beings desire them or feel compelled to have them. As a matter of fact, they must be forced and driven to build cities. The stick of royal authority is what compels them, or they may be stimulated by promise of reward and compensation amounting to so large a sum that only royal authority and a dynasty can pay for it. Thus, dynasties and royal authority are absolutely necessary for the building of cities and the planning of towns.

Then, when the town has been built and is all finished, as the builder saw fit and as the climatic and geographical conditions required, the life of the dynasty is the life of the town. If the dynasty is of short duration, life in the town will stop at the end of the dynasty. Its civilization will recede, and the town will fall into ruins. On the other hand, if the dynasty is of long duration and lasts a long time, new constructions will always go up in the town, the number of large mansions will increase, and the walls of the town will extend farther and farther. Eventually, the layout of the town will cover a wide area, and the town will extend so far and so wide as to be (almost) beyond measurement. This happened in Baghdad and similar (cities).

The Khaṭib mentioned in his *History* that in the time of al-Ma'mûn the number of public baths in Baghdad reached 65,000. It included over forty of the adjacent neighbouring towns and cities. It was not just one town surrounded by one wall. Its population was much too large for that. The same was the case with al-Qayrawân, Córdoba, and al-Mahdîyah in Islamic times. It is the case with Egypt and Cairo at this time, so we are told.

The dynasty that has built a certain town may be destroyed. Now, the mountainous and flat areas surrounding the city are a desert that constantly provides for (an influx of population). This will preserve the existence of (the town), and it will continue to live after the dynasty is dead. (This situation) can be observed in Fez and Bougie in the West, and in the non-Arab 'Irâq in the East, which get their population from the mountains. When the conditions of the inhabitants of the desert reach the utmost ease and become most profitable, they look for tranquillity and quiet. Therefore, they settle in towns and cities.

Or, it may happen that a town founded (by a dynasty now destroyed) has no opportunity to replenish its population by a constant influx of settlers from a desert near the town. In this case, the destruction of the dynasty will leave it unprotected. It cannot be maintained. Its civilization will gradually decay, until its population is dispersed and gone. This happened in Baghdad and in al-Qayrawân, as well as in other cities.

Frequently it happens that after the destruction of its original builders, a town is used by another realm and dynasty as its capital and residence. This then makes it unnecessary for (the new dynasty) to build a town for itself as a settlement. In this case, the (new) dynasty will protect the town. Its buildings and constructions will increase in proportion to the improved circumstances and the luxury of the new dynasty. The life (of the new dynasty) gives (the town) another life. This has happened in contemporary Fez and Cairo.

2 Royal authority calls for urban settlement

This is because, when royal authority is acquired by tribes and groups, they are forced to take possession of cities for two reasons. One of them is that royal authority causes (the people) to seek tranquillity, restfulness, and relaxation, and to try to provide the aspects of civilization that were lacking in the desert. The second (reason) is that rivals and enemies can be expected to attack the realm, and one must defend oneself against them.

A city situated in a district where (rivals of the dynasty) are found, may often become a place of refuge for a person who wants to attack (the tribes and groups in authority) and revolt against them and deprive them of the royal authority to which they have aspired. He fortifies himself in the city and fights them. Now, it is very difficult and troublesome to overpower a city. A city is worth a great number of soldiers, in that it offers protection from behind the walls and makes attacks difficult, and no great numbers or much power are needed. Power and group support are needed in war only for the sake of the steadfastness provided by the mutual affection (tribesmen) show each other in battle. The steadfastness of (people in a city) is assured by the walls of the city. Therefore, they do not need much group support or great numbers (for defence). The existence of a city and of rivals who fortify themselves in it thus eats into the strength of a nation desiring to gain control and breaks the impetus of its efforts in this respect. Therefore, it there are cities in the tribal territory of (a dynasty, it) will bring them under its control, in order to be safe. If there are no cities, the dynasty will have to build a new city, firstly, in order to complete the civilization of its realm and to be able to lessen its efforts, and, secondly, in order to use the city as a threat against those parties and groups within the dynasty that might desire power and might wish to resist.

It is thus clear that royal authority calls for urban settlement and control of the cities.

3 Only strong royal authority is able to construct large cities and high monuments

We have mentioned this before in connection with buildings and other dynastic (monuments). (The size of monuments) is proportionate to the importance of (the various dynasties). The construction of cities can be achieved only by united effort, great numbers, and the co-operation of workers. When the dynasty is large and far-flung, workers are brought together from all regions, and their labour is employed in a common effort. Often, the work involves the help of machines, which multiply the power and strength needed to carry the loads required in building. (Unaided) human strength would be insufficient. Among such machines are pulleys and others.

Many people who view the great monuments and constructions of the ancients, such as the Reception Hall of Khosraw, the pyramids of Egypt, the arches of the Malga (at Carthage) and those of Cherchel in the Maghrib, think that the ancients erected them by their own (unaided) powers, whether (they worked) as individuals or in groups. They imagine that the ancients had bodies proportionate to (those monuments) and that their bodies, consequently, were much taller, wider, and heavier than (our bodies), so that there was the right proportion between (their bodies) and the physical strength from which such buildings resulted. They forget the importance of machines and pulleys and engineering skill implied in this connection. Many a travelled person can confirm what we have stated from his own observation of construction and of the use of mechanics to transport building materials among the non-Arab dynasties concerned with such things. . . .

4 Very large monuments are not built by one dynasty alone

The reason for this is the aforementioned need for co-operation and multiplication of human strength in any building activity. Sometimes buildings are so large that they are too much for (human) strength, whether it is on its own or multiplied by machines, as we have stated. Therefore, the repeated application of similar strength is required over successive periods, until (the building) materializes. One (ruler) starts the construction. He is followed by another and (the second by) a third. Each of them does all he can to bring workers together in a common effort. Finally, (the building) materializes, as it was planned, and then stands before our eyes. Those who live at a later period and see the building think that it was built by a single dynasty.

Something similar has been reported with regard to the construction of Carthage, its aqueduct, and the giant arches supporting it. And the same is the case with most great buildings. This is confirmed by the great buildings of our own time. We find one ruler starting by laying out their foundations. Then, if the rulers who succeed him do not follow in his steps and complete (the building), it remains as it is, and is not completed as planned.

Another confirmation of our theory is the fact that we find that (later) dynasties are unable to tear down and destroy many great architectural monuments, even though destruction is much easier than construction, because destruction is return to the origin, which is non-existence, while construction is the opposite of that. Thus, when we find a building that our human strength is too weak to tear down, even though it is easy to tear something down, we realize that the strength used in starting such a monument must have been immense and that the building could not be the monument of a single dynasty.

This is what happened to the Arabs with regard to the Reception Hall of Khosraw. Ar-Rashîd had the intention of tearing it down but was unable. The same happened to al-Ma'mûn in (his attempt) to pull down the pyramids in Egypt. He assembled workers to tear them down, but he did not have much success. The workers began by boring a hole into the pyramids, and they came to an interior chamber between the outer wall and walls farther inside. That was as far as they got in their attempt to pull (the pyramid) down. Their efforts are said to show to this day in the form of a visible hole. Some think that al-Ma'mûn found a buried treasure between the walls.

The same applies to the arches of the Malga (at Carthage, which are still standing) at this time. The people of Tunis need stones for their buildings, and the craftsmen like the quality of the stones of the arches (of the aqueduct). For a long time, they have attempted to tear them down. However, even the smallest (part) of the walls comes down only after the greatest efforts. Parties assemble for the purpose. I have seen many of them in the days of my youth.

5 Requirements for the planning of towns and the consequences of neglecting those requirements

Towns are dwelling places that nations use when they have reached the desired goal of luxury and of the things that go with it. Then, they prefer tranquillity and quiet and turn to using houses to dwell in.

The purpose of (building towns) is to have places for dwelling and shelter. Therefore, it is necessary in this connection to see to it that harmful things are kept away from the towns by protecting them against inroads by them, and that useful features are introduced and all the conveniences are made available in them.

For the protection of towns, all the houses should be situated inside a surrounding wall. Furthermore, the town should be situated in an inaccessible place, either upon a rugged hill or surrounded by the sea or by a river, so that it can be reached only by crossing some sort of bridge. Thus, it will be difficult for an enemy to take the town, and its inaccessibility will be increased many times.

To protect towns against harmful atmospheric phenomena, one should see to it that the air is wholesome, in order to be safe from illness. When the air is stagnant and bad, or close to corrupt waters or putrid pools or swamps, it is speedily affected by putrescence and it is unavoidable that all living beings who are there will speedily be affected by illness. This fact is confirmed by direct observation. Towns where no attention is paid to good air have, as a rule, much illness. In the Maghrib, Gabès is famous for that. Very few of its inhabitants or those who come there are spared the putrid fever. It has been said that this (condition) is recent there, that it did not use to be that way. Al-Bakrî gives an account of how this happened. A copper vessel was found during an excavation there. The vessel was sealed with lead. The seal was broken, and (a puff of) smoke came out of the vessel and disappeared in the air. Feverous diseases began to occur in that place from that time on.

(Al-Bakrî) meant to imply that the vessel contained some magic spell against pestilence, and that when it was gone its magic efficacy also disappeared. Therefore, putrescence and pestilence reappeared. The story is an example of the feeble beliefs and ideas of the common people. Al-Bakrî was neither learned nor enlightened enough to reject such (a story) and see through its nonsensical character. The truth lies in the fact that it mostly is the stagnancy of putrid air that causes the putrefaction of bodies and the occurrence of feverous diseases. When Ifrîqiyah enjoyed a flourishing civilization and a large population, Gabès had many inhabitants whose constant activity helped to keep the air circulating, so that there was not much putrescence or illness there at that time. But when its inhabitants became fewer, the air there became stagnant, and putrescence and the incidence of disease increased. This is the only correct explanation (of the prevalence of feverous diseases in Gabès).

In connection with the importation of useful things and conveniences into towns, one must see to a number of matters. There is the water (problem). The place should be on a river, or near springs with plenty of fresh water. The existence of water will be a general convenience to the inhabitants.

Another utility in towns, for which one must provide, is good pastures for the livestock. Each householder needs domestic animals for breeding, for milk, and for riding. If the pastures are near and good, that will be more convenient for them.

Furthermore, one has to see to it that, there are fields suitable for cultivation. Grain is the (basic) food. When the fields are near, the grain can be obtained more easily and quickly.

Then, there also is the need for woods to supply firewood and building material.

One should also see to it that the town is situated close to the sea, to facilitate the importation of foreign goods from remote countries. However, this is not on the same level with the aforementioned (requirements).

The founder (of a town) sometimes fails to make a good natural selection, or he sees only to what seems most important to him or his people, and does not think of the needs of others. The Arabs did that at the beginning of Islam when they founded towns in the 'Irâq, the Ḥijâz, and Ifrîqiyah. They saw only to what seemed important to them, namely, pastures, trees and brackish water for their camels. They did not see to it that there was water for human consumption, fields for cultivation, firewood, or pastures for domestic animals such as cattle, sheep, goats, and so on. Among the cities (founded by the Arabs) were al-Qayrawân, al-Kûfah, al-Basrah, and the like. They were, therefore, very ready to fall into ruins, inasmuch as they did not fulfil all the natural requirements of towns.

As regards coastal towns, one must see to it that they are situated on a height or amidst a people sufficiently numerous to come to the support of the town when an enemy attacks it. The reason for this is that a town which is near the sea but does not have within its area tribes who share its group feeling, or is not situated in rugged mountain territory, is in danger of being attacked at night by surprise. Its enemies can easily attack it with a fleet. They can be sure that the city has no one to call to its support and that the urban population, accustomed to tranquillity, does not know how to fight. Among cities of this type, for instance, are Alexandria in the East, and Tripoli, Bône, and Salé in the West.

This should be understood. It may be illustrated by the fact that Alexandria was designated a 'border city' by the 'Abbâsids although the 'Abbâsid propaganda extended beyond Alexandria to Barca and Ifrîqiyah. (The term 'border city' for Alexandria) expressed 'Abbâsid fears that attacks could be made against it from the sea, in view of its exposed situation. This probably was the reason Alexandria and Tripoli were attacked by the enemy in Islamic times on numerous occasions.

6 The mosques and venerated buildings of the world

God has singled out some places of the earth for special honour. He made them the homes of His worship. People who worship in them receive a much greater reward and recompense. God informed us about this situation through His messengers and prophets, as an act of kindness to His servants and for the purpose of facilitating their ways to happiness.

We know that the most excellent places on earth are the three mosques of Mecca, Medina, and Jerusalem. Mecca is the house of Abraham. God commanded Abraham to build it and to exhort the people to make the pilgrimage thither.

Jerusalem is the house of David and Solomon. God commanded them to build the mosque there and to erect its monuments. Many of the prophets, descendants of Isaac, were buried around it.

Medina is the place to which our Prophet immigrated when God commanded him to immigrate and to establish the religion of Islam there. He built his sacred mosque in Medina, and his noble burial place is on its soil.

These three mosques are the consolation of the Muslims, the desire of their hearts, and the sacred asylum of their religion. There are many well-known traditions about their excellence and the very great reward awaiting those who live near them and pray in them. . . .

We have no information about any mosque on earth other than these three, save for stories about the Mosque of Adam on the Indian island of Ceylon. But there exists no well-established information about that mosque upon which one may rely.

The ancient nations had mosques which they venerated in what they thought to be a spirit of religious devotion. There were the fire temples of the Persians and the temples of the Greeks and the houses of the Arabs in the Ḥijâz, which the Prophet ordered to be destroyed on his raids.

7 There are few cities and towns in Ifrîqiyah and the Maghrib

The reason for this is that these regions belonged to the Berbers for thousands of years before Islam. All their civilization was Bedouin. No sedentary culture existed among (the Berbers) long enough to reach any degree of perfection. The dynasties of European Christians and Arabs who ruled them did not rule long enough for their sedentary culture to take firm root. The customs and ways of Bedouin life to which they were always closer, continued among them. Therefore, they did not have many buildings. Furthermore, crafts were unfamiliar to the Berbers, because they were firmly rooted in desert life, and the crafts result from sedentary culture. Now, buildings can materialize only with the help of (the crafts). One needs skill to learn them, and since the Berbers did not practise them, they had no interest in buildings, let alone towns.

Furthermore, they have (various) group feelings and common descent. No (Berber group) lacks these things. Common descent and group feeling are more attracted to desert (than to urban life). Only tranquillity and quiet call for towns. The inhabitants of (towns) come to be dependent on their militia. Therefore, desert people dislike settling in a town or staying there. Only luxury and wealth could cause them to settle in a town, and these things are rare among men.

Thus, the whole civilization of Ifrîqiyah and the Maghrib, or the largest part of it, was a Bedouin one. People lived in tents, (camel) litters, and mountain fastnesses.

On the other hand, the whole civilization of the non-Arab countries, or the largest part of it, was one of villages, cities, and districts. This applies to Spain, Syria, Egypt, the non-Arab 'Irâq, and similar countries. Only in the rarest cases do non-Arabs have a common descent which they guard carefully and of which they are proud when it is pure and close. It is mostly people of common descent who settle in the desert, because close common descent constitutes closer and stronger bonds than any other element. Thus, the group feeling that goes with common descent likewise is (stronger). It draws those who have it to desert life and the avoidance of cities, which do away with bravery and make people dependent upon others. This should be understood and the proper conclusions be drawn from it.

8 The buildings and constructions in Islam are comparatively few considering Islam's power and as compared to preceding dynasties

The reason for this is the very same thing that we mentioned concerning the Berbers. The Arabs, too, are quite firmly rooted in the desert and quite unfamiliar with the crafts. Furthermore, before Islam, the Arabs had been strangers to the realms of which they then took possession. When they came to rule them, there was not time enough for all the institutions of sedentary culture to develop fully. Moreover, the buildings of others which they found in existence were sufficient for them.

Furthermore, at the beginning, their religion forbade them to do any excessive building or to waste too much money on building activities for no purpose.

The influence of Islam and of scrupulousness in such matters then faded. Royal authority and luxury gained the upper hand. The Arabs subjected the Persian nation and took over their constructions and buildings. The tranquillity and luxury they now enjoyed led them to (building activities). But that also was the period close to the destruction of the dynasty. There was only a little time left for extensive building activities and town and city planning. This had not been the case with other nations. The Persians had had a period of thousands of years. The same was the case with the Copts, the Nabataeans, and the Romans. They had a great deal of time, and the crafts became firmly established among them. Thus, their buildings and monuments were more numerous and left a more lasting imprint (than the buildings of the Muslim Arabs).

9 Buildings erected by Arabs, with very few exceptions, quickly fall into ruin

The reason for this is the Bedouin attitude and unfamiliarity with the crafts. The buildings (of the Arabs) are not solidly built.

There may be another aspect, more pertinent to the problem. That is, the Arabs pay little attention in town planning to making the right choice with regard to the site, the quality of the air. the water, the fields, and the pastures. Differences with respect to these things make the difference between good and bad cities as regards natural civilization. The Arabs have no interest in these things. They only see to it that they have pastures for their camels. They do not care whether the water is good or bad, whether there is little or much of it. They do not ask about the suitability of the fields, the vegetable plots, and the air, because they move about the country and import their grain from remote places. In the desert the winds blow from all directions, and the fact that the Arabs travel about guarantees them winds of good quality. Winds turn bad only when people settle and stay in one place and there are many superfluities there.

One may cite the Arabs' planning of al-Kûfah, al-Baṣrah, and al-Qayrawân. All they looked for when planning them was pasturage for their camels and nearness to the desert and the caravan routes. Thus, (those cities) do not possess a natural site. They had no sources from which to feed their population later on. Such a source must exist if civilization is to continue.

10 The beginnings of the ruin of cities

When cities are first founded, they have few dwellings and few building materials, such as stones and quicklime, or the things that serve as ornamental coverings for walls, such as tiles, marble, mosaic, jet, (mother-of-pearl), and glass. Thus, at that time, the buildings are built in Bedouin (style), and the materials used for them are perishable.

Then, the civilization of a city grows and its inhabitants increase in number. Now the materials used for (building) increase, because of the increase in (available) labour and the increased number of craftsmen. (This process goes on) until (the city) reaches the limit in that respect.

The civilization of the city then recedes, and its inhabitants decrease in number. This entails a decrease in the crafts. As a result, good and solid building and the ornamentation of buildings are no longer practised. Then, the available labour decreases, because of the lack of inhabitants. Materials such as stones, marble, and other things are now being imported scarcely at all, and (building materials) become unavailable. The materials in the existing buildings are reused for building and refinishing. They are transferred from one construction to another, since most of the (large) constructions, castles, and mansions stand empty as the result of the great decrease in (population) as compared with former times. (The same materials) continue to be used for one castle after another and for one house after another, until most of them are completely used up. People then return to the Bedouin way of building. They use adobe instead of stone and omit all ornamentation. The architecture of the city reverts to that of villages and hamlets. The mark of the desert shows in it. (The city) then gradually decays and falls into complete ruin, if it is thus destined for it.

11 With regard to the amount of prosperity and business activity in them, cities and towns differ in accordance with the different size of their population

The reason for this is that the individual human being cannot by himself obtain all the necessities of life. All human beings must co-operate to that end in their civilization. But what is obtained through the co-operation of a group of human beings satisfies the need of a number many times greater than themselves. For instance, no one, by himself, can obtain the share of the wheat he needs for food. But when six or ten persons, including a smith and a carpenter to make the tools, and others who are in charge of the oxen, the ploughing of the soil, the harvesting of the ripe grain, and all the other agricultural activities, undertake to obtain their food and work toward that purpose either separately or collectively and thus obtain through their labour a certain amount of food, (that amount) will be food for a number of people many times their own. The combined labour produces more than the needs and necessities of the workers.

If the labour of the inhabitants of a town or city is distributed in accordance with the necessities and needs of those inhabitants, a minimum of that labour will suffice. The labour (available) is more than is needed. Consequently, it is spent to provide the conditions and customs of luxury and to satisfy the needs of the inhabitants of other cities. They import (the things they need) from (people who have a surplus) through exchange or purchase. Thus, the (people who have a surplus) get a good deal of wealth.

It will become clear in the fifth chapter, which deals with profit and sustenance, that profit is the value realized from labour. When there is more labour, the value realized from it increases among the (people). Thus, their profit of necessity increases. The prosperity and wealth they enjoy leads them to luxury and the things that go with it, such as splendid houses and clothes, fine vessels and utensils, and the use of servants and mounts. All these involve activities that require their price and skilful people must be chosen to do them and be in charge of them. As a consequence, industry and the crafts thrive. The income and the expenditure of the city increase. Affluence comes to those who work and produce these things by their labour.

When population increases, the available labour again increases. In turn, luxury again increases in correspondence with the increasing profit, and the customs and needs of luxury increase. Crafts are created to obtain (luxury products). The value realized from them increases, and, as a result, profits are again multiplied in the town. Production there is thriving even more than before. And so it goes with the second and third increases. All the additional labour serves luxury and wealth, in contrast to the original labour that served (the necessities of) life. The city that is superior to another in (population) becomes superior to it also by its increased profit and prosperity and by its customs of luxury which are not found in the other city. The more numerous and the more abundant the population in a city, the more luxurious is the life of its inhabitants. This applies equally to all levels of the population.

This may be exemplified, for instance, in the Maghrib, by comparing the situation of Fez with other Maghribî cities, such as Bougie, Tlemcen, and Ceuta. A wide difference, both in general and in detail, will be found to exist between (them and Fez). The situation of a judge in Fez is better than that of a judge in Tlemcen, and the same is the case with all other population groups. The same difference exists between Tlemcen on the one hand and Oran or Algiers on the other, and between Oran or Algiers and lesser cities, until one gets down to the hamlets where people have only the necessities of life through their labour, or not even enough of them.

The only reason for this is the difference in the labour (available) in (the different cities). They all are a sort of market for their labour (products), and the money spent in each market corresponds to (the volume of business done in it). The income of a judge in Fez suffices for his expenditure, and the same is the case with a judge in Tlemcen. Wherever income and expenditure (combined) are greater, conditions are better and more favourable. (Income and expenditure) are greater in Fez, since its production thrives because of luxury requirements there. Therefore, greater opulence exists in Fez. The same applies to Oran, Constantine, Algiers, and Biskra, until, as we have stated, one gets down to the cities whose labour does not pay for their necessities. They cannot be considered cities. They belong to the category of villages and hamlets. Therefore, the inhabitants of such small cities are found to be in a weak position and all equally poor and indigent, because their labour does not pay for their necessities and does not yield them a surplus which they can accumulate as profit. They have no increasing profit. Thus, with very few exceptions, they are poor and needy.

This can be exemplified by the condition of the poor and the beggars. A beggar in Fez is better off than a beggar in Tlemcen or

Oran. I observed beggars in Fez who, at the time of the sacrifices (of the 'Íd festival), begged for enough to buy their sacrificial animals. I saw them beg for many kinds of luxuries and delicacies such as meat, butter, cooked dishes, garments, and utensils, such as sieves and vessels. If a beggar were to ask for such things in Tlemcen or Oran, he would be considered with disapproval and treated harshly and chased away. At this time, we hear astonishing things about conditions in Cairo and Egypt as regards luxury and wealth in the customs of the inhabitants there. Many of the poor in the Maghrib even want to move to Egypt on account of that and because they hear that prosperity in Egypt is greater than anywhere else. The common people believe that this is so because property is abundant in those regions, and (their inhabitants) have much property hoarded, and are more charitable and bountiful than the inhabitants of any other city. However, this is not so, but, as one knows, the reason is that the population of Egypt and Cairo is larger than that of any other city one might think of.

Income and expenditure balance each other in every city. If the income is large, the expenditure is large, and vice versa. And if both income and expenditure are large, the inhabitants become more favourably situated, and the city grows.

No (phenomenon) of this sort one may hear about should be denied, but all these things should be understood to be the result of much civilization and the resulting great profits which facilitate spending and giving bounties to those who ask for them. This might be compared with the difference existing in one and the same town with regard to the houses dumb animals keep away from or frequent. The premises and courtyards of the houses of the prosperous and wealthy (inhabitants of the town), who set a good table and where grain and breadcrumbs lie scattered around, are frequented by swarms of ants and insects. There are many large rats in their cellars, and cats repair to them. Flocks of birds circle over them and eventually leave, satiated and full with food and drink. In the premises of the houses of the indigent and the poor who have little sustenance, no insect crawls about and no bird hovers in the air, and no rat or cat takes refuge in the cellars of such houses.

God's secret design in this respect should be scrutinized. One may compare the swarms of human beings with the swarms of dumb animals, and the crumbs from tables with the surplus of sustenance and luxury and the ease with which it can be given away by the people who have it, because as a rule they can do without it, since they have more of it. It should be known that favourable conditions and much prosperity in civilization are the results of its large size.

12 Prices in towns

All markets cater for the needs of people. Some of these needs are necessities, foodstuffs, for instance, such as wheat and barley; corresponding foods, such as beans, chick-peas, peas, and other edible grains; and wholesome foods such as onions, garlic, and the like. Other things are conveniences or luxuries, such as seasonings, fruits, clothes, utensils, mounts, all the crafts, and buildings. When a city is highly developed and has many inhabitants, the prices of necessary foodstuffs and corresponding items are low, and the prices for luxuries, such as seasonings, fruits, and the things that go with them, are high. When the inhabitants of a city are few and its civilization weak, the opposite is the case.

The reason for this is that the different kinds of grains belong among the necessary foodstuffs. The demand for them, therefore, is very large. Nobody would neglect (to provide for) his own food or that of his establishment for a month or a year. Thus, the procurement of (grain) concerns the entire population of a city, or the largest part of them, both in the city itself and in its environs. This is inevitable. Everybody who procures food for himself has a great surplus beyond his own and his family's needs. This surplus is able to satisfy the needs of many of the inhabitants of that particular city. No doubt, then, the inhabitants of a city have more food than they need. Consequently, the price of food is low, as a rule, except when misfortunes occur owing to celestial conditions that may affect the food supply in certain years. If people did not have to store food against such possible mishaps, it could be given away entirely gratis, since it would be plentiful because of the large population (of the city).

All other conveniences, such as seasonings, fruits, and whatever else belongs to them, are not matters of general concern. Their procurement does not engage the labour of all the inhabitants of a city or the largest part of them. Then, when a city has a highly developed, abundant civilization and is full of luxuries, there is a very large demand for those conveniences and for having as many of them as a person can expect in view of his situation. This results in a very great shortage of such things. Many will bid for them, but they will be in short supply. They will be needed for many purposes, and prosperous people used to luxuries will pay exorbitant prices for them, because they need them more than others. Thus, as one can see, prices come to be high.

Crafts and labour also are expensive in cities with an abundant civilization. There are three reasons for this. First, they are much needed, because of the place luxury occupies in the city on account

276

of its large population. Second, industrial workers place a high value on their services and employment, (for they do not have to work) since live is easy in a town because of the abundance of food there. Third, the number of people with money to waste is great, and these people have many needs for which they have to employ the services of others and have to use many workers and their skills. Therefore, they pay more for (the services of) workers than their labour is (ordinarily considered) worth, because there is competition for (their services) and the wish to have exclusive use of them. Thus, workers, craftsmen, and professional people become arrogant, their labour becomes expensive, and the expenditure of the inhabitants of the city for these things increases.

Foodstuffs in small cities that have few inhabitants are few, because they have a small (supply) of labour and because, in view of the small size of the city, the people fear food shortages. Therefore, they hold on to (the food) that comes into their hands and store it. It thus becomes something precious to them, and those who want to buy it have to pay higher prices. They also have no demand for conveniences, because the inhabitants are few and their condition is weak. Little business is done by them, and the prices there, consequently, become particularly low.

Customs duties and other duties that are levied on (foods) in the markets and at the city gates on behalf of the ruler, and that tax collectors levy on profits from business transactions in their own interest, enter into the price of foodstuffs. Prices in cities, thus, are higher than prices in the desert, because customs duties and other duties and levies are few or nonexistent among (the Bedouins), while the opposite is the case in cities, especially in the later (years) of a dynasty.

The cost of agricultural labour also enters into the price of foodstuffs. It is reflected in these prices. This has happened in Spain at the present time. The Christians pushed the Muslims back to the sea coast and the rugged territory there, where (the soil) is poor for the cultivation of grain and little suited for (the growth of) vegetables. They themselves took possession of the fine soil and the good land. Thus, (the Muslims) had to treat the fields and tracts of land, in order to improve the plants and agriculture there. This treatment required expensive labour (products) and materials, such as fertilizer and other things that had to be procured. Thus, their agricultural activities required considerable expenditure. They calculated this expenditure in fixing their prices, and thus Spain has become an especially expensive region, ever since the Christians forced (the Muslims) to withdraw to the Muslim-held coastal regions, for the reason mentioned.

When they hear about the high prices in (Spain), people think that they are caused by the small amount of foodstuffs and grain in the country. This is not so. As we know, the (people of Spain), of all civilized people, are the ones most devoted to agriculture. It rarely happens among them that a man in authority or an ordinary person has no tract of land or field, or does not do some farming. The only exceptions are a few craftsmen and professional people, or fighters in the holy war who are newcomers to the country. The ruler, therefore includes, in the allowances these men receive, rations consisting of the grain for food and for fodder.

The Berber countries are in the contrary position. Their fields are fine and their soil is good. Therefore, they did not have to procure anything (from outside) for their agriculture, which is widely and generally practised there. This is the reason for the cheapness of foodstuffs in their country.

13 Bedouins are unable to settle in a city with a large population

The reason for this is that luxury increases in a city with a large population, as we have stated before. The needs of the inhabitants increase on account of the luxury. Because of the demand for (luxury articles), they become customary, and thus come to be necessities. In addition, all labour becomes costly in the city, and the conveniences become expensive, because there are many purposes for which they are in demand in view of the prevailing luxury and because the government makes levies on market and business transactions. This is reflected in the sales prices. Conveniences, foodstuffs, and labour thus become very expensive. As a result, the expenditure of the inhabitants increases tremendously in proportion to the population of the city. Under these circumstances, they need a great deal of money for expenditure, to procure the necessities of life for themselves and their families, as well as all their other requirements.

The income of the Bedouins, on the other hand, is not large, because they live where there is little demand for labour, and labour is the cause of profit. Bedouins, therefore, do not accumulate any profit or property. For this reason, it is difficult for them to settle in a big city, because conveniences there are expensive and things to buy are dear. In the desert, they can satisfy their needs with a minimum of labour, because they are little used to luxuries.

Every Bedouin who is attracted to city life quickly shows himself unable (to compete) and is disgraced. The only exceptions are such as have previously accumulated property and obtained more of it than they needed and therefore achieved the amount of tranquillity and luxury that is natural to civilized people. They, then, may move to a city, and their condition, as regards customs and luxury, can blend with that of its inhabitants. This is the way the civilization of cities begins.

14 Differences with regard to prosperity and poverty are the same in countries as in cities

The condition of the inhabitants in regions that have an abundant civilization and contain numerous nations and many inhabitants is favourable. They have much property and many cities. Their dynasties and realms are large. The reason for all this is the great amount of available labour and the fact that it brings wealth. A great surplus of products remains after the necessities of the inhabitants have been satisfied. This provides for a population far beyond the size and extent of the actual one, and comes back to the people as profit that they can accumulate. Prosperity, thus, increases, and conditions become favourable. There are luxury and wealth. The tax revenues of the ruling dynasty increase on account of business prosperity. Its property increases, and its authority grows. It comes to use fortresses and castles, to found towns, and to construct cities.

This may be exemplified by the eastern regions, such as Egypt, Syria, India, China, and the whole northern region, beyond the Mediterranean. When their civilization increased, the property of the inhabitants increased, and their dynasties became great. Their towns and settlements became numerous, and their commerce and conditions improved.

At this time, we can observe the condition of the merchants of the Christian nations who come to the Muslims in the Maghrib. Their prosperity and affluence cannot be fully described because it is so great. The same applies to the merchants from the East and what we hear about their conditions, and even more so to the Far Eastern merchants from the countries of the non-Arab 'Irâq, India, and China. We hear remarkable stories reported by travellers about their wealth and prosperity. These stories are usually received with scepticism. The common people who hear them think that the prosperity of these peoples is the result of the greater amount of property owned by them, or of the existence of gold and silver mines in their country in larger number (than elsewhere), or of the fact that they, to the exclusion of others, appropriated the gold of the ancient nations. This is not so. The only gold mine about whose existence in these regions we have information, lies in the Sudan, which is nearer to the Maghrib (than to any other country). Furthermore, all the merchandise that is in their country is exported by them for commerce. If they possessed ready property in abundance, they would not export their merchandise in search of money, and they would have altogether no need of other people's property.

Astrologers have noticed this and been amazed by the favourable conditions and abundance of property in the East. They came and said that the gifts of the stars and the shares (of good fortune) were larger in the nativities of the East than in those of the West. This is correct from the point of view of the correspondence between astrological judgments and terrestrial conditions. But astrologers give us only the astrological reason. They ought also to give us the terrestrial reason; this being the large extent and concentration of civilization in the eastern regions. A large civilization yields large profits because of the large amount of available labour, which is the cause of (profit). Therefore, the East enjoys more prosperity than all other regions. This is not exclusively the result of the influence of the stars. Our previous indications have made it clear that the influence of the stars cannot produce such a result all by itself. A correspondence between astrological judgments and terrestrial civilization and nature is something inevitable.

The relationship between prosperity and civilization may be exemplified by the regions of Ifrîqiyah and Barca. When their population decreased and their civilization shrank, the condition of their inhabitants decayed. They became poor and indigent. The tax revenues decreased. The property of the dynasties that ruled there became small. . . .

15 The accumulation of estates and farms in cities. Their uses and yields

The accumulation of numerous estates and farms by the inhabitants of towns and cities does not come all at once. No one person would have enough wealth to acquire limitless (real) property. Even if prosperity were as great as possible, the acquisition and accumulation of (real) property would be gradual. It may come about through inheritance from one's forefathers and blood relatives, so that eventually the property of many comes to one person, who thus possesses much. Or it may be through fluctuation in the (real-estate) market. When one dynasty ends and another begins, the militia vanishes. There is no protection, and the city collapses and is ruined. At that time, real estate does not make a person happy, because it is of little use in the general upheaval. (Real-estate) values fall, and real estate can be acquired for low prices. It then passes through inheritance into the possession of someone else. By that time the city has regained its youthful vigour as the new dynasty flourishes, and conditions in it are in excellent shape. The result is that one may be happy with the possession of estates and farms, because they will then be very useful. Their value increases, and they assume an importance they did not have before. This is the meaning of 'fluctuation in (the real-estate market)'. The owner of (real estate) now turns out to be one of the wealthiest men in the city. That is not the result of his own effort and business activity, because he would be unable to achieve such a thing by himself.

Estates and farms do not yield their owner a sufficient income for his needs; the income from them will not pay for the customs of luxury and the things that go with it. As a rule, it serves only to help provide for the necessities of life.

We have heard from scholars that the motive in the acquisition of estates and farms is a concern for the helpless children a person may leave behind. Income from (real estate) serves to provide for their education, care, and upbringing, as long as they are unable to earn their own living. When they are able to earn their own living, they will do it by themselves. But there often are children who are unable to earn their own living because of some weakness of the body or some defect in the mind. Real property then becomes their support. This is the motive of persons who spend a great deal of money acquiring it.

(The motive is) not to accumulate capital through such acquisitions or to provide for extravagant living. This is achieved only by a few and is achieved only rarely through market fluctuations, through the acquisition of a great deal of (real estate), and through the up-grading of real estate as such and its value in a certain city. But then, if someone achieves it, the eyes of amirs and governors are directed to him. As a rule, they take it away, or they urge him to sell it to them. It spells harm and hardship to its owners.

16 Capitalists among the inhabitants of cities need rank and protection

This is because a sedentary person who has a great deal of capital and has acquired a great number of estates and farms and become one of the wealthiest inhabitants of a particular city, who is looked upon as such and lives in great luxury and is accustomed to luxury, competes in this respect with amirs and rulers. The latter become jealous of him. The aggressiveness that is natural to human beings makes them cast their eyes upon his possessions. They envy him and try every possible trick to catch him in the net of a government decision and to find an obvious reason for punishing him, so as to confiscate his property. Government decisions are as a rule unjust, because pure justice is found only in the legal caliphate that lasted only a short while. Muḥammad said: 'The caliphate after me will last thirty years; then, it will revert to being tyrannic royal authority.'

Therefore, the owner of property and conspicuous wealth in a given community needs a protective force to defend him, as well as a rank on which he may rely. (This purpose may be met by) a person related to the ruler, or a close friend of (the ruler), or a group feeling that the ruler will respect. In its shade, he may rest and live peacefully, safe from hostile attacks. If he does not have that, he will find himself robbed by all kinds of tricks and legal pretexts.

17 Sedentary culture in cities comes from the dynasties. It is firmly rooted when the dynasty is continuous and firmly rooted

The reason for this is that sedentary culture is a condition that is the result of custom and goes beyond the necessary conditions of civilization. How far beyond, differs in accordance with unlimited differences in the prosperity and the numerical strength or weakness of the nations. (Sedentary culture) occurs in nations when much diversity develops among its various subdivisions. It is thus on the same level as the crafts. Each particular kind of craft needs persons to be in charge of it and skilled in it. The more numerous the various subdivisions of a craft are, the larger the number of people who practise that craft. In the course of time, as each craft becomes more distinct, the craftsmen become experienced in their various crafts. Long periods of time and the repetition of similar (experiences) add to establishing the crafts and to causing them to be firmly rooted.

This happens mostly in cities, because cities have a highly developed civilization and their inhabitants are very prosperous, and the dynasty is at the root of it, because the dynasty collects the property of the subjects and spends it on its inner circle and on the men connected with it who are more influential by reason of their position than by reason of their property. The money comes from the subjects and is spent among the people of the dynasty and then among those inhabitants who are connected with them. They are the largest part (of the population). Their wealth, therefore, increases and their riches grow. The customs and ways of luxury multiply, and all the various kinds of crafts are firmly established among them. This is sedentary culture.

Therefore, cities in remote parts of the realm, even if they have a large population, are found to be predominantly Bedouin and remote from sedentary culture in all their ways. This is in contrast with towns that lie in the middle, the centre and the seat of the dynasty. The only reason is that the government is near them and pours its money into them, like the water (of a river) that makes green everything around it, and fertilizes the soil adjacent to it, while in the distance everything remains dry. For dynasty and government are the world's market-place. All kinds of merchandise are found in the market and near it. Far from the market, however, goods are altogether nonexistent. As a particular dynasty continues to rule and its rulers succeed each other in a particular city, sedentary culture becomes increasingly firmly established and rooted among the inhabitants of that city.

This may be exemplified by the Jews. Their rule in Syria lasted about 1,400 years. Sedentary culture thus became firmly established among them. They became skilled in the customary ways and means of making a living and in the manifold crafts belonging to it as regards food, clothing, and all the other parts of (domestic) economy, so much so that these things, as a rule, can still be learned from them to this day. Sedentary culture and its customs became firmly rooted in Syria through them and through the Roman dynasties which succeeded them for six hundred years. Thus, they had the most developed sedentary culture possible.

The same was the case with the Copts. Their political power lasted three thousand years. The customs of sedentary culture were thus firmly rooted in their country, Egypt. They were succeeded there by the Greeks and the Romans, and then by Islam, which abrogated everything. The customs of sedentary culture have, thus, always continued in Egypt.

The same was the case with the sedentary culture in the 'Irâq which, for thousands of years, was ruled continuously by the Nabataeans and the Persians, that is, the Chaldaeans, the Achaemenids, the Sassanians, and, after them, the Arabs. Down to this time there has never been upon the face of the earth a people with more sedentary culture than the inhabitants of Syria, the 'Irâq, and Egypt.

The customs of sedentary culture also became firmly rooted in Spain, which, for thousands of years, was ruled continuously by the great Gothic dynasty, later succeeded by the Umayyad realm. Both dynasties were great.

Ifrîqiyah and the Maghrib had no great royal authority before Islam. The Romans and European Christians had crossed the sea to Ifrîqiyah and had taken possession of the coast. The allegiance the Berbers who lived there paid them was not firmly grounded. They were there only temporarily. No dynasty was close to the people of the Maghrib. From time to time, they offered their obedience to the Goths across the sea. When the Arabs took possession of Ifrîqiyah and the Maghrib, Arab rule lasted for only a short while at the beginning of Islam. At that time they were in the stage of Bedouin life. Those who stayed in Ifrîqiyah and the Maghrib did not find there any old tradition of sedentary culture, because the original population had been Berbers immersed in Bedouin life. Very soon, the Berbers of Morocco revolted and never again later reverted to Arab rule. They were independent. If they rendered the oath of allegiance to Idrîs, his rule over them cannot be considered an Arab rule, because the Berbers were in charge of it, and there were not many Arabs in it. Ifrîqiyah remained in the possession of the Aghlabids and the Arabs who were with them. They had some sedentary culture as the result of the luxury and prosperity of the royal authority and the large civilization of al-Qayrawân that were theirs. The Kutâmah and then the Ṣinhâjah after them inherited it from the Aghlabids. But all that was brief and lasted less than four hundred years. Their dynasty ended, and the stamp of sedentary culture changed, as it had not been firmly established. The Hilâl, who were Arab Bedouins, gained power over the country and ruined it.

Some obscure traces of sedentary culture have remained there down to the present time. They can be found in the (domestic) economy and the customs of these people. They are mixed with other things, but the person who comes from a sedentary environment and knows about (sedentary culture) can discern them. That is the case with most cities in Ifrîqiyah, but not in the Maghrib and the cities there, because since the time of the Aghlabids, the Fâṭimids, and the Ṣinhâjah, the ruling dynasty in Ifrîqiyah has been firmly rooted there for a longer period (than the dynasties in the Maghrib).

The Maghrib, on the other hand, has received a good deal of sedentary culture from Spain since the dynasty of the Almohads, and the customs of sedentary culture became established there through the control that the ruling dynasty of the Maghrib exercised over Spain. A good many of the inhabitants of (Spain) went over to the Almohads in the Maghrib, voluntarily or involuntarily. One knows how far-flung the influence (of the Almohad dynasty) was. It possessed a good deal of firmly established sedentary culture, most of it due to the inhabitants of Spain. Later on, the inhabitants of Eastern Spain were expelled by the Christians and moved to Ifrîqiyah. In the cities there, they left traces of sedentary culture. Most of it is in Tunis, where it mixed with the sedentary culture of Egypt and Egyptian customs imported by travellers. Thus, the Maghrib and Ifrîqiyah had a good deal of sedentary culture. But emptiness took its place, and it disappeared. The Berbers in the Maghrib reverted to their Bedouin ways and Bedouin toughness. But, at any rate, the traces of sedentary culture are more numerous in Ifrîqiyah than in the Maghrib. The old dynasties had lasted longer in Ifrîqiyah than in the Maghrib, and the customs of the people of Ifrîqiyah had been close to the customs of the Egyptians because of the great amount of intercourse between them.

This secret should be understood, because it is not generally known. It should be recognized that these are related matters: The strength and weakness of a dynasty, the numerical strength of a nation or race, the size of a town or city, and the amount of prosperity and wealth. This is because dynasty and royal authority constitute the form of the world and of civilization, which, in turn, together with the subjects, cities, and all other things, constitute the matter of dynasty and royal authority. The tax money reverts to the people. Their wealth, as a rule, comes from their business and commercial activities. If the ruler pours out gifts and money upon his people, it spreads among them and reverts to him, and again from him to them. It comes from them through taxation and the land tax, and reverts to them through gifts. The wealth of the subjects corresponds to the finances of the dynasty. The finances of the dynasty, in turn, correspond to the wealth and number of the subjects. The origin of it all is civilization and its extensiveness. If this is considered and examined in connection with the dynasties, it will be found to be so.

18 Sedentary culture is the goal of civilization. It means the end of its life span and brings about its corruption

We have explained before that royal authority and the foundation of dynasties are the goal of group feeling, that sedentary culture is the goal of Bedouin life, and that any civilization, be it a Bedouin civilization or sedentary culture, whether it concerns ruler or commoner, has a physical life, just as any individual has a physical life.

Reason and tradition make it clear that forty years mean the end of the increase of an individual's powers and growth. When a man has reached the age of forty, nature stops growing for a while, then starts to decline. It should be known that the same is the case with sedentary culture in civilization, because there is a limit that cannot be overstepped. When luxury and prosperity come to civilized people, it naturally causes them to follow the ways of sedentary culture and adopt its customs. As one knows, sedentary culture is the adoption of diversified luxuries, the cultivation of the things that go with them, and addiction to the crafts that give elegance to all refinements, such as the crafts of cooking, dressmaking, building, and (making) carpets, vessels, and all other parts of (domestic) economy. For the elegant execution of all these things, there exist many crafts not needed in desert life with its lack of elegance. When elegance in (domestic) economy has reached the limit, it is followed by subservience to desires. From all these customs, the human soul receives a multiple stamp that undermines its religion and worldly well-being.

It cannot preserve its religion, because it has now been firmly stamped by customs that are difficult to discard. (It cannot preserve) its worldly (well-being), because the customs (of luxury) demand a great many things and (entail) many requirements for which (a man's) income is not sufficient.

This is explained by the fact that the expenditure of the inhabitants of a city mounts with the diversification of sedentary culture. Sedentary culture differs according to the differences in civilization. When a civilization grows, sedentary culture becomes more perfect. We have stated before that a city with a large population is characterized by high prices in business and high prices for its needs. These are then raised still higher through customs duties; for sedentary culture reaches perfection at the time when the dynasty has reached its greatest flourishing, and that is the time when the dynasty levies customs duties because then it has large expenditure. The customs duties raise the sale prices, because small businessmen and merchants include all their expenses, even their personal requirements, in the price of their stock and merchandise. Thus, customs duties enter into the sale price. The expenditure of sedentary people, therefore, grows and is no longer reasonable but extravagant. The people cannot escape this because they are dominated by and subservient to their customs. All their profits go into their expenditure. One person after another becomes reduced in circumstances and indigent. Poverty takes hold of them. Few persons bid for the available goods. Business decreases, and the situation of the town deteriorates.

All this is caused by excessive sedentary culture and luxury. They corrupt the city generally in respect to business and civilization. Corruption of the individual inhabitants is the result of painful and trying efforts to satisfy the needs caused by their (luxury) customs; (the result) of the bad qualities they have acquired in the process of satisfying (those needs); and of the damage the soul suffers after it has obtained them. Immorality, wrongdoing, insincerity, and trickery, for the purposes of making a living in a proper or an improper manner, increase among them. The soul comes to think about (making a living), to study it, and to use all possible trickery for the purpose. People are now devoted to lying, gambling, cheating, fraud, theft, perjury, and usury. Because of the many desires and pleasures resulting from luxury, they are found to know everything about the ways and means of immorality, they talk openly about it and its causes, and give up all restraint in discussing it, even among relatives and close female relations, where the Bedouin attitude requires modesty (and avoidance of) obscenities. They also know everything about fraud and deceit, which they employ to defend themselves against the possible use of force against them and against the

286

punishment expected for their evil deeds. Eventually, this becomes a custom and trait of character with most of them, except those whom God protects.

The city, then, teems with low people of blameworthy character. They encounter competition from many members of the younger generation of the dynasty, whose education has been neglected and whom the dynasty has neglected to accept. They, therefore, adopt the qualities of their environment and company, even though they may be people of noble descent and ancestry. Men are human beings and as such resemble one another. They differ in merit and are distinguished by their character, by their acquisition of virtues and avoidance of vices. The person who is strongly coloured by any kind of vice and whose character is corrupted, is not helped by his good descent and fine origin. Thus, one finds that many descendants of great families, men of a highly esteemed origin, members of the dynasty, get into deep water and adopt low occupations in order to make a living, because their character is corrupt and they are coloured by wrongdoing and insincerity. If this (situation) spreads in a town or nation, God permits it to be ruined and destroyed. This is the meaning of the word of God: 'When we want to destroy a village, we order those of its inhabitants who live in luxury to act wickedly therein. Thus, the word becomes true for it, and we do destroy it.'[1]

A possible explanation of this (situation) is that the profits (the people) make do not pay for their needs, because of the great number of (luxury) customs and the desire of the soul to satisfy them. Thus, the affairs of the people are disordered, and if the affairs of individuals one by one deteriorate, the town becomes disorganized and falls into ruin.

This is the meaning of the statement by certain experts, that if orange trees are much grown in a town, the town invites its own ruin. Many common people avoided the growing of orange trees around their houses on account of this ominous statement. But this is not the meaning intended. What is meant is that gardens and irrigation are the results of sedentary culture. Orange trees, lime trees, cypresses, and similar plants having no edible fruits[2] and being of no use, are the ultimate in sedentary culture, since they are planted in gardens only for the sake of their appearance, and they are planted only after the ways of luxury have become diversified. This is the stage in which one must fear the destruction and ruin of a city, as we have

[1] Qur'ân 17. 16 (17).
[2] This is what Ibn Khaldûn says, but since the various citrus plants can be used for some kind of nourishment, he is apparently thinking of their seeming lack of basic nutritive qualities.

stated. The same has been said with regard to oleander, which is in the same category. Its only purpose is to give colour to gardens with its red and white flowers. That is a luxury.

Among the things that corrupt sedentary culture, there is the disposition toward pleasures and indulgence in them, because of the great luxury (that prevails). It leads to diversification of the desires of the belly for pleasurable food and drink. This is followed by diversification of the pleasures of sex through various ways of sexual intercourse, such as adultery and homosexuality. This leads to destruction of the species. It may come about indirectly, through the confusion concerning one's descent caused by adultery. Nobody knows his own son, since he is illegitimate and since the sperm (of different men) got mixed up in the womb. The natural compassion a man feels for his children and his feeling of responsibility for them is lost. Thus, they perish, and this leads to the end of the species. Or, the destruction of the species may come about directly, as is the case with homosexuality, which leads directly to the nonexistence of offspring. It contributes more to the destruction of the species (than adultery), since it leads to no human beings being brought into existence, while adultery only leads to the (social) nonexistence of those who are in existence. Therefore, the school of Mâlik is more explicit and correct with regard to homosexuality than the other schools. This shows that it understands the intentions of the religious law and their bearing upon the (public) interest better (than the other legal schools).

This should be understood. It shows that the goal of civilization is sedentary culture and luxury. When civilization reaches that goal, it turns toward corruption and starts being senile, as happens in the natural life of living beings. Indeed, we may say that the qualities of character resulting from sedentary culture and luxury are identical with corruption. Man is a man only inasmuch as he is able to procure for himself useful things and to repel harmful things, and inasmuch as his character is suited to making efforts to this effect. The sedentary person cannot take care of his needs personally. He may be too weak, because of the tranquillity he enjoys. Or he may be too proud, because he was brought up in prosperity and luxury. Both things are blameworthy. He also is not able to repel harmful things, because he has no courage as the result of luxury and his upbringing under the impact of education and instruction. He thus becomes dependent upon a protective force to defend him.

He then usually becomes corrupt with regard to his religion, also. The (luxury) customs and his subservience to them have corrupted him, and his soul has been stamped by habits of luxury, as we have stated. There are only very rare exceptions. When the strength of a man and then his character and religion are corrupted, his humanity is corrupted, and he becomes, in effect, transformed into an animal.

It is in this sense that those government soldiers who are close to Bedouin life and toughness are more useful than those who have grown up in a sedentary culture and have adopted its character traits. This can be found in every dynasty. It has thus become clear that the stage of sedentary culture is the stopping point in the life of civilization and dynastics.

19 Cities that are the seats of royal authority fall into ruin when the ruling dynasty crumbles and falls into ruin

We have found out with regard to civilization that, when a dynasty disintegrates and crumbles, the civilization of the city that is the seat of the ruler also crumbles and in this process often suffers complete ruin. There hardly ever is any delay. The reasons for it are several:

First: At the beginning of the dynasty, its necessary Bedouin outlook requires it not to take away people's property and to eschew (too great) cleverness. This causes the taxes and imposts, which provide the dynasty with its substance, to be kept low. The expenditure is small, and there is little luxury. When a city that was a royal capital comes into the possession of a new dynasty that knows little of luxury, luxury decreases among the inhabitants of that city controlled by it, because the subjects follow the dynasty. They revert to the character of the dynasty, either voluntarily, because it is human nature to follow the tradition of their masters, or involuntarily, because the character of the dynasty calls for abstention from luxury in all situations and allows little profit, which is what constitutes the material for (the formation of luxury) customs. As a result, the sedentary culture of the city decreases, and many luxury customs disappear from it. That is what we mean when we speak about the ruin of a city.

Second: Royal authority and power are acquired by a dynasty only through superiority, which comes only after hostilities and wars. Hostility implies incompatibility between the people of two dynasties and mutual disapproval with regard to (luxury) customs and conditions. The victory of one of the two rivals causes the disappearance of the other. Thus, the conditions of the previous dynasty, especially the conditions of luxury, are disapproved of and considered detestable and evil by the people of the new dynasty. They disappear among them, because the (new) dynasty disapproves of them. Eventually, however, new luxury customs gradually originate among them. They produce a new sedentary culture. The period in between sees a dwindling and decrease of the first sedentary culture. This is what is meant by disintegration of civilization in a city.

Third: Each nation must have a home, where it grows up and from which the realm takes its origin. When (its members) take possession of another home, (the latter) is ranked second to the first (home), and its cities are ranked second to those of the first. When the realm expands and its influence grows, it is inevitable that the seat of government be amidst the provinces belonging to the dynasty, because it is a sort of centre for the whole area. Thus, the (new seat of government) is remote from the site of the former seat of government. The hearts of the people are attracted to the (new seat of government), because the dynasty and government (are centred there). The population moves there and disappears slowly from the city that was the former seat of government. Sedentary culture depends upon an abundant population. (With the transfer of the population), the sedentary and urban culture (of the former seat of government) decreases. This is what is meant by its disintegration.

This happened to the Saljûqs when they moved their seat of government from Baghdad to Iṣfahân; to the Arabs before them when they moved from al-Madâ'in to al-Kûfah and al-Basrah; to the 'Abbâsids when they moved from Damascus to Baghdad; and to the Merinids in the Maghrib when they moved from Marrakech to Fez. In general, when a dynasty chooses a city for its seat of government, it causes disintegration of the civilization in the former seat of government.

Fourth: When the new dynasty achieves superiority over the previous dynasty, it must attempt to transfer the people and partisans of the previous dynasty to another region where it can be sure that it will not be secretly attacked by them. Most of the inhabitants of a capital city are partisans of the (ruling) dynasty. They belong either to the militia who settled there at the beginning of the dynasty, or they are the dignitaries of the city. All their various classes and types have, as a rule, some contact with the dynasty. Most of them have grown up in the dynasty and are partisans of it. Even though they may not be (connected with the dynasty) through power and group feelings, they are (connected with it) through inclination, love, and faith. It is the nature of a new dynasty to wipe out all traces of the previous dynasty. Therefore, it transfers (the population) from the capital city (of the old dynasty) to its own home, which is firmly in its possession. Some are brought there as exiles and prisoners, others as honoured and well-treated guests, so that no antagonism can arise. Eventually, the capital city (of the previous dynasty) holds only salesmen, itinerant farm workers, hoodlums, and the great mass of common people. The place of the (transferred population) is taken by the militia and partisans of (the new dynasty). They will be sufficient to fill the city. When the various classes of dignitaries have left the city, its inhabitants decrease. This is what is meant by disintegration of civilization in a (capital city).

Then, (the former capital city) must produce a new civilization under the shadow of the new dynasty. Another sedentary culture corresponding to the importance of the dynasty arises in it. This may be compared to a person who has a house the interior of which is dilapidated. Most of the installations and conveniences of the rooms do not agree with his plans. He has the power to change these installations and to rebuild them according to his wishes and plans. Thus, he will tear down the house and build it up again. Much the same sort of thing happens in cities that once were seats of government. We have personally seen it and know it.

In sum, the primary natural reason for this (situation) is the fact that dynasty and royal authority have the same relationship to civilization as form has to matter. (The form) is the shape that preserves the existence of (matter) through the kind (of phenomenon) it represents. It has been established in philosophy that the one cannot be separated from the other. One cannot imagine a dynasty without civilization, while a civilization without dynasty and royal authority is impossible, because human beings must by nature cooperate, and that calls for a restraining influence. Political leadership, based either on religious or royal authority, is inevitable. This is what is meant by dynasty. Since the two cannot be separated, the disintegration of one of them must influence the other, just as its nonexistence would entail the nonexistence of the other.

A major disintegration results only from the disintegration of the entire dynasty. This happened to the dynasties of the Persians, the Byzantines, and the Arabs in general as well as the Umayyads and the 'Abbâsids. An individual reign, such as those of Anôsharwân, Heraclius, 'Abd-al-Malik b. Marwân, or ar-Rashîd, cannot exercise a sweeping disintegrating influence. Individuals follow upon each other and take over the (existing) civilization. They preserve its existence and duration, and they are very similar to each other. The real dynasty, the one that acts upon the matter of civilization, belongs to group feeling and power. These remain with the individual members of the dynasty. But when the group feeling is lost and replaced by another group feeling, a great disintegration sets in.

20 Certain cities have crafts that others lack

This is because it is clear that the activities of the inhabitants of a city necessitate each other, since mutual co-operation is innate in civilization. The necessary activities are restricted to certain inhabitants of the city. They are in charge of them and become experts in the crafts belonging to them. These activities become their particular job. They make their living through them and derive their sustenance from them, because these are matters of general concern in the city and generally needed. On the other hand, activities not required in a city are not regarded, since there is no profit in them for those who practise them.

The activities required for the necessities of life, such as those of tailors, smiths, carpenters, and similar occupations, exist in every city. But activities required for luxury customs and conditions exist only in cities of a highly developed culture, that have taken to luxury customs and sedentary culture. Among such activities are those of glassblowers, goldsmiths, perfumers, cooks, coppersmiths, biscuit bakers, weavers of brocade, and the like. (These activities) exist in different degrees. In accordance with increase in the customs of sedentary culture and the requirements of luxury conditions, there originate crafts for this kind (of luxury requirements). Such crafts will exist in a particular city but not in others.

(Public) baths fall into this category. They exist only in densely settled cities of a highly developed civilization as a kind of indulgence resulting from luxury and wealth. Therefore, public baths do not exist in medium-sized towns. It is true that some rulers and chiefs desire (to have baths in their medium-sized cities). They construct them and put them into operation. However, since there is no demand for them from the mass of the people, they are soon neglected and fall into ruin. Those in charge of them speedily leave them, because they have little profit and income from them.

21   The existence of group feeling in cities and the superiority of some of the inhabitants over others

It is clear that it is in the nature of human beings to enter into close contact and to associate with each other, even though they may not have a common descent. However, such association is weaker than one based upon common descent, and the resulting group feeling is proportionately weaker too. Many inhabitants of cities come into close contact through intermarriage. This draws them together and, eventually, they constitute individual related groups. The same friendship or hostility that is found among tribes and families, is found among them, and they split into parties and groups.

When senility befalls a dynasty and its shadow recedes from the remote regions, the inhabitants of the cities of that dynasty have to take care of their own affairs and to look after the protection of their own place. Souls, by their very nature, are prone to seek superiority and domination. Because the air is clear of forceful government and dynasty, the elders desire to gain complete control. Everybody vies with everybody else. They try to have followers, such as clients, partisans, and allies, join them. They spend whatever they possess on the rabble and the mob. Everybody forms a group with his fellows, and one of them achieves superiority. He then turns against his equals, and persecutes them with assassination or exile. Eventually, he takes away all executive power from them and renders them innocuous. He obtains sole control of the entire city. He then comes to believe he has created a realm that he may leave to his descendants, but the same symptoms of power and senility to be found in a large realm are also to be found in his smaller realm.

Some of these people occasionally aspire to the ways of the great rulers who are masters of tribes and families and group feelings, who go into combat and wage wars, and who control large regions and provinces. They adopt the custom of sitting upon a throne. They use an 'outfit', organize cavalcades for travelling about the country, use seal rings, are greeted (ceremoniously), and are addressed as Sire, which is ridiculous in the eyes of all who can observe the situation for themselves. They adopt royal emblems to which they are not entitled. They were pushed into following such (improper aspirations) only by the dwindling influence of the (ruling) dynasty and the close relationships they had established and that eventually resulted in group feeling. Some refrained from (improper aspirations) and lived simply, because they did not want to make themselves the butt of jokes and ridicule.

This happened in our own time in the later (years) of the Hafsid dynasty in Ifrîqiyah to inhabitants of places in the Jarîd, including Tripoli, Gabès, Tozeur, Nafta, Gafsa, Biskra and the Zâb, and adjacent regions. They acquired such aspirations when the shadow of the dynasty had been receding from them for some decades. They seized power in their respective cities and took control of the judicial and tax administration away from the dynasty. They paid (the ruling dynasty) some allegiance and treated it with some politeness, kindness, and submissiveness. However, they did not mean it. They passed their position on to their descendants, who (are living) at this time. Among their successors, there originated that cruelty and tyranny which is common among the descendants and successors of rulers. They thought that they ranked with (true) rulers, despite the fact that they had only recently been common people.

As a rule, such leadership goes to members of great and noble houses who are eligible for the positions of elders and leaders in a city. Sometimes, it goes to some person from the lowest class of people. He obtains group feeling and close contact with the mob for reasons that fate produces for him. He, then, achieves superiority over the elders and people of the higher class when they have lost their own group support.

22 The dialects of the urban population

The dialects of the urban population follow the language of the nation or race that has control of (the cities) or has founded them. Therefore, the dialects spoken in all Muslim cities in the East and the West at this time are Arabic, even though the habit of the classical Arabic language has become corrupted and its vowel endings (*i'ráb*) have changed. The reason for this is the fact that the Muslim dynasty gained power over foreign nations. Religion and religious organization constitute the form for existence and royal authority, which together constitute the matter for religion. Form is prior to matter. Religion is derived from the religious law, which is in Arabic, because the Prophet was an Arab. Therefore, it is necessary to avoid using any language but Arabic in all the provinces of Islam.

This may be exemplified by 'Umar's prohibition against using the idiom native among the non-Arabs. Since Islam avoided the non-Arab dialects, and the language of the supporters of the Muslim dynasty was Arabic, those dialects were avoided altogether in all its provinces, because people follow the government and adopt its ways. Use of the Arabic language became a symbol of Islam and of obedience to the Arabs. The (foreign) nations avoided using their own dialects and languages in all the cities and provinces, and the Arabic language became their language. Eventually, it became firmly rooted as the (spoken) language in all their cities and towns. The non-Arab languages came to seem imported and foreign there. The Arabic language became corrupt through contact with (foreign languages) in some of its rules and through changes of the word endings, even though it remained unchanged semantically. (This type of Arabic) was called 'the sedentary language' (and was used) in all the cities of Islam.

Furthermore, most of the inhabitants of the cities of Islam at this time are descendants of the Arabs who were in possession of these cities and perished in their luxury. They outnumbered the non-Arabs who lived there and inherited their land and country. Now, languages are inherited. Thus, the language spoken by the descendants has remained close to that of their forefathers, even though its rules have gradually become corrupted by contact with non-Arabs. It was called 'sedentary' with reference to the inhabitants of settled regions and cities, in contrast to the language of the desert Arabs, which is more deeply rooted in Arabism.

When non-Arabs became the rulers and obtained royal authority and control over the whole Muslim realm, the Arabic language suffered corruption. It would almost have disappeared, if the concern of Muslims with the Qur'ân and the Sunnah, which preserve Islam, had not also preserved the Arabic language. This (concern) became an element in favour of the persistence of the sedentary dialect used in the cities. But when the Tatars and Mongols, who were not Muslims, became the rulers in the East, this element in favour of the Arabic language disappeared, and the Arabic language was absolutely doomed. No trace of it has remained in these Muslim provinces: the non-Arab 'Irâq, Khurâsân, Southern Persia, eastern and western India, Transoxania, the northern countries, and Anatolia. The Arabic style of poetry and speech has disappeared, save for a (remnant). Instruction in (what little Arabic is known) is a technical matter using rules learned from the sciences of the Arabs and through memorizing their speech. (It is restricted) to those persons whom God has equipped for it. The sedentary Arabic dialect has largely remained in Egypt, Syria, Spain, and the Maghrib, because Islam still remains and requires it. Therefore, it has been preserved to some degree. But in the provinces of the non-Arab 'Irâq and beyond to the East, no trace or source of (the Arabic language) has remained. Even scientific books have come to be written in the Persian language, which is also used for teaching Arabic in class.

Chapter 5

On the various aspects of making a living, such as profit and the crafts. The conditions that occur in this connection. A number of problems are connected with this subject

1 The real meaning and explanation of sustenance and profit. Profit is the value realized from human labour

Man, by nature, needs something to feed him and to provide for him in all the conditions and stages of his life, from the time of his early growth to his maturity and on to his old age. God created everything in the world for man and gave it to him, as indicated in several verses of the Qur'ân. Man's hand stretches out over the whole world and all that is in it, since God made man His representative on earth.

Every man tries to get things; in this all men are alike. Thus, whatever is obtained by one is denied to the other, unless he gives something in exchange. When he has control of himself and is beyond the stage of (his original) weakness, he strives to make a profit, so that he may spend what God gives him to obtain his requirements and necessities through barter.

Man obtains (some profit) through no efforts of his own, as, for instance, through rain that makes the fields thrive, and similar things. However, these things are only contributory. His own efforts must be combined with them. His profits will constitute his livelihood, if they correspond to his necessities and needs. They will be capital accumulation, if they are greater than (his needs). When the use of such accruing or acquired (gain) reverts to a particular human being and he enjoys its fruits by spending it upon his interests and needs, it is called 'sustenance'.

When a person does not use (his income) for any of his interests and needs, it is not called 'sustenance'. (The part of the income) that is obtained by a person through his own effort and strength is called 'profit'. For instance, the estate of a deceased person is called 'profit' with reference to the deceased person. It is not called 'sustenance', because the deceased person has no use for it. But with reference to the heirs, when they use it, it is called 'sustenance'.

It should further be known that profit results from the effort to acquire (things) and the intention to obtain them. Sustenance requires effort and work. The effort to (obtain sustenance) depends on God's determination and inspiration. Everything comes from God. But human labour is necessary for every profit and capital accumulation. When (the source of profit) is work as such, as, for instance, (the exercise of) a craft, this is obvious. When the source of gain is animals, plants, or minerals, human labour is still necessary. Without it, no gain will be obtained, and there will be no useful (result).

Furthermore, God created the two minerals, gold and silver, as the measure of value for all capital accumulations. These the inhabitants of the world, by preference, consider treasure and property. Even if, under certain circumstances, other things are acquired, it is only for the purpose of ultimately obtaining (gold and silver). All other things are subject to market fluctuations, from which (gold and silver) are exempt. They are the basis of profit, property, and treasure.

If all this has been established, it should be further known that the capital a person earns and acquires, if resulting from a craft, is the value realized from his labour. This is the meaning of 'acquired (capital)'. There is nothing here (originally) except the labour, and it is not desired by itself as acquired (capital, but as the value realized from it).

Some crafts are partly associated with others. Carpentry and weaving, for instance, are associated with wood and yarn. However, in these two crafts, the labour (that goes into them) is more important, and its value is greater.

If the profit results from something other than a craft, the value of the resulting profit and acquired (capital) must include the value of the labour by which it was obtained. Without labour, it would not have been acquired.

In most such cases, the share of labour (in the profit) is obvious. A portion of the value, whether large or small, comes from (the labour). The share of labour may be concealed. This is the case, for instance, with the prices of foodstuffs. The labour and expenditure that have gone into them show themselves in the price of grain. But they are concealed (items) in regions where farming requires little care and few implements. Thus, only a few farmers are conscious of this element.

It has thus become clear that gains and profits, in their entirety or for the most part, are value realized from human labour. The meaning of the word 'sustenance' has become clear. It is (the part of the profit) that is utilized. Thus, the meaning of the words 'profit' and 'sustenance' has become clear.

It should be known that when the (available) labour is all gone or decreases because of a decrease in civilization, God permits profits to be abolished. Cities with few inhabitants can be observed to offer little sustenance and profit, or none whatever, because little human labour (is available). Likewise, in cities with a larger (supply of) labour, the inhabitants enjoy more favourable conditions and have more luxuries.

This is why the common people say that, with the decrease of its civilization, the sustenance of a country disappears. This goes so far that even the flow of springs and rivers stops in waste areas. Springs flow only if they are dug out and the water drawn. This requires human labour. (The conditions) may be compared with the udders of animals. Springs that are not dug out and from which no water is drawn are absorbed and disappear in the ground completely. In the same way, udders dry up when they are not milked. This can be observed in countries where springs existed in the days of their civilization. Then, they fell into ruin, and the water of the springs disappeared completely in the ground, as if it had never existed.

2 The various ways, means, and methods of making a living

It should be known that 'livelihood' means the desire for sustenance and the effort to obtain it.

Sustenance and profit may be obtained through having the power to take them away from others and to appropriate them according to a generally recognized norm. This is called imposts and taxation. Or from wild animals by killing or catching them whole on land or in the sea. Or either from domesticated animals by extracting surplus products which are used by people, such as milk from animals, silk from silkworms, and honey from bees; or from plants such as are planted in fields or grow as trees, through cultivating and preparing them for the production of their fruits. All this is called agriculture.

Or profit may be the result of human labour as applied to specific materials. Then it is called a craft, such as writing, carpentry, tailoring, weaving, and horsemanship. Or it may be applied to non-specific materials. This, then, includes all the other professions and activities.

Or profit may come from merchandise and its use in barter; merchants can make such profit either by travelling around with (merchandise) or by hoarding it and observing the market fluctuations that affect it. This is called commerce.

Agriculture is prior to all the other (ways of making a living) by its very nature, since it is something simple and innately natural. It needs no speculation or (theoretical) knowledge. Therefore, (invention) of it is ascribed to Adam, the father of mankind. He is said to have taught and practised agriculture.

The crafts are secondary and posterior to agriculture. They are composite and scientific. Thinking and speculation are applied to them. Therefore, as a rule, crafts exist only among sedentary peoples. (Sedentary culture) is posterior to Bedouin life, and secondary to it.

Commerce is a natural way of making profits. However, most of its practices and methods are tricky and designed to obtain the (profit) margin between purchase prices and sale prices. This surplus makes it possible to earn a profit. Therefore, the law permits cunning in commerce, since (commerce) contains an element of gambling. It does not, however, mean taking away the property of others without giving anything in return. Therefore, it is legal.

3 Being a servant is not a natural way of making a living

The ruler must use the services of men, such as soldiers, policemen, and secretaries, in all the departments of political power and royal authority with which he has to do. For each department, he will be satisfied with men who, he knows, are adequate, and he will provide for their sustenance from the treasury. All this belongs to political power and the living made out of it. The authority of political administration extends to all these men, and the highest royal authority is the source of (power for) their various branches.

The reason for the existence of servants on a lower level is the fact that most of those who live in luxury are too proud to take care of their own personal needs or are unable to do so, because they were brought up accustomed to indulgence and luxury. Therefore, they employ people who will take charge of such things for them. They give these people wages out of their own (money). This situation is not praiseworthy from the point of view of manliness, which is natural to man, since it is weakness to rely on persons (other than oneself). It also adds to one's duties and expenditure, and indicates a weakness and effeminacy that ought to be avoided in the interest of manliness. However, custom causes human nature to incline toward the things to which it becomes used. Man is the child of customs, not the child of his ancestors.

Moreover, satisfactory and trustworthy servants are almost non-existent. There are just four categories according to which a servant of this (description) can be classified. He may be capable of doing what he has to do, and trustworthy with regard to the things that come into his hands. Or, he may be the opposite in both respects, that is, he may be neither capable nor trustworthy. Or, he may be the opposite in one respect only, that is, he may be capable and not trustworthy, or trustworthy and not capable.

As to the first, the capable and trustworthy servant, no one would in any way be able to secure the employment of such a person. With his capability and trustworthiness, he would have no need of persons of low rank, and he would disdain to accept the wages (they could) offer for service, because he could get more. Therefore, such a person is employed only by amirs who have high ranks, because the need for rank is general.

The second kind, the servant who is neither capable nor trustworthy, should not be employed by any intelligent person, because he will do damage to his master on both counts.

No one would employ these two kinds of servants. Thus, the only thing that remains is to employ servants of the two other kinds, servants who are trustworthy but not capable, and servants who are capable but not trustworthy. There are two opinions among people as to which of the two kinds is preferable. Each has something in his favour. However, the capable (servant), even when he is not trustworthy, is preferable. One can be sure that he will not cause any damage, and one can arrange to be on guard as far as possible against being defrauded by him. (The servant) who may cause damage, even when he is reliable, is more harmful than useful, because of the damage caused by him. This should be realized and taken as the norm for finding satisfactory servants.

4 Trying to make money from buried and other treasures is not a natural way of making a living

Many weak-minded persons in cities hope to discover property under the surface of the earth and to make some profit from it. They believe that all the property of the nations of the past was stored underground and sealed with magic talismans. These seals, they believe, can be broken only by those who may chance upon the (necessary) knowledge and can offer the proper incense, prayers, and sacrifices to break them.

The inhabitants of the cities in Ifrîqiyah believe that the European Christians who lived in Ifrîqiyah before Islam, buried their property and entrusted its (hiding place) to inventories, until such time as they might find a way to dig it up again. The inhabitants of the cities in the East hold similar beliefs with regard to the nations of the Copts, the Byzantines, and the Persians. They circulate stories to this effect that sound like idle talk. Thus, a treasure hunter comes to dig where there was money buried, but does not know the talisman or the story connected with it. As a result, he finds the place empty or inhabited by worms. Or, he sees the money and jewels lying there, but guards stand over them with drawn swords. Or the earth shakes, so that he believes that he will be swallowed up, and similar nonsense.

In the Maghrib there are many Berber 'students' who are unable to make a living by natural ways and means. They approach well-to-do people with papers that have torn margins and contain either non-Arabic writing or what they claim to be the translation of a document written by the owner of buried treasures, giving the clue to the hiding place. In this way, they try to get their sustenance by (persuading the well-to-do) to send them out to dig and hunt for treasure. They fool them by saying that their only motive in asking for help is their wish to find influential protection against seizure and punishment by the authorities. Occasionally, one of these treasure hunters displays strange information or some remarkable trick of magic with which he fools people into believing his other claims, although, in fact, he knows nothing of magic and its procedures.

In addition to a weak mind, a motive that leads people to hunt for treasure is their inability to make a living in one of the natural ways that earn a profit, such as commerce, agriculture, or the crafts. Therefore, they try to make a living in devious ways, such as (treasure hunting) and the like. For they are unable to make the effort necessary to earn something, and they trust that they can gain their sustenance without effort or trouble. They do not realize that by trying to make a living in an improper manner, they plunge themselves into much greater trouble, hardship, and expenditure of energy than otherwise. In addition, they expose themselves to (the risk of) punishment.

Occasionally, a principal motive leading people to hunt for treasure is the fact that they have become used to ever-increasing luxury. As a result, the various ways and means of earning money cannot keep pace with and do not pay for their requirements. When such a person cannot earn enough in a natural way, his only way out is to wish that at one stroke, without any effort, he might find sufficient money to pay for the habits in which he has become caught. Thus, he becomes eager to find (treasure) and concentrates all his effort upon that. Among the inhabitants of cities such as Cairo, where there is much luxury, many are engrossed in the search for (treasure). They question travellers about extraordinary tales of (hidden treasure) with the same eagerness they show for the practice of alchemy. They investigate (the possibility of) making water disappear in the soil, because they believe that the majority of all buried treasures are to be found in the canals of the Nile and that the Nile largely covers the buried or hoarded treasures in those regions. They are fooled by those who possess the (aforementioned) forged records. . . .

The things that have been said about (treasure hunting) have no scientific basis, nor are they based upon (factual) information. It should be realized that although treasures are found, this happens rarely and by chance, not by systematic search.

Furthermore, why should anyone who hoards his money and seals it with magical operations, thus making extraordinary efforts to keep it concealed, set up hints and clues as to how it may be found by anyone who cares to? Why make an inventory of it, so that the people of any period and region could find his treasure? This would contradict the intention of keeping it concealed.

The question has been asked: Where is the property of the nations that came before us, and where are the abundant riches known to have existed among those nations? In reply, it should be known that treasures of gold, silver, precious stones, and utensils are no different from other minerals and acquired (capital), from iron, copper, lead, and any other real property or (ordinary) minerals. It is civilization that causes them to appear, with the help of human labour, and that makes them increase or decrease. All such things in people's possession may be transferred and passed on by inheritance. They have often been transferred from one region to another, and from one dynasty to another, in accordance with the purposes they were to serve and the particular civilization that required them. If money is scarce in the Maghrib and Ifrîqiyah, it is not scarce in the countries of the Slavs and the European Christians. If it is scarce in Egypt and Syria, it is not scarce in India and China. Such things are merely materials (*âlât*) and acquired (capital). It is civilization that produces them in abundance or causes them to be in short supply. Moreover, minerals are affected by destruction like all other existent things. Pearls and jewels deteriorate more quickly than anything else. Gold, silver, copper, iron, lead, and tin are also affected by destruction and complete annihilation, which destroy their substances in a very short time.

The occurrence of finds and treasures in Egypt is explained by the fact that Egypt was in the possession of the Copts for two thousand or more years. Their dead were buried with their possessions of gold, silver, precious stones, and pearls. This was the custom of the people of the old dynasties. When the dynasty of the Copts ended and the Persians ruled Egypt, they searched the graves for such objects and discovered them. They took an indescribably large amount of such objects from ordinary graves, and from the pyramids, which were the royal graves. The same was done by the Greeks after them. Those graves afforded opportunities for treasure hunting and have continued to do so down to this time. One frequently comes upon buried treasure in them. This may either consist of money buried by the Copts, or it may be the specially prepared vessels and sarcophagi of gold and silver with which they honoured their dead when they buried them. Because of the existence of (treasures in graves) the Egyptians have been concerned with the search for treasures and their discovery. When, in the later (years) of a dynasty, duties come to be levied upon various things, they are even levied upon treasure hunters, and a tax has to be paid by those stupid and deluded persons who occupy themselves thus.

Those who are deluded or afflicted by these things must take refuge in God from their inability to make a living and their laziness in this respect. They should not occupy themselves with absurdities and untrue stories.

5 Ranks are useful in securing property

This is as follows. We find that the person of rank who is highly esteemed is in every material aspect more fortunate and wealthier than a person who has no rank. The reason for this is that the person of rank is served by the labour (of others). They try to approach him with their labour, since they want to be close to him and are in need of (the protection) his rank affords. People help him with their labour in all his needs, whether these are necessities, conveniences, or luxuries. The value realized from all such labour becomes part of his profit. For tasks that usually require giving some compensation (to the persons who perform them), he always employs people without giving anything in return. He realizes a very high value from their labour. It is (the difference) between the value he realizes from the (free) labour (products) and the prices he must pay for things he needs. He thus makes a very great (profit). A person of rank receives much (free) labour which makes him rich in a very short time. With the passing of days, his fortune and wealth increase. It is in this sense that (the possession of) political power is one of the ways of making a living.

The person who has no rank whatever, even though he may have property, acquires a fortune only in proportion to the property he owns and in accordance with the efforts he himself makes. Most merchants are in this position. Therefore, (merchants) who have a rank are far better off than those who have not.

Evidence for this is the fact that many jurists and religious scholars and pious persons acquire a good reputation. Then, the great mass believes that when they give them presents, they serve God. People, therefore, are willing to help them in their worldly affairs and to work for their interests. As a result, they quickly become wealthy and turn out to be very well off although they have acquired no property but have only the value realized from the labour with which the people have supported them. We have seen much of this in cities and towns as well as in the desert. People do farm work and business for these men, who sit at home and do not leave their places. But still their property grows and their profits increase. Without effort, they accumulate wealth, to the surprise of those who do not understand what the secret of their affluence is, what the reasons for their wealth and fortune are.

6 Happiness and profit are achieved mostly by people who are obsequious and use flattery. Such character disposition is one of the reasons for happiness

We have stated before that the profit human beings make is the value realized from their labour. If someone could be assumed to have no ability whatever to do any labour, he would have no profit whatever. The value realized from one's labour corresponds to the value of one's labour and the value of this labour as compared to the value of other labour and the need of the people for it. The growth or decrease of one's profit, in turn, depends on that. We have also explained that ranks are useful in securing property. A person of rank has the people approach him with their labour and property. They do that in order to avoid harm and to obtain advantages. The labour and property through which they attempt to approach him are, in a way, given in exchange for the many good and bad things they may obtain or avoid with the aid of his rank. Such labour becomes part of the profit of the man of rank, and the value realized from it means property and wealth for him. He thus gains wealth and a fortune in a very short time.

Ranks are widely distributed among people, and there are various levels of rank among them. This is God's wise plan with regard to His creation. It regulates their livelihood, takes care of their interests, and ensures their permanency.

The existence and persistence of the human species can materialize only through the co-operation of all men in behalf of what is good for them. It has been established that a single human being could not fully exist by himself, and even if, hypothetically, it might happen as a rare exception, his existence would be precarious. Now, such co-operation is obtained by the use of force, since people are largely ignorant of the interests of the human species, and since they are given freedom of choice and their actions are the result of thinking and reflection, not of natural instinct. They thus refrain from co-operating. Therefore, it is imperative to make them co-operate, and there must be some motive forcing human beings to take care of their interests, so that God's wise plan as to the preservation of mankind can materialize.

It has, thus, become clear that rank means the power enabling human beings to be active among the fellow men under their control with permission and prohibition, and to have forceful superiority over them, in order to make them avoid things harmful to them and seize their advantages. They may act in justice and apply the laws of religion and politics, and also follow their own purposes in everything else.

However, (the just use of rank) was intended by the divine providence as something essential, whereas the (self-seeking use of rank) enters into it as something accidental, as is the case with all evils decreed by God. Much good can fully exist only in conjunction with the existence of some little evil, which is the result of matter. The good does not disappear with the (admixture of evil), but attaches itself to the little evil that gathers around it. This is the meaning of the occurrence of injustice in the world.

Each class among the inhabitants of a town or zone of civilization has power over the classes lower than itself. Each member of a lower class seeks the support of rank from members of the next higher class, and those who gain it become more active among the people under their control in proportion to the profit they get out of it. Thus, rank affects people in whatever way they make their living. Whether it is influential or restricted depends on the class and status of the person who has a particular rank. If the rank in question is influential, the profit accruing from it is correspondingly great. If it is restricted and unimportant, (the profit) is correspondingly so. A person who has no rank, even though he may have money, acquires a fortune only in proportion to the labour he is able to produce, or the property he owns, and in accordance with the efforts he makes to increase it. This is the case with most merchants and, as a rule, with farmers. It also is the case with craftsmen. If they have no rank and are restricted to the profits of their crafts, they make only a bare living, somehow fending off the distress of poverty.

If this has been established and if it further has become clear that rank is widely distributed and that one's happiness and welfare are intimately connected with the acquisition of (rank), it will be realized that it is a very great and important favour to bestow a rank on someone, and that the person who bestows it is a very great benefactor. He gives it only to people under his control. Thus, bestowal of rank implies influence and power. Consequently, a person who seeks and desires rank must be obsequious and use flattery as powerful men and rulers require. Otherwise, it will be impossible for him to obtain any (rank). Therefore, obsequiousness and flattery are the reasons why a person may be able to obtain a rank that produces happiness and profit, and that most wealthy and happy people possess this quality. Thus, too, many people who are proud and supercilious have no use for rank. Their earnings, consequently, are restricted to (the results of) their own labours, and they are reduced to poverty and indigence.

Such haughtiness and pride are blameworthy qualities: they result from the assumption by an individual that he is perfect, and that people need the scientific or technical skill he offers. Such an individual, for instance, is a scholar who is deeply versed in his science, or a scribe who writes well, or a poet who makes good poetry. Anyone who knows his craft assumes that people need what he has. Therefore, he develops a feeling of superiority to them. People of noble descent, whose forebears include a ruler or a famous scholar, or a person perfect in some position, also share this illusion. They assume that they deserve a similar position because of their relationship to such men and the fact that they are their heirs. In fact, they cling to something that is a matter of the past, since perfection is not passed on by inheritance. Such a person expects people to treat him in accordance with what he thinks of himself, and he hates those who in any respect fail to treat him as he expects to be treated. He always worries much, because people refuse to give him what he considers his due. People come to hate him, because of the egoism of human nature. Rarely will (a human being) concede perfection and superiority to another, unless he is somehow forced to do so by superior strength. Such (forcefulness and superior strength) is implied in rank. Thus, when a haughty person has no rank—and he cannot have any, as has been explained—people hate him for his haughtiness, and he receives no share of their kindness. He obtains no rank from members of the next higher class, because he is hated by them, and, therefore, he cannot associate with them and frequent their homes. In consequence, his livelihood is destroyed. He remains in a state of indigence and poverty or of one only a little better. The acquisition of wealth is altogether out of the question for him.

It is widely said that a person who is perfect in knowledge obtains no share (in worldly goods). The knowledge that is given to him is taken into account, and this is set apart as his share (in worldly goods).

In a dynasty, the character trait mentioned may cause disturbances among the ranks. Many people of the low classes come up to fill them, and many people of the higher classes have to step down on that account. The reason is that when a dynasty has reached its

307

limit of superiority and power, the royal clan claims royal and governmental authority exclusively for itself. Everybody else despairs of (getting any share in) it. (All the other people can only) hold ranks below the rank of the ruler and under the control of the government. They are a sort of servant of his. Now, when the dynasty continues and royal authority flourishes, those who go into the service of the ruler, who try to approach him with advice, or who are accepted as followers by him because of their capability in many of his important affairs, will all be equal in rank in his eyes. Many common people will make efforts to approach the ruler with zealous counsel and come close to him through all kinds of services. For this purpose, such people make much use of obseqiousness and flattery toward the ruler, his entourage, and his family, so that eventually they will be firmly entrenched and the ruler will give them a place in his (administration). Thus, they obtain a large share of happiness and are accepted among the people of the dynasty.

At such a time, the new generation of the dynasty, the children of the people who had seen the dynasty through its difficulties and had smoothed its path, are arrogant because of the noteworthy achievements of their forefathers. Because of them, they look down on the ruler. They rely on their influence and become very presumptuous. This makes the ruler hate them and keep away from them. He now leans toward those of his followers who do not rely upon any (achievements of the past) and would not think of being presumptuous and proud. Their behaviour is characterized by obsequiousness to him and flattery and willingness to work for his purposes whenever he is ready for some undertaking. Their rank, consequently, becomes important. Their stations become high. The outstanding personalities and the elite turn to them, because they receive so many favours from the ruler and have great influence with him. The new generation of the dynasty, meanwhile, keeps its proud attitude and continues to rely upon past (achievements). They gain nothing from that. It merely alienates them from the ruler and makes him hate them and give preference to his (newly gained) supporters, until the dynasty is destroyed.

7 *Persons who are in charge of offices dealing with religious matters, such as judge, mufti, teacher, prayer leader, preacher, muezzin, and the like, are not as a rule very wealthy*

The reason for this is that profit is the value realized from labour. This differs according to the (varying degrees of) need for (a particular kind of labour). Certain (types of) labour (products) may be necessary in civilization and be a matter of general concern. Then, the value realized from these products is greater and the need for them more urgent.

Now, the common people have no compelling need for the things that religious (officials) have to offer. They are needed only by those special people who take a particular interest in their religion. If the offices of mufti and judge are needed in case of disputes, it is not a compelling and general need. Mostly, they can be dispensed with. Only the ruler is concerned with (religious officials) and (religious) institutions, as part of his duty to look after the (public) interests. He assigns (the religious officials) a share of sustenance proportionate to the need that exists for them in the sense mentioned. He does not place them on an equal footing with people who have power or with people who ply the necessary crafts, even if the things that (the religious officials) have to offer are nobler, as they deal with religion and the legal institutions. Their portion, therefore, can only be small.

Furthermore, because the things (the religious officials) have to offer are so noble, they feel superior to the people and are proud of themselves. Therefore, they are not obsequious to persons of rank, in order to obtain something to improve their sustenance. In fact, they would not have time for that. They are occupied with those noble things they have to offer and which tax both the mind and the body. Indeed, the noble character of the things they have to offer does not permit them to prostitute themselves openly. They would not do such a thing. As a consequence, they do not, as a rule, become very wealthy.

I discussed this with an excellent man. He disagreed with me about it. But some stray leaves from the account books of the government offices in the palace of al-Ma'mûn came into my hand. They gave a good deal of information about income and expenditure at that time. Among the things I noticed, were the salaries of judges, prayer leaders, and muezzins. I called the attention of the person mentioned to it, and he realized that what I had said was correct.

8 Agriculture is a way of making a living for weak people and Bedouins in search of subsistence

This is because agriculture is a natural and simple procedure. Therefore, as a rule, sedentary people, or people who live in luxury, do not practise it. Those who practise it are characterized by humility. . . .

9 The meaning, methods, and different kinds of commerce

Commerce means the attempt to make a profit by increasing capital, through buying goods at a low price and selling them at a high price, whether these goods consist of slaves, grain, animals, weapons, or clothing material. The accrued (amount) is called 'profit'.

The attempt to make such a profit may be undertaken by storing goods and holding them until the market has fluctuated from low prices to high prices. This will bring a large profit. Or, the merchant may transport his goods to another country where they are more in demand than in his own, where he bought them. This will bring a large profit.

Therefore, an old merchant said to a person who wanted to find out the truth about commerce: 'I shall give it to you in two words: Buy cheap and sell dear. There is commerce for you.' By this, he meant the same thing that we have just established.

10 The transportation of goods by merchants

The merchant who knows his business will travel only with such goods as are generally needed by rich and poor, rulers and commoners alike. (General need) makes for a large demand for his goods. If he restricts his goods to those needed only by a few, it may be impossible for him to sell them, since these few may for some reason find it difficult to buy them. Then, his business would slump, and he would make no profit.

Also, a merchant who travels with needed goods should do so only with medium quality goods. The best quality of any type of goods is restricted to wealthy people and the entourage of the ruler. They are very few in number. As is well known, the medium quality of anything is what suits most people. This should by all means be kept in mind by the merchant, because it makes the difference between selling his goods and not selling them.

Likewise, it is more advantageous and more profitable for the merchant's enterprise, if he brings goods from a country that is far away and where there is danger on the road. In such a case, the goods transported will be few and rare, because the place where they come from is far away or because the road over which they come is beset with perils, so that there are few who would bring them, and they are very rare. When goods are few and rare, their prices go up. On the other hand, when the country is near and the road safe for travelling, they will be found in large quantities, and the prices will go down.

Therefore, the merchants who dare to enter the Sudan country are the most prosperous and wealthy of all people. The distance and the difficulty of the road they travel are great. They have to cross a difficult desert which is made almost inaccessible by fear (of danger) and beset by thirst. Therefore, the goods of the Sudan country are found only in small quantities among us, and they are particularly expensive. The same applies to our goods among them.

Thus, merchandise becomes more valuable when merchants transport it from one country to another. They get rich quickly. The same applies to merchants who travel from our country to the East, also because of the great distance to be traversed. On the other hand, those who travel back and forth between the cities and countries of one particular region earn little and make a very small profit, because their goods are available in large quantities and there is a great number of merchants who travel with them.

11 Hoarding

Intelligent and experienced people in the cities know that it is inauspicious to hoard grain and to wait for high prices, and that the profit (expected) may be spoiled or lost through (hoarding). The reason may perhaps lie in the facts that people need food, and that they are forced to spend money on it.

For things that are traded, other than foodstuffs, people have no compelling need. It is merely the diversification of desires that calls their attention to them. On things not really needed they spend their money willingly and eagerly, and feel no attachment to the money they have spent. Thus, the person known to be a hoarder is persecuted by the combined psychic powers of the people whose money he takes away. Therefore, he loses his profit. . . .

12 Continued low prices are harmful to merchants who have to trade at low prices

This is because profit and livelihood result from the crafts or from commerce. Commerce means the buying of merchandise and goods, storing them, and waiting until fluctuation of the market brings about an increase in the prices of these goods. This is called profit. It provides a profit and a livelihood for professional traders. When the prices of any type of goods, food, clothing material, or anything else that may bring in capital, remain low and the merchant cannot profit from any fluctuation of the market affecting these things, his profit stops if the situation goes on for a long period. Business in this particular line slumps, no trading is done, and the merchants lose their capital.

This may be exemplified in the instance of grain. While it remains cheap, the condition of all farmers and grain producers who have to do with any of the various stages of grain production is adversely affected, the profit they make being small, insignificant, or non-existent. They cannot increase their capital, or they find (such increase) small. They have to spend their capital. Their condition is adversely affected, and they are reduced to poverty and indigence. This then, in turn, affects the condition of millers, bakers, and all the other occupations that are connected with grain from the time it is sown to the time it can be eaten. Likewise, the condition of soldiers is adversely affected. Their sustenance is provided by the ruler in the form of grain from farmers, through the grant of fiefs. Thus, the income from taxation is small, and soldiers are unable to render the military service for which they exist and for which they receive sustenance from the ruler. Thus, (the ruler) discontinues their sustenance, and their condition is adversely affected.

Low prices for grain, and of other things that are traded, are praised, because the need for grain is general, and people, rich as well as poor, are compelled to buy food. Dependent people constitute the majority of people in civilization. Therefore, (low prices for foodstuffs) are of general usefulness, and food, as far as grain is concerned, weighs more heavily than commerce.

13 The kind of people who should practise commerce, and those who should not

We have stated before that commerce means increasing one's capital by buying merchandise and attempting to sell it for a price higher than its purchase price, either by waiting for market fluctuations or by transporting the merchandise to a country where that particular merchandise is more in demand and brings higher prices, or by selling it for a high price to be paid at a future date. The profit is small in relation to the capital (invested). However, when the capital is large, the profit becomes great, because many times a little is much.

In the attempt to earn the increase (of capital) that constitutes profit, it is unavoidable that one's capital gets into the hands of traders, in the process of buying and selling and waiting for payment. Now, honest traders are few. It is unavoidable that there should be cheating, tampering with the merchandise which may ruin it, and delay in payment which may ruin the profit, since (such delay) while it lasts prevents any activity that could bring profit. There will also be nonacknowledgment or denial of obligations, which may prove destructive of one's capital unless (the obligation) has been stated in writing and properly witnessed. The judiciary is of little use in this connection, since the law requires clear evidence.

All this causes the merchant a great deal of trouble. He may make a small profit, but only with great trouble and difficulty, or he may make no profit at all, or his capital may be lost. If he is not afraid of quarrels, knows (how to settle) an account, and is always willing to enter into a dispute and go to court, he stands a better chance of being treated fairly by (traders), because he is not afraid and always ready to enter into a dispute. Otherwise, he must have the protection of rank. It will give him respect in the eyes of traders and cause the magistrates to uphold his rights against his debtors. In this way, he will obtain justice and recover his capital from them, voluntarily in the first case, forcibly in the second.

On the other hand, the person who is afraid or unaggressive, and who, in addition, lacks the influence (of rank) with the judiciary, must avoid commerce. He risks the loss of his capital. He will become the prey of traders, and he may not get his rights from them. People as a rule covet the possessions of other people. Without the restraining influence of the laws, nobody's property would be safe. This applies especially to traders and the low-class mob.

14 The character traits of merchants are inferior to those of leading personalities and remote from manliness

In the preceding section, we stated that a merchant must concern himself with buying and selling, earning money and making a profit. This requires cunning, willingness to enter into disputes, cleverness, constant quarrelling, and great persistence. These are things that belong to commerce. They are qualities detrimental to and destructive of virtuousness and manliness, because it is unavoidable that actions influence the soul. If evil and deceitful actions come first and good qualities later, the former become firmly and deeply rooted and detract from the good qualities, since the blameworthy influence of the evil actions has left its imprint upon the soul, as is the case with all habits that originate from actions.

These influences differ according to the different types of merchants. Those who are of a very low type and associated closely with bad traders who cheat and defraud and perjure themselves, asserting and denying statements concerning transactions and prices, are much more strongly affected by these bad qualities. Deceitfulness becomes their main characteristic. Manliness is completely alien to them, beyond their power to acquire.

There exists a second kind of merchant, which we mentioned in the preceding section, namely, those who have the protection of rank and are thus spared having anything to do personally with such (business manipulations). They are most uncommon. For they are people who have all of a sudden come into the possession of a good deal of money in some unusual way, or have inherited money from a member of their family. Thus, they have obtained the wealth that helps them to associate with the people of the dynasty and to gain prominence and renown among their contemporaries. Therefore, they are too proud to have anything personally to do with such (business manipulations), and they leave them to the care of their agents and servants. It is easy for them to have the magistrates confirm their rights, because (the magistrates) are familiar with their beneficence and gifts. . . .

15 The crafts require teachers

Some crafts are simple, and others are composite. The simple ones concern the necessities. The composite ones belong to the luxuries. The simple crafts are the ones to be taught first, firstly because they are simple, and then because they concern the necessities and there is a large demand for having them transmitted. Therefore, they take precedence in instruction. The instruction in them, as a consequence, is something inferior.

The mind does not cease transforming all kinds of (crafts), including the composite ones, from potentiality into actuality through the gradual discovery of one thing after the other, until they are perfect. This is achieved in the course of time and of generations. Things are not transformed from potentiality into actuality in one stroke, especially technical matters. Consequently, a certain amount of time is unavoidable. Therefore, the crafts are found to be inferior in small cities, and only the simple crafts are found there. When sedentary civilization in (those cities) increases, and luxury conditions there cause the use of the crafts, they are transformed from potentiality into actuality.

16 The crafts are perfected only if there exists a large and perfect sedentary civilization

The reason for this is that, as long as sedentary civilization is not complete and the city not fully organized, people are concerned only with the necessities of life, that is, with the obtaining of food, such as wheat and other things. Then, when the city is organized and the (available) labour increases and pays for the necessities and is more than enough (for the inhabitants), the surplus is spent on luxuries.

The crafts and sciences are the result of man's ability to think, through which he is distinguished from the animals. (His desire for) food, on the other hand, is the result of his animal and nutritive power. It is prior to sciences and crafts because of its necessary

314

character. (The sciences and crafts) come after the necessities. The (susceptibility) of the crafts to refinement, and the quality of (the purposes) they are to serve in view of the demands made by luxury and wealth, then correspond to the civilization of a given country.

A small or Bedouin civilization needs only the simple crafts, such as those of the carpenter, the smith, the tailor, the butcher, or the weaver. They exist there. Still, they are neither perfect nor well developed. They exist only inasmuch as they are needed, since all of them are means to an end and are not intended for their own sake.

When civilization flourishes and the luxuries are in demand, it includes the refinement and development of the crafts. Consequently, these are perfected with every finesse, and a number of other crafts, in addition to them, are added as luxury customs and conditions demand. Among them are those of the cobbler, the tanner, the silk weaver, the goldsmith, and others. When the civilization is fully developed, these different kinds are perfected and refined to the limit. In the cities, they become ways of making a living for those who practise them. In fact, they become the most lucrative activities, because urban luxury demands them. Other such crafts are those of the perfumer, the coppersmith, the bath attendant, the cook, the biscuit baker, the teacher of singing, dancing, and rhythmical drum beating. There are also the book producers who ply the craft of copying, binding, and correcting books. This (last-mentioned) craft is demanded by the urban luxury of occupation with intellectual matters. Crafts become excessive when civilization develops excessively. Thus, we learn that there are Egyptians who teach dumb creatures like birds and domestic donkeys, who produce marvellous spectacles which give the illusion that objects are transformed, and who teach how to dance and walk on ropes stretched in the air, how to lift heavy animals and stones, and other things. These crafts do not exist among us in the Maghrib, because the civilization of (Maghribî) cities does not compare with the civilization of Egypt and Cairo.

17 The crafts are firmly rooted in a city only when sedentary culture is firmly rooted and of long duration

The reason for this is obvious. All crafts are customs and colours of civilization. Customs become firmly rooted only through much repetition and long duration. Then, their colouring becomes firmly established and rooted in (successive) generations. Once such colouring is firmly established, it is difficult to remove it. Therefore, we find that cities with a highly developed sedentary culture, the civilization of which has receded and decreased, retain traces o crafts that do not exist in other more recently civilized cities, even though they may have reached the largest (population). This is only because conditions in cities with the old civilization had become well established and firmly rooted through their long duration and constant repetition, whereas the (other recently civilized cities) have not yet reached the limit.

This is the situation, for instance, in contemporary Spain. There we find the crafts and their institutions still in existence. They are well established and firmly rooted, as far as the things required by the customs of Spanish cities are concerned. (They include), for instance, building, cooking, the various kinds of singing and entertainment, such as instrumental music, string instruments and dancing, the use of carpets in palaces, the construction of well-planned, well-constructed houses, the production of metal and pottery vessels, all kinds of utensils, the giving of banquets and weddings, and all the other crafts required by luxury and luxury customs. One finds that they practise and understand these things better than any other nation, even though civilization in Spain has receded and most of it does not equal that which exists in the other countries of the (Mediterranean) shore. This is only because sedentary culture had become deeply rooted in Spain through the stability given it by the Umayyad dynasty, the preceding Gothic dynasty, and the *reyes de taïfas*, successors to the Umayyads and so on. . . .

18 Crafts can improve and increase only when many people demand them

The reason for this is that man cannot afford to give away his labour for nothing, because it is his (source of) profit and livelihood. Throughout his life, he has no advantage from anything else. Therefore, he must employ his labour only on whatever has value in his city, if it is to be profitable to him.

If a particular craft is in demand and there are buyers for it, that craft, then, corresponds to a type of goods that is in great demand and imported for sale. People in the towns, therefore, are eager to learn that craft, in order to make a living through it. On the other hand, if a particular craft is not in demand, there are no buyers for it, and no one is interested in learning it. As a result, it is destined to be left alone and disappears because of neglect.

There is another secret to be understood in this connection. That is, that it is the ruling dynasty that demands crafts and their improvement. It causes the demand for them and makes them desirable. Crafts not in demand with the dynasty may be in demand with the other inhabitants of a city. However, that would not be the same thing, for the dynasty is the biggest market. Whatever is in demand with the dynasty is of necessity a major article.

19 The crafts recede from cities that are close to ruin

The crafts can improve only when they are needed and when they are in demand with many people. When the condition of a city weakens and senility sets in as the result of a decrease of its civilization and the small number of its inhabitants, luxury in the city decreases, and (its inhabitants) revert to restricting themselves to the necessities. The crafts belonging to luxury conditions become few. The master of (a particular craft) is no longer assured of making a living from it. Therefore, he deserts it for another, or he dies and leaves no successor. As a result, the institutions of the crafts disappear altogether. Thus, for instance, painters, goldsmiths, calligraphers, copyists, and similar artisans who cater to luxury needs disappear.

20 The Arabs, of all people, are least familiar with crafts

The reason for this is that the Arabs are more firmly rooted in desert life and more remote from sedentary civilization, the crafts, and the other things which sedentary civilization calls for. The non-Arabs in the East and the Christian nations along the shores of the Mediterranean are very well versed in (crafts), because they are more deeply rooted in sedentary civilization and more remote from the desert and desert civilization.

Therefore, we find that the homelands of the Arabs and the places they took possession of in Islam had few crafts altogether, so that they had to be imported from other regions. One may observe the great number of crafts in non-Arab countries such as China, India, the lands of the Turks, and the Christian nations, and the fact that other nations imported (their own crafts) from them.

The non-Arabs in the West, the Berbers, are like the Arabs in this respect, because for a very long period they remained firmly rooted in desert life. This is attested by the small number of cities in the (Berber) region. The crafts in the Maghrib, therefore, are few in number and are not well established. Exceptions are the weaving of wool and the tanning and stitching of leather. For, when they settled down, they developed these greatly, because they were matters of general concern and (the wool and leather) needed for them were the most common raw materials in their region, on account of the Bedouin conditions prevailing among them.

On the other hand, the crafts had been firmly rooted in the East for a very long period, ever since the rule of the ancient nations, the

317

Persians, the Nabataeans, the Copts, the Israelites, the Greeks, and the Romans (Rûm). Thus, the conditions of sedentary culture became firmly rooted among them.

The Yemen, al-Baḥrayn, Oman, and the Jazîrah have long been in Arab possession, but for thousands of years, the rule of these areas has belonged to different (Arab) nations in succession. They also founded cities and towns there and promoted the development of sedentary culture and luxury to the highest degree. There was a long period of royal authority and sedentary culture. The imprint of (sedentary culture) established itself firmly. The crafts became abundant and firmly rooted. They have remained and have always renewed themselves down to this time, and they have become the specialty of that area. Such (Yemenite) crafts are embroidered fabrics, striped cloth, and finely woven garments and silks.

21   The person who has gained the habit of a particular craft is rarely able afterwards to master another

A tailor, for instance, who has acquired the habit of tailoring and knows it well and has that habit firmly rooted in his soul, will not afterwards master the habit of carpentry or construction, unless the first habit was not yet firmly established and its imprint not yet firmly rooted.

The reason for this is that habits are qualities of the soul. They do not come all at once. A person who is still in his natural state has an easier time acquiring certain habits and is better prepared to gain them. When the soul has been impressed by a habit, it is no longer in its natural state, and it is less prepared (to master another habit), because it has taken on a certain imprint from that habit.

This is clear and attested by (the facts of) existence. One rarely finds a craftsman who, knowing his craft well, afterwards acquires a good knowledge of another craft and masters both equally well. This extends even to scholars whose habit has to do with thinking. (The scholar) who has acquired the habit of one particular science and masters it completely will rarely achieve the same mastery of the habit of another science, and if he were to study another science, he would, except under very rare circumstances, be deficient in it.

22   A brief enumeration of the basic crafts

The crafts practised by the human species are numerous, because so much labour is continually available in civilization. They are so numerous as to defy complete enumeration. However, some of them are necessary in civilization or occupy a noble (position) because of their object. We shall single these two kinds out for mention and leave all others.

Necessary (crafts) are agriculture, architecture, tailoring, carpentry, and weaving. Crafts noble because of their object are midwifery, the art of writing, book production, singing, and medicine.

Midwifery is something necessary in civilization and a matter of general concern, because it assures, as a rule, the life of the new-born child.

Medicine preserves the health of man and repels disease. It is a branch of physics. Its object is the human body.

The art of writing, and book production, which depends on it, preserve the things that are of concern to man and keep them from being forgotten. It enables the innermost thoughts of the soul to reach those who are far and absent. It perpetuates in books the results of thinking and scholarship.

Singing is the harmony of sounds and the manifestation of their beauty to the ears.

All these three crafts call for contact with great rulers in their privacy and at their intimate parties. Thus, they have nobility that other crafts do not have. The other crafts are, as a rule, secondary and subordinate.

23 The craft of agriculture

The object of this craft is to obtain foodstuffs and grains. People must undertake to dig the earth, sow, cultivate the plants, see to it that they are watered and that they grow until they reach their full growth, then, harvest the ears, and get the grain out of the husks. They also must understand all the related activities, and procure all the things required in this connection.

Agriculture is the oldest of all crafts, inasmuch as it provides the food that is the main factor in perfecting human life, since man can exist without anything else but not without food. Therefore, this craft has existed especially in the desert, since it is prior to and older than sedentary life.

24 The craft of architecture

This is the first and oldest craft of sedentary civilization. It is the knowledge of how to go about using houses and mansions for cover and shelter. This is because man has the natural disposition to reflect upon the outcome of things. Thus, it is unavoidable that he must reflect upon how to avert the harm arising from heat and cold by using houses which have walls and roofs to intervene between him and those things on all sides. This natural disposition to think, which is the real meaning of humanity, exists among men in different degrees. Some men are more or less temperate in this respect; they use (housing) with moderation. Others, on the other hand, are unfamiliar with the use of (housing), because they are intemperate, and their thinking does not go far enough to enable them to practise human crafts. Therefore, they take shelter in caverns and caves, just as they eat unprepared and uncooked food.

Now, the temperate people who use houses for shelter become very numerous and have many houses in one area. They become strangers to each other and no longer know each other. They fear surprise attacks at night. Therefore, they must protect their community by surrounding it with a wall to guard them. The whole thing thus becomes a single town or city in which they are guarded by authorities which keep them apart. They also need protection against the enemy. Thus, they use fortresses and castles for themselves and for the people under their control. These men are like rulers or amirs or tribal chieftains of a corresponding position.

Also, building conditions are different in various towns. Each city follows in this respect the procedure known to and within the technical (competence) of (its inhabitants) and corresponding to the climate and the different conditions of (the inhabitants) with regard to wealth and poverty. The situation of the inhabitants within each individual city also (differs). Some use castles and far-flung constructions comprising a number of dwellings and houses and rooms, because they have a great number of children, servants, dependants, and followers. They make their walls of stones, which they join together with quicklime. They cover them with paint and plaster and do the utmost to furnish and decorate everything—in order to show how greatly they are concerned for their shelter. In addition, they prepare cellars and underground rooms for the storage of their food, and also stables for tying up their horses, if they are military men and have many followers and guests, such as amirs and people of a corresponding position.

Others build a small dwelling or house for themselves and for their children to live in. Their desire goes no farther, because their situation permits them no more. Thus, they restrict themselves to a mere shelter, which is natural to human beings. Between the two (extremes), there are innumerable degrees.

Architecture is also needed when rulers and people of a dynasty build large towns and high monuments. They try their utmost to make good plans and build tall structures with technical perfection, so that (architecture) can reach its highest development. Architecture is the craft that satisfies requirements in all these respects. It is found mostly in the temperate zones. In the intemperate zones, there is no building activity. The people there use enclosures of reeds and clay as houses, or take shelter in caverns and caves.

The architects who exercise the craft differ. Some are intelligent and skilful. Others are inferior. . . .

Their quality depends on the (ruling) dynasties and their power. At the beginning, the dynasty is a Bedouin one, and therefore needs for its construction activities (the help of) other regions. This was the case when al-Walîd b. 'Abd-al-Malik decided to build the mosques of Medina and Jerusalem and his own mosque in Damascus. He sent to the Byzantine emperor in Constantinople for workmen skilled in construction work, and the emperor sent him enough men to build these mosques as he had planned them.

Architects also make some use of geometry and engineering. For instance, they use the plumb to make walls perpendicular, and they use devices for lifting water, to make it flow, and similar things. Thus, they must know something about the problems connected with (engineering). They also must know how to move heavy loads with the help of machines. Big blocks of large stones cannot be lifted into place on a wall by the unaided strength of workmen alone. Therefore, the architect must contrive to multiply the strength of the rope by passing it through holes, constructed according to geometrical proportions, of the attachments called 'pulleys'. They make the load easier to lift, so that the intended work can be completed without difficulty. This can be achieved only with the help of engineering principles which are commonly known among men. Such things made it possible to build the monuments that are standing to this day, believed to have been built in pre-Islamic times.

25 The craft of carpentry

This craft is one of the necessities of civilization. Its material is wood. This is as follows: God made all created things useful for man, so as to supply his necessities and needs. Trees belong among these things. They are used as firewood and as supports for loads.

Bedouins use wood for tent poles and pegs, for camel litters for their women, and for the lances, bows, and arrows they use for weapons. Sedentary people use wood for the roofs of their houses, for the locks of their doors, and for chairs to sit on. The particular form needed in each case is the result of craftsmanship. The craft concerned with that and which gives every wooden object its form is carpentry in all its different grades.

The man in charge of this craft is the carpenter. He is necessary to civilization. When sedentary culture increases and luxury makes its appearance and people want to use elegant types of roofs, doors, chairs, and furniture, these things come to be produced in a most elegant way through mastery of remarkable techniques which are luxuries and in no way necessities. Such include, for instance, the use of carvings for doors and chairs. Or one skilfully turns and shapes pieces of wood in a lathe, and then one puts these pieces together in certain symmetrical arrangements and nails them together, so that they appear to the eye to be of one piece. Carpentry is also needed for the construction of ships, which are made of boards and nails.

In view of its origin, carpentry needs a good deal of geometry of all kinds. It requires either a general or a specialized knowledge of proportion and measurement, in order to bring forms from potentiality into actuality in the proper manner, and for the knowledge of proportions one must have recourse to the geometrician. Therefore, the leading Greek geometricians were all master carpenters. Euclid, the author of the *Book of the Principles*, on geometry, was a carpenter and was known as such. The same was the case with Apollonius, the author of the book on *Conic Sections*, and Menelaus, and others. . . .

26 The craft of weaving and tailoring

People who are temperate in their humanity cannot avoid giving some thought to keeping warm, as they do to shelter. One manages to keep warm by using woven material as protective cover against both heat and cold. This requires the interlacing of yarn, until it turns out to be a complete garment. This is spinning and weaving.

Desert people restrict themselves to this. But people who are inclined toward sedentary culture cut the woven material into pieces of the right size to cover the form of the body and all of its numerous limbs in their various locations. They then put the different pieces together with thread, until they turn out to be a complete garment that fits the body and can be worn by people. The craft that makes things fit is tailoring.

These two crafts are necessary in civilization, because human beings must keep warm.

Tailoring is restricted to sedentary culture, since the inhabitants of the desert can dispense with it. They merely cover themselves with cloth. The tailoring of clothes, the cutting, fitting, and sewing of the material, is one of the various methods and aspects of sedentary culture.

This should be understood, in order to appreciate the reason why the wearing of sewn garments is forbidden on the pilgrimage. According to the religious law, the pilgrimage requires, among other things, the discarding of all worldly attachments and the return to

God as He created us in the beginning. Man should not set his heart upon any of his luxury customs, such as perfume, women, sewn garments, or boots. He should not go hunting or expose himself to any other of the customs with which his soul and character have been affected. When he dies, he will necessarily lose them. He should come (to the pilgrimage) as if he were going to the Last Judgment, humble in his heart, sincerely devoted to his Lord. . . .

27 The craft of midwifery

Midwifery is a craft that shows how to proceed in bringing the new-born child gently out of the womb of his mother and how to prepare the things that go with that. It also shows what is good for (a new-born child) after it is born. The craft is as a rule restricted to women, since they, as women, may see the pudenda of other women. The woman who exercises this craft is called midwife.

This is as follows: When the embryo has gone through all its stages and is completely and perfectly formed in the womb—the period God determined for its remaining in the womb is as a rule nine months—it seeks to come out, because God implanted such a desire in (unborn children). But the opening is too narrow for it, and it is difficult for (the embryo to come out). It often splits one of the walls of the vagina by its pressure, and often the close connection and attachment of its covering membranes with the uterus are ruptured. All this is painful and hurts very much. This is the meaning of labour pains. In this connection, the midwife may offer some succour by massaging the back, the buttocks, and the lower extremities adjacent to the uterus. She thus stimulates the force pushing the embryo out, and facilitates the difficulties encountered in this connection as much as she can. She uses as much strength as she thinks is required by the difficulty of (the process). When the embryo has come out, it remains connected with the uterus by the umbilical cord at its stomach, through which it was fed. That cord is a superfluous special limb for feeding the child. The midwife cuts it but so that she does not go beyond the place where it starts to be superfluous and does not harm the stomach of the child or the uterus of the mother. She then treats the place of the operation with cauterization or whatever other treatment she sees fit.

When the embryo comes out of that narrow opening with its humid bones that can easily be bent and curved, it may happen that its limbs and joints change their shape, because they were only recently formed and because the substances are humid. Therefore, the midwife undertakes to massage and correct (the new-born child) until every limb has resumed its natural shape and the position destined for it, and (the child) has regained its normal form. After that she goes back to the woman in labour and massages and kneads her, so that the membranes of the embryo may come out. They are sometimes somewhat late in coming out. On such an occasion, it is feared that the constricting muscle might resume its natural position before all the membranes are brought out. They are superfluities. They might become putrid, and their putridity might enter the uterus, which could be fatal. The midwife takes precautions against that. She tries to stimulate the ejection, until all the membranes come out.

She then returns to the child. She anoints its limbs with oils and dusts it with astringent powders, to strengthen it and to dry up the fluids of the uterus. She smears something upon the child's palate to lift its uvula. She puts something into its nose, in order to empty the cavities of its brain. She makes it swallow an electuary, in order to prevent its bowels from becoming obstructed and their walls from sticking together.

Then, she treats the woman in labour for the weakness caused by the labour pains and the pain that the separation causes her uterus. Although the child is no natural limb (of the mother), still, the way it is created in the uterus causes it to become attached as if it were an inseparable limb (of her body). Therefore, its separation causes a pain similar to that caused by the amputation (of a limb). The midwife also treats the pain of the vagina that was torn and wounded by the pressure of (the child's) coming out.

We likewise find midwives better acquainted than a skilful physician with the means of treating the ills affecting the bodies of little children from the time they are sucklings until they are weaned. After the child is weaned, its need for a physician is greater than its need for a midwife.

One can see that this craft is necessary to the human species in civilization. Without it, the individuals of the species could not, as a rule, come into being. . . .

28 The craft of medicine. The craft of medicine is needed in settled areas and cities but not in the desert

This craft is necessary in towns and cities because of its recognized usefulness. Its fruit is the preservation of health among those who are healthy, and the repulsion of illness among those who are ill, with the help of medical treatment, until they are cured of their illnesses.

It should be known that the origin of all illnesses is in food, as Muḥammad said in the comprehensive tradition on medicine, that is reported among physicians but suspected by the religious scholars.

He said: 'The stomach is the home of disease. Dieting is the main medicine. The origin of every disease is indigestion.' The statement: 'The stomach is the home of disease', is obvious. The statement: 'Dieting is the main medicine', is to be understood in the sense that 'dieting' means 'going hungry', since hunger means abstinence from food. Thus, the meaning is that hunger is the greatest medicine, the origin of all medicines. The statement: 'The origin of every disease is indigestion', is to be understood in the sense that 'indigestion' is the addition of new food to the food already in the stomach before it has been digested.

God created man and preserves his life through nourishment. He gets it through eating, and he applies to it the digestive and nutritive powers, until it becomes blood fitting for the flesh and bone parts of the body. Then, the growing power takes it over, and it is turned into flesh and bones. Digestion means that the nourishment is boiled by natural heat, stage by stage, until it actually becomes a part of the body. This is to be explained as follows. The nourishment that enters the mouth and is chewed by the jaws undergoes the influence of the heat of the mouth, which boils it slightly. Thus, its composition is slightly altered. This can be observed in a bit of food that is taken and chewed well. Its composition then can be observed to be different from that of the original food.

The food then gets into the stomach, and the heat of the stomach boils it, until it becomes chyme, that is, the essence of the boiled (food). (The stomach) sends (the chyme) on into the liver, and ejects the part of the food that has become solid sediment in the bowels, through the two body openings. The heat of the liver then boils the chyme, until it becomes fresh blood. On it, there swims a kind of foam as the result of the boiling. (That foam) is yellow bile. Parts of it become dry and solid. They are black bile. The natural heat is not quite sufficient to boil the coarse parts. They are phlegm. The liver then sends all (these substances) into the veins and arteries. There, the natural heat starts to boil them. The pure blood thus generates a hot and humid vapour that sustains the animal spirit. The growing power acts upon the blood, and it becomes flesh. The thick part of it then becomes bones. Then, the body eliminates the (elements of the digested food) it does not need as the various superfluities, such as sweat, saliva, mucus, and tears. This is the process of nourishment, and the transformation of food from potential into actual flesh.

Now, illnesses originate from fevers, and most illnesses are fevers. The reason for fevers is that the natural heat is too weak to complete the process of boiling in each of those stages. The nourishment thus is not fully assimilated. The reason for that, as a rule, is either that

325

there is a great amount of food in the stomach that becomes too much for the natural heat, or that food is put into the stomach before the first food has been completely boiled. In such a case, the natural heat either devotes itself exclusively to the new food, so that the first food is left in its (half-digested) state, or it divides itself between the old and the new food, and then is insufficient to boil and assimilate them completely. The stomach sends the (food) in that state into the liver, and the heat of the liver likewise is not strong enough to assimilate it. Often, an unassimilated superfluity, resulting from food that had been taken in earlier, has also remained in the liver. The liver sends all of it to the veins unassimilated. When the body has received what it properly needs, it eliminates the (unassimilated superfluity) together with the other superfluities such as sweat, tears, and saliva, if it can. Often, (the body) cannot cope with the greater part of the (unassimilated superfluity). Thus, it remains in the veins, the liver, and the stomach, and increases with time. Any composite humid (substance) that is not boiled and assimilated undergoes putrefaction. Consequently, the unassimilated nourishment becomes putrid. Anything in the process of putrefaction develops a strange heat. This heat is what, in the human body, is called fever.

This may be exemplified by food that is left over and eventually becomes putrid, and by dung that has become putrid. Heat develops in it and takes its course. This is what fevers in the human body mean. Fevers are the main cause and origin of illness, as was mentioned in the Prophetic tradition. Such fevers can be cured by not giving a sick person any nourishment for a certain number of weeks; then, he must take the proper nourishment until he is completely cured. In a state of health, the same procedure serves as a preventive treatment for this and other illnesses.

Putrefaction may be localized in a particular limb. Then, a disease will develop in that limb, or the body will be affected either in the principal limbs or in others, because that particular limb is ill, and its illness produces an illness of its powers. This covers all illnesses. Their origin as a rule is in the nourishment.

All this is left to the physician.

The incidence of such illnesses is most frequent among the inhabitants of sedentary areas and cities, because they live a life of plenty. They eat a great deal and rarely restrict themselves to one particular kind of food. They lack caution in taking food, and they prepare their food, when they cook it, with an admixture of a good many things, such as spices, herbs, and fruits, both fresh and dry. They do not restrict themselves in this respect to one or even a few kinds. We have on occasion counted forty different kinds of vegetables and meats in a single cooked dish. This gives the nourishment a strange temper and often does not agree with the body and its parts.

Furthermore, the air in cities becomes corrupt through admixture of putrid vapours because of the great number of superfluities. It is the air that gives energy to the spirit and thus strengthens the influence of the natural heat upon digestion.

Furthermore, the inhabitants of cities lack exercise. As a rule, they rest and remain quiet. Thus, the incidence of illness is great in towns and cities, and the inhabitants' need for medicine is correspondingly great.

On the other hand, the inhabitants of the desert, as a rule, eat little. Hunger prevails among them, because they have little grain. It eventually becomes a custom of theirs which is often thought to be something natural to them because it is so lasting. Of seasonings they have few or none. Thus, they take their nourishment plain and without admixtures, and its temper comes close to being agreeable to the body. The air they breathe has little putrescence. They take exercise, and there is a lot of movement when they race horses, or go hunting, or search for things they need. For all these reasons, their digestion is very good. Thus, their temper is healthier and more remote from illness. As a result, their need for medicine is small. Therefore, physicians are nowhere to be found in the desert. The only reason for this is the lack of need for them, because if physicians were needed in the desert they would be there. There would then be a livelihood for them to lead them to settle there.

29 Calligraphy, the art of writing, is one of the human crafts

Writing is the outlining and shaping of letters to indicate audible words which, in turn, indicate what is in the soul. It comes second after oral expression. It is a noble craft, since it is one of the special qualities of man by which he distinguishes himself from the animals. Furthermore, it reveals what is in the minds. It enables the intention (of a person) to be carried to distant places, and, thus, the needs (of that person) may be executed without his personally taking care of them. It enables people to become acquainted with science, learning, with the books of the ancients, and with the sciences and information written down by them.

The transformation of writing in man from potentiality into actuality takes place through instruction. The quality of writing in a town corresponds to the social organization, civilization, and competition for luxuries (among its inhabitants), since (writing) is a craft. For this reason, we find that most Bedouins are illiterate. They are not able to read or write. Those of them who do read or write have inferior handwriting or read haltingly. We find that instruction in handwriting in cities with an extraordinarily developed civilization is more proficient, easier, and methodically better than elsewhere. Thus, we are told that in contemporary Cairo there are experts who are specialized in the teaching of calligraphy. They teach the pupil by norms and laws how to write each letter. . . .

30 The craft of book production

Formerly, (people) were concerned with scholarly writings and (official) records. These were copied, bound, and corrected with the help of a transmission technique and with accuracy. The reason for this was the importance of the (ruling) dynasty and the existence of the things that depend on sedentary culture. All that has disappeared at the present time as the result of the disappearance of the dynasties and the decrease of civilization. In Islam it had formerly reached tremendous proportions in the 'Irâq and in Spain. Scholarly works and writings were numerous. People were desirous of transmitting them everywhere and at any time. They were copied and bound. The craft of book producers thus made its appearance. These craftsmen are concerned with copying, correcting, and binding books, and with all the other matters pertaining to books and writings. The craft of book production was restricted to cities of a large civilization.

Originally, copies of scholarly works, government correspondence, and diplomas were written on parchment especially prepared from animal skins by craftsmen, because there was great prosperity at the beginning of Islam and the works that were written were few. In addition, government documents and diplomas were few in number. The production of books and writings then developed greatly. Government documents and diplomas increased in number. There was not enough parchment for all that. Therefore, al-Faḍl b. Yaḥyâ[1] suggested the manufacture of paper. Thus, paper was used for government documents and diplomas. Afterwards, people used paper in sheets for government and scholarly writings, and its manufacture reached a considerable degree of excellence. . . .

31 The craft of singing and music

This craft is concerned with the setting of poems to music by scanning the sounds according to well-known fixed proportions, which

---

[1] Paper came into use more widely at the time of the Barmecides, in the early ninth century. However, ascribing the official introduction of paper into government offices to the Barmecides may be part of the legend woven around them.

causes any sound (complex) thus scanned to constitute a tune, a rhythmic mode. These modes are then combined with each other according to accepted proportions. The result is pleasant to listen to because of its harmony and the quality that harmony gives to the sounds.

The music produced by the rhythmic modes of singing may be supplemented by scanning other sounds that come from solids and are produced by either beating or blowing into instruments used for the purpose. Such (instrumental music) adds to the pleasure of listening. . . .

Let us explain the reason for the pleasure resulting from music. Pleasure is the attainment of something that is agreeable. In sensual perception, this can only be a quality. If such a quality is proportionate and agreeable to the person who has the perception, it is pleasant. If it is repugnant to him or discordant, it is painful. Agreeable foods are those whose quality corresponds to the temper of the sense of taste. The same applies to agreeable sensations of touch. Agreeable smells are those that correspond to the temper of the vaporous cordial spirit, because that spirit is what perceives and receives them through the sense (of smell). Thus, aromatic plants and flowers smell better and are more agreeable to the spirit, because heat, which is the temper of the cordial spirit, is preponderant in them. Agreeable sensations of vision and hearing are caused by harmonious arrangement in the forms and qualities of (the things seen or heard).

If an object of vision is harmonious in the forms and lines given to it in accordance with the matter from which it is made, so that the requirements of its particular matter as to perfect harmony and arrangement are not disregarded—that being the meaning of beauty and loveliness whenever these terms are used for any object of sensual perception—that (object of vision) is then in harmony with the soul that perceives it, and the soul, thus, feels pleasure as the result of perceiving something that is agreeable to it. Therefore, lovers who are most deeply in love express their extreme infatuation by saying that their spirit is commingled with that of the beloved. In another sense, the meaning of it is that existence is shared by all existent things, as the philosophers say. Therefore, (existent things) love to commingle with something in which they observe perfection, in order to become one with it.

The object that is most suited to man and in which he is most likely to perceive perfect harmony, is the human form. Therefore, it is most congenial to him to perceive beauty and loveliness in the lines and sounds of the human form. Thus, every man desires beauty in the objects of vision and hearing, as a requirement of his nature.

Beauty in the objects of hearing is harmony and lack of discordance in the sounds.

Sounds have certain qualities. They may be whispered or loud, soft or strong, vibrant or constrained, and so on. Harmony between them is what gives them beauty.

Such harmony may be a simple one. Many people are gifted to achieve it by nature. They do not need any special instruction or training for it, for we find people who are gifted by nature for the metres of poetry, the rhythms of the dance, and similar things.

Harmony may also result from composition. Not all human beings are alike in their knowledge of it, nor are they all equally able by nature to practise it, if they know it. This is the melodious music with which the science of music has to deal. . . .

Singing originates in a civilization when it becomes abundant and people progress from necessities to conveniences, and then to a great diversity of luxuries; because it is required only by those who are free from all the necessary and urgent needs of making a living and care for domestic and other needs. It is in demand only by those who are free from all other worries and seek various ways of having pleasure. In the non-Arab states before Islam, music was highly developed in cities and towns. The (non-Arab) rulers cultivated it eagerly. It went so far that the Persian rulers felt a great concern for musicians. Musicians had a place in their dynasty and attended their sessions and gatherings and sang for them. The same is still the case with the non-Arabs at this time in all their regions and provinces.

The Arabs originally had only poetry, which they appreciated very highly. It was distinguished in their speech by a certain nobility, because it alone possessed harmony. They made poetry the archive of their history, their wisdom, and their nobility, and the touchstone of their natural gift for expressing themselves correctly, choosing the best mode (of expression). They have continued to do so. Now, camel drivers sang when they drove their camels, and young men sang when they were alone. They repeated sounds and hummed them. When such humming was applied to poetry, it was called singing.

Then, when Islam had made its appearance, the Arabs took possession of the realms of the world. They deprived the non-Arabs of their rule and took it over. They had their well-known desert attitude and low standard of living. In addition, they possessed the thriving religion of Islam and that Muslim religious severity which is directed against all activities of leisure and all the things that are of no utility in one's religion or livelihood. Therefore, (music) was avoided to some degree. In their opinion, only the cadenced recitation of the Qur'ân and the humming of poetry which had always been their way and custom, were pleasurable things.

Then, luxury and prosperity came to them, because they obtained the spoils of the nations. They came to lead splendid and refined lives and to appreciate leisure. The singers now left the Persians and Byzantines. They descended upon the Ḥijâz and became clients of the Arabs. They all sang accompanied by lutes, pandores, lyres, and flutes. The Arabs heard their melodious use of sound, and they set their poems to music accordingly. Continual and gradual progress was made in the craft of singing. Eventually, in the days of the 'Abbâsids, singing reached its perfection.

The craft of singing is the last of the crafts attained to in civilization, because it constitutes (the last development toward) luxury with regard to no occupation in particular save that of leisure and gaiety. It also is the first to disappear from a given civilization when it disintegrates and retrogresses.

32 The crafts, especially writing and calculation, give intelligence to the person who practises them

We have already mentioned that the rational soul exists in man only potentially. Its transformation from potentiality into actuality is effected first by new sciences and perceptions derived from the *sensibilia*, and then by the later acquisition (of knowledge) through the speculative power. Eventually, it comes to be actual perception and pure intellect. Thus, it becomes a spiritual essence, and its existence then reaches perfection.

Therefore it is necessary that each kind of learning and speculation should provide (the rational soul) with additional intelligence. Now, the crafts and their habit always lead to the acquisition of scientific norms, which result from the habit. Therefore, any experience provides intelligence. The habits of the crafts provide intelligence. Perfect sedentary culture provides intelligence, because it is a conglomerate of crafts characterized by concern for the (domestic) economy, contact with one's fellow men, attainment of education through mixing with (one's fellow men), and also administration of religious matters and understanding the ways and conditions governing them. All these (factors) are norms which, properly arranged, constitute scientific disciplines. Thus, an increase in intelligence results from them.

In this respect, writing is the most useful craft because, in contrast to the other crafts, it deals with matters of theoretical, scientific interest. Writing involves a transition from the forms of the written letters to the verbal expressions in the imagination, and thence to the concepts underlying them, which are in the soul. The writer always goes from one symbol to another, as long as he is wrapped up in writing, and the soul becomes used to the constant (repetition of the process). Thus, it acquires the habit of going over from the symbols to the things meant by them. This is what is meant by intellectual speculation, by means of which the knowledge of hitherto unknown sciences is provided. As the result of being accustomed to this process people acquire the habit of intellection, which constitutes an increase in intelligence and provides an additional insight into affairs and a shrewd understanding of them.

Calculation is connected with (writing). It entails a kind of working with numbers, 'combining' and 'separating' them, which requires much deductive reasoning. Thus, (the person occupied with it) gets used to deductive reasoning and speculation, and this is what is meant by intelligence.

Chapter 6

The various kinds of sciences. The methods
of instruction. The conditions that obtain
in these connections

PREFATORY DISCUSSION

On man's ability to think, which distinguishes human beings from
animals and which enables them to obtain their livelihood, to co-operate
to this end with their fellow men, and to study the Master whom
they worship, and the revelations that the Messengers transmitted
from Him. God thus caused all animals to obey man and to be
in the grasp of his power. Through his ability to think,
God gave man superiority over many of His creatures

1   Man's ability to think

God distinguished man from all the other animals by an ability to think which He made the beginning of human perfection and the end of man's noble superiority over existing things.

This comes about as follows. Perception—that is, consciousness on the part of the person who perceives—is something peculiar to living beings to the exclusion of all other possible and existent things. Living beings may obtain consciousness of things that are outside their essence through the external senses God has given them, that is, the senses of hearing, vision, smell, taste, and touch. Man has this advantage over other beings: he can perceive things outside his essence through his ability to think, which is something beyond his senses. It is the result of (special) powers placed in the cavities of his brain. With the help of these powers, man takes the pictures of the *sensibilia*, applies his mind to them, and thus abstracts from them other pictures. The ability to think is the occupation with pictures that are beyond sense perception, and the application of the mind to them for analysis and synthesis.

The ability to think has several degrees. The first degree is man's intellectual understanding of the things that exist in the outside

333

world in a natural or arbitrary order, so that he may try to arrange them with the help of his own power. This kind of thinking mostly consists of perceptions. It is the discerning intellect, with the help of which man obtains the things that are useful for him and his livelihood, and repels the things that are harmful to him.

The second degree is the ability to think which provides man with the ideas and the behaviour needed in dealing with his fellow men and in leading them. It mostly conveys apperceptions, which are obtained one by one through experience, until they have become really useful. This is called the experimental intellect.

The third degree is the ability to think which provides the knowledge, or hypothetical knowledge, of an object beyond sense perception without any practical activity (going with it). This is the speculative intellect. It consists of both perceptions and apperceptions. They are arranged according to a special order, following special conditions, and thus provide some other knowledge of the same kind, that is, either perceptive or apperceptive. Then, they are again combined with something else, and again provide some other knowledge. The end of the process is to be provided with the perception of existence as it is, with its various genera, differences, reasons, and causes. By thinking about these things, man achieves perfection in his reality and becomes pure intellect and perceptive soul. This is the meaning of human reality.

2 The world of the things that come into being as the result of action, materializes through thinking

The world of existent things comprises pure essences, such as the elements, the things resulting from their influence, and the three things that come into being from the elements, namely, minerals, plants, and animals. All these things are connected with the divine power.

It also comprises actions proceeding from living beings, that happen through their intentions, and are connected with the power that God has given them. Some of their actions are well arranged and orderly. Such are human actions. Others are not well arranged and orderly. They are the actions of living beings other than man.

This is because thinking perceives the order that exists among the things that come into being either by nature or through arbitrary arrangement. When it intends to create something, it must understand the reason or cause of that thing, or the conditions governing it, for the sake of the order that exists among the things that come into being. (Reason, cause, or conditions) are, in general, the principles of that particular thing, since it is secondary to them, and it is not possible to arrange for something that comes earlier to come later, or for something that comes later to come earlier. Such a principle must have another principle to which its own existence is posterior. This (regression) may go on in an ascending order (from principle to principle), or it may come to an end. Now, when man, in his thinking, has reached the last principle on two, three, or more levels, and starts the action that will bring the (planned) thing into existence, he will start with the last principle that has been reached by his thinking. Thus, (that last principle) will be the beginning of action. He, then, will follow things up to the last element in the causal chain that had been the starting point of his thinking activity.

For instance, if a man thinks of bringing into existence a roof to shelter him, he will progress in his mind (from the roof) to the wall supporting the roof, and then to the foundation upon which the wall stands. Here, his thinking will end, and he will then start to work on the foundation, then (go on to) the wall, and then to the roof, with which his action will end. This is what is meant by the saying: 'The beginning of action is the end of thinking, and the beginning of thinking is the end of action.'

Thus, human action in the outside world materializes only through thinking about the order of things, since things are based upon each other. After (he has finished thinking), he starts doing things. His thinking starts with the thing that comes last in the causal chain and is done last. His action starts with the first thing in the causal chain, which thinking reaches last. Once this order is taken into consideration, human actions proceed in a well-arranged manner.

On the other hand, the actions of living beings other than man are not well arranged. They lack the thinking that acquaints the agent with the order of things governing his actions. Animals perceive only with the senses. Their perceptions are disconnected and lack a connecting link, since only thinking can constitute such (a link).

Now, the things that come into being that are of consequence in the world of existent things, are those that are orderly. Those that are not orderly are secondary to them. The actions of animals, therefore, are subordinate to (orderly human actions). Consequently, their services are forcibly utilized by man. Thus, human actions control the whole world of things that come into being and all it contains. Everything is subservient to man and works for him.

The ability to think is the quality of man by which human beings are distinguished from other living beings. The degree to which a human being is able to establish an orderly causal chain determines his degree of humanity. Some people are able to establish a causal nexus for two or three levels. Some are not able to go beyond that.

Others may reach five or six. Their humanity, consequently, is higher. For instance, some chess players are able to perceive (in advance) three or five moves, the order of which is arbitrary. Others are unable to do that, because their mind is not good enough for it. This example is not quite to the point, because (the knowledge of) chess is a habit, whereas the knowledge of causal chains is something natural. However, it is an example the student may use to gain an intellectual understanding of the basic facts mentioned here.

3 The experimental intellect and how it comes into being

One knows from philosophical works the statement that 'man is political by nature'. The philosophers cite that statement in connection with establishing the existence of prophecy and other things. The adjective 'political' refers to the 'town' (*polis*), which they use as another word for human social organization.

The statement means that a single human being cannot live by himself, and his existence can materialize only in association with his fellow men. Alone he would be unable to have a complete existence and lead a complete life. By his very nature, he needs the co-operation of others to satisfy all his needs. Such co-operation requires, firstly, consultation, and, then, association and the things that follow after it. Dealings with other people, when there is oneness of purpose, may lead to mutual affection, and when purposes differ, they may lead to strife and altercation. Thus, mutual dislike and mutual affection, friendship and hostility, originate. This leads to war and peace among nations and tribes.

(Among human beings) this does not happen haphazardly, as is the case among stray animals. God enabled them to arrange for (their activities) under political aspects and according to philosophical norms. They lead human beings from the things that are detrimental to them, to those that are in their interest, and from evil to good. First, however, they must recognize the things that are evil, and the detrimental effect of doing them, from sound experience and current customs. Thus, they are distinguished from stray animals. The result of their ability to think shows itself in the fact that their actions are orderly and not likely to be detrimental.

The concepts bringing this about are not completely divorced from sensual perception and do not require very deep study. All of them are obtained through experience and derived from it. They are particular concepts connected with the *sensibilia*. Their truth or falsehood soon comes out in events. From events the student of these concepts can learn them. Each human being can learn as much of them as he is able to. He can pick up (his knowledge) with the help of experience among the events that occur in his dealings with his fellow men. Eventually, he will have what is necessary and must be done, and must not be done, fixed in his (mind). By knowing this well, then, the proper habit of dealing with his fellow men will be obtained by him.

Those who follow this (procedure) during their whole life become acquainted with every single problem; things that depend on experience require time. God made it easy for many human beings to obtain this (social knowledge) in a time shorter than the time required to obtain it through experience, if they will follow the experience of their fathers, teachers, and elders, learn from them, and accept their instruction. People can, thus, dispense with lengthy and careful (personal) study of events and need not attempt to pick out concepts from them. But people who have no knowledge or tradition in this respect, or people who are not willing to learn and to follow others, need long and careful study in order to be educated in these things. They are unfamiliar to them, and the knowledge they obtain of them is uneven. Their manners and dealings with others will be badly planned and show defects. Their chances of making a living among their fellow men will be spoiled.

This is the meaning of the famous saying: 'He who is not educated by his parents will be educated by time.' That is, he who does not acquire the manners needed in dealing with human beings from his parents—which includes teachers and elders—and does not learn these things from them, has to fall back upon learning them with the help of nature from the events that happen in the course of time. Thus, time will teach and educate him, because he needs that education, since, by his very nature, he needs the co-operation of others.

Such is the experimental intellect. It is obtained after the discerning intellect that leads to action, as we have explained. After these two intellects, there is the (higher) degree of the speculative intellect. Many scholars have undertaken to explain it, and it is, therefore, not necessary to explain it in this book.

4 The knowledge of human beings and the knowledge of angels

We observe in ourselves through sound intuition the existence of three worlds.

The first of them is the world of sensual perception. We become aware of it by means of the perception of the senses, which the animals share with us.

Then, we become aware of the ability to think which is a special quality of human beings. We learn from it that the human soul exists. This knowledge is necessitated by the fact that we have in us scientific perceptions which are above the perceptions of the senses. They must thus be considered as another world, above the world of the senses.

Then, we deduce (the existence of) a third world, above us, from the influences that we find it leaves in our hearts, such as volition and an inclination toward active motions. Thus, we know that there exists an agent there who directs us toward those things from a world above our world. That world is the world of spirits and angels. It contains essences that can be perceived because of the existence of influences they exercise upon us, despite the gap between us and them.

Often, we may deduce (the existence of) that high spiritual world and the essences it contains, from visions and things we had not been aware of while awake but which we find in our sleep and which are brought to our attention in it and which, if they are true dreams, conform with actuality. We thus know that they are true and come from the world of truth. 'Confused dreams', on the other hand, are pictures of the imagination that are stored inside by perception and to which the ability to think is applied, after man has retired from sense perception.

Of the (three) worlds, the one we can perceive best is the world of human beings, since it is existential and attested by our corporeal and spiritual perceptions. The world of the senses is shared by us with the animals, but the world of the intellect and the spirits is shared by us with the angels, whose essences are of the same kind as the essences of that world. They are essences free from corporeality and matter, and they are pure intellect in which intellect, thinker, and the object of thinking are one. It is, in a way, an essence the reality of which is perception and intellect. . . .

5   The knowledge of the prophets

We find that this kind of human being is in a divine condition that is different from (ordinary) human ambitions and conditions. In prophets, the trend toward the divine is more powerful than their humanity, as far as the powers of perception, the powers of desire—that is, concupiscence and wrath—and the other conditions of the body are concerned. Prophets keep away from things human, except inasmuch as they are necessary for life. They turn toward divine matters, such as worship and the remembrance of God, as their knowledge of Him requires. They give information about Him and (transmit) the revelation for the guidance of believers which they received in (their divine) condition. They do that according to one particular method and in a manner known to be peculiar to them.

338

It undergoes no change in them and is like a natural disposition which God has given them.

Above the human world, there is a spiritual world. It is known to us by its influence upon us, in that it gives us the powers of perception and volition. The essences of that spiritual world are pure perception and absolute intellection. It is the world of the angels.

It follows from all this that the human soul must be prepared to exchange humanity for angelicality, in order actually to become part of the angelic species at any time, in a single instant. It will afterwards resume its humanity. But in the world of angelicality, it has meanwhile accepted (ideas) that it is charged to transmit to its fellow human beings. That is the meaning of revelation and being addressed by the angels.

All prophets possess this predisposition. It is like a natural disposition for them. In exchanging their humanity for angelicality, they experience strain and sensations of choking, as is known in this connection.

Their knowledge is one of direct observation and vision. No mistake or slip attaches itself to it, and it is not affected by errors or unfounded assumptions. The agreement in it is an essential one, because the veil of the supernatural is gone, and clear and direct observation has been attained. When (the prophets) quit that state and reassume their humanity, this clarity does not quit the knowledge they have, for it has become attached to it in the former condition. And because they possess the virtue that brings them to that condition, their (experience) constantly repeats itself, until their guidance of believers, which was the purpose for which they were sent, is accomplished. . . .

6 Man is essentially ignorant, and becomes learned through acquiring knowledge

We have already explained that man belongs to the genus of animals and that God distinguished him from them by the ability to think, which He gave man and through which man is able to arrange his actions in an orderly manner. This is the discerning intellect. Or, when it helps him to acquire from his fellow men a knowledge of ideas and of the things that are useful or detrimental to him, it is the experimental intellect. Or, when it helps him to obtain perception of the existent things as they are, whether they are absent or present, it is the speculative intellect.

Man's ability to think comes to him only after the animality in him has reached perfection. It starts from discernment. Before man has discernment, he has no knowledge whatever, and is counted one of the animals. His origin, the way in which he was created from a drop of sperm, a clot of blood, and a lump of flesh, still determines his (mental make-up). Whatever he attains subsequently is the result of sensual perception and the ability to think God has given him.

In his first condition, before he has attained discernment, man is simply matter, inasmuch as he is devoid of all knowledge. He reaches perfection of his form through knowledge, which he acquires through his own organs. Thus, his human essence reaches perfection of existence.

Man's nature and essence reveal to us the essential ignorance and acquired (character of the) knowledge that man possesses. . . .

7 Scientific instruction is a craft

This is because skill in a science, knowledge of its diverse aspects, and mastery of it are the result of a habit which enables its possessor to comprehend all the basic principles of that particular science, to become acquainted with its problems, and to evolve the details of it from its principles. As long as such a habit has not been obtained, skill in a particular discipline is not forthcoming.

Habit is different from understanding and knowing by memory. Understanding of a single problem in a single discipline may be found equally in someone well versed in the particular discipline and in the beginner, in the common man who has no scientific knowledge whatever, and in the accomplished scholar. Habit, on the other hand, belongs solely and exclusively to the scholar or the person well versed in scientific disciplines. This shows that (scientific) habit is different from understanding.

All habits are corporeal, whether they are of the body, or, like arithmetic, of the brain and resulting from man's ability to think and so on. All corporeal things are *sensibilia*. Thus, they require instruction. Therefore, a tradition of famous teachers with regard to instruction in any science or craft is acknowledged (to be necessary) by the people of every race and region.

The fact that scientific instruction is a craft is also shown by the differences in technical terminologies. Every famous authority has his own technical terminology for scientific instruction, as is the case with all crafts. This shows that technical terminology is not a part of science itself. If it were, it would be one and the same with all scholars. One knows how much the technical terminology used in the teaching of speculative theology differs between the ancients and the moderns. The same applies to any science one undertakes to study. . . .

The easiest method of acquiring the scientific habit is through acquiring the ability to express oneself clearly in discussing and disputing scientific problems. This is what clarifies their import and makes them understandable. Some students spend most of their lives attending scholarly sessions. Still, one finds them silent. They do not talk and do not discuss matters. More than is necessary, they are concerned with memorizing. Thus, they do not obtain much of a habit in the practice of science and scientific instruction. Some of them think that they have obtained (the habit). But when they enter into a discussion or disputation, or do some teaching, their scientific habit is found to be defective. Their memorized knowledge may be more extensive than that of other scholars, because they are so much concerned with memorizing. They think that scientific habit is identical with memorized knowledge. But that is not so.

The institution of scientific instruction has disappeared among the inhabitants of Spain. Their former concern with the sciences is gone, because Muslim civilization in Spain has been decreasing for hundreds of years. The only scholarly discipline remaining there is Arabic (philology) and literature, to which the (Spanish Muslims) restrict themselves. The tradition of teaching these disciplines is preserved among them, and thus the disciplines as such are preserved. Jurisprudence is an empty institution among them and a mere shadow of its real self. Of the intellectual disciplines, not even a shadow remains. The only reason for that is that the tradition of scientific instruction has ceased (to be cultivated) in Spain, because civilization there has deteriorated and the enemy has gained control over most of it, except for a few people along the coast who are more concerned with making a living than with the things that come after it.

In the East, the tradition of scientific instruction has not ceased to be cultivated. Scientific instruction is very much in demand because of the continuity of an abundant civilization and the continuity of the tradition (of scientific instruction) there. It is true that the old cities, such as Baghdad, al-Baṣrah, and al-Kûfah, which were the (original) mines of scholarship, are in ruin. However, God has replaced them with cities even greater than they were. Science was transplanted to the non-Arab 'Irâq of Khurâsân, to Transoxania in the East, and to Cairo and adjacent regions in the West. These cities have never ceased to have an abundant and continuous civilization, and the tradition of scientific instruction has always persisted in them.

The inhabitants of the East are, in general, more firmly rooted in the craft of scientific instruction and, indeed, in all the other crafts (than Maghribîs). The superiority of the inhabitants of the East over those of the West lies in the additional intelligence that accrues to

341

the soul from the influences of sedentary culture, as has been stated before in connection with the crafts. We are now going to comment on that and to verify it. It is as follows:

Sedentary people observe a particular code of manners in everything they undertake and do or do not do, and they thus acquire certain ways of making a living, finding dwellings, building houses, and handling their religious and worldly matters, including their customary affairs, their dealings with others, and all the rest of their activities. These manners constitute a kind of limitation which may not be transgressed, and, at the same time, they are crafts that later generations take over from the earlier ones. No doubt, each craft that has its proper place within the arrangement of the crafts, influences the soul and causes it to acquire an additional intelligence, which prepares the soul for accepting still other crafts. The intellect is thus conditioned for a quick reception of knowledge.

We hear that the Egyptians have achieved things hardly possible in the teaching of the crafts. For instance, they teach domestic donkeys and other dumb animals, quadrupeds and birds, to speak words and to do things that are remarkable for their rarity and that the inhabitants of the Maghrib would not be capable of understanding, let alone teaching.

Good habits in scientific instruction, in the crafts, and in all the other customary activities, add insight to the intellect of a man and enlightenment to his thinking, since the soul thus obtains a great number of habits. We have stated before that the soul grows under the influence of the perceptions it receives and the habits accruing to it. Thus, (the people of the East) become more clever, because their souls are influenced by scientific activity. The common people then suppose that it is a difference in the reality of humanity. This is not so. If one compares sedentary people with Bedouins, one notices how much more insight and cleverness sedentary people have. One might, thus, come to think that they really differ from the Bedouins in the reality of humanity and in intelligence. This is not so. The only reason for the difference is that sedentary people have refined technical habits and manners as far as customary activities and sedentary conditions are concerned, all of them things that are unknown to the Bedouins. Sedentary people possess numerous crafts, as well as the habits that go with them, and good (methods of) teaching the crafts. Therefore, those who do not have such habits think that they indicate an intellectual perfection possessed (exclusively) by sedentary people, and that the natural qualifications of the Bedouins are inferior to those of sedentary people. This is not so. We find Bedouins whose understanding, intellectual perfection, and natural qualifications are of the highest order. The seeming (superiority of) sedentary people is merely the result of a certain polish the crafts and scientific instruction give them.

8 The sciences are numerous only where civilization is large and sedentary culture highly developed

The reason for this is that scientific instruction is one of the crafts. We have stated before that the crafts are numerous only in cities. The quality and the number of the crafts depend on the greater or lesser extent of civilization in the cities and on the sedentary culture and luxury they enjoy, because (highly developed crafts) are something additional to just making a living. When civilized people have more labour available than they need for mere subsistence, such (surplus) labour is used for activities over and above making a living. These activities are man's prerogative. They are the sciences and the crafts.

People who grow up in villages and uncivilized (thinly populated) cities and who have an innate desire for scientific activity, cannot find scientific instruction in those places. For scientific instruction is something technical, and there are no crafts among the inhabitants of the desert. These people, therefore, must travel and seek scientific instruction in cities where (civilization) is highly developed, as is the case with all crafts.

We, at this time, notice that science and scientific instruction exist in Cairo in Egypt, because the civilization is greatly developed and its sedentary culture has been well established for thousands of years. Therefore, the crafts are firmly established there and exist in many varieties. One of them is scientific instruction. . . .

9 The various sciences that exist in contemporary civilization

The sciences with which people concern themselves in cities, and which they acquire and pass on through instruction, are of two kinds: one that is natural to man and to which he is guided by his own ability to think, and a traditional kind that he learns from those who invented it.

The first kind comprises the philosophical sciences. They are the ones with which man can become acquainted through the very nature of his ability to think and to whose objects, problems, arguments, and methods of instruction he is guided by his human perceptions, so that he is made aware of the distinction between what is correct and what is wrong in them by his own speculation and research, inasmuch as he is a thinking human being.

The second kind comprises the traditional, conventional sciences.

All of them depend upon information based on the authority of the given religious law. There is no place for the intellect in them, save that the intellect may be used in connection with them to relate problems of detail with basic principles. Particulars that constantly come into being are not included in the general tradition by the mere fact of its existence. Therefore, they need to be related (to the general principles) by some kind of analogical reasoning. However, such analogical reasoning is derived from the (traditional) information, while the character of the basic principle, which is traditional, remains valid (unchanged). Thus, analogical reasoning of this type reverts to being tradition itself, because it is derived from it.

The basis of all the traditional sciences is the legal material of the Qur'ân and the Sunnah, which is the law given us by God and His messenger, as well as the sciences connected with that material, by means of which we are enabled to utilize it. This, further, requires as auxiliary sciences the sciences of the Arabic language. Arabic is the language of Islam, and the Qur'ân was revealed in it.

The different kinds of traditional sciences are numerous, because it is the duty of the responsible Muslim to know the legal obligations God placed upon him and upon his fellow men. They are derived from the Qur'ân and the Sunnah, either from the text, or through general consensus, or through combination. . . .

The traditional legal sciences were cultivated in Islam in a way that permitted no further increase. The students of those sciences reached the farthest possible limit in knowledge of them. The various technical terminologies were refined, and order was brought into the various disciplines. The traditional sciences thus achieved exceeding excellence and refinement. Each discipline had its authorities to whom one referred, and its rules that were used for instruction. . . .

10 The sciences of Qur'ân interpretation and Qur'ân reading

The Qur'ân is the word of God that was revealed to His Prophet.

Its transmission has been continuous in Islam. However, the men around Muḥammad transmitted it on the authority of the Messenger of God in different ways. These differences affect certain of the words in it and the manner in which the letters were pronounced. They were handed down and became famous. Eventually, seven specific ways of reading the Qur'ân became established. . . .

12 Jurisprudence and its subdivision, inheritance laws

Jurisprudence is the knowledge of the classification of the laws of God, which concern the actions of all responsible Muslims, as obligatory, forbidden, recommendable, disliked, or permissible. These are derived from the Qur'ân and the Sunnah (traditions), and from the evidence Muḥammad has established. The laws evolved from this evidence are called 'jurisprudence'.

The early Muslims evolved from that evidence, though, unavoidably, they differed in its interpretation. The evidence is mainly derived from Arabic texts. In many instances, and especially with regard to legal concepts, there are well-known differences among them as to the meaning implicit in the words. Furthermore, the traditions differ widely in respect of the reliability of the recensions. Their legal contents, as a rule, are contradictory. Therefore, a decision is needed. This makes for differences of opinion. Furthermore, evidence not derived from texts causes (still other) differences of opinion. Then, there are new cases which arise and are not covered by the texts. They are referred by analogy to things that are covered by the texts. All of this serves to stir up unavoidable differences of opinion, and this is why controversy occurred among the early Muslims and the religious leaders after them.

Moreover, not all of the men around Muḥammad were qualified to give legal decisions. Not all of them could serve as sources for religious practice. That was restricted to men who knew the Qur'ân and were acquainted with the abrogating and abrogated, the ambiguous and unambiguous verses, and with all the rest of the evidence that can be derived from the Qur'ân, since they had learned these matters from the Prophet directly or from their higher ranking colleagues who had learned it from him. These men, therefore, were called 'readers', that is, men (able to) read the Qur'ân, since the Arabs were an illiterate nation. Their ability to read was a remarkable thing in those days.

It continued to be that way at the beginning of Islam. Then, the cities of Islam grew, and illiteracy disappeared from among the Arabs because of their constant occupation with the Qur'ân. Now the development (of jurisprudence) took place. It was perfected and came to be a craft and a science. The Qur'ân readers were no longer called Qur'ân readers but jurists and religious scholars.

The jurists developed two different approaches to jurisprudence. One was based on reasoning and analogy. It was represented by the 'Irâqîs. The other was based on traditions. It was represented by the Ḥijâzîs.

The leader of the 'Irâqîs, around whom and whose followers their school centred, was the imam Abû Ḥanîfah. The leader of the Ḥijâzîs was Mâlik b. Anas and, after him, ash-Shâfi'î.

Later on, a group of religious scholars disapproved of analogy and rejected its use. They were the Ẓâhirites. They restricted the sources

345

of the law to the texts and the general consensus. They considered obvious analogy and causality suggested by the texts as resting in the texts themselves, because a text that indicates a *ratio legis* permits legal decision for all the cases covered by (such a kind of reasoning). The leaders of this school were Dâwûd b. 'Alî and his son and their followers.

These were the three schools famous among the greet mass of Muslims. The 'Alids invented their own school and had their own jurisprudence. They based it upon their dogma requiring abuse of some of the men around Muḥammad, and upon their stated opinion concerning the infallibility of the imams and the inadmissibility of differences in their statements. All these are futile principles. The Khârijites similarly had their own school. The great mass did not care for these (unorthodox) schools, but greatly disapproved of them and abused them. Nothing is known of the opinions of these schools. Their books are not being transmitted. No trace of them can be found except in regions inhabited (by these sectarians). The (legal) books of the Shî'ah are thus found in Shî'ah countries and wherever Shî'ah dynasties exist, in the West, the East, and in the Yemen. The same applies to the Khârijites.

The Zâhirite school has become extinct today as the result of the extinction of their religious leaders and disapproval of their adherents by the great mass of Muslims.

Nothing has remained except the schools of the representatives of opinion (reasoning) in the 'Irâq and of the representatives of traditions in the Ḥijâz. . . .

The science of inheritance laws

The science of inheritance laws is the knowledge of estate division and the correct determination of the proper shares in an estate with regard to the relation of the individual shares to the basic divisions. It also includes (knowledge of) the readjustment of shares (*munâsakhah*). (Such readjustment) is necessary when one of the (original) heirs dies and his portion is to be distributed among his heirs.

Also, the division of an estate may have to consider two possibilities, in that, for instance, one heir may acknowledge another heir, while a third heir does not acknowledge (that second heir). Then, the division of the estate is adjusted (and figured out) according to the two possibilities, and the amount of the shares is considered. Then, the estate is divided among the heirs in shares proportionate to the basic fractions. All this requires calculation. Therefore, jurists made of it a separate subject, because, in addition to jurisprudence, it requires calculation as the predominant element in it. They considered it a discipline in its own right.

Religious scholars in the Muslim cities have paid much attention to it. Some authors are inclined to exaggerate the mathematical side of the discipline and to pose problems requiring for their solution various branches of arithmetic, such as algebra, the use of roots, and similar things. It is of no practical use in inheritance matters, because it deals with unusual and rare cases. . . .

13 The science of the principles of jurisprudence and its subdivisions, dialectics and controversial questions

The science of the principles of jurisprudence is one of the greatest, most important, and most useful disciplines of the religious law. It is concerned with the evidence of the religious law from which the laws and legal obligations of the Muslims are derived.

The basic sources of legal evidence are the Qur'ân and, then, the traditions which clarify the Qur'ân.

Then, general consensus took its place next to the Qur'ân and the traditions (Sunnah). Now many of the things that happened after the Prophet are not included in the established texts. Therefore, they compared and combined them with the established evidence that is found in the texts, (and drew their conclusions from analogy) according to certain rules that governed their combinations. This assured the soundness of their comparison of two similar (cases), so that it could be assumed that one and the same divine law covered both cases. This became (another kind of) legal evidence, because the (early Muslims) all agreed upon it. This is analogy, the fourth kind of evidence.

The great mass of religious scholars are agreed that these are the four basic kinds of evidence. Some scholars differed on the matters of general consensus and analogy. But this is exceptional. Others added further kinds of evidence to the four. We do not have to mention them here, because the basis (upon which they rest) is weak, and they are rarely referred to. . . .

After that comes the study of the meaning of words. This is because one depends upon knowledge of the conventional meanings of single or composite utterances, for deriving ideas in general from word combinations in general. The philological norms needed in this connection are found in the sciences of grammar, inflection, and syntax and style. Now, when speech was a habit of those who used it, these (linguistic matters) were neither sciences nor norms. At that time, jurists did not need them, because linguistic matters were familiar to them by natural habit. But when the habit of the Arabic language was lost, the experts who made it their speciality determined it once and for all with the help of a sound tradition and of

347

sound rules of analogy they evolved. (Linguistic matters) thus became sciences the jurists had to master, in order to know the divine laws. . . .

Controversial questions

The jurisprudence described, which is based upon religious evidence, involves many differences of opinion among scholars of independent judgement. Differences of opinion result from the different sources they use and their different outlooks, and are unavoidable. This kind of scholarship was called 'controversial questions'. . . .

Dialectics

'Dialectics' involves knowledge of the proper behaviour in disputations among the adherents of the legal schools and others. The choices of rejection and acceptance in disputations are numerous. In arguing and answering, each disputant lets himself go. Some of the argument is correct; some of it is wrong. Therefore, the authorities had to lay down the proper rules of behaviour by which the disputants would have to abide. These concern rejection and acceptance; how the person advancing an argument should behave and how the person replying to it should behave; when it is permissible for a disputant to advance an argument; how he (should admit) defeat and stop; when he should interrupt or contradict his opponent; and where he should be silent and permit his opponent to talk and advance his arguments. It has, therefore, been said that this discipline is the knowledge of the basic rules of proper behaviour in arguing, which help either to safeguard an opinion or to demolish it, whether that opinion concerns jurisprudence or any other subject. . . .

14 The science of speculative theology

This is a science that involves arguing with logical proofs in defence of the articles of faith and refuting innovators who deviate in their dogmas from the early Muslims and Muslim orthodoxy.

The real core of the articles of faith is the oneness of God. Therefore, we shall present here, first, a nice specimen of logical argumentation that will show us the oneness of God in the most direct method and manner. We shall then return and give a correct description of speculative theology and the (subjects) it studies. We shall also indicate the reason why it developed in Islam and what it was that called for its invention.

We say: It should be known that the things that come into being in the world of existing things, whether they belong to essences or to either human or animal actions, require appropriate causes which are prior to (their existence). They introduce the things that come into being into the realm dominated by custom, and effect their coming into being. Each one of these causes, in turn, comes into being and, thus, requires other causes. Causes continue to follow upon causes in an ascending order, until they reach the Causer of causes, Him who brings them into existence and creates them.

In the process, the causes multiply and widen in extent vertically and horizontally. The intellect becomes confused in the attempt to perceive and enumerate them. Only a comprehensive knowledge can encompass them all, especially human and animal actions. Among the causes of (action), there evidently belong the various kinds of intention and volition, since no action can materialize except through volition and intention. The various kinds of intention and volition are matters pertaining to the soul. As a rule, they originate from previous consecutive perceptions. These perceptions cause the intention to act. The causes of such perceptions are, again, other perceptions. Now, the cause of all the perceptions taking place in the soul is unknown, since no one is able to know the beginnings or order of matters pertaining to the soul. They are consecutive notions that God puts into the mind of man, who is unable to understand their beginnings and ends. As a rule, man is able only to comprehend the causes that are natural and obvious and that present themselves to our perception in an orderly and well-arranged manner, because nature is encompassed by the soul and on a lower level than it. The range of perceptions, however, is too large for the soul, because they belong to the intellect, which is on a higher level than the soul. The soul, therefore, can scarcely perceive very many of them, let alone all of them. Man often stops (to speculate about causes); his feet slip, and he becomes one of those who go astray and perish.

One should not think that man has the power, or can choose at will, to stop or to retrace his steps. No, one must be on guard by completely abandoning any speculation about (causes).

Furthermore, the way in which causes exercise their influence upon the majority of things caused is unknown. They are only known through customary (experience) and through conclusions which attest to (the existence of an) apparent (causal) relationship. What that influence really is and how it takes place is not known. Therefore, we have been commanded completely to abandon and suppress any speculation about them and to direct ourselves to the Causer of all causes, so that the soul will be firmly coloured with the oneness of God.

A man who stops at the causes is frustrated. He is rightly (said to

349

be) an unbeliever. If he ventures to swim in the ocean of speculation and of research, (seeking) each one of the causes that cause them and the influence they exercise, I can guarantee him that he will return unsuccessful. Therefore, we were forbidden by Muḥammad to study causes. We were commanded to recognize the absolute oneness of God.

Man should not trust the suggestion his mind makes, that it is able to comprehend all existing things and their causes, and to know all the details of existence. Such a suggestion of the mind should be dismissed as stupid. Every person with perception has the superficial impression that the (whole of) existence is comprised by his perceptions, and that it does not extend beyond them. The matter is different in fact. The truth lies beyond that. One knows that a deaf person feels that the whole of existence is comprised in the perceptions of his four senses and his intellect. The whole group of audible things constitutes no part of existence for him. The same applies to a blind person. The whole group of visible things constitutes no part of existence for him. If (people with such defects) were not set right by their adherence to information they receive from their fathers and teachers and from the majority of people in general, they would not admit (the existence of those things). They follow the majority in admitting the existence of these groups (of *sensibilia*), but (the admission) is not in their natural disposition nor in the nature of their sense perception. If dumb animals were asked and could speak, we would find that they would ignore the whole group of *intelligibilia*. It would simply not exist for them.

Now, it might be assumed that there exists another kind of perception different from ours, since our sense perceptions are created and brought into existence. God's creation extends beyond the creation of man. Complete knowledge does not exist in man. The world of existence is too vast for him. Therefore, everyone should be suspicious of the comprehensiveness of his perceptions and the results of his perception. This does not speak against the intellect and intellectual perceptions. The intellect, indeed, is a correct scale. Its indications are completely certain and in no way wrong. However, the intellect should not be used to weigh such matters as the oneness of God, the other world, the truth of prophecy, the real character of the divine attributes, or anything else that lies beyond the level of the intellect. That would mean to desire the impossible. One might compare it with a man who sees a scale in which gold is being weighed, and wants to weigh mountains in it. The (fact that this is impossible) does not prove that the indications of the scale are not true. Thus, the intellect cannot comprehend God and His attributes. It is but one of the atoms of the world of existence which results from God.

If this is clear, it is possible that the ascending sequence of causes reaches the point where it transcends the realm of human perception and existence and thus ceases to be perceivable. The intellect would here become lost, confused, and cut off in the wilderness of conjectures. Thus, (recognition of the) oneness of God is identical with inability to perceive the causes and the ways in which they exercise their influence, and with reliance in this respect upon the Creator of the causes who comprises them. There is no maker but Him. All (causes) lead up to Him and go back to His power. We know about Him only inasmuch as we have issued from Him. This is the meaning of the statement transmitted on the authority of a certain truthful (person): 'The inability to perceive is perception.'[1]

Such (declaration of the) oneness of God does not merely refer to faith, which is affirmation based upon judgment. The object of (all human) actions and divine worship is acquisition of the habit of obedience and submissiveness, and the freeing of the heart from all preoccupations save the worshipped Master, until the novice on the path to God becomes a holy person.

The difference between 'state' and knowledge in questions of dogma is the same as that between talking (about attributes) and having them. This may be explained as follows: Many people know that mercy to the orphans and the poor brings (a human being) close to God and is recommendable. They say so and acknowledge the fact. They quote the sources for it from the religious law. But if they were to see an orphan or a poor person they would run away from him and disdain to touch him, let alone show mercy to him. Their mercy for the orphan was the result of having reached the station of knowledge. It was not the result of the station of 'state' nor of an attribute of theirs. Now, there are people who, in addition to the station of knowledge and the realization of the fact that mercy to the poor brings one close to God, have attained another, higher 'station': they have attained the attribute and habit of mercy. When they see an orphan or a poor person, they approach him and show him (mercy). They wish to receive the (heavenly) reward for the compassion they show him.

The relationship of man's knowledge of the oneness of God to his possession of it as an attribute, is of the same character. Knowledge results by necessity from possession of an attribute. It is a kind of knowledge that exists on a more solid basis than knowledge attained previous to the possession of the attribute. An attribute is not obtained from knowledge alone. There must be an action, and it must be

[1] While Ibn Khaldûn ascribes the statement to 'a certain truthful person', al-Ghazzâlî mentions as its author 'the master of those who are truthful', i.e., 'Alî, rather than Abû Bakr.

THE VARIOUS KINDS OF SCIENCES

repeated innumerable times. Only this results in a firmly rooted habit, in the acquisition of the attribute and real (knowledge). Another kind of knowledge thus makes its appearance. It is the kind that is useful in the other world. The original knowledge which was devoid of being an attribute is of little advantage or use. It is the knowledge that most thinkers (possess). But the real object is knowledge as a 'state', and it originates from divine worship.

It is clear that the object of all (religious) obligations is the acquisition of a habit firmly rooted in the soul, from which a necessary knowledge results for the soul. It is the (recognition of the) oneness of God which is the (principal) article of faith and the thing through which happiness is attained.

Faith, which is the basis and source of all (religious) obligations, has several degrees. The first degree is the affirmation by the heart of what the tongue says. The highest degree is the acquisition, from the belief of the heart and the resulting actions, of a quality that has complete control over the heart. It commands the actions of the limbs. Every activity takes place in submissiveness to it. Thus, all actions, eventually, become subservient to this affirmation by faith, and this is the highest degree of faith. It is perfect faith. The believer who has it will commit neither a great nor a small sin. . . .

In time, the science of logic spread in Islam. People studied it. They made a distinction between it and the philosophical sciences, in that logic was merely a norm and yardstick for arguments and served to probe the arguments of the (philosophical sciences) as well as (those of) all other (disciplines).

(Scholars) studied the basic premises the earlier theologians had established. They refuted most of them with the help of arguments leading them to (a different opinion). Many of these were derived from philosophical discussions of physics and metaphysics. When they probed them with the yardstick of logic, it showed that they were applicable only to those (other disciplines and not to theology, but) they did not believe that if the arguments were wrong, the thing proven (by the arguments) was also wrong. This approach differed in its technical terminology from the older one. It was called 'the school of recent scholars'. Their approach often included refutation of the philosophers where the (opinions of the) latter differed from the articles of faith. They considered the (philosophers) enemies of the articles of faith, because, in most respects, there is a relationship between the opinions of the innovators and the opinions of the philosophers.

The first (scholar) to write in accordance with the new theological approach was al-Ghazzâlî. He was followed by the imam Ibn al-

Khaṭīb. A large number of scholars followed in their steps and adhered to their tradition.

The later scholars were very intent upon meddling with philosophical works. The subjects of the two disciplines (theology and philosophy) were thus confused by them. They thought that there was one and the same (subject) in both disciplines, because the problems of each discipline were similar.

The theologians most often deduced the existence and attributes of the Creator from the existing things and their conditions. As a rule, this was their line of argument. The physical bodies form part of the existing things, and they are the subject of the philosophical study of physics. However, the philosophical study of them differs from the theological. The philosophers study bodies in so far as they move or are stationary. The theologians, on the other hand, study them in so far as they serve as an argument for the Maker. In the same way, the philosophical study of metaphysics studies existence as such and what it requires for its essence. The theological study (of metaphysics), on the other hand, is concerned with the *existentia*, in so far as they serve as argument for Him who causes existence. In general, to the theologians, the object of theology is (to find out) how the articles of faith which the religious law has laid down as correct, can be proven with the help of logical arguments, so that innovations may be repulsed and doubts and misgivings concerning the articles of faith be removed.

If one considers how this discipline originated and how scholarly discussion was incorporated within it step by step, and how, during that process, scholars always assumed the correctness of the articles of faith and paraded proofs and arguments (in their defence), one will realize that the character of the subject of this discipline is as we have established it, and one will realize that (the discipline) cannot go beyond it. However, the two approaches have been mixed up by recent scholars. The problems of theology have been confused with those of philosophy. This has gone so far that the one discipline is no longer distinguishable from the other.

The approach of the early Muslims can be reconciled with the beliefs of the science of speculative theology only if one follows the old approach of the theologians (and not the mixed approach of recent scholars). In general, it must be known that this science—the science of speculative theology—is not something that is necessary to the contemporary student. Heretics and innovators have been destroyed. The orthodox religious leaders have given us protection against heretics and innovators in their systematic works and treatments.

However, the usefulness of speculative theology for certain individuals and students is considerable. Orthodox Muslims should not be ignorant of speculative argumentation in defence of the articles of orthodox faith.

15 An exposition of ambiguity in the Qur'ân and the Sunnah and of the resulting dogmatic schools among both the orthodox and the innovators

God sent our Prophet Muḥammad to us, in order to call us to salvation and bliss. He revealed to him His noble book in the clear Arabic language. He told us in it about the (religious) obligations that would enable us to attain (salvation and bliss). This process included and necessitated references to God's names and attributes, in order to make us acquainted with His essence; also references to the spirit attaching itself to us, and to the revelation and the angels constituting the connection between God and His messengers who were sent to us. The Day of Resurrection and its warning signs have been mentioned to us (in the Qur'ân), but the exact time when any of these things is to take place is not indicated. Also, at the beginning of certain sûrahs, the noble Qur'ân contains, scattered in various places, combinations of individual letters of the alphabet the meaning of which we are not able to understand.

All these particulars of the Qur'ân were described as 'ambiguous'. Those who followed them were censured, as indicated in the verse: 'It is He who revealed the Book to you. It contains unambiguous verses that are the mother of the Book, and other verses that are ambiguous. Those who are inclined in their hearts toward deviation follow that which is ambiguous in the Qur'ân, because they desire trouble, and they desire to interpret it. But only God knows how to interpret it. Those who are firmly rooted in knowledge say, "We believe in it. It is all from our Lord." Only those who have a heart remember.'[1]

The early Muslim scholars from among the men around Muḥammad and the men of the second generation understood this verse to mean that the 'unambiguous verses' are those that are clear and definite. The jurists, therefore, define 'unambiguous' in their terminology as 'clear in meaning'.

Concerning the 'ambiguous verses', people have different notions. It has been said that they require study and interpretation in order to establish their correct meaning, because they contradict other verses or logic. Therefore, their meaning is obscure and 'ambiguous'. In this sense, Ibn 'Abbâs said: 'One must believe in the "ambiguous verses", but one need not act in accordance with them.'

The phrase 'Mother of the Book', in the verse quoted, means 'the largest and most prominent part of (the Book)', whereas the 'am-

[1] Qur'ân 3. 6 (5).

354

biguous verses' constitute the smallest part of it, and they have no meaning except with reference to the unambiguous verses. The verse, then, censures those who follow the 'ambiguous verses' and interpret them or give them a meaning they do not have in the Arabic language which the Qur'ân addresses us in. The verse calls those persons 'deviators'—that is, people who turn away from the truth—unbelievers, heretics, stupid innovators. The verse says that they act so in order to cause trouble—that is, idolatry and confusion among the believers—or in order to be able to interpret the ambiguous verses to suit their desires. . . .

It should be known that the world of man is the most noble and exalted of the worlds of existent things. Even though human reality is uniform in the world, it contains different levels which differ from each other through conditions peculiar to them, to such a degree that the realities at each level are different ones.

The first level is constituted by the human world of the body including man's external sense perception, his thinking which is directed toward making a living, and all the other activities which are granted to him by his present existence.

The second level is constituted by the world of sleep (dream visions). It involves perception by the imagination. Man lets the perceptions of his imagination rove in his inward being. With his external senses, he perceives some of them as unencumbered by time, place, or any other condition of the body. He sees them in places where he himself is not. If they are good, they present him with the glad tidings of pleasure he may expect in this world and the other world as our truthful Prophet promised.

These two levels are shared by all human individuals, but, as one has seen, they differ as to the way perceptions are attained in them.

The third level is that of prophecy. It is restricted to the noblest representatives of humankind by virtue of the fact that God has distinguished them through the knowledge of Himself and (the declaration of) His oneness, through His revelation brought to them by His angels, and through the obligation to achieve the improvement of mankind with respect to conditions altogether different from the outward human conditions.

The fourth level is that of death. Here, human individuals leave their outward life for another existence before the Resurrection. It is called Purgatory. In it, they enjoy bliss or receive punishment, depending on their activities (while alive). Then, they come to the Great Resurrection, where they receive the great reward, that is, either bliss in Paradise or punishment in Hell.

The first two levels are attested by intuition. The third level, that of prophecy, is attested to by the prophetic miracles and the conditions peculiar to the prophets. The fourth level, attested to by the divine revelation given to the prophets, concerns revivification, the conditions of Purgatory, and the Resurrection. Moreover, logic requires its (existence). God has called our attention to that in many verses concerned with the rising (of the dead). The best argumen for their correctness is that if, apart from their visible existence in this world, human individuals had no existence after death, where they will encounter conditions befitting them, it would have been something frivolous to create them in the first place. If death is non-existence, it would mean the return of the individual to nonexistence. In that case, there would have been no sense in creating them in the first place. It is, however, absurd to assume that the wise Deity would act frivolously.

Now that the four levels have been established, we should explain how human perceptions with regard to those four levels clearly differ. This will reveal the intricacy of (the problem of) ambiguity.

At the first level, human perceptions are clear and obvious. With the help of these perceptions, man is able to master the habits of knowledge, to perfect his human reality, and to satisfy the requirements of divine worship which brings him to salvation.

At the second level—that of sleep or (dream visions)—human perceptions are the same as those of external sense perception. Although the limbs of the body are not used as they are in the waking state, yet the person who has a vision ascertains everything perceived by him in his sleep without any doubt or misgiving. The limbs of the body are not employed in their ordinary manner.

Concerning the real character of this state, people are divided into two groups:

Philosophers assume that imaginary pictures are transmitted by the imagination through the motion of thinking to the 'common sense' which constitutes the connecting link between external and inner sensual perception. As a result, (these pictures) are represented as something perceived in the external world by all the senses. The difficulty here is that true visions from God or the angels are more firmly and definitely perceived than visions of Satanic origin, although the imagination active in both is one and the same, as the (philosophers) have established.

The second group is that of the speculative theologians. Their summary statement of the problem is that it is a kind of perception created by God in (the realm of) the senses, and thus takes place in the same way that perception takes place in the waking state.

Perception in sleep is the clearest evidence for the fact that sensual perception operates at the subsequent levels.

It is not known to us how sensual perception takes place on the third level—that of the prophets—but they themselves have a more than certain knowledge of perception through intuition. The Prophet sees God and the angels. He hears God's speech from God Himself or from the angels. He sees Paradise, Hell, and the divine throne and chair. He breaks through the seven heavens in his ascension. He meets the prophets in (the heavens) and prays with them. He perceives all kinds of sensual perceptions, exactly as he perceives them at the levels of body and sleep, but through a kind of necessary knowledge that God creates for him, and not through ordinary human perception by means of the limbs of the body.

In this connection, no attention should be paid to Avicenna's remarks. He brings prophecy down to the level of sleep and says that the imagination transmits a picture to the 'common sense'. The argument against the (philosophers) in this connection is stronger in the case of dream visions. As we have established, that process of transmission by the imagination is by nature one and the same. In this way, revelation and prophetic dream vision would in reality be identical as to their certainty and reality. However, this is not so, as one knows from the dream vision of the Prophet just six months before the Revelation. The dream was the beginning of the Revelation and the prelude to it, which shows that, in reality, it is inferior to (revelation).

At the fourth level—that of the dead in Purgatory, which starts with the grave when they are free from the body, or during their rising when they reassume a body—the dead do have sensual perceptions. In his grave, a dead person sees two angels who question him. With the two eyes of his head, he sees the seat he will occupy in either Paradise or Hell. He sees the persons who attend the burial and hears what they say, and he hears the tapping of their shoes when they leave him. He hears the oneness of God or the affirmation of the two confessions of faith which they suggest to him, and other things.

Furthermore, during the rising of the dead and on the Day of Resurrection, the dead behold the different grades of bliss in Paradise and punishment in Hell with their own eyes and ears, exactly as they used to behold things during their life. They see the angels and they see their Lord.

The dead did not have such perceptions while they were alive. (Still), they are sensual perceptions like those (they had while they were alive). They take place in the limbs of the body by means of necessary knowledge that God creates, as we have stated. The secret of it lies in the knowledge that the human soul grows in the body and through the perceptions of the body. When it leaves the body in sleep or in death, or when a prophet, in the state of revelation, changes from human perceptions to angelic ones, the soul takes its means of perceptions along, but free of the limbs of the body. With (these means of perception), the soul perceives, on the (other) level, whatever perceptions it wants to perceive, but these perceptions are on a higher plane than those that the soul had while it was in the body. This was stated by al-Ghazzâlî, who added that the human soul has a form that it retains after its separation (from the body) and that, just like the body's own structure, includes two eyes, two ears, and all the rest of the limbs of the body serving (man) to attain perception. I would say that al-Ghazzâlî here refers to the habits obtained through using all those limbs of the body in addition to perception.

When one understands all this, one will realize that perceptions exist on all four levels. However, they are not everywhere the same as in the life of this world. They differ in intensity according to the conditions affecting them. The theologians have indicated this fact in the summary statement that God creates in (the senses) a necessary knowledge of the thing perceived, whatever it may be. By that, they are referring to the same thing we have been explaining.

16 Sufism

Sufism belongs to the sciences of the religious law that orignated in Islam. It is based on the assumption that the practices of its adherents had always been considered by the important early Muslims, the men around Muḥammad and the men of the second generation, as well as those who came after them, as the path of truth and right guidance. The Sufi approach is based upon constant application to divine worship, complete devotion to God, aversion to the false splendour of the world, abstinence from the pleasure, property, and position to which the great mass aspire, and retirement from the world into solitude for divine worship. These things were general among the men around Muḥammad and the early Muslims.

Then, worldly aspirations increased in the second [eighth] century and after. At that time, the special name of Sufis was given to those who aspired to divine worship.

The Sufis came to represent asceticism. They developed a particular kind of perception which comes about through ecstatic experience, as follows. Man, as man, is distinguished from all the other animals by his ability to perceive. His perception is of two kinds. He can perceive sciences and matters of knowledge, and these may be certain, hypothetical, doubtful, or imaginary. Also, he can perceive 'states' persisting in himself, such as joy and grief, anxiety and relaxation, satisfaction, anger, patience, gratefulness, and similar things. The reasoning part active in the body originates from perceptions, volitions, and states. It is through them that man is distinguished from the other animals. Knowledge originates from evidence, grief and joy from the perception of what is painful or pleasurable, energy from rest, and inertia from being tired. In the same way, the exertion and worship of the Sufi novice must lead to a 'state' that is the result of his exertion. That state may be a kind of divine worship. Then, it will be firmly rooted in the Sufi novice and become a 'station' for him. Or, it may not be divine worship, but merely an attribute affecting the soul, such as joy or gladness, energy or inertia, or something else.

The 'stations' (form an ascending order). The Sufi novice continues to progress from station to station, until he reaches the (recognition of the) oneness of God and the gnosis (ma'rifah) which is the desired goal of happiness.

Thus, the novice must progress by such stages. The basis of all of them is obedience and sincerity. Faith precedes and accompanies all of them. Their result and fruit are states and attributes. They lead to others, and again others, up to the station of the (recognition of the) oneness of God and of gnosis ('irfân). If the result shows some shortcoming or defect, one can be sure that it comes from some shortcoming that existed in the previous stage. The same applies to the ideas of the soul and the inspirations of the heart.

The novice, therefore, must scrutinize himself in all his actions and study their concealed import, because the results, of necessity, originate from actions, and shortcomings in the results, thus, originate from defects in the actions. The Sufi novice finds out about that through his mystical experience, and he scrutinizes himself as to its reasons.

Very few people share the self-scrutiny of the Sufis, for negligence in this respect is almost universal. Pious people who do not get that far perform, at best, acts of obedience. The Sufis, however, investigate the results of acts of obedience with the help of mystical and ecstatic experience, in order to learn whether they are free from deficiency or not. Thus, it is evident that the Sufis' path in its entirety depends upon self-scrutiny with regard to what they do or do not do, and upon discussion of the various kinds of mystical and ecstatic experience that result from their exertions. This, then, crystallizes for the Sufi novice in a 'station'. From that station, he can progress to another, higher one.

Furthermore, the Sufis have their peculiar form of behaviour and a linguistic terminology which they use in instruction. Linguistic data apply only to commonly accepted ideas. When there occur ideas not commonly accepted, technical terms facilitating the understanding of those ideas are coined to express them.

Thus, the Sufis had their special discipline, which is not discussed by other representatives of the religious law. As a consequence, the science of the religious law came to consist of two kinds. One is the special field of jurists and muftis. It is concerned with the general laws governing the acts of divine worship, customary actions, and mutual dealings. The other is the special field of the Sufis. It is concerned with pious exertion, self-scrutiny with regard to it, discussion of the different kinds of mystical and ecstatic experience occurring in the course of (self-scrutiny), the mode of ascent from one mystical experience to another, and the interpretation of the technical terminology of mysticism in use among them.

When the sciences were written down systematically and when the jurists wrote works on jurisprudence and the principles of jurisprudence, on speculative theology, Qur'ân interpretation, and other subjects, the Sufis, too, wrote on their subject. Some Sufis wrote on the laws governing asceticism and self-scrutiny, how to act and not act in imitation of (saints).

Al-Ghazzâlî, in the *Kitâb al-Iḥyâ'*, dealt systematically with the laws governing asceticism and the imitation of models. Then, he explained the behaviour and customs of the Sufis and commented on their technical vocabulary.

The science of Sufism became a systematically treated discipline in Islam. Before that, mysticism had merely consisted of divine worship, and its laws had existed in the breasts of men. The same had been the case with all other disciplines, such as Qur'ân interpretation, the science of tradition, jurisprudence, and the principles of jurisprudence.

Mystical exertion, retirement, and spiritual exercises are as a rule followed by the removal of the veil of sensual perception. The Sufi beholds divine worlds which a person subject to the senses cannot perceive at all. The spirit belongs to those worlds. The reason for the removal of (the veil) is the following. When the spirit turns from external sense perception to inner (perception), the senses weaken, and the spirit grows strong. It gains predominance and a new growth. The spiritual exercise helps to bring that about. It is like food to make the spirit grow. The spirit continues to grow and to increase. It had been knowledge. Now, it becomes vision. The veil of sensual perception is removed, and the soul realizes its essential existence. This is identical with perception. (The spirit) now is ready for the holy gifts, for the sciences of the divine presence, and for the outpourings of the Deity. Its essence realizes its own true character and draws close to the highest sphere, the sphere of the angels. The removal of (the veil) often happens to people who exert themselves (in mystical exercise). They perceive the realities of existence as no one else does.

They also perceive many future happenings. With the help of their minds and psychic powers they are active among the lower *existentia*, which thus become obedient to their will. The great Sufis do not think much of the removal (of the veil) and of activity (among the low *existentia*). They give no information about the reality of anything they have not been ordered to discuss. They consider it a tribulation, when things of that sort happen to them, and try to escape them whenever they afflict them.

The men around Muḥammad practised that kind of mystical exertion. They had a very abundant share in the acts of divine grace, but they did not bother with them.

Recent mystics, then, have turned their attention to the removal of the veil and the discussion of perceptions beyond (sensual perception). Their ways of mystical exercise in this respect differ. They have taught different methods of mortifying the powers of sensual perception and nourishing the reasoning spirit with exercises, so that the soul might fully grow and attain its own essential perception. When this happens, they believe that the whole of existence is encompassed by the perceptions of the soul, that the essences of existence are revealed to them, and that they perceive the reality of all the essences from the (divine) throne to light rain. This was said by al-Ghazzâlî in the *Kitâb al-Iḥyâ*', after he had mentioned the forms of mystical exercise.

The Sufis do not consider removal (of the veil) sound unless it originates in straightforwardness. People who do not eat and who retire (from the world), such as sorcerers, Christians, and other ascetics, may obtain removal without the existence of straightforwardness. However, we mean only that removal which originates in straightforwardness. It may be compared with (the reflections of) a mirror. If it is convex or concave, the object reflected by it appears in a distorted form different from the actual form of the object, but if the mirror is flat, the object appears in its correct form. As far as the 'states' impressed upon the soul are concerned, straightforwardness means to the soul what flatness means in a mirror.

Recent Sufis who have occupied themselves with this kind of removal talk about the real character of the higher and lower *existentia* and about the real character of the divine kingdom, the spirit, the divine throne, the divine seat, and similar things. Those who did not share their approach were not able to understand their mystical and ecstatic experiences in this respect. The muftis partly disapprove of these Sufis and partly accept them. Arguments and proofs are of no use in deciding whether the Sufi approach should be rejected or accepted, since it belongs to intuitive experience.

Some details in explanation:

Hadîth scholars and jurists who discuss the articles of faith often mention that God is separate from His creatures. The speculative theologians say that He is neither separate nor connected. The philosophers say that He is neither in the world nor outside it. The recent Sufis say that He is one with the creatures, in the sense that He is incarnate in them, or in the sense that He is identical with them and there exists nothing but Himself either in the whole or in any part of it.

Let us explain in detail these dogmatic opinions and the real meaning of each of them, so that their significance will be clarified. We say:

Separateness has two meanings. It may mean 'separateness in space and direction'. The opposite, then, would be connectedness. In this sense, the statement of (separation) implies (that God is in some) place, either directly—which would be direct anthropomorphism—or indirectly—which would be indirect anthropomorphism—in the way in which one speaks about (God's) direction. It has been reported that an early Muslim scholar similarly professed the separateness of God, but a different interpretation is possible.

The speculative theologians, therefore, did not acknowledge this separateness. They said: It cannot be said that the Creator is separate from His creatures, and it cannot be said that He is connected with them, because such a statement can be made only about things in space. The statement that a particular thing can be described as devoid of one concept and at the same time of the opposite of that concept depends upon whether the description is found or not. If it is impossible, the statement is not correct. It is, in sact, permissible to describe a thing as devoid of one concept and at the same time of the opposite of that concept. Thus, a solid substance may be described as not wise and not ignorant, not powerful and not weak, not causing harm and not being harmed. Now, the correctness of describing God as separate in the way mentioned is predicated upon the possibility of ascribing direction to Him in the proper meaning of the word, but this cannot be done with the Creator, who is free from such a description.

The other meaning of separateness is 'being distinct and different'. The Creator is called separate from His creatures in His essence, identity, existence, and attributes. The opposite is being one, mingled, and merged with something else.

God's separateness in this sense is assumed in the dogmas of all orthodox people, such as the great mass of early Muslims, the religious scholars, the speculative theologians, and the ancient Sufis.

A number of recent Sufis who consider intuitive perceptions to be scientific and logical, hold the opinion that the Creator is one with His creatures in His identity, His existence, and His attributes. They often assume that this was the opinion of the philosophers before Aristotle, such as Plato and Socrates.

That is what the speculative theologians mean when they speak about the (oneness of God with His creatures) in theology and try to refute it. They do not mean that there could be a question of two essences, one of which must be negated or comprised in the other as a part in the whole. That would be clear distinctness, and they do not maintain that to be the case.

The oneness (assumed by the Sufis) is identical with the incarnation the Christians claim for the Messiah. It is even stranger, in that it is the incarnation of something primeval in something created and the oneness of the former with the latter. . . .

Authors have occasionally tried to explain the Sufi opinions concerning the revelation of existence and the order of the realities of existence according to the approach of the people who (have the theory of) 'manifestations'. As compared to people who cultivate speculation, technical terminology, and the sciences, it must be said that they have always added obscurity to obscurity. An example is al-Farghânî, the commentator on Ibn al-Fâriḍ's *Poem*. He wrote a preface at the beginning of his commentary. In connection with the origin of the world of existence from the Maker and its order, he mentions that all existence comes forth from the attribute of uniqueness which is the manifestation of unity. Both of them together issue from the noble essence identical with oneness and nothing else. This process is called 'revelation'. The first degree of revelation, in Sufi opinion, is the revelation, as such, of the essence. . . .

This school is called that of the people of revelation, manifestations, and presences. It is a theory that people cultivating (logical) speculation cannot properly grasp, because it is obscure and cryptic. There also is a great gap between the theories of people who have vision and intuitive experience and those of people who cultivate logical reasoning. (Sufi) systems (like the one mentioned) are often disapproved of on the strength of the plain wording of the religious law, for no indication of them can be found in it anywhere.

Other Sufis turned to affirming absolute oneness. This is a theory stranger than the first one to understand in its implications and details. They believe the components of everything in existence to possess powers that bring the realities, forms, and matters of the existing things into being. The elements come into being through the powers that are in them. The same is the case with matter, which has in itself a power that has brought about its existence. Composite things contain such powers implicit in the power that brought about their composition. For instance, the mineral power contains the powers of the elements of matter and, in addition, the mineral power. The animal power contains the mineral power and, in addition, its own power. The same is the case with the human power as compared to animal power. The firmament contains the human power and something in addition. The same applies to the spiritual essences.

Now, the power combining everything without any particularization is the divine power. It is the power distributed over all existing things, whether they are universals or particulars, combining and comprising them in every aspect, with regard to appearance and hiddenness and with regard to form and matter. Everything is one. Oneness is identical with the divine essence, which, in reality, is one and simple. The thing that divides it is the way we look at it. For instance, as to the relationship of humanity to animality, it is clear that the former is included under the latter and comes into being when it comes into being. At times, the Sufis represent the relationship as that of genus to species in every existing thing. Or, they represent it as that of the universal to the particular, according to the theory of ideas. At any rate, they always try to get away from any thought of composition or manifoldness, which they think is brought about by fancy and imagination.

It appears that what the Sufis say about oneness is actually similar to what the philosophers say about colours, namely, that their existence is predicated upon light. When there is no light, no colours whatever exist. Thus, the Sufis think that all existing *sensibilia* are predicated upon the existence of some (faculty of) sensual perception and, in fact, that all existing *intelligibilia* and objects of imagination are predicated upon intellectual perception. Thus, every particular in existence is predicated upon the human (faculty) that perceives it. If we assumed that no human being with perception exists, there would be no particularization in existence. Existence would be simple and one.

Thus, heat and cold, solidity and softness, and, indeed, earth, water, fire, heaven, and the stars, exist only because the senses perceiving them exist, because particularization that does not exist in existence is made possible for the person who perceives. It exists only in perception. If there were no perceptions to create distinctions, there would be no particularization, but just one single perception, namely, the 'I' and nothing else. They consider this comparable to the condition of a sleeper. When he sleeps and has no external sense perception, he loses in that condition all (perception of) *sensibilia*, with the exception of the things that the imagination particularizes for him. They continued by saying that a person who is awake likewise experiences particularized perceptions only through the type oi human perception (that exists) in him. If he had not that something in him that perceives, there would be no particularization. This is what the Sufis mean when they say 'imaginary'. They do not mean 'imaginary' as a part (in the sequence) of human perceptions.

This exposition of Sufi opinion is most erroneous. We know for certain that a country that we have quitted on our travels or to which we are travelling, exists, despite the fact that we do not see it any more. We also have definite knowledge of the existence of heaven that overlooks (everything), and of the stars, and of all the other things that are remote from us. Man knows these things for certain. No one would deny to himself the existence of certain knowledge. In addition, competent recent Sufis say that during the removal of the veil, the Sufi novice often has a feeling of the oneness of existence. Sufis call that the station of 'combination'. But then, he progresses to distinguishing between existent things. That is considered by the Sufis the station of 'differentiation'. That is the station of the competent gnostic. The Sufis believe that the novice cannot avoid the ravine of 'combination', and this ravine causes difficulties for him because there is danger that he might be arrested at it and his enterprise thus come to nought.

The different kinds of mystics have thus been explained.

Many jurists and muftis have undertaken to refute statements by recent Sufis. They summarily disapproved of everything they came across in the Sufi path. The truth is that discussion with the Sufis requires making a distinction. The Sufis discuss four topics. (1) Firstly, they discuss pious exertions, the resulting mystical and ecstatic experiences, and self-scrutiny concerning one's actions. (They discuss these things) in order to obtain mystical experiences, which then become a station from which one progresses to the next higher one. (2) Secondly, they discuss the removal (of the veil) and the perceivable supernatural realities, such as the divine attributes, the divine throne, the divine seat, the angels, revelation, prophecy, the spirit, and the realities of everything in existence, be it supernatural or visible; furthermore, they discuss the order of created things, how they issue from the Creator who brings them into being, as mentioned before. (3) The third topic is concerned with activities in the various worlds and among the various created things connected with different kinds of acts of divine grace. (4) The fourth topic is concerned with expressions that are suspect in their plain meaning. These have been uttered by most Sufi leaders. In Sufi technical terminology, they are called 'ecstatic utterances'. Their plain meaning is difficult to understand. They may be something that must be disapproved of, or something that can be approved, or something that requires interpretation.

As for their discussion of pious exertions and stations, of the mystical and ecstatic experiences that result, and of self-scrutiny with regard to (possible) shortcomings in the things that cause these (experiences), this is something that nobody ought to reject. These mystical experiences of the Sufis are sound ones. Their realization is the very essence of happiness.

As for their discussion of the acts of divine grace experienced by Sufis, the information they give about supernatural things, and their activity among the created things, these also are sound and cannot be disapproved of, even though some religious scholars tend to disapprove.

Most of the Sufi discussion of the removal (of the veil), of the reception of the realities of the higher things, and of the order in which the created things issue, falls, in a way, under the category of ambiguous statements. It is based upon their intuitive experience, and those who lack such intuitive experience cannot have the same mystical experience. No language can express the things that Sufis want to say in this connection, because languages have been invented only for the expression of commonly accepted concepts, most of which apply to the *sensibilia*. Therefore, we must not bother with the Sufi discussion of those matters. Those to whom God grants some understanding of those utterances in a way that agrees with the plain meaning of the religious law do, indeed, enjoy happiness.

There are the suspect expressions which the Sufis call 'ecstatic utterances' and which provoke the censure of orthodox Muslims. As to them, it should be known that the attitude that would be fair to the Sufis is that they are people who are removed from sense perception. Inspiration grips them. Eventually, they say things about their inspiration that they do not intend to say. A person who is removed (from sense perception) cannot be spoken to. He who is forced (to act) is excused (when he acts, no matter what he does). Sufis who are known for their excellence and exemplary character are considered to act in good faith in this and similar respects. It is difficult to express ecstatic experiences, because there are no conventional ways of expressing them. Sufis whose excellence is not known and famous deserve censure for utterances of this kind, since the (data) that might cause us to interpret their statements (so as to remove any suspicion attached to them) are not clear to us. Sufis who are not removed from sense perception and are not in the grip of a state when they make utterances of this kind, also deserve censure.

Therefore, the jurists and the great Sufis decided that al-Ḥallâj[1] was to be killed, because he spoke (ecstatically) while not removed (from sense perception) but in control of his state.

And God knows better.

The early Sufis, those outstanding Muslims to whom we have referred above, had no desire to remove the veil and to have such (supernatural) perception. Their concern was to follow their models and to lead an exemplary life as far as possible. Whenever they had a supernatural experience, they turned away from it and paid no attention to it. Indeed, they tried to avoid it. They were of the opinion that it was an obstacle and a tribulation and belonged to the (ordinary) perceptions of the soul, and, as such, was something created. They also thought that human perception could not comprise all the *existentia* and that the knowledge of God was wider, His creation greater, and His religious law more certain for guidance (than any mystical experience). Therefore, they did not speak about any of their supernatural perceptions. In fact, they forbade the discussion of those things and prevented their companions, for whom the veil (of sense perception) was removed, from discussing the matter or from giving it the slightest consideration. They continued following their models and leading exemplary lives as they had done in the world of sensual perception before the removal of the veil, and they commanded their companions to do the same. Such ought to be the state of the Sufi novice.

17 The science of dream interpretation

This is one of the sciences of the religious law. It originated in Islam when the sciences became crafts and scholars wrote books on them. Dream visions and dream interpretation existed among the ancients, as among later generations. It existed among former (pre-Islamic) religious groups and nations. However, their dream interpretation did not reach us,[2] because we have been satisfied with the discussions of Muslim dream interpreters. In any case, all human beings can have dream visions, and these visions must be interpreted.

Joseph already interpreted visions, as is mentioned in the Qur'ân.[3] A dream vision is a kind of supernatural perception. Muḥammad said: 'A good dream vision is the forty-sixth part of prophecy.' He also said: 'The only remaining bearer of glad tidings is a good dream

---

[1] Al-Ḥusayn b. Manṣûr, 244–309 [858/59–922].

[2] Of course, Greek works on dream interpretation, such as the book by Artemidorus, were translated into Arabic. A fourteenth-century copy of this work, containing the first three books, is preserved in Istanbul University.

[3] Cf. *sûrah* 12.

vision, beheld by—or shown to—a good man.' The revelation given to the Prophet began with a dream vision. Every dream vision he saw appeared to him like the break of dawn. When Muḥammad went away from the morning prayer, he used to ask the men around him, 'Did any one of you see a dream vision during the night?' He asked this question in order to derive good news from dream visions, which might refer to the victory of Islam and the growth of its power.

The reason for perception of the supernatural in dream visions is as follows: The spirit of the heart, which is the fine vapour coming from the cavity in the flesh of the heart, spreads into the veins and, through the blood, to all the rest of the body. It serves to perfect the actions and sensations of the animal powers. The spirit may be affected by lassitude, because it is very busy with the sensual perception of the five senses and with the employment of the external powers. When the surface of the body, then, is covered by the chill of night, the spirit withdraws from all the other regions of the body to its centre, the heart. It rests, in order to be able to resume its activity, and all the external senses are for the time being unemployed. This is the meaning of sleep, as was mentioned before at the beginning of the book. Now, the spirit of the heart is the vehicle of man's rational spirit. Through its essence, the rational spirit perceives everything that is in the divine world, since its reality and its essence are identical with perception. It is prevented from assimilating any supernatural perception by the veil of its preoccupation with the body and the corporeal powers and senses. If it were without that veil or stripped of it, it would return to its reality, which is identical with perception. It would thus be able to assimilate any object of perception. If it were stripped of part of it, its preoccupation would be less. It is thus able to catch a glimpse of its own world, since external sense perception, its greatest preoccupation, now occupies it less. Its supernatural perception corresponds in intensity to the degree to which the veil is withdrawn from it. Thus it becomes prepared to receive the available perceptions from its own world that are appropriate for it. When it has perceived these perceptions from its own world, it returns with them to its body, since, as long as it remains in its corporeal body, it cannot be active except through corporeal means of perception.

The faculties through which the body perceives knowledge are all connected with the brain. The active part among them is the imagination. It derives imaginary pictures from the pictures perceived by the senses and turns them over to the power of memory, which retains them until they are needed in connection with speculation and deduction. From the imaginary pictures, the soul also abstracts other spiritual-intellectual pictures. In this way, abstraction ascends from the *sensibilia* to the *intelligibilia*. The imagination is the intermediary between them. Also, when the soul has received a certain number of perceptions from its own world, it passes them on to the imagination, which forms them into appropriate pictures and turns those perceptions over to the common sense. As a result, the sleeper sees them as if they were perceived by the senses. Thus, the perceptions come down from the rational spirit to the level of sensual perception, with the imagination again being the intermediary. This is what dream visions actually are.

The preceding exposition shows the difference between true dream visions and false, 'confused dreams'. All of them are pictures in the imagination while an individual is asleep. However, if these pictures come down from the rational spirit that perceives them, they are dream visions. But if they are derived from the pictures preserved in the power of memory, where the imagination deposits them when the individual is awake, they are 'confused dreams'.

True dream visions have signs indicating their truthfulness and attesting their soundness, so that the person who has the dream vision becomes conscious of the glad tidings from God given him in his sleep.

The first of these signs is that the person who has the dream vision wakes up quickly, as soon as he has perceived it. It seems as if he is in a hurry to get back to being awake and having sensual perception. Were he to continue to sleep soundly, the perception given him would weigh heavily on him. Therefore, he tries to escape from the state in which he has supernatural perception to the state of sensual perception in which the soul is always fully immersed in the body and in corporeal accidents.

Another sign is that the dream vision stays and remains impressed with all its details in the memory. Neither neglect nor forgetfulness affects it. No thinking or remembering is required, in order to have it present to one's mind. The dream vision remains pictured in the mind of the dreamer when he awakes. Nothing of it is lost to him. This is because perception by the soul does not take place in time and requires no consecutive order, but takes place all at once and within a single time element. 'Confused dreams', on the other hand, take place in time, because they rest in the powers of the brain and are brought from the power of memory to the common sense by the imagination. The process is an action of the body, and all actions of the body take place in time. Thus, they require a consecutive order, in order to perceive anything, with something coming first and something else coming later. Forgetfulness, which always affects the powers of the brain, affects them. That is not the case with the perceptions of the rational soul. They do not take place in time and have no consecutive order. Perceptions that are impressed in the rational soul are impressed all at once in the briefest moment. Thus, after the sleeper is awake, his dream vision remains present in his memory for quite some time. In no way does it slip his mind as the result of neglect, if it originally made a strong impression. However, if it requires thinking and application to remember a dream vision after a sleeper is awake, and if he has forgotten many of its details before he can remember them again, the dream vision is not a true one but a 'confused dream'.

These signs belong in particular to prophetic revelation.

As for dream interpretation, the following should be known. The rational spirit has its perceptions and passes them on to the imagination. The imagination then forms them into pictures but it forms them only into such pictures as are somehow related to the perceived idea. For instance, if the idea of a mighty ruler is perceived, the imagination depicts it in the form of an ocean. Or, the idea of hostility is depicted by the imagination in the form of a serpent. A person wakes up and knows only that he saw an ocean or a serpent. Then, the dream interpreter, who is certain that the ocean is the picture conveyed by the senses and that the perceived idea is something beyond that picture, puts the power of comparison to work. He is guided by further data that establish the character of the perceived idea for him. Thus, he will say, for instance, that the ocean means a ruler, because an ocean is something big with which a ruler can appropriately be compared. Likewise, a serpent can appropriately be compared with an enemy, because it does great harm. Also, vessels can be compared with women, because they are receptacles, and so on.

Dream visions may be evident and require no interpretation, because they are clear and distinct, or because the ideas perceived in them may be very similar to the pictures by which they are represented.

When the spirit passes its perceptions on to the imagination, the latter depicts them in the customary moulds of sensual perception. Where such moulds never existed in sensual perception, the imagination cannot form any pictures. A person who was born blind could not depict a ruler by an ocean, an enemy by a serpent, or women by vessels, because he had never perceived any such things. For him, the imagination would depict those things through similarly appropriate pictures derived from the type of perceptions with which he is familiar—that is, things which can be heard or smelled. The dream interpreter must be on guard against such things. They often cause confusion in dream interpretation and spoil its rules.

The science of dream interpretation implies a knowledge of general norms upon which the dream interpreter bases the interpretation and explanation of what he is told. For instance, they say that an ocean represents a ruler. Elsewhere, they say that an ocean represents wrath. Again, elsewhere, they say that it represents worry and calamity. Or, they say that a serpent represents an enemy, but elsewhere they say that it represents one who conceals a secret. Elsewhere again, they say that it represents life, and so on.

The dream interpreter knows these general norms by heart and interprets the dreams in each case as required by the data establishing which of these norms fits a particular dream vision best. The data may originate in the waking state. They may originate in the sleeping state. Or, they may be created in the soul of the dream interpreter himself by the special quality with which he is endowed.

Dream interpretation is a science resplendent with the light of prophecy, because prophecy and dreams are related to each other.

18 The various kinds of intellectual sciences

The intellectual sciences are natural to man, inasmuch as he is a thinking being. They are not restricted to any particular religious group. They are studied by the people of all religious groups who are all equally qualified to learn them and to do research in them. They have existed (and been known) to the human species since civilization had its beginning in the world. They are called the sciences of philosophy and wisdom. They comprise four different sciences.

(1) The first science is logic. It is a science protecting the mind from error in the process of evolving unknown facts one wants to know from the available, known facts. Its use enables the student to distinguish right from wrong wherever he so desires in his study of the essential and accidental perceptions and apperceptions. Thus, he will be able to ascertain the truth concerning created things, negatively or positively, within the limits of his ability to think.

(2) Then, philosophers may study the elemental substances perceivable by the senses, namely, the minerals, the plants, and the animals which are created from (the elemental substances), the heavenly bodies, natural motions, and the soul from which the motions originate, and other things. This discipline is called 'physics'. It is the second of the intellectual sciences.

(3) Or they may study metaphysical, spiritual matters. This science is called 'metaphysics'. It is the third of the intellectual sciences.

(4) The fourth science is the study of measurements. It comprises four different sciences, which are called the 'mathematical sciences'.

The first mathematical science is geometry. It is the study of quantities (measurements) in general, which may be either discontinuous, inasmuch as they constitute numbers, or continuous (as geometrical figures). They may be of one dimension—the line; of two dimensions—the plane; or of three dimensions—the mathematical solid. These measurements and the qualities they possess, either by themselves or in combination with each other, are what is studied (in geometry).

The second mathematical science is arithmetic. It is the knowledge of the essential and accidental properties of the discontinuous quantity, number.

The third mathematical science is music. It is the knowledge of the proportions of sounds and modes and their numerical measurements. Its fruit is the knowledge of musical melodies.

The fourth mathematical science is astronomy. It fixes the shapes of the spheres, determines the position and number of each planet and fixed star, and makes it possible to learn these things from the visible heavenly motions of each (sphere), their motions, both retrograde and direct, their precession and recession.

These are the seven basic philosophical sciences. Logic comes first. Then comes mathematics, beginning with arithmetic, followed in succession by geometry, astronomy, and music. Then comes physics and, finally, metaphysics. Each of these sciences has subdivisions. One subdivision of physics is medicine. Subdivisions of arithmetic are calculation, the inheritance laws, and business arithmetic. A subdivision of astronomy is covered by the astronomical tables. They are norms for computing the motions of the stars and adjusting (the data) in order to be able to know their positions, whenever desired. Another subdivision of the study of the stars is the science of stellar judgments (astrology).

We shall discuss all these sciences, one by one.

As far as our historical information goes, these sciences were most extensively cultivated by the two great pre-Islamic nations, the Persians and the Greeks (Rûm). According to the information we have, the sciences were greatly in demand among them, because they possessed an abundant civilization and were the ruling nations immediately before Islam and its time. In their regions and cities, the sciences flourished greatly.

The Chaldeans and, before them, the Syrians, as well as their contemporaries, the Copts, were much concerned with sorcery and astrology and the related subjects of powerful (charms) and talismans. The Persian and Greek nations learned these things from them. The Copts especially cultivated those things, which enjoyed great prominence among them. Later on, these things were declared forbidden and illegal by successive religious groups. As a result, the sciences concerned with them were wiped out and vanished, as if they had never been. Only a small remnant, transmitted by the practitioners of those crafts, has remained. And God knows better whether those crafts are sound. The sword of the religious law hangs over them and prevents choice of them (as a subject of study).

Among the Persians, the intellectual sciences played a large and important role, since the Persian dynasties were powerful and ruled without interruption. The intellectual sciences are said to have come to the Greeks from the Persians, when Alexander killed Darius and gained control of the Achaemenid empire. At that time, he appropriated the books and sciences of the Persians. However, when the Muslims conquered Persia and came upon an indescribably large number of books and scientific papers, Sa'd b. Abî Waqqâṣ wrote to 'Umar b. al-Khaṭṭâb, asking him for permission to take them and distribute them as booty among the Muslims. On that occasion, 'Umar wrote him: 'Throw them into the water. If what they contain is right guidance, God has given us better guidance. If it is error, God has protected us against it.'[1] Thus, the (Muslims) threw them into the water or into the fire, and the sciences of the Persians were lost and did not reach us.

The dynasty of the Byzantines originally belonged to the Greeks, among whom the intellectual sciences occupied a large place. They were cultivated by famous Greek personalities, among them the pillars of philosophy, and others. The Peripatetic philosophers, in particular the Stoics, possessed a good method of instruction in the intellectual sciences. It has been assumed that they used to study in a stoa, which protected them from the sun and the cold. Their school tradition is assumed to have passed from the sage Luqmân and his pupils to Socrates of the barrel,[2] and then, in succession, to Socrates' pupil, Plato, to Plato's pupil, Aristotle, to Aristotle's pupils, Alexander of Aphrodisias and Themistius, and others.

Aristotle was the teacher of Alexander, who defeated the Persians and deprived them of their realm. He was the greatest Greek scientist and enjoyed the greatest prestige and fame. He has been called 'the First Teacher'. He became world-famous.

When the Greek dynasty was destroyed and the Roman emperors seized power and adopted Christianity, the intellectual sciences were shunned by them, as religious groups and their laws require. They continued to have a permanent life in scientific writings and works that were preserved in their libraries.

[1] This is a variant of the famous legend, according to which 'Umar ordered the destruction of the celebrated library in Alexandria.
[2] Socrates was commonly confused with Diogenes.

The (Roman emperors) later on took possession of Syria. The ancient scientific books continued to exist during their rule. Then God brought Islam, and its adherents gained their incomparable victory. They deprived the Byzantines, as well as all other nations, of their realms. At the beginning, they were simple and disregarded the crafts. Eventually, however, the Muslim rule and dynasty flourished. The Muslims developed a sedentary culture, such as no other nation had ever possessed. They became versed in many different crafts and sciences. Then they desired to study the philosophical disciplines. They had heard some mention of them by the bishops and priests among their Christian subjects, and man's ability to think has aspirations in the direction of the intellectual sciences. Abû Ja'far al-Manṣûr, therefore, sent to the Byzantine Emperor and asked him to send him translations of mathematical works. The Emperor sent him Euclid's book and some works on physics. The Muslims read them and studied their contents. Their desire to obtain the rest of them grew. Later on, al-Ma'mûn came. He had some (scientific knowledge). Therefore, he had a desire for science. His desire aroused him to action in behalf of the intellectual sciences. He sent ambassadors to the Byzantine emperors; they were to discover the Greek sciences and have them copied in Arabic writing; he sent translators for that purpose. As a result, a good deal of the material was preserved and collected.

Muslim scientists assiduously studied the (Greek sciences). They became skilled in the various branches. The (progress they made in the) study of those sciences could not have been better. They contradicted the First Teacher (Aristotle) on many points. They considered him the decisive authority as to whether an opinion should be rejected or accepted, because he possessed the greatest fame. They wrote systematic works on the subject. They surpassed their predecessors in the intellectual sciences.

Abû Naṣr al-Fârâbî and Abû 'Alî Ibn Sînâ (Avicenna) in the East, and Judge Abû l-Walîd b. Rushd (Averroës) and the wazir Abû Bakr b. aṣ-Ṣâ'igh (Avempace) in Spain, were among the greatest Muslim philosophers, and there were others who reached the limit in the intellectual sciences. The men mentioned enjoy especial fame and prestige.

Many scientists restricted themselves to cultivating the mathematical disciplines and the related sciences of astrology, sorcery, and talismans. The most famous practitioners of these sciences were Jâbir b. Ḥayyân in the East, and the Spaniard, Maslamah b. Aḥmad al-Majrîṭî, and his pupils.

The intellectual sciences and their representatives succeeded to some degree in penetrating Islam. They seduced many people who were eager to study those sciences and accept the opinions expressed in them. In this respect, the sin falls upon the person who commits it. Later on, civilizing activity stopped in the Maghrib and in Spain. The sciences decreased with the decrease of civilization. As a consequence, scientific activity disappeared there, save for a few remnants that may be found among scattered individuals and that are controlled by orthodox religious scholars.

We hear that the intellectual sciences are still amply represented among the inhabitants of the East, in particular in the non-Arab 'Irâq and, farther east, in Transoxania. The people there are said to be very successful in the intellectual and traditional sciences, because their civilization is abundant and their sedentary culture firmly established.

We further hear now that the philosophical sciences are greatly cultivated in the land of Rome and along the adjacent northern shore of the country of the European Christians. They are said to be studied there again and to be taught in numerous classes. Existing systematic expositions of them are said to be comprehensive, the people who know them numerous, and the students of them very many. God knows better what exists there.

19 The sciences concerned with numbers

The first of them is arithmetic. Arithmetic is the knowledge of the properties of numbers combined in arithmetic or geometric progressions. . . .

The craft of calculation

A subdivision of arithmetic is the craft of calculation. It is a scientific craft concerned with the counting operations of 'combining' and 'separating'. The 'combining' may take place by (adding the) units. This is addition. Or it may take place by increasing a number as many times as there are units in another number. This is multiplication. The 'separating' may take place by taking away one number from another and seeing what remains. This is subtraction. Or it may take place by separating a number into equal parts of a given number. This is division.

These operations may concern either whole numbers or fractions. A fraction is the relationship of one number to another number. Or they may concern 'roots'. 'Roots' are numbers that, when multiplied by themselves, lead to square numbers. Numbers that are clearly expressed are called 'rational', and so are their squares. They do not require (special) operations in calculation. Numbers that are not clearly expressed are called 'surds'. Their squares may be

375

rational, as, for instance, the root of three whose square is three. Or, they may be surds, such as the root of the root of three, which is a surd. They require special operations in calculation. Such roots are also included in the operations of 'combining' and 'separating'.

This craft is something newly created. It is needed for business calculations. Scholars have written many works on it. They are used in the cities for the instruction of children. The best method of instruction is to begin with calculation, because it is concerned with lucid knowledge and systematic proofs. As a rule, it produces an enlightened intellect that is trained along correct lines. It has been said that whoever applies himself to the study of calculation early in his life will as a rule be truthful, because calculation has a sound basis and requires self-discipline. (Soundness and self-discipline) will thus become character qualities of such a person. He will get accustomed to truthfulness and adhere to it methodically. . . .

Algebra

Another subdivision of arithmetic is algebra. This is a craft that makes it possible to discover the unknown from the known data, if there exists a relationship between them requiring it. Special technical terms have been invented in algebra for the various multiples (powers) of the unknown. The first of them is called 'number', because by means of it one determines the unknown one is looking for, discovering its value from the relationship of the unknown to it. The second is called 'thing', because every unknown as such refers to some 'thing'. It also is called 'root', because (the same element) requires multiplication in second-degree (equations). The third is called 'property'. It is the square of the unknown. Everything beyond that depends on the exponents of the two elements multiplied.

Then, there is the operation that is conditioned by the problem. One proceeds to create an equation between two or more different units of the (three) elements mentioned. The various elements are 'confronted', and 'broken' portions (in the equation) are 'set' and thus become 'healthy'. The degrees of equations are reduced to the fewest possible basic forms. Thus, they come to be three. Algebra revolves around these three basic forms. They are 'number', 'thing', and 'property'.

When an equation consists of one (element) on each side, the value of the unknown is fixed. The value of 'property' or 'root' becomes known and fixed, when equated with 'number'. A 'property' equated with 'roots' is fixed by the multiples of those 'roots'.

When an equation consists of one (element) on one side and two on the other, there is a geometrical solution for it by multiplication in part on the unknown side of the equation with the two elements. Such multiplication in part fixes the (value) of (the equation). Equations with two elements on one side and two on the other are not possible.

The largest number of equations recognized by algebraists is six. The simple and composite equations of 'numbers', 'roots', and 'properties' come to six.

We have heard that great eastern mathematicians have extended the algebraic operations beyond the six types and brought them up to more than twenty. For all of them, they discovered solutions based on solid geometrical proofs.

Business arithmetic

Another subdivision of arithmetic is business (arithmetic). This is the application of arithmetic to business dealings in cities. These business dealings may concern the sale (of merchandise), the measuring (of land), the charity taxes, as well as other business dealings that have something to do with numbers. In this connection, one uses both arithmetical techniques, (and one has to deal) with the unknown and the known, and with fractions, whole numbers, roots, and other things.

Spanish mathematicians have written numerous works on the subject.

Inheritance laws

Another subdivision of arithmetic is inheritance laws. It is a craft concerned with calculation, that deals with determining the correct shares of an estate for the legal heirs. It may happen that there is a large number of heirs, and one of the heirs dies and his portions have to be redistributed among his heirs. Or, the individual portions, when they are counted together and added up, may exceed the whole estate. Or, there may be a problem when one heir acknowledges, but the others do not acknowledge, (another heir, and vice versa). All this requires solution, in order to determine the correct amount of the shares in an estate and the correct share that goes to each relative, so that the heirs get the amounts of the estate to which they are entitled in view of the total amount of the shares of the estate. A good deal of calculation comes in here. It is concerned with whole (numbers), fractions, roots, and knowns and unknowns; it is arranged according to the chapters and problems of inheritance law.

This craft, therefore, has something to do with jurisprudence, namely, with inheritance law, as far as it is concerned with the laws concerning the legal shares of inheritance, the reduction of the individual shares, the acknowledgment or nonacknowledgment (of heirs), wills, manumission by will, and other problems. And it has also a good deal to do with arithmetic, inasmuch as it is concerned with determining the correct amount of the shares in accordance with the law evolved by the jurists.

It is a very important discipline. Scholars, in early and late times, have written extensive works on it.

20 The geometrical sciences

This science studies quantities (measurements). Measurements may be continuous, like lines, planes, and geometrical solids, or discontinuous, like numbers. It also studies the essential properties of the measurements, as, for instance:

The angles of any triangle are equal to two right angles.

Parallel lines do not intersect anywhere, even when they extend to infinity.

The opposite angles formed when two lines intersect are equal to each other.

The Greek work on this craft which has been translated into Arabic is the book of Euclid. It is entitled *Kitāb al-uṣūl wa-l-arkān*, 'Book of Basic Principles and Pillars'. It is the simplest book on the subject for students. It was the first Greek work to be translated in Islam in the days of Abū Ja'far al-Manṣūr. The existing recensions differ, depending on the respective translators, (of whom there are at least three).

The work contains fifteen books, four on the planes, one on proportions, another one on the relationship of planes to each other, three on numbers, the tenth on rational and irrational (quantities) —the 'roots'—and five on solids.

Many abridgments of Euclid's work have been written. Avicenna, for instance, devoted a special monograph treatment to it. Many scholars have also written commentaries on it. It is the starting point of the geometrical sciences in general.

Geometry enlightens the intellect and sets one's mind right. All its proofs are very clear and orderly. It is hardly possible for errors to enter into geometrical reasoning, because it is well arranged and orderly. Thus, the mind that constantly applies itself to geometry is not likely to fall into error. In this convenient way, the person who knows geometry acquires intelligence. It has been assumed that the following statement was written upon Plato's door: 'No one who is not a geometrician may enter our house.'[1]

[1] The famous ἀγεωμέτρητος μηδεὶς εἰσίτω, which appears in Elias' commentary on the *Categories* and was well known to the Arabs. It entered Arabic literature in connection with the introductions to Aristotelian philosophy.

Our teachers used to say that one's application to geometry does to the mind what soap does to a garment. It washes off stains and cleanses it of grease and dirt. The reason for this is that geometry is well arranged and orderly, as we have mentioned.

Spherical figures, conic sections, and mechanics

A subdivision of this discipline is the geometrical study of spherical figures (spherical trigonometry) and conic sections. There are two Greek works on spherical figures, namely, the works of Theodosius and Menelaus on planes and sections of spherical figures. In mathematical instruction, the book by Theodosius is studied before the book by Menelaus, since many of the latter's proofs depend on the former. Both works are needed by those who want to study astronomy, because the astronomical proofs depend on (the material contained in) them. All astronomical discussion is concerned with the heavenly spheres and the sections and circles found in connection with them as the result of the various motions, as we shall mention. Astronomy therefore depends on knowledge of the laws governing planes and sections of spherical figures.

Conic sections also are a branch of geometry. This discipline is concerned with study of the figures and sections occurring in connection with cones. It proves the properties of cones by means of geometrical proofs based upon elementary geometry. Its usefulness is apparent in practical crafts that have to do with bodies, such as carpentry and architecture. It is also useful for making remarkable statues and rare large objects and for moving loads and transporting large objects with the help of mechanical contrivances, engineering techniques, pulleys, and similar things.

There exists a book on mechanics that mentions every astonishing, remarkable technique and nice mechanical contrivance. It is often difficult to understand, because the geometrical proofs occurring in it are difficult. People have copies of it.

Surveying

Another subdivision of geometry is surveying. This discipline is needed to survey the land. This means that it serves to find the measurements of a given piece of land in terms of spans, cubits, or other units, or to establish the relationship of one piece of land to another when they are compared in this way. Such surveying is needed to determine the land tax on (wheat) fields, lands, and orchards. It is also needed for dividing enclosures and lands among partners or heirs, and similar things.

Scholars have written many good works on the subject.

Optics

Another subdivision of geometry is optics. This science explains the reasons for errors in visual perception, on the basis of knowledge as to how they occur. Visual perception takes place through a cone formed by rays, the top of which is the point of vision and the base of which is the object seen. Now, errors often occur. Nearby things appear large. Things that are far away appear small. Furthermore, small objects appear large under water or behind transparent bodies. Drops of rain as they fall appear to form a straight line, flame a circle, and so on.

This discipline explains with geometrical proofs the reasons for these things and how they come about. Among many other similar things, optics also explains the difference in the view of the moon at different latitudes.[1] Knowledge of the visibility of the new moon and of the occurrence of eclipses is based on that. There are many other such things.

21 Astronomy

This science studies the motions of the fixed stars and the planets. From the manner in which these motions take place, astronomy deduces by geometrical methods the existence of certain shapes and positions of the spheres requiring the occurrence of those motions which can be perceived by the senses. Astronomy thus proves, for instance, by the existence of the precession of the equinoxes, that the centre of the earth is not identical with the centre of the sphere of the sun. Furthermore, from the retrograde and direct motions of the stars, astronomy deduces the existence of small spheres (epicycles) carrying the (stars) and moving inside their great spheres. Through the motion of the fixed stars, astronomy then proves the existence of the eighth sphere. It also proves that a single star has a number of spheres, from the (observation) that it has a number of declinations, and similar things.

Only astronomical observation can show the existing motions and how they take place, and their various types. It is only by this means that we know the precession of the equinoxes and the order of the spheres in their different layers as well as the retrograde and direct motions (of the stars), and similar things. The Greeks occupied themselves very much with astronomical observation. They used instruments that were invented for the observation of the motion of a given star. They called them astrolabes. The technique and theory

[1] De Slane notes that Ibn Khaldûn should have said 'longitudes'.

of how to make them, so that their motion conforms to the motion of the sphere, are a tradition among the people.

In Islam, only very little attention has been paid to astronomical observation. In the days of al-Ma'mûn, there was some interest in it. The construction of the instrument known as the astrolabe was begun but was not completed. When al-Ma'mûn died, the institution of astronomical observation was lost and neglected. Later on, (scholars) based themselves upon the ancient observations. These were of no use because of the change in the sidereal motions over the course of time. The motion of the instrument used in astronomical observations conforms only approximately to the motion of the spheres and the stars and is not absolutely exact. When a certain amount of time has elapsed, the differences are revealed.

Astronomy is a noble craft. It does not, as is generally thought, teach the real form of the heavens nor the order of the spheres, but it teaches that the forms and shapes of the spheres are the result of those motions. As one knows, it is not improbable that one and the same thing may produce two different results. Therefore, when we say that the motions produce a result, we deduce from what produces the result that the result exists, but the statement in no way teaches us the real character (of the resulting thing). Still, astronomy is an important science. It is one of the pillars of the mathematical disciplines.

One of the best works on the subject is the *Majisṭî* (*Almagest*).[1] It is ascribed to Ptolemy, who, as the commentators of the work have established, was not one of the Greek rulers called Ptolemy. Leading Muslim philosophers, such as Avicenna and Averroës, have abridged Ptolemy's work.

Astronomical tables

A subdivision of astronomy is the science of astronomical tables. This is based upon calculations according to arithmetical rules. It is concerned with the courses of motions peculiar to each star and with the character of that motion, fast, slow, direct, retrograde, and so on, as proven by astronomical means. This serves to show the positions of the stars in their spheres at any given time, by calculating their motions according to the rules evolved from astronomical works.

This craft follows certain norms. They constitute a sort of introductory and basic material for it. They deal with months and days and past eras.

It follows established basic principles. They deal with apogee and perigee, declinations, the different kinds of motions, and how these things shed light upon each other. They are written down in

[1] i.e., Ptolemy's *Syntaxis Astronomica*.

well-arranged tables, in order to make it easy for students. The determination of the positions of the stars at a given time by means of this craft is called 'adjustment and tabulation'.

Both early and later scholars have written many works on the subject.

Recent contemporary Maghribî scholars are using, as their reference work, the *zîj* that is ascribed to Ibn Isḥâq.[1] It is thought that Ibn Isḥâq based his work on astronomical observations. A Jew in Sicily who was skilled in astronomy and the mathematical sciences, and who occupied himself with astronomical observation, sent him information on the conditions and motions of the stars he had ascertained.

(Knowledge of the) positions of the stars in the spheres is the necessary basis for astrological judgments, that is, knowledge of the various kinds of influence over the world of man that are exercised by the stars depending on their positions and that affect religious groups, dynasties, human activities, and all events.

22 The science of logic

(Logic concerns) the norms enabling a person to distinguish between right and wrong, both in definitions that give information about the essence of things, and in arguments that assure apperception.

This comes about as follows: The basis of perception is the *sensibilia* that are perceived by the five senses. All living beings, those which are rational as well as the others, participate in this kind of perception. Man is distinguished from the animals by his ability to perceive universals, which are things abstracted from the *sensibilia*. Man is enabled to do this by virtue of the fact that his imagination obtains, from individual objects perceived by the senses and which agree with each other, a picture conforming to all these individual objects. Such a picture is a universal. The mind then compares the individual objects that agree with each other, with other objects that also agree with them in some respects. It thus obtains a picture conforming to both of the two groups of objects compared, inasmuch as they agree with each other. In this way, abstraction continues to progress. Eventually, it reaches the universal (concept), which admits no other universal (concept) that would agree with it, and is, therefore, simple.

For instance, from the individual specimens of man, the picture of the species to which all the individual specimens conform is abstracted. Then, man is compared with the animals, and the picture of the genus to which both men and animals conform is abstracted.

[1] Abû l-'Abbâs 'Alî b. Isḥâq, who made astronomical observations in 619 [1222].

Then, this is compared with the plants, until, eventually, the highest genus is reached, which is 'substance'. There is no other universal (concept) that would in any way agree with it. Therefore, the intellect stops here and makes no further abstraction.

God created in man the ability to think. Through it, he perceives the sciences and crafts. Knowledge is either a perception of the essence of things—a primitive kind of perception not accompanied by (the exercise of) judgment—or it is apperception: that is, the judgment that a thing is so.

Man's ability to think may try to obtain the desired (information) by combining the universals with each other, with the result that the mind obtains a universal picture that conforms to details outside. Such a picture in the mind assures a knowledge of the quiddity of the individual objects. Or man's ability to think may judge one thing by another and draw conclusions. Thus, (the other thing) is established in (the mind). This is apperception, which ultimately reverts to perception, because the only use of having perception is (to achieve) knowledge of the realities of things, which is the required goal of apperceptive knowledge.

Man's ability to think may embark on this (process) in either the right or the wrong way. Selection of the way to be followed by man's ability to think in its effort to attain the knowledge desired, requires discernment, so that man can distinguish between right and wrong. This (process) became the canon of logic.

When the ancients first began to discuss (logic), they did so in a sentèntious, disconnected manner by selecting certain stray propositions. Logical methods were unimproved. The problems of logic were not seen together. Eventually, Aristotle appeared among the Greeks. He improved the methods of logic and systematized its problems and details. He assigned to logic its proper place as the first philosophical discipline and the introduction to philosophy. Therefore he is called 'the First Teacher'. His work on logic is called 'the Text'. It comprises eight books, three on the forms of analogical reasoning, and five on the matter (to which analogical reasoning is applied).

This is because the objects of apperception are of different kinds. Some of them concern things that are certain by nature. Others concern things that are hypothetical in various degrees. Therefore, logic studies analogical reasoning from the point of view of the desired (information) it is expected to yield. It studies what the premises (of the desired information) ought to be, as seen in this light, and to which kind of certain or hypothetical knowledge the (desired information) belongs. Logic studies analogical reasoning (the syllogism), not with some particular object in mind but exclusively with regard to the way in which it is produced. Therefore, the first study, it is said, is undertaken with regard to matter, that is, the matter that produces some particular certain or hypothetical information. The second study, it is said, is undertaken with regard to the form and the manner in which analogical reasoning (the syllogism) in general is produced. Thus, the number of the books on logic came to be eight.

The first book deals with the highest genera that abstraction among the *sensibilia* may attain in the mind and that admit no (more universal) genera above them. It is called *Kitâb al-Maqûlât* (*Categories*).

The second book deals with the various kinds of apperceptive propositions. It is called *Kitâb al-'Ibârah* (*Hermeneutics*).

The third book deals with analogical reasoning (the syllogism) and the form in which it is produced in general. It is called *Kitâb al-Qiyâs* (*Analytics*). Here ends the logical study from the point of view of its form.

The fourth book is the *Kitâb al-Burhân* (*Apodeictica*). It studies the kind of analogical reasoning (the syllogism) that produces certain (knowledge). It also studies (the problem of) why its premises must be certain ones. In particular, it mentions other conditions for yielding certain knowledge. For instance, the (premises) must be essential, primary, and so on. This book contains a discussion of determinatives and definitions, because one wants them to be certain, since it is necessary—nothing else is possible—that a definition conform to the thing defined. Therefore, (definitions) were treated by the ancients in this book.

The fifth book is the *Kitâb al-Jadl* (*Topics*). *Jadl* ('disputation') is the kind of analogical reasoning that shows how to cut off a troublesome adversary and silence one's opponent, and teaches the famous (methods) to be employed to this end. It is also concerned with other conditions required in this connection. They are mentioned here. The book deals with the 'places' (*topoi*) from which the syllogism is evolved by using them to clarify the so-called middle term that brings the two ends of the desired information together. It also deals with the conversion of terms.

The sixth book is the *Kitâb as-Safsatah* (*Sophistici Elenchi*). Sophistry is the kind of analogical reasoning that teaches the opposite of the truth and enables a disputant to confuse his opponent. The book is bad because of its purpose. It was written only so that one might know sophistical reasoning and be on guard against it.

The seventh book is the *Kitâb al-Khitâbah* (*Rhetoric*). Rhetoric is the kind of analogical reasoning that teaches how to influence the great mass and get them to do what one wants them to do. It also teaches the forms of speech to be employed in this connection.

The eighth book is the *Kitâb ash-Shi'r* (*Poetics*). Poetics is the kind of analogical reasoning that teaches the invention of parables and similes, especially for the purpose of (encouraging oneself and others) to undertake something or avoid doing something. It also teaches the imginary propositions to be employed in this connection.

These are the eight books on logic according to the ancients.

After logic had been improved and systematized, the Greek philosophers were of the opinion that it was necessary to discuss the five universals providing the perception that conforms to the quiddities outside or to their parts or accidents. The five are genus, difference, species, property, and general accident. Therefore, they took the subject up in a special book concerned with the five universals, which serves as an introduction to the discipline. Thus, the books on logic came to be nine.

All of them were translated in Islam. The Muslim philosophers wrote commentaries and abridgments of them. Al-Fârâbî and Avicenna, for instance, did this, and, later on, the Spanish philosopher, Averroës.

Later on, more recent scholars have changed the terminology of logic. They added to the study of the five universals the study of its fruit, namely, the discussion of definitions and descriptions which they took over from the *Apodeictica*. They discarded the *Categories*, because (the logicians') study of the book is accidental and not essential. To the *Hermeneutics* they added the discussion of the conversion (of terms), whereas the ancient books included that subject in the *Topics*, but, in some respects, it does fall under the discussion of propositions.

Then, they discussed analogical reasoning inasmuch as it produces the desired information in general, and without regard to any matter. They discarded study of the matter to which analogical reasoning (is applied). That concerned five books, the *Apodeictica*, the *Topics*, the *Rhetoric*, the *Poetics*, and the *Sophistici Elenchi*. Some of them occasionally touched a little on those books (but in general) they neglected them, as if they had never been, whereas they are a very important basis of the discipline.

Then, they thoroughly discussed their writings on logic and studied them as a discipline in its own right, not as an instrument for the sciences. This resulted in a long and extensive discussion of the subject. . . .

23 Physics

This is a science that investigates bodies from the point of view of the motion and stationariness which attach to them. It studies the heavenly bodies and the elementary (substances), as well as the human beings, the animals, the plants, and the minerals created from them. It also studies the springs and earthquakes that come into being in the earth, as well as the clouds, vapours, thunder, lightning, and storms that are in the atmosphere, and other things. It further studies the beginning of motion in bodies—that is, the soul in the different forms in which it appears in human beings, animals, and plants.

The books of Aristotle on the subject are available to scholars. They were translated together with the other books on the philosophical sciences in the days of al-Ma'mûn. Scholars wrote books along the same lines and followed them up with explanation and comment. The most comprehensive work written on the subject is Avicenna's *Kitâb ash-Shifâ'*. In it, Avicenna treats all the seven philosophical sciences, as we have mentioned before. Avicenna later on abridged the *Kitâb ash-Shifâ'* in the *Kitâb an-Najâh* and the *Kitâb al-Ishârât*. In a way, he opposed Aristotle on most problems and expressed his own opinion on them. Averroës, on the other hand, abridged the books of Aristotle and commented on them, but followed him and did not oppose him.

24 The science of medicine

Medicine is a craft that studies the human body in its illness and health. The physician attempts to preserve health and to cure illness with the help of medicines and diets, but first he ascertains the illnesses peculiar to each limb of the body and the reasons causing them. He also ascertains the medicines existing for each illness. Physicians deduce the (effectiveness of) medicines from their composition and powers. They deduce (the stage of) an illness from signs indicating whether the illness is ripe and will accept the medicine or not. (These signs show themselves) in the colour (of the patient), the excretions, and the pulse. The physicians in this imitate the power of nature, which is the controlling element in both health and illness. They imitate nature and help it a little, as the nature of the matter (underlying the illness), the season of the year, and the age of the patient may require in each particular case. The science dealing with all these things is called medicine.

Certain limbs are occasionally discussed as individual subjects and are considered to (form the subjects of) special sciences. This is the case, for instance, with the eye, the diseases of the eye, and the collyria (used in the treatment of eye diseases).

Scholars have also added to this discipline the (study of the) uses of the parts of the body, that is, the useful purpose for which each limb of the animal body was created. This is not a medical subject, but it has been made into an annex and subdivision of medicine. Galen has written an important and very useful work on this discipline.

Galen is the leading ancient authority on medicine. His works have been translated into Arabic. He is said to have been a contemporary of Jesus and to have died in Sicily on his wanderings while in voluntary exile.[1] His works on medicine are classics which have been models for all later physicians.

There have been leading physicians in Islam of surpassing skill, such as, for instance, ar-Râzî,[2] al-Majûsî,[3] and Avicenna. There have also been many Spanish physicians. Most famous among them was Ibn Zuhr.[4]

In contemporary Muslim cities, the craft of medicine seems to have deteriorated, because the population has decreased and shrunk. Medicine is a craft required only by sedentary culture and luxury.

Civilized Bedouins have a kind of medicine which is mainly based upon individual experience. They inherit its use from the *shaykhs* and old women of the tribe. Some of it may occasionally be correct. However, it is not based upon any natural norm or upon any conformity (of the treatment) to the temper of the humours. Much of this sort of medicine existed among the Arabs.

The medicine mentioned in religious tradition is of the Bedouin type. It is in no way part of the divine revelation. (Such medical matters) were merely part of Arab custom and happened to be mentioned in connection with the circumstances of the Prophet, like other things that were customary in his generation. They were not mentioned in order to imply that that particular way of practising medicine is stipulated by the religious law. Muhammad was sent to teach us the religious law. He was not sent to teach us medicine or any other ordinary matter.

None of the statements concerning medicine that occur in sound traditions should be considered as (having the force of) law. The only thing is that if that type of medicine is used for the sake of a divine blessing and in true religious faith, it may be very useful. However, that would have nothing to do with humoral medicine but be the result of true faith. This happened in the case of the person

---

[1] The Arabs had more historically accurate data on Galen's life, but the misinformation that Ibn Khaldûn presents was widely known, although usually rejected as wrong.
[2] Muḥammad b. Zakariyâ' (Rhazes), 251–313 [865–925].
[3] 'Alî b. al-'Abbâs [tenth century].
[4] 'Abd-al-Malik b. Zuhr (Avenzoar), d. 557 [1162]

who had a stomach-ache and was treated with honey, and similar stories.

25 The science of agriculture

This craft is a branch of physics. It concerns the study of the cultivation and growth of plants through irrigation, proper treatment, improvement of the soil, (observance of) the suitable season, and the care for them by applying these things in a way that will benefit them and help them to grow.

The ancients were very much concerned with agriculture. Their study of agriculture was general. They considered the plants both from the point of view of planting and cultivation and from the point of view of their properties, their spirituality, and the relationship of (their spirituality) to the spiritualities of the stars and the great (heavenly) bodies, which is something also used in sorcery. Thus, they were very much concerned with the subject.

One of the Greek works, the *Kitâb al-Falâhah an-Nabaṭîyah*,[1] was translated. It is ascribed to Nabataean scholars. It contains much information of the type mentioned. The Muslims who studied the contents of the work (noticed that it belonged to) sorcery, which is barred (by the religious law), the study being forbidden. Therefore, they restricted themselves to the part of the book dealing with plants from the point of view of their planting and treatment and the things connected with that.

There are many books on agriculture by recent scholars. They do not go beyond discussion of the planting and treatment of plants, their preservation from things that might harm them or affect their growth, and all the things connected with that.

26 The science of metaphysics

Metaphysics is a science that studies existence as such. First, it studies general matters affecting corporeal and spiritual things, such as the quiddities, oneness, plurality, necessity, possibility, and so on. Then, it studies the beginnings of existing things and (finds) that they are spiritual things. It goes on to study the way existing things issue from (spiritual things), and also studies their order. Then, it studies the conditions of the soul after its separation from the body and its return to its beginning.

(Metaphysicians) are of the opinion that metaphysics is a noble discipline. They assume that it gives them a knowledge of existence

[1] The famous *Nabataean Agriculture*, which is ascribed to Abû Bakr Muḥammad b. 'Alî Ibn Waḥshîyah.

THE METHODS OF INSTRUCTION

as it is. This, they think, is identical with happiness. In their arrangements, metaphysics comes after physics. Therefore, they called it 'that which comes after physics' (metaphysics).

The books of Aristotle on the subject are available to scholars. They were abridged by Avicenna in the *Kitâb ash-Shifâ'* and the *Najâh*. They were also abridged by the Spanish philosopher, Averroës.

Recent scholars wrote systematic treatments of the sciences of (the Muslims). Al-Ghazzâli, at that time, refuted a good many of the (opinions of the metaphysicians). Recent speculative theologians, then, confused the problems of theology with those of philosophy, because the investigations of theology and philosophy go in the same direction, and the subject and problems of theology are similar to the subject and problems of metaphysics. (Theology and metaphysics) thus in a way came to be one and the same discipline. (Recent theologians), then, changed the order in which the philosophers had treated the problems of physics and metaphysics. They merged the two sciences in one and the same discipline. Now, in (that discipline), they first discussed general matters. This was followed, successively, by (the discussion of) the corporeal things and the matters that belong to them, the spiritual things and the matters that belong to them, and so on to the end of the discipline. The science of speculative theology thus merged with the problems of philosophy, and theological works were filled with the latter. It seemed as if the purpose which theology and philosophy followed in their respective subjects and problems was one and the same.

This confused people, but it is not correct. The problems with which the science of speculative theology deals are articles of faith derived from the religious law as transmitted by the early Muslims. They have no reference to the intellect and do not depend on it in the sense that they could not be established except through it. The intellect has nothing to do with the religious law and its views. Speculative theologians do not use the (rational) arguments they talk about as do the philosophers, in order to investigate the truth of the (articles of faith), to prove the truth of what had previously not been known, and to make it known. (Their use of rational arguments) merely expresses a desire to have rational arguments with which to bolster the articles of faith and the opinions of the early Muslims concerning them, and to refute the doubts of innovators who believe that their perceptions of (the articles of faith in their interpretation) are rational ones. (Rational arguments were used only) after the correctness of the articles of faith, as they had been received and believed in by the early Muslims, had been stipulated by traditional evidence.

389

There is a great difference between the two positions. The perceptions that Muhammad had are wider (than those of philosophers), because they go beyond rational views. They are above them and include them, because they draw their support from the divine light. Thus, they do not fall into the canon of weak speculation and circumscribed perceptions. When Muḥammad guides us toward some perception, we must prefer that to our own perceptions. We must have more confidence in it than in them. We must not seek to prove its correctness rationally, even if (rational intelligence) contradicts it. We must believe and know what we have been commanded (to believe and to know). We must be silent with regard to things of this sort that we do not understand. We must leave them to Muḥammad and keep the intellect out of it.

The only thing that caused the theologians to use rational arguments was the discussions of heretics who opposed the early Muslim articles of faith with speculative innovations. Thus, they had to refute these heretics with the same kind of arguments. This situation called for using speculative arguments and checking on the early Muslim articles of faith with these arguments.

The verification or rejection of physical and metaphysical problems, on the other hand, is not part of the subject of speculative theology and does not belong to the same kind of speculations as those of the theologians. This should be known, so that one may be able to distinguish between the two disciplines, as they have been confused in the works of recent scholars. The truth is that they are different from each other in their respective subjects and problems. The confusion arose from the sameness of the topics discussed. The argumentation of the theologians thus came to look as though it were inaugurating a search for faith through (rational) evidence. This is not so. (Speculative theology) merely wants to refute heretics. The things it investigates are stipulated (by the religious law) and known to be true. Likewise, recent extremist Sufis, those who speak about ecstatic experiences, have confused the problems of (metaphysics and speculative theology) with their own discipline. They discussed all these things as part of one and the same subject. Thus, they discussed prophecy, union, incarnation, oneness, and other things. In fact, however, the perceptions of the three disciplines are distinct and different from each other. The Sufi perceptions are the ones that are least scientific. The Sufis claim intuitive experience in connection with their perceptions and shun (rational) evidence. But intuitive experience is far removed from scientific perceptions and methods.

27 The sciences of sorcery and talismans

These are sciences showing how human souls may become prepared to exercise an influence upon the world of the elements, either without any aid or with the aid of celestial matters. The first kind is sorcery. The second kind is talismans.

These sciences are forbidden by the religious laws, because they are harmful and require (their practitioners) to direct themselves to (beings) other than God, such as stars and other things. Therefore, books dealing with them are almost nonexistent among the people. The only exceptions are the books of the ancient nations from before the time of Moses' prophecy, such as the Nabataeans and the Chaldeans. None of the prophets who preceded Moses made or brought any laws. Their books were concerned with exhortations, with the recognition of the oneness of God, and with references to Paradise and Hell.

The (magical) sciences were cultivated among the Syrian and Chaldean inhabitants of Babel and among the Copts of Egypt, and others. They composed books dealing with them and left information (concerning their occupation with them). Only very few of their books have been translated for us.

Later on, Jâbir b. Ḥayyân,[1] the chief sorcerer of Islam, appeared in the East. He scrutinized the scholarly books and discovered the craft of sorcery and alchemy. He studied its essence and brought it out. He wrote a number of works on sorcery. He lengthily discussed both sorcery and the craft of alchemy which goes together with sorcery, because the transformation of specific bodies (substances) from one form into another is effected by psychic powers, and not by a practical technique. Thus it is a sort of sorcery.

Let us present here some prefatory remarks that will explain the real meaning of sorcery. It is as follows. Human souls are one in species. However, they differ in view of their particular qualities. They are of different kinds. Each kind is distinguished by a particular quality which does not exist in any other kind of soul. These qualities come to constitute a natural disposition belonging exclusively to its particular kind of soul.

The souls of the prophets have a particular quality through which they are prepared to have divine knowledge, to be addressed by the angels in the name of God, and to exercise the influence upon created beings that goes with all that.

The souls of certain sorcerers also have the quality (of being able) to exercise influence upon created beings and to attract the spirituality of the stars, so that they can use it to exercise an influence

---

[1] The legendary founder of Muslim alchemy.

391

through either a psychic or a Satanic power. Now, the prophets are able to exercise their influence with the help of God and by means of a divine quality. The souls of soothsayers, on the other hand, have a quality enabling them to observe supernatural things by means of Satanic powers. Thus, every kind of soul is distinguished by its particular quality, which does not exist in any other kind.

The souls that have magical ability are of three degrees. These three degrees will now be explained here.

The first kind exercises its influence merely through mental power, without any instrument or aid. This is what the philosophers call sorcery.

The second kind exercises its influence with the aid of the temper of the spheres and the elements, or with the aid of the properties of numbers. This is called talismans. It is weaker in degree than the first kind.

The third kind exercises its influence upon the powers of imagination. The person who exercises this kind of influence relies upon the powers of imagination. He is somehow active in them. He plants among them different sorts of phantasms, images, and pictures, whichever he intends to use. Then, he brings them down to the level of the sensual perception of the observers with the help of the power of his soul that exercises an influence over that (sensual perception). As a result, the (phantasms, etc.) appear to the observers to exist in the external world, while, in fact, there is nothing (of the sort). For instance, a person is said to have seen gardens, rivers, and castles, while, in fact, there was nothing of the sort. This is what the philosophers call 'prestidigitation'.

Those are the different degrees of (sorcery).

Now, the sorcerer possesses his particular quality in potentiality, as is the case with all human powers. It is transformed (from potentiality) into actuality by exercise. All magical exercise consists of directing oneself to the spheres, the stars, the higher worlds, or to the devils by means of various kinds of veneration and worship and submissiveness and humiliation. Thus magical exercise is devotion, and adoration directed to beings other than God. Such devotion is unbelief. Therefore, sorcery is unbelief, or unbelief forms part of the substance and motives of sorcery, as has been seen. Consequently, (sorcerers must be killed). Jurists differ only as to whether they must be killed because of the unbelief which is antecedent to the practice of sorcery, or because of their corrupting activity and the resulting corruption of created beings.

Furthermore, since the first two degrees of sorcery are real and the third and last degree is not real, scholars differ as to whether sorcery is real or merely imaginary. Those who say that it is real have the first two degrees in mind. Those who say that it is not real have the third and last degree in mind. There is no difference of opinion among them about the matter itself, but (the difference of opinion) results from confusing the different degrees of sorcery.

No intelligent person doubts the existence of sorcery, because of the influence mentioned, which sorcery exercises. The Qur'ân refers to it.

The Messenger of God [Muhammad], according to (tradition), was put under a magic spell, so that he imagined that he was doing a thing while, in fact, he was not doing it. The spell against him was placed in a comb, in flakes of wool, and in the spathe of a palm, and buried in the well of Dharwân. Therefore, God revealed to him the following verses: 'I take refuge in God from the evil of the women who blow into knots.'[1] 'Â'ishah said, 'As soon as he recited the Qur'ân over one of those knots into which a spell against him had been placed, that particular knot became untied.'

There was much sorcery among the inhabitants of Babel, that is, the Nabataean and Syrian Chaldeans. The Qur'ân mentions much of it, and there are traditions about it. Sorcery was greatly cultivated in Babel and in Egypt at the time of Moses' prophetic mission. Therefore, the miracle Moses performed (as a proof of his prophecy) was of the kind claimed and bragged about by sorcerers. The temples in Upper Egypt are monuments attesting to the cultivation of sorcery in ancient Egypt.

We have seen with our own eyes (how a sorcerer) formed the picture of a person who was to be cast under a spell. He represented in it the characteristics of things he intended and planned (to make) that person adopt, as already existing in him in the shape of symbols of names and attributes. Then he spoke (magic words) over the picture he had made to take the place of the person who was to be cast under a spell, concretely or symbolically. During the repeated pronunciation of the evil words, he collected spittle in his mouth and spat upon the picture. Then he tied a knot over the symbol in an object that he had prepared for the purpose, since he considered tying knots auspicious (and effective in magical operations). He also entered into a pact with the jinn, asking them to participate in his spitting during the operation, intending to make the spell forceful. This (human) figure and the evil names have a harmful spirit. It issues from (the sorcerer) with his breath and attaches to the spittle he spits out. It produces more evil spirits. As a result, the things that the sorcerer intends for the person who is cast under a spell, actually befall him.

We have also observed how people who practise sorcery point at

[1] Qur'ân 113. 4 (4). The verb translated as 'blow' could also mean 'spit'.

393

a garment or a piece of leather and inwardly speak magic words over it, and behold! the object is torn to shreds. Others point in the same way at the bellies of sheep and goats at pasture with a ripping (gesture), and behold! the guts of the animals fall out of their bellies to the ground.

We have also heard that in contemporary India, there still are sorcerers who point at a man, and his heart is extracted and he falls dead. When someone looks for his heart, he cannot find it among his inner parts. Or, they point to a pomegranate. When someone opens it, no seeds are found in it. . . .

The philosophers made a distinction between sorcery and talismans. First, however, they affirmed that both (derive their effectiveness) from influences of the human soul. They deduced the existence of an influence of the human soul from the fact that the soul exercises an influence upon its own body that cannot be explained by the natural course of affairs or from corporeal reasons. At times, it results from the qualities of the spirits—such as heat, which originates from pleasure and joy—and at other times, it results from other psychic perceptions, such as the things that result from imagination. Thus, a person who walks upon the ledge of a wall or upon a high tightrope will certainly fall down if the idea of falling down is strongly present in his imagination. Therefore, there are many people who train themselves to get used to such things, so that they are not troubled by their imagination. They can walk upon the ledge of a wall or a high tightrope without fear of falling down. It is thus definite that we have here the result of an influence of the human soul and of the soul's imagining of the idea of falling down. If the soul can thus influence its own body without any natural corporeal causes, it is also possible that it can exercise a similar influence upon bodies other than its own. Its position with regard to its ability to exercise this type of influence is the same with regard to all bodies, since it is neither inherent nor firmly impressed in a (particular) body. Therefore, it is definite that the soul is able to exercise an influence upon other bodies.

Now, the distinction the (philosophers) make between sorcery and talismans is this. In sorcery, the sorcerer does not need any aid, while those who work with talismans seek the aid of the spiritualities of the stars, the secrets of numbers, the particular qualities of existing things, and the positions of the sphere that exercise an influence upon the world of the elements, as the astrologers maintain. The (philosophers) say that sorcery is a union of spirit with spirit, while the talisman is a union of spirit with body (substance). As they understand it, that means that the high celestial natures are tied together with the low (terrestrial) natures, the high natures being the spiritualities of the stars. Those who work with (talismans), therefore, as a rule seek the aid of astrology.

(The philosophers) think that a sorcerer does not acquire his magical ability but has, by nature, the particular disposition needed for exercising that type of influence.

They think that the difference between miracles and sorcery is this. A miracle is a divine power that arouses in the soul (the ability) to exercise influence. The (worker of miracles) is supported in his activity by the spirit of God. The sorcerer, on the other hand, does his work by himself and with the help of his own psychic power, and, under certain conditions, with the support of devils. The difference between the two actually concerns the idea, reality, and essence of the matter. We, however, deduce the differentiation merely from obvious signs. That is, miracles are found (to be wrought) by good persons for good purposes and by souls that are entirely devoted to good deeds. Moreover, they include the 'advance challenge' of the claim to prophecy. Sorcery, on the other hand, is found practised only by evil persons and as a rule is used for evil actions, such as causing discord between husband and wife, doing harm to enemies, and similar things. And it is found (practised) by souls that are entirely devoted to evil deeds. This is the difference between (prophecy and sorcery) in the opinion of metaphysicians.

Among the Sufis some who are favoured by acts of divine grace are also able to exercise an influence upon worldly conditions. This, however, is not counted as a kind of sorcery. It is effected with divine support, because the attitude and approach of these men result from prophecy and are a consequence of it. . . .

The religious law puts sorcery, talismans, and prestidigitation into cne and the same class, because they may cause harm. It brands them as forbidden and illegal.

Philosophers assume that the difference between miracles and sorcery is the difference between the two extremes of good and evil. Nothing good issues from a sorcerer, and sorcery is not employed in good causes. Nothing evil issues from a worker of miracles, and miracles are not employed in evil causes.

The evil eye

Another psychic influence is that of the eye—that is, an influence exercised by the soul of the person who has the evil eye. A thing or situation appears pleasing to the eye of a person, and he likes it very much. This (circumstance) creates in him envy and the desire to take it away from its owner. Therefore, he prefers to destroy him.

It is a natural gift—I mean, the eye. The difference between it and the other psychic influences is that it appears (and acts) as something natural and innate. It cannot be left alone. It does not depend on the free choice of its possessor. It is not acquired by him. Some of the other (psychic) influences may also not be acquired ones, but their appearance (in action) depends on the free choice of the person who exercises them. The thing that characterizes them as natural is their (possessors') potential ability to exercise them, not their (automatic) action. Therefore it has been said: 'A person who kills by means of sorcery or a miraculous act must be killed, but the person who kills with the eye must not be killed.' The (person who kills with the eye) did not want or intend to do so, nor could he have avoided doing so.

28 The science of the secrets of letters

At the present time, this science is called *símiyá*: 'letter magic'.[1] The word was transferred from talismans to this science and used in this conventional meaning in the technical terminology of Sufi practitioners of magic. Thus, a general magical term came to be used for some particular aspect of magic.

It is an unfathomable subject with innumerable problems. Authors who wrote about it assume that the result and fruit of letter magic is that the divine souls are active in the world of nature by means of the beautiful names of God and the divine expressions that originate from the letters comprising the secrets that are alive in the created things.

The authorities on letter magic then differed as to the secret of the magic activity lying in the letters. Some of them assumed that it was due to inherent temper. Others assumed that the secret of the activity that lies in the letters was their numerical proportion. . . .

It has been thought that this activity and the activity of people who work with talismans are one and the same thing. But it is not so. . . .

One should realize that all magic activity in the world of nature comes from the human soul and the human mind, because the human soul essentially encompasses and governs nature. Consequently, the real difference between the activity of people who work with talismans and people who work with words is as follows. The activity of people who work with talismans consists in bringing down the spirituality of the spheres and tying it down with the help of pictures or numerical proportions. The result is a kind of composition that, through its nature, effects a transformation and change comparable to those effected by a ferment in the thing into which it gets. The

[1] From Greek σημεῖα.

activity of people who work with words, on the other hand, is the effect of the divine light and the support of the Lord which they obtain through exertion and the removal (of the veil). Thus, nature is forced to work (for them) and does so willingly with no attempt at disobedience. . . .

29 The science of alchemy

This is a science that studies the substance through which the generation of gold and silver may be artificially accomplished, and comments on the operation leading to it. The (alchemists) acquire knowledge of the tempers and powers of all created things and investigate them critically. They hope that they may thus come upon the substance that is prepared to (produce gold and silver). They even investigate the waste matter of animals, such as bones, feathers, hair, eggs, and excrements, not to mention minerals.

Alchemy, then, comments on the operations through which such a substance may be transformed from potentiality into actuality, as, for instance, by the dissolution of bodies (substances) into their natural components through sublimation and distillation, by the solidification of meltable substances through calcification, by the pulverization of solid materials with the help of pestles and mullers and similar things. The (alchemists) assume that all these techniques lead to the production of a natural substance which they call 'the elixir'.[1] When some mineral substance, such as lead, tin, or copper, which is prepared for receiving the form of gold or silver, is heated in the fire and some quantity of the elixir is added to it, that substance turns into pure gold. In the technical terminology that the alchemists use for purposes of mystification, they give the cover name of 'spirit' to the elixir and that of 'body' to the substance to which the elixir is added.

The science that comments on this technical terminology and on the form of the technical operation by which predisposed substances are turned into the form of gold and silver, is the science of alchemy. In both ancient and modern times, people have written works on alchemy. Discussions of alchemy are occasionally ascribed to people who were not alchemists.

The chief systematic writer on alchemy, according to the alchemists, is Jâbir b. Hayyân. Alchemists even consider alchemy Jâbir's special preserve and call it 'the science of Jâbir'. He wrote seventy treatises on alchemy. All of them read like puzzles. It is thought that only those who know all that is in his treatises can unlock the secrets of alchemy. . . .

[1] Al-iksîr, from Greek ξήριον.

397

Works on alchemy are attributed to al-Ghazzâlî, but this attribution is not correct, because al-Ghazzâlî's lofty perceptions would not have permitted him to study, or, eventually, to adopt the errors of alchemical theories. . . .

One can see [from their writings] how all the expressions used by alchemists tend to be secret hints and puzzles, scarcely to be explained or understood. This is proof of the fact that alchemy is not a natural craft.

The truth with regard to alchemy, which is to be believed and which is supported by actual fact, is that alchemy is one of the ways in which the spiritual souls exercise an influence and are active in the world of nature. (It may) belong among the (miraculous) acts of divine grace, if the souls are good. Or it may be a kind of sorcery, if the souls are bad and wicked. It is obvious that (alchemy may materialize) as a miraculous act of divine grace. It may be sorcery, because the sorcerer, as has been established in the proper place, may change the identity of matter by means of his magic power.

Now, since alchemy is the creation of gold in a substance other than that of gold, it is a kind of sorcery. The famous sages who discussed the subject followed this line. Therefore, they used puzzling expressions. They wanted to protect alchemy from the disapproval that religious laws express for the various kinds of sorcery. It was not because they were reluctant to communicate it to others, as was thought by people who did not investigate the matter thoroughly.

30 A refutation of philosophy. The corruption of the students of philosophy

This and the following two sections are important. The sciences (of philosophy, astrology, and alchemy) occur in civilization. They are much cultivated in the cities. The harm they can do to religion is great. Therefore, it is necessary that we make it clear what they are about and that we reveal the right attitude concerning them.

There are certain intelligent representatives of the human species who think that the essences and conditions of the whole of existence, both the part of it perceivable by the senses and that beyond sensual perception, as well as the reasons and causes of (those essences and conditions), can be perceived by mental speculation and intellectual reasoning. They also think that the articles of faith are established as correct thr ugh (intellectual) speculation and not through tradition, because they belong among the intellectual perceptions. Such people are called 'philosophers'—*falâsifah*, plural of *faylasûf*—which is Greek and means 'lover of wisdom'.[1]

---

[1] This correct translation of φιλόσοφος was well known to the Arabs.

They did research on the (problem of perception). With great energy, they tried to find the purpose of it. They laid down a norm enabling intellectual speculation to distinguish between true and false which they called 'logic'. The quintessence of it is that the mental speculation which makes it possible to distinguish between true and false, concentrates on ideas abstracted from the individual *existentia*. From these (individual *existentia*), one first abstracts pictures that conform to all the individual (manifestations of the *existentia*), just as a seal conforms to all the impressions it makes in clay or wax. The abstractions derived from the *sensibilia* are called 'primary *intelligibilia*'. These universal ideas may be associated with other ideas, from which, however, they are distinguished in the mind. Then, other ideas, namely those that are associated (and have ideas in common) with (the primary *intelligibilia*), are abstracted from them. Then, if still other ideas are associated with them, a second and third abstraction is made, until the process of abstraction reaches the simple universal ideas, which conform to all ideas and individual (manifestations of the *existentia*). No further abstraction is possible. They are the highest genera. All abstract (ideas) that are not derived from the *sensibilia* serve, if combined with each other, to produce the sciences. They are called 'secondary *intelligibilia*'.

(Man through his) ability to think studies these abstract *intelligibilia* and seeks through them to perceive existence as it is. For this purpose, the mind must combine some of them with others or keep them apart with the help of unequivocal rational argumentation. This should give (the mind) a correct and conformable perception of existence, if the (process) takes place according to a sound norm, as mentioned before.

The combination of (abstract *intelligibilia*) and the judgment (concerning them) is apperception. At the end, philosophers give apperception precedence over perception, but at the beginning and during the process of instruction, they give perception precedence over apperception, because they think that perfected perception is the goal of the search for understanding and that apperception is merely a means for (undertaking that search). In the books of the logicians, one finds a statement to the effect that perception has precedence and that apperception depends upon it. This statement must be understood in the sense of (arriving at) consciousness and not in the sense of (achieving) complete knowledge. This is the opinion of Aristotle, the greatest of them.

Then, philosophers think that happiness consists in arriving at perception of all existing things, both the *sensibilia* and the (things) beyond sensual perception, with the help of (rational) speculation and argumentation. The sum total of their perceptions of existence,

399

the result to which (their perceptions) lead, that is, the detailed conclusions of their speculative propositions, is the following. First, they conclude from observation and sensual perception that there is a lower substance. Then, their perception progresses a little. (The existence of) motion and sensual perception in animals makes them conscious of the existence of the soul. The powers of the soul, then, make them aware of the dominant position of the intellect. Here, their perception stops. They draw their conclusions with regard to the most high celestial body in the same way they drew their conclusions with regard to the human essence. They thus consider it necessary that the (celestial) sphere must have a soul and an intellect, like human beings.

They assume that happiness consists in the perception of existence with the help of such conclusions (if, at the same time, such perception is) combined with the improvement of the soul and the soul's acceptance of a virtuous character. Even if no religious law had been revealed (to help man to distinguish between virtue and vice), they think the (acquisition of virtue) possible by man because he is able to distinguish between vice and virtue in his actions by means of his intellect, his (ability to) speculate, and his natural inclination toward praiseworthy actions, his natural disinclination for blameworthy actions. They assume that when the soul becomes (virtuous), it attains joy and pleasure, and that ignorance of (moral qualities) means eternal pain. This, in their opinion, is the meaning of bliss or punishment in the other world. They go further in this manner, and by the words they use, they display their well-known obtuseness as far as details are concerned.

The leading representative of these doctrines, who presented the problems connected with them, wrote books on them as a systematic science, and penned the arguments in favour of them, as far as we presently know, was Aristotle the Macedonian, from Macedonia in Byzantine territory, a pupil of Plato and the teacher of Alexander. He is called 'the First Teacher', with no further qualification. It means 'teacher of logic', because logic did not exist in an improved form before Aristotle. He was the first to systematize the norms of logic and to deal with all its problems and to give a good and extensive treatment of it. He would, in fact, have done very well with his norm of logic if only it had absolved him of responsibility for the philosophical tendencies that concern metaphysics.

Later, in Islam, there were men who adopted these doctrines and followed Aristotle's opinion with respect to them very closely except on a few points. This came about as follows. The 'Abbâsid caliphs had the works of the ancient philosophers translated from Greek into Arabic. Many Muslims investigated them critically. Scholars whom God led astray adopted their doctrines and defended them in disputations. They held different opinions on some points of detail. The most famous of these (Muslim philosophers) were Abû Naṣr al-Fârâbî in the fourth [tenth] century, and Abû 'Alî Ibn Sînâ (Avicenna) in the fifth [eleventh] century.

It should be known that the (opinion) the (philosophers) hold is wrong in all its aspects. They refer all *existentia* to the first intellect and are satisfied with (the theory of the first intellect) in their progress toward the Necessary One (the Deity). This means that they disregard all the degrees of divine creation beyond the (first intellect). Existence, however, is too wide to (be explained by so narrow a view). The philosophers, who restrict themselves to affirming the intellect and neglect everything beyond it, are in a way comparable to physicists who restrict themselves to affirming the body and who disregard both soul and intellect in the belief that there is nothing beyond the body in God's wise plan concerning (the world of) existence.

The arguments that (the philosophers) parade for their claims regarding the *existentia*, and that they offer to the test of the norms of logic, are insufficient for the purpose.

The arguments concerning the corporeal *existentia* constitute what they call the science of physics. The insufficiency lies in the fact that conformity between the results of thinking—which, as they assume, are produced by rational norms and reasoning—and the outside world, is not unequivocal. All the judgments of the mind are general ones, whereas the *existentia* of the outside world are individual in their substances. Perhaps, there is something in those substances that prevents conformity between the universal (judgments) of the mind and the individual (substances) of the outside world. At any rate, however, whatever (conformity) is attested by sensual perception has its proof in the fact that it is observable. (It does not have its proof) in (logical) arguments. Where, then, is the unequivocal character they find in (their arguments)?

The mind is also often applied to the primary *intelligibilia*, which conform to the individual (*existentia*), with the help of pictures of the imagination, but not to the secondary *intelligibilia*, which are abstractions of the second degree. In this case, judgment becomes unequivocal, comparable to (judgment in the case of) *sensibilia*, since the primary *intelligibilia* are more likely to agree with the outside world, because they conform perfectly (by definition, to the individual manifestations of the *existentia*). Therefore, in this case, one must concede (the philosophers') claims in this respect. However, we must refrain from studying these things, since such (restraint) falls under (the duty of) the Muslim not to do what does not concern him. The problems of physics are of no importance for us in our religious affairs or our livelihoods. Therefore, we must leave them alone.

The arguments concerning the *existentia* beyond sensual perception—the *spiritualia*—constitute what the (philosophers) call 'the divine science' or science of metaphysics. The essences of (the *spiritualia*) are completely unknown. One cannot get at them, nor can they be proven by logical arguments, because an abstraction of *intelligibilia* from the individual *existentia* of the outside world is possible only in the case of things we can perceive by the senses, from which the universals are thus derived. We cannot perceive the spiritual essences and abstract further quiddities from them, because the senses constitute a veil between us and them. We have, thus, no (logical) arguments for them, and we have no way whatever of affirming their existence. There are only available to us (in this connection) the situations in which perceptions of the human soul take place, and especially the dream visions which are within the intuitive experience of all. But beyond that, the reality and attributes of the (*spiritualia*) are an obscure matter, and there is no way to learn about them. Competent (philosophers) have clearly said so. They have expressed the opinion that whatever is immaterial cannot be proved by logical arguments, because it is a condition of logical arguments that their premises must be essential ones. The great philosopher Plato said that no certainty can be achieved with regard to the Divine, and one can state about the Divine only what is most suitable and proper—that is, conjectures. If, after all the toil and trouble, we find only conjectures, the conjectures that we had at the beginning may as well suffice us. What use, then, do these sciences and the pursuit of them have? We want certainty about the *existentia* that are beyond sensual perception, while, in their philosophy, those conjectures are the limit that human thinking can reach.

The philosophers say that happiness consists in coming to perceive existence as it is, by means of logical arguments. This is a fraudulent statement that must be rejected. The matter is as follows. Man is composed of two parts. One is corporeal. The other is spiritual, and mixed with the former. Each one of these parts has its own perceptions, though the part that perceives is the same in both cases, namely, the spiritual part. At times, it perceives spiritual perceptions. At other times, it perceives corporeal perceptions. However, it perceives the spiritual perceptions through its own essence without any intermediary, while it perceives the corporeal perceptions through the intermediary of organs of the body, such as the brain and the senses.

Now, anybody who has perceptions greatly enjoys whatever he perceives. For example, a child having its first corporeal perceptions, which like all corporeal perceptions come through an intermediary, greatly enjoys the light it sees and the sounds it hears. Thus, there can be no doubt that the soul finds even greater joy and pleasure in perceptions that come from its own essence without an intermediary. When the spiritual soul becomes conscious of the perception coming to it from its own essence without an intermediary, it derives from it inexpressible joy and pleasure. Such perception cannot be achieved by (intellectual) speculation and science. It is achieved by the removal of the veil of sensual perception and by forgetting all corporeal perceptions. The Sufis are very much concerned with achieving this great joy through having the soul achieve that kind of perception. They attempt to kill the bodily powers and perceptions through exercise, and even the thinking power of the brain. In this way, the soul is to achieve the perception that comes to it from its own essence, when all the disturbances and hindrances caused by the body are removed. (The Sufis) thus achieve inexpressible joy and pleasure. This, (the philosophers) imply, is a correct assumption, and must be conceded them; yet it does not account for the idea they had in mind.

Their statement that logical arguments and proofs produce this kind of perception and the resulting great joy is false, as one can see. The arguments and proofs belong in the category of corporeal perceptions, because they are produced by the powers of the brain, which are imagination, thinking, and memory. The first thing we are concerned with when we want to attain this kind of perception is to kill all these powers of the brain, because they object to such (perception) and work against it. One finds able (philosophers) poring over the *Kitâb ash-Shifâ'*, the *Ishârât*, the *Najâh* (of Avicenna), and over Averroës' abridgments of the 'Text' (*Organon*) and other works by Aristotle. They wear out the pages of these works. They firmly ground themselves in the arguments they contain, and they desire to find in them that portion of happiness (they believe they contain). They do not realize that in this way they only add to the obstacles on (the road to happiness). They base themselves on statements reported on the authority of Aristotle, al-Fârâbî, and Avicenna, to the effect that those who have attained perception of the active intellect and are united with it in their life in this world have attained their share of happiness. To them, the active intellect means the first (highest) of the degrees of the *spiritualia* from which (the veil of) sensual perception is removed. They assume union with the active intellect to be (the result of) scientific perception. One has seen that this is wrong. When Aristotle and his colleagues speak about union and perception in this way, they mean the perception of the soul that comes to it from its own essence and without an intermediary, but such is attained only by the removal of the veil of sensual perception.

Furthermore, (philosophers) state that the great joy originating in that kind of perception is identical with the happiness promised in the world to come. This, too, is wrong. The things that have been established by the (philosophers) make it clear to us that, beyond sensual perception, there is something else perceived by the soul without an intermediary. This causes very great joy to the soul, but we do not think that this makes it definite that it is identical with the happiness of the other world, although it must be one of the pleasures that constitute that happiness. Their statement that happiness consists in coming to perceive the *existentia* as they are, is wrong. It is based upon the erroneous supposition, which we mentioned before in connection with the principle of divine oneness, that anybody who has perception comprises (the whole) of existence in his perceptions. We explained that this (assumption) is wrong, and that existence is too vast to be completely encompassed or perceived, either spiritually or corporeally.

The sum total of all the (philosophical) doctrines we have set down here is that the spiritual part of man, when it separates from the powers of the body, has an essential perception belonging to a special kind of perceptions, namely, the *existentia* that are encompassed by our knowledge. It does not have a general perception of all the *existentia*, since they cannot be encompassed in their totality. It greatly enjoys this kind of perception, exactly as a child is pleased with its sensual perceptions when it begins to grow up. Nobody, then, (should try to tell) us that it is possible to perceive all the *existentia* or to achieve the happiness Muḥammad promised us, if we do not work for it.

(Philosophers) further state that man is able, by himself, to refine and improve his soul by adopting praiseworthy character qualities and avoiding blameworthy ones. This is connected with the assumption that the great joy that the soul has through the perception coming to it from its own essence, is identical with the promised happiness. For vices give the soul corporeal habits and the resulting colouring. Thus, they impede it in the realization of that perception.

Now, we have already explained that happiness and unhappiness are found beyond corporeal and spiritual perceptions. The improvement (of the soul that the philosophers) have come to know is useful only in that it (produces) great joy, originating from the spiritual perception that takes place according to rational and established norms. But the happiness beyond such (joy), which Muḥammad promised us if we would act and behave as he commanded us, is something that cannot be encompassed by anybody's perceptions.

The leading philosopher, Abû 'Alî Ibn Sînâ (Avicenna), was aware of this. He expressed himself in the following sense in his *Kitâb al-Mabda' wa-l-ma'âd*: 'The spiritual resurrection and its circumstances are something that we may come to know by means of rational arguments and reasoning, because it proceeds in a safely natural and uniform manner. Thus, we can use logical arguments for it. But the bodily resurrection and its circumstances cannot be perceived by means of logical arguments, because it does not proceed in a uniform manner. It has been explained to us by the true Muḥammadan religious law. The religious law should therefore be considered and consulted with regard to those circumstances.'

Thus, as one has seen, the science (of logic) is not adequate to achieve the avowed intentions (of the philosophers). In addition, it contains things that are contrary to the religious laws and their obvious meaning. As far as we know, this science has only a single advantage, namely, it sharpens the mind in the orderly presentation of proofs and arguments, so that the habit of excellent and correct arguing is obtained. This is because the orderly process and the solid and exact method of reasoning are as the philosophers have prescribed them in their science of logic. They employ it a good deal in the physical and mathematical sciences as well as in the science that comes after them (metaphysics). Since logical arguments are much employed in those sciences in the way they should be employed, the student of them is able to master the habit of exact and correct arguing and deducing. Even if (those sciences) are not adequate to achieve the intentions of the (philosophers), they constitute the soundest norm of (philosophical) speculation that we know of.

Such is the fruit of logic. It also affords acquaintance with the doctrines and opinions of the people of the world. One knows what harm it can do. Therefore, the student should beware of its pernicious aspects as much as he can. Whoever studies it should do so only after he is saturated with the religious law and has studied the interpretation of the Qur'ân and jurisprudence. No one who has no knowledge of the Muslim religious sciences should apply himself to it. Without that knowledge, he can hardly remain safe from its pernicious aspects.

31 A refutation of astrology. The weakness of its achievements. The harmfulness of its goal

Astrologers think that astrology, with the knowledge it gives of astral powers, individually or in combination, and of astral influences upon elemental creations, enables them to know the things that are going to be in the world of the elements, before they are created. The positions of the spheres and the stars are thus (taken to) indicate every single kind of future event, both universal and individual.

The ancient (astrologers) were of the opinion that the knowledge of astral powers and influence is acquired through experience. It is something that all human lives combined would not be able to achieve, because experience is obtained through numerous repetitions which make the attainment of (empirical) knowledge or conjectures possible. Astral revolutions may be very long. Greatly extended periods of time are required for their repetition. Even all the lives in the world combined would be too short for (observing) them.

Some weak-minded (astrologers) take the view that the knowledge of astral powers and influences comes through revelation. This is a fallacy. They themselves have furnished us with arguments sufficient to refute it. The clearest proof is that, as one knows, of all people, the prophets are least familiar with the crafts. They do not undertake to give information about the supernatural, unless it comes to them from God. Why, then, should they claim to produce (supernatural information) through a craft (such as astrology) and make it the law for their followers to do so?

Ptolemy and his followers were of the opinion that the stars are able to indicate the future as the natural result of a temper they produce in the elemental existing things. He said: 'The activity of sun and moon and their influence upon elemental things are so obvious that no one can deny them. For instance, the sun influences the changes and tempers of the seasons, the ripening of fruits and grains, and so on. The moon influences humidity, the water, the process of putrefaction in substances and cucumbers, and so on.' Ptolemy continued: 'With regard to the stars that come after sun and moon, we have two approaches. One—which, however, is unsatisfactory—is to follow the tradition of the astrological authorities. The other is to rely upon conjecture and empirical knowledge gained through comparing each star to the sun, whose nature and influence is clearly known to us. We thus note whether a given star increases the power and temper of the sun at its conjunction with it. If this is the case, we know that the nature of that particular star agrees with that of the sun. If, on the other hand, the star diminishes the power and temper of the sun, we know that its nature is opposite to that of the sun. Then, when we know the individual powers of the stars, we can also know them in combination. That happens when they look upon each other in the trine, the quartile, or other aspects. The knowledge here is derived from the natures of the signs of the zodiac, which similarly are known through comparison with the sun.

'Thus, we get to know all the astral powers. They exercise an influence upon the air. This is obvious. The resulting temper of the air communicates itself to the created things below the air, and shapes sperm and seeds. Thus, this temper comes to underlie the body created from sperm or seed, the soul which attaches itself to the body, pours itself into the body, and acquires its perfection from the body, and all the conditions depending on soul and body. The qualities of sperm and seed are the qualities of the things that are created and produced from sperm and seed.'

Ptolemy continued: 'Still, astrology remains conjectural and is not certain in any respect. It also forms no part of the divine decree—that is, predestination. It is just one of the natural causes common to all existing things, whereas the divine decree is prior to everything.' This is the sum total of the discussion by Ptolemy and his colleagues. It is found in the *Quadripartitum* and other works.

It makes the weakness of the achievements of astrology clear. Knowledge of, or conjectures about, things that come into being can only result from knowledge of all their causes, that is, agent, recipient, form, and end. According to (the astrologers), the astral powers are merely agents. The elemental part is the recipient. Furthermore, the astral powers are not the sole agents. There are other powers that act together with (the astral powers) upon the material element (involved), such as the generative power of father and species contained in the sperm, the powers of the particular quality distinguishing each variety within the species, and other things. When the astral powers reach perfection and are known, they still are only one among many causes that go into the making of a thing that comes into being.

Furthermore, in addition to a knowledge of astral powers and influences, a great amount of conjecturing and guesswork is required. Only then is (the astrologer) able to guess that a thing might happen. Now, conjecturing and guesswork are powers in the mind of the student. They are not causes or reasons of the things that come into being. Without conjectures and guesswork, (astrology) steps down from conjecture to doubtfulness.

Such is the situation even if one's knowledge of the astral powers is accurate and without defect. Now, that is difficult. The ability to calculate the courses of the stars is required in order to know their positions. Moreover, it is not proven that every star has its own particular power. The method Ptolemy used in establishing the powers of the five planets, that is, comparison with the sun, is a weak one, because the power of the sun is superior to all other astral powers and dominates them. Thus, one hardly ever becomes aware of an increase or decrease in the (powers of the sun) at its conjunction (with a given star), as Ptolemy said. All this speaks against the assumption that it is possible to predict things that will happen in the world of the elements with the help of astrology.

Furthermore, it is wrong to assume that the stars exercise an influence on the world below them. It has been proven that there is no agent but God. In this connection, speculative theologians use the self-evident argument that how causes are related to the things caused is not known, and suspicion attaches to the conclusions of the intellect regarding what appears superficially to be (due to some definite) influence. Perhaps, the relationship of (the causes to the things caused) is effected by some other than the ordinary form of influence. The divine power (would seem to) tie the two together, as it does with all created things, both high and low, especially since the religious law attributes all happenings to the power of God and does not want to have anything to do with anything else.

Prophecy also denies the importance and influence of the stars. For instance, (Muḥammad) said: 'No eclipse of either sun or moon takes place to indicate the death or life of anybody.'

Thus, the worthlessness of astrology from the point of view of the religious law, as well as the weakness of its achievements from the rational point of view, are evident. In addition, astrology does harm to human civilization. It hurts the faith of the common people when an astrological judgment occasionally happens to come true in some unexplainable and unverifiable manner. Ignorant people are taken in by that and suppose that all the other (astrological) judgments must be true, which is not the case. Thus, they are led to attribute things to some being other than their Creator.

Further, astrology often produces the expectation that signs of crisis will appear in a dynasty. This encourages the enemies and rivals of the dynasty to attack it and revolt against it. We have (personally) observed much of the sort. It is, therefore, necessary that astrology be forbidden to all civilized people, because it may cause harm to religion and dynasty. It is our duty to try to acquire goodness with the help of the things that cause it, and to avoid the causes of evil and harm. That is what those who realize the corruption and harmfulness of this science must do.

This situation should make one realize that even if astrology were in itself sound, no Muslim could acquire the knowledge and habit of it. He who studies it and thinks that he knows it fully is most ignorant of the actual situation. Those who are eager to learn it—and they are very, very few—have to read the books and treatises on astrology in a secluded corner of their houses. They have to hide from the people and are under the watchful eye of the great mass. And then, astrology is a very complicated subject with many branches and subdivisions and is difficult to understand. How could people under such conditions acquire a mastery of it? Jurisprudence is of general usefulness in both religious and worldly affairs; its sources are easily available in the Qur'ân and the accepted Sunnah, and it has been studied and taught by the great mass of Muslims. There have been classes and seminars on jurisprudence. There has been much instruction in it and a great many lectures. Still, only an occasional individual in each age and generation (race) has been able to master it. How, then, can anyone learn a subject (such as astrology) that is discarded by the religious law, banned as forbidden and illegal, concealed from the great mass, its sources difficult of access, and that, after the study and acquisition of its basic principles and details, requires a great amount of support from conjecture and guesswork on the part of the student? How could anyone become skilled in such a subject in the face of all (these difficulties)? When all this is taken into consideration, the soundness of our opinion (with regard to astrology) will become clear. . . .

32 A denial of the effectiveness of alchemy. The impossibility of its existence. The harm that arises from practising it

Many people who are unable to earn their living are led by greed to cultivate alchemy. They are of the opinion that is is a (proper) means of making a living and that its practitioners find it easier and simpler (than other people) to acquire property. In fact, however, they have to pay for (their efforts) in the form of trouble, hardship, and difficulties, and in the form of persecution by the authorities and loss of property through expenditure.

They think that (in practising alchemy) they know some gainful craft. However, they have been stimulated (to practise alchemy) solely by the thought that some minerals may be changed and transformed artificially into others, because of the matter common (to all minerals). Thus, they try to treat silver and transform it into gold; copper and tin (they try to transform) into silver. They think that it is possible in the realm of nature to do this. . . .

Certain (alchemists) restricted themselves to mere forgery. It may be of an obvious type, such as covering silver with gold, or copper with silver, or mixing the (two metals) in the ratio of one to two, or one to three. Or it may be a concealed type of forgery, such as treating a mineral to make it look like another similar one. Copper, for instance, may be blanched and softened with sublimate of mercury. Thus, it turns into a mineral that looks like silver to anyone but an expert assayer.

Such forgers use their product to coin money with the official imprint, which they circulate among the people. Thus, they cheat the great mass with impunity. Theirs is the most contemptible and pernicious profession. The forgers conspire to steal the property of the people, for they give copper for silver, and silver for gold, so as to get exclusive possession of (other people's property). They are thieves, or worse than thieves. . . .

However, it is possible for us to talk with alchemists who do not like such forgeries, but avoid them and refrain from corrupting the currency and coinage of the Muslims. Yet, we know of not one in the world who has attained the goal (of alchemy) or got any desirable result out of it. They tell stories about other alchemists who attained the goal of alchemy or were successful. They are like people who are infatuated with something and taken in by fanciful stories about the subject of their infatuation. When they are asked whether the story has been verified by actual observation, they do not know. They say, 'We have heard about it, but have not seen it.' This has been the case with alchemists in every age and of every race (generation). . . .

Those who claim to have made gold with the help of alchemy are like those who might claim the artificial creation of man from semen. If we grant to someone an all-comprehensive knowledge of the parts of man, his proportions, the stages of his (development), the way he is created in the womb, if he could know all this in every detail, so that nothing escapes his knowledge, then we would grant him the (ability to) create a human being. But where does anyone possess such knowledge? . . .

There is another aspect to alchemy proving its impossibility. It concerns the result of alchemy. This is as follows. It was God's wise plan that gold and silver, being rare, should be the standard of value by which the profits and capital accumulation of human beings are measured. If it were possible to obtain gold and silver artificially, God's wise plan in this respect would be foiled. Gold and silver would exist in such large quantities that it would be no use to acquire them.

There is still another aspect to alchemy proving its impossibility. Nature always takes the shortest way in what it does. It does not take the longest and most complicated one. If, as the alchemists suppose, the artificial method were sound, shorter, and took less time than that which nature follows in the mine, nature would not have abandoned it in favour of the method it has chosen for the generation and creation of gold and silver. . . .

The most common cause of the desire to practise alchemy is, as we have stated, a person's inability to make his living in a natural way and the wish to make a living in some way that, unlike agriculture, commerce, and handicraft, is not natural. A person without ability finds it difficult to make his living in such (legitimate occupations). He wants to get rich all at once through some occupation that is not natural, such as alchemy and other things. Alchemy is cultivated mostly by the poor among civilized people.

33 The purposes that must be borne in mind in literary composition and that alone are to be considered valid

It should be known that the storehouse of human science is the soul of man. In it God has implanted perception, enabling it to think and, thus, to acquire (scientific knowledge). (The process) starts with perception (*taṣawwur*) of the realities and is then continued by affirmation or negation of the essential attributes of the (realities), either directly or through an intermediary.

Man's ability to think thus eventually produces a problematic situation which it tries to solve affirmatively or negatively. When a scientific picture has been established in the mind through these (efforts), it must, of necessity, be communicated to someone else, either through instruction or through discussion, in order to polish the mind by trying to show its soundness.

Such communication takes place through 'verbal expression', that is, speech composed of spoken words which God created in a limb (of the human body), the tongue, as combinations of sounds—that is, the various qualities of sound as broken by uvula and tongue—so that the thoughts of people can be communicated in speech. This is the first step in the communication of thoughts. As its most important and noble part, it includes the sciences. However, it comprises every statement or wish (command) that in general enters the mind.

After this first step in communication, there is a second. It is the communication of one's thoughts to persons who are out of sight or bodily far away, or to persons who live later and whom one has not met, since they are not contemporaries. This is written communication. Writing is figures made by the hand, whose shapes and forms, by convention, indicate the individual letters (sounds) and words of speech. Thus, they communicate thought through the medium of speech. Writing, therefore, constitutes the second step of communication and is one of its two parts. It gives information about the noblest part of thinking, namely, science and knowledge. Scholars take care to deposit all their scientific thoughts in books by means of writing, so that all those who are absent and live at a later time may have the benefit of them. People who do that are authors. Everywhere in the world, written works are numerous. They are handed down among all races and in all ages. They differ as the result of differences in religious laws and organizations and in the information available about nations and dynasties. The philosophical sciences do not show such differences. They have developed uniformly, as required by the very nature of thinking, which is concerned with the perception of existing things as they are, whether corporeal, spiritual, celestial, elemental, abstract, or material. These sciences show no differences. Differences occur in the religious sciences because of differences a:nong the various religions, and in the historical sciences because of differences in the outward character of historical information.

Writing differs in that human beings have come to use different forms and shapes of it. (These differences) are called 'pen' and script. There is the Ḥimyarite script, which is called *musnad*. It is the script of the Ḥimyar and the ancient inhabitants of the Yemen. It differs from the writing of the later Muḍar Arabs, exactly as the (language written in the Ḥimyarite script) is different from the language of (the Muḍar Arabs), though all of them are Arabs. Both have their own general norms, which are evolved inductively from their (ways of linguistic) expression, and are different from the norms of the other group.

Another script is the Syrian script. This is the writing of the Nabataeans and Chaldeans. Ignorant people often think that because these were the most powerful nations (in antiquity), and the (Syrian script) is of great antiquity, it is the natural script (whereas all other scripts are conventional ones). This is a fanciful, vulgar idea. No action resulting from choice is a natural one. The fact is simply that the Syrian script is so old and was used for so long that it became a firmly rooted habit, thought by the observer to be a natural one. Many simpletons have the same idea about the Arabic language. They say that the Arabs express themselves in good Arabic and speak it by nature. This is a fanciful idea.

Another script is the Hebrew script. It is the writing of the children of Eber, the son of Shelah, who are Israelites, and of other people.

Another script is the Latin script, the script of the Latin Byzantines. They also have their own language.

Each nation has its own particular form of writing, which is attributed to it in particular. (This applies), for instance, to the Turks, the European Christians, the Indians, and others. Only three scripts are of interest. First, Syrian, because of its antiquity, as we have mentioned. Then there are Arabic and Hebrew, since the Qur'ân and the Torah were revealed in the Arabic and Hebrew scripts and languages, respectively.

Then, thirdly there is Latin, the language of the Romans. When they adopted Christianity, which is entirely based upon the Torah, they translated the Torah and the books of the Israelite prophets into their language, in order to be able to derive the law from Scripture as easily as possible. Thus, they came to be more interested in their own language and writing than in any other.

The other scripts are of no interest. Every people employs its own particular kind of script.

Now, the purposes that must be borne in mind in literary composition and that alone are to be considered valid were restricted to seven.

(1) The invention of a science with its subject, its division into chapters and sections, and the discussion of its problems. Or the invention of problems and topics of research which occur to a competent scholar and which he wants to communicate to someone else, so that they may become generally known and useful. This, then, is deposited in a written volume, so that a later (generation) may have the benefit of it. This is what happened, for instance, with the principles of jurisprudence. Ash-Shâfi'î was the first to discuss, and briefly to describe, the legal arguments based on the wording (of the traditions). Then, the Ḥanafites appeared and invented the problems of analogical reasoning and presented them fully. This (material has been used by subsequent generations down to the present time.

(2) (A scholar) may find the discussion and works of ancient (scholars) difficult to understand. God may open understanding of them to him. He will then wish to communicate his (knowledge) to someone else who may perhaps have difficulties with (the same problems), so that all those who are worthy may have the benefit of (his knowledge). This is the interpretational approach to books on the intellectual and traditional (sciences). It is a noble chapter.

(3) Some later scholar may come across an error or mistake in discussions by ancient scholars of renowned merit and famous authority as teachers. He may have clear proof for it, admitting of no doubt. He will then wish to communicate this (discovery) to those after him, since it is impossible to eradicate a mistake (in the work in question) in view of its wide dissemination in space and time, the fame of its author, and the reliance people place in his learning. Therefore, he deposits this (discovery of the mistake) in writing, so that (future) students may learn the explanation of it.

(4) A particular discipline may be incomplete, certain problems or details indicated by the division of the subject of the discipline requiring treatment. The (scholar) who becomes aware of the fact will want to supply these lacking problems, in order to perfect the discipline by having all its problems and details treated and leaving no room for deficiency in it.

(5) The problems of a particular science may have been treated

without (the proper) arrangement into chapters and without order. The (scholar) who becomes aware of that situation will arrange and improve on the problems and put every problem in the chapter where it belongs.

(6) The problems of a certain science may only exist scattered among the proper chapters of other sciences. Some excellent scholar will then become aware of the subject of that particular discipline (as a subject in its own right) and of (the need of) collecting its problems. He will do that, and a (new) discipline will make its appearance. He will give it its place among the sciences that mankind, with its ability to think, cultivates. This happened with the science of literary criticism (*bayân*).

(7) Something in the main scholarly works may be too long and prolix. One will then try to compose a brief and succinct abridgment, omitting all repetitions. However, one has to be careful not to eliminate anything essential, so that the purpose of the first author will not be vitiated.

These are the purposes that must be borne in mind and not lost sight of in literary composition. All else is unnecessary, a mistake (or deviation) from the road that all intelligent (scholars) think must be followed. For instance, (someone may try) to ascribe the work of an earlier author to himself with the aid of certain tricks, such as changing the wording and the arrangement of the contents. Or, someone may eliminate material essential to a particular discipline, or mention unnecessary material, or replace correct (statements) with wrong ones, or mention useless material. All this shows ignorance and impudence.

Aristotle, when he enumerated the purposes (by which an author must be guided) and had come to the last one, therefore said: 'Everything else is either superfluousness or greed', by which he meant ignorance and insolence.

34 *The great number of scholarly works available is an obstacle on the path to attaining scholarship*

It should be known that among the things that are harmful to the human quest for knowledge and to the attainment of a thorough scholarship are the great number of works available, the large variety in technical terminology (needed for purposes) of instruction, and the numerous methods (used in those works). The student is required to have a ready knowledge of all that. Only then is he considered an accomplished scholar.

Thus, the student must know all the works, or most of them, and observe the methods used in them. His whole lifetime would not suffice to know all the literature that exists in a single discipline, even if he were to devote himself entirely to it. Thus, he must of necessity fall short of attaining scholarship. . . .

All are variations of one and the same subject. The student is required to have a ready knowledge of all of them and to be able to distinguish between them. A whole lifetime could be spent on but one of them. If teachers and students were to restrict themselves to the school problems, (the task) would be much easier and (scholarly) instruction would be simple and easily accessible. However, this is an evil that cannot be cured, because it has become firmly engrained through custom. In a way, it has become something natural, which cannot be moved or transformed. . . .

35 The great number of brief handbooks available on scholarly subjects is detrimental to the process of instruction

Many recent scholars have turned to brief presentations of the methods and contents of the sciences. They want to know (the methods and contents), and they present them systematically in the form of brief programmes for each science. These brief handbooks express all the problems of a given discipline and the evidence for them in a few brief words that are full of meaning. This procedure is detrimental to good style and makes difficulties for the understanding.

Scholars often approach the main scholarly works on the various disciplines, which are very lengthy, intending to interpret and explain (them). They abridge them, in order to make it easier (for students) to acquire expert knowledge of them. This has a corrupting influence upon the process of instruction and is detrimental to the attainment of scholarship. For it confuses the beginner by presenting the final results of a discipline to him before he is prepared for them. This is a bad method of instruction. It also involves a great deal of work for the student. He must study carefully the words of the abridgment, which are complicated to understand because they are crowded with ideas, and try to find out from them what the problems of the given discipline are. Thus, the texts of such brief handbooks are found to be difficult and complicated. A good deal of time must be spent on trying to understand them.

Moreover, after all these (difficulties), the (scholarly) habit that results from receiving instruction from brief handbooks, even when it is at its best and is not accompanied by any flaw, is inferior to the habits resulting from the study of more extensive and lengthy works. The latter contain a great amount of repetition and lengthiness, but both are useful for the acquisition of a perfect habit. When there is little repetition, an inferior habit is the result. This is the case with the abridgments. The intention was to make it easy for students to acquire expert knowledge (of scholarly subjects), but the result is that it has become more difficult for them, because they are prevented from acquiring useful and firmly established habits.

36 *The right attitude in scientific instruction and toward the method of giving such instruction*

It should be known that the teaching of scientific subjects to students is effective only when it proceeds gradually and little by little. At first, (the teacher) presents (the student) with the principal problems within each chapter of a given discipline. He acquaints him with them by commenting on them in a summary fashion. In the course of doing so, he observes the student's intellectual potential and his preparedness for understanding the material that will come his way until the end of the discipline under consideration is reached. In the process, the student acquires the habit of the science he studies. However, that habit will be an approximate and weak one. The most it can do is to enable the student to understand the discipline and to know its problems.

The teacher, then, leads the student back over the discipline a second time. He gives him instruction in it on a higher level. He no longer gives a summary but full commentaries and explanations. He mentions to him the existing differences of opinion and the form these differences take all the way through to the end of the discipline under consideration. Thus, the student's (scholarly) habit is improved. Then, the teacher leads the student back again, now that he is solidly grounded. He leaves nothing that is complicated, vague, or obscure, unexplained. He bares all the secrets of the discipline to him. As a result, the student, when he finishes with the discipline, has acquired the habit of it.

This is the effective method of instruction. As one can see, it requires a threefold repetition. Some students can get through it with less than that, depending on their natural dispositions and qualifications.

We have observed that many teachers of the time in which we are living are ignorant of this effective method of instruction. They begin their instruction by confronting the student with obscure scientific problems. They require him to concentrate on solving them. They think that that is experienced and correct teaching, and they make it the task of the student to comprehend and know such things. In actual fact, they confuse him by exposing him to the final results of a discipline at the beginning (of his studies) and before he is prepared to understand them. Preparedness for and receptivity to scientific knowledge and understanding grow gradually. At the beginning, the student is completely unable to understand any but a very few (points). (His understanding is) only approximate and general and (can be achieved only) with the help of pictures (*muthul*) derived from sensual perception. His preparedness, then, keeps growing gradually and little by little when he faces the problems of the discipline under consideration and has them repeated to him and advances from approximate understanding of them to a complete, higher knowledge. Thus the habit of preparedness and, eventually, that of attainment materialize in the student, until he has a comprehensive knowledge of the problems of the discipline he studies. But if a student is exposed to the final results at the beginning, while he is still unable to understand and comprehend anything and is still far from being prepared to understand, his mind is not acute enough to grasp them. He gets the impression that scholarship is difficult and becomes loath to occupy himself with it. He constantly dodges and avoids it. That is the result of poor instruction, and nothing else.

The teacher should not ask more from a student than that he understand the book he is engaged in studying, in accordance with his class (age group) and his receptivity to instruction, whether he is at the start or at the end of his studies. The teacher should not bring in problems other than those found in that particular book, until the student knows the whole (book) from beginning to end, is acquainted with its purpose, and has gained a habit from it, which he then can apply to other (books). When the student has acquired the scholarly habit in one discipline, he is prepared for learning all the others. He also has become interested in looking for more and in advancing to higher (learning). Thus, he eventually acquires a complete mastery of scholarship. But if one confuses a student, he will be unable to understand. He becomes indolent and stops thinking. He despairs of becoming a scholar and avoids scholarship and instruction.

It is also necessary (for the teacher) to avoid prolonging the period of instruction in a single discipline or book, by breaks in the sessions and long intervals between them. This causes (the student) to forget and disrupts the nexus between the different problems (of the discipline being studied). The result of such interruptions is that attainment of the (scholarly) habit becomes difficult. If the first and last things of a discipline are present in the mind and prevent the effects of forgetfulness, the (scholarly) habit is more easily acquired, more firmly established, and closer to becoming a (true) colouring.

or habits are acquired by continuous and repeated activity. When

417

one forgets to act, one forgets the habit that results from that particular action.

A good and necessary method and approach in instruction is not to expose the student to two disciplines at the same time. Otherwise, he will rarely master one of them, since he has to divide his attention and is diverted from each of them by his attempt to understand the other. Thus, he will consider both of them obscure and difficult, and be unsuccessful in both. But if his mind is free to study the subject that he is out (to study) and can restrict himself to it, that (fact) often makes it simpler for him to learn (the subject in question).

You, student, should realize that I am here giving you useful (hints) for your study. If you accept them and follow them assiduously, you will find a great and noble treasure. As an introduction that will help you to understand them, I shall tell you the following:

Man's ability to think is a special natural gift that God created exactly as He created all His other creations. It is an action and motion in the soul by means of a power in the middle cavity of the brain. At times, (thinking) means the beginning of orderly and well-arranged human actions. At other times, it means the beginning of the knowledge of something that had not been available (before). The (ability to think) is directed toward some objective whose two extremes it has perceived, and (now) it desires to affirm or deny it. In almost no time, it recognizes the middle term which combines the two (extremes), if (the objective) is uniform. Or, it goes on to obtain another middle term, if (the objective) is manifold. It thus finds its objective. It is in this way that the ability to think, by which man is distinguished from all the other animals, works.

Now, the craft of logic is (knowledge of the) way in which the natural ability to think and speculate operates. Logic describes it, so that correct operation can be distinguished from erroneous. To be right, though, is in the essence of the ability to think. However, in very rare cases, it is affected by error. This comes from perceiving the two extremes in forms other than are properly theirs, as the result of confusion in the order and arrangement of the propositions from which the conclusion is drawn. Logic helps to avoid such traps. Thus, it is a technical procedure which parallels man's natural ability to think and conforms to the way in which it functions. Since it is a technical procedure, it can be dispensed with in most cases. Therefore, one finds that many of the world's most excellent thinkers have achieved scholarly results without employing the craft of logic, especially when their intention was sincere and they entrusted themselves to the mercy of God, which is the greatest help. They proceeded with the aid of the natural ability to think at its best, and this, as it was created by God, permitted them by its nature to find the middle term and knowledge of their objective.

Besides the technical procedure called logic, the (process of) study involves another introductory (discipline), namely, the knowledge of words and the way in which they indicate ideas in the mind by deriving them from what the forms (of the letters) say, in the case of writing, and from what the tongue—speech—says in the case of spoken utterances. You, the student, must pass through all these veils, in order to reach (the state where you can) think about your objective.

First, there is the way in which writing indicates spoken words. This is the easiest part of it. Then, there is the way in which the spoken words indicate the ideas one is seeking. Further, there are the rules for arranging the ideas in their proper moulds, as they are known from the craft of logic, in order to make deductions. Then, there are those ideas in the mind that are abstract—nets with which one goes hunting for the (desired) objective with the help of one's natural ability to think and entrusting oneself to the mercy and generosity of God.

Not everyone is able to pass through all these stages quickly and to cut through all these veils easily during the (process of) instruction. Disputes often cause the mind to stop at the veils of words. Disturbing quarrels and doubts cause it to fall into the nets of argument, so that the mind is prevented from attaining its objective. Rarely do more than a few, who are guided by God, succeed in extricating themselves from this abyss.

If you are afflicted by such (difficulties) and hampered in your understanding (of the problems) by misgivings or disturbing doubts in your mind, cast them off! Discard the veils of words and the obstacles of doubt! Leave all the technical procedures and take refuge in the realm of the natural ability to think given to you by nature! Let your speculation roam in it and let your mind freely delve in it, according to whatever you desire from it! Set foot in the places where the greatest thinkers before you did! Entrust yourself to God's aid, as in His mercy He aided them and taught them what they did not know! If you do that, God's helpful light will shine upon you and show you your objective. Inspiration will indicate to you the middle term that God made a natural requirement of thinking. At that particular moment, return with (the middle term) to the moulds and forms for the arguments, dip it into them, and give it its due of the technical norm (of logic)! Then, clothe it with the forms of words and bring it forth into the world of spoken utterances, firmly girt and soundly constructed!

Verbal disputes and doubts concerning the distinction between right and wrong logical evidence are all technical and conventional matters. Their numerous aspects are all alike or similar, because of their conventional and technical character. If they stop you, (you will not be able) to distinguish the truth in them, for the truth becomes distinguishable only if it exists by nature. All the doubts and uncertainties will remain. The veils will cover the objective sought and prevent the thinker from attaining it. That has been the case with most recent thinkers, especially with those who formerly spoke a language other than Arabic, which was a mental handicap, or those who were enamoured with logic and partial to it. They believe that logic is a natural means for the perception of the truth. They become confused when doubts and misgivings arise concerning the evidence, and they are scarcely able to free themselves from (such doubts).

As a matter of fact, the natural means for the perception of the truth is, as we have stated, man's natural ability to think, when it is free from all imaginings, and when the thinker entrusts himself to the mercy of God. Logic merely describes the process of thinking and mostly parallels it. Take that into consideration and ask for God's mercy when you have difficulty in understanding problems! Then, the divine light will shine upon you and give you the right inspiration.

37 Study of the auxiliary sciences should not be prolonged, and their problems should not be treated in detail

The sciences customarily known among civilized people are of two kinds. There are the sciences that are wanted *per se*, such as the religious sciences of Qur'ân interpretation, Prophetic traditions, jurisprudence, and speculative theology, and the physical and metaphysical sciences of philosophy. In addition, there are sciences that are instrumental and auxiliary to the sciences mentioned. Among such auxiliary sciences are Arabic philology, arithmetic, and others, which are auxiliary to the religious sciences, and logic which is auxiliary to philosophy and often also to speculative theology and the science of the principles of jurisprudence (when treated) according to the method of recent scholars.

In the case of the sciences that are wanted (*per se*), it does no harm to extend their discussion, to treat their problems in detail, and to present all the evidence and (all the different) views (which exist concerning them). It gives the student of them a firmer habit and clarifies the ideas they contain which one wants to know. But the sciences that are auxiliary to other sciences, such as Arabic philology, logic, and the like, should be studied only in so far as they are aids to the other sciences. Discussion of them should not be prolonged, and the problems should not be treated in detail, as this would lead away from their purpose, and their purpose is (to facilitate understanding of) the sciences to which they are auxiliary, nothing else. Whenever the (auxiliary sciences) cease to be auxiliary to other sciences, they abandon their purpose, and occupation with them becomes an idle pastime.

Moreover, it is (also) difficult to acquire the habit of them, because they are large subjects with many details. Their (difficulty) is often an obstacle to acquiring the sciences wanted *per se*, because it takes so long to get to them. However, they are more important, and life is too short to acquire a knowledge of everything in this (thorough) form. Thus, occupation with the auxiliary sciences constitutes a waste of one's life, occupation with something that is of no concern.

Recent scholars have done this with grammar and logic and even with the principles of jurisprudence. They have prolonged the discussion of these disciplines both by transmitting (more material) and (by adding) it through deductive reasoning. They have increased the number of details and problems, causing them to be no longer auxiliary sciences, but disciplines that are wanted *per se*. In consequence, (the auxiliary sciences) often deal with views and problems for which there is no need in the disciplines that are wanted *per se* (and are the sole *raison d'être* of the auxiliary sciences). Thus, they are a sort of idle pastime and also do outright harm to students, because the sciences that are wanted (*per se*) are more important for them than the auxiliary and instrumental sciences. If they spend all their lives on the auxiliary sciences, when will they get around to those which are wanted (*per se*)? Therefore, teachers of the auxiliary sciences ought not to delve too deeply in them and increase the number of their problems. They must advise the student concerning their purpose and have him stop there. Those who have the mind to go more deeply into them and consider themselves capable and able to do so, may choose (such a course) for themselves. Everyone is successful at the things for which he was created.

38 The instruction of children and the different methods employed in the Muslim cities

Instructing children in the Qur'ân is a symbol of Islam. Muslims have, and practise, such instruction in all their cities, because it imbues the heart with a firm belief in Islam and its articles of faith, which are derived from the verses of the Qur'ân and certain Prophetic traditions. The Qur'ân has become the basis of instruction, the foundation for all habits that may be acquired later on. The reason for this is that the things one is taught in one's youth take root more deeply (than anything else). They are the basis of all later (knowledge). The first impression the heart receives is, in a way, the foundation of (all scholarly) habits. The character of the foundation determines the condition of the building. The methods of instructing children in the Qur'ân differ according to differences of opinion as to the habits that are to result from that instruction.

The Maghribî method is to restrict the education of children to instruction in the Qur'ân and to practise, during the course (of instruction), in Qur'ân orthography and its problems and the differences among Qur'ân experts on this score. The (Maghribîs) do not bring up any other subjects in their classes, such as traditions, jurisprudence, poetry, or Arabic philology, until the pupil is skilled in (the Qur'ân), or drops out before becoming skilled in it. In the latter case, it means, as a rule, that he will not learn anything. This is the method the urban population in the Maghrib and the native Berber Qur'ân teachers who follow their (urban compatriots), use in educating their children up to the age of manhood. They use it also with old people who study the Qur'ân after part of their life has passed. Consequently, (Maghribîs) know the orthography of the Qur'ân, and know it by heart, better than any other (Muslim group).

The Spanish method is instruction in reading and writing as such. That is what they pay attention to in the instruction (of children). However, since the Qur'ân is the basis and foundation of all that and the source of Islam and all the sciences, they make it the basis of instruction, but they do not restrict the instruction of their children exclusively to the Qur'ân. They also bring in (other subjects), mainly poetry and composition, and they give the children an expert knowledge of Arabic and teach them good handwriting. They do not stress teaching the Qur'ân more than the other subjects. In fact, they are more concerned with teaching handwriting than anything else, until the child reaches manhood. He then has some experience and knowledge of the Arabic language and poetry. He has an excellent knowledge of handwriting, and he would have a thorough acquaintance with scholarship in general, if the tradition of scholarly instruction still existed in Spain, but he does not, because the tradition no longer exists there. Thus, (present-day Spanish children) obtain no further (knowledge) than what their primary instruction provides. It is enough for those whom God guides. It prepares (them for further studies), in the event that a teacher can be found for them.

The people of Ifrîqiyah combine the instruction of children in the Qur'ân, usually, with the teaching of traditions. They also teach basic scientific norms and certain scientific problems. However, they stress giving their children a good knowledge of the Qur'ân and acquainting them with its various recensions and readings more than anything else. Next they stress handwriting. In general, their method of instruction in the Qur'ân is closer to the Spanish method (than to Maghribî or Eastern methods), because their (educational tradition) derives from the Spanish *shaykhs* who crossed over when the Christians conquered Spain, and asked for hospitality in Tunis. From that time on, they were the teachers of (Tunisian) children.

The people of the East, as far as we know, likewise have a mixed curriculum. I do not know what they stress (primarily). We have been told that they are concerned with teaching the Qur'ân and the works and basic norms of (religious) scholarship once (the children) are grown up. They do not combine (instruction in the Qur'ân) with instruction in handwriting. They have (special) rules for teaching it, and there are special teachers for it, just like any other craft which is taught (separately) and not included in the school curriculum for children. The children's slates (on which they practise) exhibit an inferior form of handwriting. Those who want to learn (good) handwriting may do so later on from professional (calligraphers), to the extent of their interest in it and desire.

The fact that the people of Ifrîqiyah and the Maghrib restrict themselves to the Qur'ân makes them altogether incapable of mastering the linguistic habit. For as a rule, no (scholarly) habit can originate from the (study of the) Qur'ân, because no human being can produce anything like it. Thus, human beings are unable to employ or imitate its style, and they also can form no habit in any other respect. Consequently, a person who knows the Qur'ân does not acquire the habit of the Arabic language. It will be his lot to be awkward in expression and to have little fluency in speaking. This situation is not quite so pronounced among the people of Ifrîqiyah as among the Maghribîs, because, as we have stated, the former combine instruction in the Qur'ân with instruction in the terminology of scientific norms. Thus, they get some practice and have some examples to imitate. However, their habit in this respect does not amount to a good style (eloquence), because their knowledge mostly consists of scholarly terminology which falls short of good style.

As for the Spaniards, their varied curriculum with its great amount of instruction in poetry, composition, and Arabic philology gave them, from their early years on, a habit providing for a better acquaintance with the Arabic language. They were less proficient in all the other (religious) sciences, because they were little familiar with study of the Qur'ân and the traditions that are the basis and foundation of the religious sciences. Thus, they were people who knew how to write and who had a literary education that was either excellent or deficient, depending on the secondary education they received after their childhood education.

In his *Riḥlah*, Judge Abû Bakr b. al-'Arabî[1] makes a remarkable statement about instruction, which retains (the best of) the old, and presents (some good) new features. He places instruction in Arabic and poetry ahead of all the other sciences, as in the Spanish method, since, he says, 'Poetry is the archive of the Arabs. Poetry and Arabic philology should be taught first because of the existing corruption of the language. From there, the student should go on to arithmetic and study it assiduously, until he knows its basic norms. He should then go on to the study of the Qur'ân, because with his (previous) preparation, it will be easy for him.' Ibn-al-'Arabî continues: 'How thoughtless are our compatriots in that they teach children the Qur'ân when they are first starting out. They read things they do not understand and work hard at something that is not as important for them as other matters.' He concludes: 'The student should study successively the principles of Islam, the principles of jurisprudence, disputation, and then the Prophetic traditions and the sciences connected with them.' He also forbids teaching two disciplines at the same time, save to the student with a good mind and sufficient energy.

This is Judge Abû Bakr's advice. It is a good method indeed. However, accepted custom is not favourable to it, and custom has greater power over conditions than anything else. Accepted custom gives preference to the teaching of the Qur'ân. The reason is the desire for the blessing and reward (in the other world) and a fear of the things that might affect children in 'the folly of youth' and harm them and keep them from acquiring knowledge. They might miss the chance to learn the Qur'ân. As long as they remain at home, they are amenable to authority. When they have grown up and shaken off the yoke of authority, the tempests of young manhood often cast them upon the shores of wrongdoing. Therefore, while the children are still at home and under the yoke of authority, one seizes the opportunity to teach them the Qur'ân, so that they will not remain without knowledge of it. If one could be certain that a child would continue to study and accept instruction (when he has grown up), the method mentioned by the Judge would be the most suitable one ever devised in East or West.

39 Severity to students does them harm

This comes about as follows. Severe punishment in the course of instruction does harm to the student, especially to little children,

1 Muḥammad b. Abdallah, 469–543 [1076/77–1148].

because it belongs among (the things that make for a) bad habit. Students, slaves, and servants who are brought up with injustice and (tyrannical) force are overcome by it. It makes them feel oppressed and causes them to lose their energy. It makes them lazy and induces them to lie and be insincere. That is, their outward behaviour differs from what they are thinking, because they are afraid that they will have to suffer tyrannical treatment (if they tell the truth). Thus, they are taught deceit and trickery. This becomes their custom and character. They lose the quality that goes with social and political organization and makes people human, namely, (the desire to) protect and defend themselves and their homes, and they become dependent on others. Indeed, their souls become too indolent to (attempt to) acquire the virtues and good character qualities. Thus, they fall short of their potentialities and do not reach the limit of their humanity. As a result, they revert to the stage of 'the lowest of the low'.

That is what happened to every nation that fell under the yoke of tyranny and learned through it the meaning of injustice. One may check this by (observing) any person who is not in control of his own affairs and has no authority on his side to guarantee his (safety). One may look at the Jews and the bad character they have acquired, such that they are described in every region and period as having the quality of *khurj*,[1] which, according to well-known technical terminology, means 'insincerity and trickery'. The reason is what we have said.

Thus, a teacher must not be too severe toward his pupil, nor a father toward his son, in educating them. In the book that Abû Muḥammad b. Abî Zayd wrote on the laws governing teachers and pupils, he said: 'If children must be beaten, their educator must not strike them more than three times.' 'Umar said: 'Those who are not educated (disciplined) by the religious law are not educated by God.' He spoke out of a desire to preserve the souls from the humiliation of disciplinary punishment and in the knowledge that the amount (of disciplinary punishment) that the religious law has stipulated is fully adequate to keep (a person) under control, because the (religious law) knows best what is good for him.

One of the best methods of education was suggested by ar-Rashîd to Khalaf b. Aḥmar, the teacher of his son al-Amîn. Khalaf b. Aḥmar said: 'Ar-Rashîd told me to come and educate his son al-Amîn, and he said to me: "O Aḥmar, the Commander of the

---

[1] This vocalization is indicated in B, C, and D. However, no such word in the meaning required seems to exist in Arabic dictionaries. Is it, perhaps, a dialect variant of Arabic *khurq* 'charlatanry, foolishness', or a Spanish or North-west African dialect expression?

Faithful is entrusting his son to you, the life of his soul and the fruit of his heart. Take firm hold of him and make him obey you. Occupy in relation to him the place that the Commander of the Faithful has given you. Teach him to read the Qur'ân. Instruct him in history. Let him transmit poems and teach him the Sunnah of the Prophet. Give him insight into the proper occasions for speech and how to begin a (speech). Forbid him to laugh, save at times when it is proper. Accustom him to honour his relatives when they come to him, and to give the military leaders places of honour when they come to his salon. Let no hour pass in which you do not seize the opportunity to teach him something useful. But do so without vexing him, which would kill his mind. Do not always be too lenient with him, or he will get to like leisure and become used to it. As much as possible, correct him kindly and gently. If he does not want it that way, you must then use severity and harshness." '

40 *A scholar's education is greatly improved by travelling in quest of knowledge and meeting the authoritative teachers of his time*

The reason for this is that human beings obtain their knowledge and character qualities and all their opinions and virtues either through study, instruction, and lectures, or through imitation of a teacher and personal contact with him. The only difference here is that habits acquired through personal contact with a teacher are more strongly and firmly rooted. Thus, the greater the number of authoritative teachers, the more deeply rooted is the habit one acquires.

Furthermore, the technical terminologies used in scientific instruction are confusing to the student. Many students even suppose them to be part of a given science. The only way to deliver them from that (wrong notion) is by personal contact with teachers, for different teachers employ different terminologies. Thus, meeting scholars and having many authoritative teachers enables the student to notice the difference in the terminologies used by different teachers and to distinguish among them. He will thus be able to recognize the science itself behind the (technical terminologies it uses). He will realize that they are but means and methods for imparting knowledge. His powers will work toward acquiring strongly and firmly rooted habits. He will improve the knowledge he has and be able to distinguish it from other knowledge. In addition, his habits will be strengthened through his intensive personal contact with teachers, when they are many and of various types. This is for those for whom God facilitated the ways of scholarship and right guidance. Thus, travelling in quest of knowledge is absolutely necessary for the acquisition of useful knowledge and perfection through meeting authoritative teachers and having contact with (scholarly) personalities.

41 Scholars are, of all people, those least familiar with the ways of politics

The reason for this is that scholars are used to mental speculation and to a searching study of ideas which they abstract from the *sensibilia* and conceive in their minds as general universals, so that they may be applicable to some matter in general but not to any particular matter, individual, race, nation, or group of people. Scholars, then, make such universal ideas conform (in their minds) to facts of the outside world. They also compare things with others that are similar to or like them, with the help of analogical reasoning as used in jurisprudence, which is something familiar to them. All their conclusions and views continue to be something in the mind. They come to conform to the facts of the outside world only after research and speculation has come to an end, or they may never come to conform to them. The facts of the outside world are merely special cases of the (ideas) in the mind. For instance, the religious laws are special cases derived from the well-known (texts) of the Qur'ân and the Sunnah. In their case, one expects the facts of the outside world to conform to them, in contrast with the intellectual sciences, where, to (prove) the soundness of views, one expects those views to conform to the facts of the outside world.

Thus, in all their intellectual activity, scholars are accustomed to dealing with matters of the mind and with thoughts. They do not know anything else. Politicians, on the other hand, must pay attention to the facts of the outside world and the conditions attaching to and depending on (politics). These facts and conditions are obscure. They may contain some (element) making it impossible to refer them to something like and similar, or contradicting the universal (idea) to which one would like them to conform. The conditions existing in civilization cannot (always) be compared with each other. They may be alike in one respect, but they may differ in other respects.

Scholars are accustomed to generalizations and analogical conclusions. When they look at politics, they press (their observations) into the mould of their views and their way of making deductions. Thus, they commit many errors, or they cannot be trusted (not to commit errors). The intelligent and alert (segment) of civilized people falls into the same category as (scholars). Their penetrating minds drive them toward a searching occupation with ideas, analogy, and comparison, as is the case with jurists. Thus, they too commit errors.

The average person of a healthy disposition and a mediocre intelligence has not got the mind for (such speculation) and does not think of it. Therefore, he restricts himself to considering every matter as it is, and to judging every kind of situation and every type of individual by its particular (circumstances). His judgment is not infected with analogy and generalization. Most of his speculation stops at matters perceivable by the senses, and he does not go beyond them in his mind.

Such a man, therefore, can be trusted when he reflects upon his political activities. He has the right outlook in dealing with his fellow men. Thus, he makes a good living and suffers no damage or harm in the (process) because he has the right outlook.

This (situation) makes one realize that logic cannot be trusted to prevent the commission of errors, because it is too abstract and remote from the *sensibilia*. Logic considers the secondary *intelligibilia*. It is possible that material things contain something that does not admit of logical conclusions and contradicts them, when one looks for unequivocal conformity (between them and the facts of the outside world). It is different with speculation about the primary *intelligibilia*, which are less abstract. They are matters of the imagination and pictures of the *sensibilia*. They retain (certain features of the *sensibilia*) and permit verification of the conformity of (the *sensibilia* to the primary *intelligibilia*).

42 Most of the scholars in Islam have been non-Arabs

It is a remarkable fact that, with few exceptions, most Muslim scholars both in the religious and in the intellectual sciences have been non-Arabs. When a scholar is of Arab origin, he is non-Arab in language and upbringing and has non-Arab teachers. This is so in spite of the fact that Islam is an Arab religion, and its founder was an Arab.

The reason for it is that at the beginning Islam had no sciences or crafts, because of the simple conditions and the desert attitude. The religious laws, which are the commands and prohibitions of God, were in the breasts of the authorities. They knew their sources, the Qur'ân and the Sunnah, from information they had received directly from Muḥammad himself and from the men around him. The people at that time were Arabs. They did not know anything about scientific instruction or the writing of books and systematic works. There was no incentive or need for that. This was the situation during the time of the men around Muḥammad and the men of the second generation. The persons who were concerned with knowing and transmitting the (religious laws) were called 'Qur'ân readers', that is, people who were able to read the Qur'ân and were not illiterate. Illiteracy was general at that time among the men around Muḥammad, since they were Bedouins.

By the time of the reign of ar-Rashîd, (oral) tradition had become far removed (from its starting point). It was thus necessary to write commentaries on the Qur'ân and to fix the traditions in writing, because it was feared that they might be lost. It was also necessary to know the chains of transmitters and to assess their reliability, in order to be able to distinguish sound chains of transmitters from inferior ones. Then, more and more laws concerning actual cases were derived from the Qur'ân and the Sunnah. Moreover, the Arabic language became corrupt, and it was necessary to lay down grammatical rules.

All the religious sciences had thus become habits connected with producing and deriving (laws and norms) and with comparison and analogical reasoning. Other, auxiliary sciences became necessary, such as knowledge of the rules of the Arabic language, (knowledge of) the rules that govern the derivation (of laws) and analogical reasoning, and defence of the articles of faith by means of arguments, because a great number of innovations and heresies (had come into existence). All these things developed into sciences with their own habits, requiring instruction (for their acquisition). Thus, they came to fall under the category of crafts.

We have mentioned before that the crafts are cultivated by sedentary people and that of all peoples the Bedouins are least familiar with the crafts. Thus, the sciences came to belong to sedentary culture, and the Arabs were not familiar with them or with their cultivation. Now, the only sedentary people at that time were non-Arabs and, what amounts to the same thing, the clients and sedentary people who followed the non-Arabs at that time in all matters of sedentary culture, including the crafts and professions. They were most versed in those things, because sedentary culture had been firmly rooted among them from the time of the Persian Empire.

Thus, the founders of grammar were Sîbawayh and, after him, al-Fârisî and az-Zajjâj.[1] All of them were of non-Arab (Persian) descent. They were brought up in the Arabic language and acquired the knowledge of it through their upbringing and through contact with Arabs. They invented the rules of (grammar) and made it into a discipline (in its own right) for later (generations to use).

Most of the *ḥadîth* scholars who preserved traditions for the Muslims also were Persians, or Persian in language and upbringing, because the discipline was widely cultivated in the 'Irâq and the

[1] Sîbawayh died around 800, az-Zajjâj around 923, and al-Fârisî in 987.

regions beyond. Furthermore, all the scholars who worked in the science of the principles of jurisprudence were Persians. The same applies to speculative theologians and to most Qur'ân commentators. Only the Persians engaged in the task of preserving knowledge and writing systematic scholarly works. Thus, the truth of the following statement by the Prophet becomes apparent: 'If scholarship hung suspended in the highest parts of heaven, the Persians would attain it.'

The Arabs who came into contact with that flourishing sedentary culture and exchanged their Bedouin attitude for it, were diverted from occupying themselves with scholarship and study by their leading position in the 'Abbâsid dynasty and the tasks that confronted them in government. They were the men of the dynasty, at once its protectors and the executors of its policy. In addition, at that time, they considered it a lowly thing to be a scholar, because scholarship is a craft, and political leaders are always contemptuous of the crafts and professions and everything that leads to them. Thus, they left such things to non-Arabs and persons of mixed Arab and non-Arab parentage. The latter cultivated them, and the Arabs always considered it their right to cultivate them, as they were their custom and their sciences, and never felt complete contempt for the men learned in them. The final result, however, was that when the Arabs lost power and the non-Arabs took over, the religious sciences had no place with the men in power, because the latter had no relations with (scholarship). Scholars were viewed with contempt, because the men in power saw that scholars had no contact with them and were occupying themselves with things that were of no interest to the men in power in governmental and political matters. This is why all scholars in the religious sciences, or most of them, are non-Arabs.

The intellectual sciences, as well, made their appearance in Islam only after scholars and authors had become a distinct group of people and all scholarship had become a craft. (The intellectual sciences) were then the special preserve of non-Arabs, left alone by the Arabs, who did not cultivate them.

This situation continued in the cities as long as the Persians and the Persian countries, the 'Irâq, Khurâsân, and Transoxania, retained their sedentary culture. But when those cities fell into ruin, sedentary culture, which God has devised for the attainment of sciences and crafts, disappeared from them. Along with it, scholarship altogether disappeared from among the Persians, who were now engulfed by the desert attitude. Scholarship was restricted to cities with an abundant sedentary culture. Today, no city has a more abundant sedentary culture than Cairo. It is the mother of the world, the great centre of Islam, and the mainspring of the sciences and the crafts.

43 A person whose first language was not Arabic finds it harder than the native speaker of Arabic to acquire the sciences

This is explained by the fact that all scientific research deals with ideas of the mind and the imagination. This applies to the religious sciences in which research is mostly concerned with the meaning of words. These are matters of the imagination. The same fact also applies to the intellectual sciences, which are matters of the mind.

Linguistic expression is merely the interpreter of ideas that are in the mind. One person conveys them to another in oral discussion, instruction, and constant scientific research. Words and expressions are media and veils between the ideas. They constitute the bonds between them and give them their final imprint. The student of ideas must extract them from the words that express them. For this he needs a knowledge of their linguistic meaning and a good (linguistic) habit. Otherwise, it is difficult for him to get (the ideas), apart from the usual difficulties inherent in mental investigation of them. When he has a firmly rooted habit as far as semantics is concerned, so that the (correct) ideas present themselves to his mind when he hears certain words used, spontaneously and naturally, the veil between the ideas and the understanding is either totally removed, or becomes less heavy, and the only task that remains is to investigate the problems inherent in the ideas.

All this applies to instruction by personal contact in the form of oral address and explanation. But when the student has to rely upon the study of books and written material and must understand scientific problems from the forms of written letters in books, he is confronted with another veil, (namely, the veil) that separates handwriting and the form of letters found in writing from the spoken words found in the imagination. The written letters have their own way of indicating the spoken words. As long as that way is not known, it is impossible to know what they express. If it is known imperfectly, (the meaning) expressed by the letters is known imperfectly. Thus, the student is confronted with another veil standing between him and his objective of attaining scientific habits, one that is more difficult to cope with than the first one. Now, if his habit, as far as the meaning of words and writing goes, is firmly established, the veils between him and the ideas are lifted. He has merely to occupy himself with understanding the problems inherent in the (ideas). The same relationship of ideas with words and writing exists in every

431

language. The habits of students who learn these things while they are young, are more firmly established (than those of other people).

Furthermore, the Muslim realm was far-flung and included many nations. The sciences of the ancients were wiped out through the prophecy of (Islam) and its holy book. Illiteracy was the proper thing and symbol of Islam. Islam then gained royal authority and power. (Foreign) nations served the (Muslims) with their sedentary culture and refinement. The religious sciences, which had been traditional, were turned by the Muslims into crafts. Thus, (scholarly) habits originated among them. Many systematic works and books were written. The Muslims desired to learn the sciences of the foreign nations. They made them their own through translations. They pressed them into the mould of their own views. They took them over into their own language from the non-Arab languages and surpassed the achievements of the non-Arabs in them. The manuscripts in the non-Arabic language were forgotten, abandoned, and scattered. All the sciences came to exist in Arabic. The systematic works on them were written in Arabic writing. Thus, students of the sciences needed a knowledge of the meaning of Arabic words and Arabic writing. They could dispense with all other languages, because they had been wiped out and there was no longer any interest in them.

Language is a habit of the tongue. Likewise, handwriting is a craft, the habit of which is located in the hand. The tongue which had at first the habit of speaking a language other than Arabic, becomes deficient in (its mastery of) Arabic, because the person whose habit has advanced to a certain point in a particular craft is rarely able to master another one. This is obvious. If a person is deficient in his mastery of Arabic, in the meaning of its words and its writing, it is difficult for him to derive the ideas from Arabic words and (Arabic writing). Only if the early habit of speaking a non-Arab language is not yet firmly established in a person when he makes the transition from it to Arabic, as is the case with small non-Arab children who grow up with Arabs before their (habit) of speaking a non-Arab language is firmly established, only then does the Arabic language come to be like a first native language, and his ability to derive the ideas from the words of the Arabic language is not deficient. The same applies to persons who learned non-Arabic writing before Arabic writing.

This is why we find that most non-Arab scholars in their research and classes do not copy comments from books but read them aloud. In this way they are less disturbed by the veils (between words and ideas), so that they can get more easily at the ideas. When a person possesses the perfect habit as far as verbal and written expression is concerned, he does not have to (read aloud). For him, it has become like a firmly engrained natural disposition to derive an understanding of words from writing and of ideas from words. The veils between him and the ideas are lifted.

Intensive study and constant practice of the language and of writing may lead a person to a firmly rooted habit, as we find in most non-Arab scholars. However, this occurs rarely. When one compares such a person with an Arabic scholar of equal merit, the latter is the more efficient, and his habit the stronger. The non-Arab has trouble because his early use of a non-Arab language necessarily makes him inferior.

This is not in contradiction with the aforementioned fact that most Muslim scholars are non-Arabs. In that connection, 'non-Arab' meant non-Arab by descent. Such non-Arabs had a lengthy sedentary culture. Being non-Arab in language is something quite different, and this is what is meant here.

It is also not in contradiction with the fact that the Greeks were highly accomplished scholars. They learned their sciences in their own native language and in their own writing, such as was customarily used among them. The non-Arab Muslim who studies to become a scholar learns his subject in a language other than his native one and from a writing other than the one whose habit he has mastered. This, then, becomes an impediment to him. This applies quite generally to all kinds of speakers of non-Arab languages, such as the Persians, the Turks, the Berbers, the European Christians, and all others whose language is not Arabic.

44 The sciences concerned with the Arabic language

The pillars of the Arabic language are four: lexicography, grammar, syntax and style (bayân), and literature. Knowledge of them all is necessary for religious scholars, since the source of all religious laws is the Qur'ân and the Sunnah, which are in Arabic. Their transmitters, the men around Muḥammad and the men of the second generation, were Arabs. Their difficulties are to be explained from the language they used. Thus, those who want to be religious scholars must know the sciences connected with the Arabic language.

These sciences differ in emphasis (as to their importance) according to the different degrees (of usefulness) they possess for conveying the intended meaning of speech. The first and most important of them is grammar, since it gives a clear indication of the basic principles (used in expressing) the various intended meanings. Thus, one can distinguish between subject and object, as well as between the subject of a nominal sentence and its predicate.

Lexicography would deserve to be first, were not most of its data constant (and restricted) to their (conventional) meanings, incapable of changing, in contrast to the case endings (in grammar) which indicate dependence, the (person or thing) that is dependent, and the person or thing on which (something else) depends. They always change completely and leave no trace. Thus, grammar is more important than lexicography, since ignorance of grammar is very harmful to mutual understanding. This is not the case with lexicography.

Grammar

It should be known that language, as the term is customarily used, is the expression by a speaker of his intention. Such expression is an act of the tongue which originates in an intention to convey the meaning of speech. Therefore, (language) must become an established habit in the part of the body that produces it, namely, the tongue.

In every nation, the formation of language takes place according to their own terminology. The linguistic habit that the Arabs obtained in that way is the best there is. It is the one most clearly expressing the intended meaning, since many ideas are indicated in it by something other than words. There are, for instance, vowels to distinguish the subject from object and *i*-case—that is, the genitive —and there are letters to transform actions (verbs)—that is, motions —into essences, without need of other words. These (features) are found in no other language but Arabic. All other languages need special words to indicate a particular idea or situation. Therefore, we find non-Arabs lengthier in their speech than we would consider necessary in Arabic.

When Islam came, the Arabs left the Ḥijâz to seek the royal authority that was in the hands of (foreign) nations and dynasties. They came into contact with non-Arabs. As a result, their linguistic habit changed under the influence of the solecisms they heard non-Arab speakers of Arabic make, and it is hearing that begets the linguistic habit. Thus, the (Arab linguistic habit began to) incline toward adopting forms of speech at variance with it, because the Arabs became used to hearing them spoken, and their linguistic habit became corrupted.

Cultured people feared that the Arab linguistic habit would become entirely corrupted and that, if the (process) went on for a long time, the Qur'ân and the traditions would no longer be understood. Therefore, they derived certain norms for the Arab linguistic habit from their way of speaking. These norms are of general applicability, like universals and basic principles. They checked all the other parts of speech with them and combined like with like. . . .

Later on, scholars wrote books on grammar. Among the pioneers were al-Khalîl b. Aḥmad al-Farâhîdî and Sîbawayh. There was much grammatical discussion. Divergent opinions originated among the grammarians of al-Kûfah and al-Baṣrah, the two old cities of the Arabs. They used an increasing number of proofs and arguments. The methods of grammatical instruction also became different. Then recent scholars came, with their method of being brief. They cut short a good deal of the long discussion, though they included everything that had been transmitted. They restricted themselves to elementary rules for beginners.

Grammar has come to the point of being allowed to disappear, along with the decrease in the other sciences and crafts which we have noted and which is the result of a decrease in civilization. . . .

The science of lexicography

This science is concerned with explaining the (conventional) meanings of the (words of the) language. This comes about as follows. The habit of the Arabic language became corrupted. Rules for protecting the (vowel endings) were developed. However, the (process of) corruption continued on account of the close contact (of the Muslims) with non-Arabs. Eventually, it affected the conventional meanings of words. Many Arabic words were no longer used in their proper meaning. This was the result of indulgence shown to the incorrect language used by non-Arab speakers of Arabic in their terminologies, in contradiction to the pure Arabic language. It was, therefore, necessary to protect the conventional meanings of the words of the language with the help of writing and systematic works, because it was to be feared that they might be wiped out and that ignorance of the Qur'ân and the traditions would result.

Many leading philologists set out eagerly on this task and dictated systematic works on the subject. The champion in this respect was al-Khalîl b. Aḥmad al-Farâhîdî, with his *Kitâb al-'Ayn* on lexicography. In it, he dealt with all (possible) combinations of the letters of the alphabet, that is, with words of two, three, four, and five consonants. Five-consonant words are the longest letter combinations found in Arabic. . . .

He did not, however, arrange the chapters of the book according to the customary sequence of the letters of the alphabet. . . .

Abû Bakr az-Zubaydî, the teacher of Hishâm al-Mu'ayyad in Spain in the fourth [tenth] century, abridged the *Kitâb al-'Ayn* but preserved its complete character. He omitted all the words that are not used. Among eastern scholars, al-Jawharî composed the *Kitâb as-Ṣiḥāḥ*, which was the first to follow the ordinary alphabetical sequence. . . .

The science of syntax and style and literary criticism

This is a science which originated in Islam after Arabic philology and lexicography. It belongs among the philological sciences, because it is concerned with words and the ideas they convey and are intended to indicate. This is as follows:

The thing that the speaker intends to convey to the listener through speech may be a perception regarding individual words which are dependent and on which (something else) depends and from which one leads to the other. These (concepts) are indicated by individual nouns, verbs, and particles. Or, (what the speaker intends to convey) may be the distinction between the things that are dependent and those that depend on them and (the distinction between) tenses. These (concepts) are indicated by the change of vowel endings and the forms of the words. All this belongs to grammar.

Among the things that are part of the facts and need to be indicated, there still remain the conditions of speakers and agents and the requirements of the situation under which the action takes place. This needs to be indicated, because it completes (the information) to be conveyed. If the speaker is able to bring out these (facts), his speech conveys everything that it can possibly convey. If his speech does not have anything of that, it is not real Arabic speech. The Arabic language is vast. The Arabs have a particular expression for each situation, in addition to a perfect use of vowel endings and clarity.

It is known that 'Zayd came to me' does not mean the same as 'There came to me Zayd.' Something mentioned in the first place (such as 'Zayd' in the first example) has greater importance in the mind of the speaker. The person who says: 'There came to me Zayd', indicates that he is more concerned with the coming than with the person who comes. On the other hand, the person who says: 'Zayd came to me', indicates that he is more concerned with the person than with his coming, which (grammatically) depends on (the person who comes). . . .

The same applies to a statement such as: 'There came to me *the* man', which is then replaced by the statement: 'There came to me *a* man.' The use of the form without the article may be intended as an honour (for the man in question) and as an indication that he is a man who has no equal. . . .

Then, an expression may be used other than in its literal meaning. It may be intended to indicate some implication of it. This may apply to an individual word. For instance, in the statement: 'Zayd

436

is a lion', no actual lion, but the bravery implicit in lions, is meant and referred to Zayd. This is called metaphorical usage.

The discipline called syntax and style (*bayân*) expresses the meaning that the forms and conditions of speech have in various situations. It has been divided into three subdivisions.

The first subdivision has as its subject the investigation of forms and conditions of speech, in order to achieve conformity with all the requirements of a given situation. This is called 'the science of rhetoric' (*balâghah*).

The second subdivision has as its subject the investigation of what a word implies or is implied by it—that is, metaphor and metonymy. This is called 'the science of style'.

(Scholars) have added a third subdivision, the study of the artistic embellishment of speech. Such embellishment may be achieved through the ornamental use of rhymed prose, which divides speech into sections; or through the use of paronomasia, which establishes a similarity among the words used; or through the use of internal rhyme, which cuts down the units of rhythmic speech (into smaller units); or through the use of allusion to the intended meaning by suggesting an even more cryptic idea which is expressed by the same words; or through the use of antithesis; and similar things. They called this 'the science of rhetorical figures' (*'ilm al-badî'*).

Recent scholars have used the name of the second subdivision, syntax and style, for all three subdivisions, because the ancient scholars had discussed it first. . . .

The fruit of this discipline is understanding of the inimitability of the Qur'ân. This consists in the fact that the (language of the Qur'ân) indicates all the requirements of the situations (referred to), whether they are stated or understood. This is the highest stage of speech. In addition, (the Qur'ân) is perfect in choice of words and excellence of arrangement and combination. This is its inimitability, a quality that surpasses comprehension.

This discipline is needed most by Qur'ân commentators. Most ancient commentators disregarded it, until Jâr-Allâh az-Zamakhsharî appeared. When he wrote his Qur'ân commentary, he investigated each verse of the Qur'ân according to the rules of this discipline. . . .

The science of literature

This science has no object the accidents of which may be studied and thus be affirmed or denied. Philologists consider its purpose identical with its fruit, which is (the acquisition of) a good ability to handle prose and poetry according to the methods and ways of the Arabs. Therefore, they collect and memorize (documents) of Arabic speech that are likely to aid in acquiring the (proper linguistic) habit. Such documents include fine poetry, rhymed prose of an even quality, and certain problems of lexicography and grammar, from which the student is, as a rule, able to derive inductively most of the rules of Arabic.

(Philologists) who wanted to define this discipline said: 'Literature is expert knowledge of the poetry and history of the Arabs as well as the possession of some knowledge regarding every science.' They meant knowledge of the linguistic sciences and the religious sciences, but only the contents of the Qur'ân and the traditions. No other science has anything to do with Arab speech, save inasmuch as recent scholars who have occupied themselves with the craft of rhetorical figures have come to use allusion by means of (references to terms of) scientific terminologies, in their poetry and their straight prose. Therefore, littérateurs need to know scientific terminologies, in order to be able to understand such allusions.

At the beginning of (Islam) singing (music) belonged to this discipline. Singing depends on poetry, because it is the setting of poetry to music. Secretaries and outstanding persons in the 'Abbâsid dynasty occupied themselves with it, because they were desirous of becoming acquainted with the methods and (literary) disciplines of the Arabs. Its cultivation was no blemish on probity or manliness. The early Ḥijâzî Muslims in Medina and elsewhere, who are models for everybody else to follow, cultivated it. Such a great (scholar) as Judge Abû l-Faraj al-Iṣfahânî[1] wrote a book on songs, the *Kitâb al-Aghânî*. In it, he dealt with the whole of the history, poetry, genealogy, battle days, and ruling dynasties of the Arabs. The work was based on one hundred songs which the singers had selected for ar-Rashîd. His work is the most complete and comprehensive one there is. Indeed, it constitutes an archive of the Arabs. It is a collection of the *disjecta membra* of all the good things in Arab poetry, history, song, and all their other conditions. There exists no book comparable to it, as far as we know. It is the ultimate goal to which a littérateur can aspire and where he must stop—as though he could ever get so far!

Let us now return to the verification of our remarks about the linguistic sciences in general terms.

45 Language is a technical habit

All languages are habits similar to crafts. They are habits in the tongue and serve the purpose of expressing ideas. The good or inadequate (character of such expression) depends on the perfection or deficiency of the habit. This does not apply to individual words

[1] 'Alî b. al-Ḥusayn, 284–356 [897/98–967].

but to word combinations. A speaker who possesses a perfect (linguistic) habit and is thus able to combine individual words so as to express the ideas he wants to express, and who is able to observe the form of composition that makes his speech conform to the requirements of the situation, is as well qualified as is possible to convey to the listener what he wants to convey. This is what is meant by eloquence.

Habits result only from repeated action. An action is done once. With repetition it becomes a condition, which is an attribute that is not firmly established. After more repetition it becomes a habit, that is, a firmly established attribute.

As long as the habit of the Arabic language existed among the Arabs, an Arab speaker always heard the people of his generation speak Arabic. He hears their ways of address and how they express what they want to express. He is like a child hearing individual words employed in their proper meanings. He learns them first. Afterwards, he hears word combinations and learns them likewise. He hears something new each moment from every speaker, and his own practice is constantly repeated, until (use of proper speech) becomes a habit and a firmly established attribute. Thus, the child becomes like one of (the Arabs). In this way, Arab languages and dialects have passed from generation to generation, and both non-Arabs and children have learned them.

The (linguistic) habit of the original Arabs became corrupt when they came into contact with non-Arabs. . . .

50 The interpretation and real meaning of the word 'taste' according to the technical terminology of literary critics. An explanation of why Arabicized non-Arabs as a rule do not have it

The word 'taste' is in current use among those who are concerned with the various branches of literary criticism. It means the tongue's possession of the habit of eloquence. Eloquence is the conformity of speech to the meaning intended, in every aspect, (and this is achieved) by means of certain qualities that give this (conformity) to the word combinations. An eloquent speaker of the Arabic language chooses the form (of expression) that affords such conformity according to the methods and ways of Arab address. In this respect he hardly ever swerves from the way of Arab eloquence.

Habits that are firmly established and rooted in their proper places appear to be natural and innate in those places. Therefore, many ignorant people who are not acquainted with the importance of habits, think that the correct use of vowel endings and the proper eloquence of Arabs in their language are natural things. They say

439

that 'the Arabs speak (correct Arabic) by nature'. This is not so. Correct Arabic is a linguistic habit of (proper) speech arrangement that has become firmly established and rooted (in speakers of Arabic), so that, superficially, it appears to be something natural and innate. However, as mentioned before, this habit results from the constant practice of Arabic speech and from repeated listening to it and from understanding the peculiar qualities of its word combinations. It is not obtained through knowledge of the scientific rules evolved by literary critics. Those rules merely afford a knowledge of the Arabic language. They do not give a person possession of the actual habit in its proper place.

If this is established, (we may say that) the tongue's habit of eloquence guides an eloquent person toward the various aspects of (word) arrangement and toward use of the correct word combinations corresponding to the word combinations and arrangement used by Arabs when they speak Arabic. When a person who possesses the (Arabic linguistic) habit attempts to deviate from the specific ways and the word combinations peculiar to Arabic speech, he is not able to do so. His tongue will not go along with him, because it is not used to (improper speech), and its firmly rooted habit will not let it use it. . . .

This habit, if firmly rooted and established, is metaphorically called 'taste', a technical term of literary criticism. 'Taste' is the sensation caused by food. But, since the linguistic habit is located in the tongue, which is the seat of speech as it is the seat of the sensation caused by food, the name of 'taste' is metaphorically used for it. Furthermore, it is something intuitively observed by the tongue, just as food is something sensually perceived by it. Therefore, it is called 'taste'.

If this is clear, it will make one realize that non-Arabs, such as Persians, Byzantines, and Turks in the East, and Berbers in the West, who are strangers to the Arabic language and adopt it and are forced to speak it as the result of contact with the Arabs, do not possess such taste. They have too small a share in the linguistic habit the significance of which we have established. They formerly had another linguistic habit—their own language—and part of their lives had gone by (before they got to know Arabic). Now, the most they can do is to occupy themselves with the individual words and word combinations in current use in the conversation of the (Muslim) urban population in their midst and which they are forced to use.

The (ancient Arabic linguistic) habit is lost to the urban population, and they are strangers to it. They have another linguistic habit, which is not the desired linguistic habit (of the Arabs). Those who know the Arabic linguistic habit merely from rules codified in books are in no way in the possession of this habit. They merely know the laws governing it. The linguistic habit can be obtained only through constant practice, becoming accustomed to Arab speech, and repeatedly (using and listening to) it. . . .

51   The urban population is in general deficient in obtaining the linguistic habit that results from instruction. The more remote urban people are from the Arabic language, the more difficult it is for them to obtain it

The reason for this is that the student has previously obtained a habit incompatible with the desired Arabic linguistic habit, since he has grown up speaking the sedentary language, which was influenced by non-Arab (speech) to such a degree that eventually the original habit of the Arabic language was replaced by another. This other habit is the language of the present-day sedentary population.

Therefore, we find that teachers (attempt to) teach children the (Arabic) language first. The grammarians think that this is done through grammar. But this is not so. It is done through teaching them the linguistic habit through direct contact with the Arabic language and Arab speech. It is true that grammar comes closer (than anything else) to bringing about contact with those (things).

The more firmly rooted in non-Arab speech habits an urban language is and the more remote it is from the original language of the Arabs, the less able are its speakers to learn the original Arabic language and to obtain the habit of it. . . .

52   The division of speech into poetry and prose

The Arabic language and Arab speech are divided into two branches. One of them is rhymed poetry. It is speech with metre and rhyme, which means that every line of it ends upon a definite letter, which is called the 'rhyme'. The other branch is prose, that is, nonmetrical speech.

Each of the two branches comprises various subbranches and ways of speech. Poetry comprises laudatory and heroic poems and elegies. Prose may be rhymed prose. Rhymed prose consists of cola ending on the same rhyme throughout, or of sentences rhymed in pairs. This is called 'rhymed prose'. Prose may also be 'straight prose'. In straight prose, the speech goes on and is not divided into cola, but is continued straight through without any divisions, either of rhyme or of anything else. Prose is employed in sermons and prayers and in speeches intended to encourage or frighten the masses.[1]

---

[1] This is one of the purposes of rhetoric as defined in Aristotelian tradition.

The Qur'ân is in prose. However, it does not belong in either of the two categories. It can neither be called straight prose nor rhymed prose. It is divided into verses. One reaches breaks where taste tells one that the speech stops. It is then resumed and 'repeated' in the next verse. (Rhyme) letters which would make that (type of speech) rhymed prose are not obligatory, nor do rhymes (as used in poetry) occur. . . .

Each of the branches of poetry has its own particular methods, which are considered peculiar to it by the people who cultivate that branch and which do not apply to any other branch and cannot be employed for it.

Recent authors employ the methods of poetry in writing prose. Their writing contains a great deal of rhymed prose and obligatory rhymes. When one examines such prose, (one gets the impression that) it has actually become a kind of poetry. It differs from poetry only through the absence of metre. In recent times, secretaries took this up and employed it in government correspondence. They restricted all prose writing to this type, which they liked. They mixed up (all the different) methods in it. They avoided straight prose and affected to forget it, especially the people of the East. At the hand of stupid secretaries, present-day government correspondence is handled in the way described. From the point of view of good style, it is not correct, since in good style one looks for conformity between what is said and the requirements of the given situations in which the speaker and the person addressed find themselves. It is necessary that government correspondence be kept free from this (type of prose). The methods of poetry admit wittiness, the mixture of humour with seriousness, long descriptions, and the free use of proverbs, as well as frequent similes and metaphoric expressions, (even) where none of these are required in ordinary address. The (constant) obligatory use of rhyme is also something witty and ornamental. All of this is quite incompatible with the dignity of royal and governmental authority and with the task of encouraging or frightening the masses in the name of the ruler. In government correspondence, what deserves praise is the use of straight prose—that is, straightforward speech with only a very occasional use of rhymed prose in places where (sound linguistic) habit can use rhymed prose in an unforced manner—and (forms of) speech that conform properly to the requirements of a given situation.

Government correspondence done in the (aforementioned) way, that is, in a method proper to poetry, deserves censure. The only reason our contemporaries do it is the fact that non-Arab (speech habits) exercise a firm hold over their tongues, and, as a result, they are unable to give their speech its proper measure of conformity with the requirements of a given situation. Thus, they are unable to use straight speech. It is a difficult task and (takes) long effort to achieve eloquence in it. They eagerly use the type of rhymed prose (mentioned), in this way covering up their inability to make their speech conform to the things they want to say and to the requirements of the particular situation. They make up for their (shortcomings) by greatly embellishing their speech with rhymed prose and rhetorical figures. They neglect everything else.

Present-day secretaries and poets in the East use this method most and apply it in an exaggerated manner to all kinds of speech. They go so far as to tamper with the vowel endings and inflections of words (to achieve this end).

53 The ability to write both good poetry and good prose is only very rarely found together in one person

The reason for this is that, as we have explained, it is a habit in the tongue. If another habit previously occupied its place, the subsequent habit has not enough room to develop, because the acceptance and cultivation of habits is simpler and easier for natures in their original state. If there are other previous habits, they resist the new habit in the substance that is to receive the new habit. They prevent it from being quickly accepted. Thus, there arises incompatibility. It becomes impossible for the new habit to develop (to perfection). This is, in general, the case with all technical habits.

The same applies to languages. They are habits of the tongue which are in the same position as the crafts. It can be observed how persons with some previous non-Arab (speech habits) are always deficient in (their knowledge of) the Arabic language. Persons who previously had some good habit are rarely able to become skilled in another or to master it completely.

54 The craft of poetry and the way of learning it

This is one of the disciplines connected with Arab speech. The Arabs call it 'poetry'. It exists in all the other languages. Here, however, we speak only about Arabic poetry. It is possible that the speakers of other languages, too, find in poetry the things they desire to express in their speech. However, each language has its own particular laws concerning eloquence.

Poetry in the Arabic language is remarkable in its manner and powerful in its way. It is speech that is divided into cola having the same metre and held together by the last letter of each colon. Each of those cola is called a 'verse'. The last letter, which all the verses

443

of a poem have in common, is called the 'rhyme letter'. The whole complex is called a 'poem' (*qaṣîdah* or *kalimah*). Each verse, with its combinations of words, is by itself a meaningful unit. In a way, it is a statement by itself, and independent of what precedes and what follows. By itself it makes perfect sense, either as a laudatory or an erotic (statement), or as an elegy. It is the intention of the poet to give each verse an independent meaning. Then, in the next verse, he starts anew, in the same way, with some other (matter). He changes over from one (poetical) type to another, and from one topic to another, by preparing the first topic and the ideas expressing it in such a way that it becomes related to the next topic. Sharp contrasts are kept out of the poem. The poet thus continuously changes over from the erotic to the laudatory (verses). From a description of the desert and the traces of abandoned camps, he changes over to a description of camels on the march, or horses, or apparitions (of the beloved in a dream). From a description of the person to be praised, he changes over to a description of his people and his army. From (an expression of) grief and condolence in elegies, he changes over to praise of the deceased, and so on. Attention is paid to retaining the same metre throughout the whole poem, in order to avoid one's natural inclination to pass from one metre to another, similar one. Since the metres are similar to each other, many people do not notice (the need to retain the same metre).

The metres are governed by certain conditions and rules. They are the subject of the science of prosody. Prosodists restricted their number to fifteen, indicating that they did not find the Arabs using other natural metres in poetry.

The Arabs thought highly of poetry as a form of speech. Therefore, they made it the archive of their sciences and their history, the evidence for what they considered right and wrong, and the principal basis of reference for most of their sciences and wisdom. The poetical habit was firmly established in them, like all their other habits. The Arabic linguistic habits can be acquired only through technical (skill) and (constant) practice of (Arab) speech. Eventually, some sign of the poetical habit may be obtained.

Of the forms of speech, poetry is a difficult thing for modern people to learn, if they want to acquire the habit of it through (study as) a technique. Each verse is an independent statement of meaning suitable for (quotation) by itself. It requires a kind of refinement of the poetical habit, for the poet to be able to pour poetical speech into moulds suitable to this tendency of Arabic poetry. A poet must produce (a verse that) stands alone, and then make another verse in the same way, and again another, and thus go through all the different topics suitable to the thing he wants to express. Then, he establishes

444

harmony among the verses as they follow upon each other in accordance with the different topics occurring in the poem.

Poetry is difficult in its tendency and strange in its subject-matter. Therefore, it constitutes a severe test of a person's natural talent, if he wants to have a good knowledge of poetical methods. (The desire) to press speech into the moulds of poetry sharpens the mind. (Having) the Arabic linguistic habit in general does not suffice. In particular, a certain refinement is needed, as well as the exercise of a certain skill in observing the special poetic methods which the Arabs used.

Let us mention the significance of the word 'method' as used by poets, and what they mean by it.

It should be known that they use it to express the loom on which word combinations are woven, or the mould into which they are packed. It is not used to express the basis upon which the meaning (of a statement rests). That is the task of the vowel endings. It also is not used for perfect expression of the idea resulting from the particular word combination used. That is the task of eloquence and style. It also is not used in the sense of metre, as employed by the Arabs in (connection with poetry). That is the task of prosody. These three sciences fall outside the craft of poetry.

(Poetical method) is used to refer to a mental form for metrical word combinations which is universal in the sense of conforming with any particular word combination. This form is abstracted by the mind from the most prominent individual word combinations and given a place in the imagination comparable to a mould or loom. Word combinations that the Arabs consider sound, in the sense of having the (correct) vowel endings and the (proper) style, are then selected and packed by (the mind) into (that form), just as the builder does with the mould or the weaver with the loom. Eventually, the mould is sufficiently widened to admit the word combinations that fully express what one wants to express. It takes on the form that is sound in the sense (that it corresponds to) the Arabic linguistic habit.

Each branch of poetical speech has methods peculiar to it and existing in it in different ways. . . .

Word combinations in poetry may or may not be sentences. They may be commands or statements, nominal sentences or verbal sentences, followed by appositions or not followed by appositions, separate or connected, as is the case with the word combinations of Arabic speech and the position of individual words in respect to each other. This teaches a person the universal mould which he can learn through (constant) practice in Arabic poetry. This universal mould is an abstraction in the mind derived from specific word

445

combinations, to all of which the universal mould conforms. The author of a spoken utterance is like a builder or weaver. The proper mental form is like the mould used in building, or the loom used in weaving. The builder who abandons his mould, or the weaver who abandons his loom, is unsuccessful.

It should not be said that knowledge of the rules of eloquence suffices in this respect. We say: They are merely basic scientific rules which are the result of analogical reasoning and which indicate by means of analogical reasoning that the word combinations may be used in their particular forms. We have here scientific analogical reasoning that is sound and coherent, as is the analogical reasoning that establishes the rules concerning the vowel endings. But the (poetical) methods that we try to establish here have nothing to do with analogical reasoning. They are a form that is firmly rooted in the soul. It is the result of the continuity of word combinations in Arabic poetry when the tongue uses them. Eventually, the form of (those word combinations) becomes firmly established. It teaches (the poet) the use of similar (word combinations). (It teaches him) to imitate them for each word combination that he may use in his poetry.

The scientific rules that govern the word endings or syntax and style do not teach poetry. Not everything that is correct according to analogical reasoning, as used in connection with Arabic speech and the scientific (grammatical) rules, is used by poets. They use certain ways (of expression) which are known and studied by those who have expert knowledge of poetical speech and the forms of which fall (automatically) under those analogical rules.

Therefore, we have stated that the moulds in the mind are the result of expert knowledge of Arabic poetry and speech. Such moulds exist not only for poetry but also for prose. The Arabs used their speech for both poetry and prose, and they used certain types of divisions for both kinds of speech. In poetry, these are metrical cola, fixed rhymes, and the fact that each colon constitutes a statement by itself. In prose, as a rule, the Arabs observed symmetry and parallelism between the cola. Sometimes, they used prose rhymes, and sometimes straight prose. The moulds for each kind of (expression) are well known in Arabic.

The author of a spoken utterance builds his utterance in (the moulds) used by (the Arabs). They are known only to those who have expert knowledge of Arabic speech, such that in their minds they have an absolute universal mould, which is the result of abstraction from specific individual moulds. They use that universal mould as their model in composing utterances, just as builders use the mould as their model, and weavers the loom. The discipline of speech composition, therefore, differs from the studies of the grammarian, the stylist (literary critic), and the prosodist. It is true, though, that observance of the rules of those sciences is obligatory for and indispensable to the poet.

When all these qualities together are found to apply to a spoken utterance, it is distinguished by a subtle kind of insight into those moulds which are called 'methods'. Only expert knowledge of both Arab poetry and Arab prose gives (that insight).

Now that the meaning of 'method' is clear, let us give a definition or description of poetry that will make its real meaning clear to us. This is a difficult task, for, as far as we can see, there is no such definition by any older (scholar). The definition of the prosodists, according to whom poetry is metrical rhymed speech, is no definition or description of the kind of poetry we have in mind. Prosody considers poetry only under the aspect of the agreement of the verses of a poem, with respect to the number of successive syllables with and without vowels, as well as with respect to the similarity of the last foot of the first hemistich of the verses of a poem to the last foot of the second hemistich. This concerns metre alone and has nothing to do with the words and their meaning. We must have a definition that will give us the real meaning of poetry in our sense.

We say: Poetry is eloquent speech built upon metaphoric usage and descriptions; divided into cola agreeing in metre and rhyme letter, each colon being independent in purpose and meaning from what comes before and after it; and using the methods of the Arabs peculiar to it.

The phrase 'eloquent speech' in our definition takes the place of genus. The phrase 'built upon metaphoric usage and descriptions' differentiates (poetry) from (eloquent speech), which does not have that (and which must be differentiated) because it is mostly not poetry. The phrase 'divided into cola agreeing in metre and rhyme letter' differentiates (poetry) from the (kind of) prose speech that nobody would consider poetry. The phrase 'each colon being independent in purpose and meaning from what comes before and after it' explains the real character of poetry, because the verses of poetry can be only this way. This does not differentiate poetry from other things. The phrase 'using the methods . . . peculiar to it' differentiates poetry from (speech) that does not use the well-known methods of poetry. Without them, it would not be poetry but merely poetical speech, because poetry has special methods which prose does not have. Likewise, prose has methods which do not apply to poetry. Rhymed speech that does not use those methods is not poetry.

The phrase in our definition, 'using the methods of the Arabs . . .' differentiates it from the poetry of non-Arab nations. This is for those who are of the opinion that poetry exists both among Arabs and among other people. On the other hand, those who are of the opinion that poetry exists only among the Arabs would not need the phrase. They might say instead: 'using the methods peculiar to it' (omitting the words 'of the Arabs').

Having finished with the discussion of the real character of poetry, we shall now return to the discussion of how poetry is produced. We say: The production of poetry and the laws governing the poetical craft are subject to a number of conditions. The first condition is to have an expert knowledge of its genus—that is, the genus of Arabic poetry, which eventually creates a habit in the soul upon which, as on a loom, (the poet is able) to weave. The material for memorizing should be selected from the most genuine and purest and most varied poetry.

The poetry of poets who have no expert knowledge of (the old poetical material) is inferior and bad. Brilliance and sweetness is given to poetry only with the help of memorized knowledge of much old poetical material. Those who know little or nothing of it cannot (produce) any (real) poetry. They merely produce bad rhymes. They would do better to keep away from poetry.

After the poet has been saturated with memorized (poetical material) and has sharpened his talent, in order to be able to follow the great examples, he proceeds to make rhymes himself. Through more and more (practice), the habit of (rhyme making) becomes firmly established and rooted in him.

It is often said that one of the conditions governing (poetical production) is to forget the memorized material, so that its external literal forms will be wiped out of the memory, since they prevent the real use of (the poetical habit). After the soul has been conditioned by them, and they are forgotten, the method of poetry is engraved upon the (soul), as though it were a loom upon which similar such words can be woven as a matter of course.

The poet, then, needs solitude. The place he looks at should be a beautiful one with water and flowers. He likewise needs music. He must stir up his talent by refreshing it and stimulate it through pleasurable joy.

In addition to the (aforementioned) conditions, there is another. The poet must be rested and energetic. This makes him more collected and is better for his talent, so that he is able to create a loom similar to that which is in his memory. It has been said: 'The best time for it is in the morning right after waking up, when the stomach is empty and the mind energetic, and in the atmosphere of the bath.' It has often been said: 'Stimuli to poetry are love and intoxication', and: 'If the poet finds it difficult (to make a poem) after all that, he should leave it for another time. He should not force himself to do it.'

The poet should have the rhyme (in mind), when the verse is first given shape and form. He should set it down and build his speech on it all the way through to the end, because, if the poet neglects to have the rhyme in mind when he makes a verse, it may be difficult for him to get the rhyme into its proper place, for it often is loose and unstable. If a verse is satisfactory but does not fit in its context, the poet should save it for a place more fitting to it. Every verse is an independent unit, and all that is to be done is to fit (the verse into the context of the poem). Therefore, the poet may choose to do in this respect whatever he wishes.

After a poem is finished, the poet should revise it carefully and critically. He should not hesitate to throw it away, if it is not good enough. Every man is fond of his own poetry, since it is a product of his mind and a creation of his talent.

The poet should use only the most correct word combinations and a language free from all poetic licence, since (its use) is a defect as far as the linguistic habit is concerned. He should avoid it, because it might deprive his speech of eloquence. The leading authorities forbade the later-born poets to use poetic licence, since by avoiding it they might be able to obtain the most exemplary linguistic habit. The poet should also keep away, as much as he can, from involved word combinations. He should try to use only those whose meaning can be understood more quickly than the (individual) words they contain. The same applies to putting too many ideas into one verse, which make it somewhat complicated to understand. The choicest (verse) is the one whose words conform to its ideas or are more copious than its ideas. If there are many ideas, the verse becomes crowded. The mind examines the ideas and is distracted. As a result, the listener's literary taste is prevented from fully understanding, as it should, the eloquence of the verse. A poem is easy only when its ideas are more quickly grasped by the mind than its words.

The poet should also keep away from far-fetched and pretentious words. He should also keep away from vulgar words that become hackneyed through usage. (The use of such words) deprives the poem of eloquence. He should also keep away from ideas that have become hackneyed by being generally known. Their use, too, deprives the speech of eloquence. It becomes hackneyed and almost meaningless. For instance, such phrases as 'The fire is hot' and 'The heaven above us' (belong in this category). The closer a poem gets to being meaningless, the less can it claim to be eloquent, since (meaninglessness and eloquence) are (opposite) extremes. For this reason, poetry on mystical and prophetical subjects is not, as a rule, very good. Only the best poets are good at it, and even they only in small (portions of such poetry) and with great difficulty, because the ideas with which such poetry deals are generally known to the great mass and, thus, have become hackneyed. . . .

55 Poetry and prose work with words, and not with ideas

Both poetry and prose work with words, and not with ideas. The ideas are secondary to the words. The words are basic.

The craftsman who tries to acquire the habit of poetry and prose uses words for that purpose. He memorizes appropriate words from Arabic speech, so as to be able to employ it frequently and have it on his tongue. Eventually, the habit of classical Arabic becomes firmly established in him. As we have mentioned before, this comes about as follows. Language is a habit concerned with speech. One tries to acquire it by repeated practice with the tongue, until one has acquired it, as is the case with (all other) habits.

Now, tongue and speech deal only with words. Ideas are in the mind. Furthermore, everyone may have ideas. Everyone has the capacity to grasp with his mind whatever ideas his mind wants and likes. No technique is required for their composition. But the composition of speech, for the purpose of expressing ideas, requires a technique. Speech is like a mould for ideas. The vessels in which water is drawn from the sea may be of gold, silver, shells (mother-of-pearl), glass, or clay. But the water is one and the same. The quality of the vessels filled with water differs according to the material from which they are made, and not according to the water in them. In the same way, the quality of language, and eloquence in its use, differ according to different levels (of attainment) in the composition of speech, depending on the manner in which an utterance conforms to (the situation) that it wants to express. But the ideas are one and the same.

A person who is ignorant of the composition of speech and its methods, as required by the (Arabic) linguistic habit, and who unsuccessfully attempts to express what he wants to express, is like an invalid who attempts to get up but cannot, because he lacks the power to do so.

56 The linguistic habit is obtained by much memorizing. The good quality of the linguistic habit is the result of the good quality of the memorized material

We have mentioned before that those who desire to learn the Arabic language must memorize much material. The quality of the resulting habit depends on the quality, type, and amount of the memorized material. Those who memorize the poetry of the Arab (classical poets) will acquire a better habit, of a higher order of eloquence, than those who memorize the poetry and prose of recent writers, because they are inferior to their predecessors. This is obvious to the intelligent critic who has (literary) taste.

The quality of a person's own later use (of the language) depends on the quality of the material learned or memorized. By raising the level of the memorized literary material, the resulting level (of one's habit) becomes higher, since nature takes (habit) as its model, and the powers of a habit grow through nourishing it. This comes about as follows. The soul is one in species according to its natural disposition. It differs in human beings depending on its greater or lesser intensity in connection with perceptions. This difference of the soul is the result of the differing perceptions, habits, and colourings that condition the soul from the outside. (Such conditioning) causes its existence to materialize and transforms its form from potentiality into actuality.

The habits obtained by the soul are obtained only gradually, as we have mentioned before. The poetical habit originates with the memorizing of poetry. The habit of secretaryship originates with the memorizing of rhymed prose and prose correspondence. The scientific habit originates in contact with the sciences and with various perceptions, research, and speculation. The juridical habit originates in contact with jurisprudence and through comparing the problems and considering them in detail and through deriving special cases from general principles. The mystical habit originates through worship and spiritual exercises and through inactivation of the outward senses by means of solitude and as much isolation from human beings as possible, until (he who does that) acquires the habit of retiring to his inner sense and his spirit and thus becomes a mystic. The same is the case with all the other habits. Each one of them gives the soul a special colouring that conditions it.

The good or bad quality of a particular habit depends on the (condition) under which the habit originated. A first-class habit of eloquence results only from the memorizing of first-class language material. This is why all jurists and scholars are deficient in eloquence. The sole reason is in the original character of the material they memorize, in the scientific rules and juridical expressions of which their material is full and which deviate from the proper method of eloquence and are inferior to it. The expressions used for rules and sciences have nothing to do with eloquence. When such memorized material is the first to occupy the mind and is large and colours the soul, the resulting habit comes to be very deficient and the expressions connected with (that material) deviate from the methods of Arabic speech. This, we find, applies to the poetry of jurists, grammarians, speculative theologians, philosophers, and others who are not saturated with memorized knowledge of the purest and (most genuine) Arabic speech.

Secretaries and poets choose carefully the material they memorize. They have contact with the methods of Arabic speech.

One day, I had a conversation with Abû 'Abdallâh b. al-Khaṭîb, the wazir of the rulers of Spain. He was the leading authority on poetry and secretaryship. I said to him, 'I find it difficult to compose poetry when I want to, despite my understanding of poetry and my knowledge of the good language material in the Qur'ân, the traditions, and the various other branches of Arabic speech, although I know little by heart. It may be that I am affected by my knowledge of scientific poems and the rules of literary composition. That has filled my memory and harmed the habit for which I was prepared through the good material from the Qur'ân, the traditions, and (other documents of) Arabic speech. It prevented my talent from developing.' Ibn al-Khaṭîb looked at me in amazement for a while. Then he said, full of admiration: 'Would anyone but you say a thing like that?'

The remarks made in this section explain another problem. They explain why both the poetry and the prose of the Muslim Arabs are on a higher level of eloquence and literary taste than those of pre-Islamic Arabs. A sound taste and a healthy natural disposition will confirm the (correctness of this observation) to the intelligent critic of eloquence.

The reason for this is that (authors) who lived in Islam learned the highest form of speech in the Qur'ân and in the traditions, which for human beings is inimitable. It entered into their hearts. Their souls were brought up on the (linguistic) methods (of this kind of speech). As a result, their nature was lifted, and their habits with regard to eloquence were elevated, to greater heights than had ever been reached by their pre-Islamic predecessors, who had not learned the (highest) form of speech and had not been brought up on it. Therefore, their prose and poetry were better in texture and of a purer brilliance than their predecessors'. They were more solid in con-struction and more even in execution, because their authors had learned the language of the Qur'ân and the traditions.

I once asked our *shaykh*, the sharîf Abû l-Qâsim,[1] the (chief) judge of Granada in our day, why the Muslim Arabs were on a higher level (of eloquence) than the pre-Islamic Arabs. Abû l-Qâsim was the chief authority on poetry. He had studied (it) in Ceuta with

[1] Muḥammad b. Aḥmad b. Muḥammad, as-Sabtî, 697–760 [1297–1359].

certain *shaykhs* there. He had also made a profound study of philology and acquired a more than perfect knowledge of it. Thus, he
was a man who, with his taste, could be expected not to be ignorant
of (this question). He remained silent for a long while. Then he said
to me, 'By Allah, I do not know.' Whereupon I said, 'I shall suggest
to you an idea concerning this problem that has come to my mind.
Perhaps, it explains it.' And I mentioned to him what I have noted
here. He was silent in amazement. Then, he said to me: 'Doctor,
this is a remark that deserves to be written down in letters of gold.'
After that, he always treated me with deference. He listened to what
I had to say in class and acknowledged my excellence in scholarship.

57 An explanation of the meaning of natural and contrived speech. How contrived speech may be either good or deficient

It should be known that the secret and spirit of speech—that is, expression and address—lie in conveying ideas. If no effort is made to
convey ideas, speech is like 'dead land' which does not count.

The perfect way of conveying ideas is eloquence. This is shown by
the literary critics' definition of eloquence. They say that eloquence
is conformity of speech to the requirements of the situation. Knowledge of the conditions and laws governing the conformity of word
combinations to the requirements of the situation is the discipline of
eloquence (rhetoric). The conditions and laws were deduced from
the Arabic language and have become a sort of rules. The manner
in which word combinations are used indicates the relationship that
exists between two interdependent (parts of an utterance). (It does
so) with the help of conditions and laws constituting the main part
of the rules of Arabic. . . .

After the requirements of a given situation have thus been indicated, there come the diverse ways in which the mind moves among
the ideas with the help of different kinds of (word) meanings. In its
conventional meaning, a word combination indicates one particular
idea, but then the mind moves on to what might be the consequence
of, or have as its consequence, that idea, or (what might) be similar
to it and, thus, express (some idea) indirectly as metaphor or metonymy. This moving around causes pleasure to the mind, perhaps
even more than the pleasure that results from indicating (the requirements of the situation). All these things mean attainment of a
conclusion from the argument used to prove it, and attainment, as
one knows, is one of the things that cause pleasure.

The different ways the (mind) moves around in this way also have
their conditions and laws, which are like rules. They were made into
a (special) craft and called 'the (science of) style'. (This science) is

sister to the science of idea expression, which indicates the requirements of a given situation. The science of style has reference to the ideas and meanings of the word combinations. The rules of the science of idea expression have reference to the very situations that apply to the word combinations, as far as they affect the meaning. Word and idea depend on each other and stand side by side, as one knows. Thus, the science of idea expression and the science of style are both part of rhetoric, and both together produce perfect indication and conformity to the requirements of the situation. Consequently, word combinations that fall short of conformity and perfect indication are inferior in eloquence. Such word combinations are linked by rhetoricians to the sounds dumb animals make. The preferred assumption is that they are not Arabic, because Arabic is (the kind of speech) in which indications are in conformity with the requirements of the situation. Thus, eloquence is the basis, genius, spirit, and nature of Arabic speech.

It should further be known that in the usage of (philologists), 'natural speech' means the speech that conveys the intended meaning and, thus, is perfect in its nature and genius. Mere speaking is not what is meant by (natural speech) as a (kind of) expression and address; the speaker (who uses natural speech) wants to convey what is in his mind to the listeners in a complete and definite fashion.

Thus, after perfect indication (of the requirements of the situation has been achieved), the word combinations, (if expressed) according to that genius that is basic (to Arabic speech), have their different kinds of artistic embellishment. In a way, they give them the brilliance of correct speech. Such (kinds of artistic embellishment) include the ornamental use of rhymed prose, the use of phrases of identical structure at the end of successive cola, allusion to a cryptic idea by a homonym, and antithesis, so that there will be affinity between the words and ideas used. This gives brilliance to speech and pleasure to the ear, and sweetness and beauty, all in addition to indicating (the meaning). . . .

People who cultivate the craft of (rhetorical figures) distinguish numerous subdivisions and use different terminologies for the rhetorical figures. Many of them consider them part of rhetoric, although these figures are not concerned with indicating (the meaning of speech), but provide embellishment and brilliance. The early representatives of the discipline of rhetorical figures considered them not to be a part of rhetoric. Therefore, they mentioned them as part of the literary disciplines that have no (particular, defined) subject. They mentioned various conditions governing the use of the (rhetorical figures). Among them, there is the condition that they should express the intended meaning in an unforced and unstudied manner.

The spontaneous occurrence of rhetorical figures causes no comment, because (in such cases) they are in no way forced, and the speech (in which they occur) cannot therefore be criticized as (linguistically) faulty. The forced and studied use of rhetorical figures leads to disregard of the basic word combinations of speech and thus destroys all basis for indication (of the meaning of speech). It removes outright all eloquence and leaves speech only the (rhetorical) embellishments. This is the situation preponderant among our contemporaries. But people who have taste in eloquence despise them (because of) their infatuation with the various (rhetorical figures) and consider that (propensity an indication of their) inability to do better.

Another condition (governing the use of rhetorical figures) is that they be used sparingly and in no more than two or three verses of a poem, which suffices to adorn and give it brilliance, while the use of many such rhetorical figures would be a blemish.

Our *shaykh*, the sharîf Judge Abû l-Qâsim as-Sabtî, who was the chief cultivator of the Arabic language in his time, used to say: 'The different kinds of rhetorical figures may occur to a poet or a secretary, but it is ugly if he uses many of them. They belong among the things that embellish speech and constitute its beauty. They are like moles on a face. One or two make it beautiful, but many make it ugly.'

Pre-Islamic and (early) Islamic prose followed the same lines as poetry. Originally, it was straight prose, considering only creation of a balance between the larger portions of (speech) and its word combinations, to indicate that it is balanced by means of cola into which it is divided, without adherence to rhyme or concern for contrived techniques. The prose of later authors became more and more contrived. One forgot the period when straight prose had been used. Government correspondence came to be like private correspondence, and Arabic came to be like the common language. Good and bad became confused with each other.

All these (statements) show that contrived, studied, or forced speech is inferior to natural speech, because it has little concern for what is basic to eloquence. The judge in such matters is one's taste.

58 People of rank are above cultivating poetry

Poetry was the archive of the Arabs, containing their sciences, their history, and their wisdom. Leading Arabs competed in it. They used to stop at the fair of 'Ukâz to recite poetry. Each would submit his product for criticism to outstanding and intelligent personalities. Eventually, Arab poets came to vie in having their poems hung up at the corners of the Holy Sanctuary to which they made pilgrimage, the Ka'bah. Only a person who had enough power among his people and his group, and who held the proper position, was able to get so far as to have his poem hung up there.

Then, at the beginning of Islam, the Arabs gave up the (custom). They were occupied with the affairs of Islam, with prophecy and revelation. They were awed by the linguistic method and form of the Qur'ân. For a time, they no longer discussed poetry and prose. Then, those (great happenings) continued, and right guidance came to be something familiar to the Muslims. There was no revelation that poetry was forbidden or prohibited. The Prophet listened to poetry and rewarded the poet for it. Under these circumstances, the Arabs returned to their old customs with regard to poetry.

Then there came great royal authority and a mighty dynasty. The Arabs approached the (caliphs) with their laudatory poems, and the caliphs rewarded them most generously according to the quality of the poems and their position among their people. They were eager to have poems presented to them. From them they learned remarkable stories, history, lexicography, and noble speech. The Arabs saw to it that their children memorized the poems. This remained the situation during the days of the Umayyads and in the early days of the 'Abbâsid dynasty. Ar-Rashîd possessed a good knowledge of the subject and was firmly grounded in it. He was concerned with the cultivation of (poetry). He was able to discern good speech from bad speech, and knew a good deal of poetry by heart.

Later on, people came whose language was not Arabic, because they had a non-Arab (background) and a deficient knowledge of Arabic, which they had learned as a craft. Poets did write laudatory poems for the non-Arab amirs, but they did so only in order to win their favour, and not for any other reason. Thus, the predominant purpose of producing poetry came to be mere begging, because the particular use that the early Arabs had made of poetry no longer existed. This is why people of ambition and rank among later Muslims disdained poetry. Thus the situation changed. Concern with poetry came to be (considered) a blemish or fault in leaders and people holding great positions.

59 *Contemporary Arab poetry, Bedouin and urban*

Poetry is not restricted exclusively to the Arabic language. It exists in every language. There were poets among the Persians and among the Greeks. The Greek poet Homer was mentioned and praised by Aristotle in the *Logic*. The Ḥimyarites, too, had their poets in ancient times.

Later on, corruption affected the language of the Arabs. The various later dialects differed according to the (more or less close) contact with (non-Arabs) and the (larger or smaller) admixture of non-Arab (elements). As a result, the Bedouin Arabs themselves came to speak a language completely different from that of their ancestors with regard to vowel endings, and different in many respects with regard to the (conventional) meanings and forms of words. Among the urban population, too, another language originated, which was different from classical Arabic with regard to vowel endings, as well as most meanings and grammatical inflections. It differs also from the language of present-day Arab Bedouins. Again, it differs within itself according to the (different) terminologies of the inhabitants of the various regions. Thus, the urban population of the East speaks a dialect different from that of the Maghribîs. And the language of the urban population in Spain differs from both of them.

Now, poetry exists by nature among the speakers of every language, since metres of a certain harmonious arrangement, with the alternation of (fixed) numbers of consonants, with and without vowels, exist in the nature of all human beings. Therefore, poetry is never abolished as the result of the disappearance of one particular language—in this case, that of the original Arabs, who, as everybody knows, were outstanding champions of poetry. In fact, every racial and dialect group among the Arab Bedouins who have undergone some non-Arab influence, or the urban population, attempts to cultivate poetry and to fit it into the pattern of their speech, as much as it suits them.

Contemporary Arab Bedouins who gave up the language of their ancestors under non-Arab influence, produce poetry in all the metres used by their Arab ancestors. They make long poems in (those metres). Their poems represent all the ways and purposes of poetry, the erotic, the laudatory, the elegiac, and the satirical.

They have another kind of poetry which is widely in use among them. It employs four lines, of which the fourth has a rhyme different from that of the first three. The fourth rhyme, then, is continued in each stanza through the whole poem, similar to the quatrains and the stanzas of five lines which were originated by recent poets of mixed Arab and non-Arab parentage. These Arabs show an admirable eloquence in the use of this type of poetry. There are outstanding and less outstanding poets among them.

Most contemporary scholars, philologists in particular, disapprove of these types of poems when they hear them, and refuse to consider them poetry when they are recited. They believe that their (literary) taste recoils from them, because they are (linguistically) incorrect and lack vowel endings. This, however, is merely the result of the loss of the habit (of using vowel endings) in the dialect of the Arabs. If these (philologists) possessed the same speech habit, taste and natural (feeling) would prove to them that these poems are eloquent, provided that their own natural dispositions and point of view were not distorted. Vowel endings have nothing to do with eloquence. Eloquence is the conformity of speech to what one wants to express and to the requirements of a given situation, regardless of whether the *u*-ending indicates the subject and the *a*-ending the object, or vice versa. These things are indicated by syntactic combinations as used in the particular dialect used by the Arabs. The meanings are based upon the technical conventions of people who have a particular linguistic habit. When the technical terminology (as it is used) in a particular linguistic habit is generally known, the meaning comes out correctly. And if the indicated meaning is in conformity with what one wants to express and with the requirements of the situation, we have sound eloquence. The rules of the grammarians have nothing to do with that.

The poems of the Arabs show all the methods and forms of (true) poetry. They lack only the vowel endings. . . .

The Spanish muwashshaḥ and zajal

Poetry was greatly cultivated in Spain. Its various ways and types were refined. Poems came to be most artistic. As a result, recent Spaniards created the kind of poetry called *muwashshaḥ*. Like the *qaṣīdah*, the *muwashshaḥ* is used for erotic and laudatory poetry, and its authors vied to the utmost with each other in this kind of poetry. Everybody, the elite and the common people, liked and knew these poems because they were easy to grasp and understand. . . .

Muwashshaḥ poetry spread among the Spaniards. The great mass took to it because of its smoothness, artistic language, and the (many) internal rhymes found in it (which made them popular). As a result, the common people in the cities imitated them. They made poems of the *muwashshaḥ* type in their sedentary dialect, without employing vowel endings. They thus invented a new form, which they called *zajal*. They have continued to compose poems of this type down to this time. They achieved remarkable things in it. The *zajal* opened a wide field for eloquent poetry in the (Spanish-Arabic) dialect, which is influenced by non-Arab (speech habits). . . .

It should be known that taste as to what constitutes eloquence in connection with such poetry is possessed only by those who have contact with the dialect in which (a particular poem) is composed, and who have had much practice in using it among the people who speak it. Only thus do they acquire the habit of it, as we stated with regard to the Arabic language. A Spaniard has no understanding of the eloquence of Maghribî poetry. Maghribîs have none for the eloquence of the poetry of Easterners or Spaniards, and Easterners have none for the eloquence of Spaniards and Maghribîs. All of them use different dialects and word combinations. Everybody understands eloquence in his own dialect and has a taste for the beauties of the poetry of his own people.

(CONCLUDING REMARK)

We have almost strayed from our purpose. It is our intention to stop with this First Book which is concerned with the nature of civilization and the accidents that go with it. We have dealt—as we think, adequately—with the problems connected with that. Perhaps some later (scholar), aided by the divine gifts of a sound mind and of solid scholarship, will penetrate into these problems in greater detail than we did here. A person who creates a new discipline does not have the task of enumerating all the problems connected with it. His task is to specify the subject of the discipline and its various branches and the discussions connected with it. His successors, then, may gradually add more problems, until the discipline is completely (presented).

The author of the book—God forgive him!—says: I completed the composition and draft of this first part, before revision and correction, in a period of five months ending in the middle of the year 779 [November 1377]. Thereafter, I revised and corrected the book, and I added to it the history of the (various) nations, as I mentioned and proposed to do at the beginning of the work.

Knowledge comes only from God, the Mighty One, the Wise One.

Index

INDEX

Adriatic, 51; Indian Ocean, 15, 51f., 54; Red Sea, 15, 51f.; Persian Gulf, and Caspian Sea, 52
Secretaries, 190, 192, 201f., 219, 438, 442f., 451; *tawqî*, 202; epistle, 203–6
Sedentary civilization, 43; wealth and comfort, 91ff., 138ff., 221; character, 94–7, 135, 137, 176, 230, 286–9; titles, 181, 194, 196; based on dynasty, 282–286; crafts, 314–17, 319, 321f., 326; intelligence, 342f.; sciences, 343, 387; see also, dynasty, luxury
Skin pigmentation: varies in zones, 58; effect of heat, 59ff.
Sleep, 80–3, 355–8, 364f., 367–71
Soothsayers, 79f., 84, 259
Sorcery, 73, 85, 372ff., 388, 391–5, 398; talismans, 392, 394
Soul, 75–7, 79–86, 94, 331, 337, 357–361, 391–8, 400
Spain, Spaniards: loss of group feeling, 28, 123; diet, 66; imitation, 116; book-keeping, 197; agriculture, 277f.; crafts and sciences, 316, 375; teaching, 422f.; poetry, 548f.
Speculative theologians, 71f., 348–54, 356, 358, 362f., 389f.
Sufism, Sufis, 68, 73, 84ff., 258, 358–67, 390, 395f., 403
Sustenance, 297ff.
'Sword', the, 189, 196, 202, 207, 213, 249

aṭ-Ṭabarî, 6, 15, 17, 22, 24, 139
Taxation, 19f., 111, 119, 121, 134, 190f., 196f., 249, 299; Ministry of taxation, 198–201; high and low revenue, 230–236, 238, 242
Teaching, 26f., 116, 178, 375; religious, 172; crafts, 314; scientific, 341ff., 416–420; children, 421–4; advice, 424; punishment, 424ff.
Thought: ability distinguishes man, 42, 46, 75, 333–7, 382f., 418ff.; knowledge, 77, 334, 383f., 399f.; degrees of, 334f., 339; power of, 76f., 411; philosophy, 398ff.
Tools and utensils, 37, 45, 58
Torah, the, 3, 12, 14, 59, 74, 106f., 185f. 412
Tubba's of the Yemen, 14ff.

'Ubaydid-Fâtimid(s): dynasty, 194, 196; police, 175; naval war, 209ff.; emblems, 215f., 218, 220, 222; taxation, 232
'Umar, 39, 96, 162, 167, 169, 173, 180, 192, 198f., 209, 218, 222f., 294, 373, 425
Umayyad(s): historians of, 6; 28; desert attitude, 22; dynasty, 147, 164f., 168, 181, 247; wazir, 192; doorkeeper, 195; emblems, 220f.; battle order, 225; poetry, 456
Umayyad(s), Spanish: historians of, 6; judges, 27; dynasty, 124f., 181, 251f.; police, 175; wazir, 194f.; doorkeeper, 195; naval war, 209ff.; emblems, 218ff.; battle order, 225; pilgrimage forbidden, 237
'Uthmân, 162f., 165, 218

Warfare, 158, 190, 192f., 222; weapons, 46f., 95, 118, 250, 321; naval war, 208–13; origin, 223; just and unjust, 224; techniques, 224–9; luck, 229f.; trickery, 253; see also army, holy war, the 'sword'
Wazirate, wazir, 28f., 150, 190–7, 200f.
Wealth, 91, 109, 140, 233, 237, 273ff., 285, 304f.
Wine, 18, 21f., 63
Women: virtue, 18f., 22f.; religious laws, 159f., harem, 150
World: order, 74–7, 79, 334f., 337; of man, 355

Yazîd, 164, 168

465